The World: Political

1:80 000 000

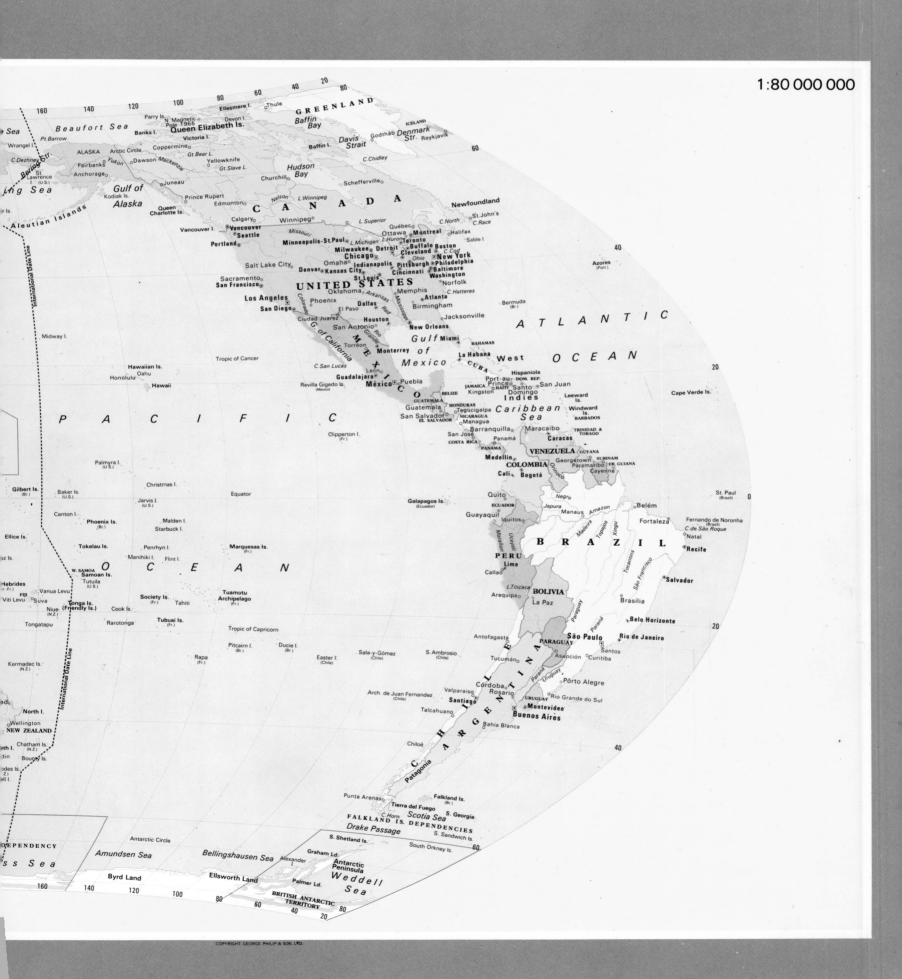

To Miriam
From Albert & Marjorie
1978.

The Pictorial Atlas of
Australia

RIGBY

Fitzroy River, near Rockhampton, Queensland

The Pictorial Atlas of
Australia

RIGBY LIMITED. SYDNEY. ADELAIDE. MELBOURNE. BRISBANE. PERTH.

First published 1977
Concept © George Philip and O'Neil Pty Ltd
Maps © as designated:
George Philip & Son Ltd and George Philip and O'Neil Pty Ltd
ISBN 0 7270 0500 6
Typesetting by The Type Shop, Melbourne
Printed in Hong Kong
Design by G. Nicholls

Simpson Desert gullies, Northern Territory

Editorial Consultants

Acknowledgments

The publishers wish to thank the many people and organisations who helped in the preparation of the *Pictorial Atlas of Australia*.

for the wildlife illustrations:
Ninon Phillips (animals)
Margot Kroyer Pedersen (birds)
Wynne Leverett Brown (flora and reptiles, amphibians and insects)

for the photography:
Robin Smith
Visair
John Carnemolla (parrot on jacket)
Michael Achurch (Ord River Scheme)
Department of Administrative Services — News and Information
Service (Lake Mungo photographs)
Bureau of Meteorology (climate and weather photographs)
CSIRO (soil profiles)

for the permission to reproduce historic maps and paintings:
The National Library of Australia
    ('The Expedition in a Desert in Australia' by T. J. Maslen,
    published in *The Friend from Australia*, 1830 — page 50 and
Thomas Luny's oil painting of *The Earl of Pembroke* — page 48).
The Nan Kivell Collection in The National Library of Australia
    ('Nova et accuratissima totius terrarum orbis tabula' by Joanne
    Blaeu — page 48).

for statistical and other information:
Joan M. Dixon, Curator of Vertebrates, National Museum of
    Victoria
James Creffield, CSIRO, Division of Building and Research,
    Highett
David Foster, Lecturer in Geography at Warrnambool Institute of
    Advanced Education (The section on tourism and recreational
    resources)
Gordon Lowing, Geography Co-ordinator, Melbourne High
    School
Dr Angus A. Martin, Senior Lecturer in Zoology, University of
    Melbourne
Australian Bureau of Statistics
Australian Tourist Commission
Department of Aboriginal Affairs
Department of Administrative Services
Department of Education
Department of Immigration
Department of National Resources
Department of Primary Industry
Department of Tourism and Recreation
Department of Transport
Department of Youth, Sport and Recreation, Victoria
National Mapping Division, Department of National Resources

Preface

Australians live in a 'lucky country' in many respects. But the rapid development that has taken place in this vast continent in recent decades has left many of us unaware of what lies beyond our own State, or even our own city.

The aim of *The Pictorial Atlas of Australia* is to present the physical, economic and social aspects of our environment in one attractive volume suitable for both home and school. The editors of this unique project, all leading educators in geography and the natural sciences, represent every State in Australia.

The world-class cartography, much of it specially commissioned for this atlas, took several years to execute. Each State is presented at a scale appropriate to its size, while the populated areas of the States, including the major cities, are represented by larger scale maps. In addition, thematic maps have been included to depict the distribution of soils, climatic and vegetation regions, fauna, population, primary production, mineral and energy resources and transport routes, to name just a few.

In every case, the maps in *The Pictorial Atlas of Australia* are accompanied by an authoritative text written by specialist authors in a clear, simple style. Significant points of the maps and text are highlighted by excellent photographs, while the section on fauna and flora has been illustrated by some of Australia's best-known wildlife artists. The statistics used are the most recent available and are in most cases based on the results of the 1976 Census. Wherever possible they have been converted into easy-to-read graphs and charts.

In devising the concept of this atlas, the editors have taken into account the increased opportunities available to Australians for recreation and travel. An interesting section has been included on tourism and recreational resources both within Australia, and in the neighbouring countries most often visited by Australians.

Place-names in Australia and the neighbouring region — South-east Asia, New Zealand, Papua New Guinea and the islands of the West Pacific — may be located by referring to the comprehensive gazetteer provided at the back of the atlas.

The Editors.

Macdonnell Range fold formations, Northern Territory.

Contents

The Australian Continent

Australia is a continent of contrasts, from the lush tropical rainforests of the north and north-east coasts to the harsh, arid centre; from the bustling cosmopolitan cities of Sydney and Melbourne to the tranquil existence of the Australian outback; from the coral playgrounds of the Barrier Reef to the mammoth oil and gas platforms in Bass Strait; from the grand performances of the Australian Opera Company at the Sydney Opera House to the beer and beef barbecues on a Sunday afternoon — Australia means many things to many people.

The popular image overseas of our island continent and its people tends to be dominated by eucalypts, koalas, sun-soaked beaches, surf riders, vast open spaces, limitless homesteads, and a strange breed of people who speak with a drawl. Though these superficial images all exist, there are many surprises for visitors to Australia.

With fourteen million people, four-fifths living in the main cities, Australia is one of the most advanced countries in the world — by whatever criterion it is judged. As a region of recent settlement, it is one of the youngest of the democratic nations, although its prehistory dates back some 30 000 years to when man first crossed the sea bridge from the South-east Asian land mass. Before European settlement in 1788 the Aborigines probably numbered about 300 000, spread throughout the continent and existing as hunters and gatherers. On 26 January 1788 Captain Arthur Phillip formally took possession of eastern Australia and Tasmania for the British crown. And so began our recent history.

With the influx of British settlers in the early nineteenth century the colonies soon developed. Queensland was the last State to obtain responsible government in 1859. Sheep, cattle and gold had transformed the early colonies into prosperous, energetic States so that by 1901 the separate colonies were federated under the name of the Commonwealth of Australia, set up under a constitutional monarchy and a member of what was then the British Empire.

The total area of Australia is 7 682 000 square kilometres, stretching between latitudes 10°41′S (Cape York) and 43°39′S (South East Cape, Tasmania) and between longitudes 113°19′E (Steep Point) and 153°39′E (Cape Byron). This represents a distance of 3680 kilometres from north to south and 4000 kilometres from west to east. The average altitude of the surface of this land mass is only 300 metres, with approximately 87 per cent of the total land mass less than 500 metres and 99.5 per cent less than 1000 metres. The highest point is Mt Kosciusko in the Eastern Highlands (2228 metres) and the lowest point is Lake Eyre (15 metres below sea level).

Considering its size, Australia's contrasting climates and vegetation patterns are to a certain extent understandable. The heavy summer monsoon rains along the north coast and the constant moderate rainfall of the south-east associated with the mid-latitude westerlies, ensure sufficient pasture for grazing pursuits. The Eastern Highlands provide a barrier to the on-shore trade winds from the Pacific. Yet 50 per cent of Australia receives a rainfall of only 300 mm or less. The vast dry interior and west coast may go for years on end without rain. The Murray River and its

tributaries form the largest river system in Australia. The catchment is about 1 057 000 square kilometres, or 16 per cent of Australia's total land area. Only 66 per cent of Australia contributes to stream flow, most of the streams being non-perennial. The main irrigation and hydro-electric works are associated with the Murray and its tributaries, while the Snowy Mountains hydro scheme, with an installed capacity of 3 740 000 kilowatts, is regarded as one of the engineering wonders of the world.

The mainstays of the rural section of the community are wool, wheat and beef which tend to be distributed over wide areas, whereas other crops and livestock are restricted to certain areas where climate and other

local conditions are suitable. Of the nearly 500 million hectares in rural holdings, crops account for over 14 million (2.8 per cent), sown pasture 26 million (5.2 per cent) and grazing and idle land 457 million (91.4 per cent. Because of Australia's climatic conditions irrigation is necessary to bring further areas into production and to enable production of crops in areas that are naturally unsuitable. Extensive grazing of beef cattle is virtually the only activity that can exist in the Australian outback.

The south-eastern coastal area, including the cities of Brisbane, Sydney, Melbourne and Adelaide, is the most heavily populated. Victoria, with 2.92 per cent of the total area, has 27.25 per cent of the total population with

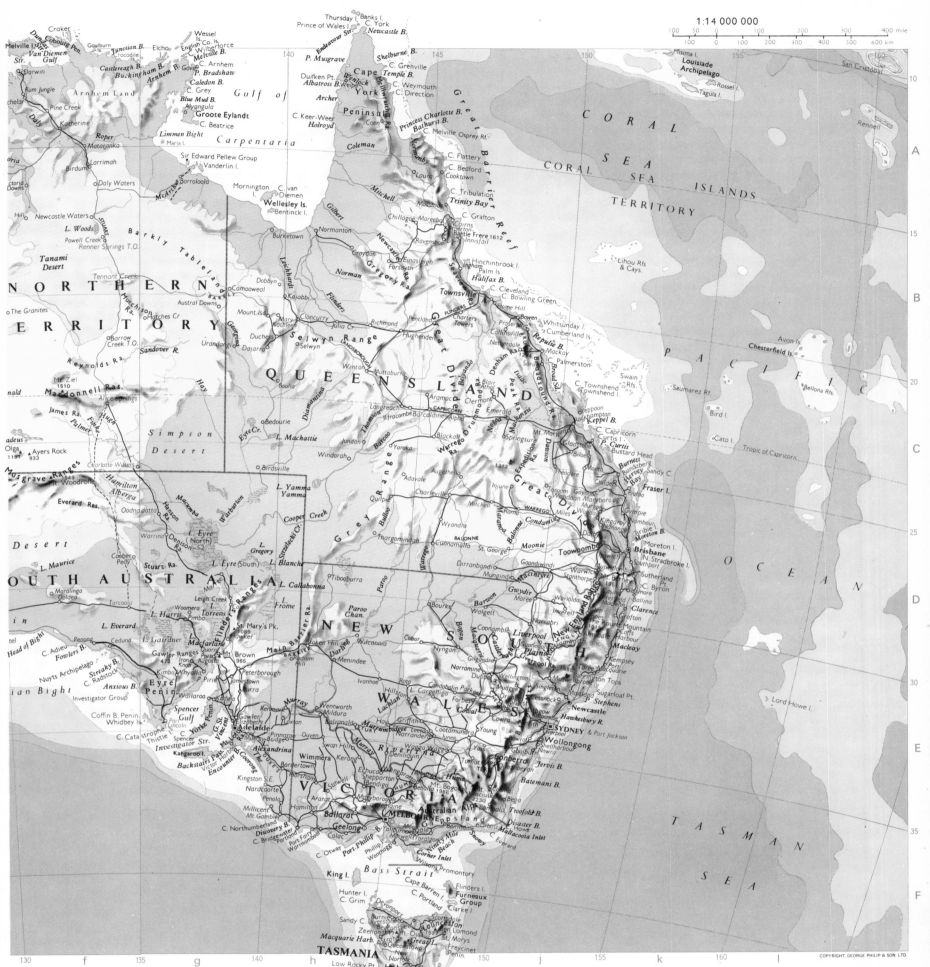

a density of 16.4 persons per square kilometre, while Western Australia on the other hand has 32.89 per cent of the total area and 8.17 per cent of the total population, with a density of only 0.43 persons per square kilometre. At the 1971 census nearly 11 million people out of 12.75 million, or 85.57 per cent, lived in cities exceeding 1000 people (64.5 per cent in cities exceeding 25 000 people). There were five urban centres exceeding 500 000 people and these accounted for 57.93 per cent of the total population. Sydney (slightly larger) and Melbourne together contain over 5.5 million people and have become vast metropolitan areas servicing the hinterlands of New South Wales and Victoria. Many urban problems of pollution, congestion and inner suburban development have been debated, rectified or controlled in the past decade. It seems that these two cities will continue to grow at the expense of lesser cities.

Since 1788 Australia has continued to develop as an urban-based society, yet even today primary production (including mining) accounts for 77.3 per cent of export income, although employing only 24 per cent of the total workforce.

One of the most significant developments of the past two decades has been the great boom in mineral production and exports. Important discoveries of the 'new' metals and fuels — bauxite, nickel and natural gas together with a revival in the more traditional minerals such as copper, lead, zinc and iron ore, have led to great prosperity for Western Australia and Queensland in particular, and for Australia as a whole. Although the boom conditions of the sixties have quietened, minerals are contributing an ever-increasing proportion of Australia's export income.

Apart from the degree of Australia's urbanisation, perhaps the most surprising fact to the visitor is the cosmopolitan nature of the country, which has been the direct result of the great post-World War II immigration scheme which brought over 3 million settlers from more than 60 different nations to Australia in a 30-year period.

How the Continents Evolved

The origin of the earth is still open to much conjecture although the most widely accepted theory is that it was formed from a solar cloud consisting mainly of hydrogen. Under gravitation, the cloud condensed and shrank to form the planets orbiting around the sun. Gravitation forced the lighter elements to the surface of the earth where they cooled to form a crust, while the inner material remained hot and molten. Earth's first rocks formed over 3500 million years ago but since then the surface has been constantly altered.

Until comparatively recently, it was believed that the primary units of the earth had remained essentially fixed throughout geological time, although the concept of moving continents appears in the Bible with the break up of the land after Noah's floods. The continental drift theory was first developed by Antonio Snider in 1858 but its most important single advocate was Alfred Wegener who, in 1915, published evidence from geology, climatology and biology, in support of his ideas. His conclusions were very similar to those reached by current research although he was wrong about the speed of break up.

The measurement of fossil magnetism found in rocks has proved to be the most influential evidence in favour of the continental drift theory. Although originally these drift theories were openly mocked, now they are considered standard doctrine.

The Jigsaw

As knowledge of the shape and structure of the earth's surface increased, several of the early geographers noticed the great similarity in shape of the coasts bordering the Atlantic. It was this remarkable similarity which led to the first detailed geological and structural comparisons. Even more accurate fits can be made by placing the edges of the continental shelves in juxtaposition.

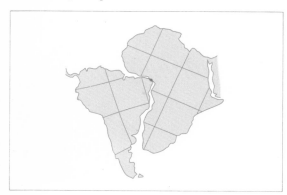

Plate Tectonics

The original debate about continental drift was a prelude to a more radical idea, plate tectonics. The basic theory is that the earth's crust is made up of a series of rigid plates which float on a soft layer of the mantle and are moved about by convection currents in the earth's interior. These plates converge and diverge along margins marked by earthquakes, volcanoes and other seismic activity. Plates diverge from mid-ocean ridges where molten lava pushes upwards and forces the plates apart at a rate of up to 30 mm a year. Converging plates form either a trench, where the oceanic plate sinks below the lighter continental rock, or mountain ranges where two continents collide. This explains the paradox that

180 million years ago.
The original Pangaea land mass had split into two major continental groups. The southern group, Gondwanaland, had itself started to break up, India and Antarctica-Australia becoming isolated. A rift had begun to appear between South America and Africa and, in the East, Africa was closing up the Tethys Sea.

135 million years ago.
Both Gondwanaland and Laurasia continued to drift northwards but the widening of the splits in the North Atlantic and Indian Oceans persisted. The South Atlantic rift continued to lengthen and a further perpendicular rift appeared which will eventually separate Greenland from North America. India continues heading northward towards Asia.

65 million years ago.
South America, completely separated from Africa, moved quickly north and westwards. Madagascar broke free from Africa but, as yet, there is no sign of the Red Sea Rift which will split Africa from the Arabian Peninsula. The Mediterranean sea is recognizable. In the south, Australia is still connected to Antarctica.

Today.
India has moved northwards and is colliding with Asia, crumpling up the sediments to form the folded mountain range of the Himalayas. South America has rotated and moved west to connect with North America. Australia has separated from Antarctica.

(After Dietz & Holden Sci. Am. 1970)

	Trench
	Rift
	New Ocean Floor
	Zones of slippage

while there have always been oceans, none of
the present oceans contains sediments more
than 150 million years old. The present
explanation for the comparative youth of the
ocean floors is that where an ocean and a continent meet the ocean plate dips under the less
dense continental plate at an angle of approximately 45°. All previous crust is then ingested
by downward convection currents.

The recent identification of the *transform,*
or *transverse, fault* proved to be one of the crucial preliminaries to the investigation of plate
tectonics. These occur when two plates slip
alongside each other without parting or approaching to any great extent. They complete
the outline of the plates delineated by the
ridges and trenches and demonstrate large
scale movements of the earth's surface.

Ocean rises or crests are basically made up
from basaltic lavas for although no gap can
exist between plates, one plate can ease itself
away from another. In that case hot, molten
rock instantly rises from below to fill in the
incipient rift and forms a *ridge.* These ridges
trace a line almost exactly through the centre
of the major oceans.

Destruction of Ocean Plates

As the ocean plate sinks below the continental
plate some of the sediment on its surface is
scraped off and piled up on the landward side.
This sediment is later incorporated in a folded
mountain range which usually appears on the
edge of the continent, such as the Andes. Similarly, if two continents collide, the sediments
are squeezed up into new mountains.

Sea Floor Spreading

Reversals in the earth's magnetic field have
occurred throughout history. As new rock em-
erges at the ocean ridges it cools and is mag-
netised in the direction of the prevailing
magnetic field.

This Skylab satellite photograph of the Alice
Springs area shows that the Central Ranges form
an almost unbroken east-west belt more than
400 km long and at its maximum 160 km from
north to south. They fall into two geomorphological
divisions: the crystalline central ranges, including
the northern part of the Macdonnell; and the
parallel strike ridges of sandstone and limestone
folded into the southern extensions of the
Macdonnell Ranges form the original deposits
of the Amadeus Trough.

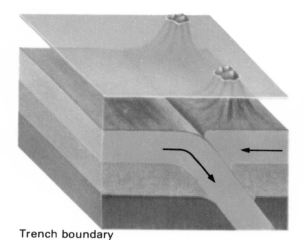

Trench boundary

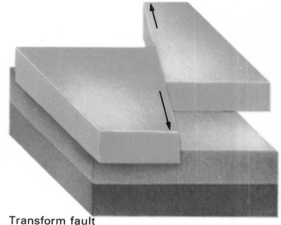

Transform fault

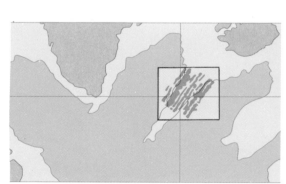

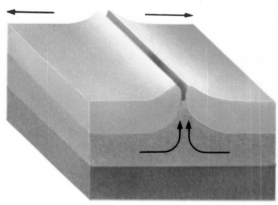

Destruction of ocean plates

Sea floor spreading

Ridge boundary

The Evolution of the Landscape

Australia is considered to be a very stable continent, relatively free from the earth movements which threaten other areas of the world. Some earth movements, however, may be occurring gradually as the surface agents of erosion and deposition create imbalances within the layers of the earth's crust. Before the origins of Australia's landforms can be fully understood, it is necessary first to consider certain aspects of the earth's structure.

The Structure of the Earth

The crust is the outer shell consisting of an upper layer of granitic rock termed *sial* from an abundance of silicon and aluminium. This layer is less dense than the underlying layer of basaltic rock, termed *sima* (silicon and magnesium), and so 'floats' in it. The sial is almost completely absent from ocean floors, but makes up the continental land masses. The crust varies in depth from about five to 80 km.

The bottom of the crust is separated from the denser mantle by a surface known as the *Mohorovicic discontinuity*, or *Moho*. The mantle layer is made up of ultrabasic rocks rich in iron-magnesium silicates. Although it appears that this layer is quite solid, it is capable of adjusting to disturbances in the pressure balance by a slow-flowing movement.

The core is the central zone, about 7000 km in diameter. There is evidence to suggest that the outer core is, at least, viscous, while the innermost core is a solid crystalline mass with rock three times as dense as that of the crust.

The Composition of the Earth

The earth, or *lithosphere*, comprises three main substances: elements, minerals and rocks. Although there are 91 natural elements, a mere eight of these comprise 98 per cent of the weight of the crust. Most minerals are a combination of two or more elements, and possess a fixed crystalline structure and chemical composition. The main rock-forming minerals are the feldspars, quartz and the ferromagnesian minerals.

Rocks are natural masses formed by the accumulation of various minerals. Depending on the way they have been formed, rocks can be classified into three main groups. *Igneous* rocks are formed by the solidification of molten magma caused by volcanic activity. Cooling beneath the surface produces *plutonic* or *hypabyssal* igneous rocks, while cooling on the surface results in *volcanic* igneous rocks. Igneous rocks which cool slowly (generally beneath the surface) exhibit large grains or crystals, while fast cooling produces a very fine-textured igneous rock.

Sedimentary rocks are formed when pre-existing rocks are broken down and redistributed by streams, wind, sea or gravity. They are usually set down in layers or beds. Sandstone, shale and mudstone are common examples of sedimentary rocks.

Metamorphic rocks are those igneous and sedimentary rocks that have undergone a change of state owing to heat, pressure and stress being applied.

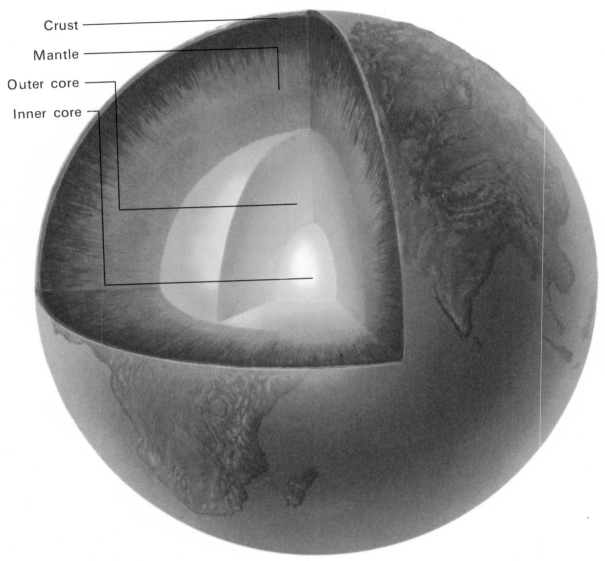

Crust
Mantle
Outer core
Inner core

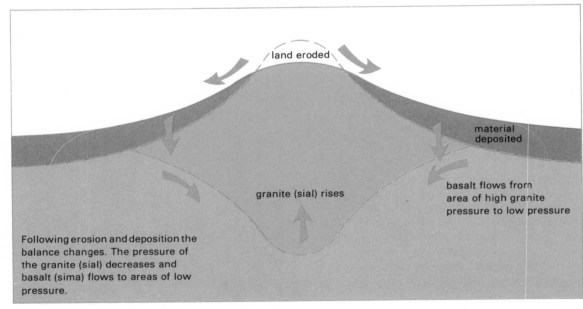

land eroded

material deposited

granite (sial) rises

basalt flows from area of high granite pressure to low pressure

Following erosion and deposition the balance changes. The pressure of the granite (sial) decreases and basalt (sima) flows to areas of low pressure.

MOST COMMON ELEMENTS IN THE CRUST

Element	Symbol	Atomic Weight	% by Weight
Oxygen	O	16.00	46.6
Silicon	SI	28.08	27.7
Aluminium	Al	26.97	8.1
Iron	Fe	55.85	5..0
Calcium	Ca	40.08	3.6
Sodium	Na	22.997	2.8
Potassium	K	39.096	2.6
Magnesium	Mg	24.32	2.1

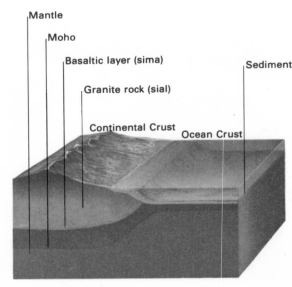

Mantle
Moho
Basaltic layer (sima)
Granite rock (sial)
Continental Crust
Ocean Crust
Sediment

Although the many different landform features seen today have been created by a variety of processes and forces over millions of years, the fact is that there has not been any significant loss or gain in the height of the surface above sea level, although particular areas have been built up or worn away. The earth's surface is therefore in a state of balance between two opposing sets of internal and external forces.

Internal Processes

These are concerned with changes in structural conditions by deformation.

Diastrophic movements are those which do not involve the flow of molten igneous material; they result in structural features called folds, faults and joints.

Folding occurs when wrinkles are produced in the rock by compressional forces, in the same way that a thin sheet of tin will bend when subjected to pressure.

Faulting in bedrock is produced when regional tension results in large-scale fractures with lateral or vertical displacement.

Joints are small fractures in the rock along which there has been no lateral or vertical movement. These can also be caused by large-scale cooling of the magma as it hardens into igneous rock.

Earthquakes are one of the common forms of diastrophic movements, although Australia is generally spared serious effects. Earthquakes are a series of rapid vibrations originating from the slipping or faulting of parts of the earth's crust, usually at depths varying from eight to 30 km, often occurring in areas of volcanic activity. Stresses build up until eventually part of the crust cracks and the two sides of the fault move, generating shock waves which travel outwards from the epicentre to the surface.

Vulcanism refers to all the processes whereby molten rock or magma moves upwards into the crust or spills out.

Sills and *dykes* are the most common forms of vulcanic intrusions, while the main extrusive features are the volcanic cones. The form of volcanoes varies considerably, according to the nature of the material emitted. If the lava is highly viscous the resultant form is a steep-sided mountain termed a *mamelon*. Fluid lava results in a flat, broad *lava dome*. Most cones are made up of alternate layers of lava and ash, hence the term *composite cone*. After the volcano has remained inactive for a period, a violent eruption may blow the top off the original cone, now termed a *caldera*.

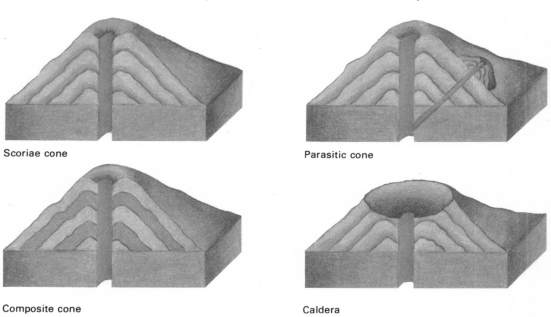

Mount Gambier crater lakes, South Australia. The crater rim was originally blown off by a volcanic eruption and has subsequently formed a crater lake. The depth of the blue lake (foreground) has not yet been determined. Part of the original crater rim can be seen on the top left.

Scoriae cone

Parasitic cone

Composite cone

Caldera

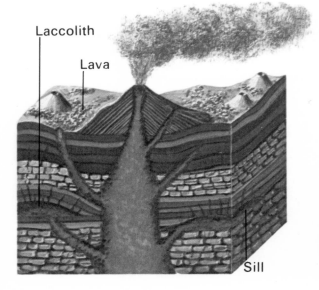

Laccolith

Lava

Sill

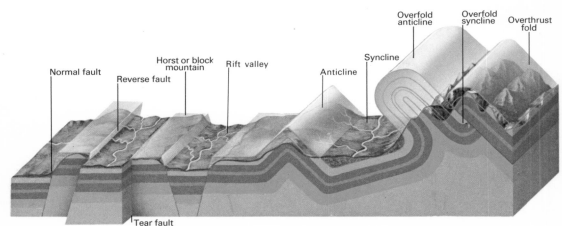

Normal fault

Reverse fault

Horst or block mountain

Rift valley

Tear fault

Anticline

Syncline

Overfold anticline

Overfold syncline

Overthrust fold

Shaping by External Forces

The surface agents of weathering, mass wasting, erosion and deposition balance the internal forces so that together they operate in a general state of equilibrium.

Rock *weathering*, or the disintegration or decomposition of rock *in situ*, generally speeds up the erosional processes as it renders the material more suitable for transporting. One of the more visible aspects of weathering is a feature termed *spheroidal* or 'onion' weathering.

Mass wasting generally refers to the movement downslope of soil or rock under its own weight, through the influence of gravity. In many cases water acts as a lubricating agent between the moving mass and the surface slope. Movements may be gradual or swift, in the form of a slump or landslide.

The erosional and depositional processes occurring on or near to the surface generally are determined by the actions of rivers, underground water, wind, waves and ice. All of these agents have influenced the current irregularities of the Australian landscape.

Rivers: Most Australian landforms have been determined by the action of rivers. If the underlying material is easily erodible and the landform steep, then rivers with a continuous supply of water over a small area will produce distinctive, deep narrow valleys. As rivers join together, the volume of water increases from a larger drainage area, so that they are capable of extending their valleys laterally and broadening their base. If the rivers are unable to carry the total load supplied to them by the agents of weathering and mass movements, then the material may be deposited in the form of a flood plain adjacent to the meandering river, or within the river in the form of islands or promontories of alluvium. If the depositional processes occur when the river meets a lake or the sea, deltas of various shapes and sizes will be created.

Underground Water: Of all the earth's water only one per cent is found on land. Of this one per cent almost 97 per cent is found beneath the surface. Most of this water derives from infiltration through the permeable soil and rocks and eventually finds its way back to the sea either by underground movement, or by running into surface streams and lakes.

In areas of extensive limestone deposits the dissolving action of underground water can create dramatic landforms, particularly if the limestone contains numerous fissures.

In certain areas particular geological formations are conducive to a special flow of ground water. If the permeable sandstone is capped by impermeable shale and the beds dip steeply away from the mountain intake zone, water will move through the sandstone by gravity. This structure is known as an artesian basin.

Onion weathering is the result of extreme daily temperature fluctuations.

The meandering Smithburne River carries its silt deposits to the Gulf of Carpentaria.

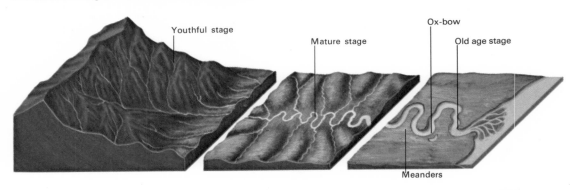
Youthful stage — Mature stage — Ox-bow — Old age stage — Meanders

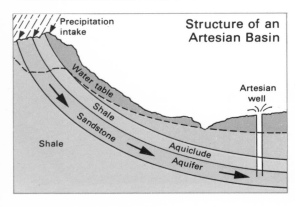
Structure of an Artesian Basin
Precipitation intake — Water table — Shale — Sandstone — Shale — Aquiclude — Aquifer — Artesian well

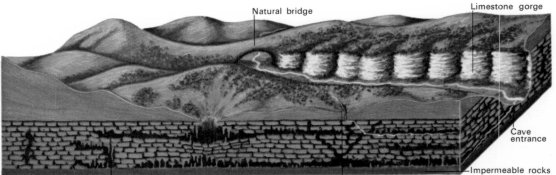
Natural bridge — Limestone gorge — Cave entrance — Impermeable rocks — Cave with stalactites and stalagmites — River disappears down swallow hole

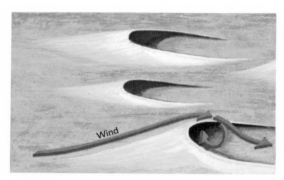

Wind: Wind is a significant sculptor of landforms in areas with a sparse vegetation cover. In these arid areas soils are not well developed, comprising an upper layer of fine, dry, sandy material. Winds are capable of removing this fine material, carrying it and depositing it where movement is obstructed, or where the wind is not strong enough to carry it further. In this process the sand particles themselves act as an abrasive agent, adding extra erosive power to the force of the wind. Many weird erosional shapes are produced, together with many forms of extensive sand dunes.

The constantly moving longitudinal sand dunes, Simpson Desert, Central Australia.

Above: Wave erosion has created the fascinating London Bridge formation which is found near the Twelve Apostles off the coast of Western Victoria.

Opposite: An aerial view of Barrenjoey and tombolo, New South Wales.

Waves: Together with wind, ocean currents and tides, waves produce the staggering variety of coastal erosional landforms seen around the Australian coastline. Cliffs, wave-cut platforms, natural arch bridges and stacks are some common examples. When the transporting power of currents and waves decreases, some of the material carried is deposited, causing beaches, bars and barriers to be built up, although the constituent sand grains change constantly. Any change in the force, direction, frequency and duration of wind and waves could increase erosive action and quickly eradicate the depositional landforms.

Ice: Although not present permanently today in Australia, rivers of ice or glaciers have left their imprint on the highland areas of southern Australia, particularly central Tasmania. As the glaciers moved downslope through gravity, they gouged out the existing landscape and carried the material with them as *moraines.* As they retreated upslope through melting, they created glacial erosional and depositional landform features.

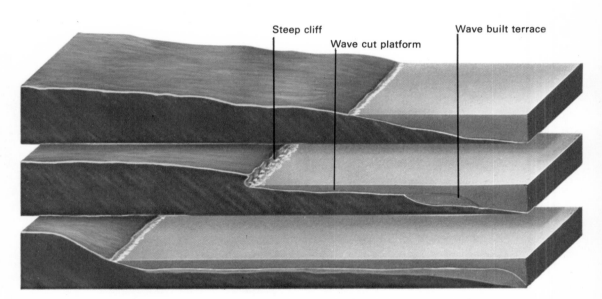

Steep cliff · Wave cut platform · Wave built terrace

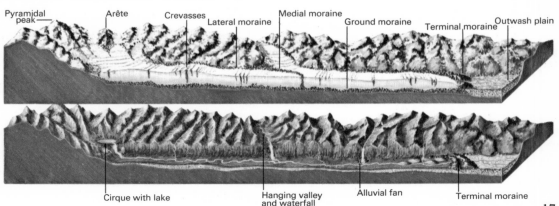

Pyramidal peak · Arête · Crevasses · Lateral moraine · Medial moraine · Ground moraine · Terminal moraine · Outwash plain

Cirque with lake · Hanging valley and waterfall · Alluvial fan · Terminal moraine

Australian Landform Structures

The Australian continent is made up of three major structures: the stable Western Shield; the gently-warped interior lowlands or Central Basin; and the Eastern Uplands.

The Western Shield

Nearly two-thirds of Australia is a plateau averaging between 300 and 600 metres high, but with smaller plateaux and ranges rising above the general level, and basins and troughs falling below it. This great plateau is in fact a complex of smaller units, but when regarded as a whole it constitutes the Pre-Cambrian Shield of the Australian continent. It is fundamentally composed of a basement complex of Archaean rocks, with some areas covered with younger rocks or extensive sand deposits.

The Central Basin

This region consists mainly of great sedimentary basins lying to the east of the Western Shield.

Great Artesian Basin: In this area, the Jurassic sandstones that crop out as intake beds in the north-east, pass beneath a thick cover of impervious Cretaceous claystones and Tertiary sands. The shallow folds have now been dissected into a landscape of rolling lowlands broken by tablelands and mesas. Nearly the whole area is less than 300 metres above sea level. In the area surrounding the Simpson Desert, gibber-strewn surfaces cover more than 160 000 km². Drainage in this area is directed to Lake Eyre. A combination of fine-textured alluvia, low slopes and irregular discharge of rivers, has produced many discontinuous trunk channels characteristic of the 'Channel Country' of south-western Queensland.

Riverine Plains: The riverine plains of the Murray-Darling system in the south are a composite alluvial fan sloping very gently from the points of entry of larger rivers of the Eastern Uplands. The many meandering channels of today are superimposed across the patterns of an earlier system of streams.

The Eastern Uplands

The Eastern Uplands consist of a broad belt of varied width extending from Cape York to Tasmania, and made up largely of tablelands, ranges and ridges with only limited mountain areas above 1000 metres. The highest summits are in the Snowy Mountains and Victorian Alps with slightly lower plateaux in New England and Tasmania.

Throughout this area a great variety of rocks of all ages is present and the geological structure is very complex. The older rocks are extensively mineralised. Most of the coal in Australia is found in or on the flanks of the highlands while the main hydro-electric schemes are of necessity also located in this region. The Main Divide separates the shorter, swifter-flowing rivers to the east coast from the internal drainage areas to the west, and those of the Murray-Darling system.

One of the uniting features of this region is the volcanic activity associated with Tertiary uplift. Basalt lava sheets form plateaux and upland plains from Queensland to western Victoria.

Folded mountains, western Macdonnell Ranges near Jay Creek Station, NT

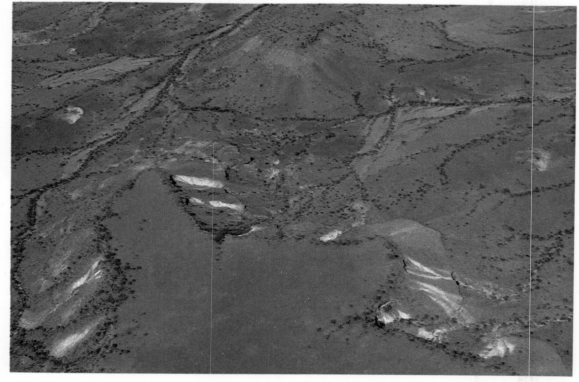

Above: Channel country, western Queensland
Below: The Black Hills, south of Alice Springs

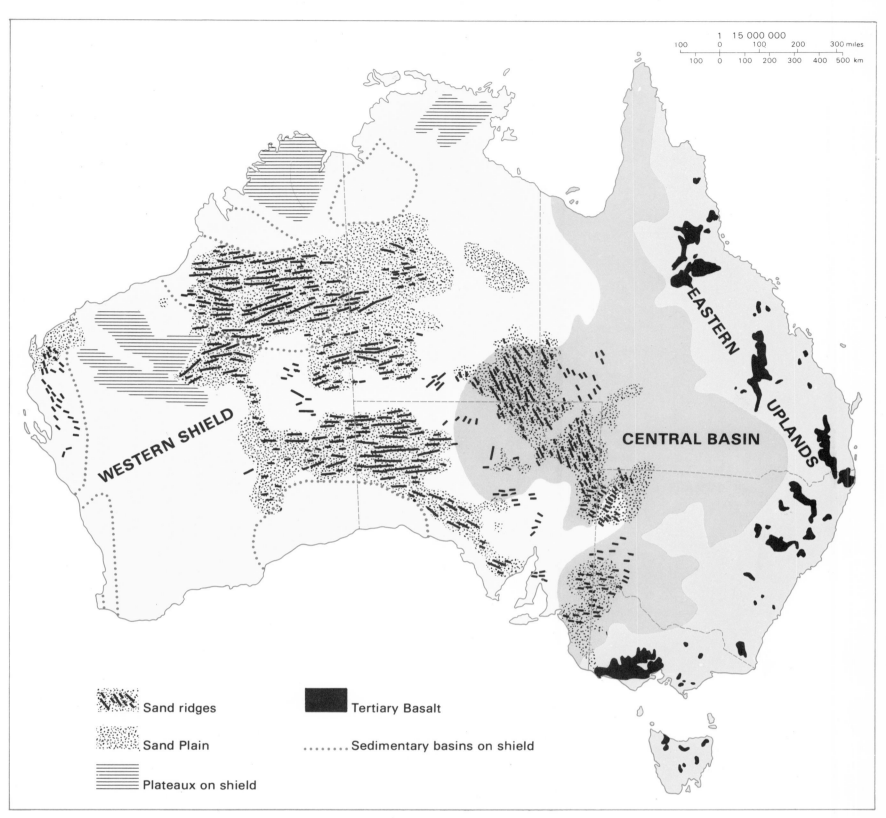

1 15 000 000

WESTERN SHIELD

CENTRAL BASIN

EASTERN UPLANDS

Sand ridges

Sand Plain

Plateaux on shield

Tertiary Basalt

.... Sedimentary basins on shield

Thredbo glacial valley, Snowy Mountains, NSW

Volcanic plugs, Glasshouse Mountains, S.E. Queensland

Australia's Geological Ages

Era	Period	Absolute Years	Major Geological and Geographical Events	Life Forms	
C A I N O Z O I C	RECENT	10 Thousand	The sea rises and falls several times, causing erosion along the coastal areas. Volcanoes are active in eastern Aust. Minor changes on the land through stream and wind erosion.	Development of present-day animals and man.	Squatting Man
	PLEIS-TOCENE	2 Million	Spread of glaciation, especially extensive in Tasmania and south-eastern Aust. Lakes and large rivers cover the centre of the continent. Some volcanic activity on the east.	Development of man. Giant kangaroos and wombats wander extensively prior to their extinction.	**AGE OF MAN**
T E R T I A R Y	PLIOCENE	8 Million	Uplifting of the Eastern Highlands and Western Plateau.	Early evolution of man. Dominance of large carnivores. Open forests spread. Marsupials and birds continue to develop.	Man Ape
	MIOCENE	25 Million	Volcanic activity widespread along the eastern coast. In the south and west the seas encroach several times. The land bridge with New Guinea disappears beneath the sea.	Rainforests, both tropical and temperate, flourish along the east coast. Mammals become dominant living creatures.	
	OLIGOCENE	40 Million	Some volcanic activity is spread throughout the south and east.	Marsupials continue to evolve. Long-legged wading birds develop. Flowering plants abound.	Diprotodon
	EOCENE	60 Million	A great deal of the land surface has now been levelled. Shallow seas in the Carnarvon area of WA.	Dinosaurs become extinct. Mammals evolve, especially marsupials. Grasses spread.	**AGE OF MAMMALS**
M E S O Z O I C	CRETA-CEOUS	135 Million	Much of the continent sinks gently. Inland seas cover the area between the Great Dividing Range and the Western Plateau. When the sea eventually retreats, swamps remain.	Flowering plants grow for the first time in Aust.	Banksia
	JURASSIC	185 Million	The sea returns over part of WA and deposits sediments of sandstone, shale and limestone.	Dinosaurs at their peak. First primitive birds evolve.	
	TRIASSIC	225 Million	Aust. possibly starts to break away from other land masses such as Asia. This process is completed in the Miocene epoch.	First dinosaurs. First primitive mammals. Reptiles now abound. Australian insects become varied.	Tyrannosaurus **AGE OF REPTILES**
P A L A E O Z O I C	PERMIAN	270 Million	The Ice Age continues. Glaciers spread over a large area. Shallow seas are formed by melting ice. Coal deposits are formed in Qld, NSW and WA. Aust. probably still connected to Asia.	Trilobites become extinct. Palm-like cycads form. Spread of insects and amphibians.	Amphicentrum
	CARBON-IFEROUS	345 Million	Extensive earth movements insert granitic rock. Seas cover north-east NSW and east Qld. An Ice Age begins.	Abundant insects. New forms of amphibians evolve. Widespread forests of tall land plants.	Eogyrinus **AGE OF AMPHIBIANS**
	DEVONIAN	400 Million	Volcanic activity. Shallow seas in the east lay down limestone deposits in Qld, NSW and Victoria. Most of the west and centre is now dry.	First amphibians. Many corals. Plant life becomes more complex.	Osteolepis
	SILURIAN	440 Million	Seas cover Qld, NSW and Victoria. Coral reefs build up extensive limestone deposits. Earth movements produce intensive folding.	First land plants appear and air-breathing animals commence. Primitive fishes and brachiopods abundant.	Brachiopod **AGE OF FISHES**
	ORDOVICIAN	500 Million	Extensive seas, deep in the east and shallow in the centre. First major palaeozoic mountain building and volcanic activity begins.	Life only in the seas. Graptolites, the possible forerunners of vertebrates, abound. Spread of molluscs. Culmination of trilobites.	
	CAMBRIAN	600 Million	Shallow seas cover north-west Qld and NT. Deeper seas cover NSW, Victoria and Tasmania.	Life still restricted to the sea. Trilobites predominant with many marine invertebrates.	Trilobite **AGE OF MARINE INVERTEBRATES**
PRE-CAMBRIAN			The surface forms a vast barren landscape of mountains, deserts and lava flows. Rocks of this period are found throughout Aust. except for Victoria.	Seaweeds and soft-bodied invertebrates originate in the warm seas. Few fossils known.	Dickinsonia Worm

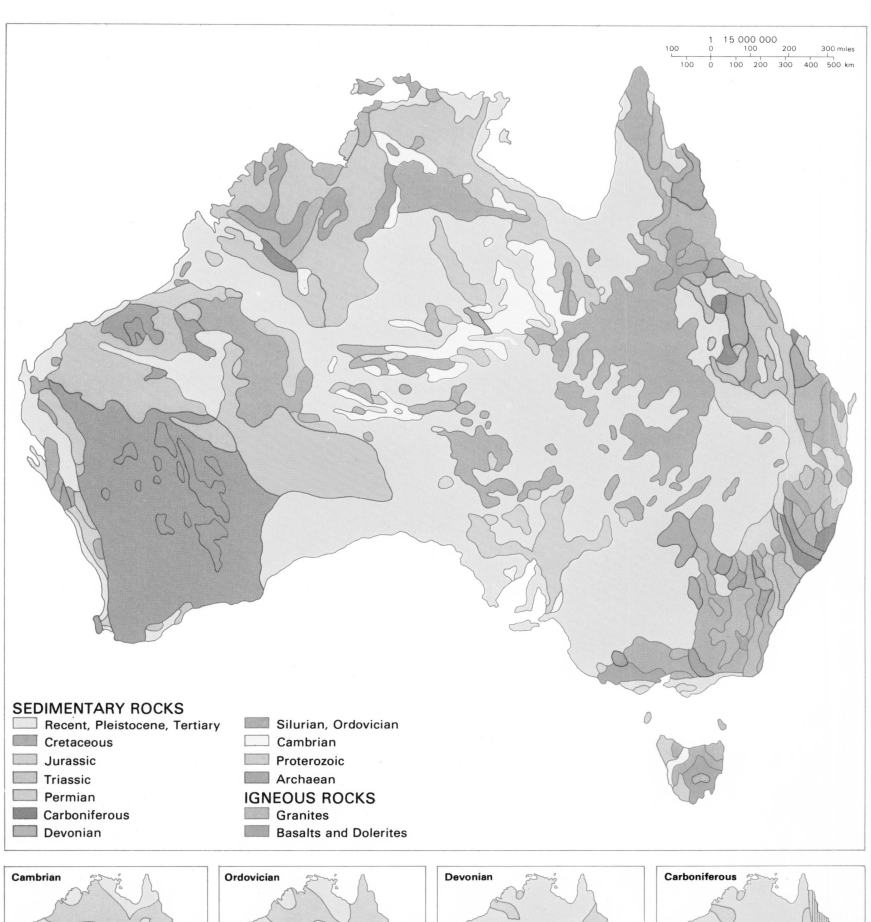

SEDIMENTARY ROCKS

- Recent, Pleistocene, Tertiary
- Cretaceous
- Jurassic
- Triassic
- Permian
- Carboniferous
- Devonian
- Silurian, Ordovician
- Cambrian
- Proterozoic
- Archaean

IGNEOUS ROCKS

- Granites
- Basalts and Dolerites

1   15 000 000

100   0   100   200   300 miles
100   0   100   200   300   400   500 km

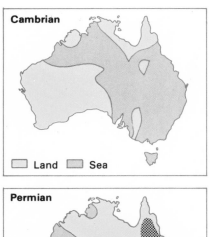

Cambrian

☐ Land ☐ Sea

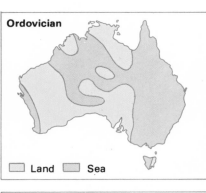

Ordovician

☐ Land ☐ Sea

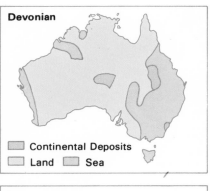

Devonian

☐ Continental Deposits
☐ Land ☐ Sea

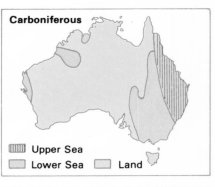

Carboniferous

☐ Upper Sea
☐ Lower Sea ☐ Land

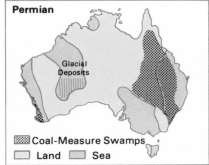

Permian

Glacial Deposits

☒ Coal-Measure Swamps
☐ Land ☐ Sea

Jurassic

☐ Continental Deposits
☐ Land ☐ Sea

Cretaceous

☐ Continental Deposits
☐ Land ☐ Sea

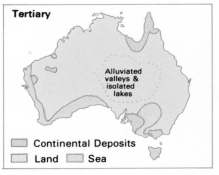

Tertiary

Alluviated valleys & isolated lakes

☐ Continental Deposits
☐ Land ☐ Sea

Prehistoric Australia

Australian prehistory has a fresh excitement. Recent finds have placed human habitation of the oldest continent as far back as 38 000 BP (Before Present), double some previous estimates. This evidence of 'modern man' — *Homo sapiens* — now compares with the earliest finds known around the world.

Many of the theories about Australia's prehistory have been reshaped by discoveries around the arid Lake Mungo region in southwest New South Wales. This ancient lake bed with its bizarre eroded landforms was best known as a local tourist attraction until 1968, when a scientist seeking information on the Australian ice ages found bones uncovered by erosion in wind-sculpted sand dunes — 'The Walls of China' — north-east of the lake.

They proved to be the broken skull of an Aboriginal woman — and 26 000 years old. The find proved to be of world significance because it was the oldest evidence in the world of a ritual cremation.

As more scientists excavated near Lake Mungo, equally rewarding discoveries were made. Another burial also dated to around 26 000 BP — and the bones were covered with ochre, earth pigments still used by Aborigines for decoration and painting. Combined with other data, this burial suggests the early Australians practised 'art' as early as any known European stone age cave painter.

Evidence has been slowly accumulated to outline how the Aborigines exploited the food sources around (and in) Lake Mungo before climate changes dried it up some 16 000 years ago. The lake yielded them fish and shellfish. Game abounded, especially the marsupials that still highlight Australian wildlife. Here is the oldest known proof of humans eating shellfish: heaps of mussels found next to hearths 36 000 years old.

Discoveries of grinding stones dated to the period when the lake was drying up support suggestions that Aborigines obtained grain from wild grasses as early as any other known 'modern man'.

If Lake Mungo has revealed facts about 'modern man', another recent investigation around Kow Swamp near the Murray River in northern Victoria has posed questions yet to be answered.

The skulls of 30 individuals found there have archaic features typical of a form of primitive man — *Homo erectus*. Yet these late Pleistocene remains date to as recently as 10 000 years ago.

As yet there is insufficient evidence to determine whether 'modern' and 'primitive' man co-existed in Australia for tens of thousands of years, or whether the groups derived from the same founding population.

A Killing of Giants

Experts have long assumed that the extinct giant fauna of Australia was hunted by man. Man — and the introduced dingo — are often blamed for contributing to this extinction. Not until recently did the first evidence of giant fauna being killed by humans in large numbers emerge, at a bone site at Lancefield in Victoria which was first noted in the 1840s by an early European settler digging a well.

Two metres beneath swampy ground lies a mass of bones, about 90 per cent of them from *Macropus titans*, an extinct giant kangaroo one-third as large again as modern kangaroos. With the bones is a large stone knife. Perhaps 1000 animals were killed in this swamp edge around 25 000 years ago.

Another notable recent 'special purpose' site was the flint mine discovered at Koonalda cave near the coast east of Eucla on the Great Australian Bight.

Tracks From the Past

Although the most exciting recent work in Australian prehistory has involved man, scientists have continued to expand the body of knowledge on other early life forms.

In 1971, for example, a university botanical expedition into the remote Genoa River gorge in eastern Victoria yielded what is believed to be 'footprints' as old as any in the world.

Preserved in sandstone were three sets of trackways made some 350 million years ago by amphibians believed to be among the earliest recorded land vertebrates (backboned animals). They are thought to have been made by animals similar to the genus *Ichthyostega* (found only in Greenland) and ranging in length from about 550 to 900 mm.

Below: The ancient beaches of the now waterless Lake Mungo, where erosion has revealed many exciting archaeological finds in recent years.

Opposite: An anthropologist studies the skull of an early Australian modern man, which dates back to 26 000 BP.

Australia's Fossil History

Fossils from before Cambrian times are rare anywhere. Australia is fortunate in having some remarkable 'jellyfish' fossils from the Pre-Cambrian, about 600 million years old. Since geologist Mr Reg Sprigg discovered the first of them in the Ediacara Range in South Australia in 1946, more than 1500 specimens have been collected and 25 species described, some with no resemblance to anything noted before.

Cambrian rocks are rich in fossils. Australia has possibly the best known examples of the interesting Archaeocyatha group, cone-shaped creatures which grew from the sea floor.

From the Palaeozoic Era, Australian fossils of significance include the graptolites found in great numbers and variety in Victoria, and the crocodile-like Triassic amphibian *Paracyclotosaurus davidi* discovered at St Peter's in New South Wales in 1910.

Australia had its dinosaurs during the Mesozoic Era, the Age of Reptiles. The largest plant-eating Australian dinosaurs *Rhaetosaurus* and *Austrosaurus*, were about 15 metres long, less impressive sizes than the North American giants.

Giant Australian swimming reptiles included the plesiosaur *Kronosaurus queenslandicus* (which grew more than 13 metres long) and *Ichthyosaurus australis* (six metres).

Mammals and Birds

Australia is famous for its variety of marsupials: the pouched mammals of past ages were even more remarkable, being in many cases far larger than their descendants.

Largest of all known marsupials was the extinct *Diprotodon optatum*, named in 1830 but known only by tantalising bone fragments until dozens of skeletons were found almost intact in 1892 in the dry bed of Lake Callabonna in South Australia. This animal was the size of a rhinoceros and weighed possibly two tonnes: other diprotodons were as small as a calf.

Other spectacular extinct creatures included the giant goanna *Megalania*, perhaps seven or more metres long; the flightless bird *Genyornis*, little taller than an emu but probably around four times its weight; a large ancestor of the echidna, and the intriguing 'pouched lion', *Thylacoleo*, whose distinctive teeth still puzzle scientists. Two pairs of wide side teeth (each up to 60 mm long) apparently acted as shears, although it is disputed whether *Thylacoleo* was a carnivore or herbivore.

The giant wombat *Phascolonus gigas* stood almost a metre high. Several huge kangaroos were significantly larger than today's kangaroos, the largest being *Procoptodon* standing about three metres tall and weighing possibly four times as much as the largest present kangaroo.

The fossil record has many gaps and innumerable questions remain. One of the most persistent queries is how much man contributed to the extinction of the giant fauna in relatively recent times.

Opposite: Stone tools found at Lake Mungo include grinding stones dating back to the period when Lake Mungo was filled with water.

Australia's Water Resources

Australia's water resources are puny by most world standards. 'Making the most of our water' has long been a national catchcry — especially from rural politicians.

One result has been that Australia currently has 48 dams and reservoirs with capacities of at least 100 million cubic metres. Lake Argyle, storage for the $100 million-plus Ord River project in Western Australia, is currently the largest storage with a gross capacity of 5679 million cubic metres. Next are Lake Eucumbene (4798 million cubic metres), heart of the $800 million Snowy Mountains Hydro-Electric Scheme in New South Wales, and Lake Eildon (3392 million cubic metres) in Victoria. Tasmania's Lake Gordon will eventually impound 11 728 million cubic metres.

But there are practical and economic limits to the building of such huge storages. In highly-populated south-eastern Australia, for example, development of surface water in some areas has already reached around 60 per cent of the total resources, close to the feasible limit.

In addition, the days of unquestioned grandiose water storage proposals are probably over. The familiar response to the problem — 'bigger and better dams' — and other long-standing assumptions about water conservation are under increasing public scrutiny. 'Damning dams' has become respectable, whether on economic or environmental grounds. Although a national outcry failed to 'Save Lake Pedder' from submersion in the name of Tasmanian hydro-electric power, other storage proposals have been defeated or modified by community pressure.

Water Sources

Australia's location in the 'dry. latitudes', together with the absence of significant mountains, is largely responsible for the continent having easily the lowest average annual rainfall of the inhabited continents. Very high evaporation rates and the lack of permanent snowfields compound the water shortage.

Australia's average rainfall is only 470 mm compared with the average 720 mm falling on the world's land surfaces, while the annual flow of all Australian rivers (345 374 million cubic metres, around 10 per cent of rainfall) represents a depth of water over the continent of only 60 mm, about one-fifth the average for the other continents. The annual discharge of Australia's largest river, the Murray, is reached in nine days by the Mississippi and only one and a half days by the Amazon.

A third of Australia has no rivers. River flows vary greatly, especially in the north where rivers carrying 30 000 cubic metres a second in flood may disappear entirely in the dry season.

Water drawn from underground provides about 20 per cent of the national water supply and is more important than surface water over 60 per cent of the country. These artesian waters, often too mineralised for irrigation or human consumption, are usually suitable for stock.

Eildon Reservoir, east-central Victoria. The Goulburn River has been regulated by Lake Eildon to provide irrigation for 145 000 hectares to the north-east.

Largest of the twelve major water-bearing basins is the Great Artesian Basin lying under almost a quarter of Australia. Some 6000 bores tap it: for almost a century it has yielded about 600 million cubic metres of low-salinity groundwater annually.

Some good quality groundwater is available, primarily near the higher rainfall areas of the east, but intense use in some regions has already made it necessary artificially to recharge depleted aquifers, notably in the Burdekin Delta whose waters are drawn on for sugar cane irrigation.

Water Uses

The long battle to 'droughtproof' Australian towns and cities is not yet finally won, although the days of restrictions on domestic water supply to the major cities are disappearing. Melbourne, for example, experienced its last significant water restrictions in 1972-73.

Irrigation is an important element of the rural scene, with some 1 600 000 hectares under irrigation, about two-thirds of them along the Murray and its tributaries.

Hydro-electricity provides about one-fifth of national annual electricity consumption, exceeding 65 million kWh. Tasmania contributes about half the hydro-electricity, thanks to the abundant and reliable rainfall which makes it the only State able to operate hydro-electric plants continuously. The Snowy Mountains Hydro-Electricity Scheme, a quarter century in the making, is the nation's greatest engineering feat. Completed in 1974 at a cost of $800 million, it has seven power stations, a pumping station, 16 large and many smaller dams, over 145 km of tunnels and 80 km of aqueducts. Total generating capacity is about 4000 MW and it also provides about 2344 million cubic metres of additional water annually for irrigation by diverting water inland from coastal watersheds to the Murray and Murrumbidgee rivers.

Artesian supplies are being increasingly exploited for town water needs and sometimes irrigation, but the most widespread use is for stock watering. Much of the nation's pastoral industry is dependent on artesian bores.

Problems

Water quality and quantity are affected by many things beyond rainfall. Within only seven years of European settlement in Australia the authorities had to issue proclamations forbidding pollution of the Tank Stream — Sydney's major water supply. Pollution continues to affect some surface waters and this often extends to groundwater supplies. Sewage, industrial and agricultural effluents and mining wastes are frequent pollutants.

Artesian waters are not inexhaustible. Reductions of flow in some basins have caused concern since the turn of the century and there are now strict controls and licensing restrictions to lessen wastage of bore water.

Equally disturbing is the incidence of salinity in groundwater and surface supplies that has resulted from expanding agricultural and irrigation schemes. In south-western Australia around 4 million hectares of land have been made sterile and difficult to till because removal of the natural vegetation caused the water table to rise, and high-salinity groundwater has affected both soil and surface water. Some urban water storages have been threatened.

A similar danger faces the Murray Valley basin in south-east Australia. Heavy flood irrigation and vegetation removal have combined to harm soil and surface water. In Victoria alone an estimated 30 000 hectares of valuable land have been laid waste. The increasing salinity of the Murray causes great concern: salt content in its upper reaches is less than 30 milligrams per litre total dissolved solids, yet during the 1967-68 drought the salt content downstream in South Australia exceeded 600 milligrams per litre. Current Victorian proposals to start correcting the salinity may cost an initial $40 million. These include pumping saline water to drying pans, and increasing the number of trees (especially the river red gum, *Eucalyptus camaldulensis*) fivefold.

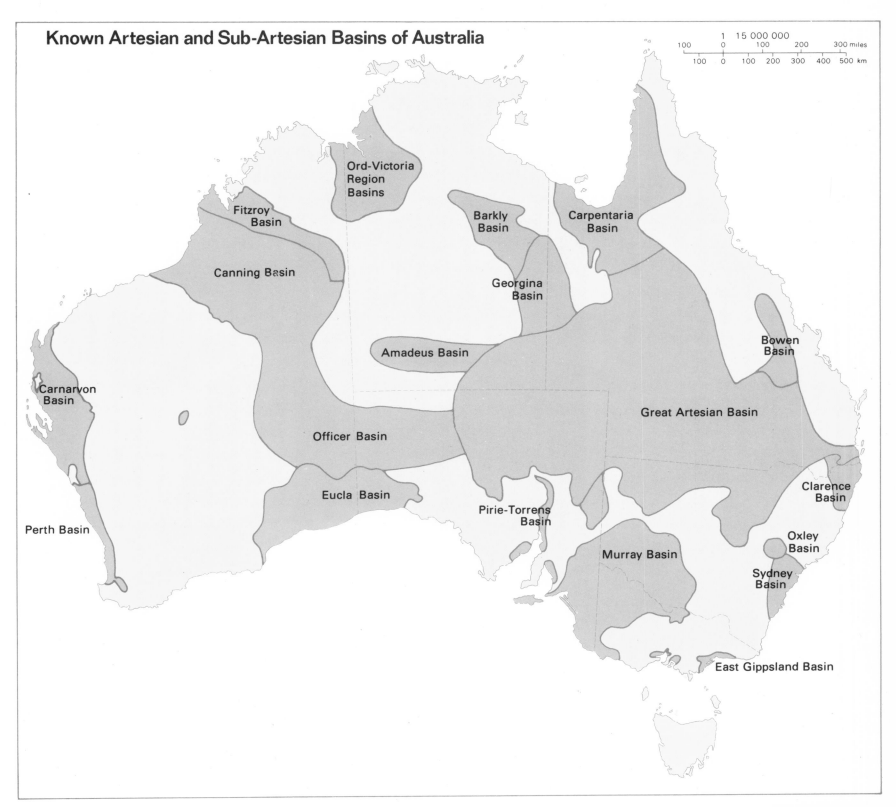

Known Artesian and Sub-Artesian Basins of Australia

1 15 000 000

100   100   200   300 miles
0
100   0   100   200   300   400   500 km

Ord-Victoria
Region
Basins

Fitzroy
Basin

Barkly
Basin

Carpentaria
Basin

Canning Basin

Georgina
Basin

Bowen
Basin

Amadeus Basin

Carnarvon
Basin

Great Artesian Basin

Officer Basin

Clarence
Basin

Eucla Basin

Pirie-Torrens
Basin

Oxley
Basin

Perth Basin

Murray Basin

Sydney
Basin

East Gippsland Basin

The Future

The national agency charged with investigating the quantity and quality of water resources through the co-operation of State and Federal authorities is the Australian Water Resources Council. The problems are complex and the solutions certain to be costly: some of the most useful answers appear to lie in the fields of more efficient management and public awareness of water conservation, rather than in expensive additional storages, the contentious possible benefits of cloud-seeding or such Space Age techniques as nuclear desalination of seawater.

A vertical infra-red photograph of irrigated vineyards near Berri, South Australia. The vegetation (leaves) can be identified by the shades of red. The areas that are patchy indicate the effects of inadequate irrigation techniques resulting in salt accumulations on the surface. Salination is a problem where evaporation is high and the water is spread by shallow gravity flows through the fields.

Irrigating a Dry Continent

Irrigation has remained something of a national article of faith since the Canadian-born Chaffey brothers drew on their Californian experiences to pioneer irrigation in Australia in 1866.

Irrigation has brought immense benefits to Australia. Yet the Chaffeys' bold venture on a run-down cattle station on the Victorian side of the Murray River at Mildura ended in their bankruptcy in 1895. Mildura endured — and now thrives as the centre of national dried fruit production — but after almost a century, irrigation is not without its troubles.

Problems of orderly marketing of the produce grown on irrigated land recur, and a traditional market shrank with Britain's entry into the Common Market. Salinity in various forms endangers some areas, and the costs of combating it will be formidable.

On the ambitious Ord River project in remote north-west Western Australia, the first large-scale attempt at tropical irrigation, the problems have so far outweighed the profits. Cotton growing has been abandoned, while the search continues for crops with sufficient return to overcome high transport costs and the hazards of insect and bird pests.

Australia now has around 1 475 000 hectares under irrigation, comprising (rounded figures) New South Wales 602 000 hectares; Victoria 557 000; Queensland 186 000; South Australia 78 000; Western Australia 28 000; Tasmania 22 000; Northern Territory 900 and Australian Capital Territory 200. Water is supplied for orchards, vineyards, pastures, vegetables, fodder and grain crops, and for domestic and stock purposes. In Victoria alone, the value of irrigation production exceeds $250 million annually.

Irrigation Methods

Flood irrigatiom is by far the most dominant form of irrigation in Australia. Other techniques are spray, furrow and trickle (drip) irrigation.

Flood irrigation is used to inundate bays of farmland, especially for pastures and rice (which has been grown since 1924 in the Murrumbidgee Irrigation Area of New South Wales). Wheat and millet are among other crops flood irrigated.

Furrow irrigation — a form of flood irrigation — is employed for vegetables and row crops, particularly tomatoes and cotton. Spray irrigation is usually used when water is pumped direct from rivers: it *must* be used over uneven ground or on sandy soils. Most citrus growers use spray irrigation and it is also commonly employed for vegetables and pastures. One sidelight of the widespread salinity problem is that some citrus growers have been forced to instal under-tree sprinklers to prevent defoliation caused by overhead sprinkling of saline water.

Murray River Valley Irrigation

About two-thirds of Australia's irrigated land is in south-east Australia, along the Murray River and its tributaries. The Murray forms the largest part of the New South Wales-Victorian border before it passes into South Australia.

Large storages on the upper reaches of the Murray, Murrumbidgee, Lachlan and Goulburn Rivers store more than nine km³ of

water for irrigation areas: an additional annual average 2.3 km³ is diverted inland to the Murray and Murrumbidgee by the Snowy Mountains Scheme, enough to irrigate an extra 2600 km² and increase productivity by around $60 million.

Generally in the upper reaches of the rivers water is tapped by weirs and gravity canals: lower down it is usually pumped out.

The irrigation season usually runs from September to April. Canneries at Shepparton in Victoria and Leeton in New South Wales process much of the fruit and vegetables. Canned fruit remains a significant export item. In South Australia, Berri and Waikerie are noted for citrus production. The Murray Valley area yields large amounts of rice, fruit, vegetables, fodder crops and wheat, wine, fat lambs, wool and dairy products from irrigated pastures.

The Ord: Expensive Experiment?

The spectacular Ord River project, conceived when 'develop the North' was a virtually unquestioned slogan, has yet to prove its economic worth. The first major tropical irrigation scheme opened for significant development with the completion in 1971 of the Lake Argyle storage, currently the nation's largest storage with a gross capacity of 5.7 km³. Federal and State spending on capital works exceeds $50 million and the project has the potential to irrigate 80 000 hectares of alluvial land east of the Kimberleys.

Until 1975 commercial agriculture production on the Ord had been almost exclusively cotton, which required large amounts of costly nitrogenous fertilisers, and pesticides to combat serious insect plagues. These factors, combined with the steep transport costs for a venture more than 2200 km from the nearest capital, Perth, forced abandonment of

cotton growing following the 1974 crop.

Currently there are 23 Ord farms with commercial production on only an estimated 2900 hectares, comprising grain sorghum (2420 hectares), rice (280), wheat (80) and peanuts (120). Future expansion will depend on scientists identifying crops with sufficient return to cover high freight charges, and not requiring excessive amounts of fertiliser or pesticide.

Research is now oriented towards assessing new varieties of sorghum and rice, sugar cane, grain legumes such as sorghum, chick peas and mung beans, and fibrous plants like kenaf used for making paper pulp, with by-products suitable for stock feed.

Other Irrigation Areas

In northern New South Wales the Keepit dam in the Namoi Valley provides irrigation for the Wee Waa-Narrabri district, Australia's most important cotton region, producing more than 100 000 bales annually.

About a third of Queensland's irrigated land grows sugar cane. Unlike other States, most water is pumped privately from rivers or underground sources.

Western Australia has more than 12 000 hectares of irrigated land in the coastal plain south of Perth, fed from dams in the nearby Darling Range. At Carnarvon 146 plantations draw water from the Gascoyne River.

Tasmania's abundant and reliable rainfall meant that the island had few irrigated areas until recent years. Spray irrigation has come into increasing use, and private pumping from streams accounts for most needs.

Above: Lake Argyle, part of the controversial Ord River Scheme, is the largest man-made lake in Australia.

Opposite: Irrigated strip pasture and the River Murray, near Mannum, South Australia.

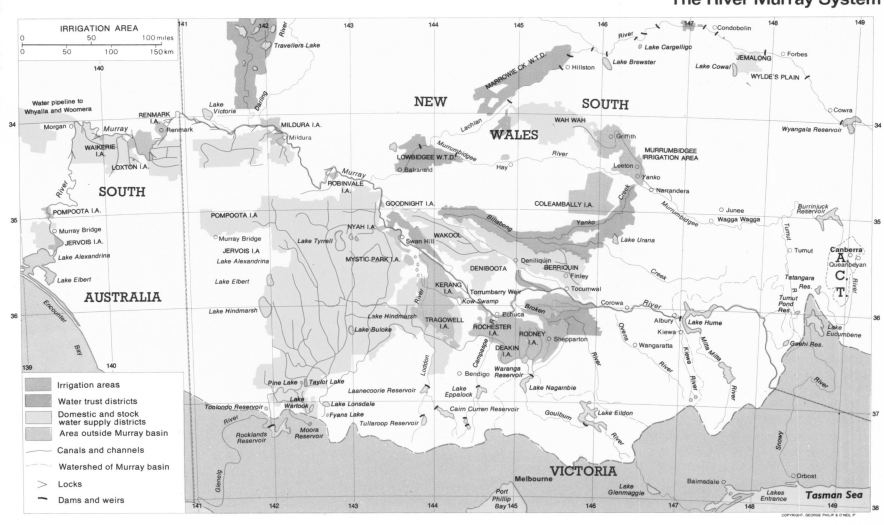

IRRIGATION AREA

0	50	100 miles	
0	50	100	150 km

Irrigation areas
Water trust districts
Domestic and stock
water supply districts
Area outside Murray basin
Canals and channels
Watershed of Murray basin
Locks
Dams and weirs

Climate and Weather Patterns

Australia's climate encourages suntans and grim jokes, not widespread human settlement. One-third of this driest of inhabited continents is desert, while another third is suitable only for grazing relatively small numbers of animals over huge areas.

To visitors from kinder climates, the seasons turn slowly, while contrast and caprice characterise the weather. The images of climate are often those of disaster: drought, floods, cyclones, and, always, heat. Cities of millions sometimes find their water supplies threatened. For three-quarters of Australia, evaporation loss exceeds rainfall in all months.

Rainfall Patterns

Fifty per cent of Australia has an annual median rainfall below 300 mm. Eighty per cent receives less than 600 mm.

Almost all Australians live along the relatively well-watered coastal fringes, especially the eastern 'fertile crescent' where the continent's only significant mountain range encourages regular rainfall. The general aridity means that Australia supports 14 000 000 people over a land mass approximating that of the USA with its population exceeding 210 000 000.

The dominant cause of this aridity is the continent's position on planet Earth, astride latitude 30°S. All the world's hot deserts lie on the 30s, the 'dry latitudes' where subtropical high pressure systems (anticyclones) prevail. Australia is also unfortunate in being the flattest continent — average elevation under 300 metres — with only the modest Eastern Highlands able to trap rain from the weather systems crossing their path. Although heat discomfort is significant over most of Australia, the continent's low relief and the moderating effects of surrounding oceans mean that low temperatures are not as extreme as in other continents.

During the winter (May-October) period, high pressure systems dominate the central and northern parts of Australia. Northern Australia is affected by mild, dry south-east trade winds and southern Australia by cool, moist westerlies associated with the Sub-Polar low pressure belt. Outbreaks of cold weather typically occur in southern Australia when intense depressions over the Southern Ocean force cold air northwards.

The summer period (November-April) sees the anticyclones taking a more southerly path from west to east, resulting in general easterly winds over the continent. Heat waves occur when an anticyclone's eastward movement is blocked and winds subsequently back northerly. Northern Australia has a monsoon season (the 'Wet') between November and April, resulting from an indraught of moist air.

Tropical cyclones (hurricanes) are random summer hazards between November and April. On average about three Coral Sea cyclones affect the Queensland coast each year while around two affect north-western Australia.

Erratic Rainfall

Australia's significant rainfall is concentrated on its east, south and north fringes with the Eastern Highlands being responsible for the heaviest regular falls. North Queensland's east coast averages around 4400 mm annually. Another very wet region is western Tasmania, with more than 2500 mm a year.

The nation's driest area comprises some 180 000 km² around Lake Eyre in South Australia, with annual rainfall averaging 130 mm. This is the forbidding zone of salt 'lakes' that may fill once in a lifetime with cyclonic rains that have drained across half a continent.

If scarcity of rainfall is the greatest check on agricultural and pastoral expansion, the general unreliability of rainfall is almost as inhibiting. Reasonably reliable rainfall is encountered only in restricted areas of southern Australia — southern Victoria, Tasmania and south-west Western Australia. Generations of Australians have complained of too many droughts broken by too many floods. Between 1864 and 1973 eight major droughts affected the greater part of Australia and at least seven other lesser droughts afflicted wide areas.

The rainfall variability over four-fifths of Australia is above the world average for comparable rainfall totals. An extreme example of erratic rainfall caused by Australia's variable weather is Onslow in Western Australia, where rain from tropical cyclones contributes randomly to wild fluctuations. Onslow's recorded annual rainfall totals range between 15 mm in 1912 to 1085 mm in 1961, while between 1921-24 its totals were successively 566, 69, 682 and 55 mm.

Even in heavy rainfall areas there may be great variability. Queensland's Tully, which has Australia's highest median rainfall (4400 mm), has had annual rainfalls as high as 7899 in 1950 and as low as 2489 mm in 1961.

Over most of Australia there are less than 50 rain-days a year when rainfall reaches 0.25 mm or more. Central Australia has less than 25 rain-days annually, while rain-day frequencies of 150 and above are known only in Tasmania, southern Victoria, areas along Queensland's north coast and in the extreme south-west of Western Australia.

Australia's record 24-hour rainfall of 907 mm occurred at Crohamhurst in Queensland on 3 February 1893.

Temperature

Australia lies between latitudes 10-40°S with more than half of Queensland, 40 per cent of Western Australia and 80 per cent of the Northern Territory in the tropics. The remaining 60 per cent of Australia is in the temperate zone.

Hot weather prevails generally. Average annual temperatures vary from around 27°C in the far north to 13°C in the far south. January (summer) and July (winter) average temperatures range from 29°C and 24°C in the north to 18°C and 10°C in the south. Average daily hours of sunshine in the major cities are Sydney 6.7, Melbourne 5.7, Brisbane 7.5, Adelaide 6.9, Perth 7.9, Hobart 5.9, Darwin 8.5 and Canberra 7.2.

Marble Bar in the north-west of Western Australia earned an unenviable place in folklore as the nation's hottest town, especially after its record unbroken spell of 160 days of at least 38.4°C (100°F) between 31 October 1923 and 7 April 1924. The highest recorded temperature was 53.1°C at Cloncurry in Queensland on 16 January 1889.

Australia's lowest temperatures have been recorded in the Snowy Mountains area of the Australian Alps, one of few regions to have snow on the ground in winter. Charlotte Pass in New South Wales (elevation 1750 metres) has twice recorded −22.2°C. Snow covers much of the Australian Alps above 1500 metres between late autumn and early spring, sometimes falling widely down to 1000 metres, but rarely below that.

Evaporation is very significant in water conservation and over about 75 per cent of Australia evaporation from a free water surface exceeds rainfall in all months. In central and north-west Australia the evaporation rate is ten times the rainfall.

The graphs below show the monthly average rainfall and max. and min. temperatures for 10 cities.

Cyclone Tracy which devastated Darwin on Xmas Day 1974, was the most destructive cyclone ever recorded on the Australian mainland.

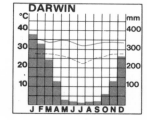

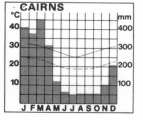

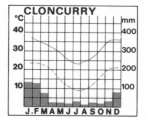

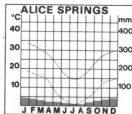

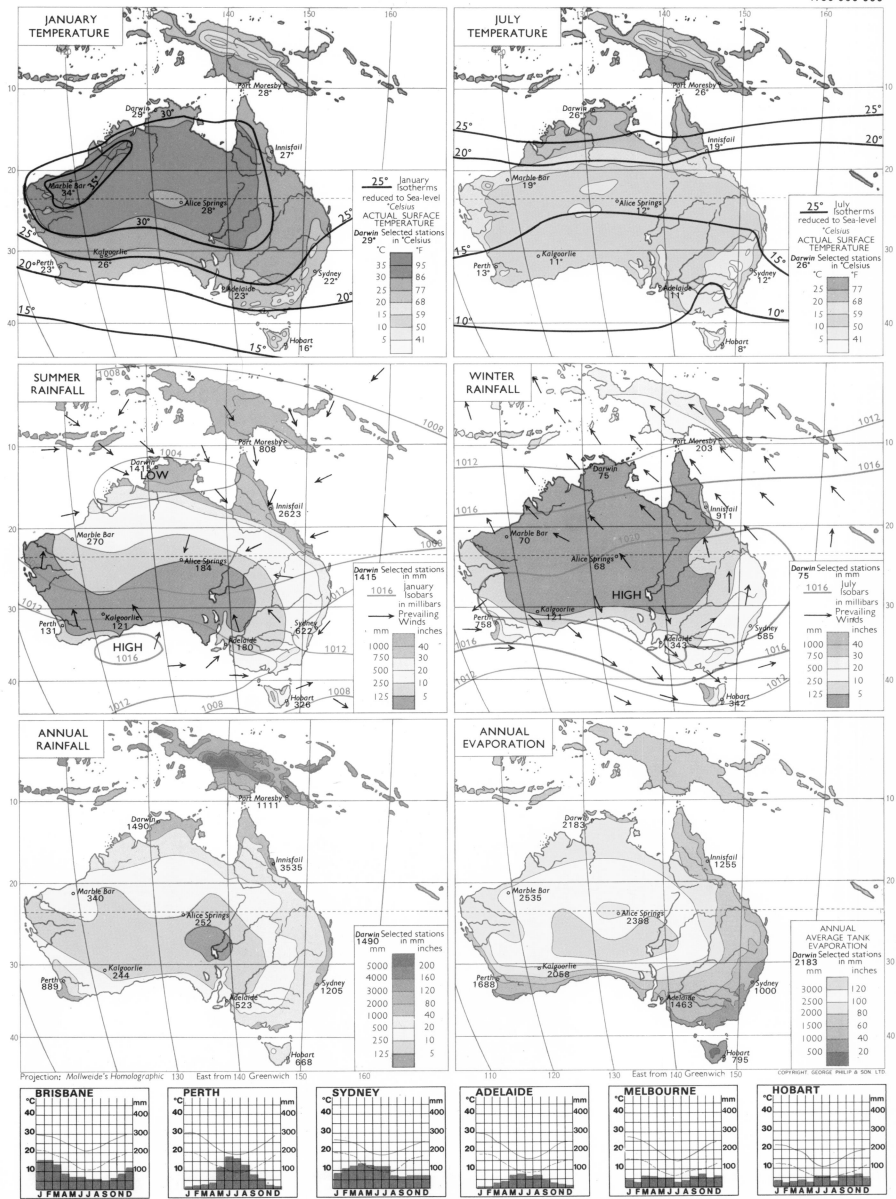

1:60 000 000

JANUARY TEMPERATURE

25° January Isotherms reduced to Sea-level °Celsius
ACTUAL SURFACE TEMPERATURE
Darwin Selected stations 29° in °Celsius

°C	°F
35	95
30	86
25	77
20	68
15	59
10	50
5	41

Port Moresby 28°
Darwin 29° 30°
Innisfail 27°
Marble Bar 34° 35°
Alice Springs 28°
Kalgoorlie 26°
Perth 23°
Sydney 22°
Adelaide 23°
Hobart 16°

JULY TEMPERATURE

25° July Isotherms reduced to Sea-level °Celsius
ACTUAL SURFACE TEMPERATURE
Darwin Selected stations 26° in °Celsius

°C	°F
25	77
20	68
15	59
10	50
5	41

Port Moresby 26°
Darwin 26°
Innisfail 19°
Marble Bar 19°
Alice Springs 12°
Kalgoorlie 11°
Perth 13°
Sydney 12°
Adelaide 11°
Hobart 8°

SUMMER RAINFALL

Darwin Selected stations 1415 in mm
1016 January Isobars in millibars
→ Prevailing Winds

mm	inches
1000	40
750	30
500	20
250	10
125	5

Port Moresby 808
Darwin 1415 LOW
Innisfail 2623
Marble Bar 270
Alice Springs 184
Perth 131
Kalgoorlie 121
HIGH 1016
Sydney 622
Adelaide 180
Hobart 326

WINTER RAINFALL

Darwin Selected stations 75 in mm
1016 July Isobars in millibars
→ Prevailing Winds

mm	inches
1000	40
750	30
500	20
250	10
125	5

Port Moresby 203
Darwin 75
Innisfail 911
Marble Bar 70
Alice Springs 68
HIGH
Perth 758
Kalgoorlie 121
Sydney 585
Adelaide 343
Hobart 342

ANNUAL RAINFALL

Darwin Selected stations 1490 in mm

mm	inches
5000	200
4000	160
3000	120
2000	80
1000	40
500	20
250	10
125	5

Port Moresby 1111
Darwin 1490
Innisfail 3535
Marble Bar 340
Alice Springs 252
Kalgoorlie 244
Perth 889
Sydney 1205
Adelaide 523
Hobart 668

ANNUAL EVAPORATION

ANNUAL AVERAGE TANK EVAPORATION
Darwin Selected stations 2183 in mm

mm	inches
3000	120
2500	100
2000	80
1500	60
1000	40
500	20

Darwin 2183
Innisfail 1255
Marble Bar 2535
Alice Springs 2388
Perth 1688
Kalgoorlie 2058
Sydney 1000
Adelaide 1463
Hobart 795

Projection: Mollweide's Homolographic   East from 140 Greenwich

BRISBANE °C mm
PERTH °C mm
SYDNEY °C mm
ADELAIDE °C mm
MELBOURNE °C mm
HOBART °C mm

J F M A M J J A S O N D

How to Read the Weather Map

The weather map seen in newspapers or on television is a simplified version of the surface synoptic weather charts and shows the distribution of the main elements of weather all over Australia.

All weather maps show the elements represented in similar ways. Atmospheric pressure is shown by a series of lines, called *isobars*, joining places of equal barometric pressure when reduced to sea level. If there are noticeable differences in air pressure then cells of relatively *high* and *low* pressure can be demarcated.

High pressure cells indicate descending air whilst low pressure cells indicate ascending air, whatever the cause of this vertical movement. Hence there is generally a greater likelihood of condensation and precipitation occurring in a low pressure system where the air rises and cools than in a high pressure system where it descends and warms up.

Much of what we call 'weather' depends on what happens to air masses of differing properties as they move over land surfaces of differing temperatures, or on the interaction of adjacent air masses at their sloping boundary, which is called a *front* or *frontal zone of transition*. Obviously a cool air mass moving over a warmer surface will increase its temperature, hence the potential of the air mass to hold water vapour increases. Similarly a warm air mass may be cooled by the colder land surface and therefore its capacity to hold moisture decreases. Condensation is more likely in this latter case.

The requirement for condensation and precipitation is for air to be cooled. Usually this is caused by the ascent of a large volume of air. As the air rises it cools and its capacity to hold moisture decreases. *Relative humidity* increases and when it equals 100 per cent, saturation is attained. Any further uplift results in cloud development, a form of condensation, and precipitation (rain, snow, etc.)

Convectional lifting is common in the tropics where the hot ground heats up the air above. *Orographic* uplift is provided by barriers to horizontal movement (usually mountain ranges) when the air stream is forced to rise. Eastern Queensland and western Tasmania receive rain by this process. *Frontal* uplift is the most common form of ascension in southern Australia. The interplay of warm and cold air masses produces endless numbers of warm fronts and cold fronts. Where the uplift is violent, as is often the case with cold fronts, cumulus clouds and showers develop quickly. If the uplift is gradual then layer clouds and light drizzle may result.

The intensity of uplift can be determined by the spacing of the isobars. If they are closely spaced then pressure changes are severe and the frontal surface steep. If the isobars are widely spaced then pressure changes are gradual, as is the lifting process.

Wind strength and direction are shown on the weather map by an arrow and feathers. The arrow indicates from which direction the wind came and the number of feathers indicates its strength. Winds aim to equalise pressure differences, so that they always blow from a high pressure (anti-cyclone) to a low pressure (cyclone). In the southern hemisphere, due to the earth's rotation and various frictional forces, the wind circulation shows clockwise flow around cyclones and anti-clockwise flow around anti-cyclones.

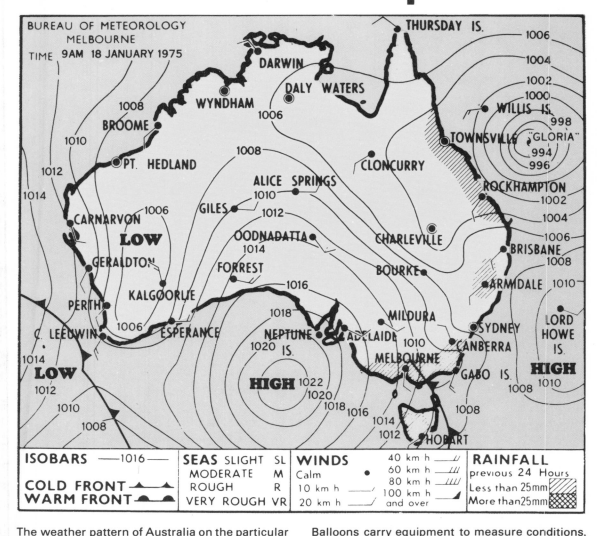

BUREAU OF METEOROLOGY MELBOURNE
TIME 9AM 18 JANUARY 1975

ISOBARS ——1016——	SEAS SLIGHT SL	WINDS	40 km h	RAINFALL
	MODERATE M	Calm •	60 km h	previous 24 Hours
COLD FRONT	ROUGH R	10 km h	80 km h	Less than 25mm
WARM FRONT	VERY ROUGH VR	20 km h	100 km h and over	More than 25mm

The weather pattern of Australia on the particular day shown by this map was dominated by three main pressure systems.

Cyclone Gloria off the north-east coast brought widespread rain to the coastal margins. Winds were from the south-west, intensifying near the low pressure system.

Another weak low pressure system was centred west of Kalgoorlie, and this would have strengthened with the arrival of a cold front at the south-west Cape. Some rain would have fallen as the cold front moved eastwards.

A ridge of high pressure extended northwards from the high pressure cell centred south of the Great Australian Bight.

A weak cold front was bringing rain to southern Victoria and Tasmania.

Balloons carry equipment to measure conditions.

Radar being used to determine cloud formation.

What Cloud Is That?

Clouds are a form of condensation, as they consist of minute particles of water or ice in suspension. As long as the droplets of water retain their individuality and do not coalesce into larger droplets, it is relatively easy for a small amount of upward air movement to keep them in suspension. Once they become too heavy for colloidal suspension, precipitation results.

The density and nature of cloud cover are good indicators of weather conditions, both prevailing and forthcoming, as they visually represent the state of condensation above the surface. The nature of the cloud cover is also determined by the amount of reflection or penetration of the sun's rays. Clouds which appear white are thin and not very dense; clouds which are grey to black are thick and dense, the greyness being a shadow from above cast on to the bottom of the cloud.

The three basic cloud types are cirrus, cumulus and stratus, the other seven varieties being combinations of these at different elevations. Clouds near the surface will be dense and dark, as most water vapour is in the lower levels of the atmosphere. Clouds at a high elevation will be thin and lightly coloured.

High Clouds (above 6000 metres)
Cirrus (Ci): Detached clouds in the form of white delicate filaments or narrow bands. Often featherlike and fibrous in appearance, these are formed entirely of ice crystals above 9150 metres and are associated with fair weather.

Cirrostratus (Cs): These are normally formed at 7500 metres entirely of ice crystals. They provide a whitish veil or sheet across the entire sky, often causing haloes to appear around the sun or moon. They often signify an approaching storm.

Cirrocumulus (CC): Composed predominantly of ice crystals, these appear as white globules or ripples across a large portion of the sky. They are not very common, being formed from the degeneration of cirrus and cirrostratus.

Middle Clouds (2000 to 6000 metres)
Altostratus (As): These are reasonably uniform sheets of bluish or greyish-white clouds, often grading imperceptibly into cirrostratus at a higher altitude. They are frequently associated with prolonged, widespread rainfall or snow.

Altocumulus (Ac): A layer or patches of cloud composed of flattened globular masses. They frequently have shadows on the under-surface, and have no vertical doming or have ordinary cumulus.

Nimbostratus (Ns): These are thick, dark, shapeless sheets associated with continuous precipitation, either rain or snow. They can form below 2000 metres.

Low Clouds (below 2000 metres)
Stratus (St): Generally a grey cloud layer with a fairly uniform base, which may give precipitation in the form of drizzle. If the wind breaks up these sheets into bands or ragged patches, they are called *fractostratus*.

Stratocumulus (Sc): These appear as bumpy, rolling bands of grey-based clouds, often occupying most of the sky. The associated weather is very light rain, drizzle or snow.

Cumulus (Cu): Detached clouds, generally dense and with sharp outlines, developing vertically in the form of rising domes, of which the upper part often resembles a cauliflower.

Cumulonimbus (Cb): These are the extension of cumulus clouds, with a vertical reach from top to base greater than 3000 metres. The rapidly rising air currents produce dense thunderhead tops and they are always associated with heavy showers or thunderstorms, lightning and hail.

Cirrus and Cirrostratus

Cirrus

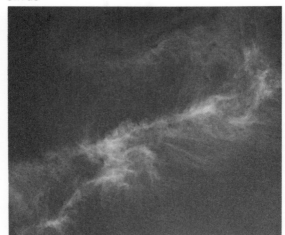

Altocumulus

Altocumulus

Altocumulus and Altostratus

Stratocumulus

Cumulus (small vertical development)

Cumulus (large vertical development)

Cumulonimbus

Australian Soil Types

Soils, like other geomorphic features, are a product of their environment, and can be viewed as a function of the independent variables of climate, organisms, topography, parent rock material and time. Variations in these factors cause a distinct change in the morphology of soils.

The classification adopted in the map opposite is based on Northcote's *A Description of Australia's Soils*, published by CSIRO.

The Soil Profile

The term *soil profile* denotes the arrangement of the soil, from surface to bedrock, into layers or *horizons*, each possessing a different colour, texture and structure. A profile is a valid means of differentiating between soil types, if the soil is *mature*; that is, if it has established an equilibrium with the prevailing conditions over a long period of time.

Soil scientists have distinguished three main horizons in the soil profile:

A Topsoil ⎤
B Subsoil ⎦—True soil
C Substratum of weathered parent rock

Within each of these horizons further zones may be distinguished. Below the C horizon is the unaltered bedrock which is commonly referred to as horizon D, although it is not soil.

The A horizon contains most of the organic matter, and is therefore dark in colour. In humid areas where rainfall is reliable and moderate the A horizon may well be a *zone of eluviation* and *leaching*, through which the percolating water carries finely-divided and soluble material.

The B horizon is commonly referred to in humid areas as the *zone of illuviation*. It is a zone of enrichment from the deposition of soluble material and particles from above, and by capillary action from below.

The C horizon is the little-changed parent material from which the soil was derived, and grades down into the unaltered bedrock. The C horizon may show evidence of weathering but the original constituents of the parent material are still recognizable.

Soil Texture

Soil texture refers to the size of soil particles. Texture determines water-holding capacity, so is important in estimating rates of plant growth. *Sandy* soils are coarsely textured, porous and can hold a large amount of water. *Loams* have approximately equal percentages of sand, silt and clay with good drainage and water retention capacity. *Clays* contain 40 per cent or more clay and relatively little sand. Due to the tightly-packed nature of clay colloids, water is prevented from moving freely through them.

Description of the Main Australian Soils

Sands: These are soils exhibiting uniform coarse-textured profiles and as a group cover 32 per cent of the Australian continent. The predominant sub-types of the sandy soils are calcareous (carbonates occur throughout the profile), bleached sands which are not calcareous (Profile 1), and brownish-earthy sands (Profile 2).

Loams: These are soils exhibiting uniform medium-textured profiles. As a group they occupy 13 per cent of Australia. Most show little or no profile development apart from some accumulation of organic matter in the surface and may be either calcareous or not calcareous (Profile 3).

Non-cracking Clays: These show uniform fine-textured profiles that do not crack open periodically. They occur in less than one per cent of the Australian continent (Profile 4).

Cracking Clays: These exhibit uniform fine-textured profiles that crack open periodically upon drying. The first main sub-type is often referred to as 'black earths', and occurs on the Darling Downs and Liverpool Plains (Profile 5). They have natural fertility but can erode easily if overworked on slopes. Other sub-types are the grey and brown, and red-brown earths (Profile 6) of the sub-humid to semi-arid zone of eastern and northern Australia. They occupy 11 per cent of Australia.

Calcareous Earths: These solonized brown soils have gradational texture profiles that are calcareous throughout (Profile 7). They have developed on calcareous materials in the semi-arid to arid regions, notably in southern Australia, and are widely used for grazing, with some irrigated crops. They occupy 6 per cent of the Australian continent.

Massive Earths: These are soils with gradational texture profiles that are not calcareous throughout and cover 17 per cent of the Australian continent. The two principal groups are the red earths (Profile 8) and yellow earths (Profile 9) and although both are used extensively for sparse natural pastures for grazing, with irrigation availability they can support intensive farming.

Structured Earths: These are similar to massive earths in that they exhibit a gradational texture profile but their B horizon development is different. The two main groups are those with smooth or non-porous B horizons (Profile 10) and those exhibiting porous B horizons (Profile 11). They are often termed *krasnozems* (red loams), *red podzols*, *prairie soils* or *chocolate soils*. Collectively they account for under 3 per cent of the Australian land mass.

Duplex Soils: Accounting collectively for about 22 per cent of the Australian continent, duplex soils are those in which the texture suddenly becomes finer (more clayey) on passing from the A to the B horizons. The *red* duplex soils (10 per cent of total land area) have predominantly red B horizons and are commonly referred to as *desert loams, red podzols* or *red-brown earths* (Profile 12). The *yellow* duplex soils have dominantly yellow B horizons with sandy or loamy A horizons. They are commonly called *yellow podzols* (Profile 13.) All the podzol soils are strongly leached in the surface and occur in fairly well-watered areas. They are primarily suited to pasture development and, although of moderate to low fertility, with good management may be highly productive.

Organic Soils: These are dominated by organic matter for at least the top 30 centimetres of the profile. Generally the black or dark brown organic matter is well decomposed and humified and under natural conditions the soils are usually saturated for long periods. *Peats* are the most common example of this group and occur in less then one per cent of the Australian land mass (Profile 14).

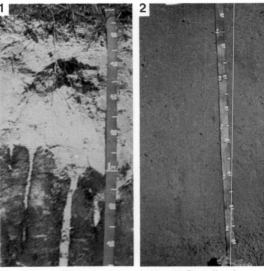

Profile 1   Bleached sand, North Stradbroke Island, Qld
Profile 2   Earthy sand, Merredin, WA

Profile 3   Shallow bleached loam, Cooroy, Qld
Profile 4   Non-cracking clay, Bundaberg, Qld

Profile 5   Black earth, Toowoomba, Qld
Profile 6   Red cracking clay, Woocalla, SA

Profile 7   Solonized brown soil, Coomealla, NSW
Profile 8   Red earth, Aramac, Qld

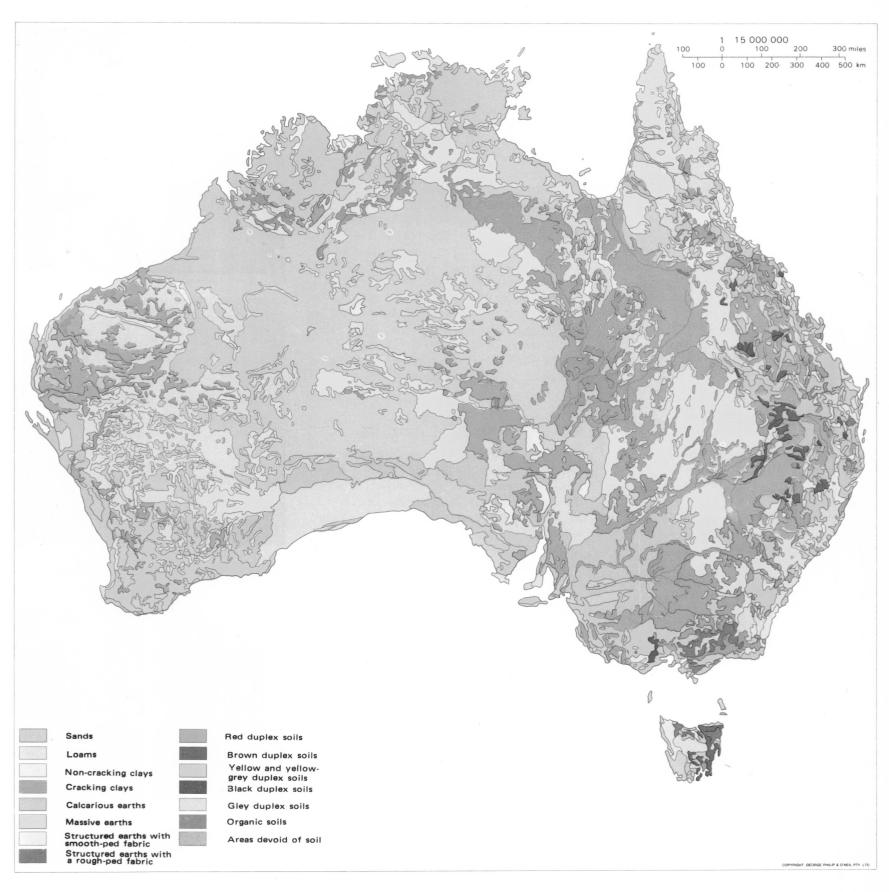

Sands	Red duplex soils
Loams	Brown duplex soils
Non-cracking clays	Yellow and yellow-grey duplex soils
Cracking clays	Black duplex soils
Calcarious earths	Gley duplex soils
Massive earths	Organic soils
Structured earths with smooth-ped fabric	Areas devoid of soil
Structured earths with a rough-ped fabric	

1 : 15 000 000

| 100 | 0 | 100 | 200 | 300 miles |
| 100 | 0 | 100 | 200 | 300 | 400 | 500 km |

COPYRIGHT GEORGE PHILIP & O'NEIL PTY LTD

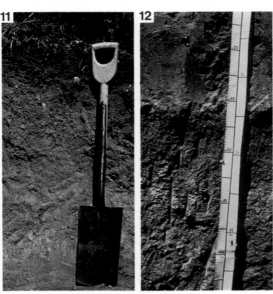

Profile 9 Yellow earth, Mareeba, Qld
Profile 10 Red podzolic soil, Mackay, Qld

Profile 11 Krasnozem, Bogong, Vic.
Profile 12 Red-brown earth, Deniliquin, NSW

Profile 13 Yellow podzolic soil, Beerwah, Qld
Profile 14 Peat soil, Breona, Tas.

33

Australian Vegetation Regions

The distinctive quality of Australian flora has been recognized since the first plant collections were made by Joseph Banks at Botany Bay in 1770. The continent has been separated from other land masses since it drifted north from Antarctica 49 million years ago. This long period of isolation has given Australia a unique flora: for example, 75 per cent of the 6000 land plants in the south-western corner of Western Australia are found nowhere else. The fact that the Australian continent was temporarily connected with New Guinea resulted in the rich tropical flora of Malaysia spreading to Australia in the Oligocene Period (about 30 million years ago) and more recently in the Pleistocene Period. Thus, many of the tropical plants in our northern forests originated in Asia and arrived here via land bridges. The Australian land flora comprises over 12 000 species of flowering plants and is dominated by such conspicuous genera as *Eucalyptus, Melaleuca, Leptospermum* (family Myrtaceae), *Banksia* (family Proteaceae), *Acacia* (family Mimosaceae), *Pulteneae* (family Papillionaceae), *Casuarina* (family Casuarinaceae) and *Xanthorrhoea* (family Xanthorrhoeaceae).

Climate is the most important factor that affects plant distribution. Rainfall and temperature are determined largely by latitude and elevation. Not only is the amount of rainfall important to an area, but the reliability and duration of precipitation are also significant influences on plant life. For example, although coastal regions of New South Wales might receive 1000 mm of rain distributed evenly throughout the year, Alice Springs might receive its annual average of 120-150 mm in one brief but heavy downpour.

There are four very broad types of vegetation in Australia: *forests* (open and closed); *woodlands* and *grasslands; scrub* (a combination of mallee and heath) and *desert*. The distribution of these types is primarily determined by climate. Very extreme localised conditions result in specialised vegetation types such as salt marshes, mangrove swamps and tundra, which will not be discussed here.

Forests

Forests are found predominantly on the eastern coast of the continent where the rainfall ranges from 1000-2500 mm per year. A forest is a plant community dominated by trees that grow very closely together. Closed forests, particularly the northern rainforests, include trees other than eucalypts, and feature buttressing tree trunks, lianes, and low light levels at the forest floor. Cabbage Fan Palms (*Livistona australis*) and Lawyer Vines (*Smilax australis*) are examples of trees found in closed forests. Open forests are less dense and are dominated by eucalypts, including Mountain Ash (*E. regnans*) and Messmate (*E. obliqua*) which are both found in south-eastern Australia, and the Spotted Gum (*E. maculata*) which grows throughout the eastern regions of the continent. Other common perennial plants found in the open forests are Prickly Moses (*Acacia verticillata*) and the Purple Coral-Pea.

Woodlands and Grasslands

Woodlands are found in drier areas than forests. Here, unlike the forests, the distance between trees is greater than the average height of the trees. In addition, the tree crowns are quite large. Woodland trees include the Darwin Stringybark (*E. tetrodonta*), the Western Australian Christmas Tree (*Nuytsia floribunda*) and two eastern species, the White Cypress Pine (*callitris glauca*) and the Yellow Box (*E. melliodora*). The River Red Gum (*E. camaldulensis*) is Australia's most widely-distributed eucalypt and is found near seasonal and permanent watercourses.

Woodlands frequently blend gradually into grasslands where trees and shrubs are more sporadic. In grassland Kangaroo Grass (*Themeda australis*) is found throughout much of the continent, Mitchell Grass (*Astrebla pectinata*) is dominant over large areas in the north, while the Common Wallaby Grass (*Danthonia caespitosa*) fills a similar role in southern Australia. The Blue Devil (*Eryngium rostratum*) and the Common Everlasting (*Helichrysum apiculatum*) are common grassland plants throughout our temperate regions.

Scrub

The area designated as scrub includes vegetations referred to as heath and mallee scrub. It is a community of shrubby plants in which the dominant individuals are less than 8 m in height. Shrubs shorter than 6 m with small evergreen leaves are common in heathlands; this vegetation is generally located on infertile soils or in areas of restricted drainage. Heath communities are often very diverse. South-west Western Australian heathlands or the Hawkesbury sandstones near Sydney may include almost as many plant species as a tropical rainforest. The Red Flowering Gum (*E. ficifolia*) and Mangle's Kangaroo Paw (*Anigozanthus manglesii*), both of Western Australia, and the eastern Saw Banksia (*Banksia serrata*) and Common Heath (*Epacris impressa*) are just a few examples of this diversity. The plant community known as mallee is dominated by eucalypts under 8 m and is restricted to the semi-arid south-western and south-eastern regions of the country. The term 'mallee' is derived from an Aboriginal word meaning 'thicket'. Mallee eucalypts consist of several slender stems rising from a single large root swelling known as a ligno tuber. Yellow Mallee (*E. incrassata*) and Erect Guinea-flower (*Hibbertia stricta*) are commonly found in mallee vegetation.

Deserts

Deserts are those regions which receive less than approximately 250 mm annual rainfall, and where evaporation exceeds precipitation throughout the year. Due to the unpredictable rainfall, flowering times are often uncertain and many plants blossom irregularly. The extreme conditions of deserts create a variety of microhabitats including saline dry lake beds and ephemeral watercourses. In addition, because so little water is available, any additional moisture can be crucial and results in a complex mosaic of plant communities. Examples of desert trees include the Coolibah (*E. microtheca*), the Ghost Gum (*E. papuana*) and the Mulga (*Acacia aneura*), while some of the perennials are Sturt's Desert Pea (*Clianthus speciosus*), Saltbush (*Atriplex vesicaria*) and Porcupine Grass (*Triodia irritans*).

Rainforest, Eastern Queensland

Wet Sclerophyll forest, Gibraltar Ranges, NSW

Dry Sclerophyll forest, Otway Ranges, Victoria
Savanna woodland (medium), Katherine, NT

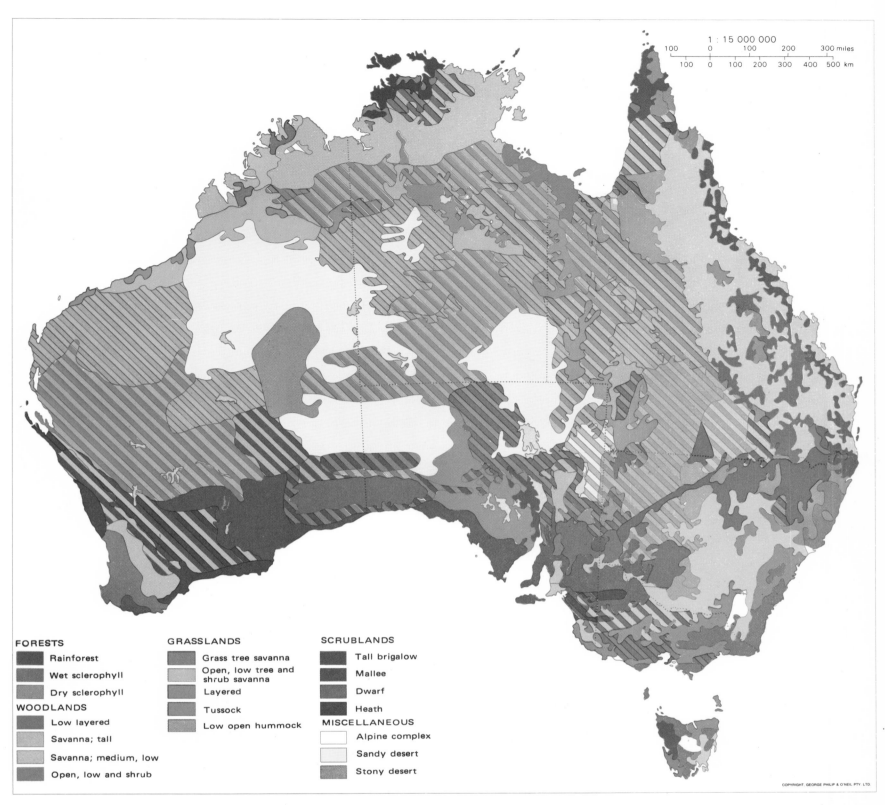

FORESTS
- Rainforest
- Wet sclerophyll
- Dry sclerophyll

WOODLANDS
- Low layered
- Savanna; tall
- Savanna; medium, low
- Open, low and shrub

GRASSLANDS
- Grass tree savanna
- Open, low tree and shrub savanna
- Layered
- Tussock
- Low open hummock

SCRUBLANDS
- Tall brigalow
- Mallee
- Dwarf
- Heath

MISCELLANEOUS
- Alpine complex
- Sandy desert
- Stony desert

Tussock grassland, Kalbarri, WA

Tall shrubland, Central Australia

Open low tree & shrub savanna, Mt Connor, NT

Trees, Grasses and Wildflowers

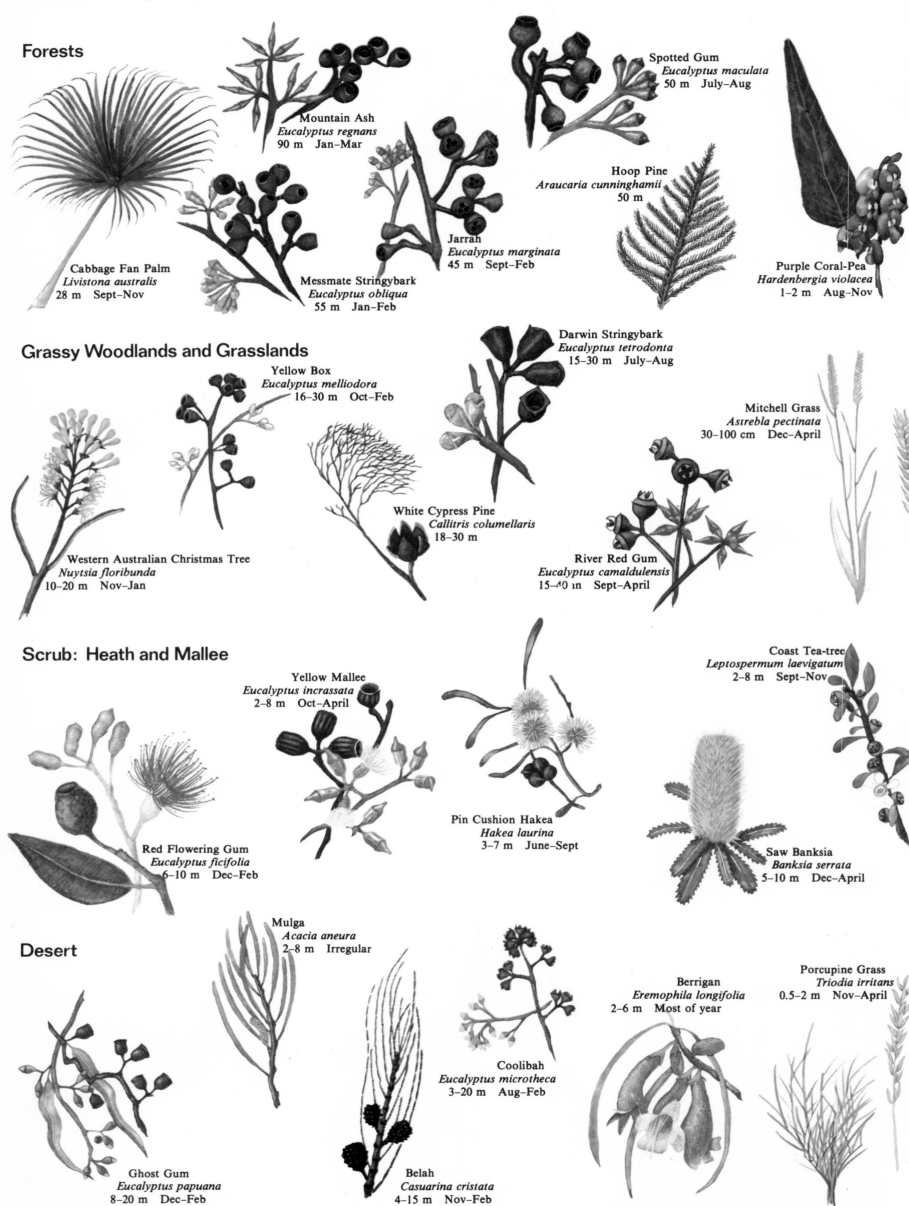

Forests

Cabbage Fan Palm
Livistona australis
28 m   Sept–Nov

Mountain Ash
Eucalyptus regnans
90 m   Jan–Mar

Messmate Stringybark
Eucalyptus obliqua
55 m   Jan–Feb

Jarrah
Eucalyptus marginata
45 m   Sept–Feb

Spotted Gum
Eucalyptus maculata
50 m   July–Aug

Hoop Pine
Araucaria cunninghamii
50 m

Purple Coral-Pea
Hardenbergia violacea
1–2 m   Aug–Nov

Grassy Woodlands and Grasslands

Yellow Box
Eucalyptus melliodora
16–30 m   Oct–Feb

Darwin Stringybark
Eucalyptus tetrodonta
15–30 m   July–Aug

Mitchell Grass
Astrebla pectinata
30–100 cm   Dec–April

Western Australian Christmas Tree
Nuytsia floribunda
10–20 m   Nov–Jan

White Cypress Pine
Callitris columellaris
18–30 m

River Red Gum
Eucalyptus camaldulensis
15–40 m   Sept–April

Scrub: Heath and Mallee

Yellow Mallee
Eucalyptus incrassata
2–8 m   Oct–April

Coast Tea-tree
Leptospermum laevigatum
2–8 m   Sept–Nov

Red Flowering Gum
Eucalyptus ficifolia
6–10 m   Dec–Feb

Pin Cushion Hakea
Hakea laurina
3–7 m   June–Sept

Saw Banksia
Banksia serrata
5–10 m   Dec–April

Desert

Mulga
Acacia aneura
2–8 m   Irregular

Coolibah
Eucalyptus microtheca
3–20 m   Aug–Feb

Berrigan
Eremophila longifolia
2–6 m   Most of year

Porcupine Grass
Triodia irritans
0.5–2 m   Nov–April

Ghost Gum
Eucalyptus papuana
8–20 m   Dec–Feb

Belah
Casuarina cristata
4–15 m   Nov–Feb

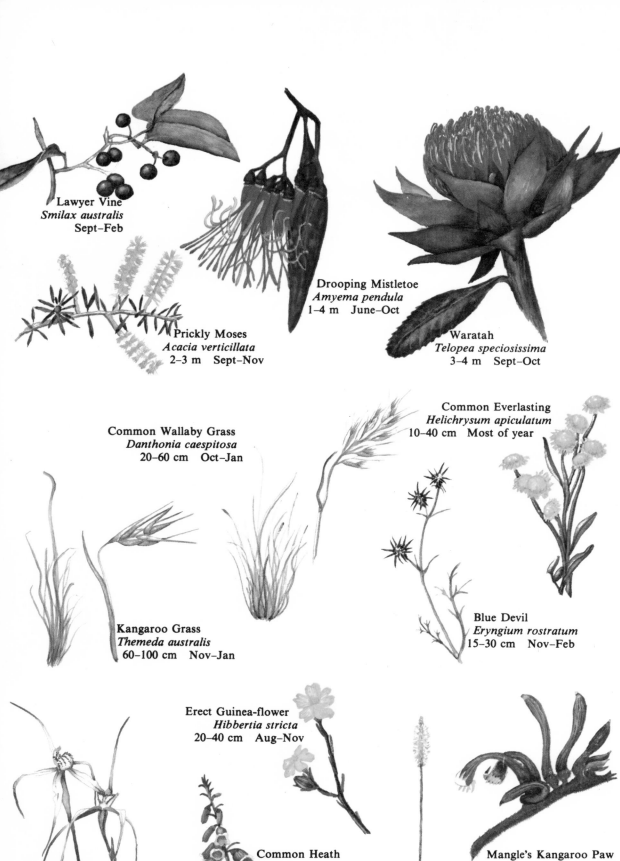

Lawyer Vine
Smilax australis
Sept–Feb

Prickly Moses
Acacia verticillata
2–3 m   Sept–Nov

Drooping Mistletoe
Amyema pendula
1–4 m   June–Oct

Waratah
Telopea speciosissima
3–4 m   Sept–Oct

Common Wallaby Grass
Danthonia caespitosa
20–60 cm   Oct–Jan

Kangaroo Grass
Themeda australis
60–100 cm   Nov–Jan

Common Everlasting
Helichrysum apiculatum
10–40 cm   Most of year

Blue Devil
Eryngium rostratum
15–30 cm   Nov–Feb

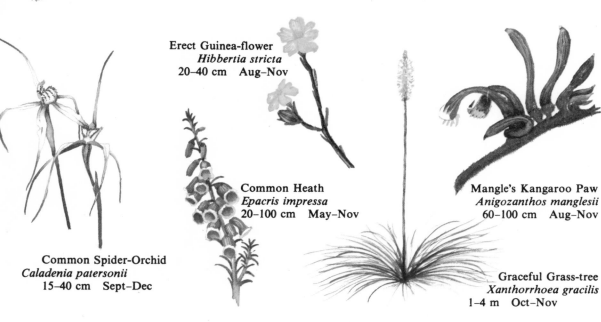

Erect Guinea-flower
Hibbertia stricta
20–40 cm   Aug–Nov

Common Heath
Epacris impressa
20–100 cm   May–Nov

Common Spider-Orchid
Caladenia patersonii
15–40 cm   Sept–Dec

Mangle's Kangaroo Paw
Anigozanthos manglesii
60–100 cm   Aug–Nov

Graceful Grass-tree
Xanthorrhoea gracilis
1–4 m   Oct–Nov

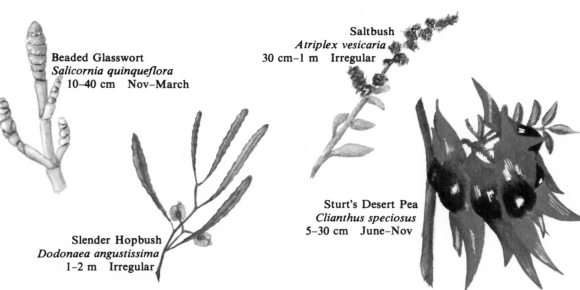

Beaded Glasswort
Salicornia quinqueflora
10–40 cm   Nov–March

Saltbush
Atriplex vesicaria
30 cm–1 m   Irregular

Slender Hopbush
Dodonaea angustissima
1–2 m   Irregular

Sturt's Desert Pea
Clianthus speciosus
5–30 cm   June–Nov

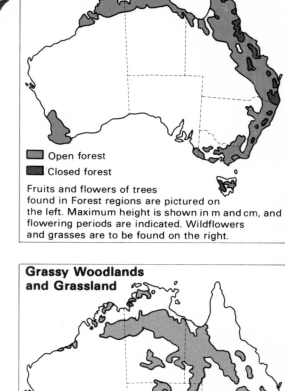

Forests

Open forest

Closed forest

Fruits and flowers of trees
found in Forest regions are pictured on
the left. Maximum height is shown in m and cm, and
flowering periods are indicated. Wildflowers
and grasses are to be found on the right.

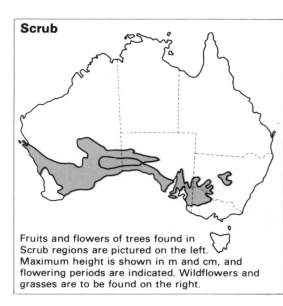

Grassy Woodlands and Grassland

Fruits and flowers
of trees found in Grassy
Woodland regions are pictured on
the left. Maximum height is shown in m and cm, and
flowering periods are indicated. Wildflowers
and grasses are to be found on the right.

Scrub

Fruits and flowers of trees found in
Scrub regions are pictured on the left.
Maximum height is shown in m and cm, and
flowering periods are indicated. Wildflowers and
grasses are to be found on the right.

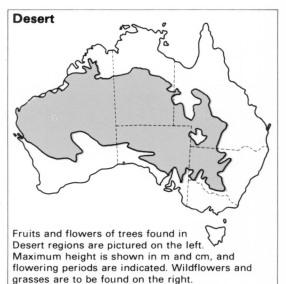

Desert

Fruits and flowers of trees found in
Desert regions are pictured on the left.
Maximum height is shown in m and cm, and
flowering periods are indicated. Wildflowers and
grasses are to be found on the right.

Australia's Unique Animals

Australia's animals seem to inspire superlatives. 'Unique ... remarkable ... missing links ... nature's strangest creatures ... the platypus seems designed by a committee ...' are typical of the comments which recur.

They enthuse the zoologist, lure the tourist, and the two best-known of them, the quaint kangaroo and the 'cuddly' koala, have become unmistakable international symbols of Australia. Australian fauna is noted for the presence of many unique animals — and the absence of many orders known elsewhere. No great apes hunt in Australian forests, hoofed animals are a recent introduction, and there are no members of the order Insectivora, among others. . .

For scores of millions of years, the fauna evolved in isolation, and many different forms came from a relatively few ancestral types. The marsupials, the pouched mammals, developed to a degree unknown elsewhere, many of them reflecting characteristics typical of mammalian orders in other continents.

In Australia the unique monotremes, platypus and echidna, the world's only egg-laying mammals, are to be found.

Links with the Reptiles

The monotremes are considered by some to be 'living fossils' which represent a stage in the evolution of mammals from reptiles. Best-known is the furred platypus (*Ornithorhynchus anatinus*) which inhabits Australia's eastern watercourses, where it finds food in the water and mud. This 'composite' creature with webbed feet, a duckbill, and a tail resembling a beaver's, lays eggs and suckles its young. Adult males (often 600 mm long) have poison spurs on their hind legs. Burrows with exits above and below water are dug many metres deep into the banks of streams.

The other monotreme is the echidna or spiny anteater (*Tachyglossus aculeatus*) of Australia and Papua New Guinea. Echidnas are land dwellers relying on their spines and their ability to burrow partly into the ground to deter predators. They do not tunnel like the platypus, but usually live under rocks or tree roots. Their long thin tongue efficiently gathers ants and insects.

Marsupials

Australia has about 230 species of mammals: almost half are marsupials, with the balance being the placental mammals and the monotremes. Marsupials lack a placenta, the womb structure which nourishes the young during pregnancy and permits the higher mammals (placental mammals) to produce almost fully-developed young. The common feature of most marsupials is the possession of a pouch in which to hold the young, which are born very early, and must find their way unaided to the pouch. Considering that the young of a large kangaroo, for example, are under 20 mm long, these are some of nature's most extraordinary journeys. Not all marsupials have pouches as prominent as that of the frequently-pictured kangaroo: some have only rudimentary pouches, while the burrowing wombat's pouch opens upside down.

Probably the best-known marsupials are the kangaroos of the family Macropodidae, some 45 species in 17 genera.

Most kangaroos are herbivorous — one reason for the slaughter of millions since Europeans introduced sheep and tried to eliminate competitors for the limited pasture. Some of the smaller kangaroos are insectivorous. With the exception of Queensland's tree-climbing kangaroos (similar to some found in Papua New Guinea) they are ground dwellers.

The largest are the red (*Megaleia rufa*) and great grey (*Macropus giganteus*) kangaroos, sometimes taller than a man. The smallest is the musky rat kangaroo (*Hypsiprymnodon moschatus*) less than 300 mm long. 'Wallaby' commonly denotes smaller kangaroos, 'wallaroo' those preferring rocky habitats.

Large kangaroos can bound briefly at speeds exceeding 45 kilometres per hour, and leap 11 metres or more. The heavy tail maintains balance in movement.

The koala, the 'teddy bear' (*Phascolarctos cinereus*) of scores of travel posters, is a tree-dwelling marsupial. Sometimes popularly called the native bear, it in fact is related to the tunnelling wombat. It reaches around 600 mm fully grown and spends most of its life in trees, although it may walk long distances in search of the species of eucalypts whose leaves form its exclusive diet. Other tree-living marsupials include tree kangaroos, the monkey-like cuscus (*Phalanger maculatus*) and various gliding possums.

The powerful, thickset wombats (*Lasiorhinus* and *Vombatus spp*) are widespread burrowing marsupials in south-eastern Australia. Far more unusual is the small blind marsupial mole (*Notoryctes typhlops*) of inland areas. Another highly specialised Western Australian marsupial is the dramatically-striped numbat or banded anteater (*Myrmecobius fasciatus*).

The few carnivorous marsupials, members of the family Dasyuridae, include insectivorous 'mice', the native 'cats', and the Tasmanian 'tiger' and 'devil'. Some of these marsupials have evolved to resemble animals of other origins, found in other countries — this trend towards similar characteristics is called 'convergent evolution'. The Tasmanian 'tiger' or thylacine (*Thylacinus cynocephalus*) is similar to unrelated wolves on other continents.

Placental Mammals

Australia's placental mammals comprise the dingo (*Canis familiaris dingo*), marine mammals, rodents and bats.

The dingo or warrigal appears to have evolved from dogs brought from Asia by the people who became the Australian Aborigines. It is now regarded as indigenous.

There are some 50 species of native rats (only the introduced species have become widespread pests) and about 50 bat species, including nine 'flying foxes' or fruit bats.

Introduced Species

Scores of species have been introduced to Australia for pastoral use, as beasts of burden, for game purposes and sometimes for curiosity's sake. Some have created new industries — others, like the rabbit which existed in plague proportions until checked by the virus disease myxomatosis in the 1950s, came close to crippling areas of the rural economy.

Echidna

Koala

Common Wombat

Hairy-nosed Wombat

Numbat

Dingo (Desert)

Platypus

Red Kangaroo

Grey Kangaroo

Short-tailed Pademelon or Quokka

Leadbeater's Possum

Potoroo

Yellow-footed
Rock Wallaby

Brushtail Possum

Ringtail Possum

Tasmanian Devil

Tasmanian Tiger

Eastern Native Cat (Quoll)

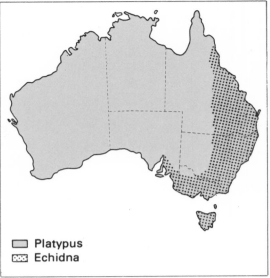

Platypus
Echidna

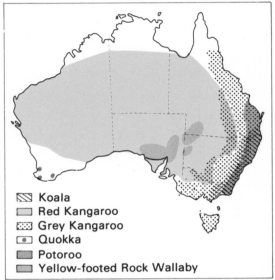

Koala
Red Kangaroo
Grey Kangaroo
Quokka
Potoroo
Yellow-footed Rock Wallaby

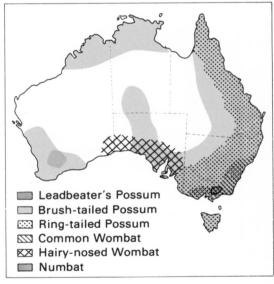

Leadbeater's Possum
Brush-tailed Possum
Ring-tailed Possum
Common Wombat
Hairy-nosed Wombat
Numbat

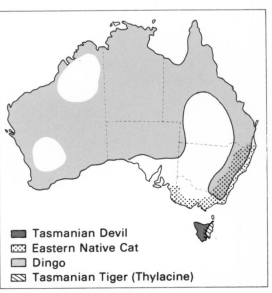

Tasmanian Devil
Eastern Native Cat
Dingo
Tasmanian Tiger (Thylacine)

Common Australian Birds

Australia's birds, frequently colourful, occasionally bizarre, appear often in the early European journals of discovery. In 1697 the startled Dutch explorer Willem de Vlamingh found swans that were black, not white — and took three back to Batavia to prove his claim. Other newcomers marvelled at birds that 'laughed', at tall flightless birds almost as high as a man, and at scores of unfamiliar parrots exploding in gaudy swarms over inland regions.

Equally remarkable were the birds that created and paraded in elaborate bowers, and others in jungle and arid country that built incubation mounds and tended them to keep the interior temperature around 33°C. Most amazing of all were the lyrebirds, delivering concerts of great vocal range and mimicry, veiled by a gauze-like tail.

Wide Representation

Of approximately 700 birds known in Australia, some 530 are regarded as endemic. Many of the latter evolved during Australia's long geographic isolation and consequently are found only in certain defined habitats.

In contrast to the limited mammal representation in Australia, the continent has most bird orders represented. Among the significant absentees are the vultures, woodpeckers and flamingoes.

Australian bird life is dominated by the insect-eaters which comprise about 70 per cent of the bird population. Many of the world's parrots are here, 50 species of great variety, some of them favoured aviary birds around the world for a century and a half. Overseas demand remains so strong that parrots form a large part of continuing bird smuggling operations.

Unusual Calls

Many Australian birds are noted for their calls. Outstanding is the raucous 'laugh' of the kookaburra (*Dacelo gigas*), the giant kingfisher which is also known as the laughing jackass. This popular bird with the 'crazed cackle', as an Australian author once wrote, is not a kingfisher in the literal sense, but a predator on small animals and young birds. Other common bush noises are the carolling of magpies (*Gymnorhina spp.*) and the harsh, melancholy cawing of crows (*Corvus spp.*). Also distinctive is the cracking of the whipbird (*Psophodes spp.*) and the sharp ring of the bellbird (*Manorina melanophrys*). But in terms of range and mimicry nothing matches the performance of the unique lyrebird. There are only two species: the Superb Lyrebird (*Menura novaehollandiae*) found in many areas of eastern Australia, and the smaller Prince Albert lyrebird (*Menura albertii*) known only in forests near the coastal junction of Queensland and New South Wales.

Males of both species are more vocal than females and give their song and dance performances around the year, except when moulting. The most spectacular concerts occur during the courting and breeding season, often on specially constructed domed mounds a metre wide. With tail extended and feathers spread forward over body and head, the lyrebird gives a performance of remarkable range that often includes mimicking the notes of other birds and even man-made noises. A single concert has been known to include up to 40 different calls.

The ancestry of lyrebirds is unknown. Their only recorded relatives are the equally remarkable Australian scrub birds (*Atrichornithidae*).

Other Distinctive Birds

Familiar from its position on the Australian Coat of Arms, the ostrich-like, flightless emu (*Dromaius novaehollandiae*) is widely distributed through inland areas, sometimes in plague proportions as far as local farmers are concerned. With the similar cassowary (*Casuarius casuarius*) of Australia and Papua New Guinea it constitutes the order Casuariiformes.

Appropriately enough, given Australia's many flowering plants, honeyeaters are well represented. Seventy species are known, ranging from pigeon-size to smaller than a canary.

Another famous group found only in Australia and Papua New Guinea comprises the bower birds (*Ptilonorhyncidae*) renowned for constructing decorated bowers for display and courtship — and for highly-developed powers of mimicry. The 16 species build bowers (separate from nests) in many forms, from the common parallel row of twigs to a leaf-paved forest clearing. Decorations also vary widely, and include flowers and berries, shining objects, shells and sometimes objects of a particular colour. Some birds mix various substances to paint parts of a bower.

Notable also are the three mound-builders, birds which incubate eggs by burial rather than by normal hatching methods. The brush turkey (*Alectura lathami*) and the scrub fowl (*Megapodius freycinet*) are from tropical and sub-tropical regions, while the mallee or lowan fowl (*Leipoa ocellata*) has adapted to arid inland conditions. The procedure is generally to cover moist decaying vegetation with soil or sand, lay eggs within the mound when the temperature is determined by the male to be suitable (around 33°C) and maintain temperature by adding or removing soil daily until the chicks hatch and dig themselves out.

One particular colony of birds forms a noted tourist attraction near Melbourne. This is the rookery of fairy or little penguins (*Eudyptula minor*) on Phillip Island. The summer 'penguin parade' at dusk when the birds, members of the only penguin species resident in Australian waters, waddle in from the surf after a day's fishing, draws tens of thousands of visitors.

Another bird noted for distinctive behaviour is the brolga or native companion (*Grus rubicunda*), sole Australian representative of the crane family. Flocks of the tall brolgas routinely perform group 'dancing', with stately formal movements, on the inland plains that are their usual habitat. They are no longer to be found in the south-east and south-west of Australia.

Australia has only one of the world's 21 bustard species, the Australian bustard or plains turkey (*Eurodotis australis*). Widespread until decimated by early settlers, subsequent sport hunting and the marauding of introduced foxes, it is now restricted to remote areas. Bustards reach almost a metre in height.

Yellow-breasted Sunbird

Purple-crowned Pigeon

Purple-capped Lorikeet

Rainbow Lorikeet

Eastern Rosella

Scarlet Robin

Orange-winged Sittella

Azure Kingfisher

Cattle Egret

Mistletoe Bird

Swallow

Brown Hawk

Silvereye

Little Thornbill

Brolga

Galah

Scarlet Honeyeater

Little Kingfisher

Blue-faced Honeyeater

Lyre Bird

Budgerigah

Zebra Finch

Emu

Yellow Weebill

Crimson Chat

Blue Wren

Rainbow Bird

Purple-crowned Wren

Orange Chat

Spur-winged Plover

Noisy Pitta

Diamond Firetail Finch

Squatter Pigeon

Aquatic Birds

The extent of bird migration within Australia is not known, but it is believed that at least 50 species are involved.

Many birds — mainly waders — migrate from Australia each year, crossing the Equator to breed in the Northern Hemisphere. Other species breed in Australia and travel north in autumn. Relatively few of the birds which migrate to the Southern Hemisphere come as far as the continent of Australia, most stopping in the islands to the north.

A number of tube-nosed seabirds, such as albatrosses, storm petrels and shearwaters, are found regularly in Australian waters, but seldom come ashore except to breed. Some visit Australia on their global wanderings, for example the muttonbird or short-tailed shearwater (*Puffinus tenuirostris*) which nests on southern coastlines.

Many of the duck-like birds — including geese, swans and shovellers — are also found in Australia. Two rare members of the goose family stand out. The magpie goose (*Anseranas semipalmata*) is found in the Northern Territory, north Queensland and southern Papua New Guinea. The Cape Barren goose (*Cereopsis novaehollandiae*) is restricted to southern coastal areas, notably Bass Strait. This grey bird, with its distinctive yellow bill, is about 600 mm long. It is not in fact a true goose and is currently in a subfamily of its own. For many years hunted and eaten, or shot as an agricultural pest, the species is now protected, although farmers are able to shoot the birds if a permit is obtained.

Some of the other aquatic birds are less well represented — there is only one species of pelican and five species of cormorants or shags in Australia.

White-eyed Duck

Black Duck

Black Swan

Frigate Bird

Gannet

Roseate Tern

Tattler

Pied Oystercatcher

Pied Cormorant

White-faced Heron

Little Penguin

Auger

Periwinkle

Distaff Spindle

Blue-winged Shoveller

Grey Teal

Pelican

Albatross

Pacific Gull

Osprey

Cape Barren Goose

Fairy Tern

Avocet

Silver Gull

White-headed Stilt

White-faced Storm Petrel

Godwit

Turnstone Non Breed

Golden Plover

Green Shank

Turnstone Breed

Hooded Dotterel

Common Sandpiper

Sanderling

Terek Sandpiper

Red-capped Dotterel

Yellow Mouthed Drupe

Double-banded Dotterel

Toad Purple

Draught Board Helmet

Jewelled Dog Whelk

Nautilus

Cowry

Yellow Sundial

Abalone

Spotted Har

Abalone

Zebra Volute

Mussel

Nerite

Reptiles, Amphibians & Insects

The cautionary tales of an Australian childhood are often remembered as warnings against snakes, sharks and spiders.

Tiger snakes, 'White Death', a shark beloved of headline writers, lurking redback spiders . . . are just some well-publicised dangers of the outdoors which regrettably lead many Australians to kill suspect creatures first, and identify them later.

While nearly 4000 Australians die annually from road accidents, about four die of snakebite, perhaps one (on average) by shark attack. Spiders have claimed only six lives in the past 15 years. But the folklore is persistent and many Australians know more about such long-odds killers than they do about natural wonders such as Australia's giant lizards, the 'living fossil' lungfish of Queensland and Gippsland earthworms growing up to 3.6 metres long.

Australia's Reptiles

These include about 140 species of snakes, 360 lizard species, two crocodiles, 15 species of freshwater tortoises and six marine turtles.

Fewer than 20 of the terrestrial snakes have venom potentially fatal to humans. Largest, and deadliest, is the taipan (*Oxyuranus scutellatus*), growing to three metres and more. Until the development of an anti-venene the bite of a large taipan was invariably fatal. Other particularly dangerous snakes are the tiger (*Notechis scutatus*), copperhead (*Australaps superbus*), death adder (*Acanthophis antarcticus*) and common brown (*Pseudonaja textilis*).

More than 30 species of sea-snakes found in northern waters are poisonous, but are fortunately rarely encountered by man. The yellow-bellied sea-snake (*Pelamis platurus*) — considered the world's most widely distributed snake — is common.

Two species of crocodiles were once common in northern Australia. One is harmless to man — the freshwater crocodile (*Crocodylus johnstoni*) which grows to three metres. The other, the saltwater crocodile (*C. porosus*) grows to seven metres and has frequently attacked cattle (and men). Both species are now protected.

Australia's lizards range in size from the giant perentie (*Varanus giganteus*) which grows to 2.4 metres — claimed as second in size only to Indonesia's Komodo dragon lizard — down to some not 50 mm long. None are venomous. Iguanas or chameleons are unknown.

Some of the dragon lizards successfully conceal a harmless nature behind a frightening facade. The best-known of the dragon lizards, the boldly-coloured thorny or mountain devil (*Moloch horridus*) has a limited ability to change colours to match background, but is well protected by many spines. The mountain devil is one of the world's most specialised dragons. Although slow of movement, its armour is so sharp that no animal could eat it without being injured itself. It has a long adhesive tongue, particularly suited to its diet of ants. The frilled lizard (*Chlamydosaurus kingii*) unfolds a vividly-coloured neck frill of membrane. The frill is normally folded back, but under attack it opens up, umbrella-style, and sways from side to side, while it opens its brightly-coloured mouth and hisses.

Unique to Australia and Papua New Guinea, the flap-footed legless lizards (Pygopodidae) are often mistaken for snakes by casual observers. They lack forelegs and their hind legs are mere flaps of skin.

Goannas, known beyond Australia as monitors, are common. These are among the most spectacular lizards. The sight of a couple of two-metre perenties fighting tooth and claw seems more in keeping with prehistoric times, than the present day.

Noteworthy among Australia's abundant skinks (*Scincidae*) is the large blue tongue skink (*Tiliqua spp.*) which discourages predators with a spectacular open-mouthed display.

Of the six turtles, the green turtle (*Chelonia mydas*) is fated to be popular as turtle soup, while the luth or leathery turtle (*Dermochelys coriacea*) is renowned as weighing half a tonne and reaching three metres in length. Both are found only in northern waters.

Australia lacks true land tortoises, but freshwater tortoises are distributed widely.

The Amphibians

Australia has approximately 130 species of frogs, but no salamanders or newts. There is only one toad, the giant South American Cane toad (*Bufo marinus*) which was introduced in 1935 to control cane-borer beetles. Since then it has spread in plague proportions along the north-east coast. Australia's native frogs include a diverse array of tree frogs, marsh frogs and burrowing frogs.

As in the case of many fish adapted to the frequent droughts of the inland, certain burrowing frogs are well-equipped to survive in dry conditions. The waterholding frog (*Cyclorana platycephalus*) fills its bladder with water, burrows into the soil, secretes a cocoon which prevents water loss, and hibernates there for months, if necessary.

Some Invertebrates

Australia has at least 50 000 insect species, many of which are endemic. There are some 350 species of butterflies and 7600 species of moths — including the world's largest moth, the giant Atlas moth (*Coscinocera hercules*) of northern Queensland. There are some 18 000 beetle species and 900 species of ants. The magnetic termite (*Amitermes meridionalis*) creates one of northern Australia's natural wonders — nests about four metres high, three metres long and a metre wide, with the narrow ends pointing approximately north-south.

The venomous red-back spider (*Latrodectus mactans*) is frequently found in rubbish heaps, old machinery and, traditionally, in outside toilets. The male red-back is almost one-third the size of the female and is reputed to be non-poisonous. The Sydney Funnel-web spider (*Atrax robustus*), possibly the world's most toxic spider, is unusually aggressive and will strike at objects of almost any size. Although the males generally die upon reaching maturity at seven or eight years, a seventeen-year-old female has been recorded.

Another curious invertebrate of startling appearance is the giant earthworm (*Megascolides australis*) of Victoria's Gippsland district, growing to 3.6 metres and 25 mm in diameter.

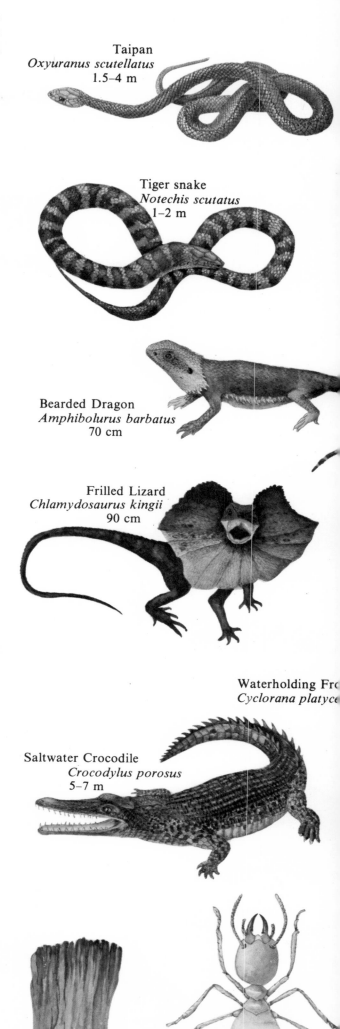

Taipan
Oxyuranus scutellatus
1.5–4 m

Tiger snake
Notechis scutatus
1–2 m

Bearded Dragon
Amphibolurus barbatus
70 cm

Frilled Lizard
Chlamydosaurus kingii
90 cm

Waterholding Fro
Cyclorana platyce

Saltwater Crocodile
Crocodylus porosus
5–7 m

east–west aspect

Magnetic termite
mound
(1–2 m in height)

north–south aspect

Magnetic Termite
Amitermes meridional
5 mm

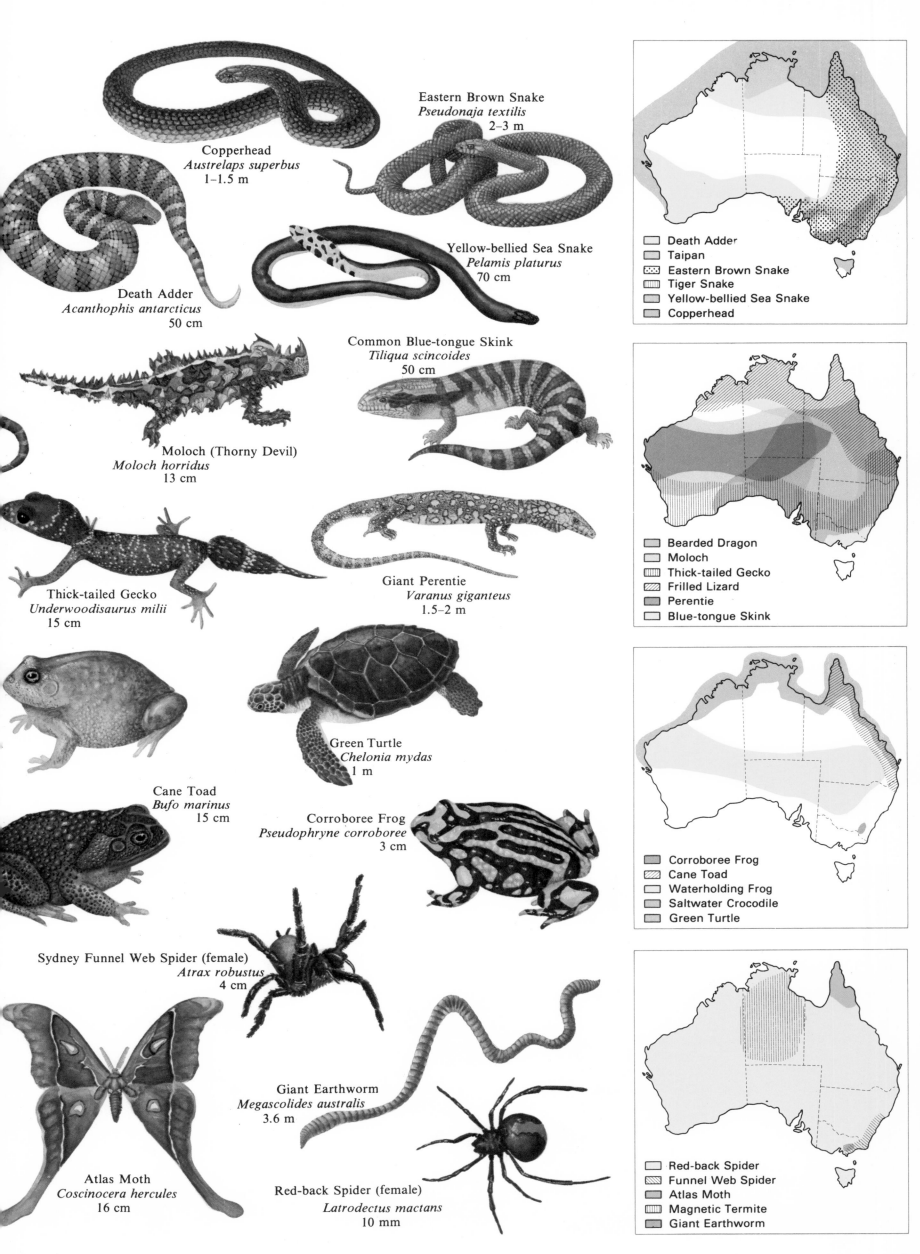

Copperhead
Austrelaps superbus
1–1.5 m

Eastern Brown Snake
Pseudonaja textilis
2–3 m

Yellow-bellied Sea Snake
Pelamis platurus
70 cm

Death Adder
Acanthophis antarcticus
50 cm

Moloch (Thorny Devil)
Moloch horridus
13 cm

Common Blue-tongue Skink
Tiliqua scincoides
50 cm

Thick-tailed Gecko
Underwoodisaurus milii
15 cm

Giant Perentie
Varanus giganteus
1.5–2 m

Green Turtle
Chelonia mydas
1 m

Cane Toad
Bufo marinus
15 cm

Corroboree Frog
Pseudophryne corroboree
3 cm

Sydney Funnel Web Spider (female)
Atrax robustus
4 cm

Giant Earthworm
Megascolides australis
3.6 m

Atlas Moth
Coscinocera hercules
16 cm

Red-back Spider (female)
Latrodectus mactans
10 mm

Death Adder
Taipan
Eastern Brown Snake
Tiger Snake
Yellow-bellied Sea Snake
Copperhead

Bearded Dragon
Moloch
Thick-tailed Gecko
Frilled Lizard
Perentie
Blue-tongue Skink

Corroboree Frog
Cane Toad
Waterholding Frog
Saltwater Crocodile
Green Turtle

Red-back Spider
Funnel Web Spider
Atlas Moth
Magnetic Termite
Giant Earthworm

45

The Australian Aborigines

The Australian Aborigines, once outcasts in their own land, have finally begun to receive the rights of other Australians. Aboriginal issues are debated as never before, and unprecedented government funding is contributing to what former Prime Minister Gough Whitlam termed the 'restoration of their lost power of self-determination in economic, social and political affairs'.

The fate of the Aborigines was almost genocide. For a long time it seemed likely that the European settlers who had seized their land and largely destroyed their unique culture, would 'smoothe their dying pillow'. But the Aborigines survived almost two centuries of oppression, neglect and racism, and their numbers are increasing so rapidly that it is probable that by the end of the century they will total around 300 000, somewhere near their population when the explorer Captain Cook 'took possession' of their land in the name of an English king in 1770. Today they number about one per cent of the Australian population, with an estimated 40 000 full-blood Aborigines and around 100 000 part-Aborigines.

Scientists believe that the Aborigines migrated to Australia from Asia about 30 000 years before European settlement. They developed in isolation, hunters and foragers with no domesticated animals but the dingo, and without crops which could be cultivated. Settled across the whole continent of Australia in some 500-600 tribal groups — each with its own territory — the Aborigines spoke about 300 distinct languages, most of which had additional dialects. Although the most common group size was a band of 20-40 people, they occasionally formed large parties for ceremonial or hunting purposes.

The men were essentially hunters or fishermen. Weapons and aids included spears and clubs, stone axes and knives, boomerangs and the woomera (throwing stick) which could propel a spear 120 metres or more. They had fish nets, traps, fish hooks, various water-craft, and often used fire to flush game. They depended on their women to provide the staple diet of small animals, seeds, roots, honey, fruit and berries.

Aboriginal culture was of an awesome complexity. It linked the Aborigines to tribal land and nature through ancestral beings — past, present and future were brought together in a framework of beliefs frequently expressed through dances, songs, verbal 'literature', art and rigidly-defined social relationships. With no written language, one measure of a man's maturity and importance was the degree of his understanding and absorption of his tribe's rituals and mythology, handed down by the older men. Life was ordered, offering individuals social, economic and psychological security.

This was the balanced, harmonious world disrupted by the Europeans who 'pioneered' beyond the first coastal villages. Given prevailing European attitudes to land, the dispossession and depopulation of the Aborigines was inevitable in the long term. In fact it came with brutal suddenness, more from epidemics of introduced disease than from gunfire, destroying random and futile resistance to the invaders. Aborigines died by the thousands of smallpox, venereal disease, tuberculosis, whooping cough, measles, influenza — killers which sometimes spread inland ahead of the first exploring parties.

In Tasmania, for example, the Aboriginal population declined from an estimated 4000 to fewer than 500 between 1800 and 1830, and was finally virtually wiped out. Three decades of European settlement in Victoria saw the Aboriginal population reduced from more than 10 000 to 2000. Disadvantaged in every way, the survivors became the 'fringe-dwellers' of Australian society, and the discriminatory pattern of poverty, health problems, high unemployment and poor education still exists in many areas.

Some Europeans had protested on behalf of the Aborigines from the earliest days of dispossession. There were well-meaning, sometimes enlightened, efforts to help. Reservations were set aside, rations issued, missions established which are still the focus of many Aboriginal settlements. But until the 1920s and 1930s the aim of much State legislation was 'protection', controlling measures which put Aborigines under the guardianship of official protectors. The result was frequently a 'reservation' philosophy, segregation which limited their movement, banned alcohol, managed property, regulated em-

ployment and often controlled interracial marriage. Public protests played a significant part in removing many of these restrictions in the 1940s, when it became obvious that improved welfare services and advanced medicines had started to reverse the population decline. In the 1950s State and Federal authorities called for assimilation, which assumed that people of Aboriginal descent would be fully integrated into the dominant European culture.

Today the policy is self-determination, and the encouraging of Aboriginal initiative, independence and identity. The increasing awareness of Aboriginal issues in the Australian community became evident after a 1967 referendum in which Australians voted in record numbers for changes in the Constitution, which resulted in the Federal government sharing responsibility for Aborigines with the States. It now dominates the field (all States but Queensland have transferred policy and coordination functions) and in consultation with elected Aboriginal spokesmen is attempting to respond to the great diversity of Aboriginal aspirations and expectations. Supplementing State funds, the Federal government allocated $153 million in 1976-77 for Aboriginal assistance programs beyond the usual social services available.

Few Aborigines live without frequent contact with elements of the European Australian community. More than 20 000 live in settlements and missions in the outback, where traditional Aboriginal culture remains strong. They have learned to put their case powerfully, especially in the controversial area of land rights. Australia has about 350 Aboriginal reserves totalling around 541 000 km²: almost half this area is in the Northern Territory, where one in four citizens is of Aboriginal descent. Some land has already been restored to Aboriginal communities, but there are still gulfs to be crossed and compromises to be reached before the 'unlucky Australians' achieve equality.

Below left: A mother and her children fishing for mussels, Arnhem Land, Northern Territory.

Below right: A nomadic Aboriginal tribesman, Northern Territory.

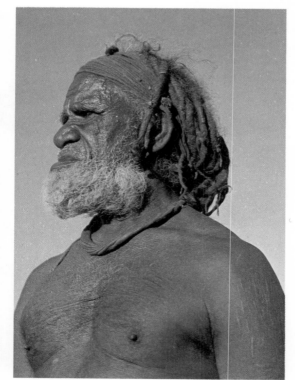

Distribution of Aborigines and Torres Strait Islanders

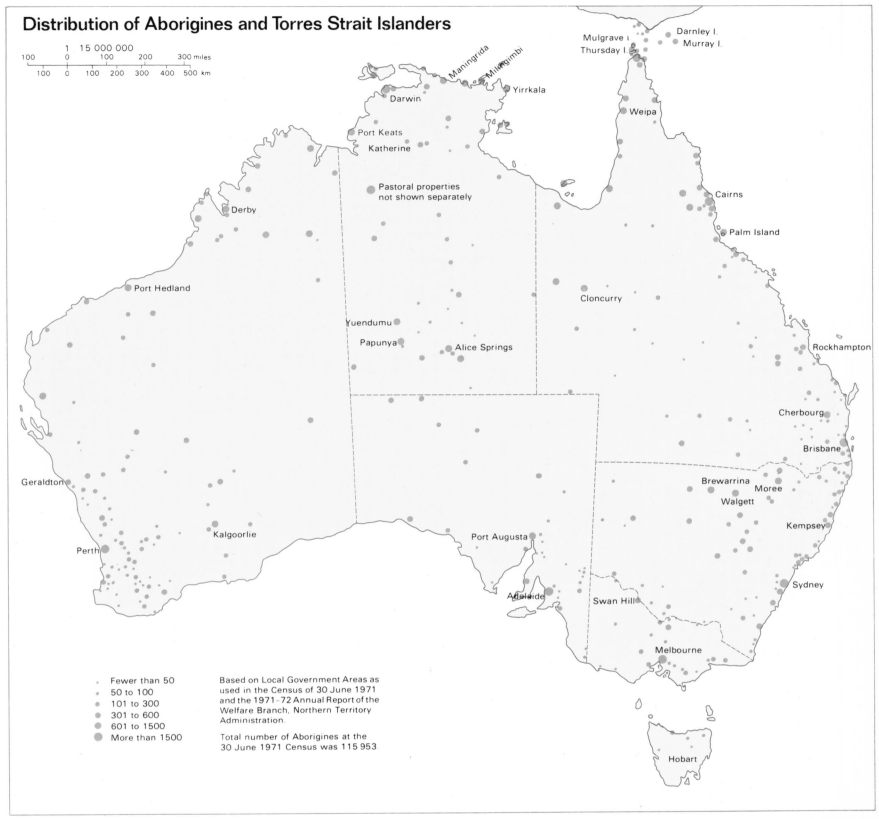

1 : 15 000 000

100   0   100   200   300 miles
100   0   100   200   300   400   500 km

Maningrida
Milingimbi
Yirrkala
Darwin
Mulgrave i.
Thursday I.
Darnley I.
Murray I.
Weipa
Port Keats
Katherine
Pastoral properties
not shown separately
Derby
Cairns
Port Hedland
Palm Island
Cloncurry
Yuendumu
Papunya
Alice Springs
Rockhampton
Cherbourg
Brisbane
Geraldton
Brewarrina
Moree
Walgett
Kempsey
Kalgoorlie
Port Augusta
Perth
Sydney
Adelaide
Swan Hill
Melbourne
Hobart

· Fewer than 50
· 50 to 100
· 101 to 300
● 301 to 600
● 601 to 1500
● More than 1500

Based on Local Government Areas as
used in the Census of 30 June 1971
and the 1971–72 Annual Report of the
Welfare Branch, Northern Territory
Administration.

Total number of Aborigines at the
30 June 1971 Census was 115 953

Aboriginal Populations and Percentages of Total Populations per State   June 1976*

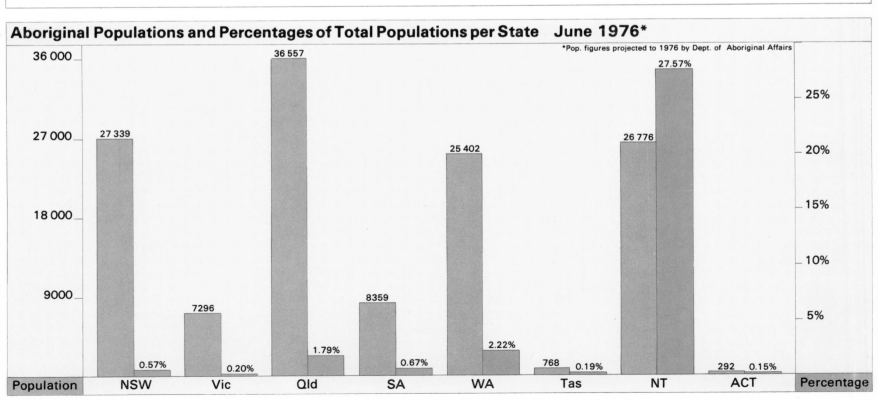

*Pop. figures projected to 1976 by Dept. of Aboriginal Affairs

Population	NSW	Vic	Qld	SA	WA	Tas	NT	ACT	Percentage
	27 339	7296	36 557	8359	25 402	768	26 776	292	
	0.57%	0.20%	1.79%	0.67%	2.22%	0.19%	27.57%	0.15%	

36 000
27 000
18 000
9000

25%
20%
15%
10%
5%

The European Discoverers

Terra Australis — the fabulous South Land that lay, perhaps, below the Equator between the Indian and Pacific Oceans — made a fine and enduring legend. Ptolemy, the Greek mathematician, sketched it south of Asia in the second century AD. Mapmakers of the Middle Ages included it on vague charts. The Chinese told fanciful tales of its riches . . .

Arabs, Indians and Chinese sailed the waters north of Australia for centuries before the Europeans appeared. There is no convincing evidence that they landed on Australia, although it is very likely that Malay fishermen were regular visitors.

Surprisingly, although the Portuguese, Spanish and Dutch were exploring the region from the early sixteenth century (northern Papua New Guinea was discovered in 1526), the first recorded European contact with Australia was not until early 1606. Sailing from Java in the pinnace *Duyfken*, the Dutch skipper Wilhelm Janszoon passed south of Papua New Guinea and sighted the west coast of Cape York peninsula. He mapped part of the coast, had a crew member killed in a skirmish with Aborigines and returned to Java unimpressed by the new land.

Later that year Luis Torres led two Spanish ships through the perilous strait, which today bears his name, between Papua New Guinea and Australia.

Seventeen years later the Dutchman Jan Carstensz retraced the *Duyfken*'s route, reporting sourly on the land and its inhabitants. Meanwhile, the Dutch captains engaged in the East Indies spice trade discovered that the quickest route to Java was by sailing east from the Cape of Good Hope with the prevailing trade winds, then turning north after some 6400 km. The first man to miscalculate and sail far enough to sight Australia was Dirk Hartog of the *Eendracht*. In 1616 he landed at Shark Bay and left the earliest memorial of European contact, a seaman's pewter plate inscribed with his name.

Other Dutchmen followed. Some lost their ships and lives on the largely uncharted coast. In three decades they discovered much of the coast from Cape York west to the Great Australian Bight — Franz Thyssen in the *Gulden Zeepart* had mapped almost as far as Spencer's Gulf in 1627 — yet New Holland had yielded nothing of value to them. Still hoping that the South Land might lie beyond New

Holland, the Governor-General of Batavia, Anthony Van Diemen, instructed Abel Tasman to search along latitude 53° South. Driven north by rough weather, Tasman came on the south-west coast of Tasmania, which he named Van Diemen's Land. Tasman explored briefly, then sailed east, discovering New Zealnd before returning to Java. A second great voyage in 1644 proved that New Holland had an unbroken coast between Cape York and North-West Cape. Dutch interest in New Holland then waned.

Top left: A mid-seventeenth century Dutch map of the world.

Top right: Statue of Matthew Flinders outside St Paul's Cathedral, Melbourne.

Below left: The collier the Earl of Pembroke, *which later became the* Endeavour.

Below right: A replica of Vlamingh's plate. In 1697 Vlamingh found the original plate which had been left by Hartog on a small island he discovered off the coast of Western Australia in 1616. Vlamingh added the details of his own visit to a new plate and took the original back to Batavia.

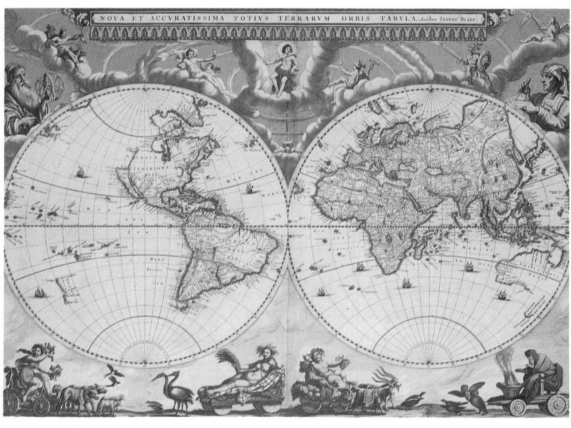

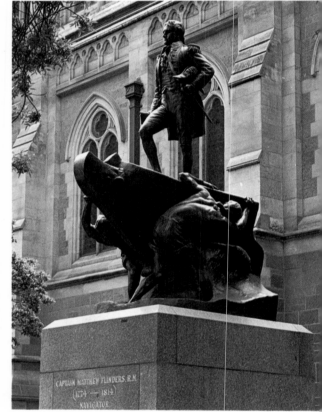

The first English ship to reach Australia was the East Indiaman *Tryal*, wrecked in 1622 on a reef north of the Monte Bello Islands off Western Australia. Captain John Daniel in the English ship *London* also sighted the west coast in 1681, but not until the voyage of the *Cygnet* along the north-west coast in 1688 — and the subsequent publication of a journal by adventurer William Dampier — did New Holland capture the English imagination. Dampier damned the inhospitable coast and its inhabitants, but as interest in the South Seas grew the incompetent former buccaneer was appointed captain of HMS *Roebuck* and sent back to continue his discoveries. It was a shambles of a voyage that added little to the charts, yet the second book which resulted helped focus English attention on the Pacific.

Cook's Triumph

Man's interest in astronomy resulted in the English claiming the fertile east coast of New Holland. Captain Cook had taken a party of scientists to Tahiti to observe the transit of Venus across the face of the sun. Following instructions to search for Terra Australis, he then sailed south in the *Endeavour* and mapped New Zealand. En route to Van Diemen's Land a southerly gale forced him north, and on 19 April 1770 he sighted the east coast of Australia at what is now Cape Everard. He sailed north, exploring Botany Bay, mapping as he went until the *Endeavour* was holed by coral on the Barrier Reef and had to be beached for repairs. After charting almost the entire northern coast, he landed on an island north of Cape York and on 22 August claimed eastern New Holland in the name of King George III. Later he gave it the name New South Wales.

Enthusiastic reports of this voyage were remembered when the rebellion of the American colonies in 1776 ended the transportation of convicts to North America. The dream of the great South Land, which had excited men for centuries, soon ended in the reality of an English prison colony. Modern Australian history started in January 1788 when Captain Phillip's First Fleet arrived in Botany Bay.

Charting the Coast

Two adventurous men who had arrived in New South Wales in 1795 were to resolve the last major uncertainty about the map of New Holland. Ship's surgeon George Bass and midshipman Matthew Flinders made their first foray south from Sydney Cove in the *Tom Thumb* — only 2.5 metres long — and followed it with other hazardous journeys. Bass then sailed as far as Westernport Bay in a whaleboat, but returned to Sydney convinced by sea conditions that there was a strait between New Holland and Van Diemen's Land. Bass and Flinders proved the theory correct by sailing the sloop *Norfolk* around Van Diemen's Land.

In 1801 Flinders commenced his great work, circumnavigating the continent in the *Investigator* and meticulously mapping both the southern and much of the north-eastern coast. He ended speculation on an inland sea dividing the continent, and suggested yet another name for the Terra Incognita of the ancients — Australia.

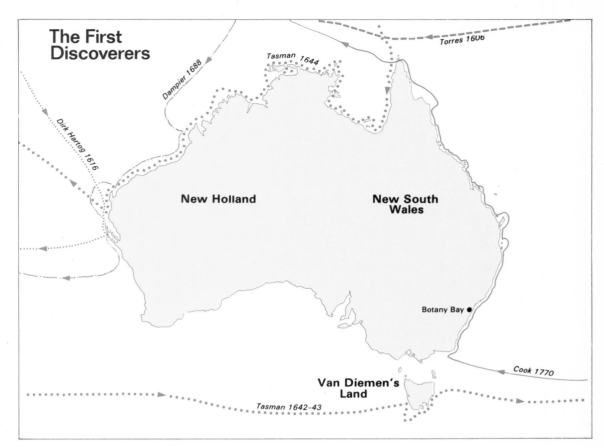

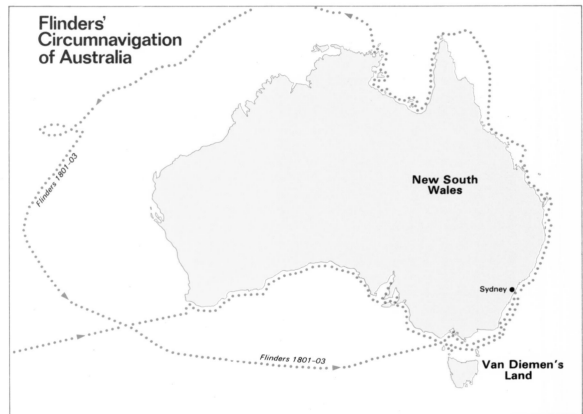

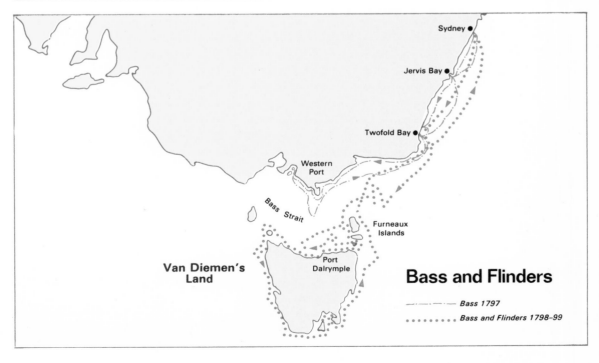

Exploring an Unknown Land

The history of Australian exploration sometimes seems as unlikely, as exaggerated, as the alien land itself: 'It does not read like history, but like the most beautiful of lies, and all of a fresh sort', Mark Twain commented. The early European settlers found the seasons reversed, the climate tending to extremes (usually heat), the animals and plants bizarre, and the geography baffling.

The sagas of exploration included men with endurance beyond belief, and also fools with no qualities other than curiosity and courage. Men carried boats towards non-existent central seas; rivers could be 40 km broad one season and then vanish for the next decade; some explorers owed their fame and lives to Aborigines, and some their lonely deaths. Some returned in triumph, or at least received a hero's burial.

The first geographic barrier facing Europeans was the Blue Mountains range — nowhere 1500 metres high — west of Sydney. For a quarter of a century its escarpments and gorges baffled expeditions, until in 1813 Gregory Blaxland, William Lawson and William Wentworth penetrated the range by following the ridges instead of the valleys. Like so many later explorers, they were driven by the need to find pastures for the colony's expanding sheep flocks. They were followed by George Evans, who completed the crossing, and John Oxley, who found rich grazing regions in 1817 and 1818 but was frustrated in attempts to follow the westward-flowing Lachlan and Macquarie Rivers.

Victoria was opened up by Hamilton Hume and William Hovell during their 1824 journey south across the Australian Alps to Corio Bay, now Geelong. The enigma of the westward-flowing rivers remained. Was there an inland sea, or perhaps a river outlet to the south coast? Part of the answer was provided by Captain Charles Sturt, who discovered the Darling in 1828 after being forced northwards by the reed beds of the Macquarie. In 1829 he was directed to explore the Murrumbidgee by boat, discovering Australia's major river, the Murray, in January 1830. His party made a remarkable voyage to its mouth near Lake Alexandrina: unable to rendezvous with a ship, they were compelled to battle back upstream for some

1450 km, a nightmare of exhaustion and near-starvation. Not daunted by the privations of that epic journey (including temporary blindness), Sturt searched for the supposed inland sea and the centre of Australia from 1844-46, enduring further hardships without finding fertile land.

By then men were probing inland from isolated coastal settlements, including Hobart in Tasmania (1803), the Brisbane River settlement in Queensland (1824), Swan River in Western Australia (1829), Melbourne in Victoria (1835) and Adelaide in South Australia (1836).

In 1836 Major Thomas Mitchell discovered much of Victoria's best land, including the famed sheep country of the Western District. In north-west Australia, George Grey made significant explorations in 1837 and 1839, incidentally becoming the first European to see the remarkable Aboriginal cave paintings of the Kimberleys. Edward John Eyre found himself a national hero in 1841 after an incredible trek of almost 1600 km across the barren southern coastline of Australia between Streaky Bay in South Australia and King George's Sound in Western Australia. Two Aborigines in the small party murdered his European companion and deserted with supplies, leaving Eyre and the remaining Aboriginal youth Wylie to continue across the near-desert. After five weeks of extreme hardship they fortunately came upon a French whaler.

Eastern Victoria — now Gippsland — was opened up by the separate discoveries of Angus McMillan and the Pole, Paul Strzelecki, who found and named Australia's highest peak, Mount Kosciusko (2228 metres). In the north, the eccentric German migrant Ludwig Leichhardt, no bushman, discovered some of the best land in central Queensland on an arduous 3200 km trek in 1844-45 from Brisbane to Port Essington, north of modern Darwin. In 1848 he set out to cross Australia from east to west — and the entire expedition vanished without trace. Another tragedy occurred that year when Edmund Kennedy penetrated Cape York peninsula. He was fatally speared by Aborigines; three men left at a depot were never found, and six of eight men at a base camp starved to death before

the relief ship arrived.

Several parties searched for the missing Leichhardt. Although unsuccessful, Augustus Gregory made two notable journeys, a west-east crossing of northern Australia in 1855-56 starting from the Victoria River, and an 1858 expedition from the Dawson Ranges in Queensland (in which he traced the Barcoo River and proved it merged into Cooper's Creek) to Adelaide.

Crossing the Continent

The first men to cross Australia from south to north were a policeman, Robert O'Hara Burke, and a surveyor, William Wills, leaders of the most costly Australian exploring party ever. They started from Melbourne with 27 camels, 23 horses and 21 tons of baggage. The impetuous Burke and three companions pushed northward from an advance base on Cooper's Creek without waiting for the main supplies to come up. In February 1861 they reached tidal waters on the north coast after a stern struggle: the return was frightful, one man dying of scurvy and the three gaunt survivors battling through to find the Cooper's Creek party had left the depot just seven hours before they arrived. A series of blunders by the three separated elements of the expedition resulted in Burke and Wills slowly starving to death in the wilderness.

John McDouall Stuart, an experienced bushman who had ridden with Sturt, came close to beating Burke and Wills to the north coast. Seeking the £2000 reward offered to the man who found a route for an overland telegraph from Adelaide to the north coast, Stuart made three gruelling journeys, discovering the arid centre of Australia and finally crossing the continent in 1862 after great suffering. In the west, John Forrest, Peter Warburton and Ernest Giles achieved fame with lengthy crossings of forbidding deserts and barren country.

Below left: One of the Aboriginal cave paintings discovered by Sir George Grey in the Kimberleys, north-west Australia.

Below right: An imaginary painting of exploration into the interior by T. J. Maslen, 1830.

Exploration Routes

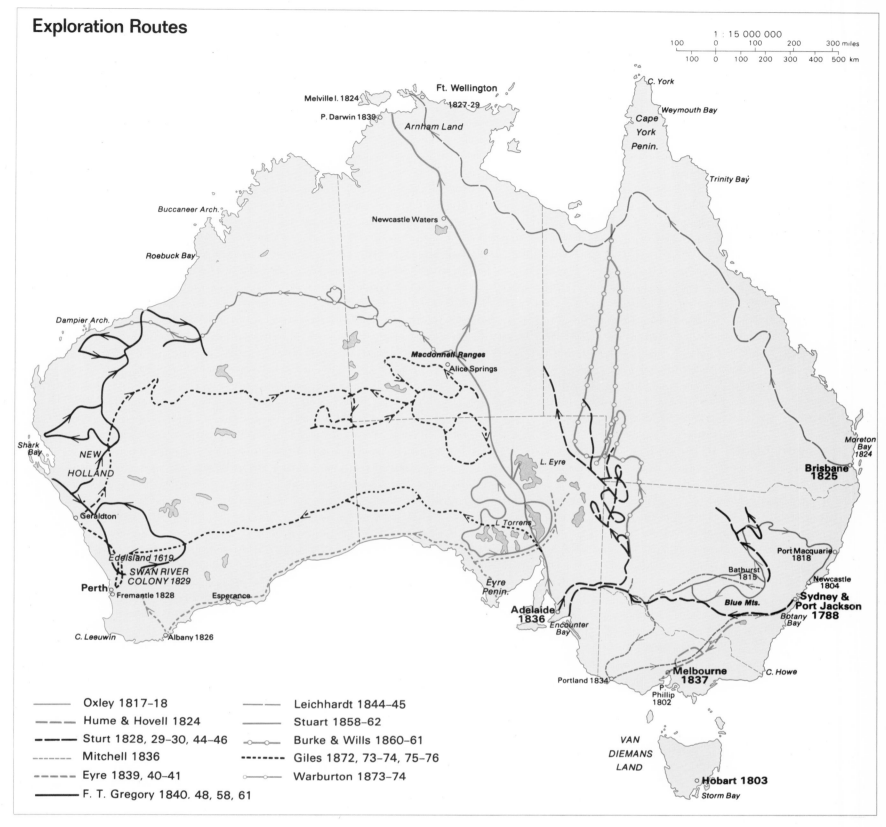

Legend (left column)	Legend (right column)
—— Oxley 1817–18	— — Leichhardt 1844–45
— — Hume & Hovell 1824	——— Stuart 1858–62
▬▬ Sturt 1828, 29–30, 44–46	—○—○— Burke & Wills 1860–61
----- Mitchell 1836	••••• Giles 1872, 73–74, 75–76
- - - Eyre 1839, 40–41	—○—○— Warburton 1873–74
——— F. T. Gregory 1840. 48, 58, 61	

Ft. Wellington 1827–29

Melville I. 1824

P. Darwin 1839

Arnhem Land

C. York

Weymouth Bay

Cape York Penin.

Trinity Bay

Buccaneer Arch.

Newcastle Waters

Roebuck Bay

Dampier Arch.

Macdonnell Ranges

Alice Springs

Moreton Bay 1824

Brisbane 1825

Shark Bay

NEW HOLLAND

L. Eyre

Port Macquarie 1818

Geraldton

Edelsland 1619

SWAN RIVER COLONY 1829

L Torrens

Bathurst 1815

Newcastle 1804

Perth

Fremantle 1828

Esperance

Eyre Penin.

Blue Mts.

Sydney & Port Jackson 1788

Botany Bay

C. Leeuwin

Albany 1826

Adelaide 1836

Encounter Bay

Melbourne 1837

C. Howe

Portland 1834

P. Phillip 1802

VAN DIEMANS LAND

Hobart 1803

Storm Bay

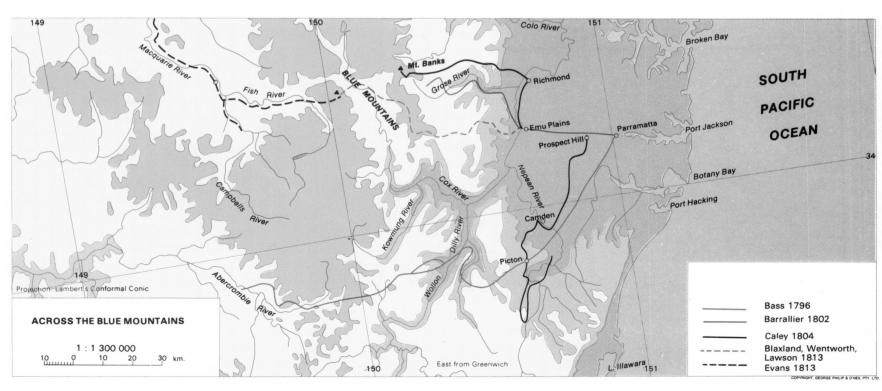

ACROSS THE BLUE MOUNTAINS

Macquarie River

Colo River

Broken Bay

BLUE MOUNTAINS

Mt. Banks

Grose River

Fish River

Richmond

SOUTH PACIFIC OCEAN

Campbells River

Kowmung River

Cox River

Dilly River

Emu Plains

Prospect Hill

Parramatta

Port Jackson

34

Napean River

Botany Bay

Port Hacking

Camden

Picton

Wollon

Abercrombie River

East from Greenwich

L. Illawara

149

Projection Lambert's Conformal Conic

1 : 1 300 000

10   0   10   20   30 km.

———	Bass 1796
———	Barrallier 1802
———	Caley 1804
- - -	Blaxland, Wentworth, Lawson 1813
— — —	Evans 1813

COPYRIGHT. GEORGE PHILIP & O'NEIL PTY. LTD.

Populating a Harsh Continent

Australia in the mid 1970s is undergoing a social change of immense significance: the sinking birthrate is approaching (and seems likely to sink below) the replacement rate required to keep the population stable.

Annual postwar rates of population increase which ranged as high as 2.5 per cent fell to one per cent in 1976. Great cuts in net migration — from 103 553 in 1971 to 22 133 in 1976 — have played the major role in these dramatic statistics.

In January 1977, Australia's population passed 14 million. Many long-standing assumptions concerning population growth, however, have been challenged by the forecasts of Australia's leading demographer, Professor W. D. Borrie. He predicts a population of about 15 900 000 by 2001 AD without immigration, and of around 17 600 000 with net immigration of 50 000 people annually. Professor Borrie believes the likely situation of virtually no natural growth will take Australia back to what existed in earlier times when the growth of the human race was only marginally above replacement level.

Australia's slide to zero population growth echoes trends in developed overseas countries. By mid 1974, 21 out of 31 countries usually regarded as highly developed had birth rates below replacement levels. West Germany, East Germany, Finland and Luxembourg experienced a population decline in 1975, while Sweden and Denmark appear likely to follow suit.

This world-wide and Australia-wide trend is emphasised by the crude birth rate figures for the State of Victoria, for the quarter ending March 1977: they number 14 800 compared with 15 925 for the same period in 1976, a fall of 7 per cent. The implications of this unexpected, and dramatic slowing down of Australia's population growth are enormous. Planning for development in education, transport, housing and other services, industry and commerce, has been based on population projections which are now proven to have been falsely optimistic. Large growth centres such as Albury-Wodonga and Monarto have been planned for an expected population growth that is now known to be non-existent.

Australia's very low population density (1.281 persons per km² in 1976) compares with 326 for the Netherlands, Britain 229, Europe 95 (excepting USSR), Asia 78 (excepting USSR), USA 24, and USSR 11. Excepting Antarctica, Australia is the world's most sparsely-settled continent. Australia's population is heavily centralised, with approximately 65 per cent living in major urban areas, 20 per cent in other urban areas and 15 per cent in rural areas. Another surprising fact revealed by the 1976 census was a trend away from the two 'giants', Sydney and Melbourne: almost all other large urban cities are growing faster.

The planned development of growth centres like Albury/Wodonga has contributed to this yet modest but applauded reversal in a long-existing pattern. The increasing popularity of Queensland's Gold Coast, with its population rising by 6.76 per cent annually, for retirement as well as holidays, is obvious.

During 1976 marriages rose by 6008 to 109 981. Divorces soared to 57 839 (more than four times the 1971 figure) a fact that is

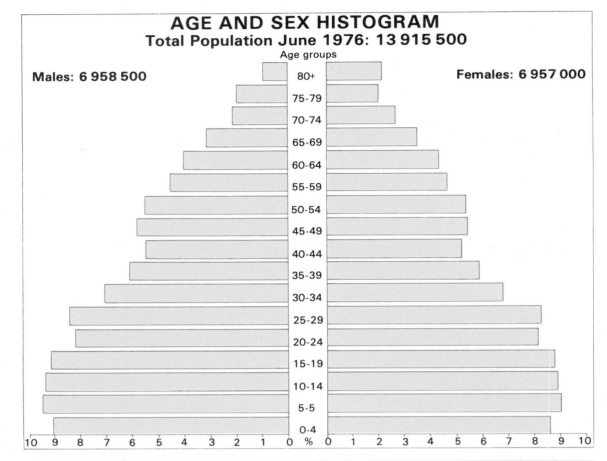

AGE AND SEX HISTOGRAM
Total Population June 1976: 13 915 500

Males: 6 958 500   Age groups   Females: 6 957 000

Age groups (top to bottom): 80+, 75-79, 70-74, 65-69, 60-64, 55-59, 50-54, 45-49, 40-44, 35-39, 30-34, 25-29, 20-24, 15-19, 10-14, 5-5, 0-4

Scale: 10 9 8 7 6 5 4 3 2 1 0 % 0 1 2 3 4 5 6 7 8 9 10

An aerial view of the Albury-Wodonga growth centre. Albury in NSW, and Wodonga in Victoria, both developed at the major bridging point of the Murray River for transport between Sydney and Melbourne. In October 1973 The Federal government and State governments of New South Wales and Victoria agreed that Albury-Wodonga would be developed as a growth centre. The Federal government promised to move sections of the public service and establish a university there. A projected population of 300 000 was to be planned for in the year 2000.

By 1977, however, with the dramatic slowing of population growth together with cuts in government expenditure, the future of this exciting exercise in decentralisation looked far from secure. Federal spending was limited to existing contracts and the population target dropped to 150 000 by the turn of the century.

accounted for by the first rush of settlements under the simplified new divorce laws.

The Decline in Fertility

The general trend of declining fertility in Australia has been evident since the 1880s, when the average married woman who had completed her family had 6.5 children. This figure dropped to 4 children in 1921 and only 2.5 children in 1961. A more conventional index, total fertility, was 6.2 children per woman in 1921, 2.2 in 1933, 3.5 in 1961 and 2.22 in 1975.

The net reproduction or replacement rate actually fell below zero in 1933 during the Depression, and it appears that Australian fertility is again close to (or possibly below) replacement level. Births per thousand of mean population have fallen from 21.62 in 1971 to 17.21 in 1975.

Reasons for the decline of the birth-rate include new attitudes to a woman's role in the home and the workforce, availability and efficiency of contraception, and the tendency to postpone first births.

Pessimistic observers see a future where a shrinking workforce supports a larger number of retired people; optimists trust that automation, national mineral wealth and other factors will improve the quality of life and lessen the demands on non-renewable resources. A vital factor will be future levels of immigration — which have yet to be decided.

Australia's Population Distribution

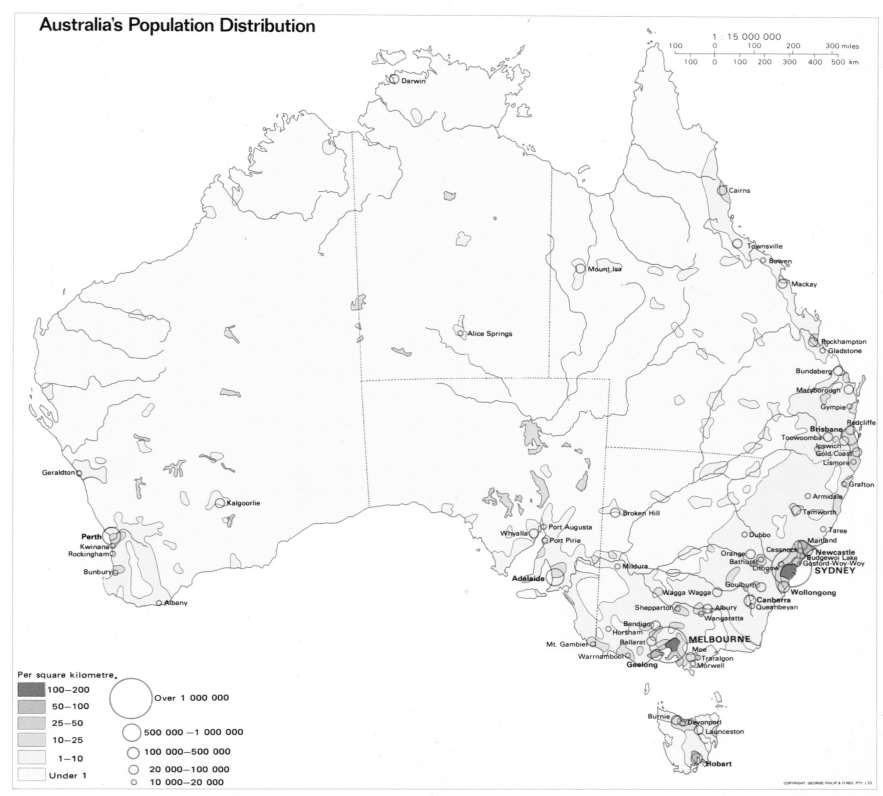

1 : 15 000 000

Per square kilometre
- 100—200
- 50—100
- 25—50
- 10—25
- 1—10
- Under 1

- Over 1 000 000
- 500 000 – 1 000 000
- 100 000 – 500 000
- 20 000 – 100 000
- 10 000 – 20 000

Population Growth in Australia 1788-1976

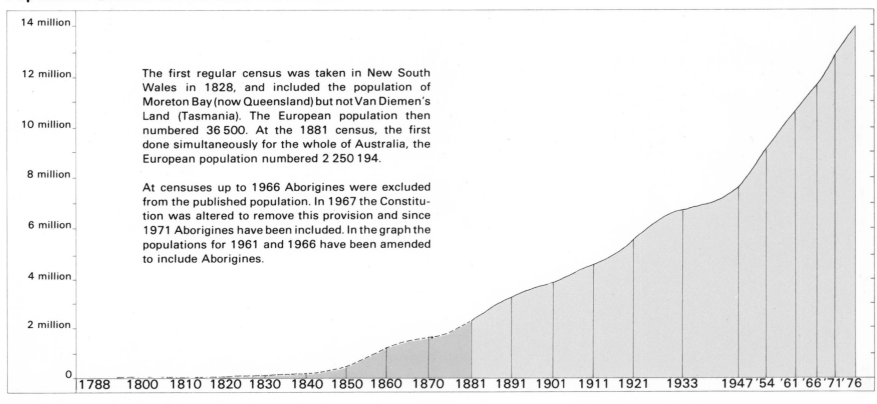

The first regular census was taken in New South Wales in 1828, and included the population of Moreton Bay (now Queensland) but not Van Diemen's Land (Tasmania). The European population then numbered 36 500. At the 1881 census, the first done simultaneously for the whole of Australia, the European population numbered 2 250 194.

At censuses up to 1966 Aborigines were excluded from the published population. In 1967 the Constitution was altered to remove this provision and since 1971 Aborigines have been included. In the graph the populations for 1961 and 1966 have been amended to include Aborigines.

The New Australians

The people who became the first Australians migrated from the Asian mainland along the Indonesian archipelago. Although sea-levels during the Pleistocene Era were lower than today, their journey probably included sea voyages. The survivors adapted to their frequently daunting homeland and were later called Aborigines.

Some 30 000 years later the second significant wave of immigrants arrived on the other side of the oldest continent. They were Caucasians, prisoners sent halfway across the world to found modern Australia. More than 160 000 of them were shipped from Britain between 1788 and 1867.

Although free settlers joined the felons and their guards, it was not until the gold rushes of the 1850s that Australia's population leapt ahead. That wild decade saw more than 500 000 people arrive.

A century later, in one of history's great mass migrations, more than 3 million people settled in Australia, during the three decades after World War 2. The population rose to more than 13 500 000, including 140 000 Aborigines, descendants of the estimated 300 000 present before the European settlers arrived.

The first European explorers and traders discovered Australia in the 1600s, usually by accident. The western fringe of the continent had nothing to offer, and it was not until 1770, when the explorer Captain Cook discovered the fertile east coast, that the long peace of the Aborigines was threatened. Only eight years after Cook rather belatedly took possession of eastern Australia in the name of George III, the first 11 shiploads of convicts and guards established the colony of New South Wales. These reluctant immigrants and their unenthusiastic gaolers were not equipped with the talents, tools or desire to tame this often inhospitable new land, and the authorities quickly sought to attract free settlers by offering free passage and other inducements. Free immigration started slowly: only 18

per cent of the 77 000 arrivals up to 1830 were free settlers. The birth of the wool industry boosted immigration, but it took the gold rushes to really open up Australia — between 1850 and 1860 the population grew from 405 000 to 1 145 000, three-quarters of the increase coming from net immigration.

They came from Britain, Germany, Poland, China, America, Scandinavia, Hungary: a torrent of free labour which hastened the end of convict transportation. Unemployment mounted as the surface gold was exhausted; the assisted immigration programs were tapered off. There was resentment against the Chinese, who were willing to accept lower employment and living standards, and increasing controversy about the indentured labour system which recruited Pacific Islanders to work in the Queensland canefields in conditions often akin to slavery.

Immigration fluctuated with the state of the economy. At two periods during the depressed 1890s more people left Australia than arrived.

Federation in 1901 led to a national immigration policy which virtually excluded non-European immigrants — the so-called 'White Australia Policy' which remained essentially unchanged until after World War 2. Immigration, interrupted by World War 1, flourished until the Depression, when once again Australia suffered a net loss of migrants.

Postwar Immigration

After World War 2 Australia launched a large-scale immigration program which changed Australian society remarkably, bringing in 3 million settlers from more that 60 nations in three decades. At the end of the war Australia had been left with 7 391 000 people (not quite one person to the km²), severe manpower shortages, fears for its continued security, and a need to develop rich natural resources. Planners aimed to recruit

new settlers at the rate of about one per cent of population a year: in fact between 1947 and 1973 the annual population increase averaged 2.12 per cent, including a net immigration rate of about 0.86 per cent. Australia spent more than $400 million on passages for more than 1 940 000 postwar settlers.

The current population of over 14 million is more than 80 per cent higher than the 1945 figure: net immigration and Australian-born children of settlers account for about 60 per cent of this.

One in five Australians was born overseas, and 25 per cent of the 6 million children born in the last quarter of a century in Australia also had at least one parent born overseas.

The workforce rose from 2 600 000 in 1947 to 5 800 000 in 1973, with migrants forming half the increase. Britain has been the largest single source of migrants, with the balance coming from more than 60 countries, particularly Italy, Greece, the Netherlands, West Germany, Yugoslavia, Poland and Austria.

With four out of ten Australians being migrants or the children of migrants, there have been far-reaching changes to the culture and attitudes of prewar Australia, with its strong British links. Some are obvious: the popularity of soccer, broadened tastes in food, even the quadrupling of table wine consumption during the 1960s owed much to migrant example. The presence of the 'New Australians' made Australians less insular, and more tolerant of people with different traditions and lifestyles.

The immigration restrictions on non-Europeans were gradually relaxed after World War 2, particularly by a 1966 review which significantly widened eligibility criteria. A further major immigration appraisal followed in the early 1970s on the cost-effectiveness of continued large-scale immigration and the nation's ability to pro-

A typically cosmopolitan scene in the Melbourne suburb of Richmond.

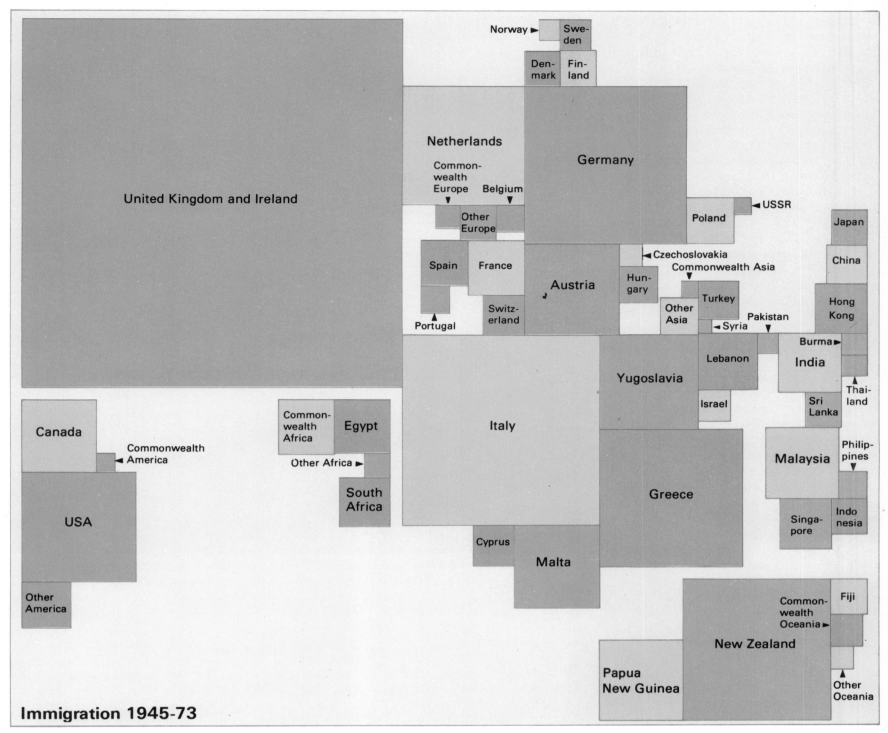

Immigration 1945-73

vide jobs and adjustment services (for example, language and orientation courses, telephone interpreters, counselling).

With much of the developed world suffering an economic recession, and Australia's unemployment the worst since the Depression, the government phased down immigration to a postwar low of 50 000 in 1975-76. (About 185 000 people arrived in 1969-70.) This trend was reversed when the 1976/77 target was raised to 70 000.

Immigration policy now emphasises family reunion and the recruiting of specific trade skills. More importance is given to the government services intended to help settlers adjust more easily.

More than 900 000 of the postwar immigrants have become Australian citizens. And as Australia's birthrate falls to zero population growth levels, the future of immigration has yet to be decided.

When countries are scaled according to their contribution of immigrants to Australia, they take on interesting new dimensions. The scale used in drawing the sides of the country 'squares' is 18 mm equalling 50 000 immigrants (approximately). The 'distorted' map of the world shows at a glance the relative importance of the major contributing countries to Australia's massive postwar migration program.

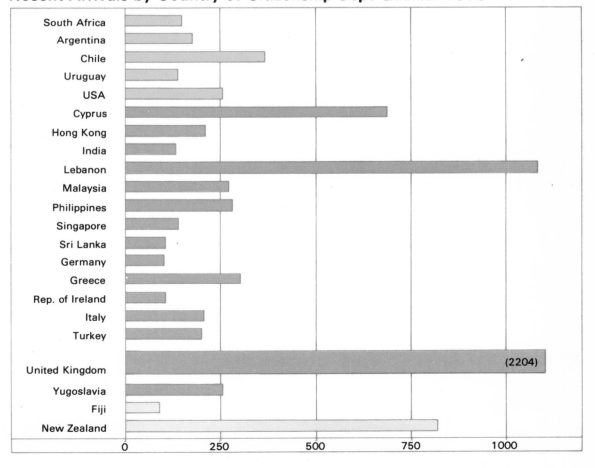

Recent Arrivals by Country of Citizenship Sept Quarter 1976

(United Kingdom bar labelled (2204))

How We Are Governed

Australia's political and administrative systems follow the Western liberal democratic tradition. They were shaped by both British and North American models.

During the nineteeth century the six British colonies in Australia attained self-government along the lines of the British ('Westminster') parliamentary system. Bicameral (two chamber) Parliaments were created — although Queensland abolished its Upper House in 1922. The five State Upper Houses are called Legislative Councils, while the Lower House is known as the Legislative Assembly in New South Wales, Victoria and Queensland, and the House of Assembly in South Australia and Tasmania.

When the States agreed to join together as one nation, they framed a Federation owing much to American and Canadian precedents. It came into effect on 1 January 1901 with a Constitution defining the powers which the Federal Government took over from the States.

Broadly, the Federation has three levels of government. The Australian Parliament (legislature) and Government are responsible for matters of national concern, primarily defence, communications, foreign affairs, transport regulation, customs, trade, social services, immigration and Treasury. The State legislatures and governments have complementary activities (especially education, agriculture, energy services, health, law enforcement) while some 900 bodies at local government level (cities, towns, shires, municipalities) have varying responsibilities that may include urban planning, road construction, water, sewerage and drainage and local community facilities and limited social services.

All government elections are by secret ballot, a world innovation pioneered in Victoria in 1856 and later widely adopted overseas as 'the Australian ballot'. Australia also pioneered compulsory voting — which results in a turnout exceeding 95 per cent of the nation's 8 million-plus electors — and was one of the first countries to give women the vote.

Federal Parliament

Federal Parliament generally follows the British model, despite having adopted the American terms 'Senate' and 'House of Representatives'.

The Government consists of the Sovereign (represented by the Governor-General, and Governors in State governments) and both Houses. Because the Constitution does not define the structure of government exhaustively, much depends on political conventions, arrangements of tradition or convenience whose fragility was especially evident during the constitutional crisis of 1975.

The Constitution's 127 sections can be changed only by referendum after proposed alterations have been passed by absolute majorities of both Houses. Referendum success then requires support from an overall majority of voters, as well as a majority in at least four of the six States.

The House of Representatives (sometimes known as the 'People's House') faces elections at least every three years. Its 127 current electorates average 65 806 voters each, although any single electorate's numbers may be up to

10 per cent above or below the average. Australia's great extremes of population density result in some remarkably large electorates, notably Kalgoorlie Division in Western Australia with only 51 161 voters in 2 271 379 square kilometres.

At present New South Wales has 45 Members of the House of Representatives, Victoria 34, Queensland 18, South Australia 12, Western Australia 10, Tasmania five, Australian Capital Territory two and the Northern Territory one. The 'alternative voting' system takes into account the voter's preference for all candidates. The number of Members must be as nearly as possible twice the number of Senators.

The Senate was conceived as a 'States' House' but few contemporary commentators concede it much power in that role, and voting is almost on party lines. There are currently 10 Senators from the six States, and two each from the Northern Territory and Australian Capital Territory. A 'preferential voting' system (in practice, representation of parties proportionate to voting in each State) elects them for six-year terms (three years for Territory senators), half retiring every three years. The Senate's role as a 'House of Review', including the potential to delay or reject money Bills essential for a Government's survival, led to the 1974 double dissolution of Parliament and consequent election, and the 1975 deadlock over other money Bills.

The Governor-General

The Governor-General represents the Crown (the Queen of Australia, not the British Government) and his powers are broadly those of the British conventions of constitutional monarchy. His role is usually limited to formalities touching decisions made by others.

However he has legal discretion in some Parliamentary matters (summoning Parliament, dissolving the House of Representatives, or both Houses).

Elections

Enrolment and voting are compulsory for British subjects aged 18 or older, resident in Australia for six months. Those ineligible are migrants not yet British subjects, people on temporary entry permits, prohibited immigrants, those of unsound mind and anyone convicted of treason or under prison sentence of a year or more.

Judiciary and State Parliaments

The Constitution created the High Court, the national Federal Supreme Court which makes all final interpretations of the Constitution and acts as court of appeal against decisions of the six State Supreme Courts.

Parliament has also created other courts with federal competence, including the Federal Court of Bankruptcy and the Australian Industrial Court whose powers include enforcing and interpreting awards made by the non-judicial Conciliation and Arbitration Commission which is charged with preventing or adjudicating industrial disputes extending beyond one State.

Above: As the functions of government increase many of the original buildings are no longer adequate. Defence is one of the departments being moved to the new Canberra growth centre of Campbell.

Opposite: Parliament Houses, Canberra, by night. This is the provisional home of the Australian Parliament as a new Parliament building is planned for Camp Hill immediately behind the present site.

1786–1824

Fort Dundas
1824

unattached

long. 135°E

New
South
Wales

Moreton Bay
1824

Sydney
1788

Lord Howe I.

Norfolk I.

Van Diemen's
Land

Hobart
1804

NZ

1829

Western
Australia

long. 129°E

New
South
Wales

Perth
1829

Brisbane

King George
Sound
1826

Sydney

Lord Howe I.

Norfolk I.

Van Diemen's
Land

Hobart

NZ

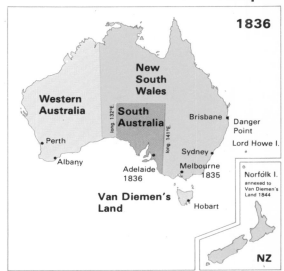

1836

Western
Australia

long. 132°E

South
Australia

long. 141°E

New
South
Wales

Perth

Brisbane

Albany

Adelaide
1836

Melbourne
1835

Sydney

Danger
Point

Lord Howe I.

Norfolk I.
annexed to
Van Diemen's
Land 1844

Van Diemen's
Land

Hobart

NZ

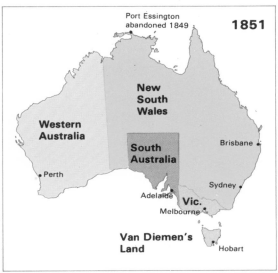

1851

Western
Australia

Port Essington
abandoned 1849

New
South
Wales

South
Australia

Brisbane

Perth

Adelaide

Sydney

Vic.

Melbourne

Van Diemen's
Land

Hobart

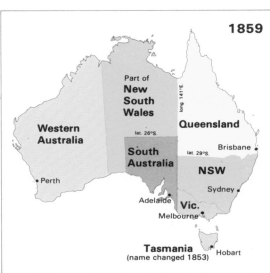

1859

Western
Australia

Part of
New
South
Wales

long. 141°E

Queensland

lat. 26°S.

South
Australia

lat. 29°S.

Brisbane

NSW

Perth

Adelaide

Sydney

Vic.

Melbourne

Tasmania
(name changed 1853)

Hobart

1931

Darwin

Western
Australia

Northern
Territory

long. 138°E

Queensland

South
Australia

Brisbane

NSW

Perth

Adelaide

Sydney

Vic.

Canberra
A.C.T.

Melbourne

Tasmania

Hobart

Agricultural Production

The Australian environment provides a broad range of settings for primary production. Since the first attempts by pioneer settlers to supply themselves with food and to establish Australia's first export market based on fine wool, primary production has developed into a major industry. It not only provides most of the populations's food and fibre requirements, but is also an important world supplier of several products, thereby securing valuable export earnings which help to finance Australia's further development.

Approximately 65 per cent of the total land area of Australia is used for agriculture, but less than four per cent of this is used for crops and sown pasture, and only 0.25 per cent is irrigated. A large proportion is used for grazing sheep and cattle on native pastures.

The major factor limiting agricultural production is the supply of moisture. An estimated 65 per cent of Australia receives an annual rainfall which is inadequate for crop-growing and much of this area has too little moisture even to support sparse grazing.

Historical Development

Wool was Australia's first important export. The discovery that Merino sheep were well suited to Australian conditions, the opening up of the western grasslands in New South Wales, and the demand created by the Industrial Revolution in England, all combined to stimulate the production and export of fine wool. During the first half of the nineteenth century vast areas were taken up for sheep grazing.

In the second half of the nineteenth century wheat-growing developed as an important industry. The advent of railways and steamships improved transport to the expanding cities of Europe, and new implements, farming techniques and breeds of grain all contributed to increased yields. As the demand for wheat-growing land increased many large grazing properties were broken up and the land cultivated.

In the 1880s the introduction of refrigerated shipping opened up an export market in meat. Refrigeration, combined with the invention of the centrifugal cream separator, made it possible to produce and export large quantities of butter and led to the rapid expansion of the dairy industry.

Patterns of Land Use

Dairying is concentrated in scattered pockets along the east, south-east and south-west coasts where rainfall and soils are suitable. Sugar is concentrated in several areas along the Queensland coast where suitable soils occur. Forested areas also occur near the coast in the highland belt of south-east Australia and Tasmania and in the south-west of Western Australia.

In a crescent stretching inland from southern Queensland to South Australia and across the south-west corner of Western Australia is a sheep-grazing zone for wool and meat. Inside this is a mixed-farming zone where lower rainfall and more suitable topography allow both wheat-growing and sheep-grazing activities.

Production of fine wool is concentrated in two large areas; one in the south-west of Western Australia, the other in a south-east belt extending from South Australia to central Queensland. Extensive grazing of beef cattle is carried out in the central and northern areas of Australia.

Agriculture and the Economy

'Australia rides on the sheep's back' was a common statement not too many years ago, indicating the importance of agricultural production, especially wool for export, to the Australian economy. However, in recent years the rural sector has played a decreasing role, in spite of the fact that the volume and value of agricultural production and exports have expanded. Between 1938-39 and 1972-73 the volume of rural production doubled and its value increased 12-fold. In the same period the volume of rural exports more than doubled and their value increased 15-fold.

The contribution of agricultural products to the Gross Domestic Product has been steadily declining over recent years. On average, for the three years ending 1950-51, gross farm production formed 23.4 per cent of the Gross Domestic Product, while by 1971-72 it had fallen to little over 6 per cent. This decline was caused mainly by expansion in other sectors of the economy, due to a rapid increase in the export of both minerals and manufactured goods.

Agriculture has also become less important as an employer of labour. In 1933, 492 000 males (28 per cent of the total male workforce) were employed in agriculture, but by 1971 this number had dropped to 298 000 (8 per cent). Farm mechanisation and the availability of more attractive employment in other sectors of the economy were important factors contributing to this trend.

Farms

In 1973 there were approximately 245 000 farms in Australia, covering a total area of 499 815 000 hectares (1 hectare = 2.47 acres). Farms range in size from less than one hectare (small market gardens, nurseries and poultry farms) to more than 1 million hectares (huge sheep or cattle stations), although in 1971 the median was 138 hectares.

Most farms are 'family farms' — they are owned and operated by the farmer and his family. However in some sectors, particularly large grazing stations, company ownership and employed management is common. Share-farming — where profits or losses are shared by the owner of the land and a farm operator — is also a common practice in industries such as dairying and the growing of wheat, potatoes and tobacoo.

Farm incomes are notoriously unstable because of variations in climatic and economic conditions. Yearly climatic changes affect production, and export prices fluctuate severely according to variations in world supply and demand.

Below: Sheep and cattle grazing on a property near Cooma NSW.

Opposite below: Wheat harvest in the Barossa Valley, SA, an important area also for wine-growing, cropping and grazing.

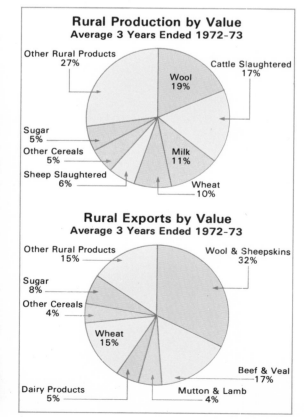

Rural Production by Value
Average 3 Years Ended 1972-73

Other Rural Products 27%
Wool 19%
Cattle Slaughtered 17%
Sugar 5%
Other Cereals 5%
Sheep Slaughtered 6%
Milk 11%
Wheat 10%

Rural Exports by Value
Average 3 Years Ended 1972-73

Other Rural Products 15%
Wool & Sheepskins 32%
Sugar 8%
Other Cereals 4%
Wheat 15%
Beef & Veal 17%
Mutton & Lamb 4%
Dairy Products 5%

Australian Land Use

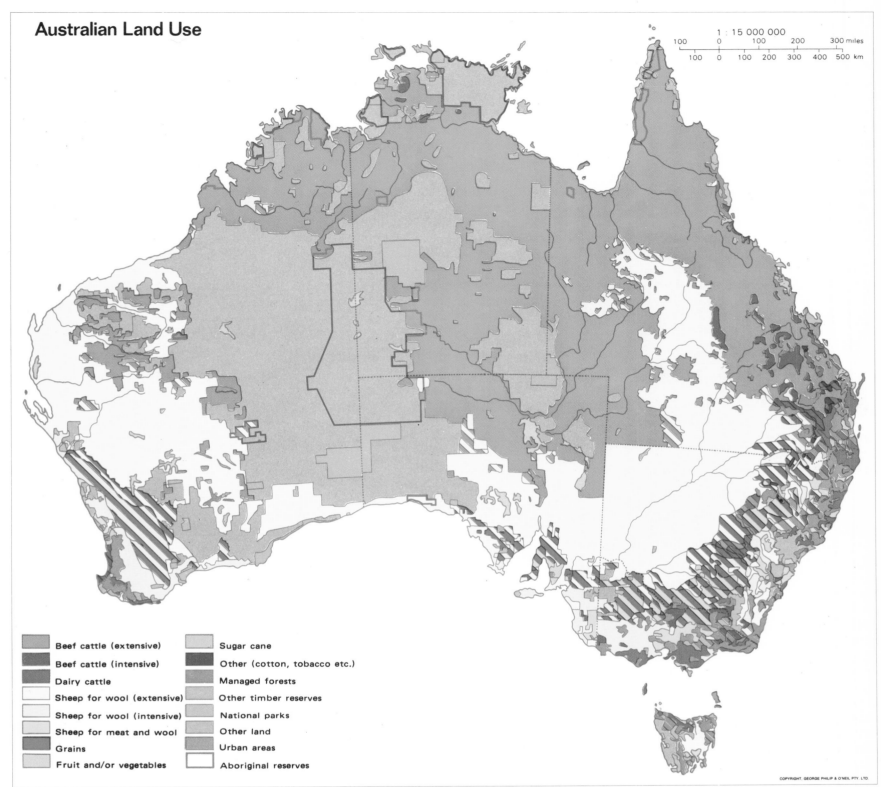

1 : 15 000 000

Beef cattle (extensive)	Sugar cane
Beef cattle (intensive)	Other (cotton, tobacco etc.)
Dairy cattle	Managed forests
Sheep for wool (extensive)	Other timber reserves
Sheep for wool (intensive)	National parks
Sheep for meat and wool	Other land
Grains	Urban areas
Fruit and/or vegetables	Aboriginal reserves

COPYRIGHT. GEORGE PHILIP & O'NEIL PTY. LTD.

Trade in Rural Production and Exports

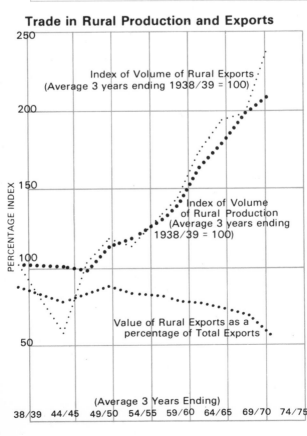

Index of Volume of Rural Exports
(Average 3 years ending 1938/39 = 100)

Index of Volume
of Rural Production
(Average 3 years ending
1938/39 = 100)

Value of Rural Exports as a
percentage of Total Exports

PERCENTAGE INDEX

(Average 3 Years Ending)

38/39 44/45 49/50 54/55 59/60 64/65 69/70 74/75

Agricultural Production

Sheep: Sheep-grazing is Australia's most important rural industry, and while wool is the major product (Australia produces about 30 per cent of the world's wool), lamb and mutton are also important income earners.

In 1975 there were about 151 700 000 sheep in Australia, 18 per cent of the world's total. Seventy-five per cent of Australia's sheep are Merinos and 90 per cent of the annual wool clip is exported.

Sheep are grazed in all States, although they are concentrated in three broad zones: pastoral, sheep-wheat, and high rainfall. Methods of farming, stocking rates and product combinations vary considerably in each zone.

The pastoral zone is the largest area and comprises the arid and semi-arid parts of New South Wales, South Australia, Western Australia and Queensland. This area carries

23 per cent of Australia's sheep, which graze on native shrubs and grasses. Holdings are large and stocking rates low, with an average of one sheep to three hectares. The emphasis is on wool production.

The sheep-wheat zone carries 44 per cent of the nation's sheep and has a more reliable rainfall. Stocking rates are higher — an average of nearly three sheep per hectare — and sheep are grazed in rotation with cereal-cropping.

In the high-rainfall zone sheep are often grazed in conjunction with beef cattle and most properties combine wool and fat-lamb production. This zone contains 33 per cent of the total sheep population and stocking rates are high, averaging six sheep per hectare.

Shearing takes place once a year, usually between autumn and spring, and the average wool yield is about 4.2 kg per sheep.

Over 80 per cent of the wool is sold at public auction, while the remainder is sold directly to buyers at private sale. The Australian Wool Corporation coordinates the marketing and promotion of wool and operates a reserve price scheme for wool sold at auction. The average price received in 1974-75 was 126.99 cents per kg.

In 1973-74 a total of 701 million kg of wool was produced, of which over 583 million kg were exported at a value of $1160 million.

Sheep and lambs slaughtered for meat in 1973-74 totalled 25 400 000, producing 465 000 tonnes of meat, of which 91 240 tonnes were exported at a value of $79 400 000. The main buyers were Japan and the USA. In 1959-60 the annual domestic consumption of lamb and mutton was 47 kg per head but by 1972-73 had fallen to 34 kg per head.

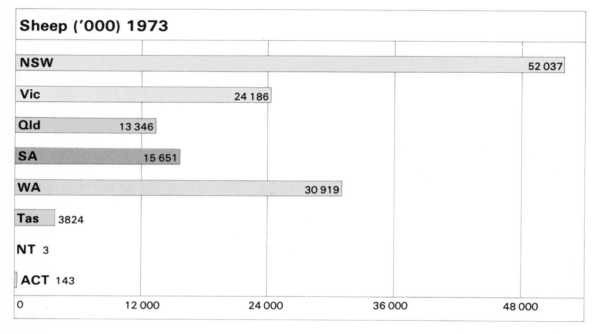

Sheep ('000) 1973

NSW	52 037
Vic	24 186
Qld	13 346
SA	15 651
WA	30 919
Tas	3824
NT	3
ACT	143

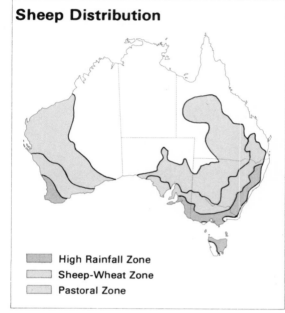

Sheep Distribution

High Rainfall Zone
Sheep-Wheat Zone
Pastoral Zone

Beef Cattle: Beef cattle are widely distributed, and in 1975 there were 29 080 000 beef cattle in Australia, with the highest proportion in Queensland. The areas in which beef cattle are most concentrated can be divided into two zones, one in the north producing meat mainly for export, and another in the south catering mainly for the domestic market.

In the north, properties are large and herds grazed on natural pastures at very low stock-

ing rates — about one animal to 15 hectares. When the cattle are ready for slaughter they are trucked along an extensive network of 'beef roads' to coastal meatworks, where they are killed and prepared for export.

In the south, the cattle are grazed more intensively on much smaller properties, usually in conjunction with other agricultural enterprises such as wheat, sheep and dairying. The animals are slaughtered locally and at a younger age, producing a higher-quality beef

which is mainly for domestic consumption.

In 1972-73, 8 112 000 cattle were killed, producing 1 434 000 tonnes of meat valued at over $1014 million. Of this meat, 584 000 tonnes were exported at a value of about $654 million. Most of Australia's export beef goes to the USA, although in 1972-73 Japan and the UK were also significant importers. In 1956-57 the annual domestic consumption of beef and veal was 60 kg per head but in 1972-73 fell to 42 kg per head.

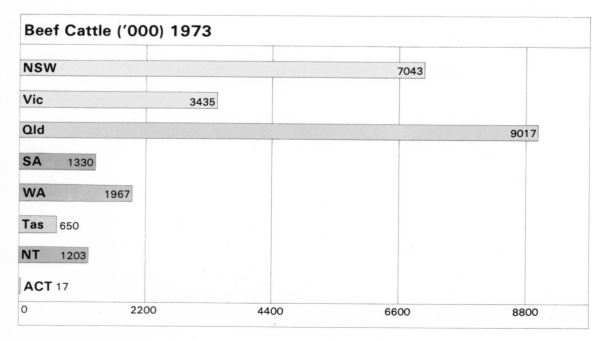

Beef Cattle ('000) 1973

NSW	7043
Vic	3435
Qld	9017
SA	1330
WA	1967
Tas	650
NT	1203
ACT	17

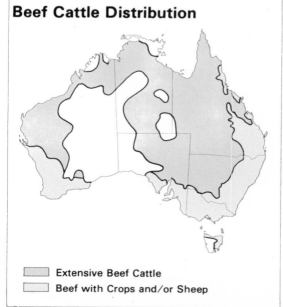

Beef Cattle Distribution

Extensive Beef Cattle
Beef with Crops and/or Sheep

Dairying: Most of Australia's dairy industry is confined to coastal areas in the south and east, where rainfall is ample and reliable and the soils and topography are suitable for the development of improved pastures. Some inland dairying occurs in irrigation areas and close to population centres.

In 1973 there were nearly 4 million dairy cattle in Australia, with 33 655 commercial herds each containing more than 30 milking cows. Dairy farms are typically small, averaging about 100 hectares and milking between 60 and 100 cows. The high labour requirement of dairy farms is usually provided by the farmer and members of his family.

Cows are machine-milked twice daily. In 1972-73 the average milk yield per cow was 2653 litres, although considerable annual variation exists between States with the Victorian average being the highest at 3153 litres per cow. Australia's total milk production in 1972-73 was 7 083 418 000 litres, Victoria producing over 50 per cent of this amount.

In 1972-73, approximately 25 per cent of milk produced was consumed as fresh milk, 54 per cent was made into butter, 12 per cent was made into cheese and 9 per cent was made into other processed products such as condensed and powdered milk. Farms close to population centres tend to supply the fresh milk requirements and receive a higher return for their milk than farms outside the urban areas, which are forced to supply the manufacturing sector for lower returns.

The Australian Dairy Corporation is responsible for the promotion of dairy products and the controlling of export sales. A price equalisation scheme operates for manufactured products, in order to average out returns from domestic and export markets.

In 1972-73 a total of 184 857 000 kg of butter was produced, of which over 57 million kg were exported at a value of $47 966 000. The United Kingdom accounted for 56 per cent of this market but since then has imported little butter from Australia. On Britain's entry to the EEC, Australia's butter exports were cut out instantly, unlike those of New Zealand which managed to negotiate a special agreement phasing out her butter exports over a period of years. Cheese exports amounted to over 29 million kg in 1972-73, valued at $21 689 000, with Japan taking 52 per cent of the shipments. Other exported milk products were valued at $58 million and went mainly to South-east Asian countries.

The Federal Government in 1977 began to implement a complete restructuring of the marketing of Australian dairy produce both locally and overseas.

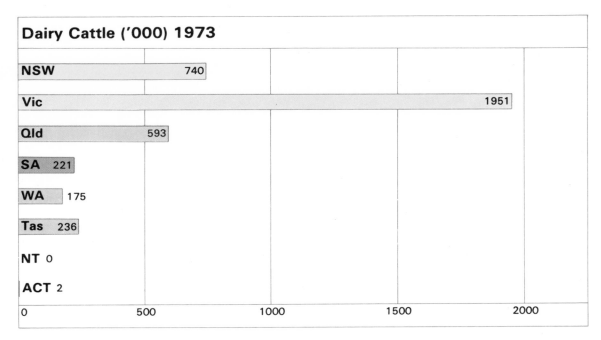

Dairy Cattle ('000) 1973

NSW	740
Vic	1951
Qld	593
SA	221
WA	175
Tas	236
NT	0
ACT	2

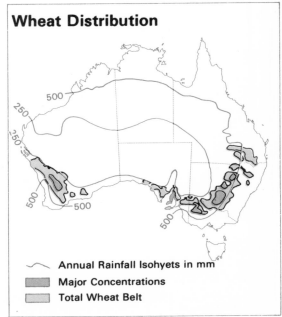

Dairy Cattle Distribution

High Density Areas
Low Density Areas

Grain Crops: Wheat is Australia's most important crop, occupying about 50 per cent of the land used for crops and contributing about 30 per cent of the gross value of all crop production.

Wheat is sown in autumn and harvested in late spring or early summer. It is mostly grown inland, in an area which extends from central Queensland to the south of South Australia and across the south-west corner of Western Australia, most of which receives an annual rainfall of 300-500 mm.

Soils in this belt vary considerably, although the topography is generally level to undulating and well suited to the use of large machines

In 1973-74, 8 956 000 hectares of wheat were sown, the largest areas being in New South Wales and Western Australia. Total production in that season was 12 094 000 tonnes for an average yield of 1.35 tonnes per hectare. Climatic variations have a significant influence on production, as indicated by the previous season's yield of only 6 434 000 tonnes (an average of 0.84 tonnes per hectare).

Wheat-growing properties numbered 48 285 in 1972-73, with an average size of approximately 1200 hectares and an average area of 200 hectares sown to wheat. Wheat growing is usually combined with the cultivation of other cereals, notably oats and barley; sheep, beef cattle and pigs are also common side-lines. A three-year system of

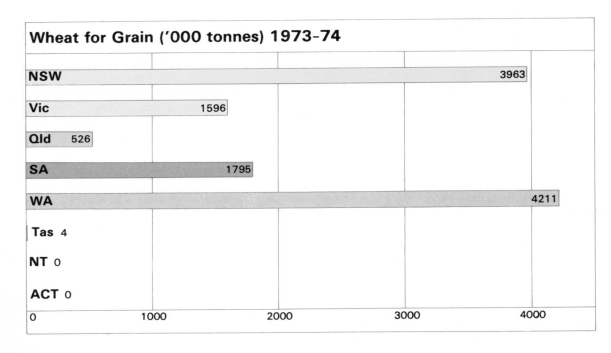

Wheat for Grain ('000 tonnes) 1973-74

NSW	3963
Vic	1596
Qld	526
SA	1795
WA	4211
Tas	4
NT	0
ACT	0

Wheat Distribution

Annual Rainfall Isohyets in mm
Major Concentrations
Total Wheat Belt

Agricultural Production

fallow-wheat-grazing is commonly used to improve wheat yields.

Other important cereal crops include oats, barley, rice, sorghum and maize. Oats are mostly grown in southern areas, providing grain and green fodder, the grain mostly for domestic use. In 1972-73, 995 100 hectares of oats were grown, producing 736 300 tonnes.

Rice is grown under irrigation, mainly in New South Wales. In 1972-73, 45 150 hectares were sown producing 309 000 tonnes.

Other Crops: Australia produced 15 421 000 kg of tobacco in 1972-73. The Mareeba-Dimbulah districts in north Queensland, and Myrtleford in north-east Victoria are the main tobacco-producing areas.

Australia is now self-sufficient in the production of most types of cotton, producing 31 690 tonnes of lint in 1972-73. The Namoi Valley in New South Wales is the main producing area.

Other crops include peanuts, flax, safflower, soybeans, sunflower and hops. A large proportion of the cultivated land in Australia is also used for hay and green fodder, for the on-farm feeding of stock.

Sugar: Sugar cane is grown on only one per cent of the land used for crops but is Australia's second most valuable crop. About 95 per cent of production occurs in Queensland, and is confined to coastal pockets there and in the north of New South Wales, in areas where soils are suitable and the annual rainfall exceeds 1000 mm. In 1972-73, 241 699 hectares were cropped producing 18 928 000 tonnes of cane which in turn yielded 2 835 202 tonnes of raw sugar.

Sugar farms average about 40 hectares in size and each crop is usually cut three times during a four year rotation; yields per hectare are high. Harvesting is done mechanically

and the crushing season extends from June to December. Areas under production are closely controlled by a system of quotas and all marketing is handled by the Queensland Sugar Board.

Approximately 75 per cent of the crop is exported, which amounted to 1 813 000 tonnes of raw sugar in 1973-74, valued at $223 199 000. Japan, the UK, Canada, the USA and the USSR were the main markets and Australia ranks second behind Cuba as a world supplier of sugar.

Fruit: The wide variety of climatic conditions in Australia means that most fruits can be cultivated. Fruit-growing occupies less than one per cent of the land under cultivation, but provides about 20 per cent of the total gross value of crop production. In 1972-73 production was valued at $253 200 000, with exports worth $109 960 000.

Australia has 115 500 hectares of fruit under cultivation. Apples are the most important fresh fruit and are concentrated in southern areas, Tasmania producing 32 per cent of the crop. Production totalled 412 338 tonnes in 1973, of which about one-third was exported.

Victoria grows 75 per cent of Australia's pears, national production being 163 139 tonnes in 1973-74. Citrus fruits — of which 80 per cent are oranges — are grown mainly on the central coast of New South Wales and the irrigation areas of the Murray and Murrumbidgee Rivers. In 1972-73, 423 800 tonnes of citrus fruits were produced.

Sixty-eight per cent of the nation's bananas are produced on the north coast of New South Wales and 28 per cent in Queensland. In 1972-73 total production was 123 833 tonnes. Southern Queensland produces most of Australia's pineapples, national production totalling 126 353 tonnes in 1972-73.

Intensive mixed citrus farms and vineyards utilising irrigation water from the Murray near Mildura in Victoria.

Peach-growing is concentrated in the irrigation areas of the Goulburn Valley in Victoria and the Murrumbidgee in New South Wales. In 1972-73, 113 510 tonnes were produced. Fruit is also canned, bottled and juiced, with about 65 per cent of canned fruit being exported.

Vineyards covered 68 502 hectares in 1972-73, occupying 30 per cent of Australia's crop area. Seventy-five per cent of this area was in Victoria and South Australia — grapes require a warm to hot climate and winter rainfall. Grapes are grown for wine, for drying as sultanas, raisins and currants, or for eating fresh. In 1971-72, 826 000 tonnes of grapes were produced, of which 55 per cent were used for drying, 42 per cent for wine and three per cent for table use.

Dried-grape products come mainly from the irrigation areas of the Mildura district in north-west Victoria and the Murray River irrigation area in the south-east of South Australia. The dry, warm climate allows sun-drying of the grapes.

South Australia is the principal producer (70 per cent) of Australia's wine. Production is concentrated in the lower Murray Valley, the Vales area south of Adelaide, and the Barossa Valley. Other notable wine-producing areas are the Murrumbidgee irrigation area and the Hunter Valley in New South Wales, the Swan Valley in Western Australia, and the Mildura, Rutherglen and Stawell districts in Victoria. In 1972-73 279 943 000 litres of wine were produced, of which 4 657 000 litres were exported, principally to Canada, the UK and Papua New Guinea. Annual domestic consumption of wine is about 10 litres per head.

Forests and Fishing

Forestry: The total area of forests and woodlands in Australia is approximately 139 million hectares, although it is estimated that only about 42 500 000 hectares of this are productive.

Forests serve a number of purposes other than the production of timber, also providing flora and fauna reserves, recreation areas and water catchments.

The main commercial forests are in the east and south-east coastal highlands, Tasmania and the south-west corner of Western Australia. These are hardwood forests, mainly eucalypts in the south and other broad-leafed species in the Queensland rainforests. About two-thirds of the wood is used as sawn timber — mainly for building — and the remainder is used for the production of paper, fibreboards and poles.

Australia is deficient in native conifers, and imports a large proportion of its softwood requirements. To overcome this shortage, government and private sources have established extensive plantations, mainly of *Pinus radiata*. By 1974, 456 600 hectares of pines had been planted in Australia.

In 1972-73, Australia's production of sawn wood was 3 433 396 cubic metres, of which 25 per cent were softwoods. Imported timber and timber products, including pulp and paper, were valued at $312 135 000 in 1972-73, while the value of exports was about $30 million.

Fishing: The waters over Australia's continental shelf contain a rich variety of marine life, which supports a substantial fishing industry. Fish, crustaceans and molluscs provide the basis of this industry.

The main commercial fish are tuna, edible shark, mullet and Australian salmon. In 1972-73, 59 428 tonnes were caught, valued at $23 497 000. Crustaceans — mainly rock lobsters, prawns and crabs — totalled 30 297 tonnes in 1972-73 and were valued at $54 424 000. In the same period a total of 32 960 tonnes of edible molluscs — mainly oysters, scallops and abalone — were caught, with a value of $18 043 000. Over 223 tonnes of pearl-shell, valued at $203 000, were also harvested.

In 1972-73, imports of edible marine products were valued at $47 million, of which canned salmon was the main component. The main sources were Japan, the UK, Norway, Malaysia and New Zealand. In the same period, exports of edible marine products — mainly rock lobsters and prawns — were valued at $74 million. The main markets were the USA, Japan, the UK, France and Hong Kong.

Above: Karri logs being transported from a forest at Pemberton, north-west of Albany in Western Australia. The Karri (Eucalyptus diversicolor) is unequalled in height and grandeur by any other broadleaved tree in the world. Pure stands of Karri grow in a belt along the coast from Albany to Cape Leeuwin.

Below: Fishing boats at Cabbage Tree Creek, Brisbane. Queensland's fishing industry is the second-largest in Australia. Mudcrabs and a wide variety of shellfish are a speciality and along with exotic reef fish such as Coral Trout and Barrimundi, are very popular with visitors from all over the world.

Fishing and Forestry

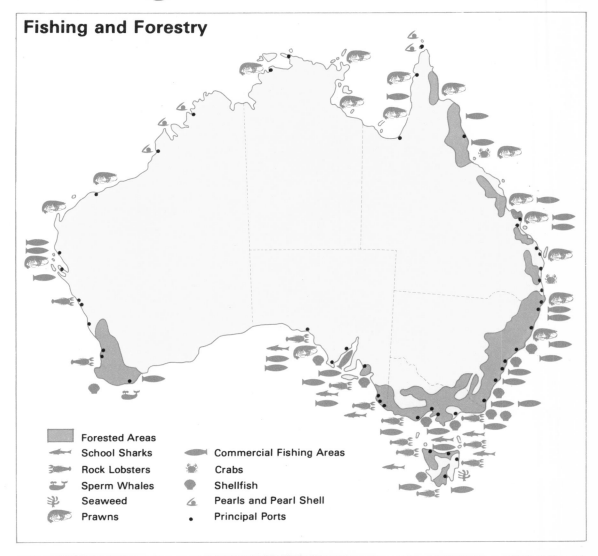

Forested Areas
School Sharks
Rock Lobsters
Sperm Whales
Seaweed
Prawns
Commercial Fishing Areas
Crabs
Shellfish
Pearls and Pearl Shell
Principal Ports

Mineral and Energy Resources

Australia and Australians have been extra-ordinarily fortunate with the mineral finds of the last two decades. The national economy has been reshaped by spiralling mineral production and exports, which have balanced setbacks in other areas, especially wool and meat.

Since the early 1950s a succession of rich finds has made Australia a major world producer of minerals and metals, with black coal, bauxite, mineral sands, iron ore, copper, nickel, manganese and uranium leading the list.

The facts and figures defy the imagination of most Australians. Investment is in billions of dollars; ore trains are more than a kilometre long; the role of Japan (which takes over 55 per cent of all mineral and metal exports) is critical.

Sydney cooks with natural gas pipelined from the Red Centre while Melbourne's supply comes from under wild Bass Strait. Indigenous petroleum is refined and available for local use but in limited amounts, unless the North-West Shelf (only a vague name to many Australians) proves to have crude oil as well as gas. And so it goes on, search and exploitation reacting to a bonanza here, a slump in the world economy there. Future triggers may be an outburst of 'resources diplomacy' on the other side of the globe, or the looming gutting of all Nauru's rock phosphate to force the opening up of more expensive Australian deposits. Meanwhile, controversies rage over sand mining versus conservation at Fraser Island, the morality of mining and exporting uranium, and Aboriginal land right claims in the Aurukun bauxite zone.

The 'minerals boom' and its implications seem certain to change Australia forever just as gold transformed the infant country in the 1850s. Mineral primary products are now the most valuable class of exports. Their export value in 1975 was $3105 million (including some smelter and refinery products), representing more than 30 per cent of the value of total exports. This figure could top 40 per cent within a decade.

Iron ore — once subject to export embargo — and black coal comprised about 45 per cent of the 1974-75 value of output of products at mine or quarry — $3305 million. Remaining minerals of economic importance include lead, zinc, bauxite, copper, construction materials, manganese, nickel, gold, limestone, tin, opals and sapphires, mineral sands (rutile, zircon, ilmenite), brown coal, salt and petroleum.

Iron Ore

Australia's known high-grade iron ore resources are estimated at around 35 000 million tonnes. Most occur in the Hamersley Iron Province (or Pilbara region) of north-west Western Australia. Iron ore provided almost a quarter of mineral export income in 1975 with exports of iron ore pellets worth over $748 million. Estimates suggest that by 1980 exports will exceed 110 million tonnes annually.

Major Western Australian deposits worked in 1975 were Mt Tom Price (23 per cent); Robe River (11 per cent); Mt Whaleback (31 per cent); Mt Goldsworthy, Shay Gap and Sunrise Hill (7 per cent); Cockatoo Island (1 per cent) and Koolan Island (3 per cent) in Yampie Sound; Koolyanobbing (2 per cent) and Paraburdoo (14 per cent). Deposits worked in South Australia's Middleback Ranges were Iron Baron and Iron Prince (3 per cent) and Iron Monarch and Iron Knob (3 per cent), while Savage River in Tasmania contributed 2 per cent.

Coal

Coal, discovered within three years of the European settlement of Australia, has been the most important mineral in the industrial growth of the nation.

Black coal is second only to iron ore in value of production and export earnings. It provides almost a quarter of mineral export income. Black coal production in 1975 totalled around 75 million tonnes, with 40 200 000 tonnes coming from New South Wales and 30 500 000 from Queensland, most from the rapidly-expanding Bowen Basin coalfields. About 4 million tonnes of sub-bituminous coal were mined in Western Australia and South Australia. Exports in 1975 totalled 30 200 000 tonnes worth $755 500 000.

Victoria's immense brown coal deposits worked in the Latrobe Valley open cuts yielded 28 200 000 tonnes valued at almost $50 million in 1975. Through complex combustion techniques this young, soft lignite is used in power stations (providing around 80 per cent of Victoria's electricity) and to provide high-grade solid fuel and char.

National reserves of black coal are estimated at not less than 200 000 million tonnes, brown coal at 66 700 million tonnes (with over 12 000 million tonnes currently considered economically recoverable).

Bauxite-Alumina

Australia is the world's largest bauxite producer, and a major exporter of bauxite and alumina. More than 20 million tonnes are mined annually from large deposits at Weipa in Queensland, the Darling Range in Western Australia and Gove in the Northern Territory. Measured and indicated reserves are about 5500 million tonnes.

Alumina is the semi-refined aluminium oxide used in the production of aluminium: in 1974 alumina production was 4 900 000 tonnes, of which exports totalled 4 700 000 tonnes worth $251 million. Exports of unworked aluminium totalled 52 700 tonnes (worth $27.8 million) in 1974.

Australia has two integrated aluminium enterprises involved in mining bauxite, producing alumina, reducing it to aluminium, and fabricating the metal. Comalco's bauxite from Weipa is shipped to the Gladstone alumina plant for reducing and export. Comalco's reduction plant at Bell Bay in Tasmania has a capacity of 95 500 tonnes annually and this is expected to increase to about 115 000 tonnes.

Alcoa of Australia (WA) Ltd refines its bauxite from Jarrahdale in Western Australia in the alumina plant at Kwinana (capacity 1 400 000 tonnes annually) and the reduction plant at Point Henry in Victoria (91 500 tonnes capacity). The second alumina plant built at Pinjarra in Western Australia (capacity 1 000 000 tonnes) uses bauxite from Del Park.

Bauxite deposits at Gove are mined by Nabalco Pty Ltd (more than 2 million tonnes annually) and Gove's alumina plant has a capacity of 1 million tonnes.

Alcan Australia Ltd uses alumina from Gladstone in its reducing plant (capacity about 50 000 tonnes annually) in the Kurri Kurri area of the Hunter Valley coalfield in New South Wales.

Lead and Zinc

Australia remains a major world producer and exporter of lead and zinc, although these metals have lost their former eminence on the Australian mineral scene with the emergence of iron ore, coal and bauxite.

Australia is the world's third-largest lead producer and fourth-largest zinc producer. Together these two metals accounted for around eight per cent of national mineral primary product exports (gold excluded) in 1975. They were valued at $247 million. Production has expanded significantly in the last quarter century, centred around Broken Hill in New South Wales, Mount Isa in Queensland and Read-Rosebery in Tasmania. Lead production in 1975 was 408 600 tonnes, zinc 502 600 tonnes.

Zinc reserves total about 37 million tonnes, lead reserves 22 million tonnes.

Copper

Copper — the first metal ever mined in Australia, in 1841 — has recently been overshadowed by the 'new' minerals, but its production is of increasing significance. Mine production of copper was 250 000 tonnes in 1974 (compared with only 12 700 tonnes in 1948) while exports of various forms of primary copper totalled 134 000 tonnes, valued at about $178 million.

Most copper comes from Mount Isa in Queensland and Mount Lyell in Tasmania, with other production at Mount Morgan and Gunpowder in Queensland, Cobar in New South Wales and Mount Gunson and Kanmantoo in South Australia. Reserves are estimated at around 5 900 000 tonnes of copper content of ore.

Nickel

Nickel, once unknown in Australia, triggered the wildest financial speculations of the mineral boom of the late sixties. Production started in 1967 in the Kalgoorlie region, ironically the setting of the decline of once-rich 'Golden Mile' gold mines. Australia currently ranks fourth in world mine output of nickel (75 794 tonnes in 1975). Kambalda and five other mines in the Kalgoorlie area produce sulphide ore, most of which is smelted at Kalgoorlie. The nickel matte is refined at

Opposite: Weipa bauxite deposits, Gulf of Carpentaria, Northern Queensland. The bauxite is mined by open cut methods, crushed, stockpiled and shipped direct to Japan or to Gladstone, eastern Queensland, for refining into aluminium.

Far opposite: Mt Tom Price, the huge open cut mine in the Pilbara area of Western Australia. Highly-mechanised methods are used for crushing, stockpiling and transport. The iron ore is railed to Dampier 294 km away, for export.

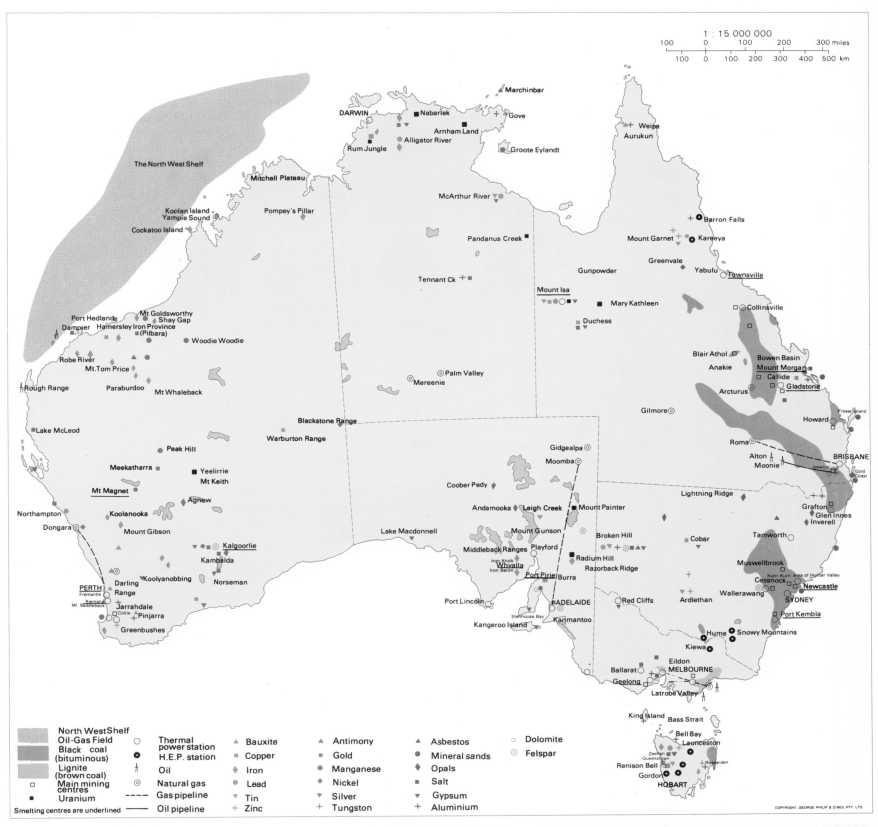

Mineral and Energy Resources

Kwinana. Another Western Australian mine is being developed at Agnew. Production from the mine at Greenvale in Queensland is treated at Yabulu near Townsville to yield various nickel compounds for export.

Uranium

Australia's future as a uranium exporter has been an extremely controversial issue in the past few years. Government and public debate on the morality and economics of Australian involvement in nuclear fuel mining, continues in the wake of the Fox Report.

Australia is estimated to have perhaps one-fifth of the world's uranium. Reasonably assured uranium reserves (resources recoverable at less than $US15 per lb of U_3O_8) are estimated at more than 300 000 tonnes. Total known resources, including sub-economic and inferred deposits, are believed to be 427 000 tonnes.

Between 1949 and 1961 Australia exported uranium worth $34 million from Rum Jungle in the Northern Territory and Radium Hill and Mount Painter in South Australia. The Mary Kathleen mine near Mount Isa in Queensland exported uranium valued at $80 million between 1958 and 1963.

Spectacular finds were made from the late 1960s, especially in Arnhem land in the Northern Territory, where the Nabarlek deposit, one of four major discoveries in the Alligator River region, is claimed as the world's richest. Another large recent find occurred at Yeelirrie in Western Australia.

In 1977 the first uranium exports for over ten years were made.

Mineral Sands

Australia provides some 95 per cent of the world's rutile, almost 80 per cent of its zircon, 40 per cent of its monazite and around 20 per cent of its ilmenite. These minerals are mined from sands on the eastern and western seaboards — operations often subject to protests by environmentalists.

Rutile production in 1975 was 344 000 tonnes (exports, $60 100 000); zircon totalled 382 000 tonnes (exports, $57 300 000); monazite totalled 3500 tonnes (exports, $428 000) and ilmenite concentrates 964 000 tonnes (exports, $8 100 000). The beach sands primarily yield titanium, a metal required to produce light, hard steels, and paint pigments.

Some Other Minerals

Manganese is of great importance in steel-making and Australian production is expanding rapidly, initially from large deposits on Groote Eylandt in the Gulf of Carpentaria. The 1975 production was 1 555 000 tonnes. High grade reserves are estimated at around 490 million tonnes.

Manganese has also been discovered at Woodie Woodie in Western Australia, east of Port Hedland.

Silver is produced chiefly as a by-product of lead, zinc and copper mining. Most of the 1975 mine production of 732 090 kg was exported.

Salt produced by solar evaporation is virtually all exported, principally to Japan. Western Australia dominated the 1975 production of 4 568 000 tonnes.

Gold production between 1851 and 1975 approached 5 388 000 kg. Production is declining with the low world price, and the last of the famous Kalgoorlie mines has closed. Production in 1975 was 16 328 kg fine gold, Western Australia providing more than 40 per cent. About 28 per cent is produced as a by-product of base-metals mining.

Tin concentrate production was 18 000 tonnes in 1975 — a tin content of 9507 tonnes. Australia is the world's sixth-largest tin producer, from mines at Renison Bell and Luina in Tasmania, Ardlethan in New South Wales and Mount Garnet in Queensland. In 1975 exports of tin in concentrates totalled 4433 tonnes ($19 800 000), tin metal 2470 tonnes ($12 300 000) and tinplate 49 574 tonnes ($14 600 000).

Tungsten used in steelmaking comes primarily from an open-cut mine on King Island in Bass Strait. Domestic production in 1975 was 2905 tonnes (65 per cent WO_3 basis), about 90 per cent of which was exported.

Opal and sapphires are valuable precious

stones. Opal production figures are likely to be understated, because so much opal is won by individuals or small groups: the 1975 export estimate was $13 600 000. Most comes from Coober Pedy and Andamooka in South Australia and Lightning Ridge in New South Wales. Sapphires won chiefly from Anakie in Queensland and Glen Innes and Inverell in New South Wales were valued at around $13 500 000 in 1975.

Phosphate rock, essential for Australia's huge superphosphate needs, has traditionally come from Christmas Island in the Indian Ocean, and Nauru and other Pacific islands. Rising import costs (more than $30 million annually) and the rapidly dwindling island reserves mean that recent large finds at Duchess in Queensland are becoming economic to mine. Australian known resources of rock phosphate total 6800 million tonnes of average grade 7.3 per cent phosphorus, and are classified as reserves.

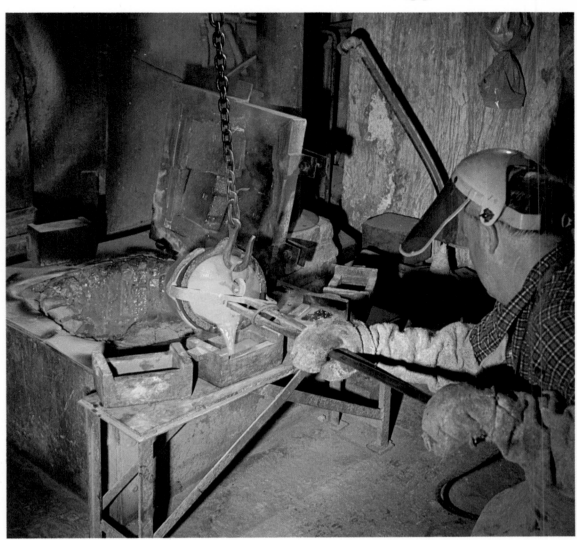

Opposite: Gold being poured at Kalgoorlie, WA, once world-famous for its Golden Mile.

Below: The uranium mine at Mary Kathleen, in the Selwyn Gorge midway between Cloncurry and Mt Isa, western Queensland.

Below opposite: Mineral sands dredge, Kingscliff, NSW.

Mineral and Energy Resources

Australia is already an important energy exporter, primarily through high grade black coal. The question of uranium exports is unresolved.

Four-fifths of Australian electricity comes from thermal power stations where coal is the most important energy source, supplemented by oil and natural gas in South Australia and Western Australia. Hydro-electric energy makes up the remaining one-fifth of total output.

Total installed generating capacity of Australian public supply systems is around 20 000 MW. Residential consumption doubled in the decade 1964-74 to 20 000 million kWh. In the same period the per capita figure rose from 3213 kWh to 4747 kWh.

Tasmania is the only State with enough water to permit continuous hydro-electric power generation. Apart from the Snowy Mountains Scheme with a generating capacity approaching 4000 MW, mainland Australia is generally too flat and has too little rainfall to make hydro-electricity possible.

Natural gas is changing the energy use pattern. One forecast is that within a decade it will supply around 19 per cent of national energy needs compared with the present 8 per cent.

Australia's per capita energy consumption is approximately level with western European countries, and about half the USA figure. Since 1960 Australian primary energy consumption has risen around 5.7 per cent annually. Evidence suggests that while there may be long-term possibilities for non-conventional sources of energy, in the immediate future Australia will obtain its energy supplies from reserves of petroleum, coal and natural gas. The government has no plans for nuclear electricity generation in Australia.

Although there are promising developments in solar energy technology, current Australian use is limited to domestic water heating (usually with conventional heat boost). Around 10 000 homes have some form of solar water heating.

Energy authorities are also seeking economic processes for deriving liquid fuels from the nation's vast black and brown coal deposits, in the hope of conserving the very limited crude oil reserves.

Some recent estimates suggest there is an 80 per cent chance that Australia may find as much oil as has already been discovered, and a 50 per cent chance the total could reach perhaps 509 million cubic metres. Even so, this would simply extend present production levels another quarter century: there seems little potential for Australia to achieve self-sufficiency.

Petroleum and Natural Gas

Australia's offshore oilfields came into production in time to blunt the potential effect of soaring world oil prices. The Bass Strait fields provide around 90 per cent of the daily output, averaging 63 000 cubic metres which supplies about 68 per cent of national crude oil needs at about one-quarter current world prices.

Yet rapidly dwindling reserves and increasing consumption mean that by the mid 1980s Australia could well be importing 70

per cent of its needs at a cost exceeding $2000 million annually. At June 1976 estimated recoverable petroleum reserves from commercial fields were: crude oil, 231 million cubic metres; well condensate and plant products, 33 million cubic metres; liquefied petroleum gas, 100 million cubic metres; and natural gas, 324 thousand million cubic metres. Additional theoretically recoverable reserves either currently uneconomic or awaiting further assessment (subject to major revisions) are crude oil, 27 million cubic metres; well condensate and plant products, 72 million cubic metres; liquefied petroleum gas, 74 million cubic metres; and natural gas, 490 thousand million cubic metres.

Crude oil production in 1975 was 23.829 million cubic metres and natural gas production was 4512 million cubic metres.

Australia's first commercial oilfield was discovered at Moonie in Queensland in 1961 and put into production in 1964. The heyday of the large Bass Strait discoveries was 1964-67. But exploration has slumped steeply from 120 wells (93 onshore, 27 offshore) in 1970 to 21 in 1976, although provisional 1977 estimates (between 30 and 44 wells likely) appear to reflect a significant revival in exploration, possibly encouraged by Federal government incentives launched in 1976. The greatest activity will be in the North West Shelf off Western Australia which contains about two-thirds of known natural gas reserves. Promising potential oil structures have been discovered but their exploration will demand advanced drilling technology to operate in depths up to 600 metres. The Fed-

eral Government is considering a North West Shelf proposal for a $2000 million scheme involving two offshore platforms, a submarine pipeline to Dampier, and onshore plants to process gas for local use and for export as liquefied natural gas.

Since March 1969 — when Brisbane was first supplied with natural gas from the Roma fields — natural gas for domestic and industrial needs has spread through the urban areas of four States. Bass Strait gas supplies Melbourne and other Victorian areas, Adelaide receives gas from the Moomba field in central Australia, and Sydney was also linked to Moomba in late 1976.

Far opposite: Hazelwood Power Station, near Morwell, Latrobe Valley, Victoria. The brown coal from the open cut mine is brought by conveyer belt to the power station. The switching station is in the foreground.

Opposite: Marlin natural gas platform, Bass Strait, near Lakes Entrance, Victoria. The gas is piped from here to Melbourne.

Opposite below: Lake Eucumbene, one of the main storage dams of the Snowy Mountains Scheme. At peak periods the Scheme supplies electricity to both New South Wales and Victoria.

Below: Oodnadatta, South Australia, where energy requirements are derived from the solar heating plant in the bottom left of picture.

Manufacturing Industry

Australia's 'Industrial Revolution' has contributed significantly to a greatly-broadened economy. Manufacturing now provides about a quarter of gross domestic product and employs some 1 265 000 people — a quarter of the workforce.

Effectively launched by BHP's pioneering steelworks at Newcastle in 1915, given real impetus by the urgent needs of World War II, and supported by the tide of postwar migration, manufacturing now forms a crucial bridge between the traditional primary industries and the growing tertiary sector.

The postwar restructuring of the economy ended a century and a half of dependence on primary production, and saw numbers of factories and employees rise by 120 per cent while net value of production increased 16 times. The vehicle, foodstuffs, chemical, construction materials and engineering industries were prominent in this expansion.

By 1975 there were 26 972 factories employing at least four people: their total employment was 1 245 200, value added production reached $15 246 million and fixed capital expenditure totalled $1 446 million. An additional 9864 smaller establishments employed 19 570 workers for value added production of $158.6 million and fixed capital expenditure of $10.5 million.

Despite State and Federal incentives to decentralise secondary industry, manufacturing remains concentrated in the large cities close to the workers and consumers. Over three-quarters of manufactures come from the two most populous States, New South Wales and Victoria, and over 80 per cent of these employees are based in the State capitals of Sydney and Melbourne.

Manufacturing uses about 60 per cent of imports and accounts for over 20 per cent of exports, primarily to South-east Asian and Pacific rim countries where Australia enjoys transport advantages. New Zealand is the largest customer, taking some 25 per cent of exported manufactures.

Manufacturing has attracted about one-third of all foreign investment — approximately $2000 million in the last ten years alone. Some industries, notably pharmaceuticals and petrochemicals, are up to 90 per cent overseas-owned.

Manufacturing has suffered along with other sectors of the flagging Western economies in the mid 1970s, with textiles, footwear and shipbuilding being particularly hard hit against a background of the worst Australian unemployment since the Depression. Rationalisation of industries receives little but lip service from governments, with the key vehicle industry frequently cited as an example of too many manufacturers chasing too few consumers. Questions of degree of tariff protection, of improving access to Australian markets for Third World goods and of taxpayer resistance to industry subsidies are among many issues yet to be resolved in the troubled manufacturing sector.

Motor Vehicles

Five main companies comprise the motor vehicle manufacturing and assembling industry, which overall is the largest in Australia. Investment exceeds $1000 million, and 1974-75 value added production for vehicles and parts was $1042 million.

More than 602 000 vehicles were produced in 1976 with around 60 000 people employed in manufacture and assembly and a further 30 000 making parts, instruments and accessories. Vehicle exports rose from the late 1960s, but have recently fallen: exports of motor vehicles and parts in 1975-76 were valued at $86 million, down 50 per cent from two years previously.

Foodstuffs

Second in the list of manufacturing industries is the foodstuffs group, with its growing emphasis on processed foods — frozen, canned, pre-cooked and convenience foods. It has attracted heavy local and foreign investment.

Australia is one of few nations able to export large amounts of foodstuffs. Food production (including agriculture) accounts for almost ten per cent of the workforce, and 1975-76 exports of foodstuffs (processed primary products, $899 million, unprocessed

Top: Burnie timber and paper mills, north coast of Tasmania.

Bottom: Aluminium refinery Gladstone, Queensland. The bauxite is brought from Weipa on the Gulf of Carpentaria, refined, then marketed overseas and locally.

$1895.9 million) formed 30 per cent of export income.

A wide range of climates, and continuing research, enables production of almost all foodstuffs, excepting some fish, nuts and a few tropical products including coffee, spices, cocoa, and tea (Australian tea production is as yet minimal).

Metals

Australia's iron and steel industry is dominated by the nation's largest private enterprise company, Broken Hill Proprietary (BHP) and its associated and subsidiary companies. Crude steel production exceeds 8

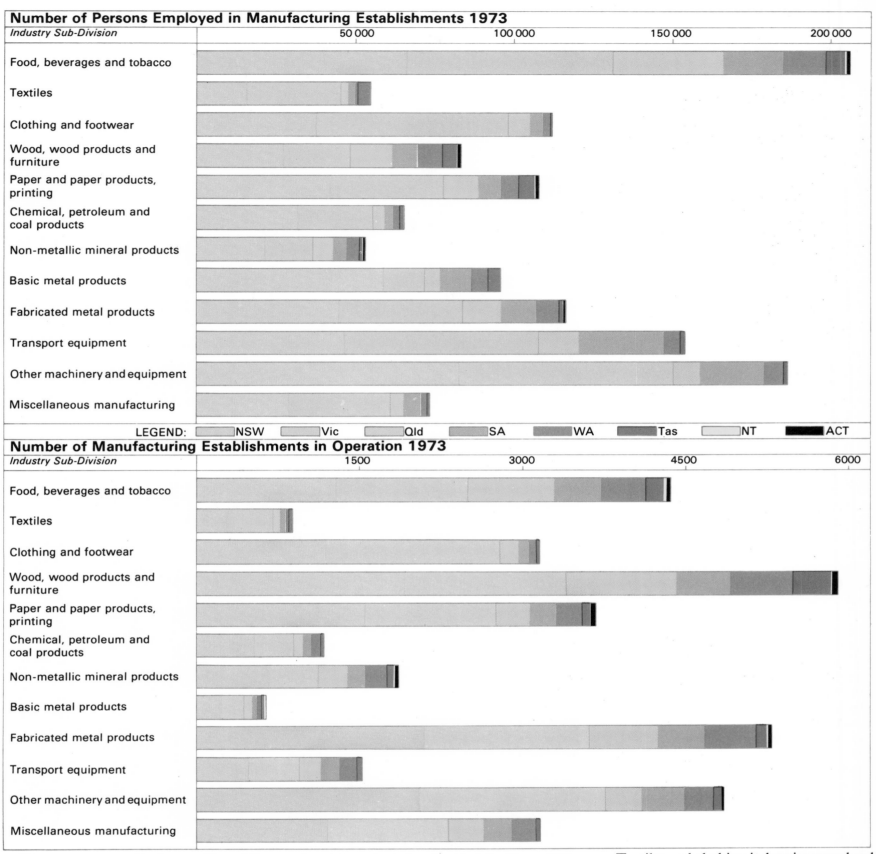

Number of Persons Employed in Manufacturing Establishments 1973

Industry Sub-Division	50 000	100 000	150 000	200 000
Food, beverages and tobacco				
Textiles				
Clothing and footwear				
Wood, wood products and furniture				
Paper and paper products, printing				
Chemical, petroleum and coal products				
Non-metallic mineral products				
Basic metal products				
Fabricated metal products				
Transport equipment				
Other machinery and equipment				
Miscellaneous manufacturing				

LEGEND: NSW Vic Qld SA WA Tas NT ACT

Number of Manufacturing Establishments in Operation 1973

Industry Sub-Division	1500	3000	4500	6000
Food, beverages and tobacco				
Textiles				
Clothing and footwear				
Wood, wood products and furniture				
Paper and paper products, printing				
Chemical, petroleum and coal products				
Non-metallic mineral products				
Basic metal products				
Fabricated metal products				
Transport equipment				
Other machinery and equipment				
Miscellaneous manufacturing				

million tonnes annually from mills at Newcastle and Port Kembla (New South Wales), Whyalla (South Australia), and Kwinana (Western Australia) which produces pig iron.

Processed metal exports totalled $520.9 million in 1975-76 while unprocessed metal exports (ores and concentrates) were worth $2235.3 million.

Chemicals

Australia's chemical industry continues to expand, using local and imported materials. The largest of the 30 petrochemical plants are at Altona in Melbourne and Botany, near Sydney. Plants produce many products including plastics, nitrogenous fertilisers, pharmaceuticals, cosmetics, explosives, paints and dyes, detergents and solvents.

Value added production of chemical and related products (excluding petroleum refining) in 1974-75 was $1172 million from 879 plants employing 64 000 people. The

breakdown includes chemical fertilisers $101 million, plastics $109 million.

Engineering and Electrical

The engineering, electrical and electronics industries are of increasing importance and sophistication. From farm machinery to diesel locomotives, from ships to colour television, from machine tools to the Australian-designed Nomad short-takeoff-and-landing aircraft, these industries supply many of Australia's requirements. Exports of metals, metal manufactures and machinery in 1975-76 totalled $843 million, averaging around 10 per cent of all exports.

Other Manufacturing Industries

Paper pulp and paperboard comes from 25 mills. Value added production of paper, paper products and printing in 1974-75 was $1279 million.

Textiles and clothing industries were hard hit by the economic slump of the mid 1970s. In 1975 there were 684 establishments producing textiles, yarns and woven fabrics, with 43 000 employees and value added production of $400 million. Another 60 000 people worked in 1960 clothing factories where value added production was $439 million. In addition, more than 40 million pairs of shoes, etc. came from 250 footwear establishments with 14 000 employees.

Shipbuilding, for years heavily subsidised, has an uncertain future, especially with the possibility of the New South Wales Dockyard closing.

The three dominant design and manufacturing companies in the aircraft industry frequently depend on component orders from overseas manufacturers, and diversification where possible, to maintain workloads. The Government Aircraft Factories have sold more than 70 of the twin turbo prop Nomad aircraft.

Transport by Land, Sea and Air

Australian historian Geoffrey Blainey chose the title *The Tyranny of Distance* for his analysis of how distance has shaped Australia's destiny. The title is still relevant for the communication problems of today.

The cost of providing rapid, reliable transport over great distances to the populations concentrated in a handful of major cities is high. About 60 per cent of the 14 million Australians live in six State capitals on the coast, varying from 640 to almost 4400 kilometres apart. The air distance from Sydney to Perth is greater than from Amsterdam to Damascus. Owing to the requirements of the long haul, the main communication systems have been created and maintained by governments. National expenditure on transport exceeds $8200 million annually — around 11 per cent of gross national expenditure — and approximately 350 000 people, about six per cent of the workforce, are employed in the transport industry.

Beyond the concerns of great distance, Australia shares transport dilemmas common to most industrialised nations, especially the demands of the private car and the general decline in public transport systems.

Road Transport

Australia is one of the world's most highly motorised nations, with more than 6 020 000 vehicles registered. There are 45 vehicles for every 100 Australians.

Australia's first road of significance was the 24 kilometre track completed in 1794 between Sydney and Parramatta: today there are 207 000 kilometres of roads paved and sealed with concrete or bitumen, 205 000 kilometres paved but unsealed and 425 000 kilometres formed of natural surface. The Federal government, State governments and local authorities spend more than $1100 million annually on roads.

More than 1 million load-carrying vehicles carry about 75 per cent of goods (freight) and passengers and account for about 20 per cent of tonne kilometres.

The road toll is regarded as a national tragedy, with 3586 deaths recorded in 1976, or approximately one person in every 4000. The only encouraging sign has been that deaths have never again reached the record total of 1970, due primarily to the progressive introduction of laws compelling the wearing of seat belts, legislation pioneered in the State of Victoria in 1970.

Sea Transport

Around Australia's 20 000 kilometres of coastline are some 70 ports of commercial significance. The largest, in terms of volume measured in millions of tonnes (tM) and millions of cubic metres (m³M) are the Western Australian iron ore export ports of Port Hedland (37 tM) and Dampier (30.9 tM), followed by Sydney (including Botany Bay) with 15.4 tM and 41.3 m³M, Newcastle (15.3 tM), Fremantle and Kwinana (12.8 tM and 0.6 m³M), Port Kembla (13.1 tM), Melbourne (5.6 tM and 7.6 m³M), Westernport (10.8 tM), Gladstone (10.6 tM), and Whyalla (6.7 tM).

Australia trades with almost 200 countries:

annual seaborne imports exceed 30 million freight tonnes and exports exceed 160 million freight tonnes. The principal trade route (by tonnage) is to Japan.

Foreign flag ships carry virtually all Australian bulk exports, and all but five per cent of overseas liner trade cargoes, although Australian flag participation in overseas trades is increasing. Australia's overseas trading fleet comprises nine vessels (with another five crewed by Australians but registered overseas) while the coastal fleet is around 100 vessels. The Australian National Line — a statutory body established by the Australian government — is easily the largest Australian shipowner, with 30 vessels. By 1978 it will be operating four new bulk carriers.

Handling of sea cargo has changed dramatically with the introduction of containerisation, bulk ships and specialised vessels (roll on-roll off). Changes include the modification of a 50 000 gross tonne oil tanker to carry 50 000 live sheep on deck for the booming Middle East meat trade.

Aviation

Great distances and a dispersed population have contributed to making Australia one of the most aviation-conscious nations in the world. Its civil aviation safety record is enviable with accidents on scheduled passenger services about one-twentieth the world average.

Australians are well represented in the history of flight. Inventor Lawrence Hargrave with his box-kites helped develop flight theory; others like Bert Hinkler, Harry Hawker and Charles Kingsford Smith were pioneers in the technology and expansion of aviation.

The Flying Doctor service has become internationally identified with Australia. Since its first flight in 1928 it has expanded to bring medical services to 3 180 000 square kilometres of the outback. Its 24 twin-engined planes operating from 12 bases in Western Australia, Queensland, South Australia, New South Wales and the Northern Territory

Australia's Highways

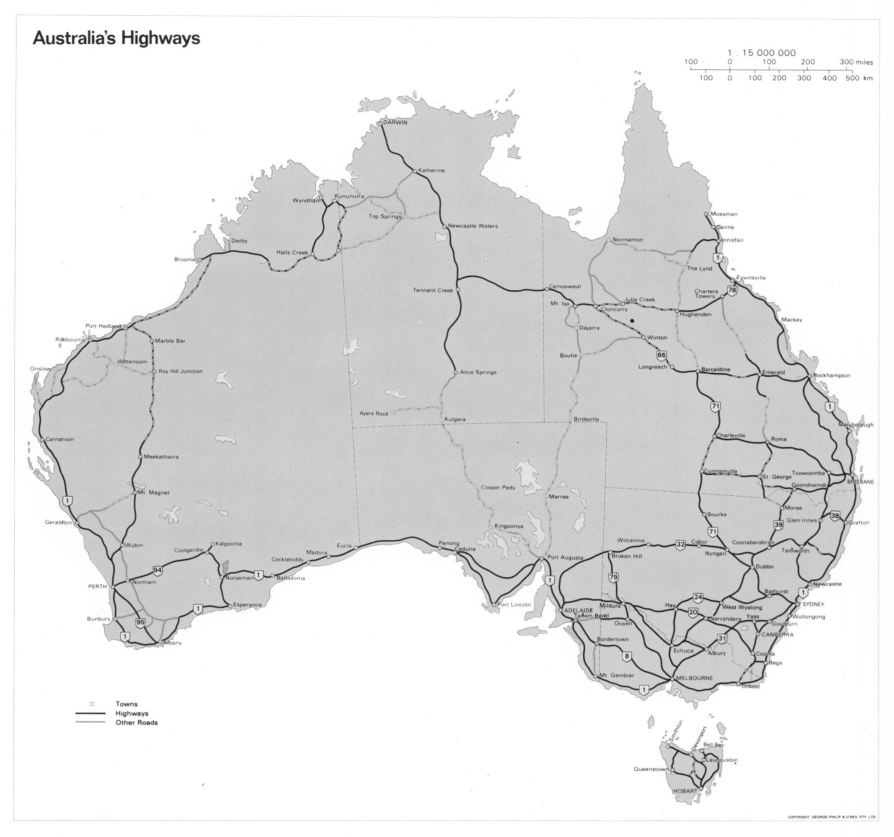

1 : 15 000 000

COPYRIGHT. GEORGE PHILIP & O'NEIL. PTY. LTD.

○ Towns
━━ Highways
── Other Roads

made 4697 flights covering 3 860 000 kilometres in 1975-76. Funding for this near-legendary service with 100 000 patient contacts annually (including emergency flights, clinics and radio consultations) comes from community contributions (35 per cent), State grants (about 45 per cent) and Federal government aid (over 20 per cent). The annual operating cost is about $3 500 000.

Domestic Aviation

Domestic aviation has experienced a mild slump in the mid 1970s. The number of passengers carried by the seven airlines in 1975-76 dropped by one per cent to 9 415 163. Total freight dropped 2.8 per cent to 106 948 tonnes and airline hours flown declined by five per cent to 275 941 hours.

Opposite above: A giant road 'train', a familiar sight in the Northern Territory.

Opposite: A liquefied gas tanker at the BP oil refinery, Western Port Bay, Victoria.

73

Transport by Land, Sea and Air

Australia's Air Routes

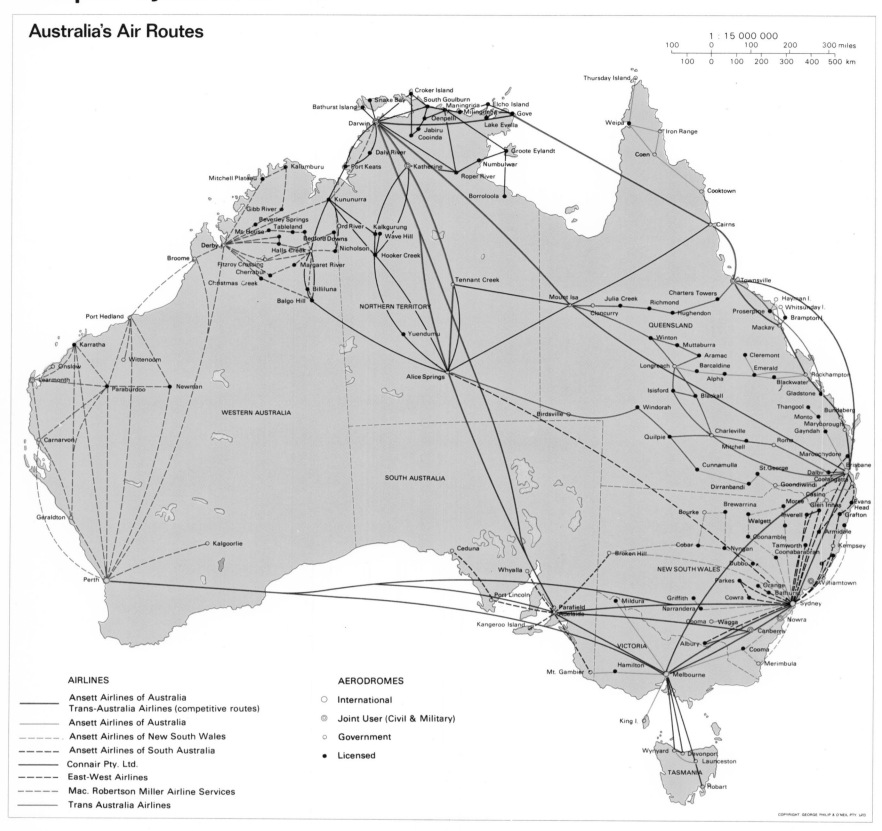

1 : 15 000 000

AIRLINES

Ansett Airlines of Australia
Trans-Australia Airlines (competitive routes)

Ansett Airlines of Australia

Ansett Airlines of New South Wales

Ansett Airlines of South Australia

Connair Pty. Ltd.

East-West Airlines

Mac. Robertson Miller Airline Services

Trans Australia Airlines

AERODROMES

○ International

◎ Joint User (Civil & Military)

○ Government

● Licensed

COPYRIGHT GEORGE PHILIP & O'NEIL PTY. LTD.

In mid 1976 the Australian register comprised 4431 aircraft: 153 regular public transport aircraft, 970 aerial work aircraft, 1035 charter aircraft and 2273 private planes. Their operations are controlled by the Federal Department of Transport, whose area of responsibility ranges from Papua New Guinea to near Antarctica, and from Cocos Island in the Indian Ocean to Norfolk Island in the east. The regular air transport network totals 145 000 kilometres and the Department operates 99 of Australia's 472 airports, including the five international domestic airports at Sydney, Melbourne, Perth, Brisbane and Darwin. In 1952 legislation on the Federal Government's 'two airline' policy provided that there shall be only two operators on the main trunk routes — the government-owned Trans-Australian Airlines (TAA) and a private enterprise airline, currently Ansett Airlines of Australia. The other five airlines have feeder services throughout the States and Northern Territory linking them to the trunk routes.

Australia's International Airline

The Australian carrier Qantas flies to 29 countries and its 13 200 employees rank it as one of the nation's largest enterprises. During 1975-76 it carried 1 324 767 passengers and flew 64 177 000 kilometres. During 1975 the 24 international airlines flying into Australia made 22 464 inward and outward flights with a total of 2 554 805 passengers and 73 595 kg of freight. Qantas, founded in 1928 as the free enterprise Queensland and Northern Territory Aerial Services, is owned and operated by the Australian government.

Rail

Australia's rail network has grown in recent years, particularly where it has been needed to transport the products of the newly established mines. The Federal and State governments manage more than 40 500 kilometres of track and there are thousands of kilometres of private railways serving mines, ports, agri-

cultural areas and industries (notably the sugar cane industry). Only since 1970 has it been possible for trains to cross the continent from Sydney to Perth on the 'standard gauge' line — a correction of the disastrous legacy of colonial confusion and short-sightedness which left Australia with three different railway gauges. The standard gauge is now being extended to Adelaide and also to Alice Springs.

Capital invested in fixed assets by government railways totals more than $2300 million; the Federal government has moved further into railway operations by accepting responsibility for the Tasmanian and non-metropolitan South Australian railways.

The Ghan, the legendary train which links Port Augusta with Alice Springs, in the Heavitree Gap. The Ghan is named after the Afghan camel drivers who were invaluable in the early days of travel in the outback.

Australia's Railways

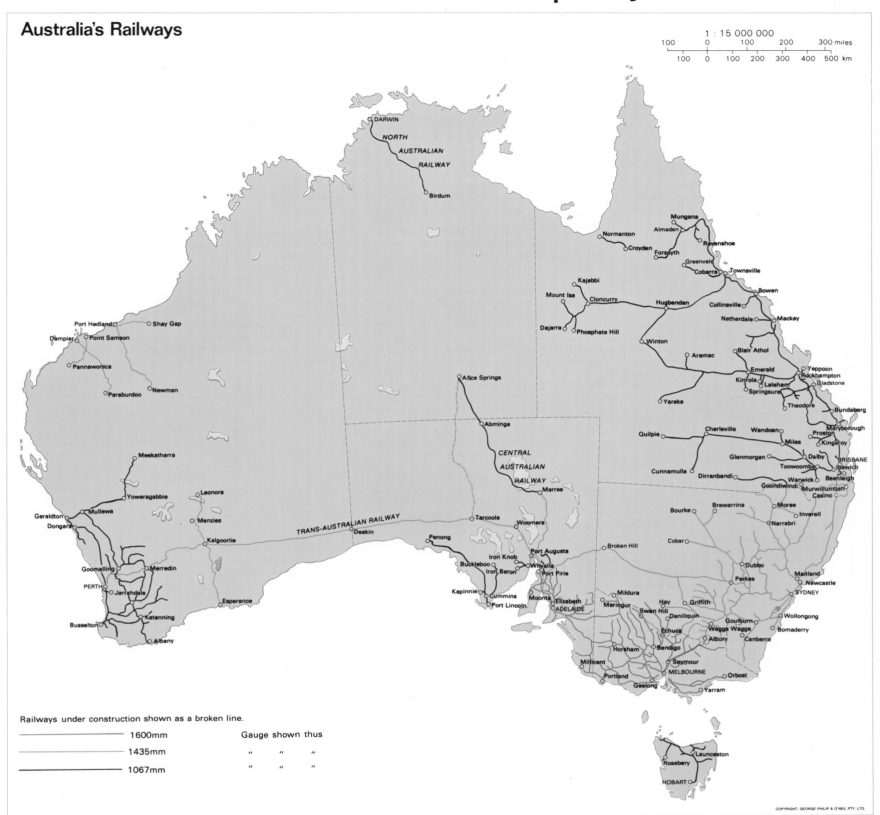

1 : 15 000 000

| 100 | 0 | 100 | 200 | | 300 miles |
| 100 | 0 | 100 | 200 | 300 | 400 | 500 km |

Railways under construction shown as a broken line.

——————— 1600mm	Gauge shown thus	
——————— 1435mm	" " "	
——————— 1067mm	" " "	

Australia's Trading Partners

Spaghetti to the Italians ... live camels to Arabs ... hamburger meat to the USA. Hardly typical exports, but they suggest the breadth and enterprise of Australian trade.

External trade has long been crucial to Australia's development. The first significant exports — whale products and seal furs in the early 1800s — were soon supplanted by wool, and generations of schoolchildren parroted 'Australia rides on the sheep's back'. From the 1850s onwards gold was a major stimulus, and indirectly led to the creation of many manufacturing industries when declining alluvial gold forced the miners to seek work elsewhere.

Since then farm and mineral products have dominated Australian exports, and still comprise about three-quarters of exports.

Australia ranks thirteenth among the world's trading nations — an impressive performance given a relatively small population and great distances from many large markets. During 1975-76 exports reached $9555.8 million and imports $8240.3 million. Freight and insurance on imports totalled almost $950 million.

Fortunately for the nation, the great surge in mineral exports since the mid 1960s and the steady expansion of manufactured exports (to their present 20 per cent of total exports) have helped to offset Britain's diminishing role as a major importer of Australian agricultural produce, as well as the threat to wool from synthetic fibres. The postwar era has also brought striking changes in the direction of trade, with the emergence of Japan as Australia's most important customer, the relatively recent appearance of the United States as Australia's major supplier of goods, and the increasing importance of nations like China and West Germany.

Patterns of Trade

Before Federation, Britain took over 70 per cent of Australian exports. This share fell to around 50 per cent before World War II, about 25 per cent in 1960 and now runs just below five per cent. British imports comprised almost half the national total into the 1950s, but have since slumped to 13 per cent in 1975-76.

Japan's purchases in Australia have risen steeply since 1957, with 1975-76 purchases totalling $3113 million, representing 30 per cent of total exports. They included coal $800 million, iron ore $609 million and greasy wool $300 million. Behind Japan with purchases of $969 million (10 per cent) is the United States, with imports including beef and veal $287 million, sugar $104 million, titanium and zirconium ores $43 million and rock lobster products $35 million. Next is New Zealand ($455 million, around five per cent of total exports) which takes one-quarter of all Australian exported manufactures.

Australia imports primarily from the USA ($1656 million, 20 per cent of all imports), predominantly vehicles, producers' equipment and other machinery. Japan is challenging the USA as chief supplier, with exports of $1609 million or 19.5 per cent. Britain, which provided almost half Australian imports into the 1950s, now supplies around 13 per cent — $1109 million in 1975-76.

Historically, Australia has exported raw materials (notably those from the pastoral, agricultural and dairying industries) and imported manufactured goods. This traditional pattern has been modified to reflect the surge of manufactures, and the greatly-enlarged minerals trade which today between them account for almost half all exports.

Imports are predominantly producers' materials and capital equipment, supplying the mining and manufacturing sectors.

Trade Relations and Policy

With export performance fluctuating with the fortunes of the mining, pastoral and agricultural industries, Australia is attempting to create greater stability in international marketing of such products. The Australian Wool Corporation's various innovative floor price and storage schemes are one such attempt.

Tariffs operate at a general rate, and a preferential rate generally applies to goods from Britain, Ireland, Canada and Papua New Guinea. Other special rates apply to some goods from specified countries (Canada, Sri Lanka, Fiji, Malawi, Malta, New Zealand, Zambia and Papua New Guinea), and a Free Trade agreement has operated with New Zealand since 1966.

In the two maps opposite, the countries of the world have been redrawn to a scale based on their importance to Australia as a market for exports and a source of imports. Since 1973 the United Kingdom has declined dramatically in importance as a trading partner for Australia partly because of its entry to the European Economic Community.

Individual countries are drawn to a scale where a side length of 20 mm equals $77 million of trade.

Below: A modern container terminal, Swanson Dock, the port of Melbourne.

Major Exports Year Ended June 1976

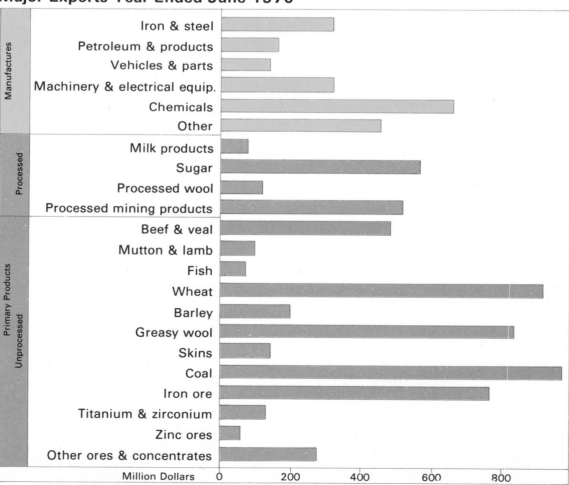

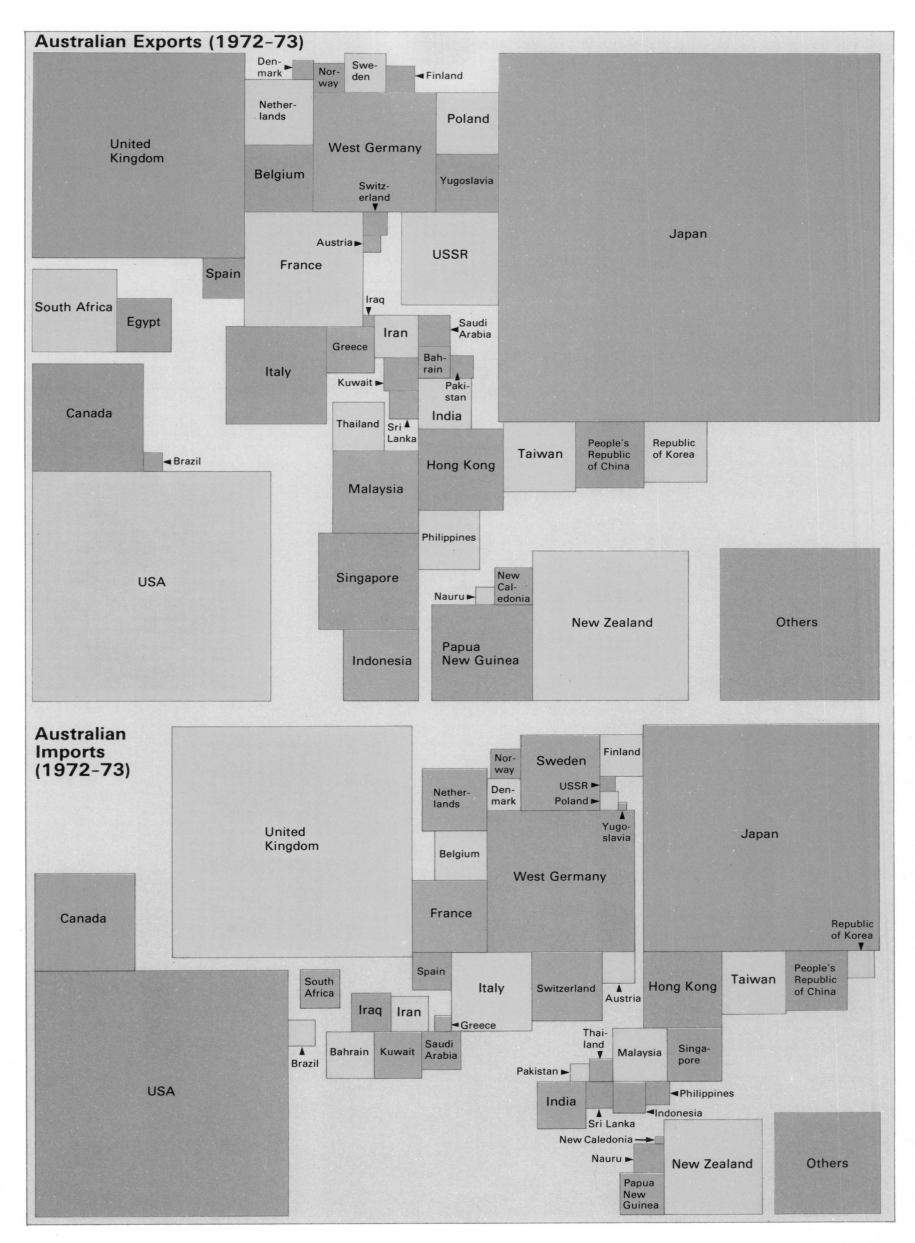

Australian Exports (1972-73)

United Kingdom
Denmark
Nor-way
Swe-den
Finland
Netherlands
Poland
West Germany
Belgium
Yugoslavia
Switzerland
Austria
France
USSR
Spain
South Africa
Egypt
Iraq
Iran
Saudi Arabia
Greece
Bahrain
Italy
Kuwait
Pakistan
India
Canada
Thailand
Sri Lanka
Hong Kong
Taiwan
People's Republic of China
Republic of Korea
Brazil
Malaysia
Japan
USA
Philippines
Singapore
Nauru
New Caledonia
New Zealand
Others
Indonesia
Papua New Guinea

Australian Imports (1972-73)

United Kingdom
Nor-way
Sweden
Finland
Netherlands
Denmark
USSR
Poland
Belgium
West Germany
Yugoslavia
France
Japan
Canada
Spain
Austria
South Africa
Italy
Switzerland
Hong Kong
Taiwan
Republic of Korea
Iraq
Iran
People's Republic of China
Brazil
Bahrain
Kuwait
Saudi Arabia
Greece
Thailand
Pakistan
Malaysia
Singapore
India
Philippines
Indonesia
USA
Sri Lanka
New Caledonia
Nauru
New Zealand
Others
Papua New Guinea

Tourism in Australia

Australia, like most other countries, has experienced a very rapid increase in both domestic and international tourism during the last two decades. Overseas visitor arrivals in Australia between 1966 and 1975 showed a steady increase from 187 000 to 519 000, an annual growth rate of over 15 per cent. In 1976 Australia again attracted well over 500 000 overseas visitors who spent in excess of $200 million in this country. Added to this are the many hundreds of thousands of Australians who visit other parts of their country during weekends, annual holidays, or long service leave. Indeed the growth in tourism has been so great that it is now a nationally important industry, one that involves a wide cross-section of component activities, including the provision of transportation, accommodation, recreation, food and related services.

History of Tourism

It has been suggested that ever since colonial days the idea of travel has been more natural to Australians than to people long established in one place. Immigrants, having once broken away from their homes, are prone to continue their search for wealth or security for a while, or, having settled down, return to their old countries to visit their kin and refresh old memories.

Around the turn of the century tourism within Australia was largely based on travel by rail and horse-drawn coach to resorts near the main population centres including the Blue Mountains in New South Wales, the Dandenongs near Melbourne and the hill and coastal resorts close to other major cities. After World War I travel for all purposes increased steadily. It continued to be mainly by rail although the family motor car began to be used for the shorter intra-State trips during the 1930s. Sea travel was also very popular at that time. A large fleet of passenger ships provided frequent and popular services between most ports on the eastern and southern coasts. The winter cruise to Queensland ports was as common in the 1930s as the flight north for a winter holiday on the Gold Coast or the Barrier Reef is today.

In the post-war period rapidly rising standards of living, and the advent of new and improved methods of transportation, especially fast, safe, and relatively cheap air travel, have turned international and domestic travel into a mass movement. Australia has shared in this world-wide expansion of travel, especially in respect of its domestic tourism. Because of the marked increase in incomes and private car ownership among large sections of the population, greater leisure time, three or four weeks paid annual holidays, and the introduction of long service leave, thousands of Australians now travel to almost every part of the country. This has led to the development of new and improved facilities, especially accommodation, of new resorts at dispersed points around Australia, and to modifications in the organisation and methods of tourist administration, development and promotion. In turn these activities have had an important influence on matters such as the improvement of highways and the opening up of national parks and foreshores.

Tourist Attractions

Australia, as yet a largely unspoiled country, has a wide variety of natural and man-made attractions for the tourist. It is one of the oldest continents and perhaps the most fascinating. Located largely in the sub-tropics and bordering the romantically regarded South Pacific, Australia has open spaces, clean air, fine beaches and its own remarkably rich flora and fauna.

In the 'outback', where time appears to have stood still, there are ranges of time-weathered mountains, enormous treeless plains crossed by dry river courses, and huge white, dry lake beds. This vast, empty area holds a special fascination for the tourist especially in the area around Alice Springs. In the 1974/75 financial year, approximately 10 000 international tourists visited Ayers Rock, the world's largest monolith, 348 metres high and about nine km around its circumference. A tourist village — named 'Yulara' — is being developed 14 km northwest of the Ayers Rock-Mount Olga National Park to accommodate and service the increasing number of visitors who go to explore the area.

The Great Barrier Reef, stretching for almost 2 000 km along the north-east coast of Queensland, is unquestionably a great natural attraction. With its myriad forms of marine life inhabiting the coral formations, the reef forms a barrier to the South Pacific breakers, sheltering a chain of beautiful tropic islands, some of which have been developed as tourist resorts. Sun-drenched Green Island, Hayman Island and Dunk Island are but a few of the many that provide a perfect base for the tourist to see and explore the wonders of one of the world's finest coral reefs. Over 640 000 people visited this coastal area north of Rockhampton in the twelve months ended June 1974.

The Gold Coast in southern Queensland is still one of Australia's most popular holiday areas for domestic and international tourists alike. Over 1 182 000 people visited the area between July 1973 and June 1974, 37 000 of whom were from overseas. The Gold Coast is particularly popular as a winter holiday area when residents of the southern States head north to escape the cold. In the period just mentioned 39 per cent of the total annual visits were made between June and September, compared with only 26 per cent for the summer months from December to February. This is in marked contrast to the pattern of visits experienced in other areas where summer crowding creates major problems for the accommodation and service industries. The influx of tourists has triggered off a building boom that has resulted in a string of hotels, motels, flats and caravan parks all along the 32 km of coast from Southport to Coolangatta.

Below left: Ayers Rock with the Olgas far in the west. The world's largest monolith, Ayers Rock exerts a strange fascination for the thousands of visitors who each year cross 435 km of desert from Alice Springs by aircraft, bus or four-wheel drive to gaze at its splendour. Energetic visitors climb the Rock's 348 metres to discover a few scraggy trees and deep round holes filled with water. Eleven km of road encircles the base of the Rock.

Below right: The Olgas, just 23 km west of Ayers Rock are a jumble of 28 massive domed boulders, the largest of which, Mount Olga itself, dominates the skyline from every direction. The Olgas cover an area 7.2 km long and 4.8 km wide and are more than half as high again as Ayers Rock. Like Ayers Rock, the Olgas are a very significant landform to the Aborigines, who call them Katajuta — 'many heads'.

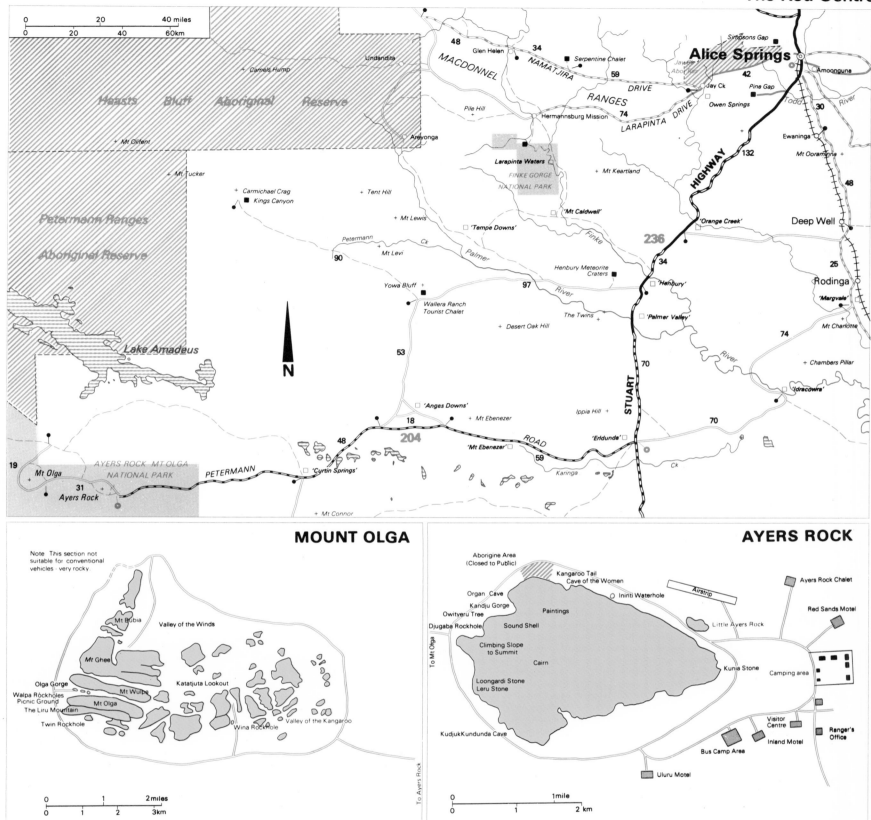

MOUNT OLGA

AYERS ROCK

Another area that is very popular for tourists is the Australian Alps in southern New South Wales and north-eastern Victoria. This very scenic mountain area has appeal in summer and winter because of both its natural beauty and the opportunities it offers for fishing, boating, walking and skiing. The latter has expanded greatly over the last few years with first class resorts being developed at Thredbo, Falls Creek and Mt Buller. In 1974 331 000 visits were made to the Victorian ski resorts alone, the number having increased by an average annual rate of 13.9 per cent in the five years prior to that date.

The island of Tasmania, with a charm and atmosphere unique amongst the Australian States, has become a popular destination for Australian holiday-makers, especially between September and April. Its appeal lies in its green, hedge-lined fields, its tranquil hamlets reminiscent of English villages, its stone bridges, and magnificent contrast mountains, cultivated valleys, river estuaries and beach-ringed bays. The vast untouched wilderness area in the south-west attracts the adventurous while the more urban-oriented traveller finds historic Hobart particularly appealing. In the period July 1973 to June 1974 approximately 1 million tourist trips had Tasmania as their main destination. Of these, 169 000 (17 per cent) had their origin either inter-State or overseas, many of them attracted to the Wrest Point Hotel, the home of Australia's first casino.

There are also the various man-made attractions that have proven appeal for both the international and domestic tourist. Port Arthur and Richmond in Tasmania, Sovereign Hill in Ballarat in Victoria and Old Sydney Town in New South Wales are examples of 'heritage attractions' that can be found in all the States. Each of the State capitals and the national capital of Canberra have their own distinctive character. Sydney with its magnificent harbour, impressive bridges and world-famous Opera House is attractive to tourists from all walks of life. Indeed Sydney has consistently remained the most popular destination for tourists, receiving an estimated 4.16 million visitors in the year ended June 1974 — 397 000 (9 per cent) of these came from overseas. Melbourne with its fine gardens, beautiful bay and impressive National Gallery is also a very popular tourist destination, receiving 1 918 000 visits in the same period. The presence of the major international airports in Melbourne and Sydney is undoubtedly partly responsible for the popularity of these centres to international visitors to Australia.

Finally, one should not overlook the attraction of the people themselves in the eyes of the international tourist. Numerous surveys have demonstrated that the factor which visitors have ranked highest, in terms of making their visit enjoyable, is Australia's 'warm and friendly' people. One must add to this the attraction of the culture of Australia's Aborigines. International visitors are always very

Tourism in Australia

eager to learn how the Aborigines managed to adapt to life in some of the most inhospitable country in the world. Moreover, Aboriginal art and artifacts (especially the boomerang) are always very popular with the souvenir-seeking tourist.

Government Involvement in Tourism

The responsibility for encouraging and providing for tourism is shared between the Federal and State Governments. The latter are primarily responsible for encouraging travel to and within each State and for the development of tourist attractions and facilities. Each State has an official Tourist Department or Authority and operates travel services through tourist bureaux and travel centres. The Federal Government, on the other hand, is primarily concerned with encouraging people from other countries to visit and travel within Australia. This is done through the Australian Tourist Commission which en-

Below: Hayman Island tourist resort in the Cumberland group of the Great Barrier Reef, offshore from Proserpine. The islands of this group once formed part of a coastal range that was subsequently drowned. Hayman has hills up to 260 metres covered with luxuriant tropical forest. Hayman, one of the best publicised resorts of the Barrier Reef, is the destination of many southerners on reasonably priced package tours to the warm winter north. Excursions are organised from Hayman Island to Lindeman, Dent and South Molle Islands, as well as coral-watching on the Reef.

gages in a wide variety of marketing activities including consumer and trade advertising, industry seminars, and familiarisation visits for travel agents, photographers and journalists. With a budget in excess of $3 million the Commission operates through offices in all Australian States as well as in a number of foreign cities including New York, Los Angeles, London and Tokyo.

International Tourism

Of the 516 000 international visitors who arrived in 1975 the main sources were New Zealand (29.9 per cent), North America (15.5 per cent), the United Kingdom and Ireland (14.1 per cent), Europe (10.2 per cent), Papua New Guinea (6.2 per cent) and Japan (4.7 per cent). The relative importance of each of these source countries has remained fairly constant since 1970 although there has been a slight tendency for Japan and New Zealand to increase their contribution to the total. The high and increasing expenditure by overseas visitors has meant that tourism has attained a high position on the list of foreign exchange earners to the Australian economy. In 1975-76 it ranked in tenth position on the list of Australian export earning industries.

Perhaps the most significant conclusion that one could draw about the places visited by international visitors is that they are very limited. Over 61 per cent of the places visited in 1974-75 were in Victoria, New South Wales and the Australian Capital Territory. Indeed the area is even more confined as 43 per cent of the places visited were in either

Melbourne or Sydney. The Gold Coast attracted 53 000 visitors (3.9 per cent of the total), the Barrier Reef and North Queensland coastal centres 49 000 (3.6 per cent), and Alice Springs and Ayers Rock 25 000 (1.8 per cent). This pattern is understandable given the reasons why tourists travel to Australia and the fact that most of the population, particularly the migrant component, lives in the south-east of the country.

Domestic Tourism

It is domestic tourism that provides the bread and butter for the industry. Indeed, it is internal travel that has provided the stimulus for most of Australia's tourist developments.

Between July 1973 and June 1974 27 million trips were made within Australia — 26 million or 98 per cent of these were made by Australians. It has been estimated that the number of Australians travelling within Australia is likely to increase in the long term by 7 per cent per annum and that this growth will provide the basis of demand for accommodation and services, especially in those areas away from the capital cities.

Nearly half of all 'main holiday' travel takes place in the summer months of December and January although there is an increasing tendency for trips to be taken in the April to May period. It is also interesting to note that some 70 per cent of domestic travellers stayed in accommodation other than hotels and motels: private houses (40 per cent), caravans or tents (17 per cent) and holiday homes (8 per cent) were the most popular

A coral cay with fringing coral reef.

Exposed coral on the Reef.

Staghorn coral on the Reef.

Tropical fish in the Reef area.

COPYRIGHT, GEORGE PHILIP & O'NEIL PTY. LTD

Tourism in Australia

forms of accommodation.

Most (85 per cent) of trips taken have their main destination in the State in which they originated. In fact domestic tourism is characterised by fairly short trips of two nights or less, although it is very difficult to generalise the origin of demand for domestic tourism in the densely-populated eastern coastal regions, particularly the urban areas of Sydney, Melbourne and Canberra. The destinations of tourists are even more varied. The Sydney and Melbourne regions receive the greatest proportion of domestic tourist trips although the coastal rim of Queensland and northern New South Wales is also very popular especially for 'main holiday' trips. The Gold Coast, for example, attracted 1 145 000 trips during the period July 1973 to June 1974, while the north coast region of New South Wales attracted 1 100 000 during the same period. Skiing resorts in south-eastern Australia are also popular, particularly for 'subsidiary holiday' travel while the 'outback' attracts continuing numbers of explorers and visitors.

The Benefits of Tourism

It is not always easy to grasp the notion that tourism is an industry, particularly one that can generate economic benefits for a country. Although it lacks easily identifiable raw materials, a processing plant and a transportable end product, tourism can still make a valuable contribution to a nation's economy. When an international visitor arrives in a country he becomes an additional consumer who demands all kinds of goods and services. Large numbers of tourists create new employment opportunities, in transportation and construction as well as the normal tourist activities.

In Australia it has been estimated that there are well over 15 000 companies, associations and organisations that draw a part or all of their earnings from travel and tourism. The travel industry employs at least 10 per cent of the Australian workforce, primarily in transportation and accommodation. Moreover, being a service industry, tourism is very labour intensive with direct labour costs representing a large percentage of total costs. This employment-generating attribute is made particularly significant by its areal distribution. Because the tourist industry is a very dispersed industry, the creation of additional direct and indirect employment and increased economic activity can mean a very real contribution to non-urban areas. In Swan Hill, where a highly successful tourist folk museum has been established, the population has increased at a time when comparable centres have declined, additional investments of at least $1.5 million have occurred, and new employment opportunities have been created for about 120 people. Tourism can certainly make a significant contribution to decentralisation.

The Australian National Travel Association, a national association of private organisations actively involved in developing and promoting tourism, estimated that the gross sales by the tourist industry were about $2 400 million in 1970, or 8 per cent of Australia's Gross National Income. Although no comparable study has been made since that time it is now expected that this figure is well in excess of $3 000 million.

The tourist industry makes a substantial contribution to government revenues at the Federal, State and local level through the direct taxation of income earned by employees, excise on goods sold, and land taxes on properties. The most recent estimate available is for 1972 when the Federal Government derived $33.2 million from overseas visitors — almost 24 per cent of total expenditure by those tourists. Revenue earned from domestic tourism is an unknown, but definitely larger, amount.

One can add to these economic benefits other less tangible, though equally important, contributions to Australia's development. Travel and tourism provide an opportunity for the constructive use of leisure time and the development of a better understanding of our history and our country. On the other hand, contact with overseas visitors can broaden each Australian's understanding and appreciation of different cultures thereby minimising parochial attitudes.

The Future of Tourism

It has already been suggested that the future of tourism seems very bright indeed. Australia is expected to attract about one million visitors in 1980 and the number of Australians travelling within the country is likely to increase in the long term by seven per cent per annum. Growth rates of this magnitude will require careful planning and management by all the private and government bodies involved in tourism.

The Federal Government is showing leadership on this. It has accepted the fact that, if tourism is to play its part in the country's social and economic development, attractions must be developed and provided with appropriate facilities so that tourists can enjoy them, learn something from their visit and understand more about the country. In order to improve the range of tourist attractions the Government has introduced a scheme of grants (worth $2.25 million in 1974-75) to assist specific tourist projects, perhaps the most famous of which is Old Sydney Town in New South Wales. Likewise, all levels of government have seen the need to manage adequately and protect outstanding natural attractions. This has meant the implementation of very strong planning controls over developments in natural areas, including on

Below: Ski slopes and lodges at Perisher Valley, a Snowy Mountains ski resort. Unlike the nearby Thredbo resort, Perisher has gentle slopes suitable for those learning to ski.

occasions some de-development as in the case of the Ayers Rock-Mount Olga National Park. Various government bodies have also been analysing the seasonality of tourist demand and moves are under way to stagger school holidays and to encourage people to take their leave outside the traditional summer holiday period. Finally, many government and private organisations have felt the need for more comprehensive and sophisticated research into travel patterns in order to provide a sound basis for a balanced national policy for tourism. Regional surveys are therefore being implemented in order to examine critically existing and planned tourist attractions and supporting facilities, to identify new opportunities and to offer planning guidelines for the future.

Opposite: A replica of the brig Perseverance *stands at anchor at the Hospital Wharf in Old Sydney Town, near Gosford in New South Wales. Behind it are the early supply stores of the colony, one of the many buildings constructed in an ambitious project to recreate Sydney as it was between 1788 and 1810. Local actors in eighteenth-century dress enact the early life of the settlement. Visitors can watch the free settlers at work in the smithy or boatshed, or ask about the production of cloth, candles and soap in the homes; they may also witness some of the more spectacular daily events of the colony — a trial, a flogging and an attempted escape by convicts.*

Below left and right: Re-creations of historic buildings at Sovereign Hill, Ballarat. Sovereign Hill, the site of a famous gold mine, has been so skilfully rebuilt that it is now one of Victoria's major attractions for Australian and overseas tourists. As well as these impressive buildings, all the details of a nineteenth-century gold-mine can be seen. It is possible for visitors to pan for gold in the creek that runs through the hill.

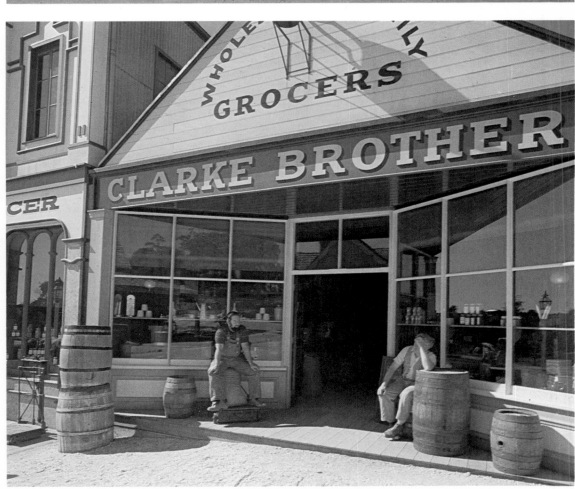

Recreational Resources

The Melbourne Cup is the Australian National Day. It would be difficult to overstate its importance . . . I can call to mind no specialised annual day, in any country, whose approach fires the whole land with the conflagration of conversation and preparation and jubilation. No day save this one, and this one does it.

Mark Twain's observation made in 1889 could still apply to Australia today. It reflects this country's popular image as a nation obsessed with leisure and sporting activities. Other countries are renowned for their national obsessions, such as Brazil with soccer and Canada with ice-hockey; but in Australia the obsession is not confined to one or two sports but rather to sport as such.

Sport, however, is just one type of recreational activity that Australians undertake during their leisure time. To avoid confusion the differences between leisure, recreation and sport should be stated at the outset. Although defining leisure has been likened to the task of trying to grasp a jelly fish, the term is usually accepted as meaning the time available to an individual when the disciplines of work, sleep and other basic needs have been met. Recreation, on the other hand, is defined as any pursuit engaged in during leisure time, other than those to which people are normally committed — the latter including such things as optional shopping, overtime, house repairs, car maintenance, further education, child-care, religion and politics. Leisure is therefore time-oriented while recreation is an activity. Finally, sport is a particular form of recreational activity, one that is usually highly structured and contains an element of competition or challenge against opponents, oneself or the environment.

The range of activities that can be described under the term recreation is very large. Five hundred separate recreational activities have been listed, including such

Wilson's Promontory, one of Victoria's most popular National Parks, is famous for its spectacular coastal scenery.

disparate things as watching television, dancing, painting, stamp collecting, window shopping, shooting, trampolining, parachuting and model building.

Leisure Time Allocation

Although there are no detailed time-budget surveys that can be used to determine how Australians divide up their time, several small-scale studies provide sufficient evidence for us to question whether Australia has really become the celebrated 'leisured society'. Indeed work has begun to consume far more of the average Australian's time than was the case two decades ago. While the nominal working week has declined from 40 hours to 35 hours, the actual length of the average working week for Australian males and females has tended to increase in recent years. The opportunity to substitute increased earnings for increased leisure time has been grasped by males in particular who are working more hours overtime than in previous years. Women are tending to remain in the workforce for longer periods, many of them returning to work after their children have reached school age. In fact married women now comprise over 20 per cent of the Australian workforce. Finally, it has been estimated that between five and ten per cent of the workforce has more than one job. These trends would suggest that Australians are devoting less effort to the pursuit of leisure and recreation.

Running counter to this, however, are a number of factors that are contributing to an increase in both leisure time and participation in recreational activities. The vast majority of workers now enjoy a five day week with Saturdays and Sundays free. Experiments in flexitime have given some the right to modify their working hours to suit themselves and have given others the opportunity to work a nine-day fortnight. The length of paid annual leave has steadily increased to the point where most workers receive four or more weeks a year. In addition to this, Australia has more public holidays than other western countries.

The average income in Australia has also increased markedly in the last few years with the average wage in December 1976 being $186 per week. Affluence has meant a very high level of personal mobility, with car ownership being the norm for most families. Indeed, the last few years have witnessed a boom in the sales of vehicles specifically designed for recreational use, many of which are bought as a family's second car.

Government Involvement in Recreation

There is a great diversity in the agencies, organisations and enterprises that provide recreational opportunities in Australia — including private clubs, youth agencies, church bodies, commercial establishments and government organisations. Governments at all levels have become increasingly involved in promoting and supporting all forms of recreational and leisure activities.

At the local level municipal authorities employ recreation workers who are responsible for the multi-purpose use of recreation facilities and for devising programs for community recreation. At the State level, departments or sections have been established to co-ordinate and be responsible for recreational activities. In New South Wales, for example, the Department of Culture, Sport and Recreation provides regional recreation officers in metropolitan and country areas to promote local recreational opportunities. This includes organising tuition in various recreational skills for interested people as well as encouraging the development of private clubs and organisations through a variety of subsidies and matching grant programs. The Department conducts outdoor educational and recreational programs and operates vacation play centres and permanent Sport and Recreation Service Centres located throughout the State. In Victoria the Department of Youth, Sport and Recreation provides advisers and consultants to promote leisure and recreation activities in metropolitan and country areas. The Department also administers an extensive program of financial grants

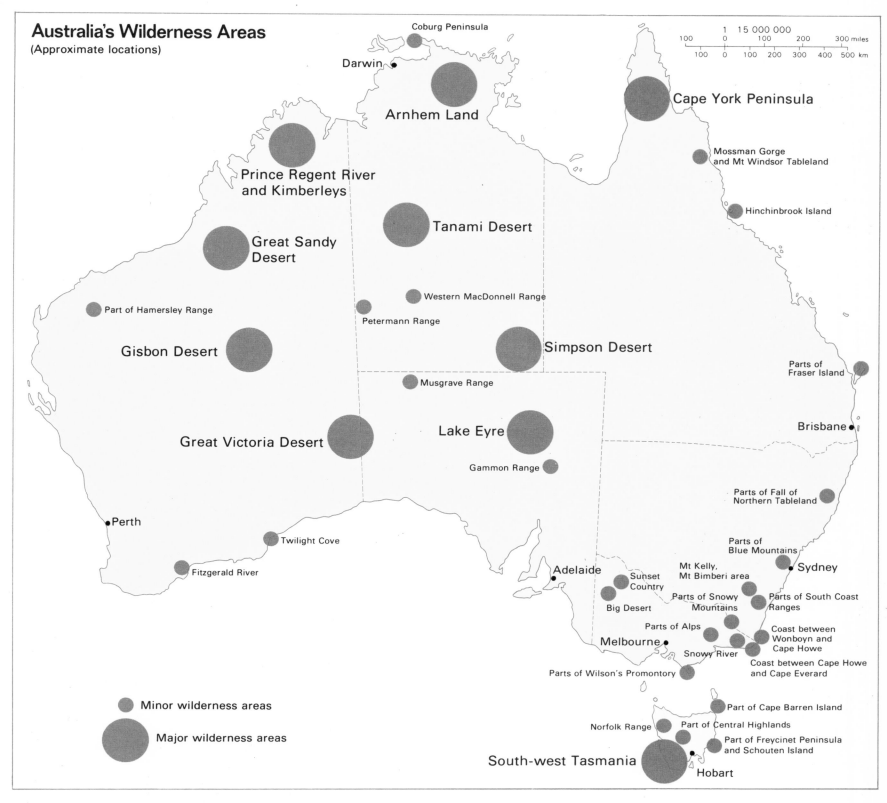

Australia's Wilderness Areas
(Approximate locations)

1 15 000 000

100   0   100   200   300 miles
100   0   100   200   300   400   500 km

Coburg Peninsula

Darwin

Arnhem Land

Cape York Peninsula

Mossman Gorge
and Mt Windsor Tableland

Prince Regent River
and Kimberleys

Hinchinbrook Island

Great Sandy
Desert

Tanami Desert

Part of Hamersley Range

Western MacDonnell Range

Petermann Range

Gisbon Desert

Simpson Desert

Parts of
Fraser Island

Musgrave Range

Great Victoria Desert

Lake Eyre

Brisbane

Gammon Range

Perth

Parts of Fall of
Northern Tableland

Twilight Cove

Parts of
Blue Mountains

Fitzgerald River

Adelaide

Mt Kelly,
Mt Bimberi area

Sydney

Sunset
Country

Parts of Snowy
Mountains

Parts of South Coast
Ranges

Big Desert

Parts of Alps

Coast between
Wonboyn and
Cape Howe

Melbourne

Snowy River

Coast between Cape Howe
and Cape Everard

Parts of Wilson's Promontory

Minor wilderness areas

Part of Cape Barren Island

Major wilderness areas

Norfolk Range

Part of Central Highlands

Part of Freycinet Peninsula
and Schouten Island

South-west Tasmania

Hobart

---

to encourage the development of local facilities, youth involvement programs, and the expansion of volunteer organisations.

In the other States, Government involvement is not as extensive. For example, the sub-department of Sport in Queensland is primarily involved in the allocation of funds to sporting associations and clubs for facility developments, coaching subsidies and team travel. Very little attempt is made to promote directly leisure and recreational activities within the State.

Until recently all of these State and local government initiatives were supported in various ways by the Federal Department of Tourism and Recreation which was established in 1972 to co-ordinate all aspects of the development of recreational opportunities in Australia. In the 1974-75 financial year this Department provided $11.5 million towards a range of community leisure facilities. A variety of research projects have also been funded by the Department including several regional demand studies and a detailed analysis of the availability and utilisation of recreational facilities for women. Although the

Department no longer exists as a separate entity, public and private recreational organisations can still receive grants either directly or indirectly from the Federal Government.

Participation in Recreation

Unfortunately there is no large body of data that can be drawn on to provide an accurate picture of the pattern of participation in various recreational activities in Australia. Sufficient studies have been conducted, however, for some general observations to be made.

A number of studies have highlighted the home and garden as a venue for leisure time activities. In the Australian Capital Territory, for example, the average person spends as much as 75 per cent of his leisure time in the home environment. A recent study in Adelaide also found that the residential garden was a major venue for the outdoor activities of most suburban dwellers. In addition to the time spent gardening, 43 per cent of householders use their garden for some sport or game once a week, 14 per cent entertaining friends, 16 per cent for barbecuing, 47 per

cent for a passive activity like reading, and 14 per cent for some other hobby. Sixty-one per cent of the adults interviewed in Adelaide maintained that half their time is spent outdoors and that of that time 57 per cent is spent in and around their gardens. Studies in Melbourne have also confirmed the importance of home-based activities. In the city of Kew, for example, it has been found that the four most common recreational activities are watching television (90.4 per cent of respondents mentioned this as a recreational activity), reading (84 per cent), listening to the radio (83.6 per cent) and attending parties (80 per cent).

Australians have been shown to be particularly sociable in their recreational activities. The popularity of a barbecue or outing with friends has been well documented. The huge Sunday crowds at picnic places close to the metropolitan centres are ample evidence of large numbers of people who enjoy getting into the open air with their family and friends.

It is easy to demonstrate that Australians spend a lot of their leisure time watching,

Recreational Resources

reading about and discussing all forms of sporting activities. On any Saturday afternoon in winter over 150 000 people in Melbourne alone watch Australian Rules League football. In 1971 a Gallup Poll found that 360 000 people over the age of eighteen, or 23 per cent of the people in Melbourne and Geelong, see all 22 matches in a season either at the ground or as a replay on television. An additional 11.2 per cent watch only two to five matches, whereas 56.5 per cent watch at least one. Indeed sport swamps the television, radio and newspapers around Australia. In 1962, for example, it was estimated that of the total amount of news space in Australian daily newspapers, 15 per cent was devoted to sport, 8.2 per cent to political-social-economic news, and 7.4 per cent to foreign news.

Despite the continuing popularity of sport, some commentators have suggested that spectator sport is relatively less important today than in earlier years. Horse-racing, for example, has experienced a 25 per cent drop in attendance rates since World War 2. Even Australian Rules football has been affected — there was very little growth in the actual number of people attending League football matches in Melbourne between 1930 and 1972 which, with population growth, means a significant decline in the proportion of the population who attend matches. During 1972 the average weekly attendance was 133 405 or just over 5 per cent of the population. Had the percentage rate of 1946 still applied, 227 000 Melburnians would have been at the football. However, to keep these and other attendance figures in perspective one must not forget the rapid rise in the number listening to sport on the radio or watching it on television.

Recent studies have consistently shown that in terms of popularity, formal sporting activities are of far less significance than informal leisure activities such as driving for pleasure, beach visits and picnicking. Indeed there is a significant trend away from many highly-structured team sports, towards the more individual activities. An extensive survey of the recreational habits and preferences of 1500 Victorian households has documented this trend. Eighty-seven per cent of respondents said that they had gone for a drive in the country during the twelve months immediately prior to the interview. During the same period 66 per cent had been on a picnic, 58 per cent had visited a National Park, and 54 per cent had been walking for pleasure through the bush. On the other hand 48 per cent had watched some competitive sport during those twelve months, and only 29 per cent had actually played competitive sport. When asked what were their preferred weekend activities 41 per cent of respondents nominated picnics and barbecues, 38 per cent pleasure drives and sightseeing, and 36 per cent preferred relaxing at home. Only 15 per cent of those interviewed nominated competitive sports as amongst their most preferred weekend activities.

It appears that the independence facilitated

by the car, money and more regular leisure time has enabled Australians of all ages to select from an almost unlimited range of recreational activities. Those that present the opportunity for greater control over one's own destiny would seem to have special appeal. Individual activities, especially those involving close contact with nature, such as surfing, hang-gliding, rock-climbing, skin-diving, bush-walking or skiing, offer this opportunity far more than team sports.

Activities associated with water have become particularly popular. In Victoria alone the number of registered power boats increased from 12 000 in 1962 to 60 000 in 1974, an increase of 500 per cent. Between 1963 and 1972 the number of boats affiliated with the Victorian Yachting Council expanded from 2600 to 8000. Boat building in Australia has become a multi-million dollar industry. The Australian Surfboard Riders Association found that in 1973 there were one-half to three-quarters of a million surfboard riders in Australia. It has been estimated that one in ten of the population fishes regularly and that people spend more on fishing than on all other sport combined.

Individual sports such as golf, bowls and squash have also grown in popularity. Golf boasts over 350 000 adherents who play on any of the 1300 golf courses throughout the country and buy an estimated 4.5 million golf balls each year. Squash has experienced in-

creased popularity with an estimated tenfold increase in the number of courts over the last decade. Lawn bowls, popular with the older age group, has an estimated 400 000 competitors at the present time.

The growth in the popularity of skiing has reached boom proportions. Although precise statistics have not been compiled, estimates of the total Australian skier population range from 180 000 to 200 000, most of them living in New South Wales, Victoria and Tasmania. Data on the total annual imports of skis and equipment provides some evidence of the rapid growth in the last few years: in 1971/72 11 705 pairs of skis, poles and stocks were imported compared with 21 126 in 1974/75.

Recreation Resources

It is generally accepted that recreational participation is very largely a function of the supply of recreational opportunities. People do not have innate recreational 'needs'; rather, they simply use whatever facilities or resources are available for them.

No one knows exactly how much of Australia's land area is devoted to recreational activities. Indeed, given the acceptance of multiple-use as a management strategy (where, for example, forests are used for both timber harvesting and recreation) it would be almost impossible to determine such a figure. What is known, however, is that Australia

Opposite: Fishing on the Tumut River, southern NSW.

Far opposite: Canoeing at Junction Dam, Bogong River, Victoria.

contains an enormous variety of recreational resources from snow-clad mountains to broad open plains, from scattered inland lakes to long sun-drenched beaches, and from large complex sports gymnasiums to small local tennis courts. In the light of this diversity it is common to classify recreational resources into three types: user-oriented, intermediate and resource-based.

User-oriented facilities are those where the activity is paramount over the characteristics of the resource. They are usually found within or in close proximity to urban areas and include such things as swimming pools, gymnasiums, football grounds, local parks, tennis courts and bowling greens. In Australia these facilities are provided by local councils as the majority of users tend to live locally. A recent study of several local government areas in the north of Melbourne found that councils provide an average of three ovals for every 10 000 people. Similar results have been found in other parts of the country although wide discrepancies do exist.

Intermediate type recreational resources are those used by people on a day's outing. They are normally environmentally attractive and very often popular because of their relative proximity to urban centres. Australia's high level of car-ownership has meant that the weekend trip into the country is a very popular activity. Recent research has indicated that most of these trips from large

urban areas are confined to a zone within two-hours' travelling time. Within this fairly large area the car provides almost unlimited flexibility of timing and movement making it possible for people to visit a whole variety of recreational resources that the area has to offer. Indeed, a common form of recreational activity is simply the Sunday drive where the trip itself becomes an integral part of the whole experience. Picnic areas, national parks and beaches within this area are therefore subjected to huge crowds particularly during summer. In a number of capital cities large 'regional parks' are being opened up close to the edge of the urban area to cater for the increasing demand for this type of recreational resource.

Finally, resource-based recreation areas are those where the type of resource determines the use that is made of the area and where development is usually at a very low level. These therefore include most of Australia's shoreline away from the capital cities, the alpine areas in the south-east, the national parks and the so-called 'wilderness areas'. In these vast areas the predominant recreational activities include hiking, canoeing, nordic skiing, camping, nature study and climbing. In the last decade Australians have demonstrated an increasing interest and concern for these areas, especially the national parks. Despite their name, national parks are controlled by each State Government usually

with the combined objective of protecting the environment within the park and encouraging the proper use of the park by the public. The almost astronomical increase in the number of visitors to these parks has initiated a strong movement for the establishment of more and bigger parks. Recent proposals have included a large national park covering much of the Cape York Peninsula as well as an Alpine National Park in Victoria to link in with the enormous Kosciusko National Park in New South Wales. Wilderness areas are large tracts of primitive country with land, waters and native plant and animal communities substantially unmodified by man. Several of these have been proposed for Australia, the most famous of which is in south-west Tasmania. The much publicised debate over the flooding of Lake Pedder was essentially about whether that area should be preserved as a wilderness area to be enjoyed by the growing numbers interested in bush-walking and climbing in remote parts of the country.

Given the trends that have been identified in both leisure time allocation and participation in different activities, it is likely that the demand for the intermediate and resource-based recreation activities will continue to increase rapidly. Not only must new areas be set aside for these types of activities but those which we already have must be managed well so that their use is guaranteed for years to come.

A Statistical Review

General Facts

	Area (km²)	Coastline (km)
NSW	801 600	1 900
Vic	227 600	1 800
Qld	1 727 200	7 400
SA	984 000	3 700
WA	2 525 500	12 500
Tas	67 800	3 200
NT	1 346 200	6 200
ACT	2 400	35
Aust	7 682 300	36 735

Australian External Territories
Australian Antarctic Territory
Christmas Island
Cocos (Keeling) Islands
Coral Sea Islands
Heard and McDonald Islands
Norfolk Island

Highest Point
Mt Kosciusko, NSW (2228 m)

Lowest Point
Lake Eyre, SA (−15 m)

Longest River
Murray River (2520 km)

Largest Lake
Lake Eyre (9500 km²)

Highest Daily Rainfall
Crohamhurst (Qld)
907 mm on 3rd Feb 1893

Highest Wind Speed
Onslow (WA)
232 kmhr⁻¹ in 1963

Maximum Temperature
Cloncurry (Qld) 53.1°C

Longest Hot Spell
Marble Bar (WA)
160 days of at least 38.4°C
31st Oct 1923 to 7th Apr 1924

Minimum Temperature
Charlotte Pass (NSW) −22.2°C

Population June 1976
Total   13 915 500

Crop Production ($'000) 1975-76

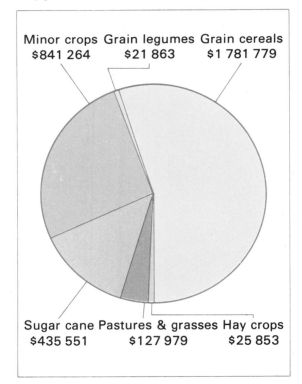

Minor crops $841 264
Grain legumes $21 863
Grain cereals $1 781 779
Sugar cane $435 551
Pastures & grasses $127 979
Hay crops $25 853

Areas of States (% of total)

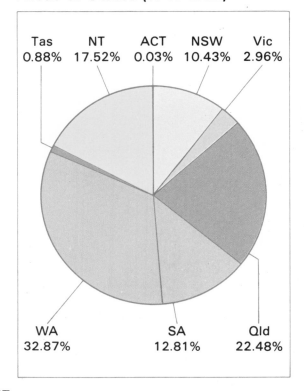

Tas 0.88%
NT 17.52%
ACT 0.03%
NSW 10.43%
Vic 2.96%
WA 32.87%
SA 12.81%
Qld 22.48%

Rural Land Use 1975-76

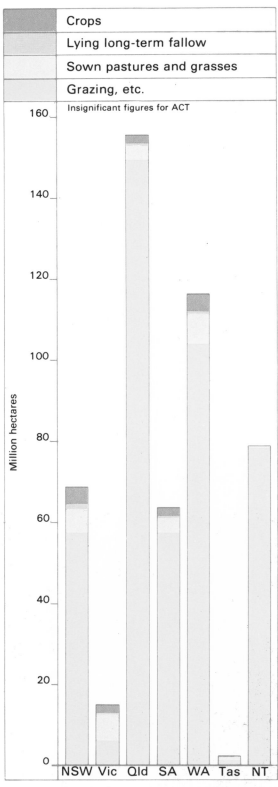

Crops
Lying long-term fallow
Sown pastures and grasses
Grazing, etc.
Insignificant figures for ACT

Million hectares

NSW Vic Qld SA WA Tas NT

Value of Minerals Produced 1974-75

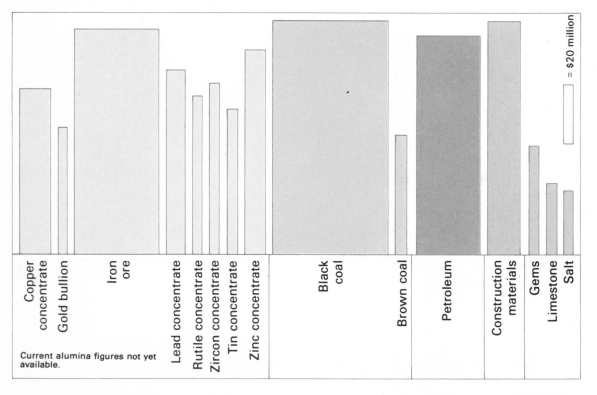

= $20 million

Copper concentrate
Gold bullion
Iron ore
Lead concentrate
Rutile concentrate
Zircon concentrate
Tin concentrate
Zinc concentrate
Black coal
Brown coal
Petroleum
Construction materials
Gems
Limestone
Salt

Current alumina figures not yet available.

Principal Mineral Exports 1976-77

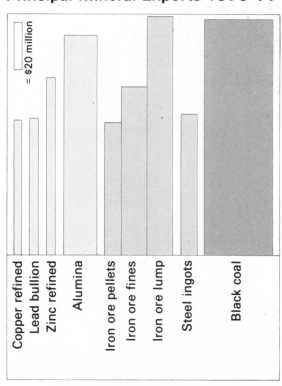

= $20 million

Copper refined
Lead bullion
Zinc refined
Alumina
Iron ore pellets
Iron ore fines
Iron ore lump
Steel ingots
Black coal

Populations of Major Urban Centres by State June 1976

NSW	Vic	Qld	SA	WA	Tas
Sydney 2 765 121	Melbourne 2 478 074	Brisbane 892 987	Adelaide 857 066	Perth 731 275	Hobart 131 524
Newcastle 251 132	Geelong 122 080	Gold Coast 94 014	Whyalla 133 426	Bunbury 19 513	Launceston 63 386
Wollongong 197 127	Ballarat 60 737	Townsville 73 961	Mt Gambier 19 292	Kalgoorlie 19 041	Devonport 19 399
Maitland 36 030	Bendigo 50 169	Toowoomba 63 956	Port Pirie 15 005	Geraldton 18 773	Burnie 16 266
Wagga Wagga 32 984	Shepparton 25 848	Rockhampton 50 132	Port Augusta 13 092	Rockingham 17 693	**NT**
Albury 31 954	Warrnambool 20 195	Cairns 39 385	Port Lincoln 9809	Albany 13 696	Darwin 41 374
Tamworth 27 887	Moe-Yallourn 18 710	Mackay 31 552		Port Hedland 11 144	Alice Springs 14 149
Broken Hill 27 647	Morwell 16 194	Bundaberg 31 189		Kwinana 10 981	**ACT**
Orange 26 254	Wangaratta 16 157	Mt Isa 25 377			Canberra 194 517
Lismore 22 082	Traralgon 15 087	Maryborough 20 670			

Note: These figures are for the centres themselves, and do not include associated administrative districts.

Urban Centres June 1971

Population size	Number of urban centres	% of Aust. pop.
500 000 and over	5	57.93
100 000–499 999	5	6.57
75 000– 99 999	0	0
50 000– 74 999	5	2.52
25 000– 49 999	12	3.20
20 000– 24 999	8	1.39
15 000– 19 999	16	2.17
10 000– 14 999	22	2.04
5 000– 9 999	66	3.66
2 500– 4 999	110	2.97
2 000– 2 499	52	0.91
1 000– 1 999	180	2.02
Less than 1 000	38	0.19
Total urban pop.	519	85.57

Note: Comparable figures based on the 1976 Census are not yet available.

Rate of Births and Deaths 1870–1976

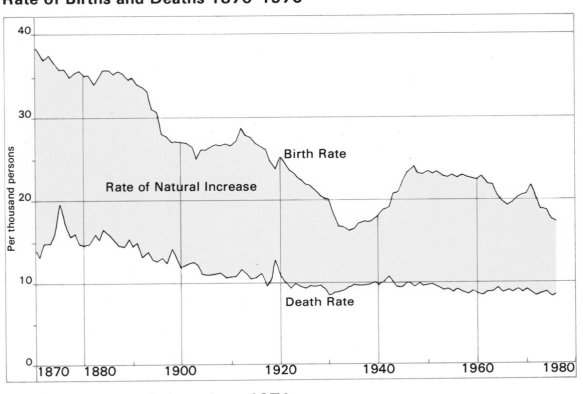

Urban & Rural Population June '76

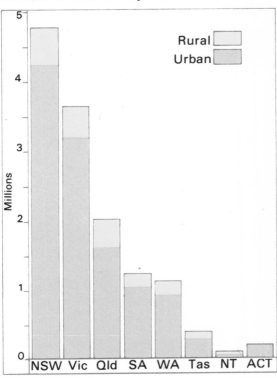

Employment Populations June 1971

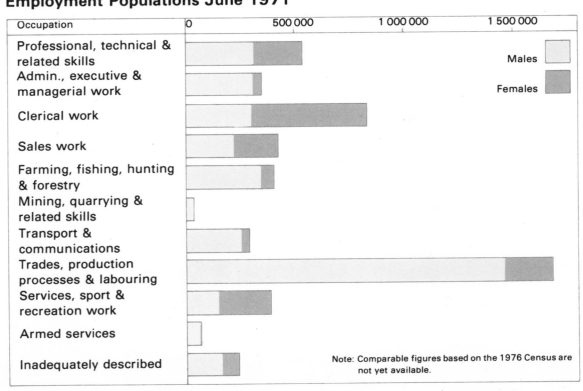

Note: Comparable figures based on the 1976 Census are not yet available.

State Population Growth

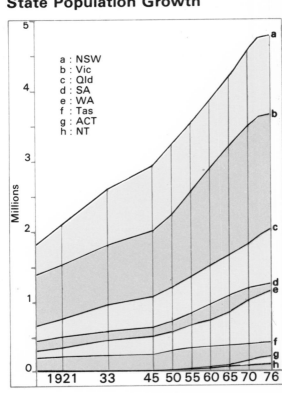

New South Wales: the Leader

Characteristics and Population

New South Wales is the oldest, most populated and most industrialised State. Its name was coined by Captain Cook in 1770 for all Australian territory east of the 135th meridian of east longitude. From that original area of 4 103 987 km² — including New Zealand — a series of adjustments reduced New South Wales to its present area of 801 428 km², including Lord Howe Island, 702 km northeast of Sydney, but excluding Australian Capital Territory. This is just over 10 per cent of the area of Australia.

New South Wales accounts for about 40 per cent of Australian secondary production (more than $12 000 million), 30 per cent of primary production (more than $1650 million) and 20 per cent of mineral production (about $785 million).

Australia's founding city is Sydney, the State capital, with a population of 3 021 300. The State's population of 4 777 000 represents about 35 per cent of the national total. Other population centres include Wollongong (165 150), Newcastle (138 700), Cessnock (36 200), Maitland (36 000), Albury (32 950), Wagga Wagga (34 300), Broken Hill (27 650), Orange (25 500), Goulburn (21 750) and Lismore (22 080).

Education is compulsory between the ages of 6 and 15 and more than 1 million students attend primary and secondary schools, about 80 per cent at free government schools and the balance at private schools. The six universities in New South Wales have enrolments totalling 52 000.

History and Government

First settled as a penal colony in 1788, New South Wales was constituted a Crown colony in 1840. More that 80 000 convicts had been sent there before public agitation forced an end to transportation in 1840. By then immigration was thriving, and the wool industry, largely pioneered by Captain John Macarthur, was already dominating Australian exports. Responsible government came in 1856 in the middle of the gold rushes which opened up so much of the nation. The State Parliament consists of an upper house (the Legislative Council) and a lower house (the Legislative Assembly).

Climate and Geography

New South Wales is in the temperate zone and its climate is generally mild and equable and mostly free from temperature extremes. The greatest temperature variations occur in the arid north-west, and the southern tablelands. On average, Sydney has sunshine for all but 23 days of the year. Its average midsummer maximum temperature is 25.7°C (average minimum is 18.3°C) and average midwinter maximum is 15.8°C (average minimum 7.8°C).

Opposite: City and mines of Broken Hill, one of the world's largest deposits of silver, lead and zinc. Although the southern mine is worked out, the northern mine is still operating.

Centre: Hat Head National Park, east of Kempsey.

Far right: Dorrigo Mountains overlooking rolling New England pastoral land, inland from Coffs Harbour.

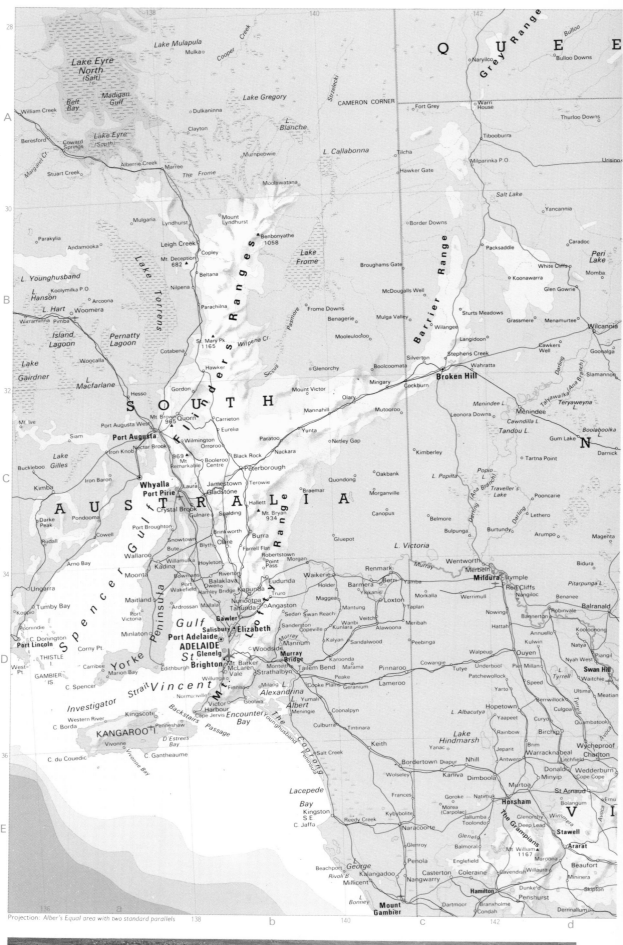

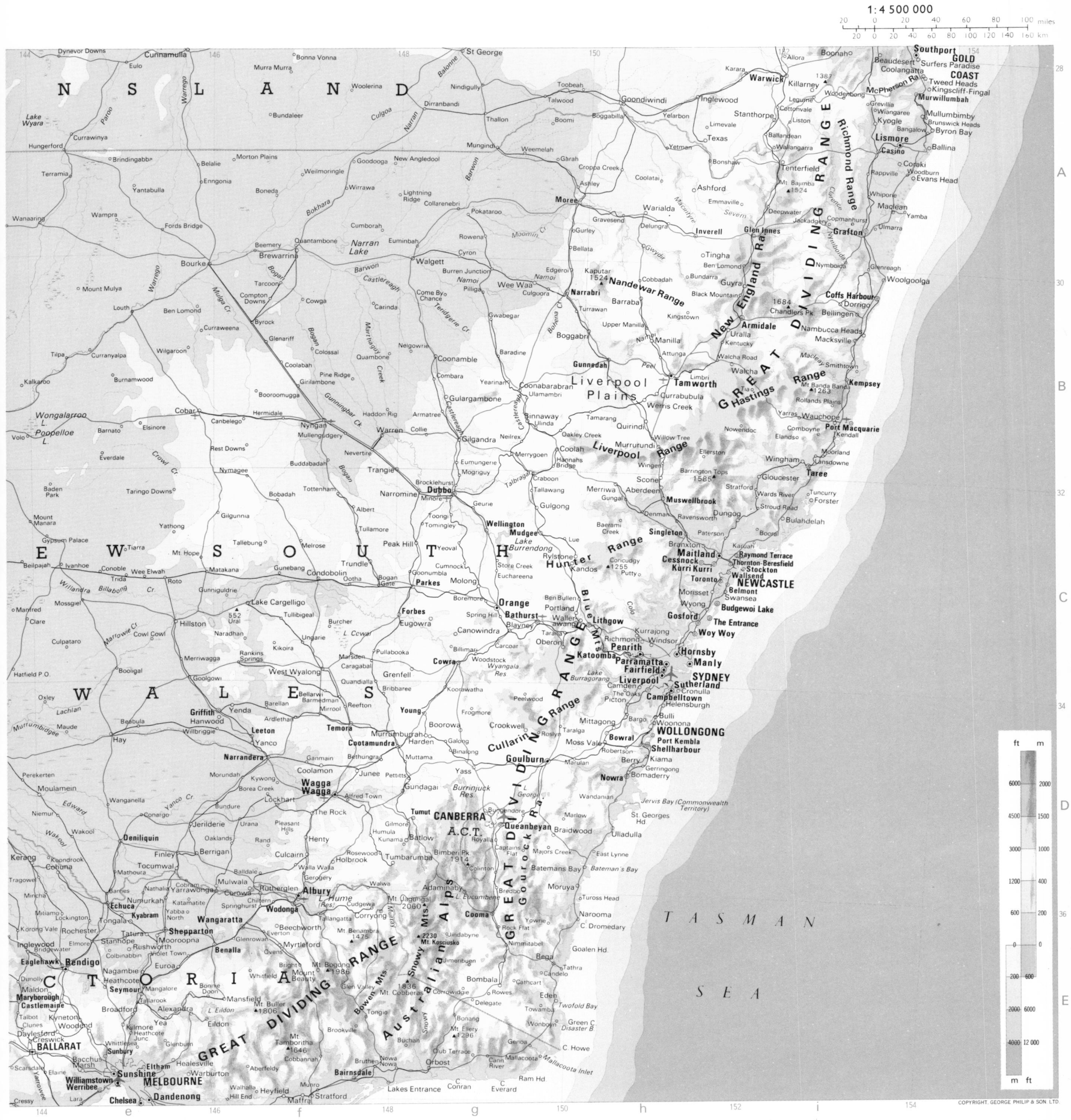

QUEENSLAND

NEW SOUTH WALES

VICTORIA

GREAT DIVIDING RANGE

Richmond Range

New England Range

Nandewar Range

Liverpool Plains

Liverpool Range

Hunter Range

Blue Mts

Cullarin Range

Gourock Ra

Great Dividing Range

Australian Alps

Snowy Mts

Great Dividing Range

T A S M A N   S E A

Cunnamulla   **St George**   **Warwick**   **Southport**   **GOLD COAST**   Surfers Paradise   Coolangatta   Tweed Heads   **Murwillumbah**   Mullumbimby   Brunswick Heads   Byron Bay   **Lismore**   **Casino**   Ballina

Bourke   **Moree**   Inverell   **Grafton**   Coffs Harbour

Narrabri   **Tamworth**   **Armidale**   Nambucca Heads   Macksville   **Kempsey**   Port Macquarie   **Taree**   Gloucester   Forster

Cobar   **Dubbo**   Mudgee   **Muswellbrook**   Singleton   **Maitland**   **NEWCASTLE**   Belmont

Parkes   **Orange**   **Bathurst**   Lithgow   Katoomba   Penrith   **Parramatta**   **SYDNEY**   Manly

Forbes   **Young**   Cowra   Goulburn   Liverpool   **Campbelltown**   **WOLLONGONG**   Port Kembla   Shellharbour   Nowra

Griffith   **Leeton**   **Narrandera**   **Wagga Wagga**   **CANBERRA**   A.C.T.   Queanbeyan   Batemans Bay   Moruya

Deniliquin   **Albury**   **Wodonga**   Cooma

Echuca   **Shepparton**   **Benalla**   **Wangaratta**   Mt Kosciusko

Bendigo   Mansfield   Bairnsdale   Lakes Entrance

BALLARAT   **MELBOURNE**   **Dandenong**   Chelsea

TASMAN SEA

Rainfall is highest in the coastal districts, varying from about 750 mm in the south to around 2000 mm in the north. Rainfall gradually diminishes towards the north-west of the State, where it averages about 200 mm annually. More than one-third of New South Wales receives less than 350 mm annually.

Natural features divide the State into four principal regions extending north-south: the fertile coastal districts, averaging between 30 and 80 km wide; the tablelands forming the Great Dividing Range; the western slopes of the Range; and the western plains which cover almost two-thirds of the State. The tablelands — an almost uninterrupted series of plateaux — form the watershed for short, fast-flowing rivers carrying more than two-thirds of the State's surface water resources. The height of the tablelands averages over 750 m in the north and slightly less in the south, where the Kosciusko Plateau includes Australia's highest peak, Mount Kosciusko (2231 m). Although Australia has no permanent snowfields, snow covers much of the Australian Alps above 1500 m for varying periods between late autumn and early spring. This area is the site of Australia's greatest engineering feat, the Snowy Mountains hydro-electric scheme, completed between 1949-74 at a cost exceeding $800 million. It has a generating capacity of 3 740 000 kilowatts (20 per cent of the State's output) and produces about 2 337 000 megalitres of additional water for irrigation via the Murray and Murrumbidgee Rivers. The Scheme has resulted in access roads being developed, which have allowed winter sports to develop in the Snowy Mountains.

Economy

The State's main primary products are beef cattle, dairy products, wool, wheat, hay, lucerne, oats, rice, maize, fruit and vegetables. The coastal districts are typically used for mixed farming, especially dairying. Sugar and bananas are grown in the warmer northern regions of the coast. The southern Riverina region contains more than 700 000 hectares of irrigated land and is the heart of fruit and vegetable production.

About 8 900 000 cattle produce 442 000 tonnes of beef and veal, 960 million litres of whole milk, and other dairy products. More than 55 million sheep (over one-third of the Australian total) produce around 255 million kg of greasy wool and 162 000 tonnes of mutton and lamb.

Some 4 120 000 hectares of crops are sown

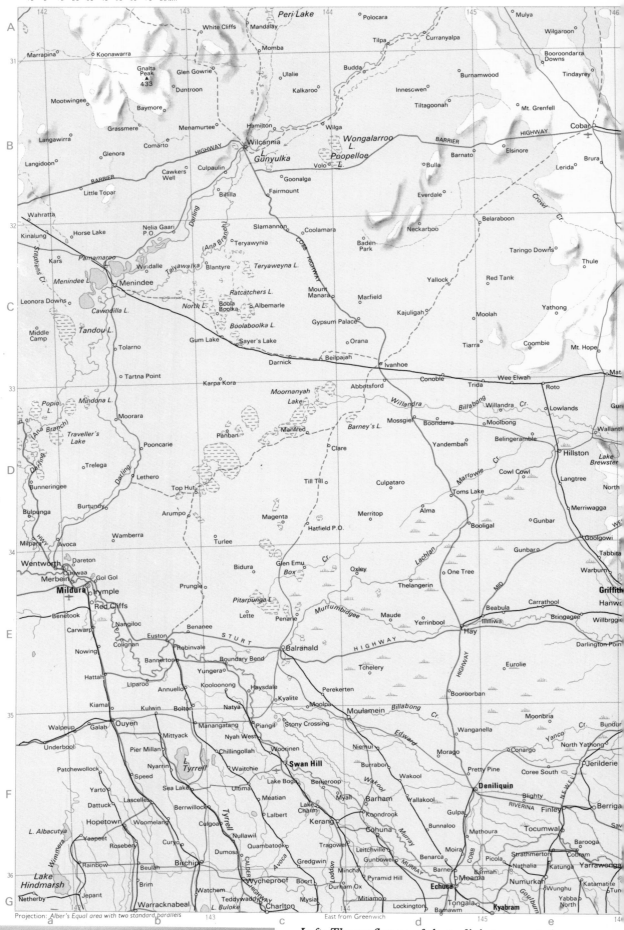

Left: The confluence of Australia's two great river systems, the Murray and the Darling, at Wentworth in the south-west corner of New South Wales.

Right: The Three Sisters, a Triassic sandstone formation rising over 300 metres from the floor of the Jamieson Valley.

Far right: King's Tableland and the Jamieson Valley, part of the Blue Mountains which for years formed an impenetrable barrier to westward exploration.

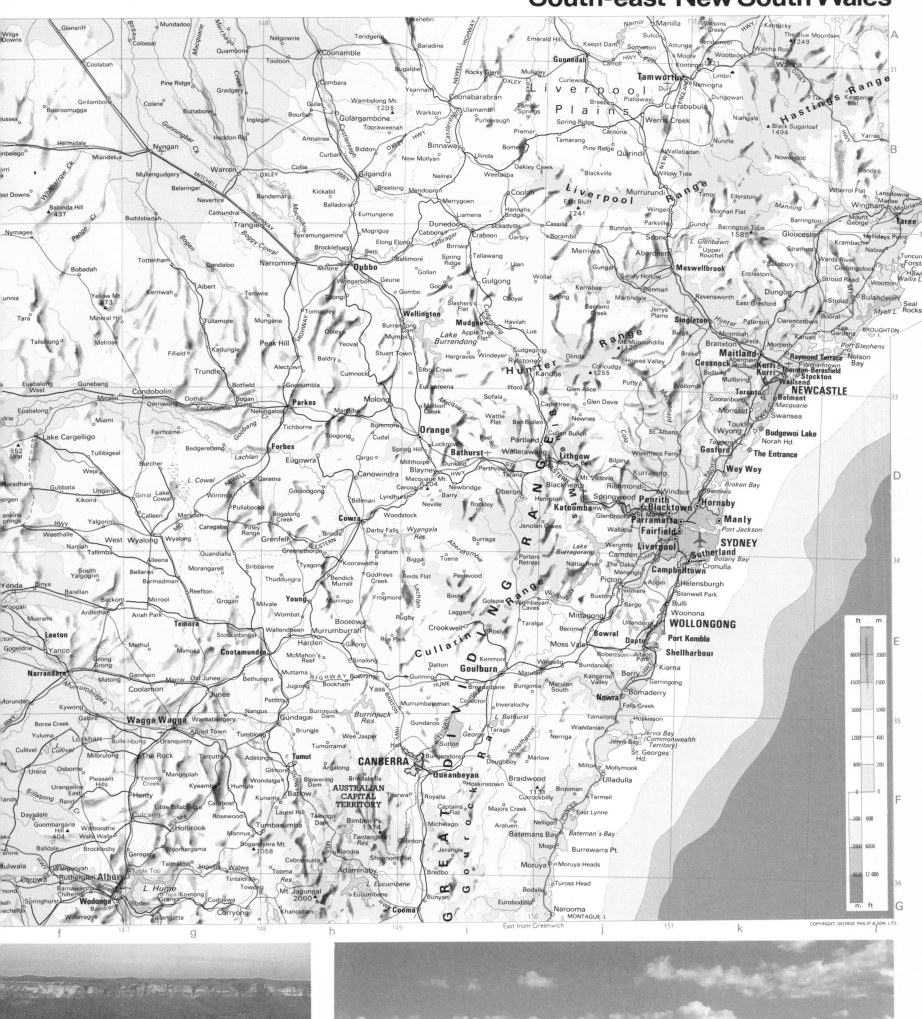

New South Wales: the Leader

annually — about 30 per cent of the national figure. New South Wales is the greatest wheat producer, with annual yields around 3 800 000 tonnes. Forestry contributes about $51 500 000 annually (including woodchipping) and fishing another $17 200 000. Oyster farming is a feature of the State's fisheries, involving 5800 leases covering 3600 hectares. There are about 13 300 hectares under grape vines (2400 hectares not yet bearing) and New South Wales is noted for its wines, especially those of the Hunter Valley region.

Manufacturing involves about 24 000 establishments employing 520 000 people. Chief manufactures include machinery, electrical goods, clothing and textiles, chemicals and fertilisers, processed food-stuffs and bev-

erages. The largest manufacturing industry is the iron and steel basic products industry, which has had a central role in the growth of the State. Steel works at Newcastle and Port Kembla produce about 85 per cent of the national steel output. Annual production is around 5 500 000 tonnes of pig iron and 6 200 000 tonnes of steel ingots.

Mineral statistics are dominated by coal, with annual black coal production exceeding 42 million tonnes, almost two-thirds of the Australian figure and half the value of New South Wales' mineral production. Next in importance is the mining of silver, lead and zinc, worth over 20 per cent of the State's mineral production. These have been mined at Broken Hill since 1883. The mineral sands

industry is important — Australia is the principal world producer of rutile and zircon — and is worth about $36 million annually.

In the half-century after Edward Hargraves discovered gold at Bathurst in 1851, almost $100 million worth of gold was mined in New South Wales: today virtually the only gold produced comes as a by-product of Broken Hill processing, around 11 000 fine oz. worth more than $400 000. Gems of significance are opal, primarily from Lightning Ridge, and sapphire, chiefly from the Glen Innes and Inverell districts. Production estimates are vague at best, given the large numbers of individual miners, but could approach $5 million of opal and $4 million of sapphire a year.

1:2 500 000

Above: Mount Warning on the border of New South Wales and Queensland in the Tweed River district, where some of Australia's best pastoral land is to be found.

Opposite: The Giant Banana at McCauley's, Coffs Harbour. A great tourist attraction, it draws attention to the importance of the banana-growing industry in this area.

Projection: Alber's Equal area with two standard parallels

COPYRIGHT. GEORGE. PHILIP & SON. LTD.

Sydney

In terms of both age and size, Sydney is the first city in Australia. Sydney's population in 1976 was 3 021 299, although its growth rate has been slower in the 1970s than most other Australian cities.

In 1788 Governor Phillip arrived from Britain with convicts and soldiers to establish the first penal colony in Australia. He chose Port Jackson as the site for Sydney in preference to Botany Bay where Captain Cook had landed and been favourably impressed 18 years earlier. Sydney Cove had the advantage of deep, sheltered waters for the fleet and the surrounding land was well-drained with plenty of fresh water.

Port Jackson is a drowned river valley. The Parramatta River became an estuarine river when the coastline sank in relation to the level of the sea. Such coastlines, known as ria coasts, usually provide ideal harbours. The steep slopes adjacent to Sydney Harbour afford excellent views and numerous deep-water inlets that benefit shipping and boating.

Today Sydney, the political and economic capital of New South Wales, contains some 62 per cent of the State's population. The city has expanded around and away from its magnificent harbour, on hilly land to the north, flatter land to the south and undulating land to the west.

The central business district of Sydney is situated on a promontory on the south shore of the harbour between Sydney Cove to the east and Darling Harbour to the west. Retail shops, commercial offices and warehouses have competed for the limited amount of land and numerous high rise buildings have been built. Banking, insurance and other businesses are dominant close to Circular Quay at the north end of the city. Retailing is concentrated in the southern area of the central business district along George, Pitt and Castlereagh Streets, while warehousing predominates to the west of the promontory near Darling Harbour. To the east are situated parklands such as Hyde Park and the Botanical Gardens.

South of the central business district there are major areas of industry. In the flatter land around Botany Bay manufacturing and refining are increasing and there are plans to improve port facilities in the area. Botany Bay must be dredged to take large vessels such as oil tankers. Industry has been established in the outer western suburbs where land is cheaper and more readily available — Liverpool, Bankstown, Parramatta and Blacktown are centres of both industry and population, forming a major area of growth.

The east and north shores of Sydney, with their hillier expensive land, have become mainly residential. Increased land prices have led to the development of high-rise flats in places such as Bondi and Manly. The north shore of the harbour has been subject to very dense flat development and an overflow of business establishments from the congested and expensive south shore. Housing development has expanded some distance from the city centre along the north coast and further inland.

Waterways, whether they be rivers or harbours, cause traffic problems in cities. In

Opposite: Bondi Beach, one of Sydney's many excellent surf beaches. The beach is the focus of high-density housing, including many flats.

1 : 250 000

| Central Business District | Urban areas | Industrial areas | Parks | Bush | Airp |

Sydney, the Harbour and Gladesville Bridges carry both road and rail traffic between the south and north shores of the city, and with increased population it is certain that a new bridge will be required in the future. Ferries are still an important form of transport between the two shores for many commuters.

Sydney — a picturesque city — is the tourist capital of Australia. The beautiful harbour is Sydney's greatest asset, and views of it are gained from many vantage points; lookouts are found in a number of city buildings. The Australia Square building overlooks the port, the central business district, central parks, the harbour and its bridge; there is another lookout from a pylon of the bridge itself. The ferries, which depart regularly from Circular Quay, give a view of the harbour coastline. The best-known of these is the Manly ferry, which passes the Opera House and travels close to the harbour entrance.

Sydney's surf beaches are world-famous and their proximity to the city makes them a popular place throughout the summer. Bondi (south of the harbour) and Manly (to the north) are probably the best-known but there are many others. Swimming in the harbour itself is recommended only where shark nets are installed.

Sydney's Opera House is a building of great interest by day with its unique architectural design and magnificent water-edge location on Benelong Point. At night, high quality performances may be heard in its opera theatre, concert hall and other theatres.

Kings Cross, located a little east of the city centre, has a number of hotels, cafes, restaurants, cinemas and night-clubs and is a popular centre for entertainment.

There are some attractive native bushland parks in Sydney. These include Lane Cove National Park, Davidson Park on the north shore and Royal National Park on the south shore. Near the city itself are the Botanical Gardens and Hyde Park. Taronga Zoological Park on the north shore is beautifully sited and developed.

There are a number of places of interest only a short distance from Sydney. About 90 km to the west are the Blue Mountains with the tourist centre of Katoomba and a deeply dissected plateau providing exciting views. To the north are Pittwater and the Tuggerah Lakes which attract sightseers as well as boating and fishing enthusiasts.

Above: An aerial view of Sydney's harbour and city showing the Bridge and the Opera House. The Opera House, situated at Bennelong Point, is based on a unique concept of interlocking shell vaults which represent the waves and sails of the Harbour.

Opposite: Typical terrace houses in Paddington, an attractive and fashionable inner suburb. Many old terraces have been restored in the past twenty years, and the local residents vigorously oppose redevelopment of the area.

Canberra

Canberra is the Federal capital of Australia and it has enjoyed the most rapid growth rate of any major city in the country. In 1949 Canberra had a population of only 20 000 but by 1976 this had increased to 197 578.

Located towards the north of the Australian Capital Territory, Canberra depends entirely upon its role as national capital for its existence and growth. Its situation between Sydney and Melbourne came about because of traditional rivalry between these two cities. Today, about one-third of the people who work in Canberra are employed directly in administration. Many people associated with the public service moved to Canberra when their departments were relocated there.

Canberra nestles in a wide valley surrounded by mountains and has an elevation of about 600 m. The main feature of the city is an artificial lake, Lake Burley Griffin, named after the man who planned the layout of Canberra. Lake Burley Griffin, completed in 1964, was formed by the damming of the Molonglo River. It is surrounded by parks and is crossed by two bridges on Commonwealth and Kings Avenues. The city today consists of crescents and wide boulevards with tracts of bushland separating the outer suburbs which are linked by modern highways.

The central business district is located on the north shore of the lake. Here, tall office buildings are found on either side of Northbourne Avenue near the City Circuit. The retail area consists of wide pedestrian malls. On the south side of the lake in the suburb of Parkes are the Houses of Parliament, the National Library and government buildings. Yarralumla and Deakin contain most of the foreign embassies as well as the Prime Minister's residence. The planning and development of Canberra is strictly controlled by the National Development Commission (N.C.D.C.).

Canberra is an important education centre, accommodating the Australian National University and Duntroon Military College.

There is very little industry in Canberra and what there is, is of a light nature, concentrated in the suburb of Fyshwick to the southeast of the city.

Canberra is a popular tourist attraction with many hotels lining Northbourne Avenue. A number of visitors also come on government business, many of them from overseas.

Canberra is particularly beautiful in autumn when the large number of deciduous trees are in full colour. There are excellent vantage points from which the city can be viewed. These include Black Mountain (812 m high), Mount Ainslie (842 m) and Red Hill (772 m).

The high altitude of Canberra gives it a much cooler climate than places of a similar latitude at sea-level.

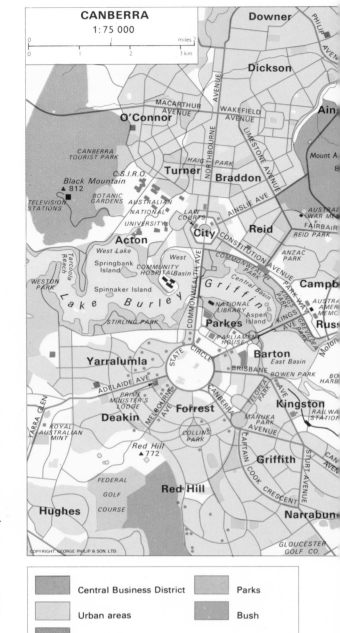

Below: An aerial view of the centre of Canberra as it was planned by Walter Burley Griffin. Griffin, who won an international competition to design the new capital in 1911, visualised a system of dramatic circles and boulevards.

Below right: The Captain Cook memorial water jet and terrestrial globe constructed by the Commonwealth Government to celebrate the bicentenary of Captain Cook's discovery of the east coast of Australia in 1770.

Opposite above: A view of Canberra Civic Centre from Mount Ainslie. The bridge to the right of the Captain Cook memorial water jet links the central business district with Parkes.

Opposite below: The Academy of Science, possibly Canberra's most striking building, is situated close to the campus of the Australian National University.

Victoria: a Fortunate State

Characteristics and Population

In 1836 Sir Thomas Mitchell, the Surveyor-General of New South Wales, an explorer, scientist and artist, journeyed south of the Murray River into good country he named '*Australia Felix*' — the fortunate land. Mitchell's description of the south-eastern corner of Australia, later named Victoria, was full of praise: 'Every variety of feature may be seen in these southern parts, from the lofty alpine region on the east, to the low grassy plains in which it terminates on the west.' . . . 'Hills, of moderate elevation, occupy the central country, between the Murray and the sea, being thinly or partially wooded, and covered with the richest pasture.' . . . 'Towards the sea coast on the south, and adjacent to the open downs . . . there is a low tract consisting of very rich black soil, apparently the best imaginable, for the cultivation of grain, in such a climate.'

Victoria's area of 227 600 km² comprises less than three per cent of Australia's land mass. Yet it produces about 25 per cent of the nation's total rural output and is one of the two major manufacturing States. It is the most densely-settled State, its population of 3 646 900 being second only to that of New South Wales. Its economy is based on the pastoral and agricultural industries, manufacturing, good energy resources and service industries, especially finance.

Most of Victoria's inhabitants live in the capital, Melbourne (population 2 603 578), a major port and the second-largest Australian city after Sydney. The largest urban area beyond Melbourne is Geelong, 70 km to the south-west, another large port within Port Phillip Bay. Geelong's heavy industry includes motor-vehicle plants and an oil refinery. With a population of more than 130 000, Geelong serves the western part of Victoria. Ballarat, 100 km north-west of Melbourne, was one of the great gold-rush centres of the 1850s, at the heart of the turbulent development which opened up so much of Australia. Today it is the State's largest inland city (population 68 450), and is known for its manufactures and nearby woolgrowing regions.

Bendigo (150 km north of Melbourne) was an equally famous gold town. Its population is now over 55 000 and the region is known for grain, sheep and dairying. Another significant urban grouping is in the brown-coal zone of the Latrobe Valley, with its main centres in Moe-Yallourn (18 000), Morwell (16 000) and Traralgon (15 000). Other cities include irrigation-oriented Mildura on the Murray River in the far north-west; Shepparton, the fruit-canning centre north of Melbourne; Warrnambool on the south-west coast, and Wodonga, sister border-city to Albury in the north-east.

Although very compact by Australian standards, Victoria offers an excellent range of recreational activities — from skiing to all forms of water sports, from bushwalking in mountains and near-desert, to hang-gliding from ocean cliffs.

Education is free and compulsory for all children between 6 and 15. Seventy-five per cent of the 820 000 children attending preschool, primary and secondary schools are at 2200 government schools. The balance attend 578 private schools, 467 of which are

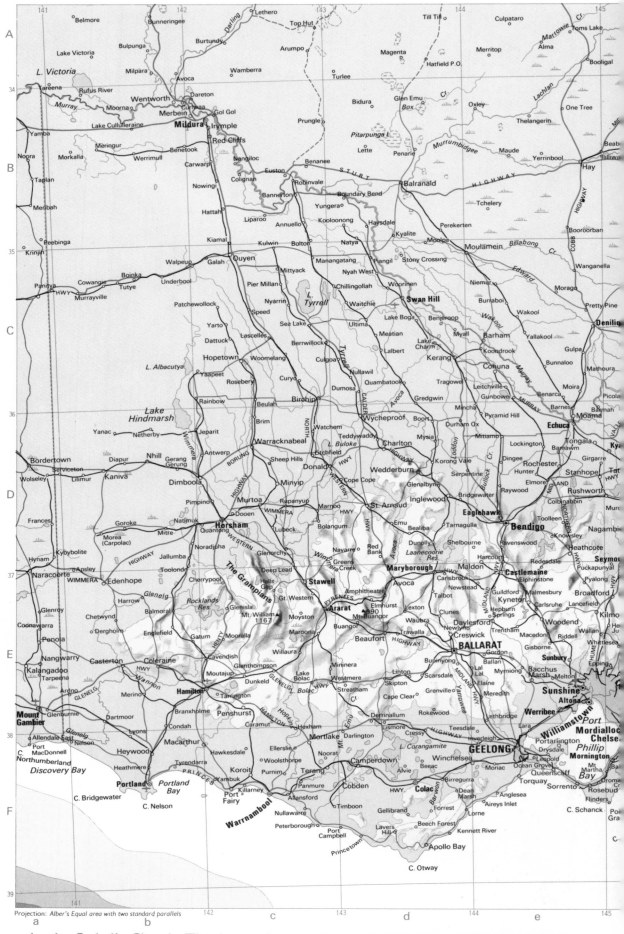

Projection: *Alber's Equal area with two standard parallels*

run by the Catholic Church. The three universities (Melbourne, Monash and La Trobe) are situated in Melbourne and have enrolments of 36 000 students. Another university, Deakin, is being established in Geelong. Another 47 000 tertiary students attend 31 colleges of advanced education throughout the State.

History and Government

After several early coastal settlements failed, it was not until 1834 — almost half a century after the First Fleet arrived — that the Henty family farm near Portland became the first permanent settlement in the Port Phillip District. Melbourne was established a year later

by Tasmanian adventurers who 'bought' vast lands from the local Aboriginal tribes with an exchange of trade goods. The colony of Victoria was created in 1851. The immense riches of the gold rushes in the 1850s gave the colony great impetus, and eventually led to the opening up of the land to small farmers. During this period the Cobb & Co. coaching system and railways were established. Many of Melbourne's grandest buildings were built at this time, including law courts, cathedrals and museums.

In 1856 responsible government was established through elections for the first Parliament comprising the upper house (Legislative Council) and the lower house (Legislative Assembly). In that year Victoria pioneered the

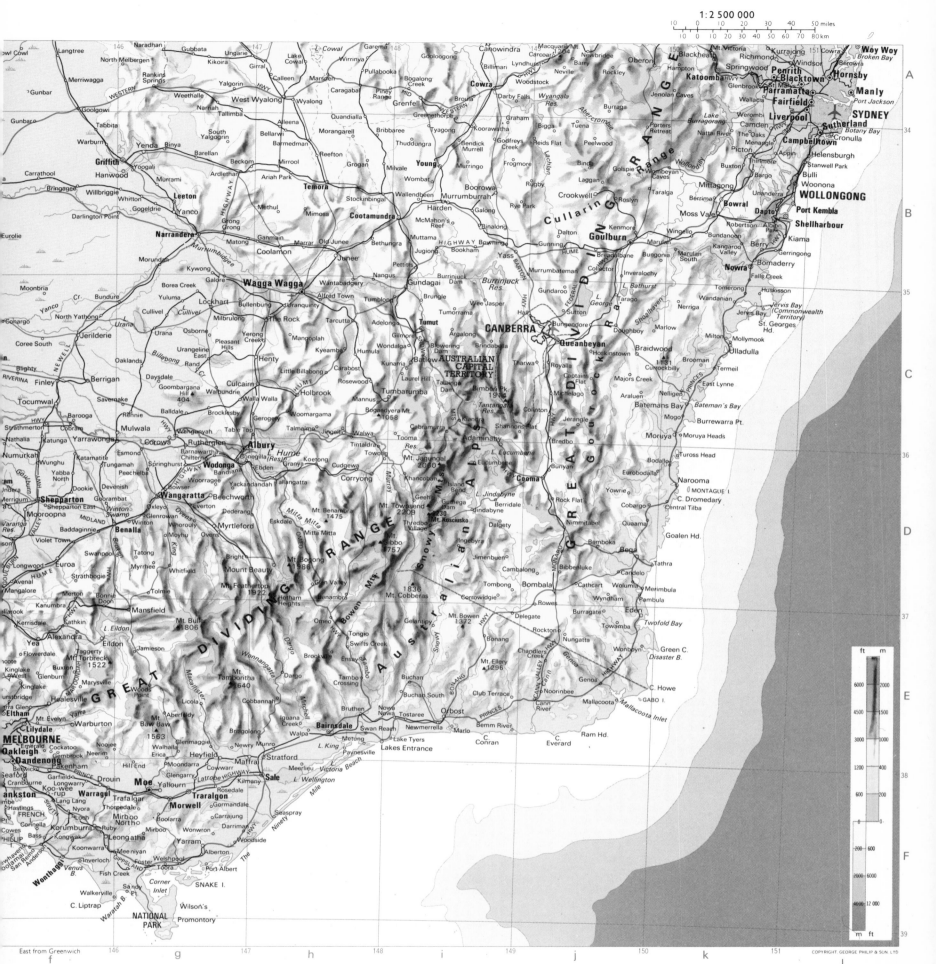

use of the secret ballot — now a system widely known overseas as the 'Australian ballot'.

Climate and Geography

The second-smallest of the six States, Victoria lies between latitudes 34° and 39° South and longitudes 141° and 150° East (an area similar to that of England, Wales and Scotland). Its coastline measures 1577 km. Most of Victoria lies in a warm temperate belt characterised by hot summers and cool to mild, wet winters. The highest north-eastern mountains are usually snow-covered between June and September. Mildura in the north-west is the warmest town, with an annual average temperature range between 23.4°C

maximum and 10.3°C minimum. The coldest place is Mount Buffalo in the north-east where the annual average temperature ranges between 11.6°C maximum and 5.0°C minimum. Rainfall is heaviest in the east and north-east (about 860 mm annual average) and lowest in the Mallee in the north-west (327 mm annual average).

Most of Victoria is open rolling country. The Great Dividing Range reaches its southernmost extension in the mountains of the north-east and east and in the isolated ranges in central-west Victoria. The highest peak is Mount Bogong, 1986 m. The longest rivers are the Murray (forming most of the northern border), the Goulburn and the Glenelg. Dry eucalypt forests are typical of

the east, centre and south-west. A zone of grassland and savannah woodland lies between these forests and the scrub and heath in the north-west corner. There are wet eucalypt forests in the north-east and on the ranges east of Melbourne, while alpine vegetation is found on the high plains country.

Economy

Victoria produces about 60 per cent of the nation's whole milk, 35 per cent of its mutton and lamb, 30 per cent of its beef and veal and over 20 per cent of its wool. It also provides 75 per cent of Australia's dried vine fruits and 40 per cent of its potatoes. More than 90 per

Victoria: a Fortunate State

cent of the rural output comes from the pastoral industry (wool, mutton and beef), agriculture (wheat, other grains, fruit and vegetables) and dairying.

Victoria's 12 000 factories employ over 450 000 people — a third of Australia's industrial workforce — and their production 'value' is about 35 per cent of the national total. The major vehicle and aircraft industries are here, along with large investments in engineering, the manufacture of chemicals, textiles, foodstuffs, paper and rubber products. The State has profited by the exploitation of the Bass Strait oil and gas fields since the mid-1960s. Currently these cater for about 60 per cent of the nation's crude-oil requirements. Immense brown coal deposits in the Latrobe Valley (140 km east of Melbourne) have long provided electricity generation and solid fuel.

Opposite: The Western Grampians Range, in western Victoria, named by the explorer Thomas Mitchell, after mountains of the same name in Scotland.

Below: Some of the Twelve Apostles along the cliffs of western Victoria near Port Campbell, some of Australia's most spectacular area of coastline.

Victoria: a Fortunate State

Above: The Murray River at Mildura in the north-west of Victoria.

Opposite right: Winter at Falls Creek alpine village in the Bogong High Country, north-eastern Victoria.

Below: The Ovens Valley at Harrietville, near Mt Feathertop in the Bogong High Country.

Melbourne

Melbourne, the capital of Victoria, is Australia's second largest city, with a population of 2 604 232 in 1976. Since World War 2 Melbourne has admitted more immigrants than any other Australian city and is reputed to have the largest Greek population of any city in the world outside Greece. However, with a reduction in both immigration and the natural rate of population increase, Melbourne's growth has slowed during the 1970s.

The settlement of Melbourne dates back to 1835 when John Batman arrived from Launceston in Tasmania and made a purchase of land from the local Aborigines — he paid with gifts such as blankets, flour, tomahawks, knives and mirrors. This land, south of the Yarra River, was chosen for its flatness. Later in that year John Pascoe Fawkner also arrived from Launceston and chose a site on the north bank of the Yarra, which he preferred because it was gently undulating and provided better drainage. It also had the advantage of clear and permanent water from the Yarra, a large, protected bay and river port, and a surrounding area of good soils. Fawkner's settlement is the site of Melbourne's present central business district.

Today about 70 per cent of Victoria's population lives in Melbourne, and the city covers some 3000 km² — a large area for such a population. The land surrounding Melbourne undulates in the east and is relatively flat to the north and west. The most rapid growth, particularly in housing, has been to the east and south-east along the shore of Port Phillip Bay, and the Government is attempting to encourage expansion to the north and west in order to reduce this sprawl.

Industry is concentrated in an inner ring of suburbs — Port Melbourne, South Melbourne, Prahran, Richmond, Collingwood, Fitzroy, Brunswick, Footscray and Spotswood — and in the outer suburbs of Altona, Sunshine, Broadmeadows, Nunawading, Scoresby and Dandenong. It is also found along the main arterial roads and rail lines.

The central business district is located close to the port of Melbourne and its streets, planned by Hoddle, surveyor to Governor La Trobe, form a regular grid pattern. This regular and parallel road pattern characterises Melbourne generally. The city centre has seen the growth of many high-rise office buildings where a number of Australia's largest companies have their headquarters. For example, companies such as BHP and Conzinc Riotinto are based in Melbourne even though their mining and manufacturing interests are elsewhere. The central business district has retained much of its retailing importance, with some excellent emporiums and many smaller shops. Large department stores such as Myer's and Buckley's are located along Bourke Street while boutiques are found in the attractive tree-lined east end of Collins Street. Numerous covered arcades provide additional shops and afford protection from Melbourne's cool, wet winter and hot summer weather.

The port of Melbourne is the busiest in Australia, handling approximately 50 per cent of the nation's imports and exports. The port facilities have been upgraded to handle

Opposite: Trams in Swanston Street, the hub of Melbourne, with Flinders Street Station on the left and St Paul's Cathedral on the right.

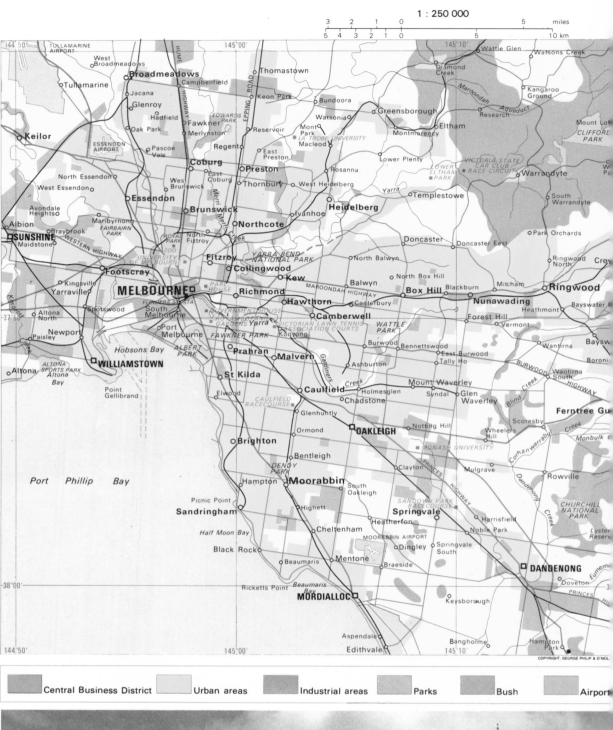

1 : 250 000

Central Business District   Urban areas   Industrial areas   Parks   Bush   Airport

COPYRIGHT. GEORGE PHILIP & O'NEIL

modern methods of loading and unloading — containerisation, roll-on-roll-off and bulk movement systems. There are a number of specialised docks along the Yarra River and in Hobson's Bay at the head of Port Phillip Bay.

Melbourne has many features which distinguish it from other cities in Australia. The magnificent parks and gardens close to the city centre have contributed to the image of a 'Garden State' which the State Government wishes to project. The Botanic Gardens south of the Yarra are of classic design, with lawns sloping to a central lake and paths lined with numerous species of trees and shrubs from various parts of Australia as well as overseas.

The city has a reputation for its love of sport and there are many fine sporting venues which reflect this enthusiasm. The Melbourne Cricket Ground, which accommodates 120 000 spectators, is used for cricket and Australian Rules football; Waverley Park is also used for football; Albert Park caters for indoor sports such as basketball as well as many outdoor sports; Kooyong is the main centre for tennis and Flemington, Moonee Valley, Caulfield and Sandown are all large horse-racing tracks. In addition, there are a number of golf courses in the sandy belt near the east shore of Port Phillip Bay.

Melbourne is also renowned for its restaurants, which are found in the central city area and in inner suburbs such as Toorak, South Yarra, Carlton and St Kilda. The cus-

tom of bringing one's own wine to restaurants is popular, although many establishments are fully licensed.

The Arts Centre in St Kilda Road houses the finest collection of European Masters in Australia, together with many Australian paintings and other works of art. Concerts, operas and plays are presented at a number of theatres and halls in the city and in the open-air Myer Music Bowl in the Alexandra Gardens. Every March the city holds a festival called Moomba, during which processions, concerts and sideshows are staged, as well as aquatic events on the Yarra River.

Melbourne has a number of historic homes which have been restored and are maintained by the National Trust. Como and Ripponlea are perhaps the best-known.

Along the eastern coast of Port Phillip Bay are sandy beaches, with calm waters ideal for swimming and boating. Only a short drive from the city are the attractive Dandenong Ranges, the Yarra Valley and the Mornington and Bellarine Peninsulas.

Above: Melbourne's ever-changing sky-line with the River Yarra winding through, and Government House, surrounded by parks.

Opposite: The dome of the Exhibition Building, erected for the Great Exhibition of 1880.

Tasmania: the Island State

Characteristics and Population

Tasmania is separated from mainland Australia by more than the shallow, stormy waters of Bass Strait. The smallest State enjoys one great advantage over the rest of the nation: reliable and abundant rainfall. Tasmania has a different environment from that of the mainland, and its intensive mixed farming results in landscapes resembling Britain rather than Australia. This difference, together with a history dating back to 1803, contributes much to its distinct character and the tourism so important to its economy. Tasmania's rainfall and predominantly mountainous terrain allow the State to produce 10 per cent of Australia's electricity through cheap hydro-electric generation which supplies some of Australia's biggest industries.

Although Tasmania has an area of only 68 331 km^2 (smaller than Scotland), the population of 402 900 rates it the second most densely settled State, behind Victoria. The inhabitants are more evenly dispersed than those in mainland States. Although 131 524 (one in three) Tasmanians live in the south-eastern capital of Hobart, the next three largest centres are on the north coast: Launceston (63 386), Burnie (19 500) and Devonport (21 000). The State includes some smaller islands (notably King, Flinders and Bruny) as well as the sub-Antarctic Macquarie Island, 1550 km south-east of Hobart and the site of a permanent scientific station.

More than 94 000 pupils attend Tasmanian preschools, primary and secondary schools. Tertiary education is provided by the University of Tasmania at Hobart (3400 students), the Tasmania College of Advanced Education (2435) and technical colleges.

History and Government

The first European to discover Tasmania, the Dutchman Abel Tasman, named it Van Diemen's Land, a name not officially changed until the colony (created 1825) was granted responsible government in 1855. First settled when Hobart was founded in 1803, Tasmania's early history was dominated by the convict system: more than 67 000 men and women were transported to Van Diemen's Land between 1803 and 1853. The Tasmanian State Parliament comprises an upper house (Legislative Council) and lower house (House of Assembly).

Climate and Geography

Tasmania's position between latitudes 40° and 43.5° South, with no point lying more than 115 km from the sea, gives it a temperate maritime climate. Its average rainfall is the highest of any Australian State, reaching as high as 3600 mm in the west down to 500 mm

Above: Bushy Park Oast House in the Derwent Valley north of Hobart, where most of the hops used in Australia's brewing industry are grown. Hops are cured in the conical-roofed oast houses which are an attractive feature amidst the fields of the tall hop vines.

Opposite: Dove Lake with the twin peaks of Cradle Mountain and Little Horn. The two peaks, situated in the Lake St Clair National Park, are the legacy of the Ice Age in Tasmania, when glaciers scoured out several lakes but left the serrated columns of the dolerite heights looking like great coxcombs.

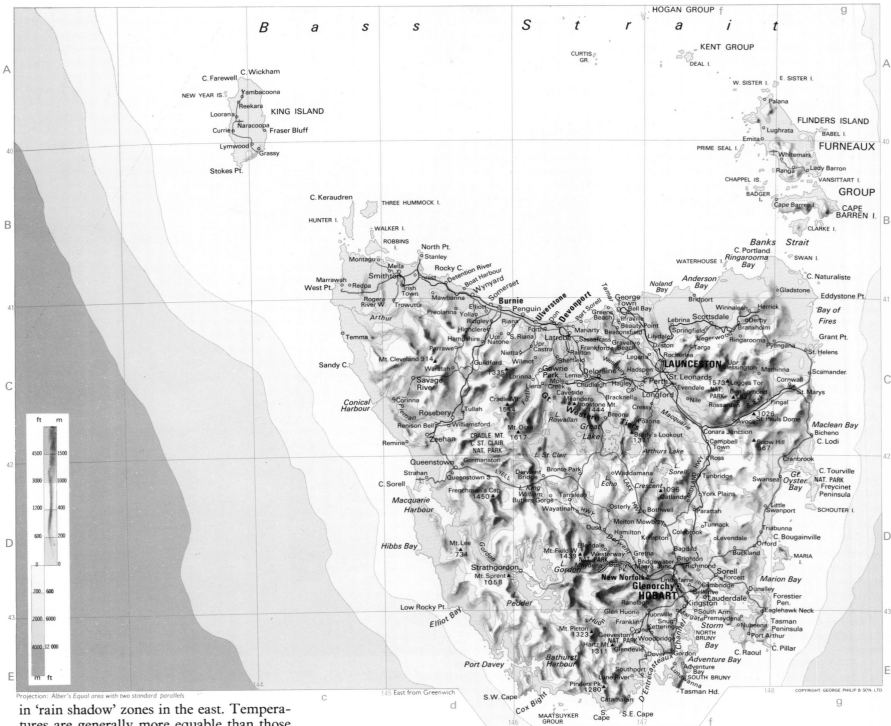

Projection: Alber's Equal area with two standard parallels

in 'rain shadow' zones in the east. Temperatures are generally more equable than those on the mainland. Summers are comparatively cool, winters mild, and seasonal temperature changes are relatively small. There is no permanent snow, but falls may occur on the highlands at any time, the heaviest being in late winter and early spring. Hobart has a midsummer average maximum temperature of 21.6°C and midwinter average maximum temperature of 11.3°C.

Tasmania, basically an extension of the mainland's Eastern Highlands, is the most mountainous State. Much of its area takes the form of rugged uplands exceeding 1000 m in height, although the highest peak, Mount Ossa, is only 1617 m. The chief geographical feature is a central plateau falling south-east from an average height of 1065 m in the north to 610 m in the south. Between this plateau and the mountains of the north-east is the rich agricultural corridor of the Midlands. Glaciation has left steep-sided flat-floored valleys in the west of the central plateau, and has gouged out the beds of over 4000 lakes in the north-west. Most of the State's mining — including the Savage River project where pulverised iron ore is mixed with water and pipelined 90 km over rough country to Port Latta on the north coast — takes place in the thinly-populated western region, parts of which are still unexplored.

Economy

Although the gross value of primary production (excluding mining) exceeds $220 million annually, Tasmania's best-known product — the apple — is experiencing troubled times. More than 1 500 000 apple trees have been bulldozed as orchard area has been more than halved (to 3200 hectares) in the face of both shrinking overseas markets and trebled sea-freight costs in the 1970s. Tasmania remains Australia's largest apple exporter however, and the annual production of apples (almost 80 000 tonnes) and pears (2000 tonnes) is worth $15 million gross. Production of berries and small fruits is also declining, but still contributes $1 500 000 annually to primary production. A further $1 230 000 came in 1974-75 from hops grown in the Derwent Valley near New Norfolk. Although this represented almost 70 per cent of national production, it was a significant decline on the previous year's figure of $3 213 000.

Agricultural holdings represent 37 per cent of the State's area. Tasmania's 4 100 000 sheep annually produce 19 million kg of wool and 17 000 tonnes of meat, while its 900 000

cattle yield 48 000 tonnes of meat and dairy products (including 10 per cent of Australia's butter). More than 47 per cent of the beef and veal, and 40 per cent of the mutton, is exported.

More than 40 per cent of Tasmania is forested and the forestry industry has a gross annual production of about $50 million. In addition to timber for construction, there is paper production (newsprint and fine papers), woodpulp, hardboard, particle board, plywood and a growing woodchip export.

Tasmania's mining industry is valued at around $73 000 000 annually, producing 50 per cent of Australia's tin and 10-15 per cent of its copper, zinc, silver and gold. The Savage River mine yields more than 2 million tonnes of iron ore annually. King Island in Bass Strait is the nation's main tungsten producer.

Hydro-electric power is plentiful and cheap (under half the average mainland cost), coming from 22 stations with a generating capacity of 1 462 400 kilowatts. The Gordon River power scheme, now under construction, will create Australia's largest reservoir, with a capacity of 14.5 cubic kilometres — three times the size of Lake Eucumbene in

Tasmania: the Island State

the Snowy Mountains. Stage 1 has a generator capacity of 288 000 kilowatts.

Manufacturing involves more than 900 establishments employing 31 000 people.

Cheap electricity has attracted some large industries with high power demands: the world's largest zinc refinery (Electrolytic Zinc, near Hobart), the Bell Bay aluminium refinery (producing 90 000 tonnes annually, each tonne requiring 16 000 kilowatt hours of electricity), three paper mills and other mining companies. Secondary industry's chief products are foodstuffs, textiles, forest products, metals, chemicals, clothing, footwear, transport equipment and industrial machinery, for an annual figure of $283 million (value added).

Tourism, always important and heavily promoted, has been a major growth industry since 1973, the year Australia's first casino opened at Wrest Point in Hobart. Each year an estimated 360 000 tourists spend about $36 million directly (travel, accommodation, etc.), with associated indirect expenditure probably doubling that figure.

Opposite: The asylum at Port Arthur, taken from the parapets of the powder magazine. Between 1830 and 1853 thirty thousand prisoners were transported to the penal settlement at Port Arthur. The picturesque ruins of this infamous settlement are one of Tasmania's major tourist attractions.

Below: Lake Pedder, which was flooded in 1973 to form a new lake behind the massive hydro-electric power generating dam on the Gordon. The flooding of Lake Pedder was the subject of bitter controversy between conservationists and the Tasmanian Government.

Hobart

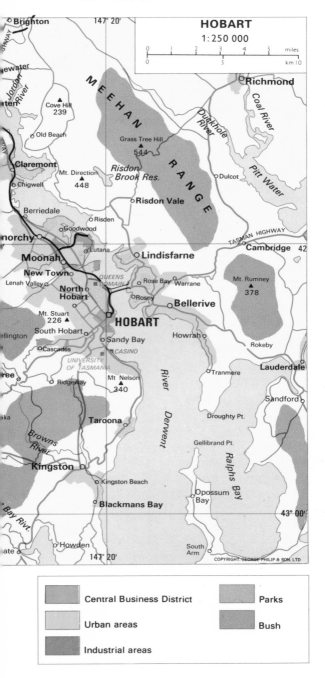

HOBART

1:250 000

COPYRIGHT GEORGE PHILIP & SON. LTD.

Central Business District	Parks
Urban areas	Bush
Industrial areas	

Hobart, with a population of 131 524 in 1976, is the smallest of Australia's State capitals. In fact it is smaller than Newcastle and Wollongong, industrial cities in New South Wales.

Hobart was founded in 1802 when Lieutenant John Bowen established a penal colony on the banks of the Derwent River at Risdon, upstream from the present city. In 1804 Lieutenant John Collins landed and chose the present site for the city of Hobart which is the second oldest of Australia's major cities. Many of its old buildings date back to the nineteenth century and have been preserved. The city was named after the Secretary of State for the Colonies, Robert Hobart.

Hobart is situated at the mouth of the Derwent River, a relatively short stream but wide and deep in its estuary. The city has developed around this picturesque valley on land which rises steeply to Mount Wellington (1300 m high) to the south-west. The east shore is also hilly, although less rugged, and it has been rapidly developed since the construction of the Tasman Bridge. The effects of the bridge's collapse in 1975 emphasised its importance to the city. The city is small, serving an island with a small population, a large proportion of which lives along the north coast and is better served by a number of smaller cities and towns such as Launceston, Devonport, Ulverstone and Burnie.

There is only a small amount of industry in Hobart, mainly along the Derwent River. The major industries are the Electrolytic Zinc Company at Risdon, the Cadbury Fry Pascall chocolate and confectionery factory at Claremont and the Australian Newsprint Mill at Boyer, some 6 km upstream. Apart from the Huon Valley — famous for its apple orchards — and the upper Derwent, little agriculture is practised because the land around the city is too rugged and the local market is too small. Tasmania's greatest attraction for industry is the availability of cheaper hydro-electric power.

Because Tasmania is an island with only a few large industries, sea transport is a vital link with the mainland. Hobart's excellent natural harbour makes it an ideal port, situated near the central business district in the heart of the city. About two-thirds of Tasmania's sea trade utilises the northern ports, however, because of their proximity to the mainland and the greater population density along the north coast.

Two of Hobart's major functions are its administrative role as State capital and its role as a centre for tourism, particularly during the summer months when temperatures are mild. Although summer temperatures are usually cooler than on the mainland, the summer of 1966-67 was exceptionally hot and resulted in several small bushfires joining to race through the Derwent Valley and the slopes of Mount Wellington, killing 62 people.

The small retail and commercial centre of the city is located on the west bank of the Derwent River and is rectangular in design.

Opposite: Hobart and the Wrest Point Casino, located at Sandy Bay, south of the city centre. The casino is a great attraction to tourists from the mainland. It is built on a small promontory in the Derwent River and has become one of Hobart's landmarks.

Housing is located around the central business district but development is concentrated in the north towards Glenorchy where the land is less rugged. On the east shore of the Derwent estuary are the suburbs of older established Bellerive and Lindisfarne and the extensive modern suburb of Howrath.

Hobart is a city with great geographical and historical appeal, to which has been added a number of more modern tourist attractions. The nineteenth century warehouses which line Salamanca Place near the city centre are of considerable interest. Their use today extends beyond that of simply warehousing, and the atmosphere of these buildings provides an ideal location for a restaurant. Behind Salamanca Place are streets such as Arthur's Circuit, lined with houses of great historic interest. Queens Domain is a pleasant park to the north of the city centre by the Derwent and there are smaller open spaces for relaxation, such as Franklin Square. The semi-covered Cat-and-Fiddle Arcade is the focal point of the retail district and a place of amusement for children as the cat plays the fiddle on the hour.

Undoubtedly, the feature which has attracted the greatest number of tourists to Hobart in recent years is the casino located at Sandy Bay, south of the city centre. The casino offers gambling, night-club entertainment, restaurants and accommodation, attracting visitors from the mainland as well as from overseas. The casino — a circular building on a small promontory in the Derwent River — has become one of Hobart's landmarks.

Only a short distance from Hobart there are many places of interest, such as Mount Wellington, approached by a steep and tortuously winding road. Along this route there are many points permitting outstanding views of Hobart and the Derwent valley. From the top of Mount Wellington one of the most magnificent views in Australia is afforded. The city of Hobart stretches from the foot of the mountain to the Derwent River and beyond, with the Meehan Range forming the horizon to the north-east.

Another famous landmark is Port Arthur, where the ruins of a penal colony provide a fascinating insight into early Australian history. It was the need for another penal colony in Australia which led to the early settlement of Tasmania. The ruins are set amidst rolling lawns and large trees just past the ill-famed Eaglehawk Neck, once guarded by dogs. Nearby there are some magnificent coastal landforms — the Blowhole, the Devil's Kitchen and many examples of cliffs, wave-cut benches and pavements. There are also a number of historic ruins on the way to Port Arthur, of which perhaps Richmond is the best.

South of Hobart is the beautiful Huon Valley. Near its centre is Huonville, a small town in an attractive setting by the Huon River. The valley is particularly appealing in spring when the apple orchards are in bloom.

To the north-west of Hobart are the upper reaches of the Derwent River, where dairying, market gardens and orchards create a pleasant landscape in the valley. Other features include the historic town of New Norfolk, which has a number of interesting buildings, and Boyer, with its paper mill and extensive pine plantations.

South Australia: Changing State

Characteristics and Population

The old tourist images of South Australia — conservative, tidy, its capital Adelaide characterised as the 'City of Churches', its economy heavily subsidised by the wine-drinkers of the nation supporting the Barossa Valley — are being swept away. Adelaide, that model of town planning, has emerged on the international cultural calendar through its highly regarded (and superbly housed) biennial arts festival. South Australia has become a pacesetter in innovative legislation. And although 'the Barossa' still thrives on its continuing role of producing almost half Australia's wine, the State's prosperity now lies more with the people who build the cars, home appliances and other factory goods than the traditional primary producer. The driest State of the driest continent is in transition.

More than 90 per cent of South Australia's 1 261 600 people (10 per cent of the national total) live in the southern coastal regions. Four-fifths of the State is virtually desert, receiving less than 250 mm of rain annually. This arid zone has appeal for tourists, the scientists of the northern Woomera rocket range, the hardy burrowers of the Coober Pedy and Andamooka opalfields, and the technicians of the north-eastern Cooper Basin natural gas fields that now supply Adelaide and Sydney by pipeline. It is also an area where large sheep stations providing high quality merino wool are found, as well as a significant beef cattle breeding area.

Adelaide, population 900 000, was established in 1836 as the first permanent European settlement in the British Crown colony created two years before. It is halfway up the eastern side of St Vincent's Gulf. Other main towns are Whyalla (population 33 800: steel works, shipbuilding), Port Pirie (15 000: smelting) and Port Augusta (14 000: pastoral, electric power), all on Spencer Gulf, and Mount Gambier (19 000) in the far south-east agricultural region.

More than 275 000 pupils receive primary and secondary education (85 per cent of whom attend government schools), and the two universities (Adelaide and Flinders) have enrolments totalling 12 300. There are seven colleges of advanced education with a student population of 14 500.

History and Government

The first European sighting of South Australia was made in 1627 when a Dutchman, Franz Thyssen, mapped much of the Great Australian Bight. Adelaide was founded by free settlers in 1836 and the colony received responsible government in 1856. Between 1863 and 1911 it also had jurisdiction over the Northern Territory.

Today's State Parliament comprises a lower house (House of Assembly) and an upper house (Legislative Council). Voting for the House of Assembly is compulsory from the age of 18, and voting for the Legislative Council is voluntary.

Climate and Geography

South Australia occupies the central area of southern Australia, an area of 984 000 km² (almost 13 per cent of the continent). It is bounded by longitudes 129° and 141° East and lies south of latitude 26° South. Almost 83 per cent of the State receives under 250 mm of rain.

The gulf lands of southern South Australia, along with the south-western corner of Western Australia, have Australia's only Mediterranean environments. Adelaide, although one of the State's higher rainfall areas, averages only 544 mm annually. It has a midsummer average maximum temperature of 29.6°C (average minimum 16.4°C), and a midwinter average maximum of 15°C (average minimum 7.3°C).

Principal topographical features include Spencer and St Vincent's Gulfs, the Flinders and Mount Lofty Ranges running north-south down much of the east of the State, and the series of saltpan 'lakes' (Eyre, Torrens, Gardiner, etc.) in the north-east which on rare occasions fill after exceptional drainage from rainfall west of the Great Dividing Range in New South Wales and Queensland. South Australia's highest point, Mount Lofty near Adelaide, is only 712m.

The Murray River's final 700 km pass through South Australia to an outlet at the sea via Lake Alexandrina. The waters of the Murray provide almost one-third of the requirements for the State's 80 000 hectares of irrigated land.

An aerial view of the Quelltaler Vineyards at Watervale, in the rich agricultural district south of Clare.

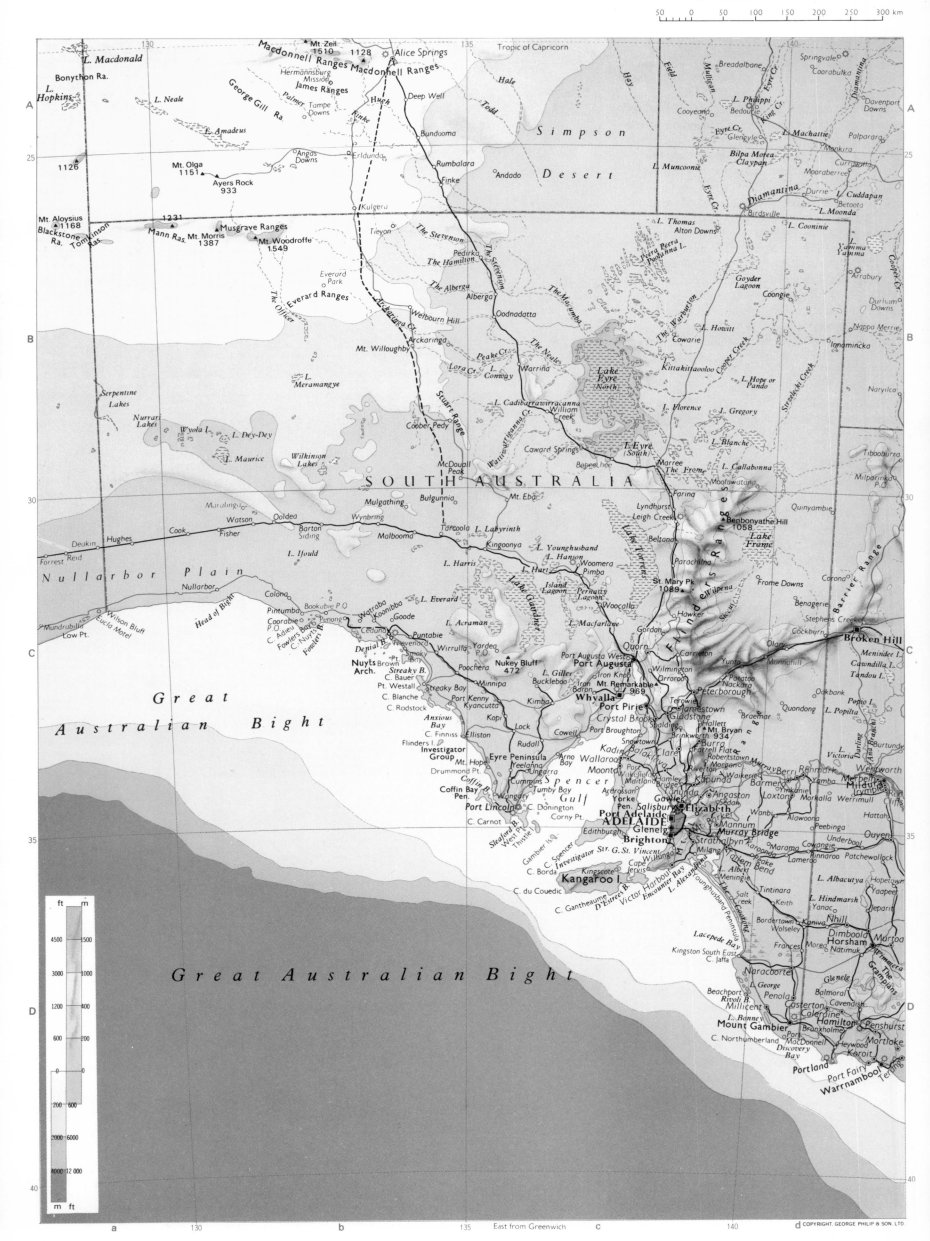

1 : 7 000 000

50 0 50 100 150 200 250 300 km

L. Macdonald

Bonython Ra.

L. Hopkins

Mt. Zeil 1510   1128   Alice Springs
Macdonnell Ranges   Macdonnell Ranges
Hermannsburg Mission
James Ranges
George Gill Ra.
Palmer   Tempe Downs
L. Neale   Hugh
Finke
Deep Well
Bundooma

Tropic of Capricorn

Springvale
Breadalbane   Coorabulka
Mulligan
L. Philippi
Cooyeana   Glengyle
Bedourie   L. Machattie
Davenport Downs
Bilpa Morea Claypan   Monkira
Moorabberee

1126

Mt. Olga 1151
Ayers Rock 933

Angas Downs   Erldunda
Rumbalara
Finke
Andado
L. Muncoonie

Durrie   Cuddapan
L. Coonie
Birdsville   L. Coonie
L. Moonda
Yerrma Yamma
Arrabury

Mt. Aloysius 1168
Blackstone Ra.   Tomkinson Ras.
Mann Ras. Mt. Morris 1387
1231   Musgrave Ranges
Mt. Woodroffe 1549

Everard Park
Everard Ranges

The Officer

Tieyon
The Stevenson
Pedirka   The Stevenson
The Hamilton
The Alberga   Alberga
Oodnadatta
The Macumba
The Neales

S i m p s o n   D e s e r t

L. Thomas
Alton Downs

Petra Peera Poolowna I.
Goyder Lagoon
Coongie

L. Howitt
Kittakittaooloo   Cooper Creek
Eowarie
L. Hope or Pando   Innamincka
Coongie   Nappa Merrie

Durham Downs

Nappa Merrie
Naryilco

Serpentine Lakes

Nurrari Lakes

L. Meramangye

Wyola I.   L. Dey-Dey
L. Maurice
Wilkinson Lakes

Mt. Willoughby   Arckaringa
Peake Cr.
Lora Cr.   L. Conway
Warrina
L. Cadibarrawirracanna
Coober Pedy   William Cr.
Stuart Range
Coward Springs
McDouall Peak
Bopeechee

L a k e   E y r e   (North)

L. Howitt

L. Hope or Pando
Strzelecki Creek

Tibooburra
Milparinka
Milparinka P.O.

S O U T H   A U S T R A L I A

L. Eyre (South)
Marree   The Frome
L. Blanche
Farina   Moolawatana
L. Callabonna

Quinyambie

Muralinguia
Watson   Ooldea   Wynbring
Barton Siding
Cook   Fisher
Deakin   Hughes
Forrest   Reid

Bulgunnia
Mulgathing   Mt. Eba
L. Labyrinth
Malbooma
Kingoonya   L. Younghusband
Tarcoola   L. Hanson
Woomera
Pimba
Lyndhurst
Leigh Creek
Beltana

Benbonyathe Hill 1058

Lake Frome

N u l l a r b o r   P l a i n
Nullarbor

Colona
Pintumba
Bookabie P.O.
Coorabie P.O.
Penong
Wilson Bluff
Eucla Motel
Mundrabilla   Low Pt.
Head of Bight

L. Ifould
L. Harris
Watraba   Koonibba
Goode
Ceduna
Denial B.   Thevenard
Puntabie
Wirrulla
Yardea P.O.
L. Everard
Nukey Bluff 472

St. Mary Pk. 1089
L. Hart
Island Lagoon
Pernatty Lagoon
Woocalla
Woomera
Port Augusta West
Port Augusta
Gordon
Hawker
Quorn
Carrieton

F l i n d e r s   R a n g e s

Parachilna

Wilpena

L a k e   T o r r e n s

Frome Downs

Corona

Benagerie

Stephens Creek

B a r r i e r   R a n g e

Broken Hill

Menindee L.
Cawndilla L.
Tandou L.

G r e a t

A u s t r a l i a n   B i g h t

Nuyts Arch.
Brown
Streaky B.   C. Bauer
Pt. Westall
C. Blanche
C. Rodstock
Smoky Bay
Streaky Bay
Port Kenny
Kyancutta
Minnipa
Poochera

L. Gilles
Buckleboo
Kimba
Iron Knob
Iron Baron
Mt. Remarkable 969
Whyalla   Port Pirie
Crystal Brook
Port Broughton

Peterborough
Terowie
Jamestown
Gladstone
Spalding
Nackara
Yunta

Oakbank
Quondong

Mannahill

Pepie I.
L. Popilta

Anxious Bay
C. Finniss
Elliston
Flinders I.
Investigator Group
Mt. Hope
Drummond Pt.
Coffin B.
Coffin Bay Pen.
Port Lincoln

Kopi
Lock
Rudall
Eyre Peninsula
Yeelanna
Ungarra
Cummins
Wangary
Tumby Bay
C. Donington
Corny Pt.

Cowell
Arno Bay
Wallaroo
Moonta

S p e n c e r

G u l f

Kadina
Balaklava
Snowtown
Brinkworth 934
Clare
Farrell Flat
Robertstown
Wakefield
Maitland
Ardrossan
Yorke Pen.

Burra

Loxton
Berri
Renmark
Morgan
Waikerie
Barmera
Morkalla
Werrimull

Mildura

Wentworth

L. Victoria

L. Darling

Merbein
Irympie
Cliffs

West Pt.
Thistle I.
Gambier Is.
C. Spencer
Edithburgh
C. Borda
Kingscote
C. du Couedic
C. Gantheaume
D'Estrees B.
C. Borda
Sleaford B.
Investigator Str.

Salisbury   Gawler
Port Adelaide   Elizabeth
ADELAIDE
Gleneig
Brighton
G. St. Vincent
Willunga
Cape Jervis
Victor Harbour
Encounter Bay

Mannum
Murray Bridge
Strathalbyn
Milang
L. Alexandrina
L. Albert
Meningie
Salt Creek

Younghusband Peninsula

Angaston
Nuriootpa
Tanunda
Hamley Bridge

Sedan

Wanbi
Alawoona
Peebinga

Karoonda
Marama
Cowangie
Lameroo
Pinnaroo
Underbool
Patchewollock

Kangaroo I.

G r e a t   A u s t r a l i a n   B i g h t

L. Coorong
Tintinara
Keith
Bordertown
Wolseley
Frances
Kingston South East
C. Jaffa
Lacepede Bay

L. Hindmarsh
Kaniva
Nhill
Jeparit
Yaapeet
Hopetoun

Dimboola
Horsham
Natimuk
Wolseley

Naracoorte
Beachport
Rivoli B.
Millicent
L. George
Penola
Glenelg
Coleraine
Mount Gambier
L. Bonney
Casterton   Cavendish
Balmoral
Hamilton
Penshurst

The Grampians

Murtoa

Port MacDonnell
C. Northumberland
Discovery Bay
Portland
Port Fairy
Warrnambool

Branxholme
Heywood
Mortlake
Koroit
Terang

ft   m
4500   1500
3000   1000
1200   400
600   200
0   0
200   600
2000   6000
4000   12 000
m   ft

East from Greenwich

COPYRIGHT. GEORGE PHILIP & SON. LTD

A
25
B
30
C
35
D
40

130   135   140
a   b   c   d

111

South Australia: Changing State

Economy

For more than a century South Australia's economy was based on primary production, principally wheat, wool, barley, fruit, wine, beef and lamb from the fertile south-east of the State. The burgeoning of manufacturing has caused factory employment to treble since 1940, but primary industry remains the major export earner, accounting for $432 million of total 1974-75 exports worth $767 million. The gross annual value of agricultural production exceeds $700 million.

The principal crops are wheat (gross production worth about $150 million from about 1 300 000 hectares), barley ($130 million from 630 000 hectares), grapes ($34 million from 30 000 hectares, over 42 per cent of national grape production) and orchard fruits ($33 million from 17 000 hectares). The State's 17 600 000 sheep yield an annual wool clip of about 100 million kg, worth more than $125 million, and 55 000 tonnes of mutton and lamb. About 85 000 tonnes of beef and veal are provided by 1 900 000 cattle. Fishing contributes about $15 million and forestry $14 million.

Secondary industry, largely set up since World War 2, employs 130 000 (45 per cent of the workforce) in 3000 establishments and is worth more than $1100 million (value added) annually. The primary industries now provide only one job in ten.

The secondary industries are dominated by vehicle and home appliance manufacturing, electronics and plastics. The State's major oil refinery is at Port Stanvac, a deep-sea port in south-west Adelaide. Ships up to 50 000 tonnes are built at Whyalla, but the future of the industry is uncertain. In 1976 a State government committee recommended that a $1400 million uranium treatment complex be built near Port Augusta — potentially Australia's largest industrial complex — but by 1977 the State Government expressed doubts about going ahead with the scheme.

Iron ore is the State's chief mineral, and more than 6 million tonnes worth over $53 million are mined annually from the Iron Knob and Iron Monarch deposits in the Middleback Ranges for blast furnaces at Whyalla and in New South Wales. Copper, mined since 1843, is worth $10 million annually. The Leigh Creek coalfield provides 1 500 000 tonnes (worth $3 500 000) annually to meet most of the State's power needs from the Port Augusta generating plants. Much of Australia's (and the world's) opal comes from the desert fields at Coober Pedy and Andamooka, where annual production may be $26 million. Given the small-scale nature of opal digging, and the secretive habits of the miners, production figures can be only speculative.

Top: The Indian-Pacific railway line crossing the Nullarbor, the world's largest open limestone plateau. The Indian-Pacific links Western Australia with the east coast 3971 km away.

Centre: The 'Coonawarra' based at Murray Bridge, one of the few remaining paddle vessels on the South Australian section of the river Murray.

Bottom: Wilpena Pound in the northern Flinders Range. Though the tops of the ridges are bare and jagged, the valleys carry a scattering of hardy trees.

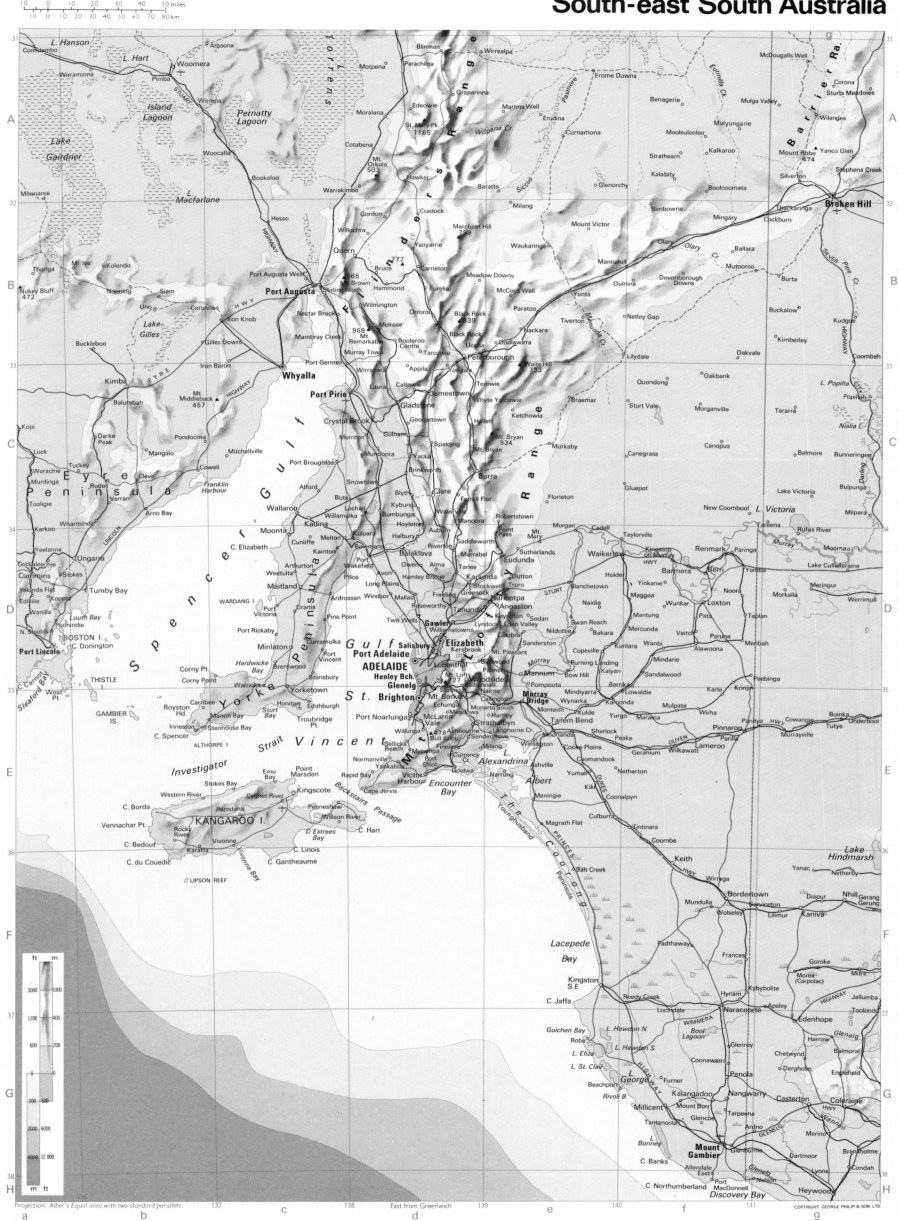

South-east South Australia

1 : 2 500 000

Projection: Alber's Equal area with two standard parallels

COPYRIGHT GEORGE PHILIP & SON. LTD.

Adelaide

Adelaide, the capital of South Australia, is Australia's fourth largest city, with a population of 900 379 in 1976.

In 1834 the idea of a colony in southern Australia — to be composed of free settlers only, with land earned in return for labour — was suggested by Edward Gibbon Wakefield. The South Australian Company was formed by George Angas in 1836 and he and the first settlers arrived in the same year. The actual site of Adelaide, at the foot of the Mount Lofty Ranges in a plain stretching to St Vincent's Gulf, was selected by Colonel Light, who arrived in the same year with a team of surveyors. He chose this site because of its flat land and soils which, although not particularly fertile, were better than areas to the north or the south where drainage was poor. It also had the advantages of a water supply and safe anchorage.

Today about 72 per cent of South Australia's population live in Adelaide, which makes it the most urbanised State in the country. The reason for this concentration is the arid nature of the land: about 90 per cent of the State receives less than 250 mm of rain. Even the remaining area — confined to the south-east corner — has hot, dry summers and mild wet winters. Adelaide is the driest of Australia's cities, with less than 500 mm average annual rainfall. The lack of water has hindered Adelaide's growth, and local supplies from the Mount Lofty Ranges are supplemented with water piped from the Murray River.

Adelaide has expanded west to the Gulf and east into the foothills of the Mount Lofty Ranges. Over recent years there has also been growth to the north and south, with the establishment of the satellite towns of Salisbury, Elizabeth and Port Stanvac. Such satellite towns have permitted the decentralisation of industries such as General Motors at Elizabeth and Chrysler in the south at Port Stanvac, which were attracted to Adelaide by the flat cheap land and State Government assistance in providing housing, and other services including factories.

Adelaide is probably the best-planned of Australia's original cities. The central business district, laid out by Colonel Light, conforms to a strict grid pattern. It contains the usual retail and commercial areas — with a limited amount of light industry and wholesale warehouses — and there are some imposing cultural and administrative buildings. The business district is surrounded by four wide terraces and extensive parkland, which separate it from residential and industrial areas. The parkland has been rigidly preserved and gives Adelaide a unique character. King William Street is a wide thoroughfare in the inner city, running north-south through the central business district and there are several wide streets running east-west. The main retail area, Rundle Street, has been converted into a pedestrian mall. The road pattern outside the central business district consists of major highways radiating outwards, while most other roads conform to a rectangular pattern. This pattern changes when the roads reach the Mount Lofty Ranges.

Inner Adelaide is in fact divided into two sections — the business district and North Adelaide — separated by the Torrens River as well as the parkland. The river is dammed to increase its width and its banks are lined with

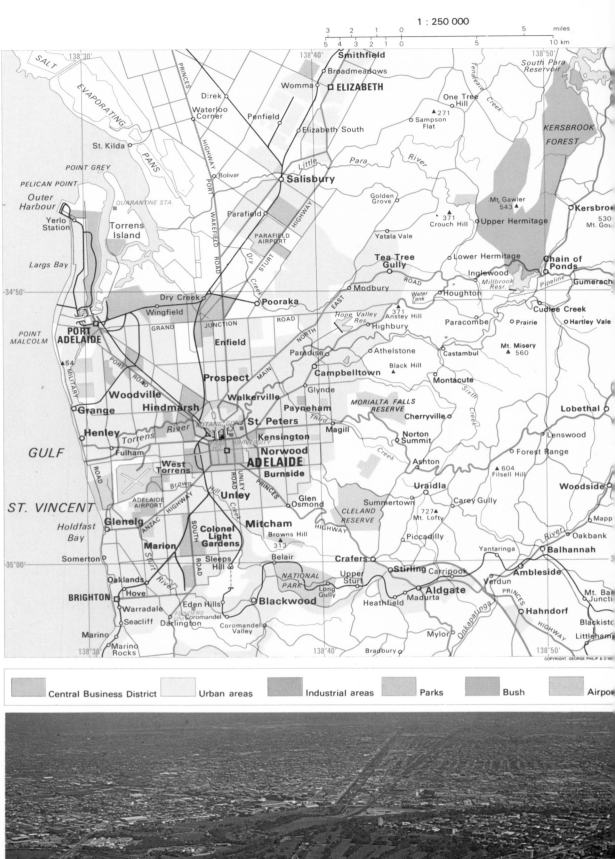

1 : 250 000

| Central Business District | Urban areas | Industrial areas | Parks | Bush | Airport |

attractively landscaped parks and gardens.

The port of Adelaide is located about 20 km from the city centre, and has attracted industry from the inner city. Adelaide has little heavy industry and the flat land around the port is highly suitable for manufacturing and warehousing. There is an inner harbour on the Port Adelaide River and an outer harbour in St Vincent's Gulf. Extensive dredging is necessary in order to accommodate large cargo vessels. Adelaide's nearby beaches — at Glenelg and Brighton — do not generally compare with those of other Australian cities, although they are very close to the residential areas and have excellent soft, white sand.

One of Adelaide's most distinguishing tourist features is the extensive parkland close to the city centre. The Botanical Gardens — with beautifully kept trees, lawns and flower gardens — are located by the Torrens River north of the central business district. Not far away stands Light's Vision, a statue commemorating the man responsible for Adelaide's design. From this point, near St Peter's Cathedral, an excellent view of the city is afforded. The Torrens River is picturesque, with rich aquatic life and many brightly-coloured paddle boats or rowing boats which can be hired throughout most of the year.

The Festival Theatre is a magnificent piece of architectural design, in terms of both its form and function. Located on the south bank of the Torrens River, the white pyramidal roof contrasts with the surrounding greenery of the park and blue waters of the river. This is the venue for Adelaide's Festival of the Arts, which is held every two years and is the most impressive occasion of its type in Australia.

Adelaide's buildings give it considerable character. Due to a shortage of local timber, the houses have traditionally been constructed of bluestone, sandstone, limestone and bricks, giving them and other structures a permanence and historic significance not found in other Australian cities. A drive through some of the older suburbs, such as North Adelaide, reveals well-preserved houses of considerable age and appeal. Many of Adelaide's restaurants owe their atmosphere to solid limestone brick walls, exposed timber beams and cellar location. Adelaide shares Melbourne's reputation for the finest restaurants in Australia.

Day-trips from Adelaide are famous. The Barossa Valley, 75 km north-east of Adelaide, is Australia's largest wine-producing district. There are many wineries for inspection and a large area under vines. The German character of the area reflects a cultural heritage derived from early settlers in the district. The Mount Lofty Ranges to the east of Adelaide have a tremendous variety of scenery and are an important area for vines, orchards and market gardens as well as large native forests. Mount Lofty is 712 m high and provides a view of Adelaide sprawling over a flat plain towards St Vincent's Gulf. The Fleurieu Peninsula south of Adelaide is a holiday area popular for its beaches and resorts such as at Victor Harbour.

Below left: An aerial view of the city of Adelaide showing the Adelaide Oval and the recently completed Festival Hall set in Montefiore Park.

Below: The central business district of Adelaide looking over the Metropolitan Golf Course from north Adelaide with the Adelaide Hills in the distance.

Opposite: A view of North Terrace, Adelaide. The University of Adelaide, Public Library, Museum and National Art Gallery are to be found in this tree-lined terrace close to the central city area.

Western Australia: Boom State

Characteristics and population

For many years Western Australia was known as the 'Cinderella State' of the Commonwealth because of its slow rate of population growth and industrial development neither of which compared favourably with the more prosperous Eastern States. Not only did the State lag behind the others economically but it was also isolated from them physically with only a single track standard gauge railway and a mainly dirt Eyre "Highway" linking it with the rest of Australia 3000 km to the east. Despite the building of a large oil refinery on the shores of Cockburn Sound (16 km south of Fremantle) in the mid 1950s and the consequent construction of ancillary industries in the area, it was not until the development of the huge mineral fields of iron ore, nickel and uranium ore, as well as the discovery of enormous reserves of natural gas on the North-West Shelf, that Western Australia emerged to become one of the most important States in the export economy of Australia. Its mineral production is worth $1351 million annually compared with other primary production totalling about $900 million and secondary production about $650 million. Development discussions continue — particularly on the future of the estimated 368 billion cubic metres of natural gas discovered offshore from Dampier in the north-west — and Western Australia's shrinking isolation was symbolically evident in September 1976 when the belated completion of the Eyre Highway at last made it possible to cross Australia on a sealed road.

The mineral development brought a rapid expansion in the State's population. By 1960 the population numbered 734 900, but this had grown to 1 144 900 by 1976 — a 55 per cent increase within 15 years. Compared to

Typical uninhabited cattle grazing land in the Carr Boyd Ranges south-east of Wyndham.

the total population of Australia, this growth was quite spectacular.

Perth has 805 489 of the State's 1 144 900 people. Other main population centres are the twin cities of Kalgoorlie-Boulder on the eastern goldfields (20 000 people); Bunbury (19 513) with its agricultural, alumina and woodchip exports, 180 km south of Perth; Geraldton (17 596), another agricultural port, 500 km north of Perth; Albany (13 000), site of the first British settlement in 1826, the port for the lower south-west agricultural areas and site of Australia's only whaling station, some 400 km south of Perth; and Port Hedland (11 772), an old port in the northwest about 1900 km from Perth, now transformed to handle iron ore from two Pilbara mines. The 1960s and 1970s saw the birth of new mining and service towns such as Mt. Newman, Paraburdoo, Karratha, Mt Tom Price, Kambalda and Windarra.

Western Australia has compulsory education between the ages of 6 and 15 and about 245 000 children attend primary and secondary school, four out of five of them at free government schools. The University of Western Australia has 9800 students; recently established Murdoch University has 1500; and the Western Australian Institute of Technology has 11 000 enrolled. There are also five teachers' colleges.

Growth Rates of WA and Aust.

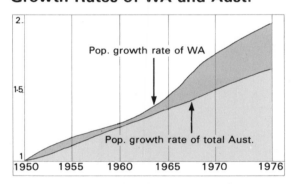

Pop. growth rate of WA

Pop. growth rate of total Aust.

1950 1955 1960 1965 1970 1976

History and Government

Although the Dutch had mapped much of the inhospitable Western Australian coast from as early as the seventeenth century, the first permanent European settlement was not until 1826 when the British sent a party from Sydney to settle at King George Sound, forestalling a feared settlement by the French. In 1829 Captain James Stirling founded the capital, Perth, as the first non-convict colony. Western Australia was constituted a separate colony from this time, although it was not granted responsible government until 1890. Western Australia has a bicameral parliamentary system: a Legislative Assembly lower house, and a Legislative Council upper house. Voting for State elections is compulsory for all citizens over 18. Voting for local government authorities is based on property qualifications and is not compulsory.

Difficult times in the infant colony eventually led to the admission of convicts, and transportation did not end until 1868. The colony's first major economic boost came when gold was discovered at Coolgardie in 1892 and nearby Kalgoorlie in 1893.

Climate and Geography

Most of Western Australia's 2 600 000 km² form a low plateau, with isolated ranges. It extends between latitudes 13° and 35° South. The south-west corner, one of two Australian regions with a Mediterranean climate, has long hot summers and wet winters. Perth is the sunniest capital (7.9 hours of sunshine daily) with an annual rainfall averaging 880 mm, an average midsummer maximum temperature of 29.5°C and an average midwinter temperature of 17.2°C. Perth's annual average minimum temperature is 13°C.

Much of the remainder of Western Australia, with the exception of the tropical north, is arid land or desert. In 1923-24 the

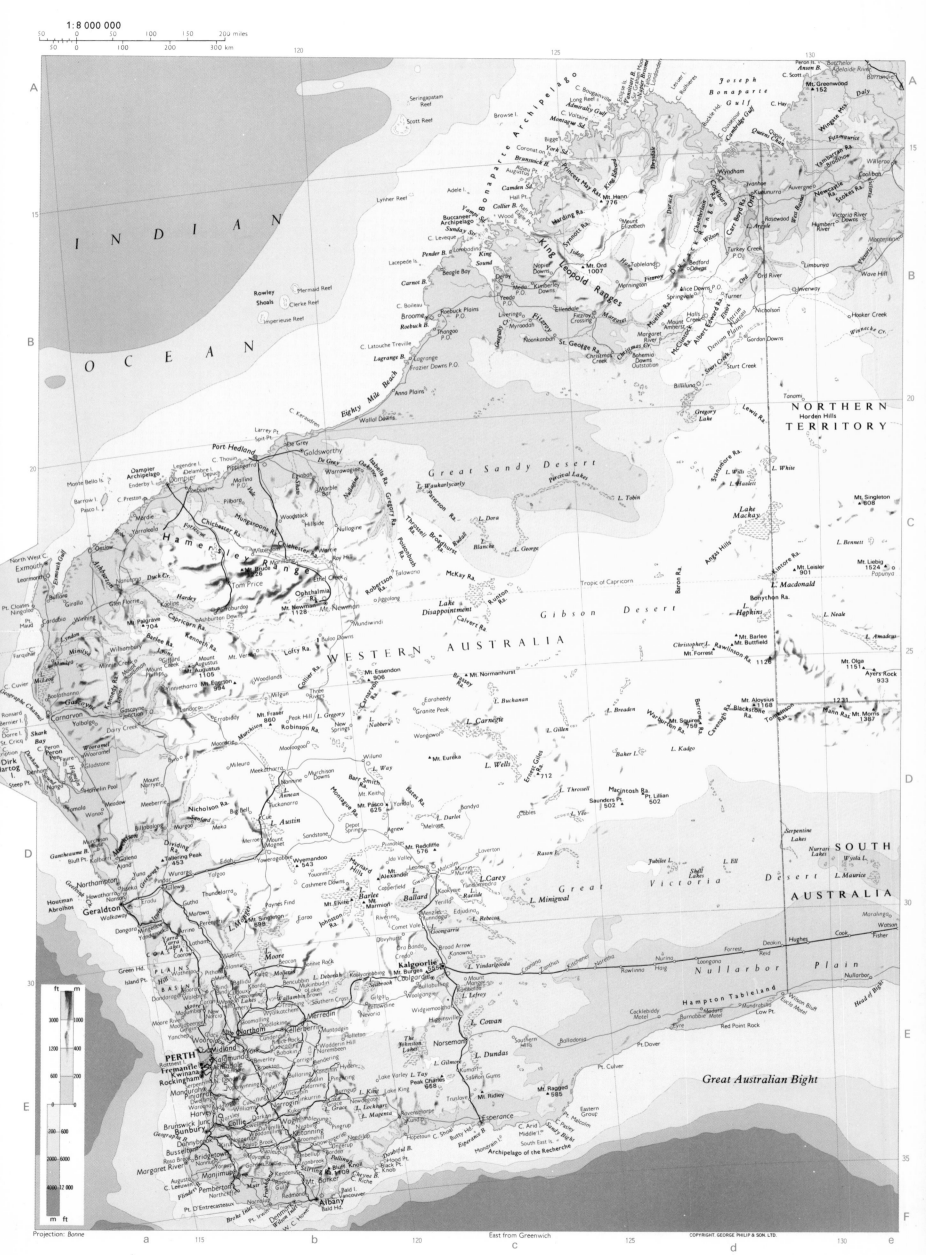

Western Australia: Boom State

former mining town of Marble Bar in the north-west broke weather records with 160 consecutive days which had maximum temperatures of at least 37.8°C.

Economy

Until the lifting of an iron ore export embargo in the 1960s, Western Australia had a primarily rural economy, and was Australia's major gold producer. Now mining dominates a generally thriving economy. About 63 per cent of its annual minerals production comes from 85 000 000 tonnes of high-grade iron ore valued at about $775 million — almost all from the four major exporters who opened up the immense deposits of the Pilbara region 1000 km north of Perth when the ore ban was lifted. Reserves of high-grade ore are estimated to exceed 26 000 million tonnes, and there are additional major reserves of lower-grade ore. In late 1976 new iron ore developments worth about $600 million were announced. These include the boosting of iron ore production by 12 000 000 tonnes annually, and large-scale secondary processing of low-grade ore.

Five nickel mines produce more than $216 million of nickel concentrates annually. Western Australian mines yield almost one-third of the nation's bauxite (valued at about $208 million annually), 83 per cent of its salt ($20 400 000) and 98 per cent of its ilmenite, from beach sands ($38 200 000). Coal mined for domestic use is worth about $18 million. Gold production is falling steeply ($24 million in 1975-76) and Mount Charlotte, last of the fabulous 'Golden Mile' mines of Kalgoorlie, has shut down. A proposed $24 million open-cut gold mine at Telfer in the Patterson Ranges desert region (400 km south-east of Port Hedland) may revive gold production. Uranium has been discovered in significant quantities at Yeelirrie, 650 km north-east of Perth. Discussions are continuing on proposals to tap the North-West Shelf gas 130 km offshore from Dampier, and build a liquefied natural gas plant at a total cost around $2000 million.

Western Australia has 34 500 000 sheep and 2 500 000 cattle. Annual wool production is about 180 000 000 kg and meat production exceeds 200 000 tonnes. Almost 30 per cent of the nation's wheat is grown here. The agricultural and pastoral industries are worth about $770 million annually, dairying, poultry and beekeeping contribute $63 million and forestry, fishing (notably rock lobsters for North America) and hunting $51 million. Western Australia has 100 000 re-

maining hectares of wet eucalypt forest containing valuable karri (which may exceed 100 m in height) and more than 400 000 hectares of jarrah, another valuable eucalypt.

The State's industrial production was only modest, chiefly linked to the requirements of agriculture, until 1955 when an oil refinery was established at Kwinana, 44 km south of Perth, the first element of what is now a major industrial centre on Cockburn Sound. It includes a steel rolling mill, an alumina refinery, a fertiliser works, a State-operated power station, a nickel refinery and a bulk grain handling terminal. The alumina refinery, along with a second later established at Pinjarra 55 km south, produces 3 400 000 tonnes annually. Construction of the $650 million first stage of a third alumina refinery (Australia's largest mining industry investment) began in 1977. Initial production will be 1 million tonnes of alumina annually. About 18 per cent of the State's workforce is engaged in secondary industry.

Below: The whaling station at King George Sound near Albany, the only station still operating in Australia. Although of slight importance now, due to international controls to prevent the species being exterminated, whaling was vital to Western Australia in the first half of the nineteenth century.

1:2 500 000

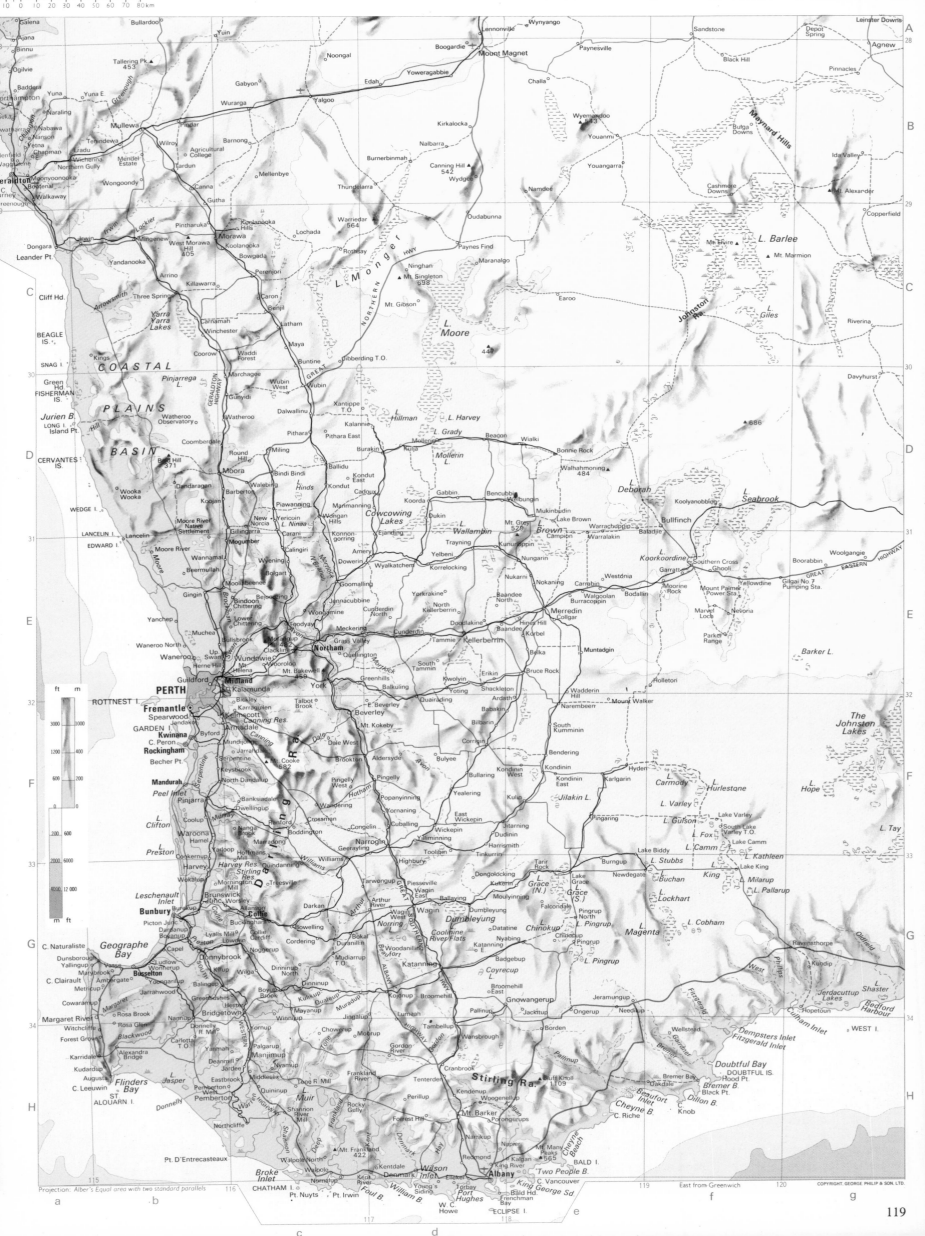

Projection: Alber's Equal area with two standard parallels

East from Greenwich

Perth

Perth, the capital of Western Australia, had a population of 805 489 in 1976. It is the fastest growing of Australia's State capitals and is presently Australia's fifth-largest city.

Perth was first settled in 1829 when Captain Fremantle hoisted the British flag on the site of the city that today bears his name. Captain Stirling returned from England in the same year with the first of the many settlers required to establish the settlement — it was generally feared that if Britain did not settle this remote part of Australia another nation, probably France, would do so. The settlement grew quickly in its early years because of the very cheap land grants. However, the soils proved to be infertile, too sandy and ridden with weeds, except for areas along the Swan and Canning Rivers, and the settlement fell on hard times.

Today, Perth extends along the beautiful lower reaches of the Swan River from Perth Water (a widening of the river) to Fremantle on the coast, some 20 km from the central business district. Perth is situated on flat and gently undulating land and there is much space for expansion. The rapid growth of Perth can be attributed primarily to the discoveries of extensive mineral deposits in Western Australia. In a State which is largely desert Perth enjoys a climate which is probably the best of any in Australia — summers are hot and dry and the winters mild and wet, as in Mediterranean countries.

The city is mainly commercial and residential, industry being less developed than in cities of the eastern States; the Western Australian market is still relatively small. The major heavy industries are located at Kwinana, some 20 km south of Fremantle, where Cockburn Sound provides a large, sheltered deep-water port. Here, among other industries, BHP has established an ironworks, Alcoa an aluminium refinery and British Petroleum a refinery. Workers travel from Perth or live at nearby centres such as Fremantle and Rockingham. Industry, together with much of the State's warehousing, is also found at Fremantle. The port of Fremantle is at the mouth of the Swan River. There are a few light industrial areas closer to Perth.

The central business district is on the north bank of Perth Water, connected to the south bank by two major bridges — the Narrows and the Causeway. The growth of the central business district is rather restricted to the south by the river, to the west by the Mitchell Freeway, and to the north by the suburban railway system, resulting in considerable high-rise development for a city with such a small population. Tall glass and concrete buildings now dwarf those built in the early days of Perth. Retail and commercial businesses are in the city centre, with open-air pedestrian malls being a feature of the shopping area. Because of the more recent development of Perth, the shops and business houses are generally more modern than those in other Australian cities. Hay Street has been turned into a pedestrian mall and is lined with flower boxes. London Court is another street of interest — an Elizabethan-style open-air court with half-timbered entrances.

Housing is developing rapidly, with growth concentrated along the beach front mainly to the north of Fremantle, as well as on the major highways which radiate out from Perth — particularly those highways

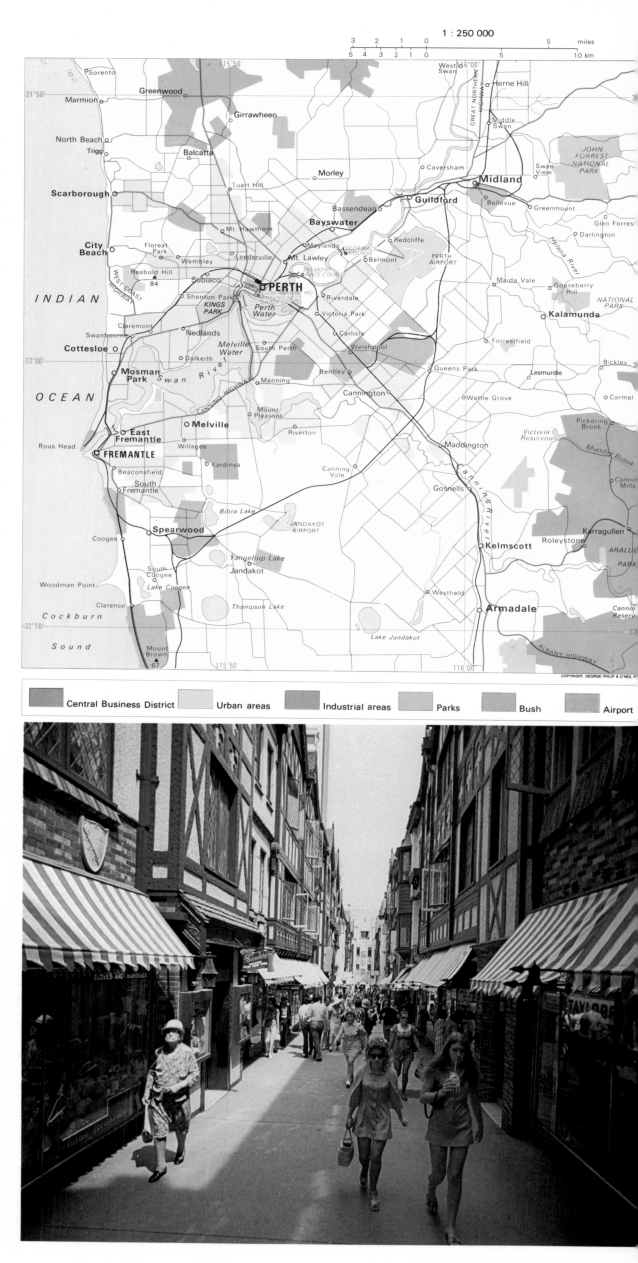

Central Business District   Urban areas   Industrial areas   Parks   Bush   Airport

that follow the course of the Swan River. Perth has probably the most efficient road system of any State capital.

Perth has surf beaches to match those of Sydney and they are far less crowded, extending from near the mouth of the Swan River to the north. The best-known are Cottesloe, City Beach, Scarborough and Trigg. Suburban development continues north, though intermittently, to the National Park at Yanchep. Rockingham beach south of Fremantle is on the sheltered shores of Cockburn Sound.

A popular drive from Perth is to the Darling Ranges (20 km from the city centre), which form the headwaters for a number of streams flowing into the Swan River. There are two large reservoirs in this area — the Mundaring and the Canning. The Swan-Avon river system, because of its salinity, is not used for metropolitan water supplies. In spring the famous wildflowers of Western Australia bloom abundantly and make the trip even more rewarding. The short journey to the upper valley of the Swan River — with its dairying, market gardens and vine cultivation — is also a popular day-trip, usually including a visit to the well-known Houghton's winery.

Opposite below: The Tudor architecture of London Court, running between Hay Street and St George's Terrace, is one of the points of interest for tourists visiting Perth.

Right: An aerial view of Perth looking over the Narrows Bridge which spans the Swan River and joins the Kwinana Freeway with the Mitchell Expressway, which is on the city side of the river.

Below: Fremantle, the chief port for Western Australia, lies on both sides of the mouth of the Swan River, some twenty kilometres from the centre of Perth.

Northern Territory: Future State

Characteristics and Population

The Northern Territory — that colourful land of extremes regarded by urban Australians as the nation's last frontier — is at last on the path to Statehood. Prime Minister Malcolm Fraser promised the Territory statehood within five years of the 1975 election campaign.

Yet even by 1980 the population of this vast area (six times the size of Britain) will only be an estimated 125 000 — about one person to 10 km². Some 60 per cent will live in the major city, Darwin (present population 46 650), Alice Springs, 1577 km to the south (21 600), Katherine (5227), Nhulunbuy (3500) and Tennant Creek (3000). Beyond such settlements the cliches of the outback live on in great distances and an isolation almost beyond comprehension. The Territory has 243 459 km² reserved for the use and benefit of its 24 000 Aborigines. And although there is no longer a cattle station 'as large as Belgium', Alexandria station on the Barkly Tableland remains Australia's largest pastoral property, reduced now to a mere 15 495 km².

The Northern Territory, Australia's most sparsely populated region, lies within the torrid zone, except for a southern strip some 300 km wide. Much of the land is arid. It covers 1 347 525 km² and occupies 17 per cent of the continent, with a population of 97 100 now that the northern port city of Darwin has largely been rebuilt following its devastation by cyclone Tracy on Christmas Day 1974.

Cyclone Tracy, like other elements of Northern Territory life (the climate, the geography, the distribution of people), fitted a pattern of extremes. The most destructive cyclone recorded on the Australian mainland, it caused the deaths of at least 66 people, completely destroyed more than 50 per cent of the houses and flats and damaged more than 45 per cent of the remainder. The cost of rebuilding Darwin could reach $600 million.

History and Government

The first abortive European settlements at Melville Island (1825), Raffles Bay (1827) and Port Essington (1838) were followed by the establishment of Palmerston — now Darwin — in 1869. The Northern Territory had been incorporated into New South Wales in 1825 when that colony was extended west to the 129th meridian of longitude East; in 1863 it was brought under South Australian jurisdiction but was transferred to the Commonwealth of Australia in 1911.

Executive authority is vested in an Administrator answerable to the Minister for Northern Australia. The Administrator's council gives advice on a range of matters and there is a Legislative Assembly of 19 elected members. The Territory has one member in the Federal House of Representatives, but no Senate representative. In January 1977 the Commonwealth transferred control of 27 boards and authorities to the Legislative Assembly as a first step towards self-government.

Climate and Geography

Northern areas of the Territory have a monsoon climate characterised by distinct wet and dry seasons. The 'Wet' usually occurs be-

tween November and April: almost all rainfall occurs in these summer months. Darwin, for example, averages almost 1500 mm of rain annually, but only 25 mm during the dry season. Darwin's average maximum temperature varies only between 33.8°C (November) and 30.4°C (July). The city averages 140 days a year with temperatures above 27°C.

The arid south, part of the 'dry centre' which defied early explorers, is largely desert. Alice Springs averages only 254 mm of rain a year. More than one-third of the Territory receives less than 250 mm annually.

Inland of the low, flat northern coastline, the land rises southwards around the 17th parallel South, where higher areas form the watershed between north and south. There

are few landmarks. Further south the land rises to about 600 m above sea-level, with several mountain ranges reaching 1000 m and more in height.

Economy

Production of beef cattle has long been the major rural industry, although in recent years depressed prices, both in Australia and throughout the world, have affected production severely. The Territory has about 1 400 000 cattle. Annual meat production slumped to 10 319 tonnes in 1975-76 from a peak of 16 500 tonnes in 1968-69.

'Open-range' grazing is the rule because of poor pasture and the lack of winter rain.

Above: An aerial view of Undoolya Station, east of Alice Springs. The lucerne crop, an unusual sight in the Northern Territory, is grown as feed for the station's cattle.

Often more than 16 hectares are required to support one animal, and herds are preferably of 50 000 head or more. Government support to the industry includes an extensive network of beef roads (road trucks can carry up to 90 cattle), an increase in the number of underground water bores, and research into improved pastures (notably Townsville-style, grown as a pasture legume in higher rainfall areas) and new breeds of cattle. There are export abattoirs at Katherine and Darwin.

Buffaloes, introduced during early settlement attempts, thrived in the tropical north and have spread as far south as Katherine. There are now believed to be more than 200 000 of them, and efforts are being made to domesticate some herds. Commercial production of buffalo meat started in 1960 (initially for pet food, later for human consumption) and more than 20 000 are slaughtered annually for meat worth more than $1 600 000. As foot and mouth disease is unknown in Australia buffaloes are occasionally exported for breeding stock.

For more than a century there have been unsuccessful attempts to grow commercial crops in the Territory. Distance from markets, poor soils and winter drought have

been the main obstacles to large-scale agriculture. Grain sorghum is one crop with potential — given good land and sufficient capital — but it is still in an early stage of development.

The Territory's main industry, in terms of productive value, is mining, in 1975 worth $130 million. The $300 million bauxite mining and treatment project at Gove contributed $62.6 million (48 per cent) of this. Manganese ore mined at Groote Eylandt in the Gulf of Carpentaria was worth $27.7 million (21 per cent) and provided exports to Japan, Europe and the USA as well as meeting Australia's needs. The underground mines at Tennant Creek annually yield gold worth about $20.1 million, copper worth $2.8

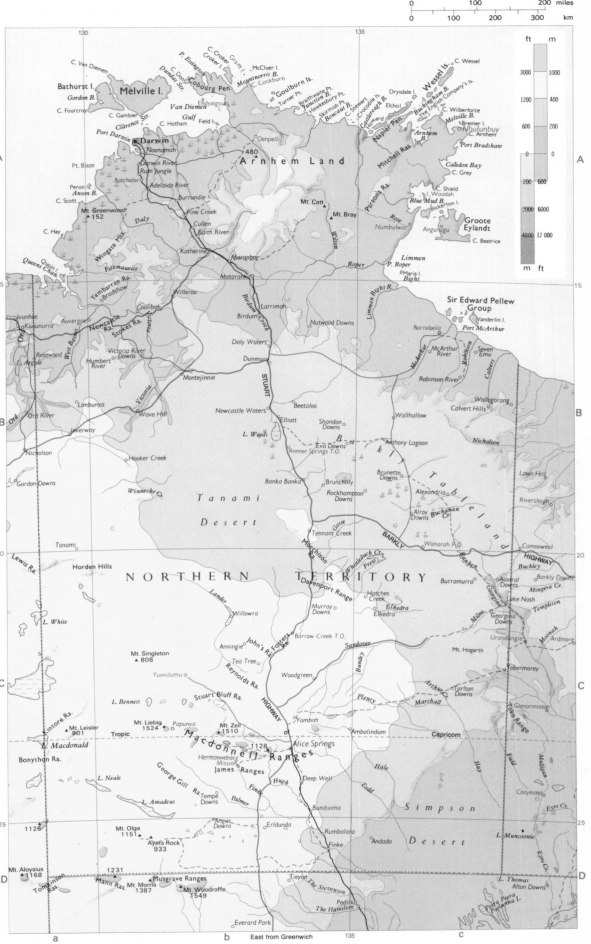

Northern Territory: Future State

million, as well as silver and bismuth. More than 700 000 tonnes of iron ore (worth over $4.3 million) is mined at Francis Creek and shipped to Japan. Uranium finds of world significance have been made in the Alligator River region some 240 km east of Darwin. Although a Federal government report has recommended the conditional mining and export of Australian uranium, the future of the Northern Territory deposits is still unclear.

Fishing is worth more than $6 million, with prawns and barramundi providing most of the catch. Tourism is also a major revenue earner, worth around $30 million annually and attracting more than 120 000 people.

Manufacturing is worth more than $50 million (value added) with about 2300 people being employed in more than 100 establishments.

Opposite: Water buffaloes at an experimental station, south of Darwin. Water buffaloes were first brought to the Northern Territory in the 1820s where they thrived and now number about 200 000. Domestication of the water buffalo is now being experimented with.

Below: Alice Springs with Heavitree Gap in the Macdonnell Ranges in the background. Alice Springs is situated on the Todd River, usually a dry river bed, but occasionally a raging torrent. Alice Springs is the starting point for tourists visiting the Centre.

Above: Katherine Gorge, east of the town of Katherine. Fresh-water crocodiles are common in the Katherine River which flows south-west from Arnhem Land.

Opposite: Central Mount Stuart, the geographical centre of Australia, is seen by travellers on the Stuart Highway, south of Barrow Creek. Central Mount Stuart was discovered by John McDouall Stuart who actually named it in honor of Sturt.

Below: Gosse's Bluff, west of Alice Springs, was discovered by W. C. Gosse the explorer who first climbed Ayers Rock. Originally thought to be a meteor crater, Gosse's Bluff is now believed to have been carved by an exploding comet above the ground.

Queensland: a Tropical State

Characteristics and Population

Queensland has always figured prominently in the annals of Australian exploration, and the days of discovery are not yet gone. In 1606 the first European known to have sighted the Great South Land — a Dutchman named Wilhelm Janszoon — came on a rather unimpressive part of Queensland, the western fringe of Cape York peninsula.

Two centuries later Matthew Flinders noted red cliffs in the same area. Another century and a half passed before a geologist recognised these cliffs as bauxite, the ore of aluminium. The discovery of what are possibly the world's largest deposits of bauxite — together with other recent mineral finds — means that the continuing prosperity of the State lies as much with these new riches as with the traditional pastoral and agricultural industries. Queensland has become an important world source of minerals such as bauxite, nickel, coal, uranium, rock phosphate and rutile. The State's annual mineral production of about $900 million is rapidly beginning to overhaul its gross annual rural production worth more than $1 200 million. Meanwhile, the geologists continue the search.

Opposite: The Darling Downs in the area between Warwick and Toowoomba where the rich soil and mainly wheat crops create a patchwork effect.

Below: Mt Ngungun in the Glasshouse Mountains, one of a group of eleven volcanic plugs that rise out of the coastal plain 80 kilometres north of Brisbane.

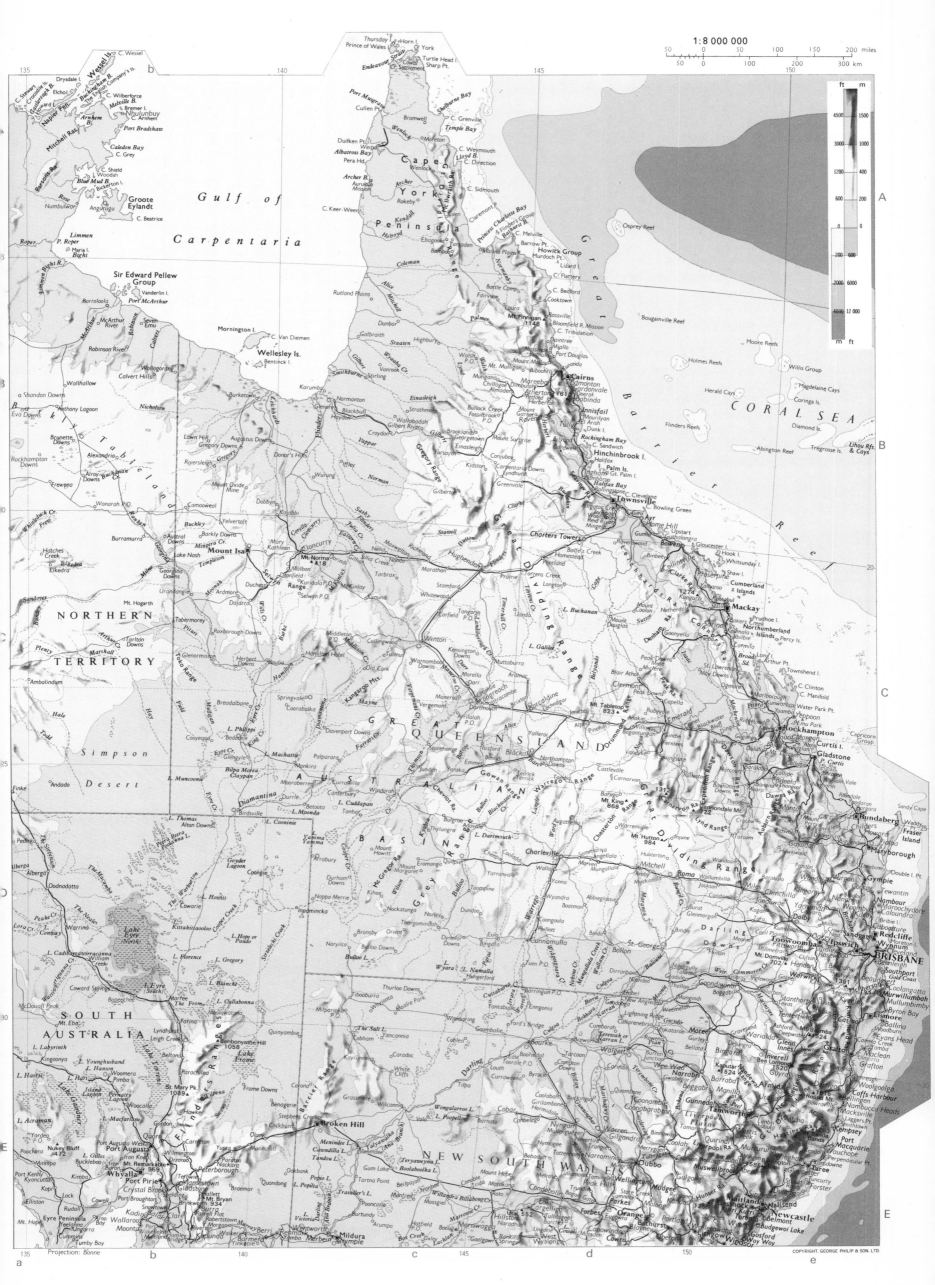

1 : 8 000 000

50   0   50   100   150   200 miles

50   0   50   100   150   200   300 km

C. Wessel

Wessel Is.

Drysdale I.

Crocodile Is.

C. Stewart

Elcho I.

Guluwuru I.

Howard I.

Buckingham B.

Napier Pen.

English Company's Is.

Bremer I.

Wilberforce B.

C. Arnhem

Melville B.

Nhulunbuy

Arnhem

Mitchell Ras.

B.

Caledon Bay

C. Grey

Shield I.

Blue Mud B.

Woodah I.

Groote Eylandt

Numbulwar

Anigurugu

C. Beatrice

Bickerton I.

Roper

Limmen

P. Roper

Maria I.

Bight

Limmen Bight R.

Sir Edward Pellew Group

Vanderlin I.

Port McArthur

Borroloola

Gulf of

Carpentaria

Mornington I.

C. Van Diemen

Wellesley Is.

Bentinck I.

Thursday I.

Prince of Wales

Horn I.

York

Turtle Head I.

Cowal

Sharp Pt.

Endeavour Str.

Port Musgrave

Cullen Pt.

Sherburne Bay

Bramwell

Duifken Pt.

Weipa

Moreton

C. Weymouth

Lloyd B.

C. Direction

Cape

York

Peninsula

Archer B.

Aurukun Mission

Kendall

Rokeby

Claremont Pt.

Princess Charlotte Bay

Bathurst B.

C. Melville

Coleman

Barrow Pt.

Howick Group

Murdoch Pt.

Lizard I.

C. Flattery

C. Bedford

Cooktown

Bloomfield R. Mission

C. Tribulation

Daintree

Mossman

Port Douglas

CORAL SEA

Osprey Reef

Bougainville Reef

Willis Group

Magdaine Cays

Holmes Reefs

Herald Cays

Coringa Is.

Moore Reefs

Flinders Reefs

Diamond Is.

Abington Reef

Lihou Rfs. & Cays

Tregrosse Is.

Cairns

Townsville

Mackay

Rockhampton

Gladstone

Bundaberg

Maryborough

BRISBANE

Newcastle

NORTHERN

TERRITORY

QUEENSLAND

SOUTH

AUSTRALIA

NEW SOUTH WALES

Simpson

Desert

Lake Eyre

GREAT

AUSTRALIAN

BASIN

Great Dividing Range

Broken Hill

Mildura

Projection: Bonne

COPYRIGHT. GEORGE PHILIP & SON. LTD.

Queensland, the second-largest State of Australia, occupies 1 728 000 km² of the north-east of the continent. This is almost 23 per cent of Australia and represents an area one-fifth the size of the USA. Queensland stretches 2100 km north-south and 1450 km east-west, with a coastline of 7400 km.

Queensland is the most decentralised of the States, having one-third of Australia's urban centres with more than 25 000 people. The State capital, Brisbane, has 957 700 of Queensland's 2 million people. Other cities include Townsville (80 000 people), the City of Gold Coast, a series of coastal resorts south of Brisbane (87 500), Ipswich (69 000), Toowoomba (66 450) and Rockhampton (51 100). The State's cities, towns and shires are managed by councils elected every third year.

There are 400 000 children at preschools, primary and secondary schools, 80 per cent of whom attend free government schools. The University of Queensland in Brisbane has 19 000 students, Townsville's James Cook University has 1900 students in five faculties oriented towards tropical studies, and Brisbane's recently established Griffith University has 820 students.

History and Government

The explorer John Oxley discovered the Brisbane River and penetrated the Moreton Bay area in 1823. A penal settlement was established at Redcliffe in 1824, but this was abandoned a few months later in favour of the present site of the capital. Land was not made officially available to free settlers until 1842, although squatters following Cunningham's route from the coast to the Darling Downs (1828) began to move into the south-east in 1840. The area north of the Tropic was settled after 1860, as first cotton and later sugar plantations were established with the help of indentured Kanaka labour.

Queensland became a separate colony with responsible government in 1859. On entering the Commonwealth, it agreed to end Kanaka labour in return for tariff protection for its sugar industry. Queensland now has the distinction of being the only State without an upper house of Parliament, having abolished the Legislative Council in 1922.

Climate and Geography

Fifty-four per cent of Queensland lies in the tropics. Rainfall varies greatly: Tully on the north-east coast is the wettest area of the nation, with the highest average annual rainfall (4400 mm); Mount Isa in the arid northwest receives only 394 mm annually. Other interesting average rainfalls on the coast are Brisbane (1148 mm), Rockhampton (947 mm) and Cairns (2190 mm). Most of the rain occurs in summer (December-March) with heavy falls often accompanying the tropical cyclones which, on average, affect Queensland's coastal areas three times a year.

The highest temperature officially recorded in Australia was 53.1°C at Cloncurry in Queensland. Brisbane in the southeast has an average midsummer maximum temperature of 29.4°C and an average midwinter maximum temperature of 20.3°C, while Cairns in the north-east records 31.5°C and 25.4°C, Longreach in central Queensland 37.8°C and 25.2°C.

Dominating Queensland's topography is the Great Dividing Range, the watershed between inland and coastal rivers, which runs the length of Australia's eastern coast. Outcrops of the Range form offshore islands. Beyond these is one of the natural wonders of the world, the coral structures of the Great Barrier Reef, which stretches some 2000 km between the Gulf of Papua and Breaksea Spit near Maryborough.

The offshore islands form part of one of the world's natural wonders, the Great Barrier Reef. The Reef stretches some 2000 km between the Gulf of Papua and Breaksea Spit near Maryborough. Its offshore distance varies from 16 to 320 km and encloses an area of about 200 000 km². The Reef is a great web of life based on the coral polyp which grows only where waters are warm, clear and shallow. Reefs develop strongly near the edge of the continental shelf, and in the Cape York area where the shelf is narrow, the reefs are close to the coast. Fringing reefs occur around the 'mainland' islands, while sand cays, barrier reefs and atolls are also common. In recent years large areas of The Reef have been destroyed by the coral-eating crown-of-thorns starfish.

To the west of the Great Dividing Range are the plains of central Queensland, falling north to the salt flats on the Gulf of Carpentaria, and merging into higher land to the north-west.

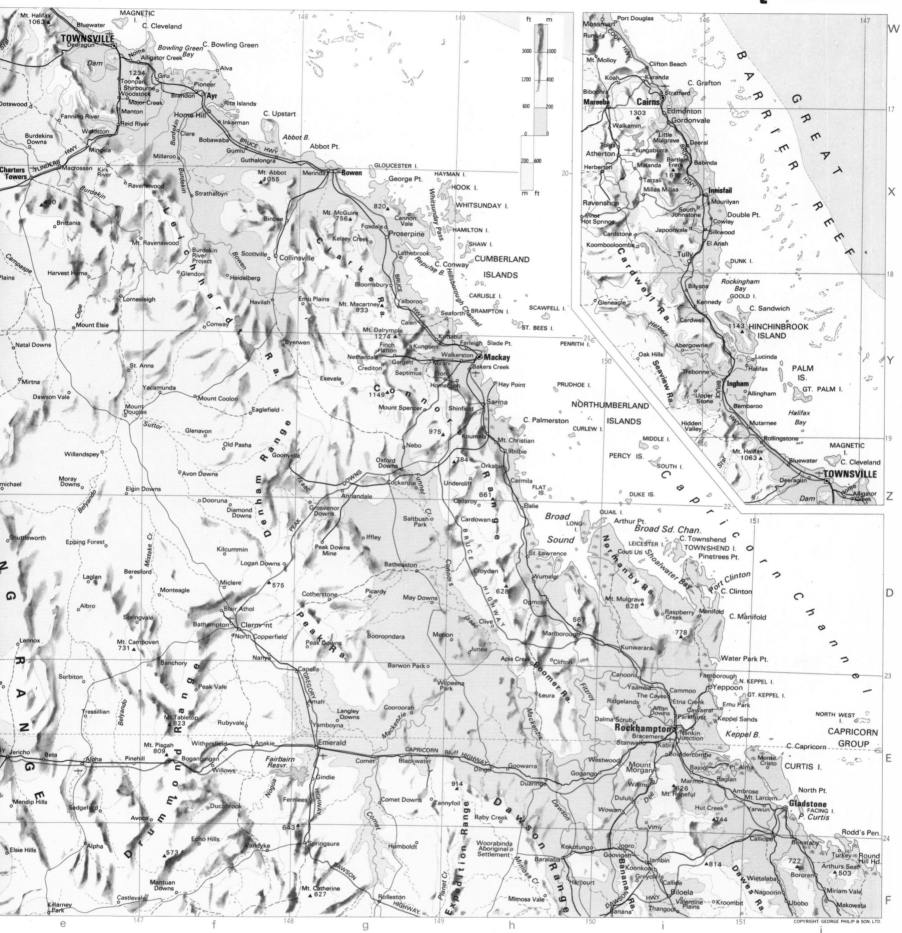

Economy

Development of the State's great natural resources has kept the economy strong, and the associated input of capital and labour has boosted industrial growth to the point where the net value of Queensland's manufacturing production is about $1650 million, with a workforce of 140 000. Products include metals, machinery, chemicals, fertilisers, motor vehicles, clothing and food.

Beef and wool dominate rural production. The State's 10 900 000 beef cattle yield 430 000 tonnes of meat annually. There are 13 540 000 sheep and 518 000 dairy cattle. Queensland produces 38 per cent of the nation's meat exports.

Sugar forms Australia's second most valuable export crop (after wheat) and comes from 280 000 hectares of farmland on Queensland's east coast, producing 24 million tonnes annually. Wheatgrowing is primarily on the Darling Downs region west of Brisbane. Annual plantings of around 700 000 hectares yield about 1 million tonnes in a good year. Fishing production is valued at $14 million, dairying and pig-farming contribute about $82 million annually, poultry and beekeeping $39 million.

Queensland's minerals have enormous export potential. There are large reserves of copper, coal, bauxite, lead, zinc, silver, rutile, nickel, uranium and rock phosphate; commercial deposits of gold, tin, zircon, silica, lime and salt, abundant supplies of natural gas, and limited oil.

The Bowen Basin coalfields of central Queensland are an important world source of coking coal. They provide most of the State's annual coal production of around 23 million tonnes worth $450 million, mostly for export. Known coal reserves exceed 10 000 million tonnes. Some 166 000 tonnes of copper (valued at $155 million) are produced annually. About 10 million tonnes of bauxite come from the Cape York fields each year, and most of it is shipped to Queensland's east coast for processing into alumina at Gladstone, the world's largest alumina plant. The nickel deposits at Greenvale currently yield 2 700 000 tonnes of unprocessed ore.

Above: Sugarcane landscape in the Maroochy River area where it is joined by the Yandina Creek north of Nambour. Sugar, which forms Australia's second most valuable export crop after wheat, is grown exclusively on the east coast of Queensland.

Below: Noosa Heads, a popular Sunshine Coast tourist resort, which is noted for its fine coastal scenery.

Right: Surfers Paradise, Australia's most highly developed tourist resort on the Gold Coast, south of Brisbane. The Gold Coast is the mecca of winter holiday makers from the Southern States as well as a popular choice for retirement.

Far right: Somerset Dam, on Lake Somerset at Kilcoy, north-west of Brisbane.

South-east Queensland

1 : 2 500 000

COPYRIGHT. GEORGE PHILIP & SON

Brisbane

Brisbane, the capital of Queensland, was established in 1824 near Moreton Bay. Its population was 957 710 in 1976, making it the third largest city in Australia today.

The Brisbane River was discovered by Surveyor-General Oxley, who was dispatched in 1823 by the Colonial Governor, Sir Thomas Brisbane, to find a site suitable for another penal settlement. Early in the next year Oxley reported his finding of the river, which was wide and deep and an ideal location, so an earlier settlement – at Redcliffe on Moreton Bay – was abandoned. In 1826 Brisbane was officially declared a penal settlement and, under the administration of a somewhat ruthless Captain Logan, received prisoners whose crimes were of a serious or repetitious nature.

During the 1830s Brisbane remained essentially a penal settlement, but from 1839-41 this function was reduced. In 1841 land in Brisbane was sold to free settlers for the first time, at an auction in Sydney. The land was sold in 13½ acre lots for £343 per acre. The growth of Brisbane accelerated from this time, with the population concentrated around the present city centre and at Ipswich – then known as Limestone – in the west. Industry was attracted to the area and farming developed nearby where the land was cleared of valuable natural timbers.

The city is located in the south-east corner of Queensland and, like Adelaide, is a great distance from the State's furthest borders. However, again like Adelaide, it is close to that part of the State with the greatest density of rural population. Some 42 per cent of Queensland's population live in Brisbane, a figure somewhat lower than for most of the other States. Sited on the Brisbane River near its mouth in Moreton Bay, most of Brisbane's development has been to the north and south on generally undulating land. Settlements close to the river have sometimes experienced severe flooding after heavy cyclonic rains, causing serious damage to housing and to the central business district's commercial, retail and warehousing establishments. Separate urban developments have taken place at Ipswich – inland on the Bremer River and also subject to flooding – and on the coast at Sandgate and Wynnum.

The city of Brisbane is of a sprawling nature and the river is an obstacle to the planning of roads and railways. Traffic congestion occurs at the three main bridges which link the central business district – concentrated on the north bank – to the suburbs south of the river. The pattern of roads is haphazard when compared with the orderly planning of Melbourne and Adelaide and, like Sydney,

Opposite above: The historic Observatory at Wickham Terrace was built by convict labour in 1829. Once dominating the Brisbane skyline, it is now dwarfed by multi-storey buildings.

Opposite right: The Brisbane River winds around the city, crossed by the South-eastern Freeway (top left) and the Captain Cook Bridge (top right) near the new Queensland Art Centre. The Botanical Gardens stretch down to the river alongside the wharves of the Harbours and Marine Department.

Opposite far right: Queensland University is located in the suburb of St Lucia on a peninsula jutting into the Brisbane River, a short distance from the central city area.

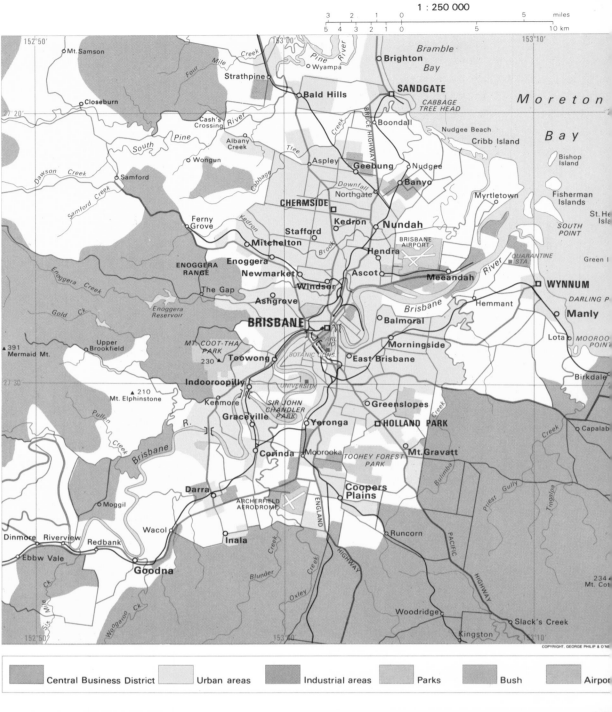

1 : 250 000

| Central Business District | Urban areas | Industrial areas | Parks | Bush | Airport |

transport routes have been influenced by the uneven terrain.

Although the Brisbane River causes flooding and transport problems, it provides the major port for the city and is dredged to take large ships, including oil tankers and ore carriers. Industries, including an oil refinery, are located along the river between the central business district and Moreton Bay, as well as in the outer suburbs to the north and south. However, manufacturing is less important in Brisbane than it is in Sydney, Melbourne or Adelaide, as there is considerable decentralisation of industry to the numerous medium-sized cities and towns in other parts of the State, particularly along the coast.

Brisbane's central business district is located on low-lying land in a meander of the river. The streets were originally laid out to resemble an English village, and as a result of this the streets are straight and narrow — little more than 20 m wide — creating considerable problems for today's motor traffic. Such streets are also unsuited to a semi-tropical climate: there are insufficient trees in the commercial and retail sections of the city to provide shelter from the weather, which is generally hot throughout the year. This problem is increased by the fact that the city frequently experiences long dry seasons, often for many successive years, so that a more conscious effort is required than in the southern states to ensure the growth of young trees and plants.

Brisbane's Botanical Gardens display tropical and sub-tropical plants native to Queensland and places with a similar climate. Other places of interest include the Town Hall, Story Bridge and Redcliffe Peninsula to the east.

A short distance from Brisbane there are many places of interest, often in fact preferred by tourists to the city itself. The Gold Coast is a tourist area stretching 30 km from Southport to Coolangatta, with its major centre at Surfers' Paradise, about 70 km south of Brisbane. There are many hotels and motels close to long sandy surf beaches, making it Australia's most popular holiday resort.

A similar distance to the north is another popular resort area known as the Sunshine Coast, where resort towns such as Caloundra, Mooloolaba and Maroochydore also attract large numbers of tourists. Between Brisbane and the Sunshine Coast are the Glass House Mountains — ancient volcanic plugs surrounded by tropical forests and crops such as pineapple. Only a short distance inland from Brisbane are mountains which are covered with rainforest and deeply dissected by river valleys. Other areas of interest are Lamington National Park in the McPherson Range to the south, the Darling Downs and the city of Toowoomba due west between the Bunya Mountains and Main Range, and the D'Aguilar Range to the north-west.

Australia's Northern Neighbours

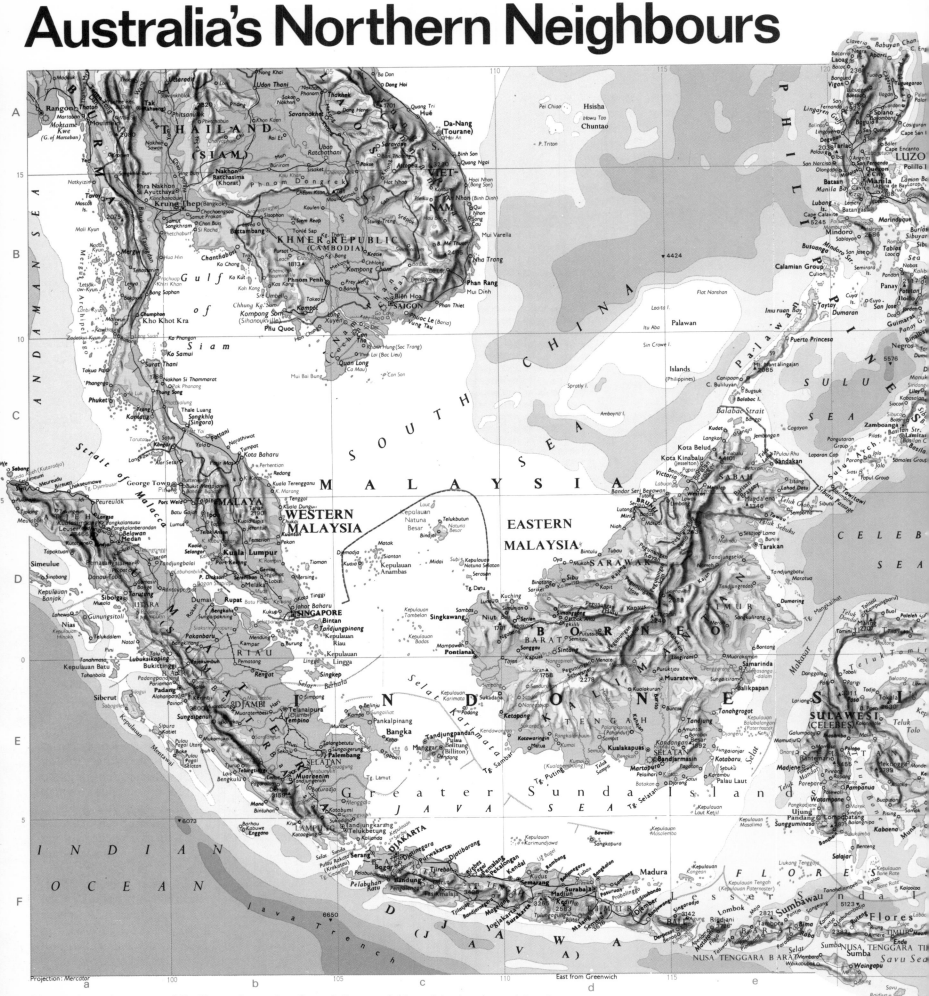

Situated to the east of India and south of China and Japan, is the region called Southeast Asia. Covering a land area of approximately 4 million km² (a little more than half the area of Australia) this region comprises nine countries, five on the mainland (Burma, Thailand, Laos, Cambodia and Vietnam), three island nations (Philippines, Indonesia and Singapore) and the Federation of Malaysia, part mainland and part island.

Much of this region is mountainous or swampy, and the large population on the mainland is concentrated in fertile river valleys associated with the Red, Mekong, Chao Phraya and Irrawaddy Rivers. The island of Java in Indonesia is also heavily populated.

The climate of South-east Asia is essen-tially tropical and is dominated by the mon-soons. These are the rain-bearing winds which change direction on passing over the equator. In summer (June-August) the low pressure system over southern Asia attracts an indraught of air known as the south-west monsoons. These bring heavy rains to Burma, Thailand, Western Malaysia and the Philip-pines. In winter (November-February) the high pressure system over the south Asian land mass forces an outdraught of air which, after its directional change over the equator, becomes the north-west monsoons for north-ern Australia. Indonesia and Singapore are essentially dominated year round by the equatorial low pressure system and the con-vectional rainfall associated with the zone of convergence. Hence, with increasing distance from the equator, uniformly distributed rain-fall gives way to a summer rainfall-winter dry situation. The same principle applies to tem-perature. Those places on or near the equator experience little fluctuation, whilst those places further north experience a peak in summer and a low in winter.

South-east Asia has approximately 270 000 000 people with an annual growth rate of about 2.5 per cent, with the exception of Burma which has only 1.0 per cent. Most of the people live in small villages and are en-gaged in agricultural pursuits. Only a small percentage live in the commercial 'primate'

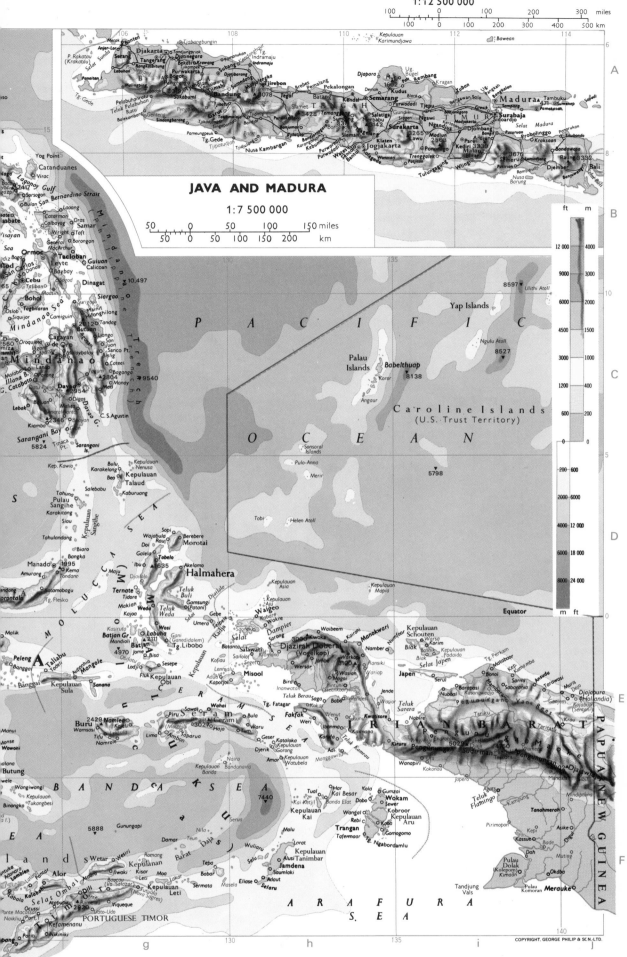

JAVA AND MADURA

1 : 7 500 000

transferred to the local inhabitants. Another form of farming, now involving only a few people and restricted almost entirely to the forested and highlands areas, is shifting cultivation. Here the areas for farming are cleared, burned and cultivated for a period of a few years, then left to return to native growth. The shifting cultivators then move on to new areas where the cycle is repeated.

Most countries rely heavily on tropical crops for their export income. Some minerals occur, notably tin, oil and iron ore, but these are restricted to small pockets. Manufacturing is not widely developed and a heavy industrial base is non-existent, which restricts the development of South-east Asia as a major economic region.

Federation of Malaysia

West Malaysia occupies the Malay Peninsula, south of Thailand and immediately north of Singapore. East Malaysia, comprising the territories of Sabah and Sarawak, lies to the north of Kalimantan. The Federation was established in 1963 and its total area is 332 240 km². West Malaysia is 749 km long and about 322 km wide.

The capital and seat of the elective constitutional monarchy within the British Commonwealth is Kuala Lumpur, with a population of over 875 000 people. West Malaysia is by far the more important of the two sections of Malaysia, economically, politically and strategically.

West Malaysia is a very mountainous area, the main range running north-south, providing a barrier to the rain-bearing winds and to east-west movement. The lowlands are almost exclusively restricted to the coastal plains and are most extensive (32 km wide) along the west coast.

The climate is equatorial modified by monsoonal influences in the north. In summer the south-west monsoon brings heavy rain to the west coast, and the east experiences a dry. In winter the monsoons are from the north-east and provide rain for the east coast. More than 90 per cent of West Malaysia receives over 2000 mm per annum, with many areas well above that figure. With a high cloud cover most of the year, the temperatures on this peninsula are moderate, averaging 25°-28°C.

Despite the abundance of highlands and rainforest (about 75 per cent of the land surface), agriculture is very important to West Malaysia's economy. It provides nearly half the national income and employs about 60 per cent of the workforce. Rubber dominates the economy. It occupies about 65 per cent of the total cultivated area and earns about 60 per cent of the total export income. About 49 per cent of the rubber is produced on large estates, the remaining 51 per cent by smallholdings (farms less than 40 hectares in size). Rubber is concentrated on the west coast from Kedah in the north to Johore in the south.

Rice occupies about 18 per cent of the cultivated area. It is the chief food crop and is grown almost exclusively by the native Malay inhabitants. Improved irrigation facilities and double-cropping have resulted in an increase in rice production but Malaysia is still not self-sufficient. The main areas of rice production are Kedah-Perlis, Perak, Selangor

cities, established generally by colonial Europeans to handle the export of tropical produce to their homelands.

Rice is the staple food crop of South-east Asia. It is ideally suited to the climatic conditions and yields more per hectare than any other crop. Wet rice or *sawah* is the predominant method of growing rice in the well-drained river valleys and terraces on low-lying hillsides, while dry rice (not requiring to stand in saturated soil) is restricted to the uplands. Wet rice producing areas coincide with the areas of greatest population density. Only Burma, Thailand and Vietnam produce sufficient quantities of rice to export

a surplus: as in the other countries of South-east Asia rice is for subsistence.

Commercial agriculture is very important to the region as a whole. Rubber, copra, palm oil, tea and coffee are the main products, together with timber. Most of these crops are grown by smallholders, often in conjunction with subsistence rice. The cash received from the sale of these crops provides necessities such as clothing, improved housing, implements and education. Apart from the widespread production by smallholders, many of these cash crops are grown on commercial estates, originally set up and operated by large European colonial companies. Now the areas of estate farming have been restricted and in the main the operations have been

Australia's Northern Neighbours

and along the Kelantan delta. Other major crops in West Malaysia are oil palm, pineapples and coconuts.

Mining is an important activity in West Malaysia which is the world's biggest tin producer, most of this being produced in the area between Ipoh and Kuala Lumpur on the west coast. Iron ore and bauxite are also mined and exported. Processing industries are the main form of manufacturing activity. There is very little true heavy industry.

Malaysia is a plural society. Of the 11 million inhabitants, 9 million are found in West Malaysia and of these 50 per cent are Malays, 37 per cent are Chinese and 11 per cent are of Indian descent. The Malays and Indians tend to be scattered throughout the rural areas whilst the Chinese concentrate in the large cities. Seventy-five per cent of Malaysia's population can be found in a 65 km-wide band along the west coast from Perlis to Johore.

Indonesia

This group of more than 3000 islands extends along the equator between Asia and Australia, south of Malaysia. With a total population in excess of 125 million the republic has a total land area of 1 491 562 km². Its capital, Jakarta, situated on the island of Java, has a population of 5 200 000.

One of the most remarkable facets of Indonesia is the contrast in population densities. Sixty per cent of the total population lives on the fertile, volcanic island of Java, with a density in excess of 3025 people per km². The other areas average only 160 people per km², with many localities as low as 15.

Java, although not the largest of the Indonesian islands, is the most important. Its temperatures are high throughout the year and its rainfall is accentuated by the monsoons, notably in November through to January. About half of Java is cultivated while the rest is unsuited to agriculture because of poor soils or steep slopes. Although various food crops are grown, wet rice is by far the most important. Double cropping and terracing on the slopes are extensive. To the Javanese smallholder coconuts are an important cash crop. On the plantations rubber is the most significant product, with tea, coffee, sugar cane, palm oil, cocoa and tobacco as other important cash crops. Jakarta, Bandung, Surabaya, Semarang and Jogjakarta are the main cities, although most people live in rural areas.

Sumatra is more than three times the size of Java, yet it has only one quarter of Java's population. Here, where the population pressure on the land is not as great, plantation agriculture is more important. Tobacco and tea are important estate crops. Shifting cultivation techniques are practised by 20 per cent of the people in the tropical forests. Padang, Bukit Tinggi, Palembang and Medan are the main urban centres.

Bali, to the east of Java, is a very small island that has developed a very successful tourist industry because of its picturesque way of life and its traditional handicrafts.

Singapore

Singapore, the tiny island (40 km wide and 24 km long) nestling 1.2 km south of West Malaysia, and only 128 km north of the equator, is the economic hub of South-east Asia.

The city of Singapore, with about 2 million people, is situated at the mouth of the Singapore River. Its ideal location has promoted the role of Singapore as one of the largest entrepot ports in the world. Many of its goods are imported in a raw or semi-processed state, then further processed, finished, packed and re-exported to world markets. Similarly, manufactured goods are imported in bulk, broken-up and re-exported in smaller units for distribution throughout South-east Asia. The import and export trade is mainly in the hands of Chinese and Indians.

The island of Singapore consists of more than the city. Although agricultural land is limited by poor soils and swamps, rubber, coconuts, vegetables and fruits are produced. Rubber occupies 66 per cent of the cultivated land. Fishing is also very important around the island.

Industry is generally limited in size and scope but with expected high levels of unemployment as a result of the relative decline of trade and other factors, the Jurong Industrial Estate, developed on former swampland in the south-west of the island, will provide many employment opportunities. Iron and steel and textiles are the basis of this development.

Philippines

This group of 7107 islands (only 2773 of which are named) has a total land area of 299 764 km². Luzon, with 104 688 km², is the largest island. Quezon City, a suburb of Manila, is now the official capital, although the seat of the republic remains in Manila, which has a metropolitan population in excess of 3 500 000, out of a national total of approximately 37 250 000.

The Philippines stretch between 5° and 20° North and experience temperatures which vary between 24°C and 30°C. The moderating effect of the sea is felt everywhere and keeps the temperature range quite small. The rainy season is from June to November associated with the south-west monsoons. To the north in December through to May north-east trade winds bring rain to the east coast. In northern Luzon typhoons are frequent.

Cultivation of the land is the most important activity in the Philippines. The crops which are cultivated are much the same as in the rest of South-east Asia with one exception. Rubber-growing is of little significance since the pronounced dry season in many parts of the islands and the cooler temperatures of the north do not favour its cultivation. Rice is the staple food crop, taking almost 40 per cent of the cultivated land. Luzon is the most important rice area, especially the Manila Plain. Maize is the second food crop of the Philippines. Coconuts cover a greater area than any other cash crop and their products are the most important export. Sugar, abaca (Manila hemp) and tobacco are other important export crops.

Other Mainland Countries

Burma: The republic of Burma has about 28 million people, nearly 2 million of them living in the capital, Rangoon. Being further from the equator than Malaysia it has more pronounced seasons, the monsoonal rains coming from May to mid-October. The heaviest population concentrations coincide with the fertile agricultural areas in the Irrawaddy valley.

Thailand: Bangkok, with approximately 3 million inhabitants out of a total population

of 36 million, is the capital of Thailand. The most important agricultural region is the Menam lowland and delta where the flat land and fertile alluvial soil form the basis for one of the most important 'rice bowls' of Asia. The monsoon forests of the north yield valuable stands of teak.

Cambodia: Phnom-Penh, with a population of about 700 000, is the capital of this picturesque country of rice paddies, sugar and rubber plantations.

Laos: The capital, Vientiane, lies on the Mekong River in the west, which is the most prosperous agricultural area and where most of the 3 million inhabitants live. Much of the country is wild and mountainous, with thick jungles and no roads.

Vietnam: At the end of the Vietnam war North and South Vietnam combined into one nation. Ho Chi Minh City (formerly Saigon) with about 2 500 000 inhabitants is the largest city on the mainland of South-east Asia. The Mekong River delta is one of the most important agricultural areas, as is the Red River Basin in the north.

Right: A section of the old Chinese quarter of Singapore which blends in with modern architectural styles in the distance. In the old areas the living quarters are very cramped. Food is bought fresh from the busy stalls.

Below: Rice terraces near Ubud, central Bali, Indonesia. The rice fields are flooded before the seedlings are transported from the nursery. The field in the foreground has been recently harvested, while other fields are in various stages of production.

Opposite below: Singapore harbour is the largest in South-east Asia and is testimony to her role as an entrepot port. Goods are brought in in a raw or semi-processed state, further processed, then re-exported throughout the world.

Islands of the West Pacific

With the exception of Guam and the Solomon Islands, which are north of the equator, all the island groups in the map opposite lie between latitudes 13° and 22° South. All can be generally classed as tropical and most are formed from coral and volcanoes.

Fiji

The Fijian islands are scattered over nearly 259 000 km² of ocean in the south-west Pacific, approximately 3200 km from Sydney and midway between Samoa and New Caledonia. The population is estimated to be about 530 000, comprising native Fijians, East Indians and Europeans.

Viti Levu, which is the largest of the 322 islands, covers 11 386 km². Suva, the capital of this independent Commonwealth nation, lies to the south-east of Viti Levu and has about 62 000 people.

The coolest period is April to November, with a possible minimum of 16°C. In the height of summer temperatures are usually pleasant at around 25-30°C. Rainfall is spread throughout the year with a slight maximum in the period January through April. Rain generally occurs in mid-afternoon after a heavy cloud build-up and is followed by periods of dazzling sunshine.

The main land use activities are the growing of tropical crops, especially copra, bananas and sugar cane.

New Caledonia

New Caledonia is situated midway between Australia and Fiji, at a latitude of 22 degrees South. The island is 400 km long and about 48 km wide. Approximately 112 000 people live on the island, half of whom are European French, the rest native Melanesians, Polynesians, Wallisians, Vietnamese and Indonesians.

New Caledonia is an overseas French Territory with its capital, Noumea, situated in the south-west of the island.

This island was discovered by Captain Cook in 1774 but annexed by the French in 1854. With its natural beauty, sandy beaches, French food and hot climate, New Caledonia has all the elements for a vacation, but the local inhabitants are also busily involved with the island's prosperous nickel mining and processing.

The climate is hot and wet throughout the year with a pronounced summer maximum of about 32°C.

Tahiti

Tahiti is a tropical island in the south-central Pacific Ocean, belonging to France. It is one of the Society Islands group, a part of French Polynesia. The island covers an area of 1036 km² and has a population of about 76 000 people, mainly Polynesians and mixed Polynesian and French. The capital, Papeete, has only 24 500 people.

The island of Moorea, the top of an extinct volcano which rises steeply from the bed of the Pacific Ocean. It is separated from the island of Tahiti by a 12 km-wide channel. Pinnacles of basalt dominate the skyline while palm-fringed bays owe their placid beauty to the reef which lies just off shore.

Tahiti is mountainous, volcanic in origin, and is encircled by a coral reef. Swimming, skin diving and fishing are ideally suited to this setting. The combination of French sophistication and unquenchable Polynesian gaiety, together with the scenic beauty, makes Tahiti a haven for tourists, who are now the island's main source of income.

The climate is warm and inviting with an average high temperature for each month of 30°-32°C. Rain is spread fairly evenly throughout the year although if there is a 'dry' season, it is from April to October.

The English navigator, Samuel Wallis, discovered Tahiti in 1767. Captain Cook later visited it and named the group the Society Islands, while France made them a protectorate in 1843 and a colony in 1880.

Samoan Islands

Samoa is a group of 16 islands in the South Pacific Ocean with a total area of 3039 km². The islands are mountainous and have fertile volcanic soil.

Samoa is divided politically into two parts. The western islands form the independent nation of Western Samoa. Its capital Apia, on Upolu Island, has about 29 500 people out of a total population of 145 000. Western Samoa belonged to Germany from 1900 to 1914, then New Zealand administered it until independence in 1962. It is now a member of the British Commonwealth. Its main sources of income, apart from tourism, are bananas and copra.

The eastern islands in the group comprise American Samoa, a territory administered by the United States Department of the Interior, which appoints a Governor. The US acquired these islands in 1900 and Swains Island was added in 1925. American Samoa has approximately 28 500 people, with 10 000 of these in Pago Pago, the capital on Tutuila Island. Again the main income is derived from tourism.

The climate is beautiful with a year long summer, averaging 30°C each month. Heaviest rainfall occurs from December to March.

New Hebrides

The New Hebrides comprise 73 islands with 14 763 km² of land area, approximately 17° South of the equator. The islands are mountainous with fine sandy coral beaches.

The New Hebrides are administered by Britain and France, both governments being represented by High Commissioners. There is a population of about 83 000 inhabitants, made up of Melanesians, Polynesians, Asians, French, British and Australians. Vila, the capital on the island of Efate, has a population of only 3200.

The climate is very pleasant, averaging a high of 30°C throughout the year with a fairly uniform tropical rainfall. Showers in late afternoon are frequent.

The main land use activities are copra, cocoa, coffee, timber and various other tropical crops. Tourism is a major source of the islands' income.

Tonga

Blessed with a benign climate, abundant food and a long succession of wise rulers, the small kingdom of Tonga was well named 'The Friendly Islands' by Captain Cook in 1773. Although independent, the kingdom has been under British protection since 1900.

This group is composed of 150 islands, 36 of them inhabited, which divide into three groups, Tongatapu, Haapai (low-lying coral formations) and Vavau. Nuku'alofa, on the major island of Tongatapu, is the seat of government and has 18 000 people.

Tongan handicrafts sought after by tourists include tapa cloth, handwoven baskets, woodcarving and jewellery. Copra is the chief export crop.

Solomon Islands

These are a group of islands just north of the equator in the West Pacific, to the east of Papua New Guinea. Bougainville and Buka are part of Papua New Guinea, whilst the remaining islands constitute the British

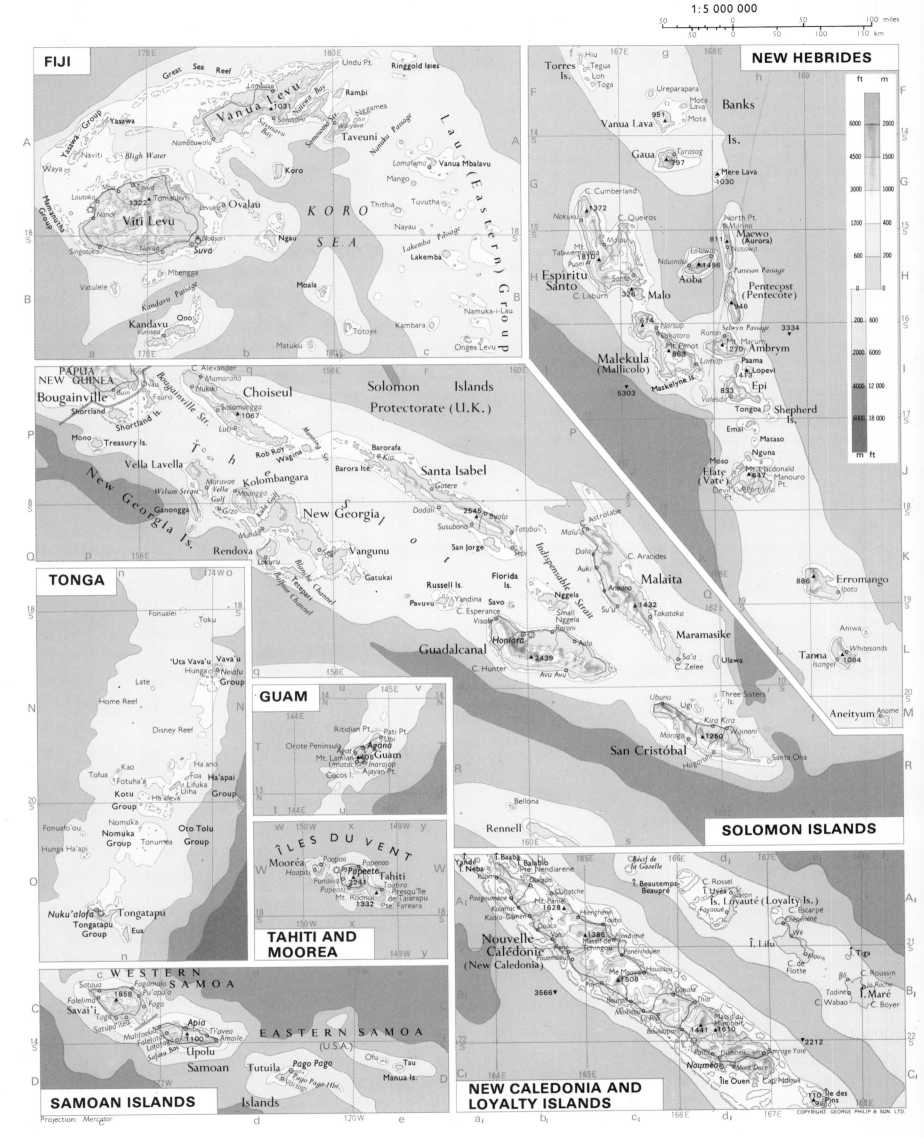

FIJI

NEW HEBRIDES

1:5 000 000

TONGA

GUAM

TAHITI AND MOOREA

SOLOMON ISLANDS

SAMOAN ISLANDS

NEW CALEDONIA AND LOYALTY ISLANDS

Solomon Islands Protectorate. It includes Ysabel, Choiseul, Guadalcanal, Malaita and numerous small islands such as the Santa Cruz and Omtong Java groups.

Ebony, sandalwood, pearl shells and copra are the main exports.

Guam

Guam is an island situated 13° North of the equator to the north of New Guinea. It is only 48 km long and 8 to 12 km wide yet has over 110 000 people, many of whom are military personnel.

The capital is Agana, with a population of 2700, and the island is an unincorporated United States Territory. The northern part of the island, closed to civilians, is occupied by Andersen Air Force Base.

Papua New Guinea: a New Nation

Papua New Guinea is a new underdeveloped nation situated in the equatorial zone immediately to the north of Australia. It is an island country, comprising the eastern half of the large island of New Guinea and over 600 smaller islands, the most significant being New Britain, New Ireland, Manus and Bougainville. In all, Papua New Guinea extends 2000 km from east to west and 1200 km from north to south.

The Physical Landscape

Papua New Guinea is dominated by its mountainous backbone and the swampy lowlands which are more extensive on the mainland.

The mountain backbone is a very steep, rugged mass dominated in the west central area by fold mountains of which Mt Wilhelm (4706 m) is the highest. In this vicinity a number of roughly parallel ranges are separated by deep, wide valleys, often 2000 m deep and 20 km wide.

North of the Central Highlands, fringing the northern coastline, are more mountain ranges. A deep trough separates these from the Central Highlands and along this flow the Sepik and Ramu rivers. These northern mountains are part of the same complex which extends into the north-eastern islands of New Britain and Bougainville.

In the south-east extension of the mainland the main cordillera is named the Owen Stanley Range. It was across this range that Australian troops made the Kokoda Trail in World War II.

Many of the mountains are recently formed and on the flanks of the northern ranges of the mainland, and in the islands, there are a number of volcanoes, some of which are still active. The last volcanic eruption, in 1951 from Mt Lamington in the Owen Stanleys, killed several thousand people and wiped out many mountainside villages. Eastern Papua New Guinea forms part of the Pacific 'Rim of Fire', stretching from Japan to New Zealand.

There are really only two great lowland areas in Papua New Guinea, lying north and south of the Central Highlands. As both areas contain vast amounts of swamp, created by the huge meandering rivers, neither are of great economic importance.

The smaller islands that are not volcanic are generally coral atolls or coral platforms. They are not well developed and are sparsely populated.

In the volcanic areas the lava weathers to a fertile soil. This process is facilitated by the high rainfall, high humidity and high temperatures. When the natural equatorial rainforests are cleared, however, the fertility is quickly lost through increased surface rain penetration and consequent erosion. Towards the upper slopes the rainforest starts to thin out, to be replaced by open woodland. In the deep valleys grasslands are dominant. Mangroves and swamp vegetation characterise the low-lying coastal areas.

Climate

Due to its position near the equator, Papua New Guinea does not experience extremes in climate. Rainfall is abundant and spread throughout the year, although January to April is generally slightly wetter than May to August. The rainfall distribution pattern is governed by the moist equatorial air mass and the highlands. A little uplift produces a lot of rain.

The period November to April sees the indraught of air from the north-west bringing the wet monsoons. In May to August the sun's relative position is over the Tropic of Cancer and Papua New Guinea experiences an airstream from the south-east, bringing rainfall to the south-eastern areas.

Generally, all places receive over 1900 mm, with many localities experiencing as much as 5000 mm. In the area north of Port Moresby, which is relatively dry (1000 mm), the ranges tend to run parallel to the prevailing winds so little uplift, and hence little precipitation, results.

Temperatures are moderately high throughout the year with little variation in any one place. The main influence on temperature variation is topography. On the lowlands the temperature range is from 24-30°C at 9.00 a.m. to 30-32°C at 3.00 p.m. At an elevation of 2000 metres temperatures are about 10-12°C cooler.

Population Distribution

About 75 per cent of Papua New Guinea's 2.5 million people live on the mainland, with the remaining 25 per cent scattered around the many small islands.

Generally the population is scattered around the coastline, or in areas of the Central Highlands above 1700 m where the climate is more pleasant. The main concentrations are: the Central Highlands (1 000 000), the Torricelli Mountains west of Wewak (150 000), the Huon Peninsula of the mainland (160 000), the Madang-Adelbert Mountains (100 000), the Gazelle Peninsula near Rabaul (70 000) and Port Moresby area (60 000).

In the Chimbu valley the population density can be as high as 120-160 persons per

Opposite: Koki and Walter Bay, Port Moresby. Koki is a large native food market on the beach at Koki Bay, a small inner bay of Walter Bay.

Below: Sawtooth mountains, Markham valley. These impressive mountains of the Saruwaged Range have been subjected to tremendous land movements which have sheered off whole ridges.

Papua New Guinea: a New Nation

km², due to the presence of fertile volcanic soils.

The People and Language

The indigenous people in Papua New Guinea can be very broadly categorised into three main groups: the Papuans (dark-skinned and longheaded); Melanesians (taller and generally lighter-skinned than Papuans); Negritos (dark-brown skins, short bodies and short fuzzy hair). Such an ethnic grouping is now not as distinct as it was since there has been a great deal of intermarriage.

More pronounced than the ethnic groupings are the many dialects spoken in Papua New Guinea. Investigators so far have classified more than 500 dialects. This has been the result of the impenetrable country providing barriers to movement. The three most common languages are Pidgin (now deemed the 'official' language), English and Motu.

Rural Land Use

Papua New Guinea is still governed by the traditional life style. The family unit and subsistence farming reign supreme. Less than five per cent of the total population are wholly or mainly dependent on a money income for the basic necessities of life.

Shifting cultivation is the most common and widespread form of farming. Here a plot of land is cleared of its forest growth, sown with root crops, harvested, then abandoned and allowed to return to natural growth. This principle ensures that soil fertility is restored in the absence of fertilisers or scientific techniques. Also it would be practically impossible to grow crops for more than a couple of years as the surface soil would be washed away by the abundant rains.

In the highlands the main root crop of the shifting cultivator is the sweet potato, while in the lowlands it tends to be taro, yams or cassava. Secondary foods are also eaten, the most widespread of these being bananas, peanuts, sugar cane, maize and coconuts.

In some areas primitive hunting and gathering continues, the emphasis being on the coastal areas where fish are freely caught.

Commercial farming is confined to a number of small areas and is restricted at this stage to about 280 000 indigenous smallholders, many adopting it as an adjunct to subsistence farming. The main cash crops produced by smallholders are copra, cocoa, coffee, pyrethrum and passionfruit.

Non-indigenous commercial agriculture is dominated by copra and operated by Europeans. There are presently about 500 plantations covering a total of about 100 000 hectares. Other important commercial crops are rubber, cocoa and coffee. Coconuts are planted on more than 90 per cent of the area of the plantations. The main plantation areas are the Bismarck Archipelago (coconuts) and inland from Port Moresby (rubber).

Mining and Manufacturing

Until the early 1970s the only mineral being mined was gold. Deposits of oil and coal are known, or still being explored, but they are either too small, too low-grade or too inaccessible to be worked profitably.

In 1972 production commenced at Pan-guna on Bougainville on an open-cut copper mine. Conzinc Riotinto of Australia spent many years investigating the quality and extent of the copper and although the ore is low grade the deposit is estimated to contain 900 million tonnes of ore.

Now Bougainville Copper are producing some 80 000 tonnes of ore a day for processing into concentrated form for sale to smelters in Japan and Europe. To facilitate the extraction of ore a new town for 4000 people was constructed at Panguna, together with a new port and power station at Arawa Bay. Copper mining is now Papua New Guinea's largest industry.

Most other manufacturing industry is on a very small scale, controlled by Europeans, and situated in small pockets in the main urban centres. Sawmilling and coconut oil production are the two main processing industries.

History

New Guinea was first sighted by Europeans in 1511 but many years passed before they settled in the country. In the seventeenth century Tasman sailed along the coast of New Ireland and Dampier discovered New Britain. Cook rediscovered Torres Strait between Australia and New Guinea in 1770. By the end of the 1870s the Germans had set up a trading station on the Gazelle Peninsula. At this time the Queensland Government claimed southern New Guinea as a British possession, as they feared the German development. The British Government rejected the claim, however, and Germany continued its exploitation by establishing the New Guinea Company. This activity caused the British Government to change its mind and in 1884 at Port Moresby Britain claimed as a protectorate what came to be called Papua. This became a crown colony in 1888.

However, the British were still not really interested in development and in 1906 Papua became an Australian Territory.

At the same time that the British acted in 1884 the Germans established a protectorate over the northern half of what is now Papua New Guinea. In 1910 Rabaul became the capital of the German administration.

After World War 1 the Australians wanted to annex German New Guinea, mainly for defence reasons against possible Japanese movements. The League of Nations granted a mandate over this area and it became Australian New Guinea or the Mandated Territory of New Guinea. By 1921 most German settlers and farmers had left and their properties were shared among Australian ex-servicemen.

During World War II the Japanese, after taking Rabaul as their operations base, aimed at Port Moresby, as a starting point for an invasion of Australia. The Australian forces managed to avert the tide and halt the Japanese advance in the Owen Stanleys. From that point the Japanese retreated along the Kokoda Trail and in September 1945 surrendered to the Allied Command near Wewak.

After the war the administrations of the two territories were combined and the Territory of Papua New Guinea created. In 1973 the country became semi-independent with the Australian Government continuing to operate the functions of defence.

Independence and the Future

In 1975 Papua New Guinea became a fully independent country and has subsequently been admitted as a member of the United Nations. However, the severance of ties pol-

itically with Australia — her protector since World War I — does not mean economic independence. Papua New Guinea still has a long way to go as a developing nation. Both the home and export markets, with their transactions based on money, need to be developed so that the local inhabitants can substitute working for wages for their subsistence existence. In essence this means changing the traditional basis of society: the family, the village and the form of cultivation.

Although the Government can provide stimuli to development in the form of improved roads and communications, agricultural machinery and educational facilities, this will be of little avail until the local people convert to a money economy.

A gradual change from subsistence production is taking place — it accounted for 35 per cent of the population in 1974, compared with 63 per cent in 1960.

The Government of Papua New Guinea is aware of the problems and is doing everything in its power to direct the new nation into a twentieth-century economy.

Below left: Manus Island is the largest of the Admiralty Group east of the main island of Papua New Guinea. The people live mostly in villages close to or over the sea and build magnificent ocean-going outrigger canoes which can carry up to four large square sails.

Opposite: Mt Koglokobugo from Mt Galmabondi. Seismic activity has produced some dramatic landscapes like this one in the Chimbu District. In spite of the steepness native women cultivate the slopes to grow sweet potatoes for their families.

Below: Rabaul, the administrative centre and major port of New Britain, is situated on magnificent Simpson Harbour and is dominated by five volcanic cones.

New Zealand: Land of Contrasts

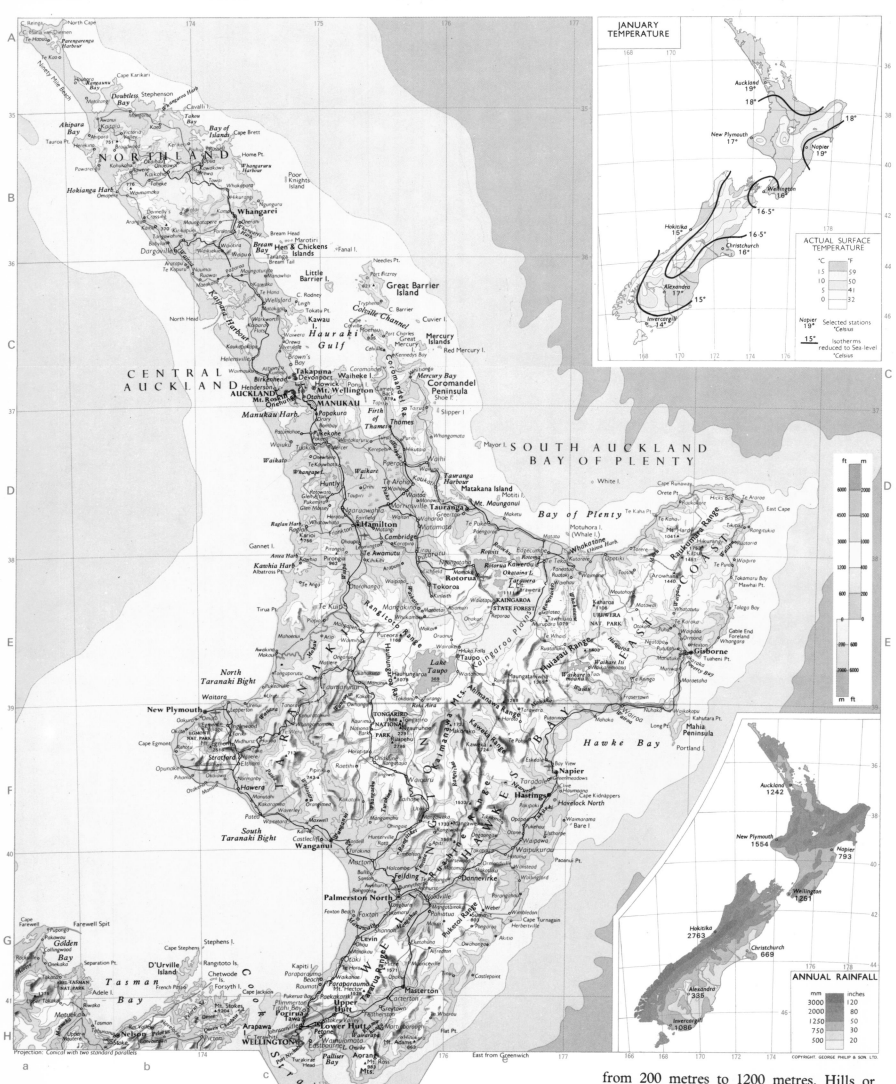

New Zealand is essentially a thriving rural area set in a situation dominated by mountains, lakes, rivers and glaciers. To the traveller, the thriving cities and small, evenly dispersed settlements provide a necessary respite from the awe-inspiring landscape, overwhelming in its magnitude.

The Physical Landscape

New Zealand is a mountainous land, with two-thirds of the country varying in height from 200 metres to 1200 metres. Hills or mountains form the background to almost every view. There are some 225 peaks over 2300 metres, with 17 peaks in the South Island exceeding 3050 metres and Mt Cook, the highest, rising to 3764 metres. Lowlands of gently undulating surface make up only nine per cent of the country.

Compared with the geological stability of

JULY
TEMPERATURE
1:16 000 000

ACTUAL SURFACE
TEMPERATURE

GEOLOGY
1:16 000 000

QUATERNARY Sands, gravels, moraines
TERTIARY Sandstone, mudstone, siltstone
CRETACEOUS ..
JURASSIC & Greywacke, argillite
TRIASSIC
PALAEOZOIC Mainly undifferentiated greywacke
PRE-CAMBRIAN ..
METAMORPHIC & Granite, gneiss, schists
PLUTONIC
VOLCANIC & Basalts
INTRUSIVE

1:2 700 000

Projection: Conical with two standard parallels

COPYRIGHT: GEORGE PHILIP & SON. LTD.

Australia, New Zealand lies on the 'mobile belt' encircling the Pacific. This belt is a narrow zone of recent mountain-building, earthquakes and volcanic activity, extending through New Guinea, the Philippines, Japan and the western slopes of North and South America. In terms of geological time the uplifting processes in New Zealand are quite recent — within the last one or two million years. Surface erosion has been particularly rapid, producing the rugged, jagged outlines so characteristic of the South Island in particular.

The detailed features of the land surface have been moulded by many processes; by huge glaciers in the South Island during the Ice Ages (some are still actively eroding and modifying the surface); by intense rainfall, high runoff and swift-flowing streams; by the intense cold in the mountains producing alternate freeze-thaw conditions in the soil and rock face; by earth movements on an unprecedented scale, especially in the North Island; and by volcanic eruptions which produced an extensive plateau and scores of volcanic cones, many still active.

New Zealand is a land of great contrast.

145

New Zealand: Land of Contrasts

Everywhere is evidence of its geological youth, serenely interspersed with the lush farming lowlands created by alluvial fill matured into fertile soil.

Climate

New Zealand experiences an insular climate modified by its rugged mountainous backbone. Its rainfall is generally high and well distributed throughout the year and extremely reliable. Together with its mild temperatures, the pattern is typical of its mid-latitude oceanic position.

Although no part of New Zealand experiences a marked dry season or prolonged drought, there are certainly great differences and rapid changes in the climatic pattern longitudinally. Totals vary from 330 mm in the sheltered basins of Central Otago to more than 7620 mm on the western slopes of the Southern Alps. Due to the north-south alignment of the mountain ranges places on the western slopes are exposed to the prevailing westerly weather systems, bringing cool wet conditions from the Tasman Sea. Those places in the intermontane basins and immediately to the east of the main range are in a rain-shadow zone, ensuring much lower total rainfalls. Topography does not have the same degree of influence on the rainfall totals in the North Island as the mountains are not as high or as continuous. In general most inhabited areas of the North and South Islands receive annual rainfalls of between 635 mm and 1520 mm.

There is a gradual decrease in the mean annual temperature from north to south, the result of a general movement away from the zone of maximum heat. In the area below 300 metres, where practically all New Zealanders live, temperatures are moderate, few extremes of heat or cold being experienced. In the South Island snow is common above 300 metres, but seldom falls on the eastern plains.

In the South Island, the western slopes often experience torrential storms of high intensity, resulting in severe flooding. The rivers, generally having a regular flow with little variation from month to month, are sometimes unable to cope with the flood discharge and damage can be severe.

Agriculture

The agricultural scene of New Zealand is dominated by the grazing industries. Arable farming, that is, the growing of crops, is much less important. The products of the pastoral industries provide 86 per cent of the value of farm production while crops, fruit-growing and market gardening account for only 14 per cent.

The great crop in New Zealand is grass. With the natural resources of the land — the fertility of the soil, the mild winters of the North Island, the adequate rainfall well distributed throughout the year and the many hours of sunshine — together with the scien-

Above: Wellington, New Zealand's wind-swept capital city, is clustered on the small amount of flat land on the harbour's edge.

Opposite: Mt Cook, New Zealand's highest peak, is a major drawcard for Australian as well as local skiers.

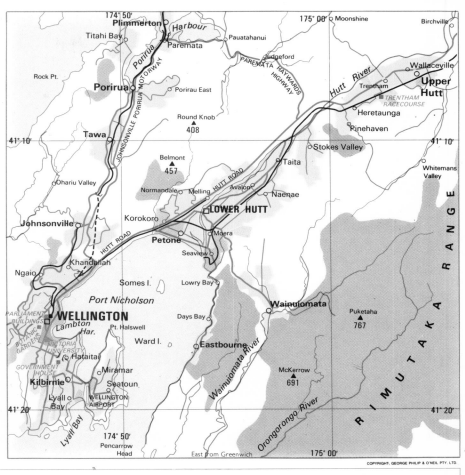

| Central Business District | Urban areas | Industrial areas | Parks | Bush | Airport |

tific development and maintenance of pastures, New Zealand is the third biggest sheep country in the world (exceeded only by Australia and the Soviet Union) and its dairy cows earn a large proportion of its export income.

Grass covers 47 per cent of the country and 71 per cent of what is classified as 'occupied farmland'. Most of the unimproved land not in farms is in the more mountainous South Island. There are two main types of grassland — grassland improved with sown grasses (mostly in the North Island), and native grasses such as tussock (mostly in the South Island). The sown grasses and clovers are by far the more important because they support 95 per cent of the livestock of the country. The most highly productive areas of sown grassland do not cover large areas; they are found in lowland areas and carry 17-25 ewes per hectare together with some cattle, or at least 2-3 dairy cows all year.

New Zealand soils are not naturally grassland soils and most were originally under a forest cover. Their fertility is a product of expert agricultural experimentation and scientific farm management. The spreading of phosphate and lime fertilisers (often by air), the sowing of seed, spraying of weeds and dropping of fencing materials by aircraft have all become standard features of New Zealand farming.

A highly-organised system of marketing has also contributed to the efficiency of New Zealand farming. The Wool Marketing Corporation, Meat Producers' Board and a dairy producers' organisation control the quality and regulate the export sales of the farmers.

The productivity of New Zealand farming is the result of capital and technological innovations rather than the application of large amounts of labour. New Zealand farms are mostly family owned and operated, encouraged by government legislation.

Sheep: New Zealand's large production of wool has been made possible by the skilful use of mountain grasslands for extensive pastoralism. The size of farm units is large and the inputs of capital and labour per hectare are low, as is the output of products per hectare. These holdings of between 2000 and 200 000 hectares, with a carrying capacity of about one sheep to 2.5 hectares, are called high country 'runs', the counterpart of Australian outback 'stations'. There are about 240 such sheep runs occupying some 3.5 million hectares in the South Island high country and producing more than half of the nation's fine wool.

A characteristic feature of high run farming is the practice of transhumance. The sheep are pastured in the summer on the higher slopes and brought down to winter quarters in April before the first of the heavy snows.

In the lower areas of the South Island, and generally throughout the North Island, sheep are also important for their meat. Fat lambs and fat sheep in many instances are taking over from sheep for wool, and have joined forces with dairy cattle in the extreme southern and northern areas of the North Island.

Dairying: The average size of the 26 000 farms classified as predominantly dairy is only 60 hectares. Because farms are so small, high outputs are required to make the units economic. Between 200 and 400 kilograms of butterfat per hectare per year are gained from these farms. To get such a high production the inputs per hectare of capital in the form of machinery, buildings, fertiliser and livestock are high.

In 1970 dairying contributed 23 per cent of New Zealand's gross farm income, second only to meat production as the major primary industry. Dairying is concentrated in the North Island: North Auckland, South Auckland, Taranaki and Wellington contain 87 per

cent of the nation's dairy cattle.

Mixed Farming in the Canterbury Plains: Mixed crop-livestock farming is a complex operation requiring a sound knowledge of livestock and of crop cultivation. It is an intensive system of agriculture requiring large amounts of capital and machinery per hectare. The intensity of farming is reflected in the high degree of investment in saleyards, freezing works, wool stores and flour mills and in the tight network of communications linking the small communities of the Canterbury Plains.

The Canterbury Plains region is located in the central east of the South Island, between the High Country and the Pacific Ocean. Generally it is quite flat with a gentle slope towards the coast.

With an annual rainfall of about 850 mm per year, this is one of the driest areas of New Zealand. It is the main crop-growing region with an increasing amount of the crops being for livestock fodder rather than for direct sale as grain. Nearly 70 per cent of the country's grain and seed crops are grown here, and the region contains more than 10 per cent of the sheep in the country.

The Movement North

Since 1900 the North Island has increased in population far more rapidly than the South Island. Seventy per cent of the people live in the North Island where the density is 16.6 persons per km² compared with 30 per cent and 5.2 persons per km² in the South Island. Ninety-five per cent of the Maori population now lives in the North Island. The reasons for this uneven distribution lie with the attractions of Auckland with its employment opportunities, its markets, its flow of traffic as the focus of world air and sea routes, as well as its warm climate.

The second major trend in New Zealand is

New Zealand: Land of Contrasts

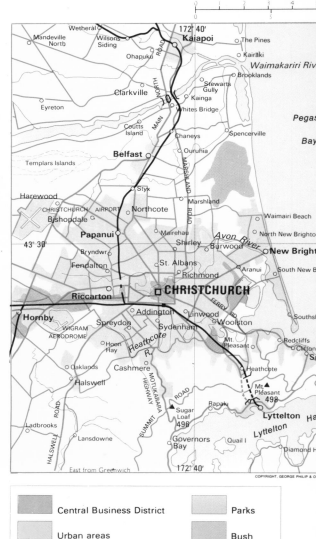

1:250 000

COPYRIGHT. GEORGE PHILIP & O'NE

Central Business District   Parks

Urban areas   Bush

Industrial areas   Airport

the movement from rural to urban areas. As in other Western countries, there has been no increase in the rural population and its density varies mainly according to the productivity of farming. The reasons for this are those that are common to all areas of Western agriculture, namely: farm mechanisation and the trend towards larger farms for the more efficient use of farm equipment, a high productivity per person and high wage levels for farm labour, the expansion of industry in the large urban centres, and the expanding desire for more and more services that are functions of urban areas.

Today, only about 14 per cent of New Zealand's labour force is required in rural pursuits or in 'primary producing' industries. Manufacturing industries account for 35 per cent of the labour force, while 51 per cent are involved in commerce, transport and service activities.

Population Growth

Although New Zealand is often termed a 'multi-racial' society, it is far more homogeneous than most countries to which this term is applied.

European settlement, long delayed after Tasman's first look at New Zealand in 1642, began after Cook's visit in the 1770s. At this time there were probably in the order of 200 000 Maoris, at least 90 per cent of them living in the North Island. Initially the relationships between the Maoris and the small numbers of missionaries, whalers, sealers and traders were quite good. Yet, through trading in flax and firearms, and with the introduction of European diseases, half the Maori population was wiped out between 1800 and 1850.

With the rapid influx of settlers, gold miners and sheepmen, land alienation took place at an unprecedented pace. The Maoris resisted and a period of continual warfare resulted (1860-1872), causing the Maori numbers to drop to about 40 000 at the end

of the nineteenth century. Since this time, however, the Maoris have been experiencing a high rate of natural increase and at the 1971 census there were 227 000, or 11 per cent of the total population. If the rate of increase continues, by the end of this century Maoris will account for about 15 per cent of the total population. A new flow of Pacific islanders into the Auckland region is adding to the ethnic diversity.

In 1971 there were 3 million people, with a fast growth rate of 2.1 per cent a year. The population is concentrated (70 per cent) in the North Island, and, even more striking, 40 per cent of the total population is grouped in the province of Auckland. Auckland city is the largest urban settlement with nearly 605 000 people. Other cities with a large population are Wellington (301 000), Christchurch (260 000) and Dunedin (110 000). The only other cities with more than 40 000 people are Hamilton (72 000), Palmerston North (53 000), Invercargill (50 000), Napier (48 000) and Hastings (41 000).

Industry

Like most other developed countries, New Zealand's industries are very important in determining the pattern of population distribution. In 1970 about 35 per cent of the labour force was engaged in manufacturing industries.

Yet, unlike most other Western countries, New Zealand is still 'rural based', in that the size of her total population (three million) and her reliance on the wool-dairy-meat sector necessarily preclude the establishment of vast heavy industries, although there are some recent new developments in this line.

Industry in New Zealand is intimately linked with and dependent on the farming sector which produces large quantities of commodities that require processing because they are bulky or perishable. Farming needs a large range of industrial products ranging from fertiliser to farm equipment.

Most factories are small units, with some notable exceptions being the paper plants in the forested areas around Kawerau and Kinleith.

Tourism

One aspect of New Zealand's economy that has reached unprecedented heights in the past decade is tourism, especially from Australia. It has often been said that to Australians 'New Zealand is a compendium of all of the best features of Europe'. It is cheaper to travel to New Zealand from Melbourne and Sydney than it is to go to Perth.

New Zealand offers much to the tourist. Its lakes, mountains, thermal areas, natural harbours, rivers, sports and peaceful settings offer all tourists the chance to seek out what interests them, without having to travel thousands of kilometres.

The following are some of the more popular natural tourist areas:

Rotorua Thermal Area: Rotorua is the leading tourist resort in New Zealand, with visitors spending nearly $30 million here each year. This thermal region has amazing variety and contrast, ranging from spectacular geysers, boiling pools, and bubbling mud-volcanoes to restful lakes and forests, and the enchanting music of the Maori people.

Milford Sound: This is the grandest of the fiords that indent the rugged coastline of New Zealand's Fiordland National Park area. The relatively shallow entrance indicates the terminal moraine of the glacier that filled the bed of Milford Sound in a remote age. The head of the sound is dominated by the sheer

rock walls of Mitre Peak (1695 metres high).

Queenstown and Lake Wakatipu: Queenstown is rightly called the place for all seasons — from skiing and ice skating in winter to swimming and boating in summer. Steeped in gold mining history, many of the old buildings and the total atmosphere have been preserved. The scenery is quite spectacular, with mountains rising steeply from Lake Wakatipu. The fissured range called the Remarkables is aptly named.

The Glaciers: Both the Franz Josef and Fox Glaciers, stretching down to the West Coast from the main Divide near Mt Cook are awesome sights. Many tourists take a scenic flight over the snow fields and crevasses.

Queen Charlotte Sound: The network of drowned valleys which form the Marlborough Sounds are poems of placid, deep water and forested peninsulas. Queen Charlotte Sound, with the township and the entry port of Picton at its head, is the busiest of these.

Mt Egmont: Fairly high annual rainfall and a mild climate combine to make Taranaki farmlands exceptionally rich. Renowned as much for its fine cheeses as its scenes of exquisite pastoral beauty, Taranaki is dominated by Mt Egmont, from whose Maori title the province takes its name.

Opposite above: Feeding out hay in the snow-covered high country, Canterbury Province.

Above: Christchurch, the largest South Island city, is a spectacular sight in winter with the Southern Alps in the background.

Opposite: Milford Harbour in Fiordland with Mitre Peak in the background. The Milford Track, said by many to be 'the finest walk in the world', is popular with New Zealanders and overseas visitors alike.

Gazetteer

The place names which appear in this gazetteer are followed by a geographical co-ordinate (latitude and longitude). To allow for speedy location of place names a grid reference has been placed after each map page number, and both of these are set in bold type.

The alphabetical order of names composed of two or more words is governed primarily by the first word and then by the second. This is an example of this rule:

North Beach
North Downs
North Manly
Northam
Northcote
Northern Territory

Names beginning with M, Mc are all indexed as if they were spelled Mac.

The following abbreviations have been used in the gazetteer:
A.C.T. — Australian Capital Territory
Aust. — Australia
B. — Bay
C. — Cape
Ck. — Creek
I. — Island
L. — Lake
Mt. — Mount

Nat. Park — National Park
N.S.W. — New South Wales
N.T. — Northern Territory
N.Z. — New Zealand
Pen. — Peninsula
Pk. — Park
P.O. — Post Office
Pt. — Point
Papua N.G. — Papua New Guinea
Qld. — Queensland
R. — River
Ra. — Range
S.A. — South Australia
Tas. — Tasmania
Vic. — Victoria
W.A. — Western Australia

A

Abau, Papua N.G. 10 11S 148 46E **149 Fe**
Abbieglassie, Qld. 27 15S 147 28 E **127 Dd**
Abbot, Mt., Qld. 20 6S 147 45E **129 Bf**
Abbot Pt., Qld. 19 53S 148 5E **129 Ag**
Abbot Bay, Qld. 19 50S 148 0E **129 Af**
Abbotsford, N.S.W. 33 0S 144 20E **92 Dd**
Abel Tasman Nat. Park, N.Z. 40 49S 172 54E **145 Ag**
Abercorn, Qld. 25 12S 151 5E **131 Cb**
Abercrombie R., N.S.W. 33 54S 149 8E **93 Di**
Aberdeen, N.S.W. 32 9S 150 56E **95 Fa**
Aberfeldy, Vic. 37 42S 146 22E **101 Eg**
Aberfoyle, Qld. 21 41S 145 16E **128 Cd**
Abergowrie, Qld. 18 29S 145 53E **129 Yw**
Abermain, N.S.W. 32 49S 151 26E **93 Ck**
Abington Reef, Aust. 18 0S 149 35E **127 Bd**
Abut Hd., N.Z. 43 7S 170 15 E **145 De**
Acheron R., N.Z. 42 16S 173 4E **145 Ch**
Acland, Qld. 27 19S 151 42E **131 Eb**
Adaminaby, N.S.W. 36 0S 148 45E **93 Fh**
Adams, Mt., N.Z. 41 20S 175 45 E **144 Hd**
Adavale, Qld. 25 52S 144 32E **127 Dc**
Adelaide, S.A. 34 52S 138 30E **111 Cc, 113 Dd**
Adelaide River, N.T. 13 15S 131 7E **123 Ab**
Adele I., N.Z. 40 59S 173 4E **145 Ah**
Adelong, N.S.W. 35 16S 148 4E **93 Fh**
Adelong, Qld. 22 26S 145 27E **128 Dd**
Adi, Indonesia 4 15S 133 30E **135 Eh**
Adieu, C., S.A. 32 0S 132 10E **111 Cb**
Adieu Pt., W.A. 15 14S 124 35E **117 Bc**
Admiralty Gulf, W.A. 14 20S 125 55E **117 Ad**
Admiralty Is. 2 0S 147 0E **141 Ad**
Adventure Bay, Tas. 43 20S 147 20E **107 Ef**
Agana, Guam 13 28N 144 45E **139 Tu**
Agat, Guam 15 38N 138 16E **139 Tu**
Agnew, W.A. 28 1S 120 30E **119 Bg**
Ahaura R., N.Z. 42 21S 171 34E **145 Cf**
Ahimanawa Ra., N.Z. 39 5S 176 30E **144 Ee**
Ahipara, N.Z. 35 10S 173 9E **144 Bb**
Ahipara B., N.Z. 35 5S 173 5E **144 Bb**
Ahuriri R., N.Z. 44 31S 170 12E **145 Ed**
Ailang, Papua N.G. 5 10S 141 20E **141 Ca**
Aireys Inlet, Vic. 38 29S 144 5E **100 Fe**
Aitape, Papua N.G. 3 11S 142 22E **141 Bb**
Ajana, W.A. 27 56S 114 35E **119 Aa**
Ajax, Mt., N.Z. 42 35S 172 5E **145 Cf**
Ajayan Pt., Guam 13 15N 144 43E **139 Tu**
Akaroa, N.Z. 43 49S 172 59E **145 Dh**
Akaroa Harbour, N.Z. 43 54S 172 59E **145 Dh**
Akitio, N.Z. 40 36S 176 25E **144 Ge**
Alahanpandjang, Indonesia 1 10S 100 45E **134 Eb**
Alawoona, S.A. 34 45S 140 30E **113 Df**
Albacutya, L., Vic. 35 45S 141 58E **100 Cb**
Albany, N.Z. 36 43S 174 42E **144 Cc**
Albany, W.A. 35 1S 117 58E **119 Hd**
Albatross Bay, Qld. 12 45S 141 30E **127 Ac**
Albatross Pt., N.Z. 38 7S 174 44E **144 Ec**
Albemarle, N.S.W. 32 32S 143 22E **92 Cc**
Alberga, S.A. 27 12S 135 28E **111 Bc**
Albert, N.S.W. 32 45S 147 31E **93 Cg**
Albert L., S.A. 35 30S 139 10E **113 Ee**
Albert Edward Ra., W.A. 18 17S 127 57E **117 Bd**
Albert Edward, Mt., Papua N.G. 20S 147 24E **141 Ed**

Alberton, Vic. 38 35S 146 40E **101 Fg**
Albion Park, N.S.W. 34 46S 150 45E **93 Ej**
Albro, Qld. 22 43S 146 35E **129 De**
Albury, N.S.W. 36 3S 146 56E **93 Gf**
Albury, N.Z. 44 14S 170 54E **145 Ee**
Aldershot, Qld. 25 28S 152 41E **131 Cc**
Aldersyde, W.A. 32 23S 117 15E **119 Fd**
Alectown, N.S.W. 32 53S 148 17E **93 Ch**
Alexander, C., Solomon Is. 6 35S 156 30E **139 Pq**
Alexander, Mt., N.Z. 44 59S 167 14E **145 Fb**
Alexander, Mt., W.A. 28 58S 120 16E **119Bg**
Alexandra, N.Z. 45 14S 169 25E **145 Fd**
Alexandra, Vic. 37 8S 145 40E **101 Ef**
Alexandra Bridge, W.A. 34 9S 115 11E **119 Hb**
Alexandria, N.T. 19 5S 136 40E **123 Bc**
Alexandrina, L., S.A. 35 25S 139 10E **113 Ee**
Alford, S.A. 33 47S 137 48E **113 Cc**
Alford, Mt., Qld. 28 4S 152 35E **131 Fc**
Alfredtown, N.S.W. 35 8S 147 30E **93 Fg**
Alfredton, N.Z. 40 41S 175 54E **144 Gd**
Alice, Qld. 23 33S 145 50E **128 Ed**
Alice R., Qld. 24 2S 144 50E **128 Ed**
Alice Downs P.O., W.A. 17 45S 127 56E **117 Bd**
Alice Springs, N.T. 32 40S 135 50E **123 Cb**
Alick Ck., Qld. 20 35S 142 10E **128 Ba**
Allansford, Vic. 38 26S 142 39E **100 Fc**
Allanson, W.A. 33 20S 116 5E **119 Gc**
Allanton, N.Z. 45 55S 170 15E **145 Fe**
Alleena, N.S.W. 34 4S 147 10E **93 Eg**
Allendale East, S.A. 38 1S 140 41E **113 Hf**
Allies Creek, Qld. 26 4S 151 6E **131 Db**
Alligator Creek, Qld. 19 23S 146 58E **129 Af**
Alligator Creek, Qld. 21 20S 149 12E **129 Ae**
Allingham, Qld. 18 43S 146 16E **129 Yx**
Allora, Qld. 28 2S 152 0E **131 Fb**
Alma, N.S.W. 33 46S 144 34E **92 Dd**
Alma, S.A. 34 17S 138 38E **113 Dd**
Alma, Pt., Qld. 23 38S 150 53E **129 Ei**
Almaden, Qld. 17 22S 144 40E **127 Bc**
Alor Setar, Malaysia 6 7N 100 22E **134 Cb**
Alotau, Papua N.G. 10 16S 150 30E **141 Ff**
Aloysius, Mt., W.A. 26 0S 128 38E **117 Dd**
Alpha, Qld. 24 8S 146 39E **129 Ee**
Alroy Downs, N.T. 19 20S 136 5E **123 Bc**
Alstonville, N.S.W 28 51S 153 27E **95 Bd**
Althorpe I., S.A. 35 21S 136 40E **113 Eb**
Alton Downs, Qld. 23 18S 150 22E **129 Ei**
Alton Downs, S.A. 26 7S 138 57E **111 Bc**
Altona, Vic. 37 51S 144 50E **100 Ee**
Alusi, Indonesia 7 35S 131 40E **135 Fh**
Alva, Qld. 19 25S 147 28E **129 Af**
Alvie, Vic. 38 14S 143 30E **100 Fd**
Amadeus, L., N.T. 24 54S 131 0E **123 Cb**
Amah, Qld. 23 16S 148 6E **129 Eg**
Amaile, Eastern Samoa 13 57S 171 23W **139 Cd**
Amaimon, Papua N.G. 5 12S 145 30E **141 Cc**
Amamoor, Qld. 26 21S 152 41E **131 Dc**
Amanab, Papua N.G. 3 40S 141 14E **141 Ba**
Amar, Indonesia 4 44S 131 40E **135 Eh**
Ambalindum, N.T. 23 23S 134 40E **123 Cb**
Ambergate, W.A. 33 45S 115 19E **119 Gb**
Amberley, N.Z. 43 9S 172 44E **145 Dg**
Ambo, Qld. 22 51S 144 30E **128 Dc**
Ambon, Indonesia 3 35S 128 20E **135 Eg**
Ambrose, Qld. 23 47S 150 56E **129 Ei**

Ambrym, I., New Hebrides 16 15S 168 10E **139 Ih**
Ambunti, Papua N.G. 4 13S 142 52E **141 Cb**
Amby, Qld. 26 30S 148 11E **127 Dd**
Amery, W.A. 31 9S 117 5E **119 Ed**
Amiens, Qld. 28 35S 151 48E **131 Fb**
Amphitheatre, Vic. 37 11S 143 22E **100 Ed**
Amuntai, Indonesia 2 28S 115 25E **135 Ee**
Amurang, Indonesia 1 5N 124 40E **135 Df**
Amuri Pass, N.Z. 42 31S 172 11E **134 Cg**
An Nhon, Vietnam 13 55N 109 7E **134 Bc**
Anakie, Qld. 23 32S 147 45E **129 Ef**
Anambas, Is., Indonesia 3 20N 106 30E **134 Dc**
Aname, New Hebrides 20 8S 169 47E **139 Mi**
Anchor I., N.Z. 45 46S 166 31E **145 Fa**
Andado, N.T. 25 25S 135 15E **123 Cc**
Anderleigh, Qld. 26 1S 152 43E **131 Dc**
Anderson, Vic. 38 32S 145 27E **101 Ff**
Anderson Bay, Tas. 40 55S 147 25E **107 Bf**
Aneityum, New Hebrides 20 12S 169 45E **139 Mi**
Angas Downs, N.T. 24 49S 132 14E **123 Db**
Angas Hills, W.A. 23 0S 127 50E **117 Cd**
Angaston, S.A. 34 30S 139 8E **113 De**
Angellala, Qld. 26 24S 146 54E **127 Dd**
Anglem, Mt., N.Z. 46 45S 167 53E **145 Gb**
Anglesea, Vic. 38 25S 144 12E **100 Fe**
Angoram, Papua N.G. 4 4S 144 4E **141 Cc**
Angurugu, N.T. 14 0S 136 25E **123 Ac**
Aniwa, I., New Hebrides 19 17S 169 35E **139 Li**
Anna Plains, W.A. 19 17S 121 37E **117 Bc**
Annanberg, Papua N.G. 4 52S 144 42E **141 Cc**
Annandale, Qld. 21 58S 148 19E **129 Cg**
Annean, L., W.A. 26 54S 118 14E **117 Db**
Anningie, N.T. 21 50S 133 7E **123 Cb**
Annuello, Vic. 34 53S 142 55E **100 Bc**
Anoano, Solomon Is. 8 59S 160 46E **139 Qs**
Anson, B., N.T. 13 20S 130 6E **123 Ab**
Ansudu, Indonesia 2 11S 139 22E **135 Ei**
Anthony Lagoon, N.T. 18 0S 135 30E **123 Bc**
Antrim Plateau, W.A. 18 8S 128 20E **117 Bd**
Antwerp, Vic. 36 17S 142 4E **100 Dc**
Anxious B., S.A. 33 24S 134 45E **111 Cb**
Aoba, New Hebrides 15 25S 167 50E **139 Hg**
Aorangi Mts., N.Z. 41 49S 175 22E **144 Hd**
Aorere R., N.Z. 40 40S 172 40E **145 Ag**
Aparima R., N.Z. 46 21S 168 0E **145 Fc**
Aparri, Philippines 18 22N 121 38E **135 Af**
Apenam, Indonesia 8 35S 116 13E **135 Fe**
Apia, Eastern Samoa 13 50S 171 50W **139 Cd**
Apis Creek, Qld. 22 59S 149 34E **129 Eh**
Apiti, N.Z. 39 58S 175 54E **144 Fd**
Apo, Mt., Philippines 6 53N 125 14E **135 Cg**
Apollo Bay, Vic. 38 45S 143 30E **100 Fd**
Appila, S.A. 33 1S 138 27E **113 Cd**
Appin, N.S.W. 34 11S 150 45E **93 Ej**
Apple Tree Flat, N.S.W. 32 40S 149 36E **93 Ci**
Apsley, Vic. 36 58S 141 5E **100 Db**
Aracides, C., Solomon Is. 8 21S 161 4E **139 Qs**
Arafura Sea 10 0S 135 0E **135 Fh**
Arahura, N.Z. 42 40S 171 2E **145 Cf**
Araluen, N.S.W. 35 36S 149 49E **93 Fi**
Aramac, Qld. 22 58S 145 14E **128 Dd**
Aramac Ck., Qld. 23 0S 144 32E **128 Dc**
Aramac Range, Qld. 23 5S 145 40E **128 Dd**
Aramara, Qld. 25 35S 152 26E **131 Cc**
Aranga, N.Z. 35 44S 173 40E **144 Bb**

Arapawa I., N.Z. 41 13S 174 20E **145 Bi**
Arapuni, N.Z. 38 3S 175 37E **144 Ed**
Ararat, Vic. 37 16S 143 0E **100 Ec**
Aratapu, N.Z. 36 1S 173 54E **144 Cb**
Aratula, Qld. 27 59S 152 34E **131 Ec**
Archer B., Qld. 13 20S 141 30E **127 Ac**
Archer R., Qld. 13 25S 142 50E **127 Ac**
Archipelago of the Recherche, W.A.
34 15S 122 50E **117 Dc**
Arckaringa, S.A. 27 56S 134 45E **111 Bb**
Arckaringa Cr., S.A. 28 10S 135 22E **111 Bb**
Arcoona, S.A. 31 2S 137 1E **113 Ac**
Ardath, W.A. 32 2S 118 4E **119 Fe**
Ardlethan, N.S.W. 34 22S 146 53E **93 Ef**
Ardmore, Qld. 21 39S 139 11E **127 Cb**
Ardno, Vic. 37 49S 141 3E **100 Eb**
Ardrossan, S.A. 34 26S 137 53E **113 Dc**
Argalong, N.S.W. 35 18S 148 27E **93 Fh**
Argyle, L., W.A. 16 20S 128 40E **117 Bd**
Aria, N.Z. 38 33S 175 0E **144 Ed**
Ariah Park, N.S.W. 34 22S 147 16E **93 Eg**
Arid, C., W.A. 34 1S 123 10E **117 Ec**
Armadale, W.A. 32 12S 116 0E **119 Fb**
Armatree, N.S.W. 31 28S 148 28E **93 Bh**
Arnhem B., N.T. 12 20S 136 10E **123 Ac**
Arnhem, C., N.T. 12 20S 137 0E **123 Ac**
Arnhem Land, N.T. 13 10S 135 0E **123 Ab**
Arno Bay, S.A. 33 54S 136 34E **113 Cb**
Arnold, N.Z. 42 29S 171 25E **145 Cf**
Arowhana, N.Z. 38 7S 177 50E **144 Ef**
Arrabury, Qld. 26 45S 141 0E **127 Dc**
Arrilalah P.O., Qld. 23 43S 143 54E **128 Eb**
Arrowsmith, Mt., N.Z. 30 7S 141 38E **145 Df**
Arrowsmith R., W.A. 29 16S 115 12E **119 Cb**
Arrowtown, N.Z. 44 57S 168 50E **145 Ec**
Arthur Ck., N.T. 22 30S 136 25E **123 Cc**
Arthur Pt., Qld. 22 7S 150 3E **129 Ci**
Arthur R., Tas. 41 2S 144 40E **107 Cc**
Arthur R., W.A. 33 25S 116 48E **119 Gc**
Arthur River, W.A. 33 20S 117 1E **119 Gc**
Arthurs Lake, Tas. 41 57S 146 55E **107 Cf**
Arthur's Pass, N.Z. 42 54S 171 35E **145 Cf**
Arthur's Pass Nat. Pk., N.Z. 42 56S 171 28E **145 Cf**
Arthurs Seat, Qld. 24 14S 151 37E **129 Fj**
Arthurton, S.A. 34 17S 137 45E **113 Dc**
Aru Is., Indonesia 6 0S 134 30E **135 Fh**
Arumpo, N.S.W. 33 48S 142 55E **92 Db**
Arundel, N.Z. 43 58S 171 17E **145 Df**
Ash Ford, N.S.W. 29 15S 151 3E **95 Cb**
Ashbourne, S.A. 35 16S 138 46E **113 Ed**
Ashburton, N.Z. 43 53S 171 48E **145 Df**
Ashburton R., N.Z. 44 2S 171 50E **145 Ef**
Ashburton R., W.A. 21 40S 114 56E **117 Cb**
Ashburton Downs, W.A. 23 25S 117 4E **117 Cb**
Ashhurst, N.Z. 40 16S 175 45E **144 Gd**
Ashley, N.S.W. 29 18S 149 52E **91 Ag**
Ashley R., N.Z. 43 17S 172 44E **145 Dg**
Ashville, S.A. 35 31S 139 20E **113 Ee**
Aspiring, Mt., N.Z. 44 23S 168 46E **145 Ec**
Aspiring Nat. Pk., Mt., N.Z. 44 23S 168 46E **145 Ec**
Astrolabe, Solomon Is. 8 20S 160 34E **139 Qs**
Atherton, Qld. 17 17S 145 30E **129 Xw**
Athol, N.Z. 45 30S 168 35E **145 Fc**
Atiamuri, N.Z. 38 24S 176 5E **144 Ee**
Attopeu, Laos 14 48N 106 50E **134 Bc**
Attunga, N.S.W. 30 55S 150 50E **93 Aj**
Auburn, Qld. 25 58S 150 37E **131 Ca**
Auburn, S.A. 34 1S 138 42E **113 Dd**
Auburn R., Qld. 25 36S 151 14E **131 Ca**
Auckland, N.Z. 36 52S 174 46E **144 Cc**
Augathella, Qld. 25 48S 146 35E **127 Dd**
Augusta, W.A. 34 22S 115 10E **119 Hb**
Augustus I., W.A. 15 20S 124 30E **117 Bc**
Augustus, Mt., W.A. 24 20S 116 50E **117 Cb**
Augustus Downs, Qld. 18 35S 139 55E **127 Bb**
Auki, Solomon Is. 8 45S 160 42E **139 Qs**
Aurukun Mission, Qld. 13 20S 141 45E **127 Ac**
Austin, L., W.A. 27 40S 118 0E **117 Db**
Austral Downs, N.T. 20 30S 137 45E **123 Cc**
Australian Alps, Vic. 36 30S 148 8E **101 Ei**
Australian Capital Territory 35 15S 149 8E **93 Fh**
Auvergne, N.T. 15 39S 130 1E **123 Bb**
Avenal, Vic. 36 53S 145 15E **101 Df**
Avoca, N.S.W. 33 55S 141 56E **92 Da**
Avoca, Qld. 23 59S 147 5E **129 Ef**
Avoca, Tas. 41 47S 147 42E **107 Cf**
Avoca, Vic. 37 5S 143 26E **100 Ed**
Avoca R., Vic. 35 40S 143 43E **100 Cd**
Avon, S.A. 34 40S 138 20E **113 Dd**
Avon R., W.A. 31 40S 116 7E **119 Ec**
Avon Downs, Qld. 21 52S 147 15E **129 Cf**
Avondale, Qld. 22 44S 152 9E **131 Bc**

Avu Avu, Solomon Is. 9 50S 160 22E **139 Qs**
Awahuri, N.Z. 40 16S 175 30E **144 Gd**
Awakina, N.Z. 38 39S 174 37E **144 Ec**
Awanui, N.Z. 35 4S 173 17E **144 Bb**
Awarua Pt., N.Z. 44 15S 168 5E **145 Ec**
Awatere R., N.Z. 41 37S 174 10E **145 Bh**
Aworro, Papua N.G. 7 43S 143 11E **141 Db**
Ayers Rock, N.T. 25 23S 131 5E **123 Db**
Ayr, Qld. 19 35S 147 25E **129 Af**
Ayrshire Downs, Qld. 21 59S 142 42E **128 Ca**

B

Baaba, I., New Caledonia 29 3S 164 59E **139 A₁b₁**
Baandee, W.A. 31 35S 117 58E **119 Ed**
Babakin, W.A. 32 7S 118 1E **119 Fe**
Babar, Indonesia 8 6S 129 30E **135 Fg**
Babel I., Aust. 39 55S 148 20E **107 Ag**
Babinda, Qld. 17 20S 145 56E **129 Xw**
Babinda Hill, N.S.W. 31 55S 146 28E **93 Bf**
Babylon, N.Z. 35 54S 173 49E **144 Bb**
Bacarra, Philippines 18 15N 120 37E **135 Af**
Bacchus Marsh, Vic. 37 43S 144 27E **100 Ee**
Back Plains, Qld. 27 53S 151 48E **131 Eb**
Backstairs Passage, S.A. 35 40S 138 5E **113 Ed**
Bacolod I., Philippines 10 40N 122 57E **135 Bf**
Badas, Malaysia 4 33N 114 25E **135 Dd**
Badas Is., Indonesia 0 45N 107 5E **134 Dc**
Baddaginnie, Vic. 36 34S 145 52E **101 Df**
Baddera, W.A. 28 17S 114 40E **119 Ba**
Baden Park, N.S.W. 32 8S 144 12E **92 Cd**
Badgebup, W.A. 33 37S 117 55E **119 Gd**
Badger I., Aust. 40 21S 147 52E **107 Bf**
Baerami Creek, N.S.W. 32 27S 150 27E **95 Fa**
Baganga, Philippines 7 34N 126 33E **135 Cg**
Bagdad, Tas. 42 38S 147 14E **107 Df**
Baguio, Philippines 16 26N 120 34E **135 Af**
Baimuru, Papua N.G. 7 35S 144 51E **141 Dc**
Bainyik, Papua N.G. 3 40S 143 4E **141 Bb**
Bairnsdale, Vic. 37 48S 147 36E **101 Eh**
Bajimba, Mt., N.S.W. 29 22S 152 0E **95 Cc**
Bajool, Qld. 23 40S 150 35E **131 Aa**
Bakara, S.A. 34 39S 139 46E **113 De**
Bake, Indonesia 3 05S 100 20E **134 Eb**
Baker, L., W.A. 26 54S 126 5E **117 Dd**
Bakers Creek, Qld. 21 13S 149 7E **129 Ch**
Bakewell, Mt., W.A. 31 51S 116 43E **119 Ec**
Baking Board, Qld. 26 43S 150 34E **131 Da**
Balabac Strait, Malaysia 7 53N 117 5E **135 Ce**
Balabalangan Is., Indonesia 2 20S 117 30E **135 Ee**
Balabio, I., New Caledonia 20 7S 164 11E **139 A₁b₁**
Baladjie, W.A. 30 58S 118 56E **119 De**
Balaklava, S.A. 34 7S 138 22E **113 Dd**
Balangnipa, Indonesia 5 15S 120 25E **135 Ff**
Balbi, Mt., Papua N.G. 5 55S 154 58E **141 Ch**
Balclutha, N.Z. 46 15S 169 45E **145 Gd**
Balcombe, Vic. 38 16S 142 2E **100 Ff**
Bald Hd., W.A. 38 16S 118 2E **119 He**
Bald I., W.A. 34 57S 118 27E **119 He**
Bald Hill, W.A. 31 36S 116 13E **119 Db**
Bald Hills, Qld. 27 17S 152 59E **131 Ec**
Baldry, N.S.W. 32 50S 148 32E **93 Ch**
Baler, Philippines 15 46N 121 34E **135 Af**
Balfe's Creek, Qld. 20 12S 145 55E **128 Bd**
Balfour, N.Z. 45 51S 168 35E **145 Fc**
Balfour Ch., Solomon Is. 8 43S 157 27E **139 Qq**
Balhannah, S.A. 35 0S 138 49E **113 Dd**
Bali, Indonesia 8 20S 115 0E **135 Fe**
Balimbing, Philippines 5 10N 120 3E **135 Ce**
Balimo, Papua N.G. 8 6S 142 57E **141 Eb**
Balingup, W.A. 33 48S 115 57E **119 Gb**
Balkuling, W.A. 31 59S 117 8E **119 Ed**
Balladonia, W.A. 32 27S 123 51E **117 Ec**
Balladoran, N.S.W. 31 52S 148 39E **93 Bh**
Ballan, Vic. 37 35S 144 13E **100 Ee**
Ballara, S.A. 32 19S 140 45E **113 Bf**
Ballarat, Vic. 37 33S 143 50E **100 Ed**
Ballaying, W.A. 33 18S 117 32E **119 Gd**
Balldale, N.S.W. 35 50S 146 31E **93 Ff**
Ballidu, W.A. 30 35S 116 45E **119 Dc**
Ballimore, N.S.W. 32 12S 148 55E **93 Ch**
Ballina, N.S.W. 28 50S 153 31E **95 Bd**
Balmoral, N.Z. 42 27S 172 42E **145 Cg**
Balmoral, Vic. 37 15S 141 48E **100 Eb**
Balranald, N.S.W. 34 38S 143 33E **92 Ec**
Balumbah, S.A. 33 13S 136 19E **113 Cb**

Bamawm, Vic. 36 18S 144 40E **100 De**
Bambaroo, Qld. 18 50S 146 10E **129 Yx**
Bamboo, Qld. 14 34S 143 20E **127 Ac**
Ban Kantang, Thailand 7 25N 99 31E **134 Ca**
Ban Thateng, Laos 15 25N 106 27E **134 Ac**
Banam, Cambodia 11 20N 105 17E **134 Bc**
Banana, Qld. 24 28S 150 8E **129 Fi**
Banana Ra., Qld. 24 25S 150 15E **129 Fi**
Banchory, Qld. 23 0S 147 7E **129 Ef**
Bancroft, Qld. 24 48S 151 12E **131 Bb**
Banda Is., 4 37S 129 50E **135 Eg**
Banda Sea, Indonesia 6 0S 130 0E **135 Fg**
Banda Banda, Mt., N.S.W. 31 10S 152 28E **95 Ec**
Bandar Seri Begawan, Malaysia
4 52N 115 0E **135 Dd**
Bandiana, Vic. 36 10S 146 55E **101 Dg**
Bandjarmasin, Indonesia 3 20S 114 35E **135 Ed**
Bandjarnegara, Indonesia 7 24S 109 42E **134 Fc**
Bandung, Indonesia 6 36S 107 48E **134 Fc**
Bandya, W.A. 27 40S 122 5E **117 Dc**
Bang Saphan, Thailand 11 14N 99 28E **134 Ba**
Bangalow, N.S.W. 28 41S 153 30E **95 Bd**
Bangeta, Mt., Papua N.G. 6 21S 147 3E **141 Dd**
Banggai, Indonesia 1 40S 123 30E **135 Ef**
Banggi, Malaysia 7 50N 117 0E **135 Ce**
Bangka, Indonesia 2 0S 105 50E **134 Ec**
Bangkalan, Indonesia 7 2S 112 46E **134 Fd**
Bangkinang, Indonesia 0 18N 100 5E **134 Db**
Bangko, Indonesia 2 5S 102 9E **135 Dg**
Bangkok, Thailand 13 45N 100 31E **134 Bb**
Bangued, Philippines 17 40N 120 37E **135 Af**
Baniara, Papua N.G. 9 44S 149 54E **141 Ee**
Banka Banka, N.T. 18 50S 134 0E **123 Bb**
Banks, C., S.A. 37 55S 140 20E **113 Gf**
Banks Is., New Hebrides 13 50S 167 30E **139 Fh**
Banks Pen., N.Z. 43 45S 173 15E **145 Dh**
Banks Strait, Tas. 40 40S 148 10E **107 Bf**
Banksiadale, W.A. 32 39S 116 6E **119 Fc**
Banyabba, N.S.W. 29 22S 153 2E **95 Cd**
Barabai, Indonesia 2 32S 115 34E **135 Ee**
Baradine, N.S.W. 30 56S 149 4E **93 Ai**
Barakula, Qld. 26 30S 150 33E **131 Da**
Baralaba, Qld. 24 13S 149 50E **129 Fh**
Barambah R., Qld. 25 33S 151 40E **131 Cb**
Barat I., Indonesia 7 30S 128 0E **135 Fe**
Barat Daja Is., Indonesia 7 30S 128 0E **135 Fg**
Baratta, S.A. 31 57S 139 5E **113 Ae**
Barberton, W.A. 30 44S 116 2E **119 Dc**
Barcaldine, Qld. 23 33S 145 13E **128 Ed**
Barcoo R., Qld. 28 29S 137 46E **128 Fc**
Bare I., N.Z. 39 30S 177 2E **144 Ff**
Barellan, N.S.W. 34 16S 146 24E **93 Ef**
Bargara, Qld. 24 50S 152 25E **131 Bc**
Bargo, N.S.W. 34 18S 150 35E **93 Ej**
Barham, N.S.W. 35 36S 144 8E **92 Fd**
Barito R., Indonesia 2 50S 114 50E **135 Ed**
Barker, L., W.A. 31 46S 120 5E **119 Eg**
Barker, Mt., S.A. 35 4S 138 55E **113 Ed**
Barker, Mt., W.A. 34 38S 117 17E **119 Hd**
Barkly Downs, Qld. 20 30S 138 30E **127 Cb**
Barkly Tablelands, N.T. 19 50S 138 40E **123 Bc**
Barlee, L., W.A. 29 15S 119 30E **119 Cf**
Barlee, Mt., W.A. 24 35S 128 10E **117 Cd**
Barlee Ra., W.A. 23 30S 116 0E **117 Cb**
Barmedman, N.S.W. 34 9S 147 21E **93 Eg**
Barmera, S.A. 34 15S 140 28E **113 Df**
Barnato, N.S.W. 31 38S 145 0E **92 Bd**
Barnawartha, Vic. 36 6S 146 44E **101 Dg**
Barnes, N.S.W. 36 2S 144 47E **92 Gd**
Barney, Mt., Qld. 28 17S 152 44E **131 Fc**
Barney's L., N.S.W. 33 14S 144 6E **92 Dd**
Barngo, Qld. 25 3S 147 20E **127 Dd**
Barnong, W.A. 28 37S 116 15E **119 Bc**
Barometer, N.Z. 41 50S 173 39E **145 Bh**
Baron Ra., W.A. 23 30S 127 45E **117 Cd**
Barooga, N.S.W. 35 53S 145 42E **92 Fe**
Barora Ite, Solomon Is. 7 36S 158 24E **139 Pr**
Barorafa, Solomon Is. 7 30S 158 20E **139 Pr**
Barr Smith Ra., W.A. 27 10S 120 15E **117 Dc**
Barraba, N.S.W. 30 21S 150 35E **95 Da**
Barram, Qld. 25 6S 150 53E **131 Ca**
Barrier, C., N.Z. 36 25S 175 32E **144 Cd**
Barrier Ra., N.S.W. 31 0S 141 30E **90 Bc**
Barrier Ra., N.Z. 44 5S 169 42E **145 Ec**
Barrington, N.S.W. 31 58S 151 55E **93 Bk**
Barrington Tops, N.S.W. 32 6S 151 28E **95 Eb**
Barrow I., W.A. 20 45S 115 20E **117 Cb**
Barrow Pt., Qld. 14 20S 144 40E **127 Ac**
Barrow Ra., W.A. 26 0S 127 40E **117 Dd**
Barrow Creek T.O., N.T. 21 30S 133 55E **123 Cb**
Barry, N.S.W. 33 38S 149 16E **93 Di**
Barrytown, N.Z. 42 14S 171 20E **145 Cf**

Gazetteer

Bartle Frere, Mt., Qld. 17 27S 145 50E **129 Xw**
Barton Siding, S.A. 30 31S 132 39E **111 Cb**
Barwon R., N.S.W. 29 10S 148 47E **91 Ag**
Barwon R., Vic. 38 8S 144 3E **100 Fd**
Barwon Park, Qld. 23 2S 148 54E **129 Eg**
Baryulgil, N.S.W. 29 12S 152 38E **95 Cc**
Basalt R., Qld. 19 35S 145 53E **128 Ad**
Basilaki I., Papua N.G. 10 35S 151 0E **141 Ff**
Basilan I., Philippines 6 35N 122 0E **135 Cf**
Basilan Str., Philippines 6 50N 122 0E **135 Cf**
Bass, Vic. 38 29S 145 28E **101 Ff**
Bataan, Philippines 14 40N 120 25E **135 Bf**
Batac, Philippines 18 3N 120 34E **135 Af**
Batangas, Philippines 13 35N 121 10E **135 Bf**
Batchelor, N.T. 13 4S 131 1E **123 Ab**
Batemans Bay, N.S.W. 35 44S 150 11E **93 Fj**
Bates Ra., W.A. 27 25S 121 0E **117 Dc**
Bathampton, Qld. 22 47S 147 36E **129 Df**
Batheaston, Qld. 22 27S 148 48E **129 Dg**
Bathurst, N.S.W. 33 25S 149 31E **93 Di**
Bathurst B., Qld. 14 16S 144 25E **127 Ac**
Bathurst I., N.T. 11 46S 130 20E **123 Ab**
Bathurst., L., N.S.W. 35 3S 149 44E **93 Fi**
Bathurst Harbour, Tas. 43 15S 146 10E **107 Ee**
Batjan I., Indonesia 0 50S 127 30E **135 Eg**
Batlow, N.S.W. 35 31S 148 9E **93 Fh**
Battambang, Cambodia 13 7N 103 12E **134 Bb**
Battle Camp, Qld. 15 20S 144 40E **127 Bc**
Batu Is., Indonesia 09 30S 98 25E **134 Ea**
Batu Pahat, Malaysia 1 50N 102 56E **134 Db**
Baturadja, Indonesia 4 11S 104 15E **134 Eb**
Baubau, Indonesia 5 25S 123 50E **135 Ff**
Bauer, C., S.A. 32 44S 134 4E **111 Cb**
Bauhinia Downs, Qld. 24 35S 149 18E **127 Cd**
Bauple, Qld. 25 49S 152 37E **131 Cc**
Baw Baw, Mt., Vic. 37 49S 146 19E **101 Eg**
Bawean I., Indonesia 5 46S 112 35E **134 Fd**
Bay of Fires, Tas. 41 5S 148 25E **107 Cg**
Bay of Islands, N.Z. 35 15S 174 6E **144 Bc**
Bay of Plenty, N.Z. 37 45S 177 0E **144 De**
Bay of Plenty, Prov., N.Z. 37 45S 177 0E **144 De**
Bayview, N.Z. 39 25S 176 50E **144 Fe**
Baybay, Philippines 10 40N 124 55E **135 Bf**
Baymore, N.S.W. 31 20S 142 48E **92 Bb**
Bayombong, Philippines 16 30N 121 10E **135 Af**
Beabula, N.S.W. 34 26S 145 9E **92 Ee**
Beachmere, Qld. 27 7S 153 3E **131 Ed**
Beachport, S.A. 37 29S 140 0E **112 Gf**
Beacon, W.A. 30 26S 117 52E **119 Dd**
Beaconsfield, Tas. 41 11S 146 48E **107 Ce**
Beagle Is., W.A. 29 49S 114 54E **119 Ca**
Beagle Bay, W.A. 16 32S 122 54E **117 Bc**
Bealiba, Vic. 36 48S 143 34E **100 Dd**
Beatrice, C., N.T. 14 20S 136 55E **123 Ac**
Beaudesert, Qld. 27 59S 153 0E **131 Ed**
Beaufort, Malaysia 5 30N 115 40E **135 Ce**
Beaufort, Vic. 37 25S 143 25E **100 Ed**
Beaufort Inlet, W.A. 34 30S 118 55E **119 He**
Beaumont, N.Z. 45 50S 169 33E **145 Ed**
Beautemps-Beaupré, I., New Caledonia 20 24S 166 9E **139 A₁c₁**
Beauty Point, Tas. 41 9S 146 49E **107 Ce**
Becher Pt., W.A. 32 23S 115 43E **119 Fb**
Beckom, N.S.W. 34 20S 146 58E **93 Ef**
Bedford, C., Qld. 15 14S 145 21E **127 Bd**
Bedford Downs, W.A. 17 19S 127 20E **117 Bd**
Bedford Harbour, W.A. 33 55S 120 35E **119 Hg**
Bedgerebong, N.S.W. 33 21S 147 43E **93 Dg**
Bedout, C., S.A. 35 58S 136 35E **113 Eb**
Bedoutie, Qld. 24 30S 139 30E **127 Cb**
Beeac, Vic. 38 13S 143 37E **100 Fd**
Beech Forest, Vic. 38 37S 143 37E **100 Fd**
Beechwood, Vic. 36 22S 146 43E **101 Dg**
Beenleigh, Qld. 27 43S 153 10E **131 Ed**
Beerburrum, Qld. 26 58S 152 58E **131 Dc**
Beermullah, W.A. 31 14S 115 45E **119 Eb**
Beerwah, Qld. 26 52S 152 58E **131 Dc**
Beetaloo, N.T. 17 15S 133 50E **123 Bb**
Beilpajah, N.S.W. 32 54S 143 52E **92 Cc**
Bejoording, W.A. 31 24S 116 30E **119 Ec**
Belaraboon, N.S.W. 32 33S 145 1E **92 Ce**
Belaringar, N.S.W. 31 45S 147 34E **92 Bg**
Belawan, Indonesia 3 33N 98 32E **134 Da**
Belfast, N.Z. 43 27S 172 38E **145 Dg**
Belgrove, N.Z. 41 27S 172 59E **145 Bh**
Belingeramble, N.S.W. 33 21S 145 22E **92 De**
Belinju, Indonesia 1 35S 105 50E **134 Ec**
Belka, W.A. 31 44S 118 9E **119 Ee**
Bell, N.S.W. 33 28S 150 17E **93 Dj**
Bell, Qld. 26 57S 151 27E **131 Db**
Bell Bay, Tas. 41 6S 146 53E **107 Ce**
Bellarwi, N.S.W. 34 6S 147 13E **93 Eg**

Bellata, N.S.W. 29 53S 149 46E **91 Ag**
Bellbird, N.S.W. 32 52S 151 19E **93 Ck**
Bellbrook, N.S.W. 30 47S 152 31E **95 Dc**
Bellerive, Tas. 42 53S 147 22E **107 Df**
Bellingen, N.S.W. 30 25S 152 50E **95 Dc**
Bellona, Solomon Is. 11 17S 159 47E **139 Rr**
Bells Bridge, Qld. 26 8S 152 34E **131 Dc**
Belmont, N.S.W. 33 4S 151 42E **93 Dk**
Belmore, N.S.W. 33 34S 141 13E **90 Cc**
Beluran, Malaysia 5 48N 117 35E **135 Ce**
Belyando R., Qld. 21 38S 146 50E **129 De**
Bemm River, Vic. 37 47S 148 58E **101 Ei**
Ben Bullen, N.S.W. 33 12S 150 2E **93 Di**
Ben Lomond, N.S.W. 30 1S 151 40E **95 Cb**
Ben Lomond, N.S.W. 30 1S 151 43E **95 Cb**
Ben Lomond, Mt., Tas. 41 38S 147 42E **107 Cf**
Ben Ohau Ra., N.Z. 44 1S 170 4E **145 Ed**
Benagerie, S.A. 31 25S 140 22E **113 Af**
Benalla, Vic. 36 30S 146 0E **101 Df**
Benambra, Vic. 36 57S 147 42E **101 Dh**
Benambra, Mt., Vic. 36 57S 147 42E **101 Dh**
Benanee, N.S.W. 34 31S 142 52E **92 Eb**
Benaraby, Qld. 24 1S 151 19E **131 Bb**
Benarca, N.S.W. 35 57S 144 42E **92 Fd**
Bencubbin, W.A. 30 48S 117 52E **119 Dd**
Bendemeer, N.S.W. 30 53S 151 8E **95 Db**
Bendemer, Qld. 21 54S 142 25E **128 Ca**
Bendering, W.A. 32 23S 118 18E **119 Fe**
Bendick Murrell, N.S.W. 34 8S 148 28E **93 Eh**
Bendigo, Vic. 36 40S 144 15E **100 De**
Benetook, Vic. 34 22S 142 0E **100 Bb**
Bengkalis, Indonesia 1 30N 102 10E **134 Db**
Bengkulu, Indonesia 3 50S 102 12E **134 Eb**
Beni, N.S.W. 32 11S 148 43E **93 Ch**
Benjeroop, Vic. 35 30S 143 50E **100 Cd**
Benlidi, Qld. 24 35S 144 50E **127 Cc**
Benmore, L., N.Z. 44 24S 170 14E **145 Ee**
Benmore Peak, N.Z. 44 24S 170 14E **145 Ee**
Benoa, Indonesia 8 50S 115 20E **135 Fe**
Bentinck I., Qld. 17 3S 139 35E **127 Bb**
Beo, Indonesia 4 25N 126 56E **135 Dg**
Berajondo, Qld. 24 38S 151 51E **131 Bb**
Berebere, Indonesia 2 25N 128 45E **135 Dg**
Bereina, Papua, N.G. 8 39S 146 30E **141 Ed**
Beresford, Qld. 22 30S 146 56E **129 De**
Bernier I., W.A. 24 50S 113 12E **117 Ca**
Berowra, N.S.W. 33 35S 151 12E **93 Dk**
Berri, S.A. 34 14S 140 35E **113 Df**
Berrigan, N.S.W. 35 38S 145 49E **92 Fe**
Berrima, N.S.W. 34 28S 150 20E **93 Ej**
Berrinba, N.S.W. 34 28S 150 20E **93 Ej**
Berry, N.S.W. 34 46S 150 43E **93 Ej**
Berrwillock, Vic. 35 36S 142 59E **100 Cc**
Berwick, Vic. 38 2S 145 23E **101 Ff**
Besar, Mt., Indonesia 2 40S 116 0E **135 Ee**
Beta, Qld. 23 37S 146 22E **129 Ee**
Bethungra, N.S.W. 34 45S 147 51E **93 Eg**
Betong, Malaysia 5 45N 101 5E **134 Dd**
Betoota, Qld. 25 40S 140 42E **127 Dc**
Beulah, Vic. 35 58S 142 29E **100 Cc**
Beverley, W.A. 32 9S 116 56E **119 Fc**
Biaro I., Indonesia 2 5N 125 26E **135 Dg**
Biboohra, Qld. 16 56S 145 25E **129 Ww**
Bicheno, Tas. 41 52S 148 18E **107 Cf**
Bickerton I., N.T. 13 45S 136 10E **123 Ac**
Bickley, W.A. 32 2S 116 5E **119 Fc**
Biddon, N.S.W. 31 30S 148 47E **93 Bh**
Bidura, N.S.W. 34 10S 143 21E **92 Ec**
Bien Hoa, Vietnam 10 57N 106 49E **134 Bc**
Big Bell, W.A. 27 21S 117 40E **117 Db**
Bigga, N.S.W. 34 4S 149 9E **93 Ei**
Bigge I., W.A. 14 35S 125 10E **117 Ad**
Biggenden, Qld. 25 31S 152 4E **131 Cc**
Bilauk Taungdan, Thailand 13 0N 99 0E **134 Ba**
Bilbarin, W.A. 32 12S 117 56E **119 Fd**
Billabong, W.A. 27 25S 115 49E **117 Db**
Billabong Ck., N.S.W. 35 5S 144 2E **93 Ff**
Billiluna, W.A. 19 37S 127 41E **117 Bd**
Billilla, N.S.W. 31 49S 143 10E **92 Bc**
Billimari, N.S.W. 33 41S 148 37E **93 Dh**
Biloela, Qld. 24 34S 150 31E **131 Ba**
Bilpa Morea Claypan, Qld. 25 0S 140 0E **127 Db**
Bilpin, N.S.W. 33 28S 150 31E **93 Dj**
Bilyana, Qld. 18 5S 145 50E **129 Yw**
Bima, Indonesia 8 22S 118 49E **135 Fe**
Bimberi Pk., Mt., A.C.T. 35 44S 148 51E **93 Fh**
Bimbowrie, S.A. 32 2S 140 10E **113 Bf**
Bimerah, Qld. 24 13S 143 33E **128 Fb**
Binalbagan I., Philippines 10 12N 122 50E **135 Bf**
Binalong, N.S.W. 34 40S 148 39E **93 Eh**
Binatang, Malaysia 2 10N 111 40E **134 Dd**
Binbee, Qld. 20 19S 147 56E **129 Bf**
Binda, N.S.W. 34 18S 149 25E **93 Ei**

Binda, Qld. 27 52S 147 21E **127 Dd**
Bindi Bindi, W.A. 30 37S 116 22E **119 Dc**
Bindjai, Indonesia 3 50N 98 30E **134 Da**
Bindle, Qld. 27 40S 148 45E **127 Dd**
Bindoon, W.A. 31 22S 116 13E **119 Ec**
Bingara, N.S.W. 29 52S 150 36E **95 Ca**
Bingara, Qld. 28 10S 144 37E **127 Dc**
Bingera, Qld. 24 54S 152 12E **131 Bc**
Bingera Plantation, Qld. 24 56S 152 13E **131 Bc**
Binh San, Vietnam 15 20N 108 40E **134 Ac**
Biniguy, N.S.W. 29 34S 150 14E **95 Ca**
Binjour, Qld. 25 30S 151 27E **131 Cb**
Binnaway, N.S.W. 31 28S 149 24E **93 Bi**
Binnu, W.A. 28 3S 114 39E **119 Ba**
Binongko I., Indonesia 5 55S 123 55E **135 Ff**
Bintan, Indonesia 1 0N 104 0E **134 Db**
Bintuhan, Indonesia 4 50S 103 25E **134 Eb**
Bintulu, Malaysia 3 10N 113 0E **134 Dd**
Binya, N.S.W. 34 13S 146 21E **93 Ef**
Bira, Indonesia 2 3S 132 2E **135 Eh**
Birchip, Vic. 35 56S 142 55E **100 Cc**
Birchwood, N.Z. 45 55S 167 53E **145 Fb**
Birdsville, Qld. 25 51S 139 20E **127 Db**
Birdum, N.T. 15 39S 133 13E **123 Bb**
Birdum Creek, N.T. 15 39S 133 13E **123 Bb**
Birdwood, S.A. 34 51S 138 58E **113 Dd**
Bireuen, Indonesia 5 14N 96 39E **134 Ca**
Birkenhead, N.Z. 36 49S 174 46E **144 Cc**
Birregurra, Vic. 38 20S 143 46E **100 Fd**
Birricania, Qld. 21 54S 144 40E **128 Cc**
Birriwa, N.S.W. 32 7S 149 28E **93 Ci**
Bisa, Indonesia 1 10S 127 40E **135 Eg**
Bislig, Philippines 8 15N 126 27E **135 Cg**
Bismarck Archipelago 2 30S 150 0E **141 Be**
Bismarck Ra., Papua N.G. 5 35S 145 0E **141 Cc**
Bismarck Sea 4 10S 146 50E **141 Cd**
Black Pt., W.A. 34 30S 119 25E **119 Hf**
Black Braes, Qld. 19 34S 144 12E **128 Ac**
Black Hill, W.A. 28 6S 119 30E **119 Bf**
Black Mountain, N.S.W. 30 18S 151 39E **95 Db**
Black Rock, S.A. 32 45S 138 49E **113 Bd**
Black Rock, Mt., S.A. 32 50S 138 44E **113 Bd**
Black Sugarloaf, Mt., N.S.W. 31 18S 151 35E **93 Bk**
Blackall, Qld. 24 25S 145 45E **128 Fd**
Blackball, N.Z. 42 22S 171 26E **145 Cf**
Blackbull, Qld. 17 55S 141 45E **127 Bc**
Blackbutt, Qld. 26 51S 152 6E **131 Dc**
Blackheath, N.S.W. 33 39S 150 17E **93 Dj**
Blackmount, Qld. 25 42S 152 36E **131 Cc**
Blackstone Ra., W.A. 26 0S 129 0E **117 Dd**
Blackstone Hill, N.Z. 44 58S 169 53E **145 Ed**
Blacktown, N.S.W. 33 48S 150 55E **93 Dj**
Blackville, N.S.W. 31 40S 150 15E **95 Ea**
Blackwater, N.S.W. 30 4S 151 53E **95 Db**
Blackwater, Qld. 23 35S 148 53E **129 Eg**
Blackwater Cr., Qld. 25 56S 144 30E **127 Dc**
Blackwood, C., Papua N.G. 7 49S 144 31E **141 Dc**
Blackwood R., W.A. 34 18S 115 10E **119 Hb**
Blair Athol, Qld. 22 42S 147 31E **129 Df**
Blanche C., S.A. 33 1S 134 9E **111 Cb**
Blanche Ch., Solomon Is. 8 30S 157 30E **139 Qq**
Blanche, L., S.A. 29 15S 139 40E **111 Bc**
Blanche, L., W.A. 22 25S 123 17E **117 Cc**
Blanchetown, S.A. 34 22S 139 36E **113 De**
Blaxland, Qld. 27 13S 151 18E **131 Eb**
Blayney, N.S.W. 33 32S 149 14E **93 Di**
Blaze, Pt., N.T. 12 56S 130 11E **123 Ab**
Blenheim, N.Z. 41 38S 174 5E **145 Bi**
Blenheim, Qld. 27 39S 152 20E **131 Ec**
Bligh Sd., N.Z. 44 47S 167 32E **145 Eb**
Bligh Water, Fiji 17 0S 178 0E **139 Aa**
Blighty, N.S.W. 35 36S 145 17E **92 Fe**
Blinman, S.A. 31 6S 138 40E **113 Ad**
Blitar, Indonesia 8 5S 112 11E **134 Fd**
Bloomfield R. Mission, Qld. 15 56S 145 22E **127 Bd**
Bloomsbury, Qld. 20 43S 148 36E **129 Bg**
Blowering Dam, N.S.W. 35 6S 148 16E **93 Fh**
Blue Mud Bay, N.T. 13 30S 136 0E **123 Ac**
Bluecliffs, N.Z. 44 31S 170 59E **145 Ef**
Bluewater, Qld. 19 10S 146 34E **129 Ae**
Bluff, N.Z. 46 37S 168 20E **145 Gc**
Bluff, Qld. 23 40S 149 0E **129 Eh**
Bluff Pt., W.A. 27 50S 114 5E **117 Da**
Bluff Harbour, N.Z. 46 36S 168 21E **145 Gc**
Bluff Knoll, Mt., W.A. 34 24S 118 15E **119 He**
Blyth, S.A. 33 49S 138 28E **113 Cd**
Bo Duc, Vietnam 11 58N 106 50E **134 Bc**
Boat Harbour, Tas. 40 56S 145 38E **107 Bd**
Boatman, Qld. 27 16S 146 55E **127 Dd**
Bobadah, N.S.W. 32 19S 146 41E **93 Cf**
Bobawaba, Qld. 19 46S 147 33E **129 Af**
Bodallin, W.A. 31 23S 118 50E **119 Ee**

152

Bodallo, N.S.W. 36 4S 150 4E **93 Gj**
Boddington, W.A. 32 50S 116 30E **119 Fc**
Bodjonegoro, Indonesia 7 11S 111 54E **134 Fd**
Bogalong Creek, N.S.W. 33 50S 148 6E **93 Dh**
Bogan R., N.S.W. 32 45S 148 8E **93 Ag**
Bogan Gate, N.S.W. 33 7S 147 49E **93 Dg**
Bogandyera Mt., N.S.W. 35 50S 147 5E **93 Fg**
Bogantungan, Qld. 23 41S 147 17E **129 Ef**
Boggabilla, N.S.W. 28 36S 150 24E **95 Ba**
Bogia, Papua N.G. 4 9S 145 0E **141 Cc**
Bogo, Philippines 11 3N 124 0E **135 Bf**
Bogong, Mt., Vic. 36 47S 147 17E **101 Dh**
Bogor, Indonesia 6 36S 106 48E **134 Fc**
Bohemia Downs O.S., W.A. 18 53S 126 14E **117 Bd**
Bohena Cr., N.S.W. 30 17S 149 42E **91 Bg**
Boholl I., Philippines 9 50N 124 10E **135 Cf**
Boileau C., W.A. 17 40S 122 7E **117 Bc**
Boinka, Vic. 35 11S 141 36E **100 Cb**
Bokal, W.A. 33 29S 116 54E **119 Gc**
Bokhara R., N.S.W. 29 55S 146 42E **91 Af**
Bolac L., Vic. 37 43S 142 57E **100 Ec**
Bolangum, Vic. 36 42S 142 54E **100 Dc**
Bolgart, W.A. 31 16S 116 30E **119 Ec**
Bolinao, C., Philippines 16 30N 119 55E **135 Af**
Bolivia, N.S.W. 29 17S 151 59E **95 Cb**
Bollon, Qld. 28 2S 147 29E **127 Dd**
Bolong, Philippines 6 6N 122 16E **135 Cf**
Bolton, Vic. 34 58S 142 54E **100 Bc**
Bolubolu, Papua N.G. 9 21S 150 20E **141 Ef**
Bomaderry, N.S.W. 34 52S 150 37E **93 Ej**
Bombay, N.Z. 37 11S 175 0E **144 Dd**
Bomera, N.S.W. 31 33S 149 49E **93 Bi**
Bonalbo, N.S.W. 28 44S 152 37E **95 Bc**
Bonang, Vic. 37 11S 148 41E **101 Ei**
Bonang R., Vic. 37 11S 148 41E **101 Ei**
Bonaparte Archipelago, W.A. 14 0S 124 30E **117 Bc**
Bone Rate, Indonesia 6 30S 121 10E **135 Ff**
Bone Rate I., Indonesia 7 25S 121 5E **135 Ff**
Bonegilla, Vic. 36 8S 146 58E **101 Dg**
Bongeen, Qld. 27 34S 151 28E **131 Eb**
Bonney, L., S.A. 37 50S 140 20E **113 Gf**
Bonnie Doon, Vic. 37 2S 145 53E **101 Ef**
Bonnie Downs, Qld. 22 7S 143 50E **128 Db**
Bonnie Rock, W.A. 30 29S 118 22E **119 De**
Bonshaw, N.S.W. 29 2S 151 16E **95 Cb**
Bontang, Indonesia 0 10N 117 30E **135 De**
Bonthain, Indonesia 5 34S 119 56E **135 Fe**
Bonython Ra., W.A. 23 40S 128 45E **117 Cd**
Boogardie, W.A. 28 2S 117 45E **119 Bd**
Bookabie P.O., S.A. 31 50S 132 41E **111 Cb**
Bookaloo, S.A. 31 54S 137 20E **113 Ac**
Bookham, N.S.W. 34 48S 148 36E **93 Eh**
Bool Lagoon, S.A. 37 7S 140 40E **113 Gf**
Boola Boolka, N.S.W. 32 34S 143 8E **92 Cc**
Boola Boolka L., N.S.W. 32 38S 143 10E **92 Cc**
Boolarra, Vic. 38 20S 146 20E **101 Fg**
Boolathanna, W.A. 21 40S 113 41E **117 Ca**
Boolboonda, Qld. 25 4S 151 42E **131 Cb**
Boolcoomata, S.A. 31 57S 140 33E **113 Af**
Booleroo Centre, S.A. 32 53S 138 21E **113 Bd**
Booligal, N.S.W. 33 58S 144 53E **92 Dd**
Booloongie, Qld. 24 50S 152 18E **131 Bc**
Boomi, N.S.W. 28 44S 149 34E **91 Ag**
Boonah, Qld. 27 58S 152 41E **131 Ec**
Boonarga, Qld. 26 48S 150 45E **131 Da**
Boondandilla, Qld. 27 53S 150 36E **131 Ea**
Boondarra, N.S.W. 33 14S 144 42E **92 Dd**
Boondooma, Qld. 26 12S 151 17E **131 Db**
Boonooroo, Qld. 25 40S 152 54E **131 Cc**
Boorabbin, W.A. 31 13S 120 15E **119 Eg**
Booral, N.S.W. 32 30S 151 56E **95 Fb**
Booroomugga, N.S.W. 31 17S 146 27E **93 Bf**
Booroondarra, Qld. 22 49S 148 30E **129 Dg**
Booroondarra Downs, N.S.W. 31 4S 145 28E **92 Be**
Booroorban, N.S.W. 34 53S 144 46E **92 Ed**
Boorowa, N.S.W. 34 28S 148 44E **93 Eh**
Boort, Vic. 36 7S 143 46E **100 Dd**
Bootenal, W.A. 28 53S 114 43E **119 Ba**
Booubyjan, Qld. 25 56S 151 54E **131 Cb**
Booyal, Qld. 25 12S 152 3E **131 Cc**
Bopeechee, S.A. 29 36S 137 22E **111 Bc**
Borambil, N.S.W. 32 4S 150 1E **95 Fa**
Borda, C., S.A. 35 45S 136 34E **113 Eb**
Borden, W.A. 34 3S 118 12E **119 He**
Border Downs, N.S.W. 30 21S 141 4E **90 Bc**
Bordertown, S.A. 36 19S 140 45E **113 Ff**
Boremore, N.S.W. 33 15S 149 0E **93 Dh**
Borea Creek, N.S.W. 35 5S 146 35E **93 Ff**
Boreen Point, Qld. 26 18S 152 58E **131 Dc**
Borneo I., Indonesia 1 0N 115 0E **134 Dd**
Borongan, Philippines 11 37N 125 26E **135 Bg**
Bororen, Qld. 24 13S 151 33E **129 Fj**

Borrika, S.A. 35 0S 140 4E **113 Df**
Borroloola, N.T. 16 4S 136 17E **123 Bc**
Bosavi, Mt., Papua N.G. 6 30S 142 49E **141 Db**
Boston I., S.A. 34 42S 135 55E **113 Da**
Botany Bay, N.S.W. 34 0S 151 14E **93 Ek**
Botfield, N.S.W. 33 1S 147 46E **93 Cg**
Bothwell, Tas. 42 28S 147 2E **107 Df**
Boucaut B., N.T. 12 0S 134 25E **123 Ab**
Bougainville, Tas. 43 32S 148 0E **107 Dg**
Bougainville, C., W.A. 13 54S 126 6E **117 Ad**
Bougainville I., Papua N.G. 6 0S 155 0E **141 Dh**
Bougainville Reef 15 30S 147 5E **127 Bd**
Bougainville Str., Solomon Is.
6 40S 156 10E **139 Pq**
Bouldercombe, Qld. 23 32S 150 29E **131 Aa**
Boulia, Qld. 22 52S 139 51E **127 Cb**
Bouloupari, New Caledonia 21 52S 166 4E **139 B_1c_1**
Boundary Bend, N.S.W. 34 43S 143 8E **92 Ec**
Bourail, New Caledonia 21 34S 165 30E **139 B_1c_1**
Bourbah, N.S.W. 31 18S 148 20E **93 Bh**
Bourke, N.S.W. 30 8S 145 55E **91 Be**
Bow Hill, S.A. 34 54S 139 36E **113 De**
Bowelling, W.A. 33 25S 116 30E **119 Gc**
Bowen, Qld. 20 0S 148 16E **129 Bg**
Bowen, Mts., Vic. 37 9S 148 35E **101 Eh**
Bowen R., Qld. 20 24S 147 20E **129 Bf**
Bowen Downs, Qld. 22 30S 145 0E **128 Dd**
Bowenville, Qld. 27 18S 151 30E **131 Eb**
Bowgada, W.A. 29 20S 116 10E **119 Cc**
Bowie, Qld. 21 47S 145 57E **128 Cd**
Bowling Green Bay, Qld. 19 20S 147 20E **129 Af**
Bowling Green C., Qld. 19 19S 147 25E **129 Af**
Bowmans, S.A. 34 10S 138 17E **113 Dd**
Bowning, N.S.W. 34 46S 148 50E **93 Eh**
Bowral, N.S.W. 34 26S 150 27E **93 Ej**
Bowraville, N.S.W. 30 37S 152 52E **95 Dc**
Bowser, Vic. 36 19S 146 23E **101 Dg**
Bowutu Mts., Papua N.G. 7 45S 147 10E **141 Dd**
Boyanup, W.A. 33 30S 115 40E **119 Gb**
Boyer, C., New Caledonia 21 37S 168 6E **139 B_1f_1**
Boyneside, Qld. 26 43S 151 34E **131 Db**
Boyup Brook, W.A. 33 50S 116 23E **119 Gc**
Bracemere, Qld. 23 22S 150 27E **131 Aa**
Bracknell, Tas. 41 38S 146 56E **107 Ce**
Bradshaw, N.T. 15 21S 139 16E **123 Bb**
Brady's Lookout, Mt., Tas. 41 52S 146 55E **107 Ce**
Braemar, S.A. 33 12S 139 35E **113 Ce**
Braidwood, N.S.W. 35 27S 149 49E **93 Fi**
Braithwaite Pt., N.T. 12 5S 133 50E **123 Ab**
Bramwell, Qld. 12 8S 142 37E **127 Ac**
Brampton I., Qld. 20 49S 149 16E **129 Bh**
Brandon, Qld. 19 32S 147 20E **129 Af**
Branxholm, Tas. 41 9S 147 44E **107 Ce**
Branxholme, Vic. 37 52S 141 49E **100 Eb**
Branxton, N.S.W. 32 38S 151 21E **93 Ck**
Brassey Ra., W.A. 25 8S 122 15E **117 Dc**
Bray, Mt., N.T. 14 0S 134 30E **123 Ab**
Breadalbane, N.S.W. 34 48S 149 28E **93 Ei**
Breadalbane, Qld. 23 50S 139 35E **127 Cb**
Breaden, L., W.A. 25 51S 125 28E **117 Dd**
Breaksea Sd., N.Z. 45 35S 166 35E **145 Fa**
Bream, B., N.Z. 35 56S 174 28E **144 Bc**
Bream Hd., N.Z. 35 51S 174 36E **144 Bc**
Bream Tail, N.Z. 36 3S 174 36E **144 Cc**
Brebes, Indonesia 6 52S 109 3E **134 Fc**
Bredbo, N.S.W. 35 58S 149 10E **93 Fi**
Breelong, N.S.W. 31 48S 148 47E **93 Bh**
Breeza, N.S.W. 31 15S 150 278E **93 Bj**
Bremer, B., W.A. 34 25S 119 27E **119 Hf**
Bremer, I., N.T. 12 5S 136 45E **123 Ac**
Bremer, R., W.A. 34 23S 119 24E **119 Hf**
Bremer Bay, W.A. 34 25S 119 24E **119 Hf**
Brentwood, S.A. 34 51S 137 29E **113 Dc**
Breona, Tas. 41 46S 146 42E **107 Ce**
Brett, C., N.Z. 35 10S 174 20E **144 Bc**
Brewarrina, N.S.W. 30 0S 146 51E **91 Af**
Brewster, L., N.S.W. 33 28S 146 0E **92 De**
Brewster, Mt., N.Z. 44 4S 169 25E **145 Ed**
Briagolong, Vic. 37 51S 147 5E **101 Eh**
Bribbaree, N.S.W. 34 10S 147 51E **93 Eg**
Bribie, Qld. 27 5S 153 8E **131 Ed**
Bribie I., Qld. 27 0S 152 58E **131 Dd**
Bridgetown, W.A. 33 58S 116 7E **119 Gc**
Bridgewater, Vic. 36 36S 143 59E **100 Dd**
Bridgewater, C., Aust. 38 23S 141 23E **100 Fb**
Bridgewater Junc., Tas. 42 44S 147 15E **107 Df**
Bridport, Tas. 40 59S 147 23E **107 Bf**
Brigalow, Qld. 26 51S 150 49E **131 Da**
Bright, Vic. 36 42S 146 56E **101 Dg**
Brighton, N.Z. 45 58S 170 20E **145 Fe**
Brighton, S.A. 35 5S 138 30E **113 Ed**
Brighton, Tas. 42 42S 147 16E **107 Df**

Brightwater, N.Z. 41 22S 173 9E **145 Bg**
Brim, Vic. 36 3S 142 27E **100 Dc**
Brindabella, N.S.W. 35 22S 148 44E **93 Fh**
Bringagee, N.S.W. 34 28S 145 44E **92 Ee**
Brinkworth, S.A. 33 42S 138 26E **113 Cd**
Brisbane, Qld. 27 25S 153 2E **131 Ed**
Brisbane R., Qld. 27 24S 153 9E **131 Dc**
Brittania, Qld. 20 23S 146 25E **129 Be**
Brixton, Qld. 23 32S 144 57E **128 Ec**
Broad Arrow, W.A. 30 23S 121 15E **117 Ec**
Broad Sound, Qld. 22 0S 149 45E **129 Dh**
Broad Sd. Channel, Qld. 22 0S 149 45E **129 Di**
Broadford, Vic. 37 14S 145 4E **100 Ef**
Broadhurst Ra., W.A. 22 30S 122 30E **117 Cc**
Broadwater, N.S.W. 28 59S 153 29E **95 Bd**
Broadwood, N.Z. 35 15S 173 23E **144 Bb**
Brocklehurst, N.S.W. 32 9S 148 38E **93 Ch**
Brocklesby, N.S.W. 35 48S 146 40E **93 Ff**
Broke, N.S.W. 32 45S 151 7E **93 Ck**
Broke Inlet, W.A. 34 55S 116 25E **119 Hc**
Broken R., Vic. 36 24S 145 24E **101 Df**
Broken Bay, N.S.W. 33 30S 151 15E **93 Dk**
Broken Hill, N.S.W. 31 58S 141 29E **90 Bc**
Bronte Park, Tas. 42 8S 146 30E **107 De**
Brooklands, Qld. 18 55S 144 0E **127 Bc**
Brookstead, Qld. 27 45S 151 28E **131 Eb**
Brookton, W.A. 32 22S 116 57E **119 Fc**
Brookville, Vic. 37 19S 147 37E **101 Eh**
Brooloo, Qld. 26 30S 152 43E **131 Dc**
Brooman, N.S.W. 35 29S 150 17E **93 Fj**
Broome, W.A. 18 0S 122 15E **117 Bc**
Broomehill, W.A. 31 51S 117 39E **119 Gd**
Broomehill East, W.A. 33 51S 117 53E **119 Gd**
Brooweena, Mt., Qld. 25 35S 152 21E **131 Cc**
Broughton I., N.S.W. 32 37S 150 20E **93 Cl**
Broula, N.S.W. 33 52S 148 34E **93 Dh**
Brovinia, Qld. 25 57S 151 7E **131 Cb**
Brown, L., W.A. 31 5S 118 15E **119 Ee**
Brown, Mt., S.A. 32 30S 138 0E **113 Bd**
Brown, Pt., S.A. 32 32S 133 50E **111 Cb**
Browns, N.Z. 46 9S 168 25E **145 Gc**
Brown's B., N.Z. 36 40S 174 40E **144 Cc**
Browse I., W.A. 14 7S 123 33E **117 Ac**
Bruce, S.A. 32 27S 138 13E **113 Bd**
Bruce, Mt., W.A. 22 37S 118 8E **117 Cb**
Bruce Bay, N.Z. 43 35S 169 42E **145 Dd**
Bruce Rock, W.A. 31 52S 118 8E **119 Ee**
Brunchilly, N.T. 18 50S 134 30E **123 Bb**
Brunei, Malaysia 4 50N 115 0E **135 Dd**
Brunette Downs, N.T. 18 40S 135 55E **123 Bc**
Brungle, N.S.W. 35 8S 148 13E **93 Fh**
Brunner, N.Z. 42 27S 171 20E **145 Cf**
Brunner, L., N.Z. 42 27S 171 20E **145 Cf**
Brunswick B., W.A. 15 15S 124 50E **117 Bc**
Brunswick Heads, N.S.W. 28 32S 153 33E **95 Bd**
Brunswick Junc., W.A. 33 15S 115 50E **119 Gb**
Brura, N.S.W. 31 41S 145 52E **92 Be**
Bruthen, Vic. 37 42S 147 50E **101 Eh**
Bryan, Mt., S.A. 33 30S 139 0E **113 Ce**
Buala, Solomon Is. 8 10S 159 35E **139 Lj**
Buangor, Vic. 37 20S 143 10E **100 Ed**
Buangor, Mt., Vic. 37 16S 143 13E **100 Ed**
Buapinang, Indonesia 4 40S 121 30E **135 Ef**
Buccaneer Archipelago, W.A. 16 7S 123 20E **117 Bc**
Buchan, Vic. 37 30S 148 12E **101 Ei**
Buchan, L., W.A. 33 10S 119 5E **119 Gf**
Buchan South, W.A. 37 34S 148 8E **101 Ei**
Buchanan L., Qld. 21 35S 145 52E **128 Cd**
Buchanan, L., W.A. 25 33S 123 2E **117 Dc**
Buchanan Ck., N.T. 17 10S 138 6E **123 Bc**
Buckingham, W.A. 33 24S 116 18E **119 Gc**
Buckingham B., N.T. 12 10S 135 40E **123 Ac**
Buckland, Tas. 43 36S 147 43E **107 Df**
Buckle Hd., W.A. 14 26S 127 52E **117 Ad**
Buckleboo, S.A. 32 54S 136 12E **113 Bb**
Buckley, R., Qld. 20 22S 137 57E **127 Cb**
Budda, N.S.W. 31 7S 144 13E **92 Bd**
Buddabadah, N.S.W. 31 56S 147 14E **93 Bg**
Budgewoi Lake, N.S.W. 33 13S 151 34E **93 Dk**
Bugaldie, N.S.W. 31 2S 149 6E **93 Bi**
Builyan, Qld. 24 30S 151 25E **131 Bb**
Buin, Papua N.G. 6 48S 155 42E **141 Dh**
Buji, Papua N.G. 9 8S 142 11E **141 Eb**
Buka I., Papua N.G. 5 10S 154 34E **141 Ch**
Bukit Mertajam, Malaysia 5 22N 100 28E **134 Cb**
Bukittinggi, Indonesia 0 20S 100 20E **134 Eb**
Bukkulla, N.S.W. 29 30S 151 8E **95 Cb**
Bulahdelah, N.S.W. 32 23S 152 13E **95 Fc**
Bulan, Philippines 12 40N 123 52E **135 Bf**
Bulga, N.S.W. 32 39S 151 2E **93 Ck**
Bulga Downs, W.A. 28 32S 119 43E **119 Bf**
Bulgroo, Qld. 25 47S 143 58E **127 Dc**

Gazetteer

Bulgunnia, S.A. 30 10S 134 53E **111 Cb**
Buli, Teluk, Indonesia 1 5N 128 25E **135 Dg**
Bull Knob, Mt., S.A. 35 18S 138 35E **113 Ed**
Bulla, N.S.W. 31 31S 144 38E **92 Bd**
Bullabulling, W.A. 31 1S 120 32E **117 Ec**
Bullara, W.A. 22 40S 114 3E **117 Ca**
Bullardoo, W.A. 27 52S 115 40E **119 Ab**
Bullaring, W.A. 32 30S 117 45E **119 Fd**
Bullenbung, N.S.W. 35 8S 146 54E **93 Ff**
Buller, Mt., Vic. 37 10S 146 28E **101 Ed**
Buller R., N.Z. 41 44S 171 36E **145 Bg**
Buller Gorge, N.Z. 41 40S 172 10E **145 Bg**
Bullfinch, W.A. 30 58S 119 3E **119 Df**
Bulli, N.S.W. 34 15S 150 57E **93 Ej**
Bullock Creek, Qld. 17 51S 143 45E **127 Bc**
Bullock Creek, Vic. 35 42S 143 54E **100 De**
Bulloo, L., Qld. 28 43S 142 25E **127 Dc**
Bulloo, R., Qld. 28 43S 142 30E **127 Dc**
Bulloo Downs, Qld. 28 31S 142 57E **127 Dc**
Bulls, N.Z. 40 10S 175 24E **144 Gd**
Bullsbrook, W.A. 31 41S 115 59E **119 Eb**
Bulolo, Papua N.G. 7 10S 146 40E **141 Dd**
Buloo Downs, W.A. 24 0S 119 32E **117 Cb**
Bulu Karakelong, Indonesia 4 35N 126 50E **135 Dg**
Buluan, Philippines 9 0N 125 30E **135 Cf**
Bulukumba, Indonesia 5 33S 120 11E **135 Ff**
Bulyee, W.A. 32 23S 117 30E **119 Fd**
Bumbunga, S.A. 33 55S 138 14E **113 Cd**
Buna, Papua N.G. 8 42S 148 27E **141 Ee**
Bunbury, W.A. 33 20S 115 35E **119 Gb**
Bundaberg, Qld. 24 54S 152 22E **131 Bc**
Bundanoon, N.S.W. 34 40S 150 16E **93 Ej**
Bundarra, N.S.W. 30 4S 151 0W **95 Db**
Bundemar, N.S.W. 31 50S 148 10E **93 Bh**
Bundey R., N.T. 21 46S 135 37E **123 Cc**
Bundooma, N.T. 24 54S 134 16E **123 Cb**
Bungendore, N.S.W. 35 14S 149 30E **93 Fi**
Bungil Cr., Qld. 27 5S 149 5E **127 Dd**
Bungonia, N.S.W. 34 51S 149 57E **93 Ei**
Buninyong, Vic. 37 36S 143 54E **100 Ed**
Bunjil, W.A. 29 39S 116 22E **119 Cc**
Bunker Group, Qld. 23 45S 152 20E **131 Ac**
Bunnaloo, N.S.W. 35 46S 144 35E **92 Fd**
Bunnan, N.S.W. 32 2S 150 37E **95 Fa**
Bunneringee, N.S.W. 33 34S 141 46E **92 Da**
Bunnythorpe, N.Z. 40 16S 175 39E **144 Gd**
Buntine, W.A. 29 59S 116 34E **119 Cc**
Buntok, Indonesia 1 40S 114 58E **135 Ed**
Bunyan, N.S.W. 36 10S 149 11E **93 Gi**
Buol, Indonesia 1 15N 121 32E **135 Df**
Burakin, W.A. 30 31S 117 10E **119 Dd**
Burcher, N.S.W. 33 30S 147 16E **93 Dg**
Burdekin R., Qld. 19 38S 147 25E **129 Be**
Burekup, W.A. 33 20S 115 48E **119 Gb**
Burges, Mt. W.A. 30 50S 121 5E **117 Ec**
Burias I., Philippines 12 55N 123 5E **135 Bf**
Burke R., Qld. 23 12S 139 33E **127 Cc**
Burketown, Qld. 17 45S 139 33E **127 Bb**
Burleigh, Qld. 20 16S 143 7E **128 Bb**
Burleigh Heads, Qld. 28 5S 153 25E **131 Fd**
Burma 21 0N 96 30E **134**
Burnabbie Motel, W.A. 32 7S 126 21E **117 Ed**
Burnamwood, N.S.W. 31 7S 144 53E **92 Bd**
Burnerbinmah, W.A. 28 45S 117 22E **119 Bd**
Burnett Heads, Qld. 24 47S 152 25E **131 Bc**
Burnett R., Qld. 24 45S 152 23E **131 Cb**
Burney, C., W.A. 28 55S 114 38E **119 Ba**
Burngup, W.A. 33 2S 118 42E **119 Ge**
Burnie, Tas. 41 4S 145 56E **107 Cd**
Burra, S.A. 33 40S 138 55E **113 Cd**
Burraboi, N.S.W. 35 22S 144 18E **92 Fd**
Burracoppin, W.A. 31 25S 118 28E **119 Ee**
Burraga, N.S.W. 33 57S 149 32E **93 Di**
Burragorang, L., N.S.W. 33 52S 150 37E **93 Dj**
Burramurra, N.T. 20 25S 137 15E **123 Cc**
Burren Junction, N.S.W. 30 7S 148 59E **91 Bg**
Burrendong, L., N.S.W. 32 45S 149 10E **93 Ci**
Burrendong Dam, N.S.W. 32 39S 149 6E **93 Ci**
Burrewarra Pt., N.S.W. 35 50S 150 15E **93 Fj**
Burrigbar, Qld. 28 25S 153 29E **131 Fd**
Burringbar, N.S.W. 28 25S 153 29E **95 Bd**
Burrinjuck Dam, N.S.W. 35 0S 148 34E **93 Eh**
Burrum Heads, Qld. 25 11S 152 35E **131 Cc**
Burrum Pt., Qld. 25 9S 152 38E **131 Cc**
Burrundie, N.T. 13 32S 131 42E **123 Ab**
Burtundy, N.S.W. 33 45S 142 15E **92 Db**
Buru I., Indonesia 3 30S 126 30E **135 Eg**
Burung, Indonesia 0 21N 108 25E **134 Db**
Bushy Pk., Tas. 42 43S 146 53E **107 De**
Busselton, W.A. 33 42S 115 15E **119 Gb**
Bustard Bay, Qld. 24 5S 151 50E **131 Bb**
Busuanga I., Philippines 12 10N 120 0E **135 Be**

Bute, S.A. 33 51S 138 2E **113 Cd**
Butlers Gorge, Tas. 42 16S 146 17E **107 De**
Buttabone, N.S.W. 31 20S 147 39E **93 Bg**
Butterworth, Malaysia 5 24N 100 23E **134 Cb**
Buttfield, Mt., W.A. 24 45S 128 9E **117 Cd**
Butty Hd., W.A. 33 54S 121 39E **117 Ec**
Butuan, Philippines 8 57N 125 33E **135 Cg**
Butung I., Indonesia 5 0S 122 45E **135 Ef**
Buxton, N.S.W. 34 15S 150 32E **93 Ej**
Buxton, Vic. 37 26S 145 42E **101 Ef**
Bwagola, Papua N.G. 10 40S 152 52E **141 Fg**
Byerwen, Qld. 21 5S 147 55E **129 Cf**
Byford, W.A. 32 15S 116 0E **119 Fb**
Bylong, N.S.W. 32 24S 150 8E **95 Fa**
Byro, W.A. 26 5S 116 11E **117 Db**
Byrock, N.S.W. 30 40S 146 27E **91 Bf**
Byron, N.S.W. 290 40S 151 7E **95 Cb**
Byron, C., N.S.W. 28 38S 153 40W **95 Bd**
Byron Bay, N.S.W. 28 30S 153 30E **95 Bd**

C

Cabarlah, Qld. 27 25S 152 0E **131 Ec**
Cabawin, Qld. 27 19S 150 15E **131 Ea**
Cabbora, N.S.W. 32 2S 149 17E **93 Ci**
Cables, W.A. 27 55S 123 25E **117 Dc**
Caboolture, Qld. 27 5S 152 58E **131 Ec**
Cabramurra, N.S.W. 35 56S 148 26E **93 Fh**
Cadell, S.A. 34 2S 139 45E **113 De**
Cadibarrawirracanna, L., S.A.
28 52S 135 27E **111 Bc**
Cadiz, Philippines 11 30N 123 15E **135 Bf**
Cadoux, W.A. 30 46S 117 7E **119 Dd**
Cagayan De Oro, Philippines 8 30N 124 40E **135 Cf**
Cairns, Qld. 16 57S 145 45E **129 Ww**
Calamian Group, Philippines
11 50N 119 55E **135 Be**
Calapan, Philippines 13 25N 121 7E **135 Bf**
Calauag, Philippines 13 55N 122 15E **135 Bf**
Calavite, C., Philippines 13 26N 120 10E **135 Be**
Caledon Bay, N.T. 12 45S 137 0E **123 Ac**
Calen, Qld. 20 56S 148 48E **129 Bg**
Calicoan, Philippines 10 59N 125 50E **135 Bg**
Calingiri, W.A. 31 5S 116 27E **119 Ec**
Callabonna, L., S.A. 29 40S 140 5E **111 Bc**
Callide, Qld. 24 18S 150 28E **131 Ba**
Callington, S.A. 35 6S 139 3E **113 Ee**
Calliope, Qld. 24 0S 151 16E **131 Bb**
Caloundra, Qld. 26 45S 153 10E **131 Dd**
Caltowie, S.A. 33 10S 138 29E **113 Cd**
Calvert Hills, N.T. 17 15S 137 20E **123 Bc**
Calvert R., N.T. 16 17S 137 44E **123 Bc**
Calvert Ra., W.A. 24 0S 122 30E **117 Cc**
Cambodia 12 15N 105 0E **134 Bc**
Camboon, Qld. 25 1S 150 26E **131 Ca**
Cambrai, S.A. 34 40S 139 16E **113 De**
Cambridge, N.Z. 37 54S 175 29E **144 Dd**
Cambridge, Tas. 42 50S 147 27E **107 Df**
Cambridge Gulf, W.A. 14 45S 128 0E **117 Ad**
Camden, N.S.W. 34 1S 150 43E **93 Dj**
Camden Sd., W.A. 15 27S 124 25E **117 Bc**
Camels Back, N.Z. 36 58S 175 34E **144 Cd**
Cameron Downs, Qld. 21 24S 144 16E **127 Cc**
Cameron Mts., N.Z. 46 1S 167 0E **145 Fb**
Camiguin I., Philippines 19 55N 122 0E **135 Cg**
Camira Creek, N.S.W. 29 15S 152 58E **95 Cc**
Camm, L., W.A. 32 57S 119 35E **119 Ff**
Cammoo, Qld. 23 10S 150 28E **131 Aa**
Camooweal, Qld. 19 56S 138 7E **127 Bb**
Campaspe R., Qld. 20 59S 146 22E **129 Be**
Campbell C., N.Z. 41 47S 174 18E **145 Bi**
Campbell Town, Tas. 41 52S 147 30E **107 Cf**
Campbelltown, N.S.W. 34 4S 150 49E **93 Ej**
Camperdown, Vic. 38 14S 143 9E **100 Fd**
Campion, W.A. 31 1S 118 28E **119 Ee**
Campoyen, Mt., Qld. 22 57S 146 58E **129 De**
Canaga, Qld. 26 41S 150 55E **131 Da**
Canala, New Caledonia 21 32S 165 57E **139 B_1c_1**
Canbelego, N.S.W. 31 32S 146 18E **93 Bf**
Canberra, A.C.T. 35 15S 149 8E **93 Fi**
Canegrass, S.A. 33 35S 140 0E **113 Cf**
Cangai, N.S.W. 29 30S 152 30E **95 Cc**
Canlaon, Philippines 9 27N 118 25E **135 Bf**
Cann R., Vic. 37 44S 149 7E **101 Ej**
Cann River, Vic. 37 35S 149 7E **101 Ej**
Canna, W.A. 38 54S 115 51E **119 Bb**
Canning Creek, Qld. 28 10S 151 12E **131 Fb**

Canning Hill, W.A. 28 44S 117 45E **119 Bd**
Canning Res., W.A. 32 10S 116 8E **119 Fc**
Canning R., W.A. 32 1S 115 51E **119 Fc**
Cannon Vale, Qld. 20 17S 148 43E **129 Bg**
Cannondale, Mt., Qld. 25 13S 148 57E **127 Dd**
Canoona, Qld. 23 7S 150 17E **129 Ei**
Canopus, S.A. 33 29S 140 42E **113 Cf**
Canowindra, N.S.W. 33 35S 148 38E **93 Dh**
Canterbury, Prov., N.Z. 43 45S 171 19E **145 De**
Canterbury, Qld. 25 23S 141 53E **127 Dc**
Canterbury Bight, N.Z. 44 16S 171 55E **145 Ef**
Canterbury Plains, N.Z. 43 55S 171 22E **145 Df**
Canvastown, N.Z. 41 17S 173 40E **145 Bh**
Cape Barren, Tas. 40 23S 148 1E **107 Bg**
Cape Clear, Vic. 37 47S 143 36E **100 Ed**
Cape Jervis, S.A. 35 40S 138 5E **113 Ed**
Cape R., Qld. 20 37S 147 1E **129 Be**
Cape Ward Hunt, Papua N.G. 8 2S 148 10E **141 Ee**
Capel, W.A. 33 34S 115 33E **119 Gb**
Capella, Qld. 23 2S 148 1E **129 Eg**
Capella, Mt., Papua N.G. 5 4S 141 8E **141 Ca**
Capertree, N.S.W. 33 6S 149 58E **93 Dj**
Capricorn, C., Qld. 23 30S 151 13E **129 Ej**
Capricorn Group, Qld. 23 30S 151 55E **129 Ej**
Capricorn Ra., W.A. 23 20S 117 0E **117 Cb**
Captains Flat, N.S.W. 35 35S 149 27E **93 Fi**
Carabost, N.S.W. 35 35S 147 43E **93 Fg**
Caradoc, N.S.W. 30 35S 143 5E **90 Bd**
Caragaba, N.S.W. 33 49S 147 45E **93 Dg**
Caramut, Vic. 37 56S 142 31E **100 Ec**
Carani, W.A. 30 57S 116 28E **119 Dc**
Carcoar, N.S.W. 33 36S 149 8E **93 Di**
Cardabia, W.A. 23 2S 113 55E **117 Ca**
Cardowan, Qld. 22 7S 149 4E **129 Dh**
Cardrona, Mt., N.Z. 44 51S 168 55E **145 Ec**
Cardwell, Qld. 18 14S 146 2E **129 Yx**
Cardwell Ra., Qld. 18 0S 145 35E **129 Yw**
Cargo, N.S.W. 33 25S 148 48E **93 Dh**
Carey L., W.A. 29 0S 122 15E **117 Dc**
Carinda, N.S.W. 30 28S 147 41E **91 Bf**
Carisbrook, Vic. 37 3S 143 49E **100 Ed**
Carlotta T.O., W.A. 34 6S 115 45E **119 Hb**
Carlsruhe, Vic. 37 16S 144 30E **100 Ee**
Carmichael, Qld. 21 59S 146 5E **129 Ce**
Carmila, Qld. 21 55S 149 24E **129 Ch**
Carmody L., W.A. 32 30S 119 10E **119 Ff**
Carnamah, W.A. 29 41S 115 53E **119 Cb**
Carnarvon, Qld. 24 48S 147 45E **127 Cd**
Carnarvon, W.A. 24 51S 113 42E **117 Ca**
Carnarvon Ra., Qld. 25 15S 148 30E **127 Dd**
Carnarvon Ra., W.A. 24 0S 120 45E **117 Dc**
Carnegie L., W.A. 26 5S 122 30E **117 Dc**
Carnot, B., W.A. 17 20S 121 30E **117 Bc**
Caroda, N.S.W. 29 59S 150 22E **95 Ca**
Caroline, N.Z. 45 50S 168 23E **145 Fc**
Caroline Peak, N.Z. 45 57S 167 15E **145 Fb**
Caron, W.A. 29 34S 116 19E **119 Cc**
Caroona, N.S.W. 31 24S 150 26E **95 Ea**
Carpentaria Downs, Qld. 18 44S 144 20E **127 Bc**
Carr Boyd Ra., W.A. 16 15S 128 35E **117 Bd**
Carrabin, W.A. 31 22S 118 40E **119 Ee**
Carrajung, Vic. 38 22S 146 44E **101 Fg**
Carrathool, N.S.W. 34 22S 145 30E **92 Ee**
Carribee, S.A. 35 7S 136 57E **113 Eb**
Carrick, Tas. 41 31S 147 1E **107 Cf**
Carrieton, S.A. 32 25S 138 31E **113 Bd**
Carroll, N.S.W. 30 58S 150 27E **95 Da**
Carterton, N.Z. 41 2S 175 31E **144 Hd**
Carwarp, Vic. 34 28S 142 11E **100 Bc**
Cascade Pt., N.Z. 44 1S 168 20E **145 Ec**
Cascade R., N.Z. 44 1S 168 22E **145 Ec**
Cashmere Downs, W.A. 28 57S 119 35E **119 Bf**
Casiguran, Philippines 16 15N 122 15E **135 Af**
Casino, N.S.W. 28 52S 153 3E **95 Bd**
Cass, N.Z. 43 2S 171 46E **145 Df**
Cassilis, N.S.W. 32 3S 149 58E **93 Bj**
Casterton, Vic. 37 30S 141 30E **100 Eb**
Castlecliff, N.Z. 39 57S 174 59E **144 Fc**
Castlemaine, Vic. 37 2S 144 12E **100 Ee**
Castlepoint, N.Z. 40 54S 176 15E **144 Ge**
Castlereagh B., N.T. 12 10S 135 10E **123 Ac**
Castlereagh R., N.S.W. 30 12S 147 32E **93 Bh**
Castlevale, Qld. 24 30S 146 48E **129 Fe**
Caswell SD, N.Z. 44 59S 167 8E **145 Eb**
Catamaran, Tas. 43 34S 146 55E **107 Ee**
Catanduanes I., Philippines 13 50N 124 20E **135 Bf**
Catarman, Philippines 12 28N 124 1E **135 Bf**
Cateel, Philippines 7 47N 126 24E **135 Cg**
Catherine, Mt., Qld. 24 26S 148 8E **129 Fg**
Cathkin, Vic. 37 10S 145 38E **101 Ef**
Cathundral, N.S.W. 31 55S 147 51E **93 Bg**
Catt, Mt., N.T. 13 49S 134 23E **123 Ab**

Cavalli I., N.Z. 35 0S 173 58E **144 Ac**
Cave, N.Z. 44 19S 170 58E **145 Ee**
Cavenagh Ra., W.A. 26 12S 127 55E **117 Dd**
Caveside, Tas. 41 35S 146 26E **107 Ce**
Cawarral, Qld. 23 14S 150 42E **129 Ei**
Cawarrat, Qld. 23 14S 150 42E **131 Aa**
Cawkers Well, N.S.W. 31 41S 142 57E **92 Bb**
Cawndilla L., N.S.W. 32 30S 142 15E **92 Cb**
Cawongla, N.S.W. 28 36S 153 6E **95 Bd**
Cebu I., Philippines 10 15N 123 40E **135 Bf**
Cecil Plains, Qld. 27 30S 151 11E **131 Eb**
Celebes I., Indonesia 3 0N 123 0E **135 Ee**
Celebes Sea 3 0N 123 0E **135 Df**
Cement Mills, Qld. 28 20S 151 31E **131 Fb**
Central Auckland (Prov.), N.Z.
37 30S 175 30E **144 Db**
Central Ra., Papua N.G. 5 0S 143 0E **141 Cb**
Centre I., N.Z. 46 28S 167 52E **145 Gb**
Ceram Sea, Indonesia 2 30S 128 30E **135 Eg**
Cervantes Is., W.A. 30 32S 115 2E **119 Da**
Cessnock, N.S.W. 32 50S 151 21E **93 Ck**
Chachaengsao, Thailand 13 42N 101 5E **134 Bb**
Chahpingah, Qld. 26 29S 151 24E **131 Db**
Chalky I., N.Z. 46 3S 166 25E **145 Ga**
Challa, W.A. 28 15S 118 19E **119 Be**
Chamberlain R., W.A. 15 58S 127 54E **117 Bd**
Chambri L., Papua N.G. 4 15S 143 10E **141 Cb**
Chandlers Creek, Vic. 37 21S 149 12E **101 Ej**
Chandlers Pk., N.S.W. 30 24S 152 10E **95 Dc**
Chanthaburi, Thailand 12 38N 102 12E **134 Bb**
Chapman, W.A. 28 41S 114 47E **119 Ba**
Chappel Is., Aust. 40 17S 147 50E **107 Bf**
Charles Sd., N.Z. 45 2S 167 4E **145 Fb**
Charleston, N.Z. 41 54S 171 27E **145 Bf**
Charleville, Qld. 26 24S 146 15E **127 Dd**
Charlton, Vic. 36 16S 143 24E **100 Dd**
Charters Towers, Qld. 20 5S 146 13E **129 Be**
Chaslands Mistake, N.Z. 46 38S 169 22E **145 Gd**
Chatsworth, Qld. 26 8S 152 38E **131 Dc**
Chatto Creek, N.Z. 45 8S 169 31E **145 Fd**
Cheepie, Qld. 26 43S 144 59E **127 Dc**
Chelsea, Vic. 38 5S 145 8E **101 Ff**
Chepénéhé, New Caledonia 20 47S 167 9E **139 A₁e₁**
Cherbourg Aboriginal Settlement, Qld.
26 18S 151 57E **131 Db**
Chermside, Qld. 27 22S 153 1E **131 Ed**
Cherry Gully, Qld. 28 25S 152 1E **131 Fc**
Cherrypool, Vic. 37 7S 142 13E **100 Ec**
Chertsey, N.Z. 43 48S 171 56E **145 Df**
Chest Peak, N.Z. 43 6S 172 1E **145 Df**
Chesterton Range, Qld. 25 30S 147 27E **127 Dd**
Chetwode I., N.Z. 40 54S 174 5E **145 Ai**
Chetwynd, Vic. 37 17S 141 23E **100 Eb**
Cheviot, N.Z. 42 49S 173 16E **145 Ch**
Cheviot Ra., Qld. 25 20S 143 45E **127 Dc**
Cheyne Beach, W.A. 34 50S 118 25E **119 He**
Cheyne, B., W.A. 34 35S 118 50E **119 He**
Chhlong, Cambodia 12 15N 105 58E **134 Bc**
Chichester Ra., W.A. 21 35S 117 45E **117 Cb**
Childers, Qld. 25 15S 152 17E **131 Cc**
Chillagoe, Qld. 17 14S 144 33E **127 Bc**
Chillingham, N.S.W. 28 30S 153 17E **95 Bd**
Chillingollah, Vic. 35 16S 143 3E **100 Cd**
Chiltern, Vic. 36 10S 146 36E **101 Dg**
Chinchilla, Qld. 26 45S 150 38E **131 Da**
Chinocup, W.A. 33 30S 118 25E **119 Ge**
Chinokup, L., W.A. 33 32S 118 21E **119 Ge**
Chittering, W.A. 31 28S 116 4E **119 Ec**
Choiseul, Solomon Is. 7 0S 156 40E **139 Pq**
Chon Buri, Thailand 13 22N 100 59E **134 Bb**
Chorregon, Qld. 22 40S 143 32E **128 Db**
Chowerup, W.A. 34 6S 116 39E **119 Hc**
Christchurch, N.Z. 43 32S 172 38E **145 Dg**
Christian, Mt., Qld. 21 40S 149 18E **129 Ch**
Christmas Creek, W.A. 18 29S 125 23E **117 Bd**
Christmas Ck., W.A. 18 53S 125 55E **117 Bd**
Christopher, L., W.A. 24 49S 127 42E **117 Cd**
Chudleigh, Tas. 41 33S 146 29E **107 Ce**
Chumphon, Thailand 10 35N 99 14E **134 Ba**
Cinnabar, Qld. 26 7S 152 12E **131 Dc**
Clackline, W.A. 31 40S 116 32E **119 Ec**
Clairault, C., W.A. 33 43S 114 58E **119 Ga**
Clara R., Qld. 19 8S 142 30E **128 Aa**
Clare, N.S.W. 33 24S 143 54E **92 Dc**
Clare, Qld. 19 47S 147 13E **129 Af**
Clare, S.A. 33 50S 138 37E **113 Cd**
Claremont, P., Qld. 14 1S 143 41E **127 Ac**
Clarence, N.Z. 42 9S 173 56E **145 Ch**
Clarence R., N.Z. 42 10S 173 56E **145 Ch**
Clarence R., N.S.W. 29 25S 153 22E **95 Cc**
Clarence Str., N.T. 12 0S 131 0E **123 Ab**

Clarencetown, N.S.W. 32 34S 151 46E **93 Ck**
Clarke I., Aust. 40 32S 148 10E **107 Bg**
Clarke Range, Qld. 20 45S 148 20E **129 Bg**
Clarke R., Qld. 19 12S 145 28E **127 Bc**
Clarke River P.O., Qld. 19 12S 145 27E **128 Ad**
Clarksville, N.Z. 46 8S 169 55E **145 Gd**
Claveria, Philippines 18 37N 121 15E **135 Af**
Clayton, Qld. 24 55S 152 22E **131 Bc**
Clermont, Qld. 22 49S 147 39E **129 Df**
Cleve, S.A. 33 43S 136 30E **113 Cb**
Cleveland, Qld. 27 31S 153 3E **131 Ed**
Cleveland, C., Qld. 19 11S 147 1E **127 Bd**
Cleveland, Mt., Tas. 41 25S 145 23E **107 Cd**
Clifden, N.Z. 46 1S 167 42E **145 Gb**
Cliff Hd., W.A. 29 33S 114 58E **119 Ca**
Clifton, Qld. 22 58S 149 43E **131 Eb**
Clifton, L., W.A. 32 50S 115 40E **119 Fb**
Clifton Beach, Qld. 16 46S 145 39E **129 Ww**
Clinton, N.Z. 46 12S 169 23E **145 Gd**
Clinton, C., Qld. 22 30S 150 45E **129 Di**
Clive, N.Z. 39 36S 176 58E **144 Fe**
Clive, Qld. 22 46S 149 18E **129 Dh**
Cloates, Pt., W.A. 22 43S 113 40E **117 Ca**
Cloncose, Qld. 25 23S 150 42E **131 Ca**
Cloncurry, Qld. 20 40S 140 28E **127 Cc**
Clouds Creek, N.S.W. 30 4S 152 42E **95 Dc**
Cloudy B., N.Z. 41 25S 174 10E **145 Bi**
Cloyna, Qld. 26 6S 151 50E **131 Db**
Club Terrace, Vic. 37 35S 148 58E **101 Ei**
Clunes, Vic. 37 20S 143 45E **100 Ed**
Clutha R., N.Z. 46 20S 169 49E **145 Ed**
Clyde, N.Z. 45 12S 169 20E **145 Fd**
Clyde Park, Qld. 20 22S 144 41E **128 Bc**
Clydevale, N.Z. 46 6S 169 32E **145 Gd**
Coal Creek, N.Z. 45 27S 169 19E **145 Fd**
Coalgate, N.Z. 43 29S 171 58E **145 Df**
Coalstoun Lakes, Qld. 25 37S 151 54E **131 Cb**
Coastal Plains Basin, W.A. 30 10S 115 30E **119 Db**
Cobar, N.S.W. 31 27S 145 48E **92 Be**
Cobba-Da-Mana, Qld. 28 24S 151 14E **131 Fb**
Cobbannah, Vic. 37 37S 147 12E **101 Eh**
Cobberas, Mt., Vic. 36 53S 148 12E **101 Di**
Cobden, Vic. 38 20S 143 3E **100 Fd**
Cobham, L., W.A. 33 52S 119 17E **119 Gf**
Cobourg Pen., N.T. 11 20S 132 15E **123 Ab**
Cobram, Vic. 35 54S 145 40E **101 Ch**
Cockaleechie, S.A. 34 12S 135 51E **113 Da**
Cockatoo, Qld. 25 32S 150 12E **131 Ca**
Cockatoo, Vic. 37 57S 145 32E **101 Ef**
Cockburn, S.A. 32 5S 141 0E **113 Bg**
Cockburn, C., N.T. 15 20S 132 52E **123 Ab**
Cockburn Ra., W.A. 15 46S 128 0E **117 Bd**
Cockenzie, Qld. 21 57S 148 48E **129 Cg**
Cocklebiddy Motel, W.A. 32 0S 126 3E **117 Ed**
Cocos I., Guam 13 14N 144 39E **139 Tu**
Coen, Qld. 13 52S 143 12E **127 Ac**
Coffin B., S.A. 34 18S 135 12E **111 Cc**
Coffin Bay Pen., S.A. 34 20S 135 10E **111 Cc**
Coffs Harbour, N.S.W. 30 16S 153 5E **95 Dd**
Cohuna, Vic. 35 45S 144 15E **100 Ce**
Colac, Vic. 38 21S 143 35E **100 Fd**
Colac Bay, N.Z. 46 22S 167 53E **145 Gb**
Colane, N.S.W. 31 14S 147 18E **93 Bg**
Colebrook, Tas. 42 31S 147 12E **107 Df**
Coleman, R., Qld. 15 6S 141 38E **127 Bc**
Coleraine, Vic. 37 36S 141 40E **100 Eb**
Coleridge, L., N.Z. 43 17S 171 30E **145 Df**
Colignan, N.S.W. 34 35S 142 25E **92 Ea**
Colinton, N.S.W. 35 50S 149 10E **93 Fi**
Colinton, Qld 26 55S 152 18E **131 Dc**
Collarenebri, N.S.W. 29 33S 148 36E **91 Ag**
Collaroy, Qld. 22 2S 149 12E **129 Dh**
Collector, N.S.W. 34 56S 149 29E **93 Ei**
Collgar, W.A. 31 34S 118 21E **119 Ee**
Collie, N.S.W. 31 41S 148 18E **93 Bh**
Collie, W.A. 33 22S 116 8E **119 Gc**
Collie R., W.A. 33 19S 115 40E **119 Gb**
Collie Cardiff, W.A. 33 26S 116 10E **119 Gc**
Collier B., W.A. 16 10S 124 15E **117 Bc**
Collier Ra., W.A. 24 45S 119 10E **117 Cb**
Collingwood, N.Z. 40 42S 172 40E **145 Ag**
Collingwood, Qld. 22 20S 142 31E **128 Da**
Collinsville, Qld. 20 30S 147 56E **127 Cd**
Colo R., N.S.W. 33 25S 150 52E **93 Dj**
Colossal, N.S.W. 30 52S 147 3E **93 Ag**
Colton, Qld. 25 25S 152 40E **131 Cc**
Colville, N.Z. 36 37S 175 28E **144 Cd**
Colville C., N.Z. 36 29S 175 21E **144 Cd**
Colville Ch., N.Z. 36 24S 175 27E **144 Cd**
Comarto, N.S.W. 31 30S 142 50E **92 Bb**
Combara, N.S.W. 31 10S 148 22E **93 Bh**
Comboyne, N.S.W. 31 34S 152 34E **95 Ec**

Comet, Qld. 23 36S 148 33E **129 Eg**
Comet R., Qld. 23 34S 148 32E **129 Eg**
Comet Downs, Qld. 23 52S 148 35E **129 Eg**
Comet Vale, W.A. 29 55S 121 4E **117 Dc**
Commoron Cr., Qld. 28 22S 150 8E **131 Fa**
Compton Downs, N.S.W. 30 28S 146 30E **91 Bf**
Con San I., Vietnam 8 41N 106 37E **134 Cc**
Conara Junction, Tas. 41 50S 147 26E **107 Cf**
Conargo, N.S.W. 35 16S 145 10E **92 Fe**
Condah, Vic. 37 57S 141 44E **100 Eb**
Condamine, Qld. 26 56S 150 9E **131 Da**
Condamine R., Qld. 26 56S 150 9E **131 Eb**
Condobolin, N.S.W. 33 4S 147 6E **93 Dg**
Congelin, W.A. 32 50S 116 53E **119 Fc**
Conical Harbour, Tas. 41 41S 144 55E **107 Cc**
Conjuboy, Qld. 18 35S 144 45E **127 Bc**
Connmara, Qld. 24 12S 142 17E **128 Fa**
Connor Range, Qld. 21 40S 149 10E **129 Cg**
Connors Ra., Qld. 21 40S 149 10E **127 Cd**
Conoble, N.S.W. 32 54S 144 42E **92 Cd**
Conran, C., Vic. 37 49S 148 44E **101 Ei**
Conway, Qld. 20 22S 148 42E **129 Bf**
Conway C., Qld. 20 33S 148 54E **129 Bg**
Conway R., N.Z. 42 37S 173 28E **145 Ch**
Coober Pedy, S.A. 29 1S 134 43E **111 Bb**
Cook, S.A. 30 42S 130 48E **111 Cb**
Cook, Mt., N.Z. 43 36S 170 9E **145 De**
Cook Nat. Pk., Mt., N.Z. 43 36S 170 9E **145 De**
Cook Str., N.Z. 41 15S 174 29E **144 Hc**
Cooke, Mt., W.A. 32 25S 116 19E **119 Fc**
Cooke Plains, S.A. 35 23S 139 34E **113 Ee**
Cookernup, W.A. 33 1S 115 53E **119 Fb**
Cooktown, Qld. 15 30S 145 16E **127 Bd**
Coolabah, N.S.W. 31 1S 146 43E **93 Bf**
Coolabunia, Qld. 26 36S 151 55E **131 Db**
Cooladdi, Qld. 26 37S 145 23E **127 Dd**
Coolah, N.S.W. 31 48S 149 41E **93 Bi**
Coolamara, N.S.W. 32 6S 143 45E **92 Cc**
Coolamon, N.S.W. 34 46S 147 8E **93 Eg**
Coolangatta, Qld. 28 11S 153 29E **131 Fd**
Coolatai, N.S.W. 29 15S 150 45E **95 Ca**
Coolgardie, W.A. 30 55S 121 8E **117 Ec**
Coolibah, N.T. 15 33S 130 56E **123 Bb**
Coolinine River Flats, W.A. 33 30S 117 35E **119 Gd**
Coolongolook, N.S.W. 32 12S 152 20E **95 Fc**
Coolum Beach, Qld. 26 32S 153 4E **131 Dd**
Coolup, W.A. 32 45S 115 52E **119 Fb**
Cooma, N.S.W. 36 12S 149 8E **93 Gi**
Coomandook, S.A. 35 29S 139 42E **113 Ee**
Coombe, S.A. 35 58S 140 11E **113 Ef**
Coomberdale, W.A. 30 28S 116 2E **119 Dc**
Coombie, N.S.W. 32 49S 145 22E **92 Ce**
Coominglah, Qld. 24 45S 150 51E **131 Ba**
Coominya, Qld. 27 23S 152 31E **131 Ec**
Coonabarabran, N.S.W. 31 14S 149 18E **93 Bi**
Coonalpyn, S.A. 35 43S 139 52E **113 Ee**
Coonamble, N.S.W. 30 56S 148 27E **93 Ah**
Coonana, W.A. 31 0S 123 0E **117 Ec**
Coonawarra, S.A. 37 20S 140 48E **113 Gf**
Coongie, S.A. 27 9S 140 8E **111 Bd**
Coongoola, Qld. 27 43S 145 47E **127 Dd**
Cooninie, L., S.A. 26 4S 139 59E **111 Bd**
Cooper I., N.Z. 45 45S 166 50E **145 Fa**
Cooper Cr., N.Z. 28 29S 137 46E **127 Dc**
Cooper Ck., S.A. 28 29S 137 46E **111 Bc**
Coorabie P.O., S.A. 31 54S 132 18E **111 Cb**
Coorabulka, Qld. 23 41S 140 20E **127 Cc**
Cooran, Qld. 26 19S 152 49E **131 Dc**
Cooranbong, N.S.W. 33 4S 151 28E **93 Dk**
Cooranga N., Qld. 26 47S 151 26E **131 Db**
Cooroorah, Qld. 27 44S 149 52E **129 Eg**
Coorow, W.A. 29 53S 116 2E **119 Cc**
Cooroy, Qld. 26 22S 152 54E **131 Dc**
Cootamundra, N.S.W. 34 36S 148 1E **93 Eg**
Cooyar, Qld. 26 59S 151 51E **131 Db**
Cooyeana, Qld. 24 29S 138 45E **127 Cb**
Cope Cope, Vic. 36 27S 143 5E **100 Dd**
Copeville, S.A. 34 47S 139 51E **113 De**
Copmanhurst, N.S.W. 29 33S 152 49E **95 Cc**
Coppabella, W.A. 29 1S 120 26E **119 Cg**
Copperfield, W.A. 29 1S 120 26E **119 Cg**
Coraki, N.S.W. 28 59S 153 17E **95 Bd**
Coral Sea, Aust. 15 0S 150 0E **127 Bd**
Coramba, N.S.W. 30 12S 153 3E **95 Dd**
Corangamite, L., Vic. 38 0S 143 30E **100 Fd**
Cordalba, Qld. 25 10S 152 13E **131 Cc**
Cordering, W.A. 33 26S 116 39E **119 Gc**
Cordon, Philippines 16 42N 121 32E **135 Af**
Corea Plains, Qld. 20 43S 145 56E **128 Bd**
Coree South, N.S.W. 35 23S 145 28E **92 Fe**
Coreena, Qld. 23 17S 145 23E **128 Ed**

155

Corella R., Qld. 19 34S 140 47E **127 Cc**
Corfield, Qld. 21 40S 143 21E **128 Cb**
Coricudgy, Mt., N.S.W. 32 51S 150 24E **93 Cj**
Corinda, Qld. 22 5S 145 21E **128 Dd**
Corindi, N.S.W. 30 1S 153 12E **95 Dd**
Corinella, Vic 38 25S 145 25E **101 Ff**
Coringa Is. 16 51S 149 58E **127 Be**
Corinna, Tas. 41 35S 145 10E **107 Cd**
Corner Inlet, Vic. 38 45S 146 20E **101 Fg**
Cornish Ck., Qld. 22 29S 144 38E **128 Dd**
Cornwall, Tas. 41 33S 148 7E **107 Cg**
Corny Point, S.A. 34 55S 137 0E **113 Dc**
Coromandel, N.Z. 36 45S 175 31E **144 Cd**
Coromandel Pen., N.Z. 37 0S 175 45E **144 Cd**
Coromandel Ra., N.Z. 37 0S 175 40E **144 Cd**
Coronation Is., W.A. 14 57S 124 55E **117 Ac**
Corowa, N.S.W. 35 58S 146 21E **93 Ff**
Corrigin, W.A. 32 20S 117 53E **119 Fd**
Corryong, Vic. 36 12S 147 53E **101 Dh**
Corunna, S.A. 32 40S 137 5E **113 Bb**
Cotabato, Philippines 7 14N 124 15E **135 Cf**
Cotabena, S.A. 31 42S 138 11E **113 Ad**
Cotherstone, Qld. 22 38S 148 14E **129 Dg**
Cottonvale, Qld. 28 31S 151 57E **131 Fb**
Couedic, C du, S.A. 36 5S 136 40E **113 Fb**
Couti Uti, Qld. 22 20S 150 6E **129 Di**
Coutts Crossing, N.S.W. 29 49S 152 55E **95 Cc**
Cowal, L., N.S.W. 33 45S 147 25E **93 Dg**
Cowal Creek Settlement, Qld.
10 54S 142 20E **127 Ac**
Cowan, L., W.A. 31 45S 121 45E **117 Ec**
Cowangie, Vic. 35 12S 141 26E **100 Cb**
Cowaramup, W.A. 33 52S 115 5E **119 Gb**
Coward Springs, S.A. 29 24S 136 48E **111 Bc**
Cowarie, S.A. 27 45S 138 15E **111 Bc**
Cowcowing Lakes, W.A. 30 55S 117 20E **119 Dd**
Cowell, S.A. 33 39S 136 56E **113 Cb**
Cowes, Vic. 38 28S 145 14E **101 Ff**
Cowl Cowl, N.S.W. 33 36S 145 18E **92 De**
Cowley, Qld. 17 41S 146 3E **129 Xx**
Cowra, N.S.W. 33 49S 148 42E **93 Dh**
Cowwarr, Vic. 38 2S 146 42E **101 Fg**
Cox Bight, Tas. 43 32S 146 15E **107 Ee**
Coyrecup L., W.A. 33 44S 117 50E **119 Gd**
Craboon, N.S.W. 32 3S 149 30E **93 Ci**
Cracow, Qld. 25 17S 150 17E **131 Ca**
Cradle Mt. L. St. Clair Nat. Pk., Tas.
41 55S 145 50E **107 Cd**
Cradle Mt., Tas. 41 40S 145 58E **107 Cd**
Cradock, S.A. 32 6S 138 31E **113 Bd**
Cramsie, Qld. 23 20S 144 15E **128 Ec**
Cranbourne, Vic. 38 7S 145 20E **101 Ff**
Cranbrook, Tas. 42 0S 148 5E **107 Cg**
Cranbrook, W.A. 34 18S 117 33E **119 Hd**
Crater Mt., Papua N.G. 6 37S 145 7E **141 Dc**
Crater Point, Papua N.G. 5 25S 152 9E **141 Cg**
Crediton, Qld. 21 12S 148 34E **129 Cg**
Credo, W.A. 30 28S 120 45E **117 Ec**
Crescent Head, N.S.W. 31 11S 152 59E **95 Ec**
Crescent, L., Tas. 42 10S 147 10E **107 Df**
Cressy, Tas. 41 41S 147 4E **107 Cf**
Cressy, Vic. 38 2S 143 40E **100 Fd**
Creswick, Vic. 37 25S 143 51E **100 Ed**
Cretin, C., Papua N.G. 6 40S 147 53E **141 Dd**
Crib Pt., Vic. 38 22S 145 13E **101 Ff**
Crocodile Is., N.T. 11 43S 135 8E **123 Ac**
Croker, C., N.T. 10 58S 132 35E **123 Ab**
Croker, I., N.T. 11 14S 132 32E **123 Ab**
Cromwell, N.Z. 45 3S 169 14E **145 Fd**
Cronadun, N.Z. 42 2S 171 51E **145 Cf**
Cronulla, N.S.W. 34 3S 151 8E **93 Ek**
Crooble, N.S.W. 29 16S 150 16E **95 Ca**
Crookwell, N.S.W. 34 28S 149 24E **93 Ei**
Croppa Creek, N.S.W. 28 9S 150 20E **95 Ca**
Croppa Cr., N.S.W. 28 48S 150 4E **95 Ca**
Crossley, Mt., N.Z. 42 50S 172 5E **145 Cg**
Crossman, W.A. 32 48S 116 35E **119 Fc**
Crowdy Hd., N.S.W. 31 48S 152 44E **95 Ec**
Crowfoot, Mt., N.Z. 44 33S 167 3E **145 Fb**
Crowl Cr., N.S.W. 32 0S 145 30E **92 Be**
Crows Nest, Qld. 27 16S 152 4E **131 Ec**
Croydon, Qld. 18 13S 142 14E **127 Bc**
Croydon, Qld. 22 28S 149 11E **129 Dh**
Crystal Brook, S.A. 33 21S 138 12E **113 Cd**
Cuballing, W.A. 32 50S 117 10E **119 Fd**
Cudal, N.S.W. 33 16S 148 46E **93 Dh**
Cuddapan, L., Qld. 25 45S 141 26E **127 Dc**
Cudgegong R., N.S.W. 32 30S 149 16E **93 Ci**
Cudgewa, Vic. 36 10S 147 42E **101 Dh**
Cue, W.A. 27 25S 117 54E **117 Db**
Culburra, S.A. 35 50S 139 58E **113 Ee**
Culcairn, N.S.W. 35 41S 147 3E **93 Fg**

Culgoa, Vic. 35 44S 143 6E **100 Cd**
Culgoora, N.S.W. 30 18S 149 35E **91 Bg**
Culham Inlet, W.A. 33 58S 120 3E **119 Hg**
Culion I., Philippines 11 54N 120 1E **135 Be**
Cullarin Ra., N.S.W. 34 30S 149 30E **93 Ei**
Cullen, N.T. 13 58S 131 54E **123 Ab**
Cullen Pt., Qld. 11 57S 141 54E **127 Ac**
Cullen Bullen, N.S.W. 33 18S 150 2E **93 Dj**
Cullivel, N.S.W. 35 14S 146 22E **93 Ff**
Cullivel, L., N.S.W. 35 13S 146 25E **93 Ff**
Culloden, Qld. 22 7S 144 18E **128 Dc**
Culpataro, N.S.W. 33 40S 144 22E **92 Dd**
Culpaulin, N.S.W. 31 42S 143 14E **92 Bc**
Culver, Pt., W.A. 32 54S 124 43E **117 Ec**
Culverden, N.Z. 42 47S 172 49E **145 Cg**
Cumberland, C., New Hebrides
14 39S 166 37E **139 Gf**
Cumberland Islands, Qld. 20 35S 149 10E **129 Bh**
Cumborah, N.S.W. 29 40S 147 45E **91 Af**
Cummins, S.A. 34 16S 135 43E **113 Da**
Cumnock, N.S.W. 32 59S 148 46E **93 Ch**
Cunderdin, W.A. 31 37S 117 12E **119 Ed**
Cunderdin Nth., W.A. 31 33S 117 12E **119 Ed**
Cunliffe, S.A. 34 5S 137 44E **113 Dc**
Cunnamulla, Qld. 28 2S 145 38E **127 Dd**
Curban, N.S.W. 31 33S 148 32E **93 Bh**
Curlew Is., Qld. 21 36S 149 48E **129 Ch**
Curlewis, N.S.W. 31 7S 150 16E **95 Ea**
Curlwaa, N.S.W. 34 2S 141 59E **92 Ea**
Curnamona, S.A. 31 37S 139 32E **113 Ae**
Currabubula, N.S.W. 31 16S 150 44E **95 Ea**
Curramulka, S.A. 34 47S 137 42E **113 Dc**
Curranyalpa, N.S.W. 30 53S 144 39E **92 Ad**
Curraweena, N.S.W. 30 47S 145 54E **91 Be**
Currawilla, Qld. 25 10S 141 20E **127 Dc**
Currency Ck., S.A. 35 26S 138 45E **113 Ed**
Currie, Tas. 39 56S 143 53E **107 Ab**
Currockbilly, N.S.W. 35 25S 150 0E **93 Fi**
Curtis Channel, Qld. 24 0S 152 20E **131 Ab**
Curtis Gr. Is., Qld. 39 30S 146 37E **107 Ae**
Curtis I., Qld. 23 35S 151 10E **131 Ab**
Curtis, Pt., Qld. 23 53S 151 21E **131 Ab**
Curyo, Vic. 35 50S 142 47E **100 Cc**
Cushnie, Qld. 26 20S 151 45E **131 Db**
Cust, N.Z. 43 19S 172 22E **145 Dg**
Cuvier, C., W.A. 23 14S 113 22E **117 Ca**
Cuvier, I., N.Z. 36 27S 175 50E **144 Cd**
Cuyo, Philippines 10 12N 121 6E **135 Bf**
Cuyo I., Philippines 10 50N 121 5E **135 Bf**
Cygnet, Tas. 43 8S 147 1E **107 Ee**
Cygnet River, S.A. 35 42S 137 30E **113 Ec**
Cynthia, Qld. 25 13S 151 8E **131 Cb**

D

Da Lat, Vietnam 11 56N 108 25E **134 Bc**
Da Nang, Vietnam 16 4N 108 13E **134 Ac**
Daandine, Qld. 27 6S 150 59E **131 Ea**
Dadali, Solomon Is. 8 7S 159 6E **139 Qr**
Dagua, Papua N.G. 3 27S 143 20E **141 Bb**
Dagupan, Philippines 16 3N 120 20E **135 Af**
Dagworth, Qld. 21 52S 142 10E **128 Ca**
Daintree, Qld. 16 20S 145 20E **127 Bd**
Dairy Creek, W.A. 25 12S 115 48E **117 Db**
Dajarra, Qld. 21 42S 139 30E **127 Cb**
Dala, Solomon Is. 8 30S 160 41E **139 Qs**
Dalby, Qld. 27 10S 151 17E **131 Eb**
Dale R., W.A. 32 5S 116 49E **119 Fc**
Dale West, W.A. 32 17S 116 45E **119 Fc**
Dallarnil, Qld. 25 19S 152 2E **131 Cc**
Dalma Scrub, Qld. 23 21S 150 15E **131 Aa**
Dalmorton, N.S.W. 29 50S 152 28E **95 Cc**
Dalrymple, Mt., Qld. 21 1S 148 39E **129 Bg**
Dalton, N.S.W. 34 43S 149 12E **93 Ei**
Dalwallinu, W.A. 30 17S 116 40E **119 Dc**
Dalwogon, Qld. 26 32S 150 6E **131 Da**
Daly R., N.T. 13 21S 130 18E **123 Ab**
Daly Waters, N.T. 16 15S 133 24E **123 Bb**
Dampier, W.A. 20 41S 116 42E **117 Cb**
Dampier Archipelago, W.A. 20 38S 116 32E **117 Cb**
Dampier St., Papua N.G. 5 50S 148 0E **141 Ce**
Danao, Philippines 10 31N 124 1E **135 Bf**
Dandaleo, N.S.W. 32 16S 147 38E **93 Cg**
Dandaraga, Qld. 23 48S 144 47E **128 Ec**
Dandaragan, W.A. 30 40S 115 40E **119 Db**
Dandenong, Vic. 38 0S 145 15E **101 Ef**

Dannevirke, N.Z. 40 12S 176 8E **144 Ge**
Dao, Philippines 10 30N 122 6E **135 Bf**
Dapto, N.S.W. 34 30S 150 47E **93 Ej**
Darby Falls, N.S.W. 33 53S 148 52E **93 Dh**
Dardanup, W.A. 33 26S 115 45E **119 Gb**
Dareton, N.S.W. 34 4S 142 3E **92 Eb**
Darfield, N.Z. 43 29S 172 7e **145 Dg**
Dargaville, N.Z. 35 57S 173 52E **144 Bb**
Dargo, Vic. 37 27S 147 15E **101 Eh**
Dargo, R., Vic. 37 32S 147 15E **101 Eh**
Darkan, W.A. 33 20S 116 43E **119 Gc**
Darke Peak, S.A. 33 27S 136 12E **113 Cb**
Darling R., N.S.W. 34 4S 141 54E **92 Cb**
Darling Downs, Qld. 38 30S 152 0E **127 Dd**
Darling R., W.A. 32 30S 116 0E **119 Gc**
Darlington, Vic. 38 2S 143 3E **100 Fd**
Darlington Point, N.S.W. 34 37S 146 1E **93 Ef**
Darlot, L., W.A. 27 48S 121 35E **117 Dc**
Darnick, N.S.W. 32 48S 143 38E **92 Cc**
Darr, Qld. 23 13S 144 7E **128 Ec**
Darr Creek, Qld. 26 32S 151 7E **131 Db**
Darr, R., Qld. 23 39S 143 50E **128 Ec**
Dartmoor, Vic. 37 56S 141 19E **100 Eb**
Dartmouth, Qld. 23 31S 144 44E **128 Ec**
Dartmouth, L., Qld. 26 4S 145 18E **127 Dd**
Darran Mts., N.Z. 44 37S 167 59E **145 Eb**
Darriman, Vic. 38 26S 146 59E **101 Fg**
Daru, Papua N.G. 9 3S 143 13E **141 Eb**
Darwin, N.T. 12 25S 130 51E **123 Ab**
Darwin River, N.T. 12 50S 130 58E **123 Ab**
Datatine, W.A. 33 28S 117 54E **119 Gd**
Dattuck, Vic. 35 34S 142 17E **100 Cc**
Davao, Philippines 7 0N 125 40E **135 Cg**
Davao G., Philippines 7 30N 125 48E **135 Cg**
Davenport Downs, Qld. 24 8S 141 7E **127 Cc**
Davenport Ra., N.T. 20 28S 134 0E **123 Cb**
Davyhurst, W.A. 30 2S 120 40E **119 Dg**
Dawes, Qld. 24 36S 150 44E **131 Ba**
Dawson Range, Qld. 24 30S 149 48E **129 Eh**
Dawes Ra., Qld. 24 40S 150 40E **131 Bb**
Dawson R., Qld. 23 25S 150 10E **131 Ba**
Dawson Vale, Qld. 21 23S 146 31E **129 Ce**
Dayboro, Qld. 27 11S 152 50E **131 Ec**
Daylesford, Vic. 37 21S 144 9E **100 Ee**
Daysdale, N.S.W. 35 38S 146 19E **93 Ff**
De Grey, W.A. 20 12S 119 12E **117 Cb**
De Grey R., W.A. 20 0S 119 13E **117 Cb**
Deakin, W.A. 30 46S 129 58E **117 Ed**
Deal I., Aust. 39 30S 147 20E **107 Af**
Deans Marsh, Vic. 38 25S 143 52E **100 Fd**
Deanmill, W.A. 34 15S 116 4E **119 Hc**
Deborah L., W.A. 30 45S 119 0E **119 De**
Dederang, Vic. 36 28S 147 1E **101 Dg**
Dee R., Qld. 24 6S 150 8E **131 Aa**
Deep R., W.A. 35 0S 116 40E **119 Hc**
Deep Lead, Vic. 37 0S 142 43E **100 Ec**
Deep Well, N.T. 24 20S 134 0E **123 Cb**
Deepwater, N.S.W. 29 25S 151 51E **95 Cb**
Deeragun, Qld. 19 15S 146 42E **129 Zx**
Deeral, Qld. 17 14S 145 55E **129 Xw**
Delambre I., W.A. 20 27S 117 4E **117 Cb**
Delegate, N.S.W. 37 4S 148 56E **101 Ei**
Deloraine, Tas. 41 30S 146 40E **107 Ce**
Delungra, N.S.W. 29 39S 150 51E **95 Ca**
Dempo Mt., Indonesia 4 10S 103 15E **134 Eb**
Dempsters Inlet, W.A. 34 5S 119 39E **119 Hf**
Denham, W.A. 25 56S 113 31E **117 Da**
Denham Range, Qld. 21 55S 147 46E **129 Df**
Denham Sound, W.A. 25 45S 113 15E **117 Da**
Denial B., S.A. 32 14S 133 32E **111 Cb**
Deniliquin, N.S.W. 35 30S 144 58E **92 Fd**
Denison Plains, W.A. 18 35S 128 0E **117 Bd**
Denman, N.S.W. 32 24S 150 42E **95 Fa**
Denmark, W.A. 34 59S 117 18E **119 Hd**
Denmark R., W.A. 34 58S 117 21E **119 Hd**
Denniston, N.Z. 41 45S 171 49E **145 Bf**
Denpasar, Indonesia 8 45S 115 5E **135 Fe**
D'Entrecasteaux I., Papua N.G. 9 0S 151 0E **141 Ef**
D'Entrecasteaux Channel, Tas.
43 20S 147 10E **107 Ef**
D'Entrecasteaux Pt., W.A. 34 50S 115 57E **119 Hb**
Depot Spring, W.A. 27 55S 120 3E **119 Ag**
Depuch I., W.A. 20 35S 117 44E **117 Cb**
Derby, Tas. 41 8S 147 48E **107 Cf**
Derby, W.A. 17 18S 123 38E **117 Bc**
Dergholm, Vic. 37 24S 141 14E **100 Eb**
Derri Derra, Qld. 25 42S 151 12E **131 Cb**
Derrinallum, Vic. 37 57S 143 15E **100 Ed**
Derriwong, N.S.W. 33 6S 147 21E **93 Dg**
Derwent Bridge, Tas. 42 8S 146 14E **107 De**
Derwent R., Tas. 42 20S 146 30E **107 De**
D'Estrees Bay, S.A. 35 55S 137 45E **113 Ec**

Gatton, Qld. 27 32S 152 17E **131 Ec**
Gatukai, Solomon Is. 8 45S 158 15E **139 Qr**
Gatum, Vic. 37 26S 141 57E **100 Eb**
Gaua, New Hebrides 14 15S 167 30E **139 Gg**
Gawler, S.A. 34 30S 138 42E **113 Dd**
Gayndah, Qld. 25 35S 151 39E **131 Cb**
Gazelle Pen., Papua N.G. 4 40S 152 0E **141 Cf**
Gazelle, Récif de la, New Caledonia
20 11S 156 27E **139 A_1c_1**
Gebe, Indonesia 0 5N 129 25E **135 Dg**
Geegully Ck., W.A. 18 0S 123 53E **117 Bc**
Geelong, Vic. 38 10S 144 22E **100 Fe**
Geerayling, W.A. 32 59S 117 2E **119 Fd**
Geeveston, Tas. 43 10S 146 56E **107 Ee**
Gelantipy, Vic. 37 8S 148 22E **101 Ei**
Gellibrand, Vic. 38 33S 143 30E **100 Fd**
Gembrook, Vic. 37 58S 145 37E **101 Ef**
Genoa, Vic. 37 29S 149 35E **101 Ej**
Genoa R., Vic. 37 31S 149 41E **101 Ej**
General Macarthur, Philippines
11 18N 125 28E **135 Bf**
General Santos, Philippines 6 12N 125 14E **135 Cf**
George L., N.S.W. 35 10S 149 25E **93 Fi**
George L., S.A. 37 25S 140 0E **113 Gf**
George L., W.A. 22 45S 123 40E **117 Cc**
George Pt., Qld. 20 5S 148 35E **129 Bg**
George Sd., N.Z. 44 52S 167 25E **145 Eb**
George Town, W. Malaysia 5 25N 100 19E **134 Cb**
George Town, Tas. 41 5S 146 49E **107 Ce**
Georgetown, S.A. 33 23S 138 27E **113 Cd**
Georgetown, Qld. 18 18S 143 32E **127 Bc**
Georgina Downs, N.T. 21 10S 137 40E **123 Cc**
Geraldine, N.Z. 44 5S 171 15E **145 Ef**
Geraldton, W.A. 28 48S 114 32E **119 Ba**
Gerang Gerung, Vic. 36 22S 141 52E **100 Db**
Geranium, S.A. 35 23S 140 11E **113 Ef**
Gerogery, N.S.W. 35 50S 147 1E **93 Fg**
Gerringong, N.S.W. 34 46S 150 47E **93 Ej**
Geser, Indonesia 3 50N 130 35E **135 Eh**
Geurie, N.S.W. 32 22S 148 50E **93 Ch**
Ghooli, W.A. 31 15S 119 27E **119 Ef**
Gibbo Mt., Vic. 36 38S 147 58E **101 Di**
Gibson Desert, W.A. 24 0S 126 0E **117 Cc**
Gibson Mt., W.A. 29 35S 117 25E **119 Cd**
Gifford Creek, W.A. 24 3S 116 16E **117 Cb**
Gilbert River, Qld. 18 9S 142 52E **127 Bc**
Gilbert R., Qld. 16 35S 141 15E **128 Ab**
Gilberton, Qld. 19 16S 143 35E **128 Ab**
Gilgai No 7 Pumping Sta., W.A.
31 18S 119 56E **119 Ef**
Gilgandra, N.S.W. 31 43S 148 39E **93 Bh**
Gilgunnia, N.S.W. 32 26S 146 2E **93 Cf**
Giles L., W.A. 29 40S 119 45E **119 Cf**
Gillen L., W.A. 26 11S 124 38E **117 Dc**
Gilles Downs, S.A. 32 52S 136 58E **113 Bc**
Gillespie Pt., N.Z. 43 24S 169 49E **145 Dd**
Gilliat, Qld. 20 40S 141 28E **127 Cc**
Gillingarra, W.A. 30 58S 116 4E **119 Dc**
Gilmore, N.S.W. 35 14S 148 12E **93 Fh**
Gilmore L., W.A. 32 39S 121 37E **117 Ec**
Giluwe Mt., Papua N.G. 6 8S 143 52E **141 Db**
Gin Gin, Qld. 25 0S 152 0E **131 Bd**
Gindie, Qld. 23 44S 148 8E **129 Eg**
Gingin, W.A. 31 22S 115 54E **119 Eb**
Giralla, W.A. 22 31S 114 15E **117 Ca**
Girgarre, Vic. 36 18S 145 2E **100 De**
Girgir C., Papua N.G. 3 50S 144 35E **141 Bc**
Girilambone, N.S.W. 31 16S 146 57E **93 Bf**
Girral, N.S.W. 33 40S 147 4E **93 Dg**
Giru, Qld. 19 30S 147 5E **127 Bd**
Gisborne, N.Z. 38 39S 178 5E **144 Eg**
Gisborne, Vic. 37 29S 144 36E **100 Ee**
Gizo, Solomon Is. 8 7S 156 50E **139 Qq**
Gladstone, Qld. 23 52S 151 16E **131 Ab**
Gladstone, S.A. 33 15S 138 22E **113 Cd**
Gladstone, Tas. 40 57S 148 2E **107 Bg**
Gladstone, W.A. 25 57S 114 17E **117 Da**
Glass House Mts., Qld. 26 54S 152 58E **131 Dc**
Glastonbury, Qld. 26 12S 152 32E **131 Dc**
Glen Afton, N.Z. 37 46S 175 4E **144 Dd**
Glen Alice, N.S.W. 33 2S 150 14E **93 Cj**
Glen Davis, N.S.W. 33 5S 150 18E **93 Dj**
Glen Emu, N.S.W. 34 8S 143 43E **92 Ec**
Glen Florrie, W.A. 22 55S 115 59E **117 Cb**
Glen Gowrie, N.S.W. 31 4S 143 10E **92 Bc**
Glen Huon, Tas. 43 1S 146 57E **107 Ee**
Glen Innes, N.S.W. 29 40S 151 39E **95 Cb**
Glen Massey, N.Z. 37 38S 175 2E **144 Dd**
Glen Valley, Vic. 36 54S 147 28E **101 Dh**
Glenalbyn, Vic. 36 30S 143 48E **100 Dd**
Glenariff, N.S.W. 30 50S 146 33E **93 Af**
Glenavon, Qld. 21 38S 147 25E **129 Cf**

Glenavy, N.Z. 44 54S 171 7E **145 Ef**
Glenbawn L., N.S.W. 32 5S 151 0E **95 Fb**
Glenbrook, N.S.W. 33 45S 150 37E **93 Dj**
Glenburn, Vic. 37 37S 145 26E **101 Ef**
Glenburnie, S.A. 37 51S 140 50E **113 Gf**
Glencoe, S.A. 37 43S 140 31E **113 Gf**
Glendevie, Tas. 43 14S 147 0E **107 Ee**
Glendon, Qld. 20 39S 147 14E **129 Bf**
Gleneagle, Qld. 18 10S 145 2QE, **129 Yw**
Glenelg, S.A. 34 58S 138 31E **113 Dd**
Glenelg R., Vic. 38 4S 140 59E **100 Eb**
Glenfield, W.A. 28 43S 114 38E **119 Ba**
Glengarry, Vic. 38 7S 146 37E **101 Fg**
Glenham, N.Z. 46 26S 168 52E **145 Gc**
Glenhope, N.Z. 41 40S 172 39E **145 Bg**
Glenhope, Qld. 26 53S 150 40E **131 Da**
Glenisla, Vic. 37 14S 142 12E **100 Ec**
Gleniti, N.Z. 44 23S 171 12E **145 Ef**
Glenmaggie, Vic. 37 54S 146 43E **101 Eg**
Glenmary Mt., N.Z. 44 0S 169 55E **145 Dd**
Glenmorgan, Qld. 27 14S 149 42E **127 Dd**
Glenora, N.S.W. 31 36S 142 21E **92 Bb**
Glenorchy, S.A. 31 55S 139 46E **113 Ae**
Glenorchy, Tas. 42 49S 147 18E **107 Df**
Glenorchy, Vic. 36 55S 142 41E **100 Dc**
Glenore, Qld. 17 50S 141 12E **127 Bc**
Glenormiston, Qld. 22 55S 138 50E **127 Cb**
Glenreagh, N.S.W. 30 2S 153 1E **95 Cc**
Glenrowan, Vic. 36 29S 146 13E **101 Dg**
Glenroy, S.A. 37 13S 140 48E **113 Gf**
Glenthompson, Vic. 37 38S 142 38E **100 Ec**
Glentunnel, N.Z. 43 29S 171 56E **145 Df**
Gloucester, N.S.W. 32 0S 151 59E **95 Fb**
Gloucester C., Papua N.G. 5 26S 148 21E **141 Ce**
Gloucester I., Qld. 20 0S 148 30E **129 Ag**
Gluepot, S.A. 33 45S 140 0E **113 Ce**
Gnalta Peak, N.S.W. 31 8S 142 41E **92 Bb**
Gnowangerup, W.A. 33 58S 117 59E **119 Gd**
Go Cong, Vietnam 10 22N 106 40E **134 Bc**
Godfreys Creek, N.S.W. 34 8S 148 43E **93 Eh**
Gogango, Qld. 23 40S 150 2E **131 Aa**
Gogeldrie, N.S.W. 34 33S 146 17E **93 Ef**
Gol Gol, N.S.W. 34 12S 142 14E **92 Eb**
Gold Coast, Qld. 28 0S 153 25E **131 Ed**
Golden B., N.Z. 40 40S 172 50E **145 Ag**
Goldsworthy, W.A. 20 21S 119 30E **117 Cb**
Gollan, N.S.W. 32 16S 149 5E **93 Ci**
Golspie, N.S.W. 34 20S 149 42E **93 Ei**
Gombo, N.S.W. 32 24S 148 56E **93 Ch**
Goobank Ck., N.S.W. 33 6S 147 10E **93 Dg**
Goodurrum, Qld. 24 52S 152 18E **131 Bc**
Goode, S.A. 31 58S 133 45E **111 Cb**
Goodenough I., Papua N.G. 9 20S 150 50E **141 Ef**
Goodna, Qld. 27 35S 152 57E **131 Ec**
Goodonga, N.S.W. 29 1S 147 28E **91 Af**
Goodwood, N.Z. 45 32S 170 43E **145 Fe**
Goodwood, Qld. 25 9S 152 25E **131 Cc**
Goolara, Qld. 24 56S 150 6E **131 Ba**
Goold Is., Qld. 18 10S 146 10E **129 Yx**
Goolgowi, N.S.W. 33 58S 145 41E **92 De**
Goolma, N.S.W. 32 18S 149 10E **93 Ci**
Gooloogong, N.S.W. 33 36S 148 26E **93 Dh**
Goolwa, S.A. 35 30S 138 47E **113 Ed**
Goomalling, W.A. 31 15S 116 42E **119 Ec**
Goombargana Hill, N.S.W. 35 43S 146 34E **93 Ff**
Goombi, Qld. 26 41S 150 26E **131 Da**
Goomboorian, Qld. 26 5S 152 50E **131 Dc**
Goomburra, Qld. 28 2S 152 5E **131 Fc**
Goomeri, Qld. 26 12S 152 6E **131 Dc**
Goonalga, N.S.W. 31 45S 143 37E **92 Bc**
Goondiwindi, Qld. 28 30S 150 21E **131 Fa**
Goongarrie L., W.A. 30 2S 121 8E **117 Ec**
Goonumbla, N.S.W. 32 59S 148 11E **93 Ch**
Goonyella, Qld. 21 47S 147 58E **129 Cf**
Goorambat, Vic. 36 24S 145 56E **101 Df**
Gooray, Qld. 28 25S 150 2E **131 Fa**
Goovigen, Qld. 24 9S 150 16E **131 Ba**
Goowarra, Qld. 23 39S 149 26E **129 Eh**
Gordon, S.A. 32 7S 138 20E **113 Bd**
Gordon, Tas. 43 16S 147 14E **107 Ef**
Gordon, Vic. 37 34S 144 6E **100 Ee**
Gordon B., N.T. 11 35S 130 10E **123 Ab**
Gordon Downs, W.A. 18 48S 128 40E **117 Bd**
Gordon L., Tas. 42 45S 146 15E **107 De**
Gordon R., Tas. 42 27S 145 30E **107 Dd**
Gordon River, W.A. 34 13S 116 59E **119 Hd**
Gordon R., W.A. 34 10S 117 15E **119 Hd**
Gordonvale, Qld. 17 5S 145 50E **129 Xw**
Gore, N.Z. 46 5S 168 58E **145 Gc**
Gore, Qld. 28 17S 151 30E **131 Fb**
Gormandale, Vic. 38 18S 146 44E **101 Fg**
Gormanston, Tas. 42 3S 145 42E **107 Dd**

Goroka, Papua N.G. 6 7S 145 25E **141 Dc**
Goroke, Vic. 36 43S 141 29E **100 Db**
Gorong Is., Indonesia 4 5S 131 15E **135 Eh**
Gorontalo, Indonesia 0 35N 123 13E **135 Df**
Gosford, N.S.W. 33 23S 151 18E **93 Dk**
Gosse R., N.T. 19 32S 134 37E **123 Bb**
Goulburn, N.S.W. 34 44S 149 44E **93 Ei**
Goulburn I., N.T. 11 40S 133 20E **123 Ab**
Goulburn R., Vic. 36 6S 144 55E **101 Df**
Gourock Ra., N.S.W. 36 0S 149 25E **93 Fi**
Gowan Range, Qld. 25 0S 145 0E **127 Cc**
Gowanbridge, N.Z. 41 43S 172 33E **145 Bg**
Gowrie Junc., Qld. 27 30S 151 54E **131 Fb**
Gowrie Park, Tas. 41 28S 146 14E **107 Ce**
Goyder Lagoon, S.A. 27 3S 139 58E **111 Bc**
Grace (N) L., W.A. 33 10S 118 20E **119 Ge**
Grace (S) L., W.A. 33 15S 118 25E **119 Ge**
Gradgery, N.S.W. 31 12S 147 52E **93 Bg**
Gradule, Qld. 28 32S 149 15E **127 Dd**
Grady L., W.A. 30 25S 117 30E **119 Dd**
Grafton, N.S.W. 29 38S 152 58E **95 Cc**
Grafton C., Qld. 16 51S 146 0E **129 Ww**
Graham, N.S.W. 34 2S 148 33E **93 Eh**
Graman, N.S.W. 29 28S 150 56E **95 Ca**
Grampians Mts., Vic. 37 0S 142 20E **100 Ec**
Grandchester, Qld. 27 40S 152 29E **131 Ec**
Granite Peak, W.A. 25 40S 121 20E **117 Dc**
Granity, N.Z. 41 39S 171 51E **145 Bf**
Grant I., N.T. 11 10S 132 52E **123 Ab**
Grant Pt., Tas. 41 16S 148 20E **107 Cg**
Grant Pt., Vic. 38 32S 145 6E **101 Ff**
Granya, Vic. 36 8S 147 15E **101 Dh**
Grass Valley, W.A. 31 39S 116 48E **119 Ec**
Grassmere, N.S.W. 31 24S 142 38E **92 Bb**
Grassmere L., N.Z. 41 43S 174 10E **145 Bi**
Grassy, King Island 40 3S 144 5E **107 Bc**
Gravelly Beach, Tas. 41 18S 146 58E **107 Ce**
Gravesend, N.S.W. 29 35S 150 20E **95 Ca**
Graysholm, Qld. 28 22S 151 22E **131 Fb**
Great I., N.Z. (S.I.) 46 0S 166 34E **145 Fa**
Great Australian Basin, Qld.
26 0S 140 0E **127 Dc**
Great Australian Bight 33 30S 130 0E **117 Ed**
Great Barrier I., N.Z. 36 11S 175 25E **144 Cd**
Great Barrier Reef, Qld. 19 0S 149 0E **129 Wx**
Great Dividing Range, Vic. 23 0S 146 0E **101 Eg**
Great Keppel I., Qld. 23 10S 150 58E **131 Ab**
Great Lake, Tas. 41 50S 146 30E **107 Ce**
Great Mercury I., N.Z. 36 37S 175 48E **144 Cd**
Great Oyster Bay, Tas. 42 10S 148 10E **107 Dg**
Great Palm I., Qld. 18 45S 146 40E **129 Yx**
Great Papuan Plateau, Papua N.G.
6 30S 142 25E **141 Db**
Great Sandy Desert, W.A. 21 0S 124 0E **117 Cc**
Great Sea Reef, Fiji 16 15S 179 0E **139 Ab**
Great Victoria Desert, W.A.
29 30S 126 30E **117 Dd**
Great Western, Vic. 37 10S 142 50E **100 Ec**
Great Western Tiers Mts., Tas.
41 45S 146 30E **107 Ce**
Gredgwin, Vic. 35 59S 143 38E **100 Cd**
Green Hd., W.A. 30 5S 114 56E **119 Da**
Green I., N.Z. 47 57S 170 25E **145 Gc**
Green Is., Papua N.G. 4 35S 154 10E **141 Ch**
Greenbank, Qld. 27 32S 152 58E **131 Ec**
Greenbushes, W.A. 33 51S 116 2E **119 Gc**
Greenhills, W.A. 31 56S 116 58E **119 Ec**
Greenmeadows, N.Z. 39 32S 176 51E **144 Fe**
Greenmount, Qld. 27 46S 151 51E **131 Eb**
Greenock, S.A. 34 27S 138 55E **113 Dd**
Greenough, W.A. 28 58S 114 43E **119 Ba**
Greenough R., W.A. 28 54S 115 36E **119 Bb**
Greens Beach, Tas. 41 4S 146 45E **107 Ce**
Greens Creek, Vic. 36 57S 143 0E **100 Dc**
Greenwood Mt., N.T. 13 48S 130 4E **123 Ab**
Greerton, N.Z. 37 43S 176 8E **144 De**
Gregory Downs, Qld. 18 35S 138 45E **127 Bb**
Gregory Lake, W.A. 25 38S 119 58E **117 Cd**
Gregory L., S.A. 20 10S 127 30E **111 Bc**
Gregory L., W.A. 28 55S 139 0E **117 Db**
Gregory Range, Qld. 19 30S 143 40E **128 Ac**
Gregory R., Qld. 17 53S 139 17E **127 Bb**
Gregory Ra., W.A. 21 20S 121 12E **117 Cc**
Gregory Springs, Qld. 19 43S 144 22E **128 Ac**
Grenfell, N.S.W. 33 52S 148 8E **93 Dh**
Grenfell Mt., N.S.W. 31 20S 145 18E **92 Be**
Grenville, Vic. 37 46S 143 52E **100 Ed**
Grenville C., Qld. 12 0S 143 13E **127 Ac**
Greta, N.S.W. 32 35S 151 24E **93 Ck**
Gretna, Tas. 42 40S 146 56E **107 De**
Grevillia, N.S.W. 28 26S 152 55E **95 Bc**
Grey C., N.T. 13 0S 136 35E **123 Ac**

Gazetteer

H

Kajabbi, Qld. 20 0S 140 1E **127 Bc**
Kajan R., Indonesia 2 40N 116 40E **135 De**
Kajeli, Indonesia 3 20S 127 10E **135 Eg**
Kajoa, Indonesia 0 1N 127 28E **135 Dg**
Kajuagung, Indonesia 32 8S 104 46E **134 Eb**
Kajuligah, N.S.W. 32 34S 144 38E **92 Cd**
Kaka Pt., N.Z. 46 23S 169 47E **145 Gd**
Kakahi, N.Z. 38 56S 175 24E **144 Ed**
Kakanui, N.Z. 45 11S 170 54E **145 Fe**
Kakanui Mts., N.Z. 45 10S 170 30E **145 Fe**
Kakapotahi, N.Z. 43 0S 170 45E **145 Ce**
Kakaramea, N.Z. 29 42S 174 27E **144 Fc**
Kakatahi, N.Z. 39 42S 175 21E **144 Fd**
Kalabity, S.A. 31 53S 140 20E **113 Af**
Kalamunda, W.A. 32 0S 116 0E **119 Ec**
Kalangadoo, S.A. 37 34S 140 41E **113 Gf**
Kalannie, W.A. 30 22S 117 5E **119 Dd**
Kalao I., Indonesia 7 21S 121 0E **135 Ff**
Kalbar, Qld. 27 56S 152 37E **131 Ec**
Kalbarri, W.A. 27 40S 114 10E **117 Da**
Kalgan, W.A. 34 54S 118 1E **119 Hd**
Kalgoorlie, W.A. 30 40S 121 22E **117 Ec**
Kalianda, Indonesia 5 50S 105 45E **134 Fc**
Kalibo, Philippines 11 43N 122 22E **135 Bf**
Kalkaroo, N.S.W. 31 12S 143 54E **92 Bc**
Kalkaroo, S.A. 31 43S 140 33E **113 Af**
Kalo, Papua N.G. 10 1S 147 48E **141 Ed**
Kalpowar, Qld. 24 42S 151 18E **131 Bb**
Kalyan, S.A. 34 55S 139 49E **113 De**
Kambalda, W.A. 31 10S 121 37E **117 Ec**
Kamo, N.Z. 35 42S 174 20E **144 Bc**
Kampa, Indonesia 1 42S 105 24E **134 Ec**
Kandanga, Qld. 26 24S 152 40E **131 Dc**
Kandavu I., Fiji 19 0S 178 15E **139 Bb**
Kandavu Pass, Fiji 18 45S 178 0E **139 Bb**
Kandep, Papua N.G. 5 54S 143 32E **141 Cb**
Kandos, N.S.W. 32 45S 149 58E **93 Ci**
Kandrian, Papua N.G. 6 14S 149 37E **141 De**
Kangaroo I., S.A. 35 45S 137 0E **113 Ec**
Kangaroo Flat, N.S.W. 31 8S 145 13E **93 Bl**
Kangaroo Flat, N.S.W. 36 45S 144 20E **95 Ec**
Kangaroo Mts., Qld. 23 25S 142 0E **127 Cc**
Kangaroo Valley, N.S.W. 34 42S 150 32E **93 Ej**
Kaniere, N.Z. 42 45S 171 0E **145 Cf**
Kaniva, Vic. 36 22S 141 18E **100 Db**
Kanowit, Malaysia 2 14N 112 20E **134 Dd**
Kanowna, W.A. 30 32S 121 31E **117 Ec**
Kanumbra, Vic. 37 3S 145 40E **101 Ef**
Kao I., Tonga 19 40S 175 1W **139 Nn**
Kapagere, Papua N.G. 9 46S 147 42E **141 Ed**
Kapit, Malaysia 2 0N 113 5E **134 Dd**
Kapiti I., N.Z. 40 50S 174 56E **144 Gc**
Kapua, N.Z. 37 59S 177 55E **144 Dg**
Kapunda, S.A. 34 20S 138 56E **113 Dd**
Kapuni, N.Z. 39 29S 174 8E **144 Fc**
Kaputar Mt., N.S.W. 30 15S 150 10E **95 Da**
Karakitang I., Indonesia 3 14N 125 28E **135 Dg**
Karambu, Indonesia 3 53S 116 6E **135 Ee**
Karamea, N.Z. 41 14S 172 6E **145 Bg**
Karamea Bight, N.Z. 41 22S 171 40E **145 Bf**
Karamea R., N.Z. 41 13S 172 25E **145 Bg**
Karangarua, N.Z. 43 33S 169 48E **145 Dd**
Karara, Qld. 28 12S 151 37E **131 Fb**
Karatta, S.A. 35 59S 136 54E **113 Eb**
Karema, Papua N.G. 9 12S 147 18E **141 Ed**
Karikari C., N.Z. 34 46S 173 24E **144 Ab**
Karimata Is., Indonesia 1 40S 109 0E **134 Ec**
Karimundjawa Is., Indonesia 5 50S 110 30E **134 Fd**
Karioi, N.Z. 37 52S 174 47E **144 Dc**
Karitane, N.Z. 45 38S 170 39E **145 Fe**
Karkar I., Papua N.G. 4 40S 146 0E **141 Cd**
Karkoo, S.A. 34 2S 135 45E **113 Da**
Karlgarin, W.A. 32 30S 118 42E **119 Fe**
Karoonda, S.A. 35 1S 139 59E **113 Ee**
Karragullen, W.A. 32 5S 116 5E **119 Fc**
Karridale, W.A. 34 13S 115 4E **119 Hb**
Karte, S.A. 35 3S 140 43E **113 Ef**
Karuah, N.S.W. 32 37S 151 56E **93 Ck**
Karufa, Indonesia 3 50S 133 20E **135 Eh**
Karumba, Qld. 17 31S 140 50E **127 Bc**
Kassue, Indonesia 6 58S 139 21E **135 Fi**
Kataloka, Indonesia 3 54S 131 27E **135 Eh**
Katamatite, Vic. 36 6S 145 41E **101 Df**
Katanning, W.A. 33 40S 117 33E **119 Gd**
Katanning E., W.A. 33 35S 117 45E **119 Gd**
Katherine, N.T. 14 27S 132 20E **123 Ab**
Katherine Ck., Qld. 23 46S 143 43E **128 Eb**
Kathleen L., W.A. 33 0S 119 22E **119 Gf**
Katiet, Indonesia 2 21S 99 44E **134 Ea**
Katikati, N.Z. 37 32S 175 57E **144 Dd**
Katoomba, N.S.W. 33 41S 150 19E **93 Dj**

Katunga, Vic. 35 58S 145 28E **101 Ch**
Kaukapakapa, N.Z. 36 37S 174 30E **144 Cc**
Kavieng, Papua N.G. 2 36S 150 51E **141 Bf**
Kawakawa, N.Z. 35 23S 174 6E **144 Bc**
Kawarau R., N.Z. 45 2S 169 13E **145 Ec**
Kawau I., N.Z. 36 25S 174 52E **144 Cc**
Kaweka, N.Z. 39 17S 176 23E **144 Fe**
Kaweka Ra., N.Z. 39 17S 176 24E **144 Fe**
Kawerau, N.Z. 38 7S 176 42E **144 Ee**
Kawhia, N.Z. 38 4S 174 49E **144 Ec**
Kawhia Harb., N.Z. 38 5S 174 51E **144 Ec**
Kediri, Indonesia 7 51S 112 1E **134 Fd**
Keepit Dam, N.S.W. 30 52S 150 29E **95 Da**
Keer-Weer C., Qld. 14 0S 141 32E **127 Ac**
Keith, S.A. 36 0S 140 20E **113 Ff**
Keith, W.A. 27 15S 120 30E **117 Dc**
Kekerengu, N.Z. 42 0S 174 0E **145 Bh**
Kellerberrin, W.A. 31 36S 117 38E **119 Ed**
Kelmscott, W.A. 32 7S 115 59E **119 Fb**
Kelsey Creek, Qld. 20 28S 148 28E **129 Bg**
Kelso, N.Z. 45 54S 169 15E **145 Fd**
Keluant, Malaysia 2 3N 103 18E **134 Db**
Kema, Indonesia 1 22N 125 8E **135 Dg**
Kempsey, N.S.W. 31 1S 152 50E **95 Ec**
Kempton, Tas 42 31S 147 12E **107 Df**
Kendal, Indonesia 6 56S 110 14E **134 Fd**
Kendall, N.S.W. 31 35S 152 44E **95 Ec**
Kendall R., Qld. 14 4S 141 35E **127 Ac**
Kendari, Indonesia 3 50S 122 30E **135 Ef**
Kendawangan, Indonesia 2 32S 110 17E **134 Ed**
Kendenup, W.A. 34 30S 117 38E **119 Hd**
Kenebri, N.S.W. 30 46S 149 1E **93 Ai**
Kenilworth, Qld. 26 34S 152 44E **131 Dc**
Kenmore, N.S.W. 34 44S 149 45E **93 Ei**
Kennedy, Qld. 18 12S 145 58E **129 Yw**
Kennedy Ra., W.A. 24 45S 115 10E **117 Cb**
Kennedy's B., N.Z. 36 40S 175 32E **144 Cd**
Kenneth Ra., W.A. 23 50S 117 8E **117 Cb**
Kennett River, Vic. 38 40S 143 52E **100 Fd**
Kensington Downs, Qld. 22 31S 144 19E **128 Dc**
Kent Group Is., Aust. 39 30S 147 20E **107 Af**
Kent R., W.A. 34 59S 117 2E **119 Hc**
Kent River, W.A. 34 58S 117 1E **119 Hc**
Kentdale, W.A. 34 54S 117 3E **119 Hd**
Kentucky, N.S.W. 30 45S 151 28E **95 Db**
Kepler Mts., N.Z. 45 25S 167 20E **145 Fb**
Keppel B., Qld. 23 21S 150 55E **131 Aa**
Keppel Sands, Qld. 23 20S 150 48E **131 Aa**
Kerang, Vic. 35 40S 143 55E **100 Cd**
Keraudren C., Tas. 40 22S 144 47E **107 Bc**
Keraudren C., W.A. 19 58S 119 45E **117 Bc**
Kerema, Papua N.G. 7 58S 145 50E **141 Dc**
Kerepehi, N.Z. 37 18S 175 33E **144 Dd**
Kerevat, Papua N.G. 4 17S 152 2E **141 Cg**
Kerikeri, N.Z. 35 12S 173 59E **144 Bb**
Kerrabee, N.S.W. 32 24S 150 19E **95 Fa**
Kerrisdale, Vic. 37 10S 145 16E **101 Ef**
Kerriwah, N.S.W. 32 26S 147 22E **93 Cg**
Kersbrook, S.A. 34 48S 138 51E **113 Dd**
Ketapang, Indonesia 1 55S 110 0E **134 Ed**
Ketchowla, S.A. 33 18S 139 12E **113 Ce**
Kettering, Tas. 43 7S 147 16E **107 Ef**
Keyneton, S.A. 34 33S 139 10E **113 De**
Keysbrook, W.A. 32 27S 115 58E **119 Fb**
Khancoban, N.S.W. 36 12S 148 7E **93 Gh**
Khemmarat, Thailand 16 10N 105 15E **134 Ac**
Khmer Republic, Asia 12 15N 105 0E **134 Bb**
Khong R., Thailand 17 45N 104 20E **134 Ab**
Kia, Solomon Is. 7 32S 158 26E **139 Kj**
Kiama, N.S.W. 34 40S 150 50E **93 Ej**
Kiamal, Vic. 34 58S 142 18E **100 Bc**
Kiandra, N.S.W. 35 53S 148 31E **93 Fh**
Kianga, Qld. 24 42S 150 1E **131 Ba**
Kickabil, N.S.W. 31 50S 148 30E **93 Bh**
Kidnappers C., N.Z. 39 38S 177 5E **144 Ff**
Kidston, Qld. 18 52S 144 8E **127 Bc**
Kieta, Papua N.G. 6 12S 155 36E **141 Dh**
Kihee, Qld. 27 23S 142 37E **127 Dc**
Kihikihi, N.Z. 38 2S 175 22E **144 Ed**
Kiki, S.A. 35 36S 139 48E **113 Ee**
Kikoira, N.S.W. 33 59S 146 40E **93 Df**
Kikori, Papua N.G. 7 13S 144 15E **141 Dc**
Kikori R., Papua N.G. 7 5S 144 0E **141 Db**
Kilcoy, Qld. 26 59S 152 30E **131 Dc**
Kilcummin, Qld. 22 22S 147 33E **129 Df**
Kilinailau Is., Papua N.G. 4 45S 155 20E **141 Ch**
Kilkivan, Qld. 26 4S 152 14E **131 Dc**
Killarney, Qld. 28 20S 152 18E **131 Fc**
Killarney, Vic. 38 21S 142 18E **100 Fc**
Killarney Park, Qld. 28 20S 152 18E **129 Fe**
Killawarra, W.A. 29 30S 116 2E **119 Cc**
Kilmany, Vic. 38 8S 146 55E **101 Fg**

Kilmore, Vic. 37 25S 144 53E **100 Ee**
Kimba, S.A. 33 8S 136 23E **113 Cb**
Kimbe, Papua N.G. 5 33S 150 11E **141 Cf**
Kimbe Bay, Papua N.G. 5 15S 150 30E **141 Cf**
Kimberley, N.S.W. 32 50S 141 4E **90 Cc**
Kimberley Downs, W.A. 17 24S 124 22E **117 Bc**
Kimbolton, N.Z. 40 4S 175 47E **144 Gd**
Kin Kin, Qld. 26 15S 152 53E **131 Dc**
Kinabalu Mt., Malaysia 6 0N 116 0E **135 Ce**
Kinalung, N.S.W. 32 2S 141 57E **92 Ca**
King Cr., Qld. 24 35S 139 30E **127 Cb**
King I., Tas. 39 50S 144 0E **107 Ac**
King L., Vic. 37 55S 147 45E **101 Eh**
King L., W.A. 33 10S 119 35 **119 Gf**
King Mt., Qld. 25 10S 147 30E **127 Dd**
King R., Vic 37 55S 147 45E **101 Dg**
King Edward R., W.A. 14 14S 126 35E **117 Bd**
King George Sd., W.A. 35 5S 118 0E **119 He**
King Leopold Ra., W.A. 17 20S 124 20E **117 Bc**
King River, W.A. 34 55S 117 53E **119 Hd**
King Sound, W.A. 16 50S 123 20E **117 Bc**
Kingaroy, Qld. 26 32S 151 51E **131 Db**
Kinglake, Vic. 37 31S 145 19E **101 Ef**
Kinglake West, Vic. 37 31S 145 19E **101 Ef**
Kings, N.Z. 29 54S 115 9E **119 Cb**
Kingscliff-Fingal, N.S.W. 28 16S 153 34E **95 Bd**
Kingscote, S.A. 35 33S 137 31E **113 Ec**
Kingston, N.Z. 45 20S 168 43E **145 Fc**
Kingston, Tas. 42 58S 147 19E **107 Df**
Kingston On Murray, S.A. 34 13S 140 20E **113 Df**
Kingston S.E., S.A. 36 52S 139 51E **113 Fe**
Kingstown, N.S.W. 30 29S 151 6E **95 Db**
Kinleith, N.Z. 38 20S 175 56E **144 Ed**
Kintap, Indonesia 3 51S 115 30E **135 Ed**
Kintore Ra., N.T. 23 15S 128 47E **123 Ca**
Kira Kira, Solomon Is. 10 27S 161 56E **139 Rs**
Kirikopuni, N.Z. 35 50S 174 1E **144 Bb**
Kirk Rivers, Qld. 19 59S 146 47E **129 Be**
Kirkalocka, W.A. 28 32S 117 46E **119 Bd**
Kirkliston Ra., N.Z. 44 25S 170 34E **145 Ee**
Kirup, W.A. 33 40S 115 50E **119 Gb**
Kiruru, Indonesia 3 55S 134 55E **135 Eh**
Kirwee, N.Z. 43 30S 172 13E **145 Dg**
Kisaran, Indonesia 2 47N 99 29E **134 Da**
Kitchener, W.A. 30 55S 124 8E **117 Ec**
Kittakittaooloo L., S.A. 28 3S 138 14E **111 Bc**
Kiwai I., Papua N.G. 8 35S 143 30E **141 Eb**
Knob C., W.A. 34 32S 119 16E **119 Hf**
Knowsley, Vic. 36 50S 144 35E **100 De**
Ko Chang I., Thailand 12 0N 102 23E **134 Bb**
Ko Kut I., Thailand 11 40N 102 35E **134 Bb**
Ko Samui I., Thailand 9 30N 100 0E **134 Cb**
Koah, Qld. 16 51S 145 29E **129 Ww**
Koba, Indonesia 2 26S 106 14E **134 Ec**
Koetong, Vic. 36 10S 147 30E **101 Dh**
Kogan, Qld. 27 2S 150 40E **131 Ea**
Koh Kong I., Thailand 11 20N 103 0E **134 Bb**
Kohukohu, N.Z. 36 31S 173 38E **144 Bb**
Kohuratahi, N.Z. 39 6S 174 47E **144 Fc**
Kojonup, W.A. 33 48S 117 10E **119 Gd**
Kokeby Mt., W.A. 32 13S 116 58E **119 Fc**
Kokoda, Papua N.G. 8 54S 147 47E **141 Ed**
Kokopo, Papua N.G. 4 22S 152 19E **141 Cg**
Kokotungo, Qld. 24 8S 150 0E **129 Fh**
Kolenda, S.A. 32 24S 136 17E **113 Bb**
Kolombangara I., Solomon Is. 8 0S 157 5E **139 Pq**
Komoda I., Indonesia 8 37S 119 20E **135 Fe**
Kompong Som, Cambodia 10 38N 103 30E **134 Bb**
Kondar, Qld. 28 5S 150 0E **131 Fa**
Kondinin, W.A. 32 34S 118 8E **119 Fe**
Kondinin East, W.A. 32 31S 118 21E **119 Fe**
Kondinin West, W.A. 32 27S 118 7E **119 Fe**
Kondut East, W.A. 30 40S 116 55E **119 Dc**
Kone, New Caledonia 21 4S 164 52E **139 B_1b_1**
Kongwak, Vic. 38 30S 145 42E **101 Ff**
Konnongorring, W.A. 31 3S 116 45E **119 Ec**
Konos, Papua N.G. 3 10S 151 44E **141 Bf**
Koo-wee-rup, Vic. 38 13S 145 28E **101 Ff**
Koojan, W.A. 30 47S 116 2E **119 Dc**
Kookynie, W.A. 29 17S 121 22E **117 Dc**
Koolanooka, W.A. 29 16S 116 4E **119 Cc**
Koolanooka Hills, W.A. 29 9S 116 10E **119 Cc**
Kooline, W.A. 22 57S 116 20E **117 Cb**
Kooloonong, Vic. 34 48S 143 10E **100 Bd**
Koolyanobbing, W.A. 30 48S 119 36E **119 Df**
Koombooloomba, Qld. 17 51S 145 36E **129 Xw**
Koonarna, N.S.W. 30 58S 142 20E **92 Ab**
Koondrook, Vic. 35 33S 144 8E **100 Ca**
Koonibba, S.A. 31 58S 133 27E **111 Cb**
Koonkool, Qld. 24 15S 150 25E **131 Ba**
Koonwarra, Vic. 30 58S 142 20E **101 Ff**
Koorawatha, N.S.W. 34 2S 148 33E **93 Eh**

Koorda, W.A. 30 48S 117 35E **119 Dd**
Koorkoordine L., W.A. 31 10S 119 17E **119 Ef**
Kootingal, N.S.W. 31 1S 151 3E **95 Eb**
Kopi, S.A. 33 24S 135 40E **113 Ca**
Koppio, S.A. 34 26S 135 51E **113 Da**
Korbel, W.A. 31 39S 118 7E **119 Ee**
Koro I., Fiji 17 19S 179 23E **139 Ab**
Koro Sea, S-W Pacific 17 30S 179 45W **139 Ab**
Koroba, Papua N.G. 5 44S 142 47E **141 Cb**
Korogoro Pt., N.S.W. 31 3S 153 4E **95 Ec**
Koroit, Vic. 38 18S 142 24E **100 Fc**
Korong Vale, Vic. 22S 143 45E **100 Dd**
Korrelocking, W.A. 31 13S 117 28E **119 Ed**
Korumburra, Vic. 38 26S 145 50E **101 Ff**
Kota Baharu, Malaysia 6 7N 102 14E **134 Cb**
Kota Kinabalu, Malaysia 6 0N 116 12E **135 Ce**
Kotaagung, Indonesia 5 38S 104 29E **134 Fb**
Kotabaru, Indonesia 3 20S 116 20E **135 Ee**
Kotabumi, Indonesia 4 49S 104 46E **134 Eb**
Kotamobagu, Indonesia 0 57N 124 31E **135 Df**
Kotawaringin, Indonesia 2 28S 111 27E **134 Ed**
Kotu Group, Tonga 20 6S 174 40W **139 Nn**
Koulen, Cambodia 13 50N 104 40E **134 Bbn**
Koumac, New Caledonia 20 33S 164 17E **139 A₁b₁**
Koumala, Qld. 21 38S 149 15E **129 Ch**
Kowai Bush, N.Z. 43 18S 171 56E **145 Df**
Kowhitirangi, N.Z. 42 53S 171 2E **145 Cf**
Koyan Pegunungan, Malaysia 3 15N 114 30E **135 Dd**
Krambach, N.S.W. 32 4S 152 16E **95 Fc**
Kratie, Cambodia 12 32N 106 10E **134 Bc**
Kratke Ra., Papua N.G. 6 45S 146 0E **141 Dc**
Krinjin, S.A. 34 58S 140 48E **113 Df**
Kroombit, Qld. 24 25S 150 48E **131 Ba**
Krui, Indonesia 5 10S 104 0E **134 Fb**
Krung Thep, Thailand 13 45N 100 35E **134 Bb**
Kuala I., Indonesia 2 46N 105 47E **134 Dc**
Kuala Dungun, Malaysia 4 45N 103 25E **134 Db**
Kuala Kerai, Malaysia 5 30N 102 12E **134 Cb**
Kuala Lipis, Malaysia 4 10N 102 3E **134 Db**
Kuala Lumpur, Malaysia 3 9N 101 41E **134 Db**
Kuala Selangor, Malaysia 3 20N 101 15E **134 Db**
Kuala Terengganu, Malaysia 5 20N 103 8E **134 Cb**
Kualakpuas, Indonesia 2 55S 114 20E **135 Ed**
Kualakurun, Indonesia 1 10S 113 50E **134 Ed**
Kuandang, Indonesia 0 56N 123 1E **135 Df**
Kuantan, Malaysia 3 49N 103 20E **134 Db**
Kubor Mt., Papua N.G. 6 10S 144 44E **141 Dc**
Kuching, Malaysia 1 33N 110 25E **134 Dd**
Kudardup, W.A. 34 17S 115 6E **119 Hb**
Kudat, Malaysia 6 55N 116 55E **135 Ce**
Kudus, Indonesia 6 48S 110 51E **134 Fd**
Kukerin, W.A. 33 13S 118 0E **119 Ge**
Kula G., Solomon Is. 8 5S 156 18E **139 Qq**
Kulde, S.A. 35 10S 139 39E **113 Ee**
Kulikup, W.A. 33 50S 116 41E **119 Gc**
Kulin, W.A. 32 40S 118 2E **119 Fe**
Kulja, W.A. 30 28S 117 18E **119 Dd**
Kulpara, S.A. 34 5S 138 2E **113 Dd**
Kulwin, Vic. 35 0S 142 42E **100 Bc**
Kumai, Indonesia 2 52S 111 45E **134 Ed**
Kumara, N.Z. 42 37S 171 12E **145 Cf**
Kumara Junction, N.Z. 42 35S 171 8E **145 Cf**
Kumarl, W.A. 32 47S 121 33E **117 Ec**
Kumbarilla, Qld. 27 15S 150 55E **131 Ea**
Kumbia, Qld. 26 41S 151 39E **131 Db**
Kumeu, N.Z. 36 46S 174 33E **144 Cc**
Kumusi R., Papua N.G. 8 16S 148 13E **141 Ed**
Kunama, N.S.W. 35 35S 148 4E **93 Fh**
Kundiawa, Papua N.G. 6 2S 145 1E **141 Dc**
Kundip, W.A. 33 42S 120 10E **119 Gg**
Kungala, N.S.W. 29 58S 153 7E **95 Cd**
Kungurri, Qld. 21 3S 148 46E **129 Cg**
Kunlara, S.A. 34 54S 139 55E **113 De**
Kununoppin, W.A. 31 6S 117 28E **119 Ed**
Kununurra, W.A. 15 40S 128 39E **117 Bd**
Kunwarara, Qld. 22 55S 150 9E **129 Di**
Kupiano, Papua N.G. 10 4S 148 14E **141 Fe**
Kuranda, Qld. 16 48S 145 35E **129 Ww**
Kuridala P.O., Qld. 21 16S 140 29E **127 Cc**
Kurow, N.Z. 44 4S 170 29E **145 Ee**
Kurrajong, N.S.W. 33 33S 150 42E **93 Dj**
Kurri Kurri, N.S.W. 32 50S 151 28E **93 Ck**
Kutajane, Indonesia 3 45N 97 50E **134 Da**
Kutarere, N.Z. 38 3S 177 6E **144 Ef**
Kuttabul, Qld. 21 5S 148 48E **129 Cg**
Kwatisore, Indonesia 3 7S 139 59E **135 Eh**
Kwikila, Papua N.G. 9 49S 147 38E **141 Ed**
Kwinana, W.A. 32 15S 115 47E **119 Fb**
Kwolyin, W.A. 31 56S 117 45E **119 Ed**
Kyabram, Vic. 36 19S 145 4E **100 Df**
Kyalite, N.S.W. 34 57S 143 30E **92 Ec**
Kybunga, S.A. 33 54S 138 31E **113 Cd**

Kybybolite, S.A. 36 53S 140 55E **113 Ff**
Kyeamba, N.S.W. 35 26S 147 40E **93 Fg**
Kyeburn, N.Z. 45 10S 170 15E **145 Fe**
Kyneton, Vic. 37 10S 144 29E **100 Ee**
Kynuna, Qld. 21 37S 141 55E **127 Cc**
Kyogle, N.S.W. 28 40S 153 0E **95 Bd**
Kywong, N.S.W. 34 58S 146 44E **93 Ef**

L

La Foa, New Caledonia 21 43S 165 50E **139 B₁c₁**
La Roche, New Caledonia 21 26S 168 2E **139 B₁f₁**
Laanecoorie Res., Vic. 36 52S 143 50E **100 Dd**
Labis, Malaysia 2 22N 103 2E **134 Db**
Labuha, Indonesia 0 30S 127 30E **135 Eg**
Labuhanbadjo, Indonesia 8 28S 120 1E **135 Fe**
Lacepede Is., W.A. 16 55S 122 0E **117 Bc**
Lacepede Bay, S.A. 36 40S 139 40E* **113 Fe**
Lachlan R., N.S.W. 34 22S 143 55E **92 Ed**
Lady Barron I., Tas. 40 12S 148 15E **107 Bg**
Lae, Papua N.G. 6 40S 147 2E **141 Dd**
Lagaip R., Papua N.G. 5 4S 141 52E **141 Cb**
Laggan, N.S.W. 34 23S 149 31E **93 Ei**
Laggers Pt., N.S.W. 30 52S 153 4E **95 Dd**
Laglan, Qld. 22 32S 146 40E **129 De**
Lagonoy Gulf, Philippines 13 50N 123 50E **135 Bf**
Lagrange, W.A. 14 13S 125 46E **117 Bc**
Lagrange B., W.A. 18 38S 121 42E **117 Bc**
Lahewa, Indonesia 1 22N 97 12E **134 Da**
Laiagam, Papua N.G. 5 33S 143 30E **141 Cb**
Laidley, Qld. 27 39S 152 20E **131 Ec**
Lais, Indonesia 3 35S 102 0E **134 Eb**
Lakatoro, New Hebrides 16 0S 167 0E **139 Ig**
Lake Biddy, W.A. 33 1S 118 56E **119 Fe**
Lake Boga, Vic. 35 26S 143 38E **100 Cd**
Lake Bolac, Vic. 37 42S 142 49E **100 Ec**
Lake Brown, W.A. 30 56S 118 20E **119 De**
Lake Buloke, Vic. 36 15S 142 58E **100 Dc**
Lake Camm, W.A. 32 57S 119 36E **119 Ff**
Lake Cargelligo, N.S.W. 33 15S 146 22E **93 Df**
Lake Charm, Vic. 35 36S 143 46E **100 Cd**
Lake Coleridge, N.Z. 43 17S 171 30E **145 Df**
Lake Cowal, N.S.W. 33 41S 147 21E **93 Dg**
Lake Cullelleraine, Vic. 34 15S 141 37E **100 Ab**
Lake Gairdner, S.A. 31 30S 136 0E **113 Aa**
Lake Gilles, S.A. 32 50S 136 45E **113 Bb**
Lake Grace, W.A. 33 7S 118 28E **119 Ge**
Lake Hindmarsh, Vic. 36 5S 141 55E **100 Cb**
Lake King, W.A. 33 5S 119 45E **119 Gf**
Lake Mackay, W.A. 22 30S 129 0E **117 Cd**
Lake Murray, Papua N.G. 6 48S 141 29E **141 Da**
Lake Nash, N.T. 20 57S 138 0E **123 Cc**
Lake Pukaki, N.Z. 44 4S 170 1E **145 Ee**
Lake Rotoiti, N.Z. 38 2S 176 35E **145 Bg**
Lake Tekapo, N.Z. 43 53S 170 33E **145 Ee**
Lake Tyers, Vic. 37 52S 148 5E **101 Ei**
Lake Varley, W.A. 32 48S 119 30E **119 Ff**
Lakemba, Fiji 33 55S 151 5E **139 Bc**
Lalemba Pass, Fiji 18 0S 181 1E **139 Bc**
Lakes Entrance, Vic. 37 50S 148 0E **101 Ei**
Lakuramau, Papua N.G. 2 54S 151 15E **141 Bf**
Lal Lal, Vic. 37 38S 144 1E **100 Ec**
Lalbert, Vic. 35 38S 143 20E **100 Cd**
Lamap, New Hebrides 16 26S 167 43E **139 Ig**
Lambasa, Fiji 15 30S 179 10E **139 Ab**
Lambert, Papua N.G. 4 11S 151 31E **141 Cf**
Lambon, Papua N.G. 4 45S 152 48E **141 Cg**
Lameroo, S.A. 35 19S 140 33E **113 Ef**
Lamitan, Philippines 6 40N 122 10E **135 Cf**
Lamlan Mt., Guam 13 20N 144 40E **139 Tu**
Lamon Bay, Philippines 14 30N 122 20E **135 Bf**
Lampung, Indonesia 1 48S 115 0E **134 Fb**
Lanao L., Philippines 7 52N 124 15E **135 Cf**
Lancefield, Vic. 37 18S 144 45E **100 Ee**
Lancelin, W.A. 31 1S 115 20E **119 Eb**
Lancelin I., W.A. 31 0S 115 18E **119 Db**
Lander R., N.T. 20 25S 132 0E **123 Cb**
Landor, W.A. 25 10S 117 0E **117 Db**
Landsborough, Qld. 26 48S 152 58E **131 Dc**
Landsborough Ck., Qld. 22 28S 144 35E **128 Cc**
Landsborough R., N.Z. 43 58S 169 31E **145 Dd**
Lang Lang, Vic. 38 15S 145 34E **101 Ff**
Langawirra, N.S.W. 31 27S 142 0E **92 Bb**
Langhorne Ck., S.A. 35 17S 139 2E **113 Ee**
Langidoon, N.S.W. 31 36S 142 2E **92 Bb**
Langkon, Malaysia 6 30N 116 40E **135 Ce**
Langley Mt., Qld. 26 46S 152 35E **131 Dc**

Langley Downs, Qld. 23 22S 148 18E **129 Eg**
Langlo R., Qld. 26 26S 146 5E **127 Dd**
Langsa, Indonesia 4 30N 97 57E **134 Da**
Langtree, N.S.W. 33 39S 145 34E **92 De**
Lansdowne, N.S.W. 31 48S 152 30E **95 Ec**
Laoag, Philippines 18 7N 120 34E **135 Af**
Laos, Asia 17 45N 105 0E **134 Ac**
Lara, Vic. 38 2S 144 26E **100 Fe**
Larap, Philippines 14 18N 122 39E **135 Bf**
Laravale, Qld. 28 6S 152 57E **131 Fc**
Larcom Mt., Qld. 23 48S 150 59E **131 Aa**
Lariang, Indonesia 1 35S 119 25E **135 Ee**
Laroona, Qld. 19 22S 145 59E **128 Ad**
Larrey Pt., W.A. 19 55S 119 7E **117 Bb**
Larrimah, N.T. 15 35S 133 12E **123 Bb**
Lascelles, Vic. 35 34S 142 34E **100 Cc**
Late I., Tonga 18 48S 174 39W **139 Nn**
Latham, W.A. 29 44S 116 20E **119 Cc**
Latouche Treville C., W.A. 18 27S 121 49E **117 Bc**
Latrobe, Tas. 41 14S 146 30E **107 Ce**
Latrobe, Tas. 41 14S 146 30E **101 Fg**
Lau (Eastern Group) Is., Fiji 17 0S 178 30W **130 Ac**
Lauderdale, Tas. 42 55S 147 29E **107 Df**
Launceston, Tas. 41 24S 147 8E **107 Cf**
Laura, S.A. 33 10S 138 18E **113 Cd**
Laurel Hill, N.S.W. 35 34S 148 6E **93 Fh**
Laurieton, N.S.W. 31 39S 152 48E **95 Ec**
Lauriston, N.Z. 43 44S 171 46E **145 Df**
Laut Ketjil Is., Indonesia 4 45S 115 40E **135 Ee**
Lautoka, Fiji 17 37S 177 27E **139 Aa**
Laverton, W.A. 28 44S 122 29E **117 Dc**
Lavers Hill, Vic. 38 40S 143 25E **100 Fd**
Lawas, Malaysia 4 55N 115 40E **135 De**
Lawele, Indonesia 5 16S 123 3E **135 Ff**
Lawn Hill, Qld. 18 36S 138 33E **127 Bb**
Lawrence, N.S.W. 29 30S 153 8E **95 Cd**
Lawrence, N.Z. 45 55S 169 41E **145 Fd**
Leadville, N.S.W. 32 1S 149 38E **93 Bi**
Leamington, N.Z. 37 55S 175 29E **144 Dd**
Leander Pt., W.A. 29 17S 114 53E **119 Ca**
Learmonth, W.A. 22 40S 114 10E **117 Ca**
Lebak, Philippines 6 32N 124 5E **135 Cf**
Lebrina, Tas. 41 10S 147 12E **107 Cf**
Lee Mt., Tas. 42 36S 145 35E **107 Dd**
Leeston, N.Z. 43 45S 172 19E **145 Dg**
Leeton, N.S.W. 34 23S 146 23E **93 Ef**
Leeuwin C., W.A. 34 20S 115 9E **119 Hb**
Lefroy L., W.A. 31 21S 121 40E **117 Ec**
Legana, Tas. 41 22S 147 3E **107 Cf**
Legendre I., W.A. 20 22S 116 55E **117 Cb**
Legerwood, Tas. 41 12S 147 41E **107 Cf**
Legges Tor Mt., Tas. 41 33S 147 39E **107 Cf**
Legume, N.S.W. 28 20S 152 12E **95 Bc**
Leicester I., Qld. 22 15S 150 25E **129 Di**
Leichardt Ra., Qld. 20 46S 147 40E **129 Bf**
Leichardt R., Qld. 16 27S 129 44E **127 Bb**
Leigh, N.Z. 36 17S 174 58E **144 Cc**
Leisler Mt., N.T. 23 23S 129 30E **123 Ca**
Leitchville, Vic. 35 54S 144 18E **100 Ce**
Leithfield, N.Z. 43 12S 172 44E **145 Dg**
Leksula, Indonesia 3 46S 126 31E **135 Eg**
Lemana, Tas. 41 31S 146 35E **107 Ce**
Lemery, Philippines 13 58N 120 56E **135 Bf**
Lennonville, W.A. 27 59S 117 50E **119 Ad**
Lennox, Qld. 22 55S 146 11E **129 De**
Lennox Head, N.S.W. 28 46S 153 37E **95 Bd**
Leongatha, Vic. 38 30S 145 58E **101 Ff**
Leonora, W.A. 28 49S 121 19E **117 Dc**
Leonora Downs, N.S.W. 32 29S 142 5E **92 Ca**
Leopold, Vic. 38 13S 144 28E **100 Fe**
Lepperton, N.Z. 39 4S 174 13E **144 Fc**
Lerida, N.S.W. 31 42S 145 42E **92 Be**
Leschenault Inlet, W.A. 33 15S 115 42E **119 Gb**
Lesuer I., W.A. 13 50S 127 17E **117 Ad**
Lethbridge, Vic. 37 58S 144 6E **100 Ee**
Lethebrook Qld. 20 32S 148 40E **129 Bg**
Lethero, N.S.W. 33 33S 142 30E **92 Db**
Leti Is., Indonesia 8 10S 128 0E **135 Fg**
Lette, N.S.W. 34 24S 143 18E **92 Ec**
Leura, Qld. 23 10S 149 36E **129 Eh**
Levels, N.Z. 44 19S 171 12E **145 Ef**
Levendale, Tas. 42 32S 147 34E **107 Df**
Leveque C., W.A. 16 20S 123 0E **117 Bc**
Levuka, Fiji 17 34S 181 0W **139 Ab**
Levin, N.Z. 40 37S 175 18E **144 Gd**
Lewis Pass, N.Z. 42 24S 172 24E **145 Cg**
Lewis Ra., W.A. 20 3S 128 50E **117 Cd**
Lexton, Vic. 37 16S 143 31E **100 Ed**
Leyburn, Qld. 28 1S 151 35E **131 Fb**
Leyte I., Philippines 11 0N 125 0E **135 Bf**
Lhokseumawe, Indonesia 5 20N 97 10E **134 Ca**
Liamena, N.S.W. 31 58S 149 22E **93 Bi**

163

Lianga, Philippines 8 34N 126 6E **135 Cg**
Lichfield, N.Z. 38 6S 175 49E **144 Ed**
Licola, Vic. 37 39S 146 39E **101 Eg**
Liena, Tas. 41 33S 146 14E **107 Ce**
Lifu I., New Caledonia 20 53S 167 13E **139 A₁e₁**
Lifuka I., Tonga 19 48S 174 21W **139 Nn**
Lightning Ridge, N.S.W. 29 22S 148 0E **91 Ag**
Lihir Group, Papua N.G. 3 0S 152 35E **141 Bg**
Lihou Reefs & Cays 17 25S 151 40E **127 Be**
Lilimur, Vic. 36 23S 141 11E **100 Db**
Lillian Pt., Mt., W.A. 27 40S 126 6E **117 Dd**
Lilydale, S.A. 32 57S 139 59E **113 Bf**
Lilydale, Tas. 41 15S 147 13E **107 Cf**
Lilydale, Vic. 37 46S 145 20E **101 Ef**
Lima, Indonesia 3 37S 128 4E **135 Eg**
Limbang, Malaysia 4 42N 115 6E **135 De**
Limbri, N.S.W. 31 3S 151 5E **95 Eb**
Limbunya, N.T. 17 14S 129 50E **123 Ba**
Limehills, N.Z. 46 4S 168 20E **145 Gc**
Limmen Bight, N.T. 14 40S 135 35E **123 Ac**
Limmen Bight R., N.T. 15 7S 135 44E **123 Bc**
Lincoln, N.Z. 43 38S 172 30E **145 Dg**
Lindis Pass, N.Z. 44 43S 169 30E **145 Ed**
Lindisfarne, Tas. 42 51S 147 23E **107 Df**
Lingayen, Philippines 16 1N 120 14E **135 Af**
Lingayen G., Philippines 16 10N 120 15E **135 Af**
Lingga Is., Indonesia 0 10S 104 30E **134 Eb**
Linois C., S.A. 36 0S 137 35E **113 Fc**
Linton, Vic. 37 41S 143 33E **100 Ed**
Linville, Qld. 26 50S 152 11E **131 Dc**
Lipson Reef, S.A. 36 12S 136 49E **113 Fb**
Liptrap C., Vic. 38 50S 145 55E **101 Ff**
Lisburn C., New Hebrides 15 40S 166 43E **139 Hf**
Lismore, N.S.W. 28 44S 153 21E **95 Bd**
Lismore, Vic. 37 58S 143 21E **100 Ed**
Liston, N.S.W. 28 39S 152 6E **95 Bc**
Litchfield, Vic. 36ˈ18S 142 52E **100 Dc**
Lithgow, N.S.W. 33 25S 150 8E **93 Dj**
Little Barrier I., N.Z. 36 12S 175 8E **144 Cc**
Little Billabong, N.S.W 35 35S 147 33E **93 Fg**
Little Mulgrave, Qld. 17 19S 145 44E **129 Xw**
Little Plain, N.S.W. 29 43S 150 59E **95 Ca**
Little River, N.Z. 43 45S 172 49E **145 Dg**
Little Swanport, Tas. 42 19S 147 57E **107 Dg**
Little Topar, N.S.W. 31 47S 142 12E **92 Bb**
Liveringa, W.A. 18 3S 124 10E **117 Bc**
Liverpool, N.S.W. 33 55S 150 52E **93 Dj**
Liverpool Plains, N.S.W. 31 15S 150 15E **95 Ea**
Liverpool Ra., N.S.W. 31 50S 150 30E **95 Ea**
Livingston Mts., N.Z. 45 15S 168 9E **145 Fc**
Lizard I., Qld. 14 42S 145 30E **127 Ad**
Llangothlin, N.S.W. 30 7S 151 41E **95 Db**
Lloyd B., Qld. 12 45S 143 27E **127 Ac**
Lobenthal, S.A. 34 54S 138 52E **113 Dd**
Loch, Vic. 38 21S 145 42E **101 Ff**
Lochada, W.A. 29 12S 116 33E **119 Cc**
Lochiel, N.Z. 46 12S 168 20E **145 Gc**
Lochiel, S.A. 33 56S 138 8E **113 Cd**
Lochnagar, Qld. 24 34S 144 52E **128 Ed**
Lock, S.A. 33 34S 135 46E **113 Ca**
Lockhart, N.S.W. 35 14S 146 40E **93 Ff**
Lockhart L., W.A. 33 15S 119 3E **119 Gf**
Lockier R., W.A. 29 12S 115 15E **119 Cb**
Lockington, Vic. 36 16S 144 34E **100 De**
Loddon R., Vic. 35 31S 143 51E **100 Dd**
Lodi C., Tas. 41 55S 148 20E **107 Cg**
Lodji, Indonesia 1 38S 127 28E **135 Eg**
Lofty, Mt., S.A. 34 59S 138 42E **113 Dd**
Lofty Ra., W.A. 24 15S 119 30E **117 Cb**
Logan Downs, Qld. 22 25S 147 56E **129 Df**
Loh, New Hebrides 13 21S 166 38E **139 Ff**
Lolowai, New Hebrides 15 18S 168 0E **139 Hg**
Lolworth Range, Qld. 20 17S 145 15E **128 Bd**
Lomok, I., Indonesia 8 35S 116 20E **135 Fe**
Lompobatang, Indonesia 5 24S 119 56E **135 Fe**
Londonderry, C., W.A. 13 45S 126 55E **117 Ad**
Long I., N.Z. 45 46S 166 41E **145 Fa**
Long I., Papua N.G. 5 20S 147 5E **141 Cd**
Long Is., Qld. 22 8S 149 53E **129 Dh**
Long I., W.A. 30 19S 115 0E **119 Da**
Long Pt., N.Z. 39 10S 177 49E **144 Ff**
Long Pt., N.Z. 46 34S 169 36E **145 Gd**
Long Plains, S.A. 34 23S 138 24E **113 Dd**
Long Reefs, W.A. 13 55S 125 45E **117 Ad**
Long Xuyen, Vietnam 10 19N 105 28E **134 Bc**
Longbeach, N.Z. 44 6S 171 41E **145 Ef**
Longburn, N.Z. 40 23S 175 35E **144 Gd**
Longford, Tas. 41 32S 147 3E **107 Cf**
Longiram, Indonesia 0 5S 115 45E **135 Ee**
Longreach, Qld. 23 28S 144 14E **128 Ec**
Longton, Qld. 21 0S 145 55E **128 Bd**
Longwarry, Vic. 38 8S 145 48E **101 Ff**

Longwood, Vic. 36 48S 145 26E **101 Df**
Looc, Philippines 12 20N 122 5E **135 Bf**
Lookout Pt., Qld. 27 25S 153 33E **131 Ed**
Loongana, W.A. 30 52S 127 5E **117 Ed**
Loorana, King Island 39 50S 143 55E **107 Ab**
Lopevi, I., New Hebrides 16 30S 168 21E **139 Ih**
Lora Ck., S.A. 28 10S 135 22E **111 Bb**
Lorengau, Manus I. 2 1S 147 15E **141 Bd**
Lorinna, Tas. 41 32S 146 9E **107 Ce**
Lorne, N.S.W. 31 36S 152 39E **95 Ec**
Lorne, Vic. 38 33S 143 59E **100 Fd**
Lornesleigh, Qld. 20 47S 146 52E **129 Be**
Lotofaga, Eastern Samoa 14 1S 171 30W **139 Cd**
Lottery, Qld. 20 42S 145 21E **128 Bd**
Louisiade Archipelago 11 10S 153 0E **141 Fg**
Louth, N.S.W. 30 30S 145 8E **91 Be**
Louth Bay, S.A. 34 35S 136 0E **113 Da**
Low Rocky Pt., Tas. 42 59S 145 29E **107 Dd**
Lowaldie, S.A. 35 2S 139 59E **113 Ef**
Lowburn Ferry, N.Z. 44 59S 169 13E **145 Ed**
Lowden, W.A. 33 33S 115 58E **119 Gb**
Lower Chittering, W.A. 31 35S 116 5E **119 Ec**
Lower Hutt, N.Z. 41 10S 174 55E **144 Hd**
Lowlands, N.S.W. 33 12S 145 28E **92 De**
Lowmead, Qld. 24 32S 151 45E **131 Bb**
Lowood, Qld. 27 28S 152 35E **131 Ec**
Loxton, S.A. 34 28S 140 31E **113 Df**
Loyalty Is., S-W Pacific 21 0S 167 30E **139 A₁d₁**
Lubang Is., Philippines 13 50N 120 12E **135 Be**
Lubeck, Vic. 36 45S 142 34E **100 Dc**
Lubuagan, Philippines 17 21N 121 10E **135 Af**
Lubuksikaping, Indonesia 0 10N 100 15E **134 Eb**
Lucinda, Qld. 18 32S 146 20E **129 Yx**
Lucindale, S.A. 36 59S 140 23E **113 Ff**
Lucknow, N.S.W. 33 21S 149 11E **93 Di**
Ludlow, W.A. 33 37S 115 28E **119 Gb**
Lue, N.S.W. 32 38S 149 50E **93 Ci**
Luggate, N.Z. 44 46S 169 18E **145 Ed**
Lughrata, Tas. 39 56S 147 55E **107 Af**
Lumeah, W.A. 34 1S 117 12E **119 Hd**
Lumi, Papua N.G. 3 30S 142 2E **141 Bb**
Lumsden, N.Z. 45 44S 168 27E **145 Fc**
Lunawanna, Tas. 43 21S 147 15E **107 Ef**
Lune River, Tas. 43 31S 146 57E **107 Ee**
Lundu, Malaysia 1 40N 109 50E **134 Dc**
Luti, Solomon Is. 7 14S 157 0E **139 Pq**
Lutong, Malaysia 4 30N 114 0E **134 Dd**
Luwuk, Indonesia 10 0S 122 40E **135 Ef**
Luzon I., Philippines 16 0N 121 0E **135 Af**
Lyall, Mt., N.Z. 45 16S 167 32E **145 Fb**
Lyall's Mill, W.A. 33 28S 116 4E **119 Gc**
Lyell, N.Z. 41 48S 172 4E **145 Bg**
Lyell Ra., N.Z. 41 38S 172 20E **145 Bg**
Lymwood, King Island 40 1S 144 2E **107 Bc**
Lynd Range, Qld. 25 30S 149 20E **127 Dd**
Lynd R., Qld. 16 28S 143 18E **127 Bc**
Lyndhurst, N.S.W. 33 41S 149 2E **93 Di**
Lyndhurst, Qld. 19 12S 144 20E **128 Ac**
Lyndock, S.A. 34 36S 138 55E **113 Dd**
Lyndon R., W.A. 23 29S 114 6E **117 Ca**
Lyons, Vic. 38 2S 141 28E **100 Fb**
Lyons R., W.A. 25 2S 115 9E **117 Cb**
Lyttelton, N.Z. 43 35S 172 44E **145 Dg**
Lyttelton Harbour, N.Z. 43 37S 172 44E **145 Dg**

M

Maatsuyker Group Is., Aust. 43 40S 146 20E **107 Ee**
Macalister R., Vic. 38 2S 146 59E **101 Eg**
Macarthur, Vic. 38 5S 142 0E **100 Fb**
McArthur R., N.T. 16 45S 136 0E **123 Bc**
McArthur River, N.T. 16 27S 137 7E **123 Bc**
Macartney, Mt., Qld. 20 50S 148 33E **129 Bg**
Maccalister, Qld. 27 3S 151 6E **131 Eb**
McClintock Ra., W.A. 18 44S 127 38E **117 Bd**
McCluer I., N.T. 11 5S 133 0E **123 Ab**
McCoys Well, S.A. 32 36S 139 10E **113 Be**
Macdonald, Mt., New Hebrides 17 36S 168 23E **139 Jh**
MacDonald R., N.S.W. 33 22S 151 0E **95 Db**
MacDonnell Ranges, N.T. 23 40S 133 0E **123 Cb**
McDouall Pk., S.A. 29 51S 134 55E **111 Bb**
McDougalls Well, N.S.W. 31 8S 141 15E **90 Bc**
Macedon, Vic. 37 24S 144 35E **100 Ee**
Macfarlane L., S.A. 32 0S 136 40E **113 Ab**
Macfarlane, Mt., N.Z. 43 56S 169 21E **145 Dd**
McGregor Ra., Qld. 27 0S 142 45E **127 Dc**
McGuire, Mt., Qld. 20 19S 148 20E **129 Bg**

Macintosh Ra., W.A. 24 45S 121 33E **117 Dd**
Macintyre R., N.S.W. 28 37S 149 40E **95 Ba**
Mackay, Qld. 21 36S 148 39E **127 Cd**
McKay Ra., W.A. 23 0S 122 30E **117 Cc**
Mackenzie R., Qld. 23 38S 149 46E **129 Eg**
Mackenzie Plains, N.Z. 44 10S 170 25E **145 Ee**
McKerrow L., N.Z. 44 25S 168 5E **145 Eb**
McKinlay, Qld. 21 16S 141 18E **127 Cc**
McKinlay R., Qld. 20 50S 141 28E **127 Cc**
Macksville, N.S.W. 30 40S 152 56E **95 Dc**
Maclagan, Qld. 27 5S 151 39E **131 Eb**
McLaren Vale, S.A. 35 13S 138 31E **113 Ed**
Maclean, N.S.W. 29 26S 153 16E **95 Cd**
Maclean Bay, Tas. 41 47S 148 20E **107 Cg**
Maclean R., N.S.W. 30 56S 153 0E **95 Dc**
Maclennan, N.Z. 46 33S 169 29E **145 Gd**
McLeod L., W.A. 24 9S 113 47E **117 Ca**
McMahon's Reef, N.S.W. 34 39S 148 26E **93 Eh**
McPherson Ra., Qld. 28 15S 153 15E **131 Fd**
Macquarie Harbour, Tas. 42 15S 145 15E **107 Dd**
Macquarie L., N.S.W. 33 4S 151 36E **93 Dk**
Macquarie, Mt., N.S.W. 33 37S 151 36E **93 Di**
Macquarie R., N.S.W. 30 50S 147 30E **93 Ag**
Macquarie R., Tas. 41 45S 147 7E **107 Cf**
Macrossan, Qld. 19 59S 146 28E **129 Be**
Madang, Papua N.G. 5 12S 145 49E **141 Cc**
Madiun, Indonesia 7 38S 111 32E **134 Fd**
Madjene, Indonesia 3 27S 118 57E **135 Ee**
Madura, W.A. 31 55S 127 0E **117 Ed**
Maewo (Aurora), New Hebrides 15 10S 168 10E **139 Hh**
Magdalena, Mt., Malaysia 4 25N 117 55E **135 De**
Magdelaine Cays, Qld. 16 33S 150 18E **127 Be**
Magelang, Indonesia 7 29S 110 13E **134 Fd**
Magenta, N.S.W. 33 51S 143 34E **92 Dc**
Magenta L., W.A. 33 30S 119 10E **119 Gf**
Maggea, S.A. 34 28S 140 2E **113 Df**
Magnetic I., Qld. 19 8S 146 50E **129 Ae**
Magnus, Mt., Qld. 28 30S 151 50E **131 Fb**
Magra, Tas. 42 54S 147 2E **107 Df**
Magrath Flat, S.A. 35 52S 139 25E **113 Ee**
Mahakam R., Indonesia 1 0N 114 40E **135 De**
Maheno, N.Z. 45 10S 170 50E **145 Fe**
Mahia Pen., N.Z. 39 9S 177 55E **144 Ff**
Mahoenui, N.Z. 38 34S 174 50E **144 Ec**
Mainit L., Philippines 9 31N 125 30E **135 Cg**
Maitland, N.S.W. 32 44S 151 36E **93 Ck**
Maitland, S.A. 34 23S 137 40E **113 Dc**
Major Creek, Qld. 19 35S 146 54E **129 Ae**
Majors Creek, N.S.W. 35 33S 149 45E **93 Fi**
Maju I., Indonesia 1 40N 126 30E **135 Dg**
Makaraka, N.Z. 38 39S 177 58E **144 Ef**
Makarewa, N.Z. 46 20S 168 21E **145 Gc**
Makarewa Junction, N.Z. 46 18S 168 20E **145 Gc**
Maketu, N.Z. 37 45S 176 28E **144 De**
Makian I., Indonesia 0 12N 127 20E **135 Dg**
Makikihi, N.Z. 44 38S 171 9E **145 Ef**
Makorako, N.Z. 39 10S 176 0E **144 Fe**
Makotuku, N.Z. 40 7S 176 14E **144 Ge**
Makowata, Qld. 24 27S 151 38E **131 Bb**
Makuri, N.Z. 40 33S 176 1E **144 Gd**
Malabang, Philippines 7 36N 124 3E **135 Cf**
Malacca, Strait of 3 0N 101 0E **134 Ca**
Malaita, Solomon Is. 9 0S 161 0E **139 Qs**
Malanda, Qld. 17 22S 145 35E **129 Xw**
Malang, Indonesia 7 59S 112 35E **134 Fd**
Malaysia, Asia 4 0N 102 0E **134 Db**
Malbon, Qld. 21 5S 140 17E **127 Cc**
Malbooma, S.A. 30 41S 134 11E **111 Cb**
Malcolm, W.A. 28 51S 121 25E **117 Dc**
Malcolm, Pt., W.A. 33 48S 123 45E **117 Ec**
Maldon, Vic. 37 0S 144 6E **100 Ee**
Malekula (Mallicolo), New Hebrides 16 15S 167 30E **139 Ig**
Maleny, Qld. 26 45S 152 52E **131 Dc**
Malik, Indonesia 0 39S 123 16E **135 Ef**
Malinau, Indonesia 3 35N 116 30E **135 De**
Maling, Mt., Indonesia 1 0N 121 0E **135 Df**
Malita, Philippines 6 19N 125 39E **135 Cg**
Mallacoota, Vic. 37 40S 149 40E **101 Ej**
Mallacoota Inlet, Vic. 37 40S 149 40E **101 Ej**
Mallala, S.A. 34 26S 138 30E **113 Dd**
Mallanganee, N.S.W. 28 54S 152 44E **95 Bc**
Mallina P.O., W.A. 20 53S 118 2E **117 Cb**
Malmesbury, Vic. 37 9S 144 25E **100 Ee**
Malo, New Hebrides 15 40S 167 11E **139 Hg**
Malpas Hut, Qld. 19 36S 142 14E **128 Aa**
Malte Brun, N.Z. 43 38S 170 14E **145 De**
Malu'a, Solomon Is. 8 0S 160 0E **139 Qs**
Maluku, Indonesia 3 0S 128 0E **135 Dg**
Malvern Hills, Qld. 24 30S 145 7E **128 Fd**
Mamaku, N.Z. 38 5S 176 8E **144 Ee**
Mamanutha Group, Fiji 17 34S 177 4E **139 Aa**

Mamarana, Solomon Is. 7 0S 157 0E **139 Pq**
Mamasa, Indonesia 2 55S 119 20E **135 Ee**
Mambray Creek, S.A. 32 49S 137 59E **113 Bc**
Mampawah, Indonesia 0 30N 109 5E **134 Dc**
Mamudju, Indonesia 2 50S 118 50E **135 Ee**
Mana, Indonesia 4 25S 102 55E **134 Eb**
Manado, Indonesia 1 40N 124 45E **135 Df**
Manaio, N.Z. 39 33S 174 8E **144 Fc**
Manakau, N.Z. 40 43S 175 13E **145 Ch**
Manam I., Papua N.G. 4 5S 145 0E **141 Cc**
Manangatang, Vic. 35 5S 142 54E **100 Cc**
Manapouri, N.Z. 45 34S 167 39E **145 Fb**
Manapouri L., N.Z. 45 32S 167 32E **145 Fb**
Manawaru, N.Z. 40 28S 175 12E **144 Dd**
Manawhai, N.Z. 36 13S 174 35E **144 Cc**
Manay, Philippines 7 17N 126 33E **135 Cg**
Mandalay, N.S.W. 30 48S 143 25E **92 Ac**
Mandeville, N.Z. 46 0S 168 48E **145 Gc**
Mandioli, Indonesia 0 40S 127 20E **135 Eg**
Mandurah, W.A. 32 36S 115 48E **119 Fb**
Maneroo, Qld. 23 22S 143 53E **128 Eb**
Maneroo Ck., Qld. 23 21S 143 53E **128 Eb**
Manfred, N.S.W. 33 19S 143 45E **92 Dc**
Mangahao R., N.Z. 40 23S 175 50E **144 Gd**
Mangalo, S.A. 33 32S 136 34E **113 Cb**
Mangalore, Vic. 36 56S 145 10E **101 Df**
Mangamahu, N.Z. 39 49S 175 22E **144 Fd**
Mangapehi, N.Z. 38 31S 175 18E **144 Ed**
Mangatainoka, N.Z. 40 25S 175 52E **144 Gd**
Manggar, Indonesia 2 50S 108 10E **134 Ec**
Mango I., Fiji 17 27S 179 9W **139 Ac**
Mangole I., Indonesia 1 50S 125 55E **135 Eg**
Mangonui, N.Z. 35 1S 173 32E **144 Bb**
Mangoplah, N.S.W. 33 25S 147 17E **93 Fg**
Manifold, Qld. 22 41S 150 40E **129 Di**
Manifold C., Qld. 22 41S 150 50E **129 Di**
Manila, Philippines 14 40N 121 3E **135 Bf**
Manila Bay, Philippines 14 0N 120 0E **135 Bf**
Manildra, N.S.W. 33 11S 148 41E **93 Dh**
Manilla, N.S.W. 30 45S 150 43E **95 Da**
Manjimup, W.A. 34 15S 116 6E **119 Hc**
Manly, N.S.W. 33 48S 151 17E **93 Dk**
Manmanning, W.A. 30 51S 117 5E **119 Dd**
Mann Ranges, S.A. 26 6S 130 5E **111 Bb**
Mannahill, S.A. 32 25S 140 0E **113 Be**
Manning R., N.S.W. 31 52S 152 43E **95 Eb**
Manning Str., Solomon Is. 7 30S 158 0E **139 Pq**
Mannum, S.A. 34 57S 139 12E **113 De**
Mannus, N.S.W. 35 45S 147 55E **93 Fg**
Manokwari, Indonesia 0 54S 134 0E **135 Eh**
Manoora, S.A. 34 1S 138 48E **113 Cd**
Manouro Pt., New Hebrides 17 41S 168 36E **139 Jh**
Mansfield, Vic. 37 0S 146 0E **101 Eg**
Manton, Qld. 19 39S 146 40E **129 Ae**
Mantuan Downs, Qld. 24 26S 147 14E **129 Ff**
Mantung, S.A. 34 35S 140 3E **113 Df**
Manua Is., Eastern Samoa 14 13S 169 35W **139 De**
Manui I., Indonesia 3 35S 123 5E **135 Ef**
Manukan, Philippines 8 14N 123 3E **135 Cf**
Manukau, N.Z. 37 1S 174 55E **144 Dd**
Manukau Harbour, N.Z. 37 3S 174 45E **144 Dc**
Manumbar Mill, Qld. 26 24S 152 16E **131 Dc**
Manunda Ck., S.A. 33 15S 139 53E **113 Be**
Manunui, N.Z. 38 54S 175 21E **144 Ed**
Manutahi, N.Z. 39 39S 174 24E **144 Fc**
Manutuke, N.Z. 38 41S 177 55E **144 Ef**
Many Peaks, Mt., W.A. 34 53S 118 15E **119 He**
Maoke, Pengunungan, Indonesia 3 40S 137 30E **135 Ei**
Mapleton, Qld. 26 32S 152 52E **131 Dc**
Maprik, Papua N.G. 3 44S 143 3E **141 Bb**
Maraetaha, N.Z. 38 53S 177 50E **144 Ef**
Maraetai, N.Z. 38 22S 175 45E **144 Ed**
Maralinga, S.A. 29 45S 131 15E **111 Cb**
Marama, S.A. 35 10S 140 10E **113 Ef**
Maramasike, Solomon Is. 9 30S 161 25E **139 Qs**
Maranalgo, W.A. 29 22S 117 50E **119 Cd**
Maranboy, N.T. 14 40S 132 40E **123 Ab**
Maranoa R., Qld. 27 50S 148 37E **127 Dd**
Mararoa R., N.Z. 45 37S 167 41E **145 Fc**
Marathon, Qld. 20 51S 143 32E **128 Bb**
Maratua I., Indonesia 2 10N 118 35E **135 Df**
Maravae, Solomon Is. 7 54S 156 44E **139 Pq**
Marble Bar, W.A. 21 9S 119 44E **117 Cb**
Marburg, Qld. 27 33S 152 28E **131 Ec**
Marchagee, W.A. 30 3S 116 5E **119 Dc**
Marchant Hill, Mt., S.A. 32 14S 138 48E **113 Bd**
Mardie, W.A. 21 12S 115 59E **117 Cb**
Maré, I., New Caledonia 21 30S 168 0E **139 B_1f_1**
Mareeba, Qld. 16 59S 145 28E **129 Ww**
Marek, Indonesia 4 41S 120 24E **135 Ef**
Margaret R., W.A. 18 38S 126 52E **119 Gb**
Margaret River, W.A. 33 57S 115 7E **119 Gb**
Margate, Tas. 43 0S 147 16E **107 Ef**
Maria I., N.T. 14 52S 135 45E **123 Ac**
Maria I., Tas. 42 35S 148 0E **107 Dg**
Maria Van Diemen C., N.Z. 34 29S 172 40E **144 Aa**
Mariarty, Tas. 41 11S 146 28E **107 Ce**
Marillana, W.A. 22 37S 119 24E **117 Cb**
Marina Plains, Qld. 14 37S 143 57E **127 Ac**
Marinduque I., Philippines 13 25N 122 0E **135 Bf**
Marino, New Hebrides 35 3S 138 31E **139 Gh**
Marion Bay, S.A. 35 12S 136 59E **113 Eb**
Marion Bay, Tas. 42 47S 147 55E **107 Df**
Markham R., Papua N.G. 6 41S 147 2E **141 Dd**
Marlborough, Qld. 22 46S 149 52E **129 Dh**
Marlborough, Prov., N.Z. 41 45S 173 33E **145 Bh**
Marlee, N.S.W. 31 47S 152 20E **95 Ec**
Marlo, Vic. 37 46S 148 31E **101 Ei**
Marlow, N.S.W. 35 17S 149 55E **93 Fi**
Marmion, Mt., W.A. 29 16S 119 50E **119 Cf**
Marmor, Qld. 23 40S 150 43E **131 Aa**
Marnoo, Vic. 36 40S 142 54E **100 Dc**
Maroochydore, Qld. 26 29S 153 5E **131 Dd**
Maroona, Vic. 37 27S 142 54E **100 Ec**
Marotiri, N.Z. 35 53S 174 44E **144 Bc**
Marrabel, S.A. 34 10S 138 54E **113 Dd**
Marradong, W.A. 32 54S 116 26E **119 Fc**
Marrapina, N.S.W. 30 56S 142 4E **92 Ab**
Marrar, N.S.W. 34 50S 147 23E **93 Eg**
Marrawah, Tas. 40 55S 144 42E **107 Bc**
Marree, S.A. 29 39S 138 1E **111 Bc**
Marrowie Ck., N.S.W. 33 23S 145 40E **92 Dd**
Marsden, Pt., S.A. 35 34S 137 37E **113 Ec**
Marshall R., N.T. 22 59S 136 59E **123 Cc**
Martaban, Burma 16 30N 97 35E **134 Aa**
Martaban, Gulf, Burma 15 40N 96 30E **134 Aa**
Martapura, Indonesia 3 22S 114 56E **135 Ed**
Martha, Mt., Vic. 38 17S 145 1E **100 Fe**
Marthagu Ck., N.S.W. 30 50S 147 45E **93 Ag**
Martinborough, N.Z. 41 14S 175 29E **144 Hd**
Martindale, N.S.W. 32 27S 150 40E **95 Fa**
Martins Well, S.A. 31 28S 139 7E **113 Ae**
Marton, N.Z. 40 4S 175 23E **144 Gd**
Marudi, Malaysia 4 10N 114 25E **135 Dd**
Marui, Papua N.G. 4 4S 143 2E **141 Cb**
Maruia, N.Z. 42 11S 172 13E **145 Cg**
Maruia R., N.Z. 41 47S 172 13E **145 Cg**
Marulan, N.S.W. 34 43S 150 3E **93 Ei**
Marulan South, N.S.W. 34 47S 150 3E **93 Ej**
Marum, Mt., New Hebrides 16 15S 168 7E **139 Ih**
Marvel Loch, W.A. 31 28S 119 29E **119 Ef**
Mary, Mt., S.A. 34 7S 139 24E **113 De**
Mary R., Qld. 25 25S 152 55E **131 Cc**
Mary Kathleen, Qld. 20 35S 139 48E **127 Cb**
Maryborough, Qld. 25 31S 152 37E **131 Cc**
Maryborough, Vic. 37 0S 143 44E **100 Ed**
Marybrook, W.A. 33 41S 115 10E **119 Gb**
Marysville, Vic. 37 33S 145 45E **101 Ef**
Maryvale, Qld. 28 4S 152 12E **131 Fc**
Masalima Is., Indonesia 5 10S 116 50E **135 Fe**
Maskelyne Is., New Hebrides 16 32S 167 49E **139 Ig**
Mason B., N.Z. 46 55S 167 45E **145 Gb**
Masterton, N.Z. 40 56S 175 39E **144 Gd**
Matak I., Indonesia 3 18N 106 16E **134 Dc**
Matakana, N.S.W. 32 59S 145 54E **92 Ce**
Matakana, N.Z. 32 59S 145 54E **144 Cc**
Matakana I., N.Z. 37 32S 176 5E **144 De**
Matakitaki, N.Z. 41 58S 172 20E **145 Bg**
Matakohe, N.Z. 36 8S 174 11E **144 Cc**
Matamata, N.Z. 37 48S 175 47E **144 Dd**
Matamau, N.Z. 40 8S 176 10E **144 Ge**
Matangi, N.Z. 37 48S 175 24E **144 Dd**
Mataram, Indonesia 8 41S 116 10E **135 Fe**
Mataranka, N.T. 14 55S 133 4E **123 Ab**
Mataso, New Hebrides 17 14S 168 26E **139 Jh**
Matata, N.Z. 37 54S 176 48E **144 De**
Mataura, N.Z. 46 11S 168 51E **145 Gc**
Mataura R., N.Z. 45 49S 168 44E **145 Gc**
Matawai, N.Z. 38 21S 177 33E **144 Ef**
Mathoura, N.S.W. 35 50S 144 55E **92 Fd**
Mati, Philippines 6 55N 126 15E **135 Cg**
Matiere, N.Z. 38 46S 175 7E **144 Ed**
Matong, N.S.W. 34 46S 146 57E **93 Ef**
Matong, Papua N.G. 5 36S 151 50E **141 Cf**
Matua, Indonesia 2 58S 110 52E **134 Ed**
Matuku I., Fiji 19 10S 179 44E **139 Bb**
Maud Pt., W.A. 23 6S 113 45E **117 Ca**
Maude, N.S.W. 34 29S 144 18E **92 Ed**
Maungataniwha, N.Z. 38 49S 176 49E **144 Ee**
Maungatapere, N.Z. 35 45S 174 12E **144 Bc**
Maungaturoto, N.Z. 36 6S 174 23E **144 Cc**
Maungawera, N.Z. 44 39S 169 13E **145 Ed**
Maurice L., S.A. 29 30S 131 0E **111 Bb**
Mauriceville, N.Z. 40 45S 175 35E **144 Gd**
Mawbanna, Tas. 40 58S 145 24E **107 Bd**
Mawhai Pt., N.Z. 38 10S 178 22E **144 Eg**
Mawheraiti, N.Z. 42 11S 171 43E **145 Cf**
Maxwelton, Qld. 20 43S 142 41E **127 Cc**
May Downs, Qld. 22 38S 148 55E **129 Dg**
May River, Papua N.G. 4 19S 141 58E **141 Ca**
Maya, W.A. 29 52S 116 30E **119 Cc**
Mayanup, W.A. 33 58S 116 25E **119 Gc**
Maydena, Tas. 42 45S 146 39E **107 De**
Mayfield, N.Z. 43 49S 171 25E **145 Df**
Maynard Hills, W.A. 28 35S 119 50E **119 Bf**
Mayne R., Qld. 23 40S 142 10E **127 Cc**
Mayneside, Qld. 23 32S 142 34E **128 Ea**
Mayor I., N.Z. 37 16S 176 17E **144 De**
Mba, Fiji 17 33S 177 41E **139 Aa**
Mbengga I., Fiji 18 23S 178 8E **139 Bb**
Mé Maoya, New Caledonia 21 22S 16 22E **139 B_1c_1**
Meadow, W.A. 26 35S 114 40E **117 Da**
Meadow Downs, S.A. 32 30S 138 57E **113 Bd**
Meadows, S.A. 35 10S 138 44E **113 Ed**
Meander, Tas. 41 39S 146 36E **107 Ce**
Meatian, Vic. 35 34S 143 21E **100 Cd**
Meckering, W.A. 31 38S 117 2E **119 Ec**
Meda P.O., W.A. 17 22S 123 59E **117 Bc**
Medan, Indonesia 3 40N 98 38E **134 Da**
Meeberrie, W.A. 26 57S 116 0E **117 Db**
Meekatharra, W.A. 26 32S 118 29E **117 Db**
Meeniyan, Vic. 38 35S 146 0E **101 Fg**
Meerlieu, Vic. 38 2S 147 24E **101 Fh**
Meka, W.A. 27 25S 116 48E **117 Db**
Mekong R., Cambodia 18 0N 104 15E **134 Bc**
Mekongga, Mt., Indonesia 3 50S 121 30E **135 Ef**
Melaka, Malaysia 2 15N 102 15E **134 Db**
Melalop, Malaysia 5 10N 116 5E **135 Ce**
Melbourne, Vic. 37 40S 145 0E **101 Ef**
Mella, Tas. 40 50S 145 4E **107 Bd**
Mellenbye, W.A. 28 50S 116 18E **119 Bc**
Melrose, N.S.W. 32 42S 146 57E **93 Cf**
Melrose, S.A. 32 48S 138 15E **113 Bd**
Melrose, W.A. 27 50S 121 15E **117 Dc**
Melton Mowbray, Tas. 42 27S 147 10E **107 Df**
Melville B., N.T. 12 0S 135 45E **123 Ac**
Melville C., Qld. 14 11S 144 30E **127 Ac**
Melville I., N.T. 11 30S 131 0E **123 Ab**
Memboro, Indonesia 9 30S 119 30E **135 Fe**
Menamurtee, N.S.W. 31 25S 143 11E **92 Bc**
Menangle, N.S.W. 34 6S 150 44E **93 Ej**
Menate, Indonesia 0 12S 112 47E **134 Ed**
Mendawai R., Indonesia 1 30S 113 0E **134 Ed**
Mendel Estate, W.A. 28 41S 115 31E **119 Bb**
Mendi, Papua N.G. 6 11S 143 47E **141 Db**
Mendip Hills, Qld. 23 54S 146 9E **129 Ee**
Mendooran, N.S.W. 31 50S 149 6E **93 Bi**
Mendung, Indonesia 0 38N 103 8E **134 Db**
Menggala, Indonesia 4 20S 105 15E **134 Ec**
Menindee, N.S.W. 32 20S 142 25E **92 Cb**
Menindee L., N.S.W. 32 20S 142 25E **92 Cb**
Meningie, S.A. 35 43S 139 20E **113 Ee**
Mentawaj Is., Indonesia 2 0S 99 0E **134 Ea**
Menyamya, Papua N.G. 7 10S 145 59E **141 Dd**
Menzies, W.A. 29 40S 120 58E **117 Dc**
Merah, Indonesia 0 53N 116 54E **135 De**
Meramangye L., S.A. 28 25S 132 13E **111 Bb**
Merauke, Indonesia 8 29S 140 24E **135 Fi**
Merbein, Vic. 34 10S 142 2E **100 Bc**
Mercer, N.Z. 37 16S 175 5E **144 Dd**
Mercunda, S.A. 34 38S 140 1E **113 Df**
Mercury Is., N.Z. 36 37S 175 52E **144 Cd**
Mere Lava I., New Hebrides 14 25S 168 3E **139 Gh**
Meredith, Vic. 37 49S 144 5E **100 Ee**
Mergui, Burma 12 30N 98 35E **134 Ba**
Meribah, S.A. 34 43S 140 51E **113 Df**
Merinda, Qld. 20 2S 148 11E **129 Bg**
Meringandan, Qld. 27 27S 151 56E **131 Eb**
Meringur, Vic. 34 20S 141 19E **100 Bd**
Merino, Vic. 37 44S 141 35E **100 Eb**
Merion, Qld. 22 52S 149 2E **129 Dh**
Merredin, W.A. 31 28S 118 18E **119 Ee**
Merrigum, Vic. 36 22S 145 8E **100 Df**
Merriwa, N.S.W. 32 6S 150 22E **95 Fa**
Merriwagga, N.S.W. 33 47S 145 43E **92 De**
Merriton, S.A. 33 27S 138 9E **113 Cd**
Merritop, N.S.W. 33 51S 144 12E **92 Dd**
Merroe, W.A. 27 53S 117 50E **117 Db**
Merrygoen, N.S.W. 31 51S 149 12E **93 Bi**
Mersing, Malaysia 2 25N 103 50E **134 Db**
Merton, Vic. 36 59S 145 43E **101 Df**
Methul, N.S.W. 34 36S 147 10E **93 Eg**
Methven, N.Z. 43 38S 171 40E **145 Df**
Metricup, W.A. 33 47S 115 6E **119 Gb**
Metung, Vic. 37 54S 147 52E **101 Eh**

Gazetteer

Meureudu, Indonesia 5 19N 96 10E **134 Ca**
Miallo, Qld. 16 28S 145 22E **127 Bd**
Miami, N.S.W. 33 13S 146 47E **93 Df**
Miandetta, N.S.W. 31 34S 146 58E **93 Bf**
Micabil, N.S.W. 33 2S 146 58E **93 Df**
Michael, Mt., Papua N.G. 6 2S 145 22E **141 Dc**
Michelago, N.S.W. 35 41S 149 11E **93 Fi**
Miclere, Qld. 22 34S 147 32E **129 Df**
Midai I., Indonesia 3 0N 107 42E **134 Dc**
Middle Camp, N.S.W. 32 38S 141 51E **92 Ca**
Middle I., Qld. 21 40S 150 15E **129 Ci**
Middle I., W.A. 28 55S 113 55E **117 Ec**
Middle Park, Qld. 19 47S 143 17E **128 Ab**
Middleback, Mt., S.A. 33 14S 137 5E **113 Cc**
Middlemarch, N.Z. 45 30S 170 9E **145 Fe**
Middlesex, W.A. 34 20S 116 9E **119 Hc**
Middleton Ck., Qld. 22 35S 141 51E **127 Cc**
Middleton P.O., Qld. 22 22S 141 32E **127 Cc**
Midhurst, N.Z. 39 17S 174 18E **144 Fc**
Midland, W.A. 31 54S 115 59E **119 Eb**
Milang, S.A. 32 2S 139 10E **113 Ed**
Milarup L., W.A. 33 10S 119 40E **119 Gf**
Milbrulong, N.S.W. 35 14S 146 50E **93 Ff**
Mildura, Vic. 34 13S 142 9E **100 Bc**
Miles, Qld. 26 37S 150 10E **131 Da**
Mileura, W.A. 26 22S 117 20E **117 Db**
Milford Sound, N.Z. 44 34S 167 47E **145 Eb**
Milford Sd., N.Z. 44 34S 167 47E **145 Eb**
Milgun, W.A. 25 6S 118 18E **117 Db**
Miling, W.A. 30 30S 116 17E **119 Dc**
Millaa Millaa, Qld. 17 32S 145 38E **129 Xw**
Millaroo, Qld. 19 56S 147 14E **129 Af**
Millers Flat, N.Z. 45 39S 169 22E **145 Fd**
Millerton, N.Z. 41 39S 171 54E **145 Bf**
Millicent, S.A. 37 34S 140 21E **113 Gf**
Millmerran, Qld. 27 53S 151 16E **131 Eb**
Millthorpe, N.S.W. 33 26S 149 12E **93 Di**
Milparinka P.O., N.S.W. 29 46S 141 57E **90 Ac**
Milton, N.S.W. 35 20S 150 27E **93 Fj**
Milton, N.Z. 46 7S 169 59E **145 Ge**
Milvale, N.S.W. 34 18S 147 56E **93 Eg**
Mimosa, N.S.W. 34 34S 147 22E **93 Eg**
Mimosa Ck., Qld. 24 30S 149 43E **129 Fh**
Mimosa Vale, Qld. 24 25S 149 42E **129 Fh**
Mincha, Vic. 36 1S 144 6E **100 De**
Mindanao I., Philippines 8 0N 125 0E **135 Cf**
Mindanao Sea, Philippines 9 0N 124 0E **135 Cf**
Mindarie, S.A. 34 48S 140 12E **113 Df**
Mindiyarra, S.A. 35 2S 139 48E **113 Ee**
Mindona L., N.S.W. 33 6S 142 6E **92 Db**
Mindoro I., Philippines 13 0N 121 0E **135 Bf**
Mindoro Str., Philippines 12 30N 120 30E **135 Bf**
Mineral Hill, N.S.W. 32 36S 147 0E **93 Cf**
Mingary, S.A. 32 8S 140 45E **113 Bf**
Mingela, Qld. 19 52S 146 38E **129 Ae**
Mingera Cr., Qld. 20 38S 138 10E **127 Cb**
Minigwal L., W.A. 29 31S 123 14E **117 Dc**
Minilya, W.A. 23 55S 114 0E **117 Ca**
Minilya R., W.A. 23 45S 114 0E **117 Ca**
Minimbah, N.S.W. 32 39S 151 15E **93 Ck**
Mininera, Vic. 37 37S 142 58E **100 Ec**
Minj, Papua N.G. 5 54S 144 30E **141 Cc**
Minlaton, S.A. 34 45S 137 35E **113 Dc**
Minnie Creek, W.A. 24 35 115 42E **117 Cb**
Minore, N.S.W. 32 14S 148 27E **93 Ch**
Minyip, Vic. 36 29S 142 36E **100 Dc**
Mirani, Qld. 21 9S 148 53E **129 Cg**
Mirboo, Vic. 38 27S 146 13E **101 Fg**
Mirboo North, Vic. 38 24S 146 10E **101 Fg**
Miri, Malaysia 4 18N 114 0E **134 Dd**
Miriam Vale, Qld. 24 20S 151 39E **131 Bb**
Miromiro, N.Z. 42 29S 172 40E **145 Cg**
Mirrool, N.S.W. 34 19S 147 10E **93 Eg**
Mirtna, Qld. 21 18S 146 12E **129 Ce**
Misima I., Papua N.G. 10 40S 152 45E **141 Fg**
Misool I., Indonesia 2 0S 130 0E **135 Eh**
Mistake Ck., Qld. 21 39S 146 50E **129 Df**
Mitchell, Qld. 26 29S 147 58E **127 Dd**
Mitchell Ra., N.T. 15 12S 141 35E **123 Ac**
Mitchell R., Qld. 15 12S 141 35E **127 Bc**
Mitchell R., Vic. 37 51S 147 38E **101 Eh**
Mitchellville, S.A. 33 35S 137 8E **113 Cc**
Mitre, N.Z. 36 44S 141 46E **144 Gd**
Mitre, Vic. 36 44S 141 46E **100 Db**
Mitre Peak, N.Z. 44 35S 167 45E **145 Eb**
Mitta Mitta, Vic. 36 34S 147 22E **101 Dh**
Mitta Mitta R., Vic. 36 14S 147 10E **101 Ee**
Mittagong, N.S.W. 34 28S 150 29E **93 Ej**
Mittyack, Vic. 35 8S 142 36E **100 Cc**
Moala I., Fiji 18 36S 179 53E **139 Bb**
Moama, N.S.W. 36 3S 144 45E **92 Gd**
Moana, N.Z. 42 35S 171 28E **145 Cf**
Moe, Vic. 38 12S 146 19E **101 Fg**
Moehau, N.Z. 36 18S 175 28E **144 Cd**
Moeraki Pt., N.Z. 45 23S 170 54E **145 Fe**
Moerewa, N.Z. 35 23S 174 1E **144 Bc**
Moffat Peak, N.Z. 45 2S 168 7E **145 Fc**
Mogriguy, N.S.W. 32 3S 148 40E **93 Ch**
Mogumber, W.A. 31 2S 116 3E **119 Ec**
Mohaka, N.Z. 39 7S 177 12E **144 Ff**
Moindou, New Caledonia 21 42S 165 41E **139 B_1c_1**
Moira, N.S.W. 35 55S 144 50E **92 Fd**
Mokai, N.Z. 38 32S 175 56E **144 Ed**
Mokau, N.Z. 38 42S 174 39E **144 Ec**
Mokau R., N.Z. 38 42S 174 39E **144 Ec**
Mokihinui R., N.Z. 41 32S 171 57E **145 Bg**
Mokotua, N.Z. 46 27S 168 34E **145 Gc**
Mole R., N.S.W. 29 0S 151 32E **95 Cb**
Mole Creek, Tas. 41 32S 146 24E **107 Ce**
Molesworth, N.Z. 42 5S 173 16E **145 Ch**
Mollerin L., W.A. 30 30S 117 35E **119 Dd**
Molloy, Mt., Qld. 16 42S 145 20E **129 Ww**
Mollymook, N.S.W. 35 21S 150 29E **93 Fj**
Molong, N.S.W. 33 5S 148 54E **93 Dh**
Molu I., Indonesia 6 45S 131 40E **135 Fh**
Momba, N.S.W. 30 58S 143 30E **92 Ac**
Monarto Sth., S.A. 35 7S 139 7E **113 Ee**
Mondeodo, Indonesia 3 21N 122 9E **135 Ef**
Mondrain I., W.A. 34 9S 122 14E **117 Ec**
Mondure, Qld. 26 11S 151 47E **131 Db**
Monger L., W.A. 29 25S 117 5E **119 Cd**
Monkira, Qld. 24 46S 140 30E **127 Cc**
Mono, Solomon Is. 7 20S 155 35E **139 Pp**
Monowai, N.Z. 45 53S 167 25E **145 Fb**
Monowai L., N.Z. 45 53S 167 25E **145 Fb**
Monse, Indonesia 4 0S 123 10E **135 Ef**
Monsildale, Qld. 26 42S 152 23E **131 Dc**
Mont Dore, New Caledonia 22 16S 166 34E **139 C_1d_1**
Montague, Tas. 40 45S 144 59E **107 Bc**
Montague I., N.S.W. 36 16S 150 13E **93 Gj**
Montague Ra., W.A. 29 15S 119 30E **117 Db**
Montague Sd., W.A. 14 28S 125 20E **117 Ad**
Monte Bello Is., W.A. 20 30S 115 45E **117 Cb**
Monte Cristo, Qld. 23 36S 151 9E **131 Ab**
Monteagle, Qld. 22 36S 147 7E **129 Df**
Monteith, S.A. 35 11S 139 23E **113 Ee**
Montejinnie, N.T. 16 40S 131 45E **123 Bb**
Moolah, N.S.W. 32 38S 144 58E **92 Cd**
Moolawatana, S.A. 29 55S 139 45E **111 Bc**
Moolbong, N.S.W. 33 17S 145 1E **92 De**
Mooleulooloo, S.A. 31 36S 140 32E **113 Af**
Mooliabeenee, W.A. 31 20S 116 2E **119 Ec**
Moolpa, N.S.W. 35 0S 143 43E **92 Ec**
Mooloogool, W.A. 26 2S 119 5E **117 Db**
Moomin Cr., N.S.W. 29 44S 149 20E **91 Ag**
Moonah R., Qld. 22 3S 138 33E **127 Cb**
Moonan Flat, N.S.W. 31 55S 151 14E **95 Eb**
Moonaree, S.A. 31 59S 135 52E **113 Aa**
Moonda L., Qld. 25 52S 140 27E **127 Dc**
Moondarra, Vic. 38 2S 145 23E **101 Fg**
Moonie R., Qld. 27 45S 150 0E **131 Ea**
Moonta, S.A. 34 6S 137 32E **113 Dc**
Moonyoonooka, W.A. 28 45S 114 45E **119 Ba**
Mooraberree, Qld. 25 13S 140 54E **127 Dc**
Mooralla, Vic. 37 25S 142 10E **100 Ec**
Moorara, N.S.W. 33 12S 142 24E **92 Db**
Moorarie, W.A. 25 56S 117 35E **117 Db**
Moore, N.S.W. 30 57S 150 52E **95 Da**
Moore, Qld. 26 54S 152 17E **131 Dc**
Moore L., W.A. 29 50S 117 35E **119 Cd**
Moore R., W.A. 31 22S 115 30E **119 Eb**
Moore Reefs 16 0S 149 5E **127 Bd**
Moore River, W.A. 31 6S 115 32E **119 Eb**
Moore River Native Sett., W.A. 31 1S 115 56E **119 Db**
Mooréa, S-W Pacific 17 32S 149 50W **139 Ww**
Moorine Rock, W.A. 31 19S 119 7E **119 Ef**
Moorland, N.S.W. 31 46S 152 38E **95 Ec**
Moorlands, S.A. 35 17S 139 37E **113 Ee**
Moornanyah L., N.S.W. 33 15S 143 42E **92 Dc**
Mooroopna, Vic. 36 25S 145 22E **101 Df**
Mootwingee, N.S.W. 31 16S 142 16E **92 Bb**
Morago, N.S.W. 35 18S 144 40E **92 Fd**
Moralana, S.A. 31 10S 138 16E **113 Ad**
Morangarell, N.S.W. 34 8S 147 42E **93 Eg**
Morangup Hill, W.A. 31 41S 116 59E **119 Ec**
Morawa, W.A. 29 13S 116 0E **119 Cc**
Moray Downs, Qld. 21 58S 146 37E **129 Ce**
Mordialloc, Vic. 38 1S 145 6E **100 Ff**
Morea (Carpolac), Vic. 36 45S 141 18E **100 Db**
Moree, N.S.W. 29 28S 149 54E **91 Ag**
Morehead, Papua N.G. 8 41S 141 41E **141 Ea**
Morella, Qld. 23 0S 143 47E **128 Db**
Moreton, Qld. 12 22S 142 30E **127 Ac**
Moreton C., Qld. 27 1S 153 28E **131 Ed**
Moreton I., Qld. 27 10S 153 25E **131 Ed**
Moreton Bay, Qld. 27 10S 153 10E **131 Ed**
Morgan, S.A. 34 0S 139 35E **113 De**
Morganville, Qld. 25 10S 152 0E **131 Cb**
Morganville, S.A. 33 10S 140 32E **113 Cf**
Moriac, Vic. 38 15S 144 10E **100 Fe**
Morisset, N.S.W. 33 6S 151 30E **93 Dk**
Morkalla, Vic. 34 23S 141 10E **100 Bb**
Mornington, Vic. 38 15S 145 5E **100 Ff**
Mornington, W.A. 17 31S 126 6E **117 Bd**
Mornington I., Qld. 16 30S 139 30E **127 Bb**
Mornington Mill, W.A. 33 10S 115 55E **119 Gb**
Moro G., Philippines 6 30N 123 0E **135 Cf**
Morobe, Papua N.G. 7 49S 147 38E **141 Dd**
Moroga, Solomon Is. 10 0S 161 0E **139 Rs**
Morotai I., Indonesia 2 10N 128 30E **136 Dg**
Morpeth, N.S.W. 32 44S 151 39E **93 Ck**
Morrinsville, N.Z. 37 40S 175 32E **144 Dd**
Morris, Mt., S.A. 26 9S 131 4E **111 Bb**
Mortlake, Vic. 38 5S 142 50E **100 Fc**
Mortlock R., W.A. 31 40S 116 40E **119 Ed**
Mortlock N. Branch R., W.A. 31 40S 116 40E **119 Ec**
Morundah, N.S.W. 34 57S 146 19E **93 Ef**
Moruya, N.S.W. 35 58S 150 3E **93 Fj**
Moruya Heads, N.S.W. 35 55S 150 9E **93 Fj**
Morven, N.Z. 44 50S 171 6E **145 Ef**
Morwell, Vic. 38 10S 146 22E **101 Fg**
Mosgiel, N.Z. 45 53S 170 21E **145 Fe**
Moso, New Hebrides 17 30S 168 15E **139 Jh**
Moss Vale, N.S.W. 34 32S 150 25E **93 Ej**
Mossburn, N.Z. 45 41S 168 15E **145 Fc**
Mossgiel, N.S.W. 33 15S 144 30E **92 Dd**
Mossman, Qld. 16 28S 145 23E **129 Ww**
Mota I., New Hebrides 13 49S 167 42E **139 Fg**
Mota Lava I., New Hebrides 13 40S 167 40E **139 Fg**
Motatapu, Mt., N.Z. 44 30S 168 57E **145 Ed**
Motpena, S.A. 31 10S 138 16E **113 Ad**
Motu R., N.Z. 37 51S 177 35E **144 Ef**
Motueka, N.Z. 41 7S 173 1E **145 Bg**
Motueka R., N.Z. 41 5S 173 1E **145 Bg**
Motuhora I. (Whale I.), N.Z. 37 51S 176 59E **144 Df**
Motunau I., N.Z. 43 4S 173 5E **145 Dh**
Motupiko, N.Z. 41 27S 172 49E **145 Bg**
Motutangi, N.Z. 35 53S 173 10E **144 Ab**
Mou, New Caledonia 21 5S 165 26E **139 B_1e_1**
Moulamein, N.S.W. 35 3S 144 1E **92 Fd**
Moulmein, Burma 16 30N 97 40E **134 Aa**
Moulyinning, W.A. 33 14S 117 55E **119 Gd**
Moungga, Solomon Is. 7 0S 156 0E **139 Pq**
Mount Amherst, W.A. 18 24S 126 58E **117 Bd**
Mount Augustus, W.A. 24 20S 116 56E **117 Cb**
Mount Beauty, Vic. 36 47S 147 10E **101 Dh**
Mount Bryan, S.A. 33 30S 139 0E **113 Cd**
Mount Burr, S.A. 37 34S 140 26E **113 Gf**
Mount Coolon, Qld. 21 25S 147 25E **127 Cd**
Mount Douglas, Qld. 21 35S 146 50E **129 Ce**
Mount Elizabeth, W.A. 16 0S 125 50E **117 Bd**
Mount Elsie, Qld. 21 0S 146 33E **129 Be**
Mount Gambier, S.A. 37 50S 140 46E **113 Gf**
Mount Garnet, Qld. 17 37S 145 6E **127 Bd**
Mount George, N.S.W. 31 53S 152 12E **95 Ec**
Mount Hagen, Papua N.G. 5 52S 144 16E **141 Cc**
Mount Howitt, Qld. 26 31S 142 16E **127 Dc**
Mount Isa, Qld. 20 42S 139 26E **127 Cb**
Mount Lofty Ranges, S.A. 34 35S 139 5E **113 Ee**
Mount Magnet, W.A. 28 2S 117 47E **119 Bd**
Mount Manara, N.S.W. 32 29S 143 58E **92 Cc**
Mount Marcella, Qld. 25 53S 151 51E **131 Cb**
Mount Margaret, Qld. 26 54S 143 21E **127 Dc**
Mount Molloy, Qld. 16 42S 145 20E **127 Bd**
Mount Monger, W.A. 31 0S 122 0E **117 Ec**
Mount Morgan, Qld. 23 40S 150 25E **131 Aa**
Mount Mulligan, Qld. 16 45S 144 47E **127 Bc**
Mount Mulya, N.S.W. 30 46S 145 16E **91 Be**
Mount Narryer, W.A. 26 32S 116 24E **117 Db**
Mount Nebo, Qld. 27 26S 152 48E **131 Ec**
Mount Newman, W.A. 23 20S 119 34E **117 Cb**
Mount Norman, Qld. 19 48S 143 9E **128 Ab**
Mount Norris B., N.T. 11 25S 132 45E **123 Ab**
Mount Oxide Mine, Qld. 19 30S 139 29E **127 Bb**
Mount Palmer Power Sta., W.A. 31 25S 119 40E **119 Ef**
Mount Perry, Qld. 25 13S 151 42E **131 Cb**
Mount Phillips, W.A. 24 25S 116 15E **117 Cb**
Mount Sandiman, W.A. 24 25S 115 30E **117 Cb**
Mount Spencer, Qld. 21 28S 148 50E **129 Cg**
Mount Sturgeon, Qld. 20 8S 144 16E **128 Bc**
Mount Surprise, Qld. 18 10S 144 17E **127 Bc**
Mount Tyson, Qld. 27 34S 151 34E **131 Eb**
Mount Victor, S.A. 32 11S 139 44E **113 Be**
Mount Walker, Qld. 27 47S 152 34E **131 Ec**
Mount Walker, W.A. 32 3S 118 44E **119 Fe**
Mourilyan, Qld. 17 35S 146 3E **129 Xx**

Moutong, Indonesia 0 28N 121 13E **135 Df**
Moyhu, Vic. 36 36S 147 11E **101 Dg**
Moyston, Vic. 37 17S 142 45E **100 Ec**
Muar, Malaysia 2 3N 102 34E **134 Db**
Muarabungo, Indonesia 1 40S 101 10E **134 Eb**
Muaradjulaoi, Indonesia 0 12S 114 3E **134 Ed**
Muaraenim, Indonesia 3 40S 103 50E **134 Eb**
Muarakaman, Indonesia 0 2S 116 45E **135 Ee**
Muaratebo, Indonesia 1 30S 102 26E **134 Eb**
Muaratembesi, Indonesia 1 42S 103 2E **134 Eb**
Muaratewe, Indonesia 0 50S 115 0E **135 Ed**
Muchea, W.A. 31 36S 115 58E **119 Eb**
Muckadilla, Qld. 26 35S 148 23E **127 Dd**
Mudgee, N.S.W. 32 32S 149 31E **93 Ci**
Mudgeeraba, Qld. 28 4S 153 21E **131 Fd**
Mudiarrup T.O., W.A. 33 37S 116 46E **119 Gc**
Mueller Ra., W.A. 18 18S 126 46E **117 Bd**
Murgoo, W.A. 27 24S 116 28E **117 Db**
Mui Bai Bung, Vietnam 3 38N 104 44E **134 Cb**
Mui Dinh, Vietnam 11 22N 109 1E **134 Bc**
Mui Varella, Vietnam 12 54N 109 26E **134 Bc**
Muir L., W.A. 34 30S 116 40E **119 Hc**
Mukah, Malaysia 2 55N 112 5E **134 Dd**
Mukinbudin, W.A. 30 55S 118 5E **119 De**
Mukomuko, Indonesia 2 20S 101 10E **134 Eb**
Mulgathing, S.A. 30 15S 134 0E **111 Cb**
Mulgildie, Qld. 24 58S 151 8E **131 Bb**
Mulgowie, Qld. 27 44S 152 23E **131 Ec**
Mulgrave, Mt., Qld. 22 37S 150 17E **129 Di**
Mulifanua, Eastern Samoa 13 50S 171 59W **139 Cc**
Mullaley, N.S.W. 31 5S 149 56E **93 Bi**
Mullbring, N.S.W. 32 54S 151 28E **93 Ck**
Mullengudgery, N.S.W. 31 43S 147 29E **93 Bg**
Muller, Pegunungan, Indonesia
  0 30N 113 30E **134 Dd**
Mullewa, W.A. 28 29S 115 30E **119 Bb**
Mulligan R., Qld. 26 40S 139 0E **127 Cb**
Mullion Creek, N.S.W. 33 7S 149 7E **93 Di**
Mullumbimby, N.S.W. 28 30S 153 30E **95 Bd**
Mulpata, S.A. 35 8S 140 24E **113 Ef**
Mulwala, N.S.W. 35 59S 146 0E **93 Ff**
Mulya, N.S.W. 30 46S 145 16E **92 Ae**
Mulyungarie, S.A. 31 34S 140 47E **113 Af**
Mumbil, N.S.W. 32 41S 149 2E **93 Ci**
Mumeng, Papua N.G. 7 1S 146 37E **141 Dd**
Mummulgum, N.S.W. 28 50S 152 50E **95 Bc**
Muna I., Indonesia 5 0S 122 30E **135 Ff**
Munbilla, Qld. 27 54S 152 39E **131 Ec**
Munbooree, Qld. 27 51S 151 24E **131 Cb**
Munda, Solomon Is. 8 20S 157 16E **139 Qq**
Mundadoo, N.S.W. 30 48S 147 14E **93 Ag**
Mundijong, W.A. 32 18S 115 58E **119 Fc**
Mundiwindi, W.A. 23 47S 120 9E **117 Cc**
Mundoora, S.A. 33 34S 138 7E **113 Cd**
Mundrabilla, W.A. 31 52S 127 51E **117 Ed**
Mundubbera, Qld. 25 34S 151 17E **131 Cb**
Mundulla, S.A. 36 22S 140 39E **113 Ff**
Mungallala, Qld. 26 25S 147 34E **127 Dd**
Mungallala Cr., Qld. 28 53S 147 5E **127 Dd**
Mungana, Qld. 17 8S 144 27E **127 Bc**
Mungar, Qld. 25 35S 152 36E **131 Cc**
Mungaroona Ra., W.A. 21 40S 118 20E **117 Cb**
Mungerie, N.S.W. 32 33S 148 1E **93 Ch**
Mungungo, Qld. 24 46S 151 10E **131 Bb**
Munnundilla, Mt., N.S.W. 32 44S 150 32E **93 Cj**
Munro, Vic. 37 56S 147 11E **101 Eh**
Muntadgin, W.A. 31 45S 118 33E **119 Ee**
Muntok, Indonesia 2 5S 105 10E **134 Ec**
Muradup, W.A. 33 51S 116 57E **119 Gc**
Murchison, N.Z. 41 49S 172 21E **145 Bg**
Murchison, Vic. 36 39S 145 14E **101 Df**
Murchison Gl., N.Z. 43 36S 170 20E **145 De**
Murchison, Mt., N.Z. 45 13S 167 23E **145 Df**
Murchison Ra., N.T. 20 0S 134 10E **123 Cb**
Murchison R., W.A. 26 45S 116 15E **117 Da**
Murchison Downs, W.A. 26 45S 118 55E **117 Db**
Murchison House, W.A. 27 39S 114 14E **117 Da**
Murdinga, S.A. 33 44S 135 43E **113 Ca**
Murdoch Pt., Qld. 14 37S 144 55E **127 Ad**
Murgon, Qld. 26 15S 151 54E **131 Db**
Muris, Indonesia 2 23S 140 5E **135 Ei**
Muriwai, N.Z. 38 45S 177 55E **144 Ef**
Murkaby, S.A. 33 30S 139 27E **113 Ce**
Murrami, N.S.W. 34 26S 146 18E **93 Ef**
Murray L., Papua N.G. 7 0S 141 35E **141 Da**
Murray R., W.A. 32 33S 115 45E **119 Fb**
Murray Bridge, S.A. 35 6S 139 14E **113 Ee**
Murray Downs, N.T. 21 4S 134 40E **123 Ca**
Murray Town, S.A. 32 55S 138 15E **113 Bd**
Murrayville, Vic. 35 16S 141 11E **100 Cb**
Murringo, N.S.W. 34 16S 148 32E **93 Eh**
Murrumba, Qld. 27 12S 152 30E **131 Ec**

Murrumbateman, N.S.W. 34 58S 149 0E **93 Ei**
Murrumbidgee R., N.S.W. 34 40S 143 0E **93 Ef**
Murrumburrah, N.S.W. 34 32S 148 22E **93 Eh**
Murrurundi, N.S.W. 31 42S 150 51E **95 Ea**
Murwillumbah, N.S.W. 28 18S 153 27E **95 Bd**
Murtoa, Vic. 36 35S 142 28E **100 Dc**
Murupara, N.Z. 38 30S 178 40E **144 Ee**
Musa R., Papua N.G. 9 3S 148 55E **141 Ee**
Musala I., Indonesia 1 41N 98 28E **134 Da**
Musgrave, Mt., N.Z. 43 48S 170 43E **145 De**
Musgrave Ras., S.A. 26 0S 132 0E **111 Bb**
Musi R., Indonesia 2 55S 103 40E **134 Eb**
Muswellbrook, N.S.W. 32 16S 150 56E **95 Fa**
Mutarnee, Qld. 18 57S 146 18E **129 Yx**
Mutooroo, S.A. 32 26S 140 55E **113 Bf**
Muttaburra, Qld. 22 38S 144 29E **128 Dc**
Muttama, N.S.W. 34 46S 148 8E **93 Eh**
Muttonbird Is., N.Z. 47 13S 167 23E **145 Hb**
Myall, Vic. 35 32S 143 55E **100 Cd**
Myall L., N.S.W. 32 30S 152 18E **95 Fc**
Myall Creek, N.S.W. 29 44S 150 47E **95 Ca**
Myponga, S.A. 35 24S 138 27E **113 Ed**
Myrniong, Vic. 37 38S 144 23E **100 Ee**
Myroodah, W.A. 18 8S 124 6E **117 Bc**
Myrrhee, Vic. 36 46S 146 17E **101 Dg**
Myrtleford, Vic. 36 34S 146 44E **101 Dg**
Mysia, Vic. 36 13S 143 46E **100 Dd**

N

Nabas, Philippines 11 47N 122 6E **135 Bf**
Nabawa, W.A. 28 30S 114 48E **119 Ba**
Nabberu L., W.A. 25 30S 120 30E **117 Dc**
Nabiac, N.S.W. 32 5S 152 25E **95 Fc**
Nackara, S.A. 32 48S 139 12E **113 Be**
Naga, Philippines 13 38N 123 15E **135 Bf**
Nagambie, Vic. 36 47S 145 10E **101 Df**
Nagoorin, Qld. 24 17S 151 15E **131 Bb**
Naidia, S.A. 34 31S 139 49E **113 De**
Nairne, S.A. 35 2S 138 56E **113 Ed**
Nakanai Mts., Papua N.G. 5 40S 151 0E **141 Cf**
Nakhon Phanom, Thailand 13 49N 100 3E **134 Ab**
Nakhon Ratchasima, Thailand 14 59N 102 12E **134 Bb**
Nakhon Sawan, Thailand 15 35N 100 10E **134 Ab**
Nakhon Si Thammarat, Thailand 8 29N 100 0E **134 Ca**
Nalbarra, W.A. 28 40S 117 37E **119 Bd**
Nam Tok, Thailand 14 14N 99 4E **134 Ba**
Namatanai, Papua N.G. 3 40S 152 29E **141 Bg**
Namber, Indonesia 1 2S 134 57E **135 Eh**
Nambour, Qld. 26 32S 152 58E **131 Dc**
Nambouwalu, Fiji 15 0S 178 0E **139 Ab**
Nambucca Heads, N.S.W. 30 37S 153 0E **95 Dd**
Namdee, W.A. 28 56S 118 10E **119 Be**
Nameh, Indonesia 2 34N 116 21E **135 De**
Namlea, Indonesia 3 10S 127 5E **135 Eg**
Namoi R., N.S.W. 30 12S 149 30E **95 Da**
Namrole, Indonesia 3 46S 126 46E **135 Eg**
Nana Glen, N.S.W. 30 8S 153 2E **95 Dd**
Nanango, Qld. 26 40S 152 0E **131 Dc**
Nandewar Ra., N.S.W. 30 15S 150 35E **95 Da**
Nandi, Fiji 17 25S 176 50e **139 Aa**
Nanga, W.A. 26 7S 113 45E **117 Da**
Nanga Brook, W.A. 32 49S 116 4E **119 Fc**
Nangapinoh, Indonesia 0 20S 111 14E **134 Ed**
Nangatajap, Indonesia 1 32S 110 34E **134 Ed**
Nangus, N.S.W. 35 0S 147 52E **93 Eg**
Nangwarry, S.A. 37 33S 140 48E **113 Gf**
Nankin Junction, Qld. 23 23S 150 38E **131 Aa**
Nannine, W.A. 26 51S 118 18E **117 Db**
Nannup, W.A. 33 59S 115 48E **119 Gb**
Nanson, W.A. 28 35S 114 45E **119 Ba**
Nanuku Pass, Fiji 16 45S 179 15W **139 Ac**
Nanutana, W.A. 22 32S 115 30E **117 Cb**
Nanya, Qld. 22 58S 147 51E **129 Df**
Napabalana, Indonesia 4 42S 127 43E **135 Ef**
Napier, N.Z. 39 30S 176 56E **144 Fe**
Napier, W.A. 34 50S 117 57E **119 Hd**
Napier Broome B., W.A. 14 25S 126 37E **117 Ad**
Napier Downs, W.A. 17 11S 124 36E **117 Bc**
Napier Pen., N.T. 12 4S 135 43E **123 Ac**
Nappa Merrie, Qld. 27 36S 141 7E **127 Dc**
Nara, Qld. 19 14S 143 1E **128 Ab**
Naracoopa, Tas. 39 56S 144 7E **107 Ac**
Naracoorte, S.A. 36 58S 140 45E **113 Ff**
Naradhan, N.S.W. 33 34S 146 17E **93 Df**
Naraling, W.A. 28 25S 114 52E **119 Ba**
Narathiwat, Thailand 6 40N 101 55E **134 Cb**

Narembeen, W.A. 32 7S 118 17E **119 Fe**
Naretha, W.A. 31 0S 124 45E **117 Ec**
Narooma, N.S.W. 36 14S 150 4E **93 Gj**
Narrabri, N.S.W. 30 19S 149 46E **91 Bg**
Narran L., N.S.W. 28 37S 148 12E **91 Af**
Narriah, N.S.W. 33 56S 146 43E **93 Df**
Narrikup, W.A. 34 47S 117 40E **119 Hd**
Narrogin, W.A. 32 58S 117 14E **119 Fd**
Narromine, N.S.W. 32 12S 148 12E **93 Ch**
Narrung, S.A. 35 32S 139 8E **113 Ee**
Naryilco, Qld. 28 37S 141 53E **127 Dc**
Nasawa, New Hebrides 15 0S 168 0E **139 Hh**
Naseby, N.Z. 45 1S 170 10E **145 Fe**
Natal, Indonesia 0 35N 99 0E **134 Da**
Natal Downs, Qld. 21 7S 146 10E **129 Ce**
Natewa B., Fiji 16 35S 179 40E **139 Ab**
Nathalia, Vic. 36 1S 145 7E **100 Df**
Natimuk, Vic. 36 42S 142 0E **100 Db**
Natkyizin, Burma 14 57N 97 59E **134 Ba**
Natuna Besar I., Indonesia 4 0N 108 15E **134 Dc**
Natuna Selatan Is., Indonesia 2 45N 109 0E **134 Dc**
Naturaliste C., Tas. 40 50S 148 15E **107 Bg**
Naturaliste C., W.A. 33 32S 115 0E **119 Ga**
Natya, Vic 34. 57S 143 13E **100 Bd**
Naumai, N.Z. 36 5S 173 59E **144 Cc**
Nausori, Fiji 18 2S 178 32E **139 Bb**
Navarre, Vic. 36 53S 143 11E **100 Dd**
Naviti I., Fiji 17 7S 177 15E **139 Aa**
Navua, Fiji 18 6S 177 43E **139 Bb**
Ndoua C., New Caledonia 22 24S 166 56E **139 C₁e₁**
Nduindui, New Hebrides 15 24S 167 46E **139 Hg**
Neale L., N.T. 24 15S 130 0E **123 Cb**
Neba I., New Caledonia 20 9S 163 56E **139 A₁a₁**
Nebine Cr., Qld. 29 7S 146 56E **127 Dd**
Nebo, Qld. 21 42S 148 42E **129 Cg**
Neckarboo, N.S.W. 32 3S 144 35E **92 Cd**
Nectar Brook, S.A. 32 43S 137 57E **113 Bc**
Needilup, W.A. 33 55S 118 45E **119 Ge**
Needles Pt., N.Z. 36 3S 175 25E **144 Cd**
Neerim, Vic. 37 59S 145 57E **101 Ef**
Negra Pt., Philippines 18 40N 120 50E **135 Af**
Negros I., Philippines 10 0N 123 0E **135 Cf**
Neiafu, Tonga 18 39S 173 59W **139 No**
Neilrex, N.S.W. 31 44S 149 20E **93 Bi**
Nelgowrie, N.S.W. 30 54S 148 7E **93 Ah**
Nelia, Qld. 20 39S 142 12E **128 Ba**
Nelia Gaari P.O., N.S.W. 32 4S 142 51E **92 Cb**
Nelligen, N.S.W. 35 39S 150 8E **93 Fj**
Nelson, Vic. 38 3S 141 2E **100 Fb**
Nelson, N.Z. 41 18S 173 16E **145 Bh**
Nelson Prov., N.Z. 42 11S 172 15E **145 Bg**
Nelson Bay, N.S.W. 32 43S 152 9E **93 Cl**
Nelson C., Australia 38 26S 141 32E **100 Fb**
Nelson C., Papua N.G. 9 0S 149 20E **141 Ee**
Nelson Lakes Nat. Pk., N.Z. 41 55S 172 44E **145 Bg**
Nelungaloo, N.S.W. 33 7S 148 0E **93 Dh**
Nemingha, N.S.W. 31 6S 151 0E **95 Eb**
Nendiarene Pt., New Caledonia
  20 14S 164 19E **139 A₁b₁**
Nenusa Is., Indonesia 4 45N 127 1E **135 Dg**
Nerang, Qld. 27 58S 153 20E **131 Ed**
Nerriga, N.S.W. 35 5S 150 6E **93 Fj**
Netherby, Vic. 36 8S 141 40E **100 Db**
Netherdale, Qld. 21 10S 148 33E **129 Cg**
Netherton, S.A. 35 30S 139 57E **113 Ee**
Netley Gap, S.A. 32 43S 139 59E **113 Bf**
Nevertire, N.S.W. 31 50S 147 44E **93 Bg**
Neville, N.S.W. 33 41S 149 12E **93 Di**
Nevoria, W.A. 31 25S 119 25E **119 Ef**
New Angledool, N.S.W. 29 10S 147 55E **91 Af**
New Brighton, N.Z. 43 29S 172 43E **145 Dg**
New Britain I., Papua N.G. 5 50S 150 20E **141 Df**
New Caledonia, S-W Pacific 21 0S 165 0E **139 A₁b₁**
New Coombool, S.A. 33 55S 140 54E **113 Cf**
New Georgia, Solomon Is. 8 15S 157 30E **139 Qq**
New Georgia Is., Solomon Is. 8 15S 159 30E **139 Pp**
New Hanover I., Papua N.G. 2 30S 150 10E **141 Be**
New Hebrides, S-W Pacific 15 0S 168 0E **139 Cg**
New Ireland I., Papua N.G. 3 20S 151 50E **141 Bf**
New Mollyan, N.S.W. 31 34S 149 14E **93 Bi**
New Moon, Qld. 19 12S 145 46E **128 Ad**
New Norcia, W.A. 30 57S 116 13E **119 Dc**
New Norfolk, Tas. 42 46S 147 2E **107 Df**
New Plymouth, N.Z. 39 4S 174 5E **144 Fb**
New Springs, W.A. 25 49S 120 1E **117 Db**
New Year Is., Aust. 39 41S 143 50E **107 Ab**
Newbridge, N.S.W. 33 35S 149 22E **93 Di**
Newcastle, N.S.W. 32 52S 151 49E **93 Ck**
Newcastle Ra., N.T. 15 45S 130 15E **123 Bb**
Newcastle Waters, N.T. 17 30S 133 28E **123 Bb**
Newdegate, W.A. 33 6S 119 0E **119 Ge**

Newhaven, Vic. 38 32S 145 20E **101 Ff**
Newlyn, Vic. 37 23S 144 0E **100 Ed**
Newman, Mt., W.A. 23 18S 119 45E **117 Cb**
Newmarket, Qld. 27 25S 152 57E **131 Ec**
Newmerrella, Vic. 37 45S 148 25E **101 Ei**
Newnes, N.S.W. 33 9S 150 16E **93 Dj**
Newry, Vic. 37 59S 146 53E **101 Eg**
Newstead, Vic. 37 7S 144 4E **100 Ee**
Newton Boyd, N.S.W. 29 45S 152 16E **95 Cc**
Ngabang, Indonesia 0 30N 109 55E **134 Dc**
Ngaere, N.Z. 39 23S 174 17E **144 Fc**
Ngahere, N.Z. 42 24S 171 26E **145 Cf**
Ngaruroro R., N.Z. 39 34S 176 55E **144 Fe**
Ngatapa, N.Z. 38 32S 177 45E **144 Ef**
Ngauruhoe, N.Z. 39 13S 175 45E **144 Fd**
Nggamea, Fiji 16 46S 179 46W **139 Ac**
Nggela, Solomon Is. 9 5S 160 15E **139 Qs**
Nguna, New Hebrides 17 26S 168 21E **139 Jh**
Ngunguru, N.Z. 35 37S 174 30E **144 Bc**
Nha Trang, Vietnam 12 16N 109 10E **134 Bc**
Nhill, Vic. 36 18S 141 40E **100 Db**
Nhulunbuy, N.T. 12 10S 136 45E **123 Ac**
Niah, Malaysia 3 58N 113 46E **134 Dd**
Niangala, N.S.W. 31 18S 151 25E **95 Eb**
Nias I., Indonesia 1 0N 97 40E **134 Da**
Nicholson, W.A. 18 2S 128 54E **117 Bd**
Nicholson Ra., W.A. 27 15S 116 30E **117 Db**
Nicholson R., N.T. 17 31S 139 36E **123 Bc**
Niemur, N.S.W. 35 17S 144 9E **92 Fd**
Nietta, Tas. 41 21S 146 4E **107 Ce**
Nightcaps, N.Z. 45 57S 168 14E **145 Fc**
Nildottie, S.A. 34 40S 139 38E **113 De**
Nile, Tas. 41 39S 147 21E **107 Cf**
Nimbin, N.S.W. 28 36S 153 13E **95 Bd**
Ninaa L., W.A. 30 57S 116 38E **119 Dc**
Nindigully, Qld. 28 21S 148 50E **127 Dd**
Ninety Mile Beach, Vic. 38 15S 147 24E **101 Fh**
Ninety Mile Beach, N.Z. 34 45S 173 0E **144 Aa**
Ningaloo, W.A. 22 41S 113 41E **117 Ca**
Ninghan, W.A. 29 25S 117 20E **119 Cd**
Nipa, Papua N.G. 6 9S 143 29E **141 Db**
Niut, Mt., Indonesia 0 55N 109 30E **134 Dc**
Nobby, Qld. 27 52S 151 54E **131 Eb**
Nockatunga, Qld. 27 42S 142 42E **127 Dc**
Noggerup, W.A. 33 32S 116 5E **119 Gc**
Nogo R., Qld. 25 5S 150 57E **131 Ba**
Nogoa R., Qld. 23 33S 148 32E **129 Ef**
Nokaning, W.A. 31 20S 118 12E **119 Ee**
Noland Bay, Tas. 40 57S 147 5E **107 Bf**
Nomad, Papua N.G. 6 19S 142 13E **141 Db**
Nome, Qld. 19 12S 146 55E **129 Ae**
Nomuka, Tonga 20 20S 174 48W **139 On**
Nomuka Group, Tonga 20 20S 174 48W **139 On**
Nonda, Qld 20 40S 142 28E **128 Ba**
Nong Khai, Thailand 17 50N 102 46E **134 Ab**
Nonning, S.A. 32 32S 136 28E **113 Bb**
Noojee, Vic. 37 57S 146 1E **101 Eg**
Noondoo, Qld 28 35S 148 30E **127 Dd**
Noongal, W.A. 28 7S 116 47E **119 Bc**
Noonkanbah, W.A. 18 30S 124 50E **117 Bc**
Noora, S.A. 34 26S 140 51E **113 Df**
Noorat, Vic. 38 12S 142 55E **100 Fc**
Noorinbee, Vic. 37 32S 149 10E **101 Ej**
Noosa Hd., Qld. 26 24S 153 5E **131 Dd**
Noradjuha, Vic. 36 50S 141 58E **100 Db**
Norah Hd., N.S.W. 33 18S 151 32E **93 Dk**
Norley, Qld. 27 45S 143 48E **127 Dc**
Norma, Mt., Qld. 20 55S 140 42E **127 Cc**
Norman R., Qld. 19 20S 142 35E **127 Bc**
Normanby, N.Z. 39 32S 174 18E **144 Fc**
Normanby I., Papua N.G. 10 55S 151 0E **141 Ff**
Normanby R., Qld. 14 23S 144 10E **127 Ac**
Normanby Ra., Qld. 22 25S 150 10E **129 Ci**
Normanhurst, Mt., W.A. 25 13S 122 30E **117 Dc**
Normanton, Qld. 17 40S 141 10E **127 Bc**
Normanville, S.A. 35 27S 138 18E **113 Ed**
Nornalup, W.A. 35 0S 116 48E **119 Hc**
Norseman, W.A. 32 8S 121 43E **117 Ec**
Norsup, New Hebrides 16 3S 167 24E **139 Ig**
North Br., N.Z. 43 30S 171 30E **145 Df**
North Head, N.Z. 36 24S 174 3E **144 Cc**
North L., N.S.W. 32 30S 143 5E **92 Cc**
North Pt., Qld. 23 45S 151 20E **131 Ab**
North Pt., Tas. 40 42S 145 17E **107 Bd**
North Bruny I., Tas. 43 10S 147 23E **107 Ef**
North Cape, Papua N.G. 2 32S 150 50E **141 Bf**
North Copperfield, Qld. 22 51S 147 36E **129 Df**
North Dandalup, W.A. 32 30S 116 2E **119 Fb**
North Kellerberrin, W.A. 31 30S 117 40E **119 Ed**
North Keppel Is., Qld. 23 45S 150 55E **129 Ej**
North Mavora L., N.Z. 45 13S 168 11E **145 Fc**
North Melbergen, N.S.W. 33 42S 146 2E **93 Df**

North Shields, S.A. 34 38S 135 52E **113 Da**
North Stradbroke I., Qld. 27 35S 153 28E **131 Ed**
North Taranaki Bight, N.Z. 38 45S 174 20E **144 Ec**
North Trap, N.Z. 47 25S 167 55E **145 Hb**
North West C., W.A. 21 45S 114 9E **117 Ca**
North West I., Qld. 23 17S 151 43E **131 Ab**
North Yathong, N.S.W. 35 14S 145 54E **92 Fe**
Northam, W.A. 31 35S 116 42E **119 Ec**
Northampton, W.A. 28 21S 114 33E **119 Ba**
Northampton Downs, Qld. 24 35S 145 48E **127 Cd**
Northcliffe, W.A. 34 39S 116 7E **119 Hc**
Northern Gully, W.A. 28 44S 114 56E **119 Ba**
Northern Territory, Aust. 16 0S 133 0E **123**
Northumberland C., S.A. 38 5S 140 40E **113 Hf**
Northumberland Islands, Qld. 21 30S 149 50E **129 Ci**
Noumea, New Caledonia 22 17S 166 30E **139 C_1d_1**
Nowa Nowa, Vic. 37 44S 148 3E **101 Ei**
Nowendoc, N.S.W. 31 32S 151 44E **95 Eb**
Nowingi, Vic. 34 33S 142 15E **100 Bc**
Nowra, N.S.W. 34 53S 150 35E **93 Ej**
Nubeena, Tas. 43 6S 147 45E **107 Ef**
Nuboai, Indonesia 2 10S 136 30E **135 Ei**
Nugget Pt., N.Z. 46 27S 169 50E **145 Gd**
Nuguria Is., Papua N.G. 3 20S 154 40E **141 Bh**
Nuhaka, N.Z. 39 3S 177 45E **144 Ff**
Nukarni, W.A. 31 17S 118 11E **119 Ee**
Nukey Bluff, Mt., S.A. 32 32S 135 40E **113 Ba**
Nukiki, Solomon Is. 6 45S 156 29E **139 Pq**
Nuku'alofa, Tonga 21 10S 174 0W **139 On**
Nulla Nulla, Qld. 19 50S 145 10E **128 Ad**
Nullagine, W.A. 21 53S 120 6E **117 Cc**
Nullarbor, S.A. 31 28S 130 55E **111 Cb**
Nullarbor Plain, S.A. 30 45S 129 0E **111 Ca**
Nullawarre, Vic. 38 30S 142 45E **100 Fc**
Nullawil, Vic. 35 49S 143 10E **100 Cd**
Numbulwar, N.T. 14 15S 135 45E **123 Ac**
Numurkah, Vic. 36 0S 145 26E **101 Df**
Nundle, N.S.W. 31 29S 151 9E **95 Eb**
Nungarin, W.A. 31 12S 118 6E **119 Ee**
Nurina, W.A. 30 44S 126 23E **117 Ed**
Nuriootpa, S.A. 34 27S 139 0E **113 De**
Nurrari Lakes, S.A. 29 1S 130 5E **111 Ba**
Nurri, Mt., N.S.W. 31 42S 146 2E **93 Bf**
Nusa Tenggara Barat, Indonesia 8 50S 117 30E **135 Fe**
Nutwood Downs, N.T. 15 49S 134 10E **123 Bb**
Nuyts Arch., S.A. 32 12S 133 20E **111 Cb**
Nuyts C., S.A. 32 2S 132 21E **111 Cb**
Nuyts Pt., W.A. 35 4S 116 38E **119 Hc**
Nyabing, W.A. 33 30S 118 7E **119 Ge**
Nyah West, Vic. 35 11S 143 21E **100 Cd**
Nyamup, W.A. 34 18S 116 19E **119 Hc**
Nyarrin, Vic. 35 22S 142 43E **100 Cc**
Nymagee, N.S.W. 32 7S 146 20E **93 Cf**
Nymboida R., N.S.W. 29 22S 152 32E **95 Cc**
Nyngan, N.S.W. 31 30S 147 8E **93 Bg**
Nyora, Vic. 38 20S 145 41E **101 Ff**

O

Oak Hills, Qld. 18 32S 145 36E **129 Yw**
Oak Vale, Qld. 20 24S 145 11E **128 Bd**
Oakbank, S.A. 33 4S 140 33E **113 Cf**
Oakdale, W.A. 34 25S 119 2E **119 Hf**
Oakey, Qld. 27 25S 151 43E **131 Eb**
Oaklands, N.S.W. 35 34S 145 10E **93 Ff**
Oakleigh, Vic. 37 54S 145 6E **101 Ef**
Oakley, Qld. 21 11S 145 5E **128 Cd**
Oakley Creek, N.S.W. 31 27S 149 46E **93 Bi**
Oakura, N.Z. 39 7S 173 57E **144 Fb**
Oakvale, S.A. 32 58S 140 48E **113 Bf**
Oakwood, N.S.W. 29 38S 151 4E **95 Cb**
Oamaru, N.Z. 45 5S 170 59E **145 Ff**
Oaro, N.Z. 42 31S 173 30E **145 Ch**
Oatlands, Tas. 42 17S 147 21E **107 Df**
Oban, N.Z. 46 55S 168 10E **145 Gc**
Oberon, N.S.W. 33 45S 149 52E **93 Di**
Obi Is., Indonesia 1 30S 127 30E **135 Eg**
O'Bil Bil, Qld. 25 31S 151 14E **131 Cb**
Obley, N.S.W. 32 40S 148 34E **93 Ch**
Ocean Grove, Vic. 38 16S 144 32E **100 Fe**
Oenpelli, N.T. 12 20S 133 4E **123 Ab**
Ofu, Eastern Samoa 14 11S 169 41W **139 De**
Ogilvie, N.Z. 28 10S 114 37E **119 Ba**
Ogmore, Qld. 22 37S 149 35E **127 Cd**
Ohaeawai, N.Z. 35 21S 173 53E **144 Bb**
Ohai, N.Z. 44 55S 168 0E **145 Fb**
Ohakune, N.Z. 39 24S 175 24E **144 Fd**

Ohau, N.Z. 40 40S 175 15E **144 Gd**
Ohau L., N.Z. 44 15S 169 53E **145 Ed**
Ohau R., N.Z. 44 15S 170 3E **145 Ee**
Ohaupo, N.Z. 37 56S 175 20E **144 Dd**
Ohingait, N.Z. 39 51S 175 44E **144 Fd**
Ohiwa Harbour, N.Z. 37 59S 177 10E **144 Df**
Ohura, N.Z. 38 51S 174 59E **144 Ec**
Okahukura, N.Z. 38 48S 175 14E **144 Ed**
Okaihau, N.Z. 35 19S 173 36E **144 Bb**
Okaiawa, N.Z. 39 32S 174 12E **144 Fc**
Okapa, Papua N.G. 6 38S 145 39E **141 Dc**
Okarito, N.Z. 43 15S 170 9E **145 De**
Okataina L., N.Z. 38 8S 176 24E **144 Ee**
Okato, N.Z. 39 12S 173 53E **144 Fb**
Okuru, N.Z. 43 55S 168 55E **145 Dc**
Olary, S.A. 32 18S 140 19E **113 Bf**
Olary Ck., S.A. 32 38S 140 48E **113 Bf**
Old Cork, Qld 22 57S 142 0E **127 Cc**
Old Junee, N.S.W. 34 49S 147 31E **93 Eg**
Old Kolonga, Qld. 24 53S 151 44E **131 Bb**
Old Pasha, Qld. 21 43S 147 32E **129 Cf**
Oldfield R., W.A. 33 53S 120 48E **119 Gg**
Olga, Mt., N.T. 25 20S 130 40E **123 Db**
Olinda, N.S.W. 32 25S 150 10E **93 Cj**
Olivine Ra., N.Z. 44 15S 168 30E **145 Ec**
Olongapo, Philippines 14 50N 120 18E **135 Bf**
Omakau, N.Z. 45 6S 169 37E **145 Fd**
Omapere, N.Z. 35 37S 173 25E **144 Bb**
Omarama, N.Z. 44 29S 169 58E **145 Ed**
Omata, N.Z. 39 6S 174 1E **144 Fc**
Omeo, Vic. 37 6S 147 36E **101 Eh**
Omihi, N.Z. 43 1S 172 51E **145 Dg**
Onang, Indonesia 3 2S 118 55E **135 Ee**
One Tree, N.S.W. 34 11S 144 43E **92 Ed**
Onehunga, N.Z. 36 55S 174 30E **144 Cd**
Onekaka, N.Z. 40 46S 172 42E **145 Ag**
Onerahi, N.Z. 35 45S 174 22E **144 Bc**
Onewhero, N.Z. 37 19S 174 55E **144 Dc**
Ongarue, N.Z. 38 42S 175 19E **144 Ed**
Ongaonga, N.Z. 39 55S 176 26E **144 Fe**
Ongea Levu, Fiji 9 8S 178 24E **139 Bc**
Ongerup, W.A. 33 58S 118 28E **119 Ge**
Ono, Fiji 18 55S 178 29E **139 Bb**
Onslow, W.A. 21 40S 115 0E **117 Cb**
Oodlawirra, S.A. 32 53S 139 4E **113 Be**
Oodnadatta, S.A. 27 33S 135 30E **111 Bc**
Ooldea, S.A. 30 27S 131 50E **111 Cb**
Oondooroo, Qld. 22 10S 143 5E **128 Db**
Oorindi, Qld. 20 40S 141 1E **127 Cc**
Ootha, N.S.W. 33 6S 147 29E **93 Dg**
Opaki, N.Z. 40 53S 175 38E **144 Gd**
Opapa, N.Z. 39 47S 176 42E **144 Fe**
Open Bay Is., N.Z. 43 51S 168 51E **145 Dc**
Ophthalmia Ra., W.A. 23 15S 119 30E **117 Cb**
Opotiki, N.Z. 38 1S 177 19E **144 Ef**
Opua, N.Z. 35 19S 174 9E **144 Bc**
Opunake, N.Z. 39 26S 173 52E **144 Fb**
Ora Banda, W.A. 30 20S 121 0E **117 Ec**
Orana, N.Z. 32 46S 144 4E **92 Cd**
Orangimea, N.Z. 39 41S 174 51E **144 Fc**
Oraparinna, S.A. 31 22S 138 45E **113 Ad**
Orara R., N.S.W. 29 37S 152 49E **95 Cc**
Orari, N.Z. 44 9S 171 18E **145 Ef**
Oras, Philippines 12 9N 125 22E **135 Bg**
Orbost, Vic. 37 40S 148 29E **101 Ei**
Ord, Mt., W.A. 17 20S 125 34E **117 Bd**
Ord River, W.A. 15 33S 128 35E **117 Bd**
Ord R., W.A. 15 33S 128 35E **117 Bd**
Orepuki, N.Z. 46 19S 167 46E **145 Gb**
Orete Pt., N.Z. 37 36S 177 54E **144 Df**
Oreti R., N.Z. 45 39S 168 14E **145 Fc**
Orewa, N.Z. 36 35S 174 42E **144 Cc**
Orford, Tas. 42 35S 147 52E **107 Df**
Orient, Qld. 28 7S 143 3E **127 Dc**
Orini, N.Z. 37 33S 175 19E **144 Dd**
Orkabie, Qld. 21 49S 149 22E **129 Ch**
Orkola, Mt., S.A. 31 52S 138 13E **113 Ad**
Ormoc I., Philippines 11 0N 124 37E **135 Bf**
Ormond, N.Z. 38 33S 177 56E **144 Ef**
Ormondville, N.Z. 40 5S 176 19E **144 Ge**
Oroquieta, Philippines 8 32N 123 44E **135 Cf**
Orote Pen., Guam 13 26N 144 38E **139 Tu**
Orroroo, S.A. 32 43S 138 38E **113 Bd**
Oruanui, N.Z. 38 34S 176 3E **144 Ee**
Osborne, N.S.W. 35 22S 146 41E **93 Ff**
Oslob, Philippines 9 31N 123 26E **135 Cf**
Ossa, Mt., Tas. 41 52S 146 3E **107 Ce**
Osterly, Tas. 42 22S 146 44E **107 De**
Otago Harbour, N.Z. 45 47S 170 42E **145 Fe**
Otago Pen., N.Z. 45 48S 170 45E **145 Fe**
Otago Prov., N.Z. 45 20S 169 20E **145 Fd**
Otahuhu, N.Z. 36 56S 174 51E **144 Cc**

Pine Creek, N.T. 13 50S 131 49E **123 Ab**
Pine Point, S.A. 34 35S 137 50E **113 Dc**
Pine Ridge, N.S.W. 31 30S 150 28E **95 Ea**
Pinehill, Qld. 23 38S 146 57E **129 Ee**
Pinetrees Pt., Qld. 22 20S 150 37E **129 Di**
Piney Range, N.S.W. 33 50S 147 58E **93 Dg**
Pingaring, W.A. 32 40S 118 32E **119 Fe**
Pingelly, W.A. 32 29S 116 59E **119 Fd**
Pingelly West, W.A. 32 34S 116 54E **119 Fc**
Pingrup, W.A. 33 32S 118 29E **119 Ge**
Pingrup L., W.A. 33 27S 118 25E **119 Ge**
Pingrup North, W.A. 33 24S 118 30E **119 Ge**
Pini I., Indonesia 0 10N 98 40E **134 Da**
Pinjarra, W.A. 32 37S 115 52E **119 Fb**
Pinjarrega L., W.A. 30 5S 115 55E **119 Db**
Pinnacle, N.Z. 41 49S 173 25E **145 Bh**
Pinnacles, W.A. 28 12S 26E **119 Bg**
Pinnaroo, S.A. 35 13S 140 56E **113 Ef**
Pinrang, Indonesia 3 46S 119 34E **135 Ee**
Pins, Is., des, New Caledonia 22 37S 167 30E **139 C₁e₁**
Pintharuka, W.A. 29 7S 115 58E **119 Cb**
Pintumba, S.A. 31 50S 132 18E **111 Cb**
Pio Pio, N.Z. 38 28S 175 1E **144 Ec**
Pioneer, Qld. 19 31S 147 20E **129 Af**
Pipiriki, N.Z. 38 28S 175 5E **144 Fc**
Pippingarra, W.A. 20 27S 118 42E **117 Cb**
Pirongia, N.Z. 38 0S 175 12E **144 Dd**
Pisa, Mt., N.Z. 44 52S 169 12E **145 Ed**
Pisa Ra., N.Z. 44 52S 169 12E **145 Ed**
Pisgah, Mt., N.Z. 45 5S 170 24E **145 Fe**
Pisgah, Mt., Qld. 23 35S 147 10E **129 Ef**
Pising, Indonesia 5 8S 121 53E **135 Ef**
Pitarpunga L., N.S.W. 34 24S 143 30E **92 Ec**
Pithara, W.A. 30 20S 116 35E **119 Dc**
Pithara East, W.A. 30 24S 116 46E **119 Dc**
Pittsworth, Qld. 27 41S 151 37E **131 Eb**
Pituri R., Qld. 22 35S 138 30E **127 Cb**
Plampang, Indonesia 8 48S 117 46E **135 Fe**
Planet Ck., Qld. 24 25S 149 2E **129 Fh**
Pleasant, Mt., S.A. 34 46S 139 4E **113 De**
Pleasant Hills, N.S.W. 35 28S 146 50E **93 Ff**
Pleasant Point, N.Z. 44 16S 171 9E **145 Ef**
Pleiku, Vietnam 14 3N 108 0E **134 Bc**
Plenty R., N.T. 23 25S 136 31E **123 Cc**
Plimmerton, N.Z. 41 4S 174 51E **144 Hc**
Poatina, Tas. 41 47S 146 56E **107 Ce**
Poh, Indonesia 0 46S 122 51E **135 Ef**
Poindimie, New Caledonia 20 56S 165 20E **139 A₁c₁**
Point Danger, Qld. 28 9S 153 30E **131 Fd**
Point Lookout, Mt., N.S.W. 30 29S 152 24E **95 Dc**
Point Vernon, Qld. 25 15S 152 49E **131 Cc**
Poisonbush Ra., W.A. 22 30S 121 30E **117 Cc**
Pokataroo, N.S.W. 29 30S 148 34E **91 Ag**
Pokeno, N.Z. 37 15S 175 1E **144 Dc**
Polewali, Indonesia 4 8S 119 43E **135 Ee**
Polillo Is., Philippines 14 56N 122 0E **135 Bf**
Polocara, N.S.W. 30 46S 144 12E **92 Ad**
Pollux, N.Z. 44 14S 168 52E **145 Ec**
Pomahaka R., N.Z. 46 8S 169 34E **145 Fd**
Pomio, Papua N.G. 5 32S 151 33E **141 Cf**
Pomona, Qld. 26 22S 152 52E **131 Dc**
Pompoota, S.A. 34 59S 139 19E **113 De**
Pondooma, S.A. 33 29S 136 59E **113 Cb**
Ponérihouen, New Caledonia 21 5S 165 24E **139 B₁c₁**
Pongaroa, N.Z. 40 33S 176 15E **144 Ge**
Pontianak, Indonesia 0 3S 109 15E **134 Dc**
Ponui I., N.Z. 36 52S 175 11E **144 Cd**
Poochera, S.A. 32 43S 134 51E **111 Cb**
Pooncarie, N.S.W. 33 22S 142 31E **92 Db**
Poonindie, S.A. 34 34S 135 54E **113 Da**
Poopelloe L., N.S.W. 31 40S 144 0E **92 Bd**
Poor Knights I., N.Z. 35 29S 174 43E **144 Bc**
Popanyinning, W.A. 32 40S 117 2E **119 Fd**
Popilta, N.S.W. 33 10S 141 42E **90 Ca**
Popio L., N.S.W. 33 10S 141 52E **92 Da**
Popondetta, Papua N.G. 8 48S 148 17E **141 Ee**
Porangahau, N.Z. 40 17S 176 37E **144 Ge**
Porirua, N.Z. 41 8S 174 52E **144 Hc**
Porongurups, W.A. 34 39S 117 53E **119 Hd**
Port Adelaide, S.A. 34 46S 138 30E **113 Dd**
Port Albert, Vic. 38 42S 146 42E **101 Fg**
Port Arthur, Tas. 43 7S 147 50E **107 Ef**
Port Augusta, S.A. 32 30S 137 50E **113 Bc**
Port Augusta West, S.A. 32 29S 137 47E **113 Bc**
Port Bradshaw, N.T. 12 30S 137 0E **123 Ac**
Port Broughton, S.A. 33 37S 137 56E **113 Cc**
Port Campbell, Vic. 35 37S 143 1E **100 Fd**
Port Chalmers, N.Z. 45 49S 170 30E **145 Fe**
Port Clinton, Qld. 22 30S 150 46E **129 Di**
Port Darwin, N.T. 12 18S 130 55E **123 Ab**
Port Davey, Tas. 43 16S 145 55E **107 Ed**
Port Dickson, Malaysia 2 30N 101 49E **134 Db**

Port Douglas, Qld. 16 30S 145 30E **129 Ww**
Port Elliot, S.A. 35 32S 138 41E **113 Ed**
Port Fairy, Vic. 38 22S 142 12E **100 Fc**
Port Fitzroy, N.Z. 36 8S 175 20E **144 Cd**
Port Germein, S.A. 33 1S 138 1E **113 Cd**
Port Hedland, W.A. 20 25S 118 35E **117 Cb**
Port Hughes, W.A. 35 5S 117 40E **119 Hd**
Port Jackson, N.S.W. 33 50S 151 18E **93 Dk**
Port Kelang, Malaysia 3 0N 101 23E **134 Db**
Port Kembla, N.S.W. 34 29S 150 56E **93 Ej**
Port Lincoln, S.A. 34 42S 135 52E **113 Da**
Port MacDonnell, S.A. 38 0S 140 39E **113 Hf**
Port Macquarie, N.S.W. 31 25S 152 54E **95 Ec**
Port Moresby, Papua N.G. 9 24S 147 8E **141 Ed**
Port Musgrave, Qld. 11 55S 141 50E **127 Ac**
Port Nicholson, N.Z. 41 20S 174 52E **144 Hc**
Port Noarlunga, S.A. 35 10S 138 26E **113 Ed**
Port Pegasus, N.Z. 47 12S 167 41E **145 Hb**
Port Phillip B., Vic. 38 10S 144 50E **100 Fe**
Port Pirie, S.A. 33 10S 137 58E **113 Cd**
Port Rickaby, S.A. 34 41S 137 29E **113 Dc**
Port Sorell, Tas. 41 9S 146 41E **107 Ce**
Port Stephens, N.S.W. 32 38S 152 12E **93 Cl**
Port Victoria, S.A. 34 30S 137 29E **113 Dc**
Port Vila, New Hebrides 17 44S 168 19E **139 Jh**
Port Vincent, S.A. 34 47S 137 49E **113 Dc**
Port Weld, Malaysia 4 50N 100 38E **134 Db**
Portarlington, Vic. 38 7S 144 40E **100 Fe**
Porters Retreat, N.S.W. 34 2S 149 49E **93 Ei**
Portland, N.S.W. 33 20S 150 0E **93 Di**
Portland, N.Z. 35 50S 174 20E **144 Bc**
Portland, Vic. 38 20S 141 35E **100 Fb**
Portland Bay, Vic. 38 15S 141 45E **100 Fb**
Portland C., Tas. 40 46S 148 0E **107 Bf**
Portland I., N.Z. 39 20S 177 51E **144 Ff**
Portobello, N.Z. 45 50S 170 39E **145 Fe**
Poteriteri L., N.Z. 46 5S 167 10E **145 Gb**
Potosi, Qld. 22 16S 144 48E **128 Dc**
Pouembout, New Caledonia 21 8S 164 53E **139 B₁b₁**
Poum, New Caledonia 20 14S 164 2E **139 A₁a₁**
Poverty Bay, N.Z. 38 43S 178 2E **144 Eg**
Prairie, Qld. 20 50S 144 35E **128 Bc**
Praja, Indonesia 8 39S 116 27E **135 Fe**
Pratten, Qld. 28 6S 151 48E **131 Fb**
Premaydena, Tas. 43 3S 147 46E **107 Ef**
Premer, N.S.W. 31 29S 149 56E **93 Bi**
Preolanna, Tas. 41 4S 145 34E **107 Cd**
Preston C., W.A. ·20 51S 116 12E **117 Cb**
Preston L., W.A. 33 0S 115 40E **119 Fb**
Preston R., W.A. 33 19S 115 40E **119 Gb**
Pretty Pine, N.S.W. 35 25S 144 53E **92 Fd**
Prey Veng, Khmer Rep. 11 35N 105 29E **134 Bc**
Price, S.A. 34 18S 138 0E **113 Dc**
Prime Seal I., Tas. 40 3S 147 43E **107 Bf**
Prince Of Wales I., Qld. 10 40S 142 10E **127 Ac**
Princess Charlotte Bay, Qld. 14 25S 144 0E **127 Ac**
Princess May Ra., W.A. 15 30S 125 30E **117 Bd**
Princetown, Vic. 38 41S 143 10E **100 Fd**
Probolinggo, Indonesia 7 46S 113 13E **134 Fd**
Proserpine, Qld. 20 21S 148 36E **129 Bg**
Proston, Qld. 26 14S 151 32E **131 Db**
Prudhoe I., Qld. 21 23S 149 45E **129 Ch**
Prungle, N.S.W. 34 14S 143 0E **92 Eb**
Pu'apu'a, Western Samoa 13 34S 172 9W **139 Cc**
Puckapunyal, Vic. 37 0S 145 3E **100 Ef**
Puha, N.Z. 38 30S 177 50E **144 Ef**
Pukaki L., N.Z. 44 4S 170 1E **145 Ee**
Pukehou, N.Z. 39 51S 176 39E **144 Fe**
Pukekohe, N.Z. 37 12S 174 55E **144 Dc**
Pukerau, N.Z. 46 6S 169 6E **145 Gd**
Pukerua Bay, N.Z. 41 2S 174 53E **144 Hc**
Puketeraki Ra., N.Z. 42 58S 172 13E **145 Dg**
Pukeuri, N.Z. 45 4S 171 2E **145 Ff**
Pulau Belitung, Indonesia 3 10S 107 50E **134 Ec**
Pullabooka, N.S.W. 33 44S 147 46E **93 Dg**
Punakaiki, N.Z. 42 7S 171 20E **145 Cf**
Punavia, Tahiti 17 38S 149 36W **139 Wx**
Puntabie, S.A. 32 12S 134 5E **111 Cb**
Puponga, N.Z. 40 31S 172 43E **145 Ag**
Purari R., Papua N.G. 7 49S 145 0E **141 Dc**
Pureora, N.Z. 38 33S 175 38E **144 Ed**
Puriri, N.Z. 37 14S 175 38E **144 Dd**
Purlewaugh, N.S.W. 31 20S 149 30E **93 Bi**
Purnim, Vic. 38 16S 142 36E **100 Fc**
Purning Landing, S.A. 34 51S 139 36E **113 De**
Pursat, Khmer Rep. 12 34N 103 50E **134 Bb**
Puruktjau, Indonesia 0 35S 114 35E **135 Ed**
Purwakarta, Indonesia 6 35S 107 29E **134 Fc**
Putaruru, N.Z. 38 2S 175 50E **144 Ed**
Putorino, N.Z. 39 4S 177 9E **144 Fe**
Putty, N.S.W. 32 57S 150 42E **93 Cj**
Putussibau, G., Indonesia 0 45N 113 50E **134 Dd**

Pyalong, Vic. 37 7S 144 51E **100 Ee**
Pyengana, Tas. 41 16S 148 0E **107 Cg**
Pyramid Hill, Vic. 36 2S 144 6E **100 De**

Q

Quail I., Qld. 22 8S 150 0E **129 Ci**
Quairading, W.A. 32 0S 117 21E **119 Fd**
Qualeup, W.A. 33 48S 116 48E **119 Gc**
Quambatook, Vic. 35 49S 143 34E **100 Cd**
Quambetook, Qld. 21 23S 142 11E **128 Ca**
Quambone, N.S.W. 30 57S 147 53E **93 Ag**
Quan Long, Vietnam 9 7N 105 8E **134 Cc**
Quang Ngai, Vietnam 15 13N 108 58E **134 Ac**
Quandialla, N.S.W. 34 1S 147 47E **93 Eg**
Quantong, Vic. 36 43S 142 3E **100 Dc**
Queen Charlotte Sd., N.Z. 41 10S 174 15E **145 Bi**
Queens Chan., N.T. 15 0S 129 30E **123 Aa**
Queenscliff, Vic. 38 16S 144 39E **100 Fe**
Queenstown, N.Z. 45 1S 168 40E **145 Fc**
Queenstown, Tas. 42 4S 145 35E **107 Dd**
Queenstown S., Tas. 42 7S 142 32E **107 Dd**
Queiros C., New Hebrides 14 55S 167 1E **139 Gg**
Quellington, W.A. 31 45S 116 50E **119 Ec**
Quezon City, Philippines 18 34N 121 0E **135 Bf**
Qui Nhon, Vietnam 13 40N 109 13E **134 Bc**
Quinalow, Qld. 27 6S 151 37E **129 EB 131 Eb**
Quindanning, W.A. 33 2S 116 32E **119 Gc**
Quininup, W.A. 34 25S 116 13E **119 Hc**
Quinyambie, S.A. 30 15S 141 0E **111 Cd**
Quirindi, N.S.W. 31 28S 150 40E **95 Ea**
Quoin I., N.T. 14 45S 129 32E **123 Aa**
Quondong, S.A. 33 6S 140 18E **113 Cf**
Quorn, S.A. 32 25S 138 0E **113 Bd**

R

Raba, Indonesia 8 36S 118 55E **135 Fe**
Rabaraba, Papua N.G. 9 58S 149 49E **141 Ee**
Rabaul, Papua N.G. 4 24S 152 18E **141 Cg**
Raby Creek, Qld. 23 56S 149 24E **129 Eh**
Radja Is., Indonesia 0 30S 129 40E **135 Eg**
Raetihi, N.Z. 39 25S 175 17E **144 Fd**
Raft Pt., W.A. 16 4S 124 26E **117 Bc**
Ragged, Mt., W.A. 33 27S 123 25E **117 Ec**
Raglan, N.Z. 37 55S 174 55E **144 Dc**
Raglan, Qld. 23 42S 150 49E **131 Aa**
Raglan Harbour, N.Z. 37 55S 174 55E **144 Dc**
Raha, Indonesia 8 20S 118 40E **135 Ef**
Rahotu, N.Z. 39 20S 173 49E **144 Fb**
Railton, Tas. 41 25S 146 28E **107 Ce**
Rainbow, Vic. 35 55S 142 0E **100 Cc**
Rainsby, Qld. 22 0S 145 16E **128 Cd**
Rajang R., Malaysia 2 30N 113 30E **134 Dd**
Rakaia, N.Z. 43 45S 172 1E **145 Dg**
Rakaia R., N.Z. 43 26S 171 47E **145 Df**
Raleigh, N.S.W. 30 27S 153 2E **95 Dd**
Ram Hd., Vic. 37 47S 149 30E **101 Ej**
Ramu R., Papua N.G. 4 0S 144 41E **141 Cc**
Ranau, Malaysia 6 2N 116 40E **135 Ce**
Rand, N.S.W. 35 33S 146 32E **93 Ff**
Ranelagh, Tas. 42 58S 147 3E **107 Df**
Ranford, W.A. 32 49S 116 30E **119 Fc**
Ranfurly, N.Z. 45 7S 170 6E **145 Fe**
Ranga, Tas. 40 10S 148 8E **107 Bg**
Rangataua, N.Z. 39 26S 175 28E **144 Fd**
Rangaunu B., N.Z. 34 51S 173 15E **144 Ab**
Rangiora, N.Z. 43 19S 172 36E **145 Dg**
Rangitaiki, N.Z. 38 52S 176 23E **144 Ee**
Rangitaiki R., N.Z. 37 54S 176 49E **144 Ee**
Rangitata Diversion, N.Z. 43 40S 171 30E **145 Df**
Rangitata R., N.Z. 43 45S 171 15E **145 Df**
Rangitikei, N.Z. 40 17S 175 15E **144 Fd**
Rangitikei R., N.Z. 40 17S 175 15E **144 Fd**
Rangitoto I., N.Z. 36 47S 174 52E **145 Ai**
Rangitoto Ra., N.Z. 38 25S 175 35E **144 Ed**
Rangiwahia, N.Z. 39 54S 175 55E **144 Fd**
Rangoon, Burma 16 45N 96 20E **134 Aa**
Rankins Springs, N.S.W. 33 49S 146 14E **93 Df**
Ranon, New Hebrides 15 59S 167 23E **139 Ih**
Ranong, Thailand 9 56N 98 40E **134 Ca**

Rantauprapat, Indonesia 2 15N 99 50E **134 Da**
Rantemario, Mt., Indonesia 3 15S 119 57E **135 Ee**
Raoul C., Tas. 43 15S 147 48E **107 Ef**
Rapahoe, N.Z. 42 22S 171 14E **145 Cf**
Rapang, Indonesia 3 45S 119 55E **135 Ee**
Rapid Bay, S.A. 35 32S 138 10E **113 Ed**
Rappville, N.S.W. 29 6S 152 57E **95 Cc**
Rason L., W.A. 28 45S 124 25E **117 Dc**
Raspberry Creek, Qld. 22 41S 150 25E **129 Di**
Rata, N.Z. 39 59S 175 27E **144 Fd**
Ratcatchers L., N.S.W. 32 30S 143 12E **92 Cc**
Rathdowney, Qld. 28 13S 152 52E **131 Fc**
Raukokore, N.Z. 37 38S 177 53E **144 Df**
Raukumara Ra., N.Z. 38 5S 177 55E **144 Df**
Raumati, N.Z. 40 55S 174 58E **144 Gc**
Raurimu, N.Z. 39 7S 175 20E **144 Fd**
Ravensbourne, Qld. 27 22S 152 10E **131 Ec**
Ravenshoe, Qld. 17 37S 145 29E **129 Xw**
Ravensthorpe, W.A. 33 35S 120 2E **119 Gg**
Ravenswood, Qld. 20 6S 146 54E **129 Be**
Ravenswood, Vic. 36 53S 144 15E **100 De**
Ravenswood, Mt., Qld. 20 26S 146 59E **129 Be**
Ravensworth, N.S.W. 32 26S 151 4E **95 Fb**
Rawbelle, Qld. 24 53S 150 44E **131 Ba**
Rawene, N.Z. 35 25S 173 32E **144 Bb**
Rawlinna, W.A. 30 58S 125 28E **117 Ed**
Rawlinson Ra., W.A. 24 40S 128 30E **117 Cd**
Raymond Terrace, N.S.W. 32 45S 151 44E **93 Ck**
Raywood, Vic. 36 30S 144 15E **100 De**
Rebecca L., W.A. 30 0S 122 30E **117 Dc**
Red Bank, Vic. 36 56S 143 21E **100 Dd**
Red Cliffs, Vic. 34 19S 142 11E **100 Bc**
Red Hill, N.Z. 41 40S 173 5E **145 Bg**
Red Point Rock, W.A. 32 13S 127 32E **117 Ed**
Red Range, N.S.W. 29 26S 151 57E **95 Cb**
Red Rock, N.S.W. 29 59S 153 14E **95 Cd**
Red Tank, N.S.W. 32 26S 145 4E **92 Ce**
Redang I., Malaysia 5 46N 103 2E **134 Cb**
Redbank, Qld. 25 30S 150 36E **131 Ca**
Redcliffe, Qld. 27 12S 153 0E **131 Ed**
Redcliffe, Mt., W.A. 28 30S 121 30E **117 Dc**
Redesdale, Vic. 37 2S 144 31E **100 Ee**
Redland Bay, Qld. 27 36S 153 18E **131 Ed**
Redmond, W.A. 34 55S 117 40E **119 Hd**
Redpa, Tas. 40 55S 144 45E **107 Bc**
Reedy Creek, S.A. 36 58S 140 2E **113 Ff**
Reedy Springs, Qld. 19 58S 144 41E **128 Ac**
Reefton, N.S.W. 34 15S 147 27E **93 Eg**
Reefton, N.Z. 42 6S 171 51E **145 Cf**
Reekara, King Island 39 45S 143 56E **107 Ab**
Reid, W.A. 30 49S 128 26E **117 Ed**
Reid River, Qld. 19 40S 146 48E **129 Ae**
Reids Flat, N.S.W. 34 7S 149 0E **93 Ei**
Reinga C., N.Z. 34 25S 172 43E **144 Aa**
Remarkable, Mt., S.A. 32 48S 138 10E **113 Bd**
Rembang, Indonesia 6 42S 111 21E **134 Fd**
Remine, Tas. 41 55S 145 10E **107 Cd**
Rendova, Solomon Is. 8 33S 157 17E **139 Qq**
Rengat, Indonesia 0 30S 102 45E **134 Eb**
Renison Bell, Tas. 41 48S 145 25E **107 Cd**
Renmark, S.A. 34 11S 140 43E **113 Df**
Rennell I., Solomon Is. 11 40S 160 10E **139 Rr**
Renner Springs T.O., N.T. 18 20S 133 47E **123 Bb**
Rennie, N.S.W. 35 49S 146 8E **93 Ff**
Renwicktown, N.Z. 41 30S 173 51E **145 Bh**
Reporoa, N.Z. 38 26S 176 20E **144 Ee**
Repulse B., Qld. 20 31S 148 45E **129 Bg**
Resolution I., N.Z. 45 40S 166 40E **145 Fa**
Rest Downs, N.S.W. 31 48S 146 21E **93 Bf**
Reynolds Ra., N.T. 22 30S 133 0E **123 Cb**
Riana, Tas. 41 10S 146 1E **107 Ce**
Riau, Indonesia 0 N 102 35E **134 Db**
Riau, Kepulauan, Indonesia 0 30N 104 20E **134 Db**
Riccarton, N.Z. 43 32S 172 37E **145 Dg**
Richardson Mts., N.Z. 44 49S 168 34E **145 Ec**
Riche C., W.A. 34 36S 118 47E **119 He**
Richmond, N.S.W. 33 35S 150 42E **93 Dj**
Richmond, N.Z. 41 4S 173 12E **145 Bh**
Richmond, Qld. 20 43S 143 8E **128 Bb**
Richmond, Tas. 42 44S 147 26E **107 Df**
Richmond R., N.S.W. 28 52S 153 35E **95 Bc**
Richmond Ra., N.S.W. 29 0S 152 45E **95 Cc**
Richmond Ra., N.Z. 41 32S 173 22E **145 Bh**
Riddell, Vic. 37 28S 144 42E **100 Ee**
Ridgelands, Qld. 23 16S 150 17E **131 Aa**
Ridgley, Tas. 41 9S 145 50E **107 Cd**
Ridley, Mt., W.A. 33 12S 122 7E **117 Ec**
Ringarooma, Tas. 41 15S 147 45E **107 Cf**
Ringarooma Bay, Tas. 40 50S 147 50E **107 Bf**
Ringgold Isle, Fiji 16 15S 179 25W **139 Ac**
Rintja I., Indonesia 8 45S 119 35E **135 Fe**
Ripley, Qld. 27 43S 152 49E **131 Ec**

Rita Islands, Qld. 19 37S 147 30E **129 Af**
Ritidian Pt., Guam 13 39N 144 51E **139 Tu**
Riverina, W.A. 29 45S 120 40E **119 Cg**
Riversleigh, Qld. 19 5S 138 48E **127 Bb**
Riverton, S.A. 34 10S 138 46E **113 Dd**
Riverton, N.Z. 46 21S 168 0E **145 Gc**
Rivoli B., S.A. 37 32S 140 3E **113 Gf**
Riwaka, N.Z. 41 5S 172 59E **145 Bh**
Rŏ, New Caledonia 21 22S 167 50E **139 B₁e₁**
Roa, N.Z. 42 21S 171, 23E **145 Cf**
Rob Roy I., Solomon Is. 7 23S 157 36E **139 Pq**
Robbins I., Tas. 40 42S 145 0E **107 Bd**
Robe R., W.A. 21 42S 115 15E **117 Cb**
Robertson, N.S.W. 34 37S 150 36E **93 Ej**
Robertson Ra., W.A. 23 15S 121 0E **117 Cc**
Robertstown, S.A. 33 58S 139 5E **113 Ce**
Robinson Ra., W.A. 25 40S 118 0E **117 Db**
Robinson R., N.T. 16 3S 137 16E **123 Bc**
Robinson River, N.T. 16 45S 136 58E **123 Bc**
Robinvale, Vic. 34 40S 142 45E **100 Bc**
Rocherlea, Tas. 41 24S 147 10E **107 Cf**
Rochester, Vic. 36 22S 144 41E **100 De**
Rock & Pillar Ra., N.Z. 45 29S 170 3E **145 Fe**
Rockhampton, Qld. 23 22S 150 32E **131 Aa**
Rockhampton Downs, N.T. 18 57S 135 10E **123 Bc**
Rockingham, W.A. 32 15S 115 38E **119 Fb**
Rockingham Bay, Qld. 18 5S 146 10E **129 Yx**
Rocklands Res., Vic. 37 15S 142 5E **100 Ec**
Rockley, N.S.W. 33 41S 149 33E **93 Di**
Rockvale, N.S.W. 30 25S 151 53E **95 Db**
Rockville, N.Z. 40 44S 172 38E **145 Ag**
Rocky C., Tas. 40 51S 145 30E **107 Bd**
Rocky Glen, N.S.W. 31 6S 149 35E **93 Bi**
Rocky Gully, W.A. 34 30S 117 0E **119 Hc**
Rocky River, N.S.W. 30 36S 151 29E **95 Db**
Rocky River, S.A. 35 57S 136 44E **113 Eb**
Rodd's Pen., Qld. 24 0S 151 45E **131 Bb**
Rodney C., N.Z. 36 17S 174 50E **144 Cc**
Rodney Downs, Qld. 23 11S 144 50E **128 Ec**
Roebourne, W.A. 20 44S 117 9E **117 Cb**
Roebuck B., W.A. 18 5S 122 20E **117 Bc**
Roebuck Plains P.O., W.A. 17 56S 122 8E **117 Bc**
Roi Et, Thailand 15 46N 103 40E **134 Ab**
Rokeby, Qld. 13 39S 142 40E **127 Ac**
Rokewood, Vic. 37 54S 143 44E **100 Ed**
Rollands Plains, N.S.W. 31 17S 152 42E **95 Ec**
Rolleston, N.Z. 43 35S 172 24E **145 Dg**
Rolleston, Qld. 24 28S 148 35E **129 Fg**
Rollingstone, Qld. 19 2S 146 24E **129 Zx**
Roma, Qld. 26 32S 148 49E **127 Dd**
Rongotea, N.Z. 40 19S 175 25E **144 Gd**
Ronsard C., W.A. 26 46S 113 10E **117 Ca**
Rooney Pt., Qld. 24 49S 153 7E **131 Bd**
Roonui, Mt., Tahiti 17 49S 149 12W **139 Wx**
Roper R., N.T. 14 43S 135 27E **123 Ab**
Rosa Brook, W.A. 33 57S 115 10E **119 Gb**
Rosa Glen, W.A. 34 1S 115 10E **119 Hb**
Rose R., N.T. 14 16S 135 45E **123 Ac**
Rosebery, Tas. 41 46S 145 33E **107 Cd**
Rosebery, Vic. 35 48S 142 27E **100 Cc**
Rosebud, Vic. 38 21S 144 54E **100 Fe**
Rosedale, Qld. 24 38S 151 53E **131 Bb**
Rosedale, Vic. 38 11S 146 48E **101 Fg**
Rosevale, Qld. 27 50S 152 59E **131 Ec**
Rosewood, N.S.W. 35 38S 147 52E **93 Fg**
Rosewood, N.T. 16 28S 128 58E **123 Ba**
Rosewood, Qld. 27 38S 152 36E **131 Ec**
Roseworthy, S.A. 34 31S 138 45E **113 Dd**
Roskill, Mt., N.Z. 36 55S 174 45E **144 Cc**
Roslyn, N.S.W. 34 31S 149 46E **93 Ei**
Ross, N.Z. 42 53S 170 49E **145 Ce**
Ross, Mt., N.Z. 41 28S 175 21E **144 Hd**
Ross, Tas. 42 2S 147 30E **107 Df**
Rossarden, Tas. 41 40S 147 44E **107 Cf**
Rossel C., New Caledonia 20 23S 166 36E **139 A₁d₁**
Rossel I., Papua N.G. 11 30S 154 30E **141 Fh**
Rossville, Qld. 15 48S 145 15E **127 Bd**
Rota Aira L., N.Z. 39 3S 175 55E **144 Fd**
Rotherham, N.Z. 42 42S 172 57E **145 Cg**
Rothsay, W.A. 29 15S 116 50E **119 Cc**
Roto, N.S.W. 33 0S 145 30E **92 De**
Rotoehu L., N.Z. 38 1S 176 32E **144 De**
Rotoiti L., N.Z. 41 51S 172 49E **145 Bg**
Rotoma, N.Z. 38 2S 176 35E **144 Ee**
Rotorua, N.Z. 38 9S 175 16E **144 Ee**
Rotorua L., N.Z. 38 5S 176 18E **144 Ee**
Rotowaro, N.Z. 37 35S 175 5E **144 Dd**
Rottnest I., W.A. 32 0S 115 27E **119 Fb**
Rough Ra., N.Z. 45 10S 169 55E **145 Fd**
Round, Mt., N.S.W. 30 26S 152 16E **95 Dc**
Round Hill, W.A. 30 34S 116 13E **119 Dc**

Round Hill Hd., Qld. 24 9S 151 53E **131 Bb**
Roussin C., New Caledonia 21 20S 167 59E **139 B₁f₁**
Rowallan L., Tas. 41 45S 146 15E **107 Ce**
Rowena, N.S.W. 29 48S 148 55E **91 Ag**
Roxas, Philippines 11 36N 122 49E **135 Bf**
Roxborough Downs, Qld. 22 20S 138 45E **127 Cb**
Roxburgh, N.Z. 45 33S 169 19E **145 Fd**
Roy Hill, W.A. 22 37S 119 58E **117 Cb**
Royalla, N.S.W. 35 30S 149 9E **93 Fi**
Royston Hd., S.A. 35 10S 136 52E **113 Eb**
Ruapehu, N.Z. 39 17S 175 35E **144 Fd**
Ruapuke I., N.Z. 46 46S 168 31E **145 Gc**
Ruatahuna, N.Z. 38 37S 176 58E **144 Ee**
Ruatapu, N.Z. 42 49S 170 54E **145 Ce**
Ruatoki, N.Z. 38 9S 177 1E **144 Ee**
Ruatoria, N.Z. 37 55S 178 20E **144 Dg**
Ruawai, N.Z. 36 15S 173 59E **144 Cc**
Ruby, Vic. 38 27S 145 55E **101 Ff**
Rubyvale, Qld. 23 25S 147 45E **129 Ef**
Rudall, S.A. 33 43S 136 17E **113 Cb**
Rugby, N.S.W. 34 23S 149 0E **93 Eh**
Rugged I., N.Z. 46 43S 167 36E **145 Gb**
Rulhieres C., W.A. 13 56S 127 22E **117 Ad**
Rum Jungle, N.T. 13 0S 130 59E **123 Ab**
Rumbalara, N.T. 25 20S 134 29E **123 Dc**
Rumbee, Mt., N.S.W. 29 55S 151 35E **95 Cb**
Rumula, Qld. 16 35S 145 20E **129 Ww**
Runanga, N.Z. 42 25S 171 15E **145 Cf**
Runaway C., N.Z. 37 32S 178 2E **144 Df**
Runton Ra., W.A. 23 35S 123 15E **117 Cc**
Rupanyup, Vic. 36 36S 142 40E **100 Dc**
Rupat I., Indonesia 1 45N 101 40E **134 Db**
Rupert Ck., Qld. 20 53S 142 23E **128 Ba**
Rushworth, Vic. 36 32S 145 1E **100 De**
Russell, N.Z. 35 16S 174 10E **144 Bc**
Russell I., Qld. 37 39S 153 23E **131 Ed**
Russell Is., Solomon Is. 9 4S 159 12E **139 Qr**
Rutherglen, Vic. 36 5S 146 29E **101 Dg**
Rutland Plains, Qld. 15 38S 141 49E **127 Bc**
Rye Park, N.S.W. 34 31S 148 56E **93 Eh**
Rylstone, N.S.W. 32 46S 149 58E **93 Ci**
Rywung, Qld. 26 42S 150 29E **131 Da**

S

Sa Dec, Vietnam 10 20N 105 46E **134 Bc**
Sa'A, Solomon Is. 9 41S 161 34E **139 Qs**
Sabagalet, Indonesia 1 36S 98 40E **134 Ea**
Sabah, Malaysia 6 0N 117 0E **135 Ce**
Sablayan, Philippines 12 5N 120 50E **135 Bf**
Saddleworth, S.A. 34 5S 138 47E **113 Dd**
Safata B., Eastern Samoa 14 0S 171 50W **139 Dd**
Sag Sag, Papua N.G. 5 32S 148 23E **141 Ce**
Sagod, Philippines 10 30N 125 0E **135 Bf**
Saidor, Papua N.G. 5 40S 146 29E **141 Cd**
Saigon (Ho Chi Minh City), Vietnam
10 58N 106 40E **134 Bc**
St. Albans, N.S.W. 33 16S 150 59E **93 Dj**
St. Alouarn Is., W.A. 34 25S 115 11E **119 Hb**
St. Andrews, N.Z. 44 33S 171 10E **145 Ef**
St. Anns, Qld. 21 15S 146 55E **129 Ce**
St. Arnaud, Vic. 36 32S 143 16E **100 Dd**
St. Arnaud R.A., N.Z. 42 1S 172 53E **145 Bg**
St. Bathans, N.Z. 44 53S 170 0E **145 Ed**
St. Bathans, Mt., N.Z. 44 45S 169 45E **145 Ed**
St. Bees I., Qld. 20 55S 149 26E **129 Bh**
St. Clair, L., S.A. 37 20S 139 55E **113 Ge**
St. Clair, L., Tas. 42 4S 146 10E **107 De**
St. Cricq, C., W.A. 25 17S 113 6E **117 Da**
St. George, Qld. 28 1S 148 41E **127 Dd**
St. George, C., Papua N.G. 4 49S 152 53E **141 Cg**
St. George Ra., W.A. 18 40S 125 0E **117 Bd**
St. George's Channel, Papua N.G.
4 10S 152 20E **141 Cg**
St. Georges Hd., N.S.W. 35 11S 150 45E **93 Fj**
St. Helens, Tas. 41 20S 148 15E **107 Cg**
St. Joseph, New Caledonia 20 27S 166 36E **139 A₁d₁**
St. Kilda, N.Z. 45 53S 170 31E **145 Fe**
St. Lawrence, Qld. 22 16S 149 31E **129 Dh**
St. Leonards, Tas. 41 29S 147 11E **107 Cf**
St. Mary, Mt., N.Z. 44 15S 169 38E **145 Ed**
Saint Mary, Mt., Papua N.G. 8 8S 146 54E **141 Ed**
St. Mary Pk., S.A. 31 32S 138 34E **113 Ad**
St. Marys, N.S.W. 33 44S 150 49E **93 Dj**
St. Marys, Tas. 41 32S 148 11E **107 Cg**
St. Omer, N.Z. 41 11S 173 57E **145 Bh**
St. Pauls Dome, Mts., Tas. 41 45S 147 51E **107 Cf**

Gazetteer

St. Vincent, G., S.A. 35 0S 138 0E **113 Dd**
Sakon Nakhon, Thailand 17 10N 104 9E **134 Ab**
Sale, Vic. 38 6S 147 6E **101 Fh**
Salebabu I., Indonesia 3 45N 125 55E **135 Dg**
Salisbury, N.S.W. 32 11S 151 33E **95 Fb**
Salisbury, S.A. 34 46S 138 40E **113 Dd**
Salmon Gums, W.A. 32 59S 121 38E **117 Ec**
Salt Creek, S.A. 36 8S 139 38E **113 Fe**
Saltbush Park, Qld. 22 8S 148 544E **129 Dg**
Samak, Indonesia 4 40S 122 26E **135 Ef**
Samales Group, Philippines 6 0N 122 0E **135 Cf**
Samar I., Philippines 12 0N 125 0E **135 Bg**
Samarai, Papua N.G. 10 39S 150 41E **141 Ff**
Sambas, Indonesia 1 20 N 109 20E **134 Dc**
Samoan Is., S-W Pacific 14 0S 171 0W **139 Cc**
Samosir Balige, Indonesia 2 20N 98 50E **134 Da**
Sampang, Indonesia 7 11S 113 13E **134 Fd**
Sampit, Indonesia 2 20S 113 0E **134 Ed**
Samut Prakan, Thailand 13 32N 100 40E **134 Bb**
Samut Songkhram, Thailand 13 24N 100 1E **134 Bb**
San R., Cambodia 13 32N 105 57E **134 Bc**
San Agustin, C., Philippines 6 20N 126 13E **135 Cg**
San Carlos, Philippines 10 29N 123 25E **135 Bf**
San Cristobal, I., Solomon Is. 10 30S 161 0E **139 Rs**
San Fernando, Philippines 15 5N 120 37E **135 Af**
San Fernando, Philippines 16 40N 120 23E **135 Af**
San Ildefonso, C., Philippines 16 0N 122 10E **135 Af**
San Jorge, Solomon Is. 8 27S 159 35E **139 Qr**
San Jose, Philippines 10 50N 122 5E **135 Bf**
San Jose, Philippines 15 45N 120 55E **135 Af**
San Juan, Philippines 8 35N 126 20E **135 Cg**
San Narcisco, Philippines 15 2N 120 3E **135 Af**
San Quinton, Philippines 16 11N 120 56E **135 Af**
San Remo, Vic. 38 33S 145 22E **101 Ff**
Sanana, Indonesia 2 5S 125 50E **135 Eg**
Sanco Pt., Philippines 8 15N 126 24 E **135 Cg**
Sandai, Indonesia 1 15S 110 31E **134 Ed**
Sandalwood, S.A. 34 55S 140 9E **113 Df**
Sandergrove, S.A. 35 19S 138 53E **113 Ed**
Sanderston, S.A. 34 46S 139 15E **113 De**
Sandgate, Qld. 27 18S 153 3E **131 Ed**
Sandon Bluffs, N.S.W. 29 41S 153 20E **95 Cd**
Sandstone, W.A. 27 59S 119 16E **119 Af**
Sandwich, C., Qld. 18 14S 146 18E **129 Yx**
Sandy Bight, W.A. 33 50gs 123 20E **117 Ec**
Sandy Cape, Qld. 24 42S 153 15E **131 Bd**
Sandy, C., Tas. 41 25S 144 45E **107 Cc**
Sandy Pt., Vic. 38 50S 146 6E **101 Fg**
Sandy Hollow, N.S.W. 32 20S 150 32E **95 Fa**
Sanford R., W.A. 27 22S 115 53E **117 Db**
Sangasangadalam, Indonesia 0 29S 117 13E **135 Ee**
Sangeang I., Indonesia 8 12S 119 6E **135 Fe**
Sanggau, Indonesia 0 5N 110 30E **134 Dd**
Sangihe, P., Indonesia 3 45N 125 30E **135 Dg**
Sangkapura, Indonesia 5 52S 112 40E **134 Fd**
Sangkurilang, Indonesia 1 0N 118 0E **135 De**
Sanson, N.Z. 40 13S 175 25E **144 Gd**
Santa Isabel, I., Solomon Is. 8 0S 159 0E **139 Pr**
Santa Ono, Solomon Is. 10 0S 162 0E **139 Rt**
Santo, New Hebrides 15 27S 166 48E **139 Hg**
Saparua, Indonesia 3 33S 128 40E **135 Eg**
Sarmi, Indonesia 1 49S 138 38E **135 Ei**
Saran, Mt., Indonesia 0 30S 111 25E **134 Ed**
Sarangani Bay, Philippines 6 0N 125 13E **135 Cf**
Sarangani Is., Philippines 5 25N 125 25E **135 Cg**
Saratok, Malaysia 3 5S 110 50E **134 Dd**
Saravane, Laos 15 43N 106 25E **134 Ac**
Sarawak, Malaysia 2 0N 113 0E **134 Dd**
Sarikei, Malaysia 2 8N 111 30E **134 Dd**
Sarina, Qld. 21 22S 149 13E **129 Ch**
Sarolangun, Indonesia 2 30S 102 30E **134 Eb**
Sasamungga, Solomon Is. 7 0S 156 50E **139 Pq**
Sassafrass, Tas. 41 17S 146 30E **107 Ce**
Satui, Indonesia 3 50S 115 20E **135 Ee**
Satun, Thailand 6 43N 100 2E **134 Cb**
Satupa'itea, Western Samoa 13 45S 172 18W **139 Cc**
Saunders, C., N.Z. 45 53S 170 45E **145 Fe**
Saunders Pt., W.A. 27 52S 125 38E **117 Dd**
Savage R., Tas. 41 31S 145 14E **107 Cd**
Savai'i, Western Samoa 13 28S 172 24W **139 Cc**
Savannakhet, Laos 16 30N 104 40E **134 Ab**
Savernake, N.S.W. 35 47S 146 3E **93 Ff**
Savo, Solomon Is. 9 8S 159 48E **139 Qr**
Savusavu, Fiji 17 34S 178 15E **139 Ab**
Savusavu B., Fiji 16 45S 179 15E **139 Ab**
Sawtell, N.S.W. 30 19S 153 6E **95 Dd**
Saxby Ck., Qld. 20 0S 142 32E **128 Aa**
Saxby, R., Qld. 18 25S 140 53E **127 Bc**
Saxby Downs, Qld. 20 4S 142 30E **128 Ba**
Sayer's Lake, N.S.W. 32 46S 143 16E **92 Cc**
Scamander, Tas. 41 29S 148 16E **107 Cg**
Scargill, N.Z. 42 56S 172 58E **145 Cg**
Scarsdale, Vic. 37 41S 143 39E **100 Ed**
Scawfell I., Qld. 20 52S 149 35E **129 Bh**
Schanck, C., Vic. 38 30S 144 55E **100 Fe**
Schouten Is., Indonesia 1 0S 136 0E **135 Ei**
Schouter I., Tas. 42 20S 148 20E **107 Dg**
Schwaner, Pegungan, Indonesia 1 0S 112 30E **134 Ed**
Scone, N.S.W. 32 0S 150 52E **95 Fa**
Scoria, Qld. 24 32S 150 35E **131 Ba**
Scott, C., N.T. 13 30S 129 49E **123 Aa**
Scottsdale, Tas. 41 9S 147 31E **107 Cf**
Scottsville, Qld. 20 35S 147 40E **129 Bf**
Sea Lake, Vic. 35 28S 142 55E **100 Cc**
Seabrook, L., W.A. 30 55S 119 40E **119 Df**
Seacliff, N.Z. 45 41S 170 37E **145 Fe**
Seaford, Vic. 38 10S 145 11E **101 Ff**
Seaforth, Qld. 20 55S 148 57E **129 Bg**
Seal Rocks, N.S.W. 32 26S 152 32E **95 Fc**
Seaspray, Vic. 38 25S 147 15E **101 Fh**
Seaview Ra., Qld. 18 40S 145 45E **129 Yw**
Seaward Kaikouras, Mts., N.Z. 42 10S 173 44E **145 Ch**
Sebuku I., Indonesia 3 30S 116 25E **135 Ee**
Secretary I., N.Z. 45 15S 166 56E **145 Fa**
Sedan, S.A. 34 34S 139 19E **113 De**
Seddon, N.Z. 41 40S 174 7E **145 Bh**
Seddonville, N.Z. 41 33S 172 1E **145 Bg**
Sedgeford, Qld. 23 56S 146 45E **129 Ee**
Sefton, N.Z. 43 15S 172 41E **145 Dg**
Sefton, Mt., N.Z. 43 40S 170 5E **145 Dd**
Segamat, Malaysia 2 30N 102 50E **134 Db**
Segi, Solomon Is. 8 34S 157 54E **139 Li**
Sekaju, Indonesia 2 58S 103 58E **134 Eb**
Selat Karimata, Indonesia 2 0S 108 20E **134 Ec**
Sellicks Beach, S.A. 35 20S 138 25E **113 Ed**
Selpele I., Indonesia 0 1S 130 5E **135 Eg**
Selwyn P.O., Qld. 21 32S 140 30E **127 Cc**
Selwyn Passage, New Hebrides 16 3S 168 12E **139 Ih**
Selwyn Range, Qld. 21 10S 140 0E **127 Cc**
Selwyn R., N.Z. 43 44S 172 26E **145 Dg**
Semeru Mt., Indonesia 8 4S 113 3E **134 Fd**
Semirara Is., Philippines 12 0N 121 20E **135 Bf**
Semitau, Indonesia 0 29N 111 57E **134 Dd**
Semuda, Indonesia 2 51S 112 58E **134 Ed**
Semudo, Indonesia 2 51S 112 58E **134 Ed**
Sen R., Khmer Rep. 13 45N 105 12E **134 Bc**
Senaja, Malaysia 6 49S 117 2E **135 Ce**
Senduruhan, Indonesia 1 0S 110 46E **134 Ed**
Senmonoram, Cambodia 12 27N 107 12E **134 Bc**
Sepi, Solomon Is. 8 33S 159 50 E **139 Qr**
Sepik R., Papua N.G. 3 49S 144 30 E **141 Cb**
Septimus, Qld. 21 13S 148 47E **129 Cg**
Seram, I., Indonesia 3 10S 129 0E **135 Eg**
Serang, Indonesia 6 8S 106 10E **134 Fc**
Serasan I., Indonesia 2 29N 109 4E **134 Dc**
Seremban, Malaysia 2 43N 101 53E **134 Db**
Serian, Malaysia 1 10N 110 40E **134 Dd**
Sermata, I., Indonesia 8 15S 128 50E **135 Fg**
Serpentine, Vic. 36 25S 144 0E **100 Dd**
Serpentine, W.A. 32 23S 115 58E **119 Fb**
Serpentine L., S.A. 28 30S 129 10E **111 Ba**
Serpentine R., W.A. 32 33S 115 45E **119 Fb**
Serviceton, Vic. 36 22S 141 0E **100 Da**
Sesepe, Indonesia 1 30S 127 59E **135 Eg**
Seven Emu, N.T. 16 20S 137 8E **123 Bc**
Severn R., N.S.W. 29 8S 150 59E **95 Cb**
Sexton, Qld. 26 0S 152 27E **131 Cc**
Seymour, Vic. 36 58S 145 10E **100 Df**
Shackleton, W.A. 31 57S 117 50E **119 Ed**
Shag Pt., N.Z. 45 29S 170 52E **145 Fe**
Shag R., N.Z. 45 29S 170 49E **145 Fe**
Shandon Downs, N.T. 17 45S 134 50E **123 Bb**
Shannon, N.Z. 40 33S 175 25E **144 Gd**
Shannon R., W.A. 34 52S 116 25E **119 Hc**
Shannons Flat, N.S.W. 35 55S 148 58E **93 Fh**
Shannon River Mill, W.A. 34 24S 116 34E **119 Hc**
Shark Bay, W.A. 25 55S 113 32E **117 Da**
Sharp Pt., Qld. 10 58S 142 43E **127 Ac**
Shaster, L., W.A. 33 52S 120 40E **119 Hg**
Shaw I., Qld. 20 30S 149 2E **129 Bh**
Shaw R., W.A. 20 21S 119 17E **117 Cb**
Sheep Hills, Vic. 36 20S 142 33E **100 Dc**
Sheffield, N.Z. 43 23S 172 2E **145 Dg**
Sheffield, Tas. 41 23S 146 20E **107 Ce**
Shelbourne, Vic. 36 53S 144 2E **100De**
Shelburne Bay, Qld. 11 50S 143 0E **127 Ac**
Shell Lakes, W.A. 29 20S 127 30E **117 Dd**
Shellharbour, N.S.W. 34 31S 150 51E **93 Ej**
Shepherd, Is., New Hebrides 16 55S 168 36E **139 Ih**
Shepparton, Vic. 36 23S 145 26E **101 Df**
Shepparton East, Vic. 36 25S 145 30E **101 Df**
Sherlock, S.A. 35 18S 139 47E **113 Ee**
Sherwood Downs, N.Z. 43 58S 170 54E **145 De**
Shield C., N.T. 13 20S 136 20E **123 Ac**
Shinfield, Qld. 21 29S 149 10E **129 Ch**
Shirbourne, Qld. 19 32S 147 5E **129 Af**
Shoal, C., W.A. 33 52S 121 10E **117 Ec**
Shoalhaven R., N.S.W. 34 54S 150 42E **93 Fi**
Shoalwater Bay, Qld. 22 52S 150 25E **129 Di**
Shoe I., N.Z. 36 59S 175 54E **144 Cd**
Shortland, Is., Solomon Is. 7 0S 155 45E **139 Pp**
Shotover R., N.Z. 44 59S 168 41E **145 Ec**
Shuttleworth, Qld. 22 17S 146 8E **129 De**
Si Racha, Thailand 13 10N 100 56E **134 Bb**
Siaksrinderapura, Indonesia 0 51N 102 0E **134 Db**
Siam, S.A. 32 35S 136 41E **113 Bb**
Siam, G. of, Thailand 11 30N 101 0E **134 Bb**
Siantan I., Indonesia 3 10N 106 15E **134 Dc**
Siargao Is., Philippines 9 52N 126 3E **135 Cg**
Siasi, Philippines 5 34N 120 50E **135 Cf**
Siassi, Papua N.G. 5 40S 147 51E **141 Cd**
Siau I., Indonesia 2 50N 125 25E **135 Dg**
Siberut I., Indonesia 1 30S 99 0E **134 Ea**
Sibolga, Indonesia 1 50N 98 45E **134 Da**
Sibuco, Philippines 7 20N 122 10E **135 Cf**
Sibugey, Philippines 7 50N 122 45E **135 Cf**
Sibuyan I., Philippines 12 25N 122 40E **135 Bf**
Siccus R., S.A. 31 42S 139 25E **113 Ae**
Sidmouth C., Qld. 13 25S 143 36E **127 Ac**
Siem Reap, Cambodia 13 20N 103 52E **134 Bb**
Silkwood, Qld. 17 45S 146 2E **129 Xx**
Silogui, Indonesia 1 10S 98 46E **134 Ea**
Silverdale, N.Z. 36 37S 174 41E **144 Cc**
Silverton, N.S.W. 31 52S 141 10E **90 Bc**
Simanggang, Malaysia 1 15N 111 25E **134 Dd**
Simpang, Indonesia 1 3S 110 6E **134 Eb**
Simpson Desert, N.T. 25 0S 137 0E **123 Cc**
Simunjan, Malaysia 1 25N 110 45E **134 Dd**
Sindangan, Philippines 8 10N 123 5E **135 Cf**
Sindjai, Indonesia 5 0S 120 20E **135 Ef**
Sinewit, Mt., Papua N.G. 4 44S 152 2E **141 Cg**
Singapore, Rep. 1 17N 103 51E **134 Db**
Singaradja, Indonesia 8 15S 115 10E **135 Fe**
Singatoka, Fiji 18 8S 177 30E **139 Ba**
Singkang, Indonesia 4 8S 120 1E **135 Ee**
Singkawang, Indonesia 1 0N 109 5E **134 Dc**
Singkep I., Indonesia 0 30S 104 20E **134 Eb**
Singleton, N.S.W. 32 33S 151 10E **93 Ck**
Singleton, Mt., N.T. 29 27S 117 15E **123 Cb**
Singleton, Mt., W.A. 29 27S 117 15E **119 Cd**
Singora, Thailand 7 12N 100 36E **134 Cb**
Sintang, Indonesia 0 5N 111 35E **134 Dd**
Siquijar, Philippines 9 12N 123 45E **135 Cf**
Sir Edward Pellew Group, N.T. 15 40S 137 10E **123 Bc**
Sisaket, Thailand 15 8N 104 23E **134 Ab**
Sisophon, Khmer Rep. 13 31N 102 59E **134 Bb**
Situbondo, Indonesia 7 45S 114 0E **134 Fd**
Skipton, Vic. 37 39S 143 21E **100 Ed**
Skirmish Pt., N.T. 11 59S 134 17E **123 Ab**
Slade Pt., Qld. 21 4S 149 14E **129 Ch**
Slamannon, N.S.W. 32 1S 143 41E **92 Cc**
Slashers Flat, N.S.W. 32 29S 149 30E **93 Ci**
Sleaford Bay, S.A. 34 55S 135 45E **113 Da**
Slipper I., N.Z. 37 3S 175 55E **144 Dd**
Small Nggela, Solomon Is. 9 0S 160 0E **139 Qs**
Smithburne, R., Qld. 17 3S 140 57E **127 Bc**
Smithton, Tas. 40 53S 145 6E **107 Bd**
Smithtown, N.S.W. 30 58S 152 56E **95 Dc**
Smoky Bay, S.A. 32 22S 133 56E **111 Cb**
Snag I., W.A. 29 56S 114 58E **119 Ca**
Snake I., Vic. 38 47S 146 33E **101 Fg**
Snow Hill, Mt., Tas. 41 55S 147 51E **107 Cf**
Snowtown, S.A. 33 46S 138 14E **113 Cd**
Snowy Mts., N.S.W. 36 30S 148 20E **93 Fh**
Snowy R., Vic. 37 46S 148 30E **101 Ei**
Snug, Tas. 43 6S 147 16E **107 Ef**
Soaker, Mt., N.Z. 45 23S 167 15E **145 Fb**
Sofala, N.S.W. 33 4S 149 43E **93 Di**
Sogeri, Papua N.G. 9 26S 147 35E **141 Ed**
Sohano, Papua N.G. 5 22S 154 37E **141Ch**
Solano, Philippines 16 25N 121 15E **135 Af**
Solok, Indonesia 0 55S 100 40E **134 Eb**
Solomon Is., S-W Pacific 6 0S 155 0E **139 Pr**
Solomon Sea, 7 0S 150 0E **141 De**
Somers, Mt., N.Z. 43 45S 171 27E **145 Df**
Somerset, Tas. 41 3S 145 50E **107 Cd**
Somerset Dam, Qld. 27 5S 152 35E **131 Ec**
Somerton, N.S.W. 30 55S 150 38E **95 Da**
Sommariva, Qld. 26 24S 146 36E **127 Dd**
Somo Somo Str., Fiji 16 0S 180 0E **139 Ab**
Song Cau, Vietnam 13 20N 109 18E **134 Bc**
Songkhla, Thailand 7 13N 100 37E **134 Cb**
Sopi, Indonesia 2 40N 128 28E **135 Dg**
Sorell, Tas. 42 47S 147 34E **107 Df**
Sorell, C., Tas. 42 11S 145 10E **107 Dd**
Sorell L., Tas. 42 5S 147 10E **107 Df**

Sorrento, Vic. 38 22S 144 47E **100 Fe**
Sorsogon, Philippines 13 0N 124 0E **135 Bf**
South Br., N.Z. 43 30S 171 15E **145 Df**
South I., Qld. 21 45S 150 20E **129 Ci**
South Arm, Tas. 43 0S 147 24E **107 Ef**
South Auckland, Prov., N:Z. 38 30S 177 0E **144 De**
South Australia, State, Aust. 32 0S 139 0E **111**
South Bruny, I., Tas. 43 25S 147 17E **107 Ef**
South Cape, Tas. 43 39S 146 42E **107 Ee**
South China Sea 7 0N 107 0E **134 Cd**
South East Cape, Tas. 43 40S 146 50E **107 Ee**
South East Is., W.A. 34 17S 123 30E **117 Ec**
South Grafton, N.S.W. 29 41S 152 47E **95 Cc**
South Invercargill, N.Z. 46 26S 168 23E **145 Gc**
South Johnstone, Qld. 17 37S 145 58E **129 Xw**
South Kummin, W.A. 32 12S 118 20E **119 Fe**
South Lake Varley T.O., W.A. 32 50S 119 33E **119 Ff**
South Riana, Tas. 41 11S 145 58E **107 Cd**
South Stradbroke I., Qld. 27 50S 153 25E **131 Ed**
South Tammin, W.A. 31 48S 117 32E **119 Ed**
South Taranaki Bight, N.Z. 39 40S 174 5E **144 Fc**
South Trap, N.Z. 47 35S 167 50E **145 Hb**
South West Cape, Tas. 43 34S 146 3E **107 Ee**
South West Rocks, N.S.W. 30 52S 153 3E **95 Dd**
South Yalgogrin, N.S.W. 34 10S 146 48E **93 Ef**
Southbridge, N.Z. 43 48S 172 16E **145 Dg**
Southbrook, N.Z. 43 20S 172 36E **145 Dg**
Southbrook, Qld. 27 41S 151 43E **131 Eb**
Southern Alps, N.Z. 42 41S 170 11E **145 Ed**
Southern Cross, W.A. 31 125S 119 15E **119 Ef**
Southland, Prov., N.Z. 45 51S 168 13E **145 Fb**
Southport, Qld. 27 58S 153 25E **131 Ed**
Southport, Tas. 43 25S 147 0E **107 Ef**
Spalding, S.A. 33 30S 138 37E **113 Cd**
Spearwood, W.A. 32 7S 115 47E **119 Fb**
Speed, Vic. 35 21S 142 27E **100 Cc**
Spencer, C., S.A. 35 20S 136 45E **113 Eb**
Spencer G., S.A. 34 0S 137 20E **113 Db**
Spenser Mts., N.Z. 42 15S 172 45E **145 Cg**
Spit Pt., W.A. 20 4S 118 59E **117 Cb**
Sprent, Mt., Tas. 42 47S 145 57E **107 Dd**
Spring Creek, N.Z. 41 28S 173 58E **145 Bi**
Spring Ridge, N.S.W. 32 15S 149 21E **95 Ea**
Springburn, N.Z. 43 40S 171 32E **145 Df**
Springfield, N.Z. 43 19S 171 56E **145 Df**
Springfield, Tas. 41 1S 147 29E **107 Cf**
Springhurst, Vic. 36 10S 146 31E **101 Dg**
Springs Junction, N.Z. 42 20S 172 11E **145 Cg**
Springsure, Qld. 24 8S 148 6E **129 Fg**
Springston, N.Z. 43 39S 172 25E **145 Dg**
Springvale, Qld. 22 47S 146 59E **129 De**
Springvale, W.A. 17 48S 127 41E **117 Bd**
Springwood, N.S.W. 33 41S 150 33E **93 Dj**
Squires, Mt., W.A. 26 14S 127 46E **117 Dd**
Srepok R., Khmer Rep. 13 33N 106 16E **134 Bc**
Staaten R., Qld. 16 24S 141 17E **127 Bc**
Stamford, Qld. 21 15S 143 46E **128 Cb**
Stanhope, Vic. 36 27S 144 59E **100 De**
Stanley, Tas. 40 46S 145 19E **107 Bd**
Stannifer, N.S.W. 29 52S 151 14E **95 Cb**
Stansbury, S.A. 34 55S 137 45E **113 Dc**
Stansmore Ra., W.A. 21 23S 128 33E **117 Cd**
Stanthorpe, Qld. 28 36S 151 59E **127 De**
Stanwell, Qld. 23 28S 150 20E **131 Aa**
Stanwell Park, N.S.W. 34 13S 150 58E **93 Ej**
Star R., Qld. 19 30S 145 54E **129 Ae**
Stawell, Vic. 37 5S 142 47E **100 Ec**
Stawell R., Qld. 20 38S 142 55E **128 Bb**
Steep Pt., W.A. 26 8S 113 8E **117 Da**
Stenhouse Bay, S.A. 35 15S 136 57E **113 Eb**
Stephens I., N.Z. 40 40S 174 1E **145 Ai**
Stephens Cr., N.S.W. 32 15S 141 55E **92 Ca**
Stephenson I., N.Z. 34 58S 173 47E **144 Ab**
Stevens, Mt., N.Z. 40 48S 172 27E **145 Ag**
Stewart, C., N.T. 11 57S 134 45E **123 Ab**
Stewart I., N.Z. 46 58S 167 54E **145 Hc**
Stirling, N.Z. 46 14S 169 49E **145 Gd**
Stirling, Qld. 17 12S 141 35E **127 Bc**
Stirling, S.A. 35 0S 138 43E **113 Ed**
Stirling Nth., S.A. 36 35S 137 50E **113 Bc**
Stirling Ra., W.A. 34 0S 118 0E **119 Hd**
Stirling Res., W.A. 33 7S 116 3E **119 Gc**
Stockinbingal, N.S.W. 34 30S 147 53E **93 Eg**
Stockton, N.S.W. 32 56S 151 47E **93 Ck**
Stockwell, S.A. 34 25S 139 6E **113 Dd**
Stoke, N.Z. 43 19S 172 29E **145 Bh**
Stokes, S.A. 34 18S 135 56E **113 Da**
Stokes, Mt., N.Z. 41 7S 174 7E **145 Bi**
Stokes Pt., Tas. 40 10S 143 56E **107 Bb**
Stokes Ra., N.T. 15 50S 130 50E **123 Bb**
Stokes Bay, S.A. 35 38S 137 10E **113 Ec**
Stokes Valley, N.Z. 41 10S 174 59E **144 Hd**
Stonehenge, Qld. 24 22S 143 17E **128 Fb**
Stony Crossing, N.S.W. 35 4S 143 33E **92 Fc**
Store Creek, N.S.W. 32 54S 149 6E **93 Ci**
Storm Bay, Tas. 43 10S 147 30E **107 Ef**
Strahan, Tas. 42 9S 145 20E **107 Dd**
Stratford, N.S.W. 32 7S 151 55E **95 Fb**
Stratford, N.Z. 39 20S 174 19E **144 Fc**
Stratford, Qld. 16 55S 145 45E **129 Ww**
Stratford, Vic. 37 59S 147 7E **101 Eh**
Strathalbyn, S.A. 35 13S 138 53E **113 Ed**
Strathalbyn, Qld. 20 10S 147 18E **129 Bf**
Strathbogie, Vic. 36 53S 145 43E **101 Df**
Strathearn, S.A. 31 43S 140 22E **113 Af**
Strathmerton, Vic. 35 54S 145 30E **101 Cf**
Strathmore, Qld. 17 50S 142 35E **127 Bc**
Strathpark, Qld. 19 36S 143 11E **128 Ab**
Streaky B., S.A. 32 51S 134 18E **111 Cb**
Streatham, Vic. 37 43S 143 5E **100 Ed**
Strickland R., Papua N.G. 7 35S 141 36E **141 Da**
Stroud, N.S.W. 32 25S 152 0E **95 Fc**
Stroud Road, N.S.W. 32 18S 151 57E **95 Fb**
Strzelecki Cr., S.A. 29 37S 139 59E **111 Bd**
Stuart Ra., S.A. 29 10S 134 56E **111 Bb**
Stuart Bluff Ra., N.T. 29 10S 134 56E **123 Cb**
Stuart Town. N.S.W. 32 44S 149 4E **93 Ci**
Stubbs, L., W.A. 33 4S 119 0E **119 Gf**
Studholme Junction, N.Z. 44 42S 171 9E **145 Ef**
Stung-Treng, Khmer Rep. 13 31N 105 58E **134 Bc**
Sturt Ck., W.A. 19 0S 128 15E **117 Bd**
Sturt Bay, S.A. 34 58S 138 31E **113 Ec**
Sturt Creek, W.A. 20 3S 127 24E **117 Bd**
Sturt Vale, S.A. 33 14S 140 1E **113 Cf**
Sturts Meadows, N.S.W. 31 18S 141 42E **90 Bc**
Suckling, Mt., Papua N.G. 9 43S 148 59E **141 Ee**
Sujeewong, Qld. 25 44S 150 36E **131 Ca**
Sukadana, Indonesia, 1 10S 110 0E **134 Ed**
Sukaradja, Indonesia 2 28S 110 25E **134 Ed**
Sula Arch., Philippines 6 0N 121 0E **135 Cf**
Sula Is., Indonesia 1 45S 125 0E **135 Eg**
Sulawesi, Indonesia 2 0S 120 0E **135 Ee**
Sulcor, N.S.W. 30 51S 150 48E **95 Da**
Sumatra I., Indonesia 0 40N 100 20E **134 Eb**
Sumalata, Indonesia 1 0N 122 37E **135 Df**
Sumba I., Indonesia 9 45S 119 35E **135 Ff**
Sumbawa, Indonesia 8 26S 117 30E **135 Fe**
Sumbawau I., Indonesia 8 34S 117 17E **135 Fe**
Summit, Pk., N.Z. 40 29S 176 7E **144 Ge**
Sumner, N.Z. 43 35S 172 48E **145 Dg**
Sumner, L., N.Z. 42 42S 172 15E **145 Cg**
Sunbury, Vic. 37 35S 144 44E **100 Ee**
Sunday Str., W.A. 16 25S 123 18E **117 Bc**
Sungaianjar, Indonesia 2 53S 116 14E **135 Ee**
Sungaipakning, Indonesia 1 19N 102 0E **134 Db**
Sungaipenuh, Indonesia 2 1S 101 20E **134 Eb**
Sungaitiram, Indonesia 0 45S 117 8E **135 Ee**
Sunny Glen, Qld. 26 55S 150 27E **131 Da**
Sunshine, Vic. 37 48S 144 52E **100 Ee**
Surabaja, Indonesia 7 17S 112 45E **134 Fd**
Surakarta, Indonesia 7 35S 110 48E **134 Fd**
Surat, Qld. 27 10S 149 6E **127 Dd**
Surat Thani, Thailand 9 6N 99 14E **134 Ca**
Surbiton, Qld. 23 8S 146 38E **129 Ee**
Surfers Paradise, Qld. 28 0S 153 25E **131 Fd**
Sussex, N.S.W. 31 23S 146 16E **93 Bf**
Susubona, Solomon Is. 8 19S 159 27E **139 Qr**
Sutherland, N.S.W. 34 2S 151 4E **93 Dk**
Sutherlands, S.A. 34 9S 139 14E **113 De**
Sutton, N.S.W. 35 10S 149 15E **93 Fi**
Sutton, N.Z. 45 34S 170 8E **145 Fe**
Suttor R., Qld. 20 36S 147 2E **129 Cf**
Su'u, Solomon Is. 9 11S 160 56E **139 Qs**
Suva, Fiji 17 40S 178 8E **139 Bb**
Swan I., Aust. 40 45S 148 7E **1097 Bg**
Swan Hill, Vic. 35 20S 143 33E **100 Cd**
Swan R., W.A. 32 3S 115 35E **119 Ec**
Swan Reach, S.A. 34 35S 139 37E **113 De**
Swan Reach, Vic. 37 49S 147 53E **101 Eh**
Swan Vale, N.S.W. 29 45S 151 27E **95 Cb**
Swanpool, Vic. 36 44S 146 2E **101 Df**
Swansea, N.S.W. 33 3S 151 35E **93 Dk**
Swansea, Tas. 42 8S 148 4E **107 Dg**
Swifts Creek, Vic. 37 17S 147 44E **101 Eh**
Sydney, N.S.W. 33 53S 151 10E **93 Dk**
Sylvia, Mt., Qld. 27 44S 152 14E **131 Ec**
Synnott Ra., W.A. 16 30S 125 20E **117 Bd**

T

Tabaco, Philippines 13 22N 123 44E **135 Bf**
Tabar Is., Papua N.G. 2 50S 152 0E **141 Bg**
Tabbita, N.S.W. 34 6S 145 51E **92 Ee**
Tablas I., Philippines 12 25N 122 2E **135 Bf**
Table Top, N.S.W. 35 58S 147 1E **93 Fg**
Tableland, W.A. 17 16S 126 51E **117 Bd**
Tabletop, Mt., Qld. 23 24S 147 11E **129 Ef**
Tabwemasana, Mt., New Hebrides 15 20S 166 44E **139 Hf**
Tadine, New Caledonia 21 33S 167 52E **139** B_1e_1
Tacloban, Philippines 11 15N 124 58E **135 Bf**
Tadmor, N.Z. 41 27S 172 45E **145 Bg**
Tadulam, N.S.W. 28 53S 152 35E **95 Bc**
Taft, Philippines 11 57N 125 30E **135 Bg**
Taga, Western Samoa 13 46N 172 28W **139 Cc**
Tagbilaran, Philippines 9 39N 123 51E **135 Cf**
Tage, Papua N.G. 6 19S 143 20E **141 Db**
Taggerty, Vic. 37 21S 145 43E **101 Ef**
Tagula I., Papua N.G. 11 30S 153 30E **141 Fg**
Tagum, Philippines 7 33N 125 53E **135 Cg**
Tahahbala I., Indonesia 0 30S 98 30E **134 Ea**
Tahakopa, N.Z. 46 30S 169 23 E **145 Gd**
Taheke, N.Z. 35 28S 173 39E **144 Bb**
Tahiti & Mooréa, S-W Pacific 17 37S 149 27W **139 Wx**
Tahora, N.Z. 39 2S 174 49E **144 Fc**
Tahulandang I., Indonesia 2 27N 125 23E **135 Dg**
Tahuna, Indonesia 3 45N 125 30E **135 Dg**
Taiaroa Hd., N.Z. 45 47N 170 44E **145 Fe**
Taieri R., N.Z. 46 3S 170 12E **145 Fd**
Taihape, N.Z. 39 41S 175 48E **144 Fd**
Tailem Bend, S.A. 35 1S 139 29E **113 Ee**
Taiping, Malaysia 4 51N 100 44E **134 Db**
Tairua, N.Z. 37 0S 175 51E **144 Dd**
Taitapu, N.Z. 43 40S 172 34E **145 Dg**
Tajan, Indonesia 0 6S 110 2E **134 Ed**
Tak, Thailand 16 52N 99 8E **134 Ab**
Taka Pau, N.Z. 40 2S 176 21E **144 Ge**
Takapuna, N.Z. 36 47S 174 47E **144 Cc**
Takataka, Solomon Is. 9 17S 161 14E **139 Qs**
Taki, Papua N.G. 6 29S 155 52E **141 Dh**
Takingeun, Indonesia 4 45N 96 50E **134 Da**
Takou B., N.Z. 35 6S 173 56E **144 Bb**
Talangbetutu, Indonesia 2 50S 104 35E **134 Eb**
Talasea, Papua N.G. 5 20S 150 2E **141 Cf**
Talaud Is., Indonesia 4 30N 127 10E **135 Dg**
Talawana, W.A. 22 51S 121 9E **117 Cc**
Talayan, Philippines 6 52N 124 24E **135 Cf**
Talbingo Dam, N.S.W. 35 40S 148 20E **93 Fh**
Talbor, Vic. 37 10S 143 44E **100 Ed**
Talbot, C., W.A. 13 48S 126 43E **117 Ad**
Talbot Brook, W.A. 32 2S 116 40E **119 Fc**
Talbragar R., N.S.W. 32 5S 149 15E **93 Ci**
Taliwang, Indonesia 8 50S 116 55E **135 Fe**
Tallangatta, Vic. 36 15S 147 10E **101 Dh**
Tallarook, Vic. 37 5S 145 6E **101 Ef**
Tallawang, N.S.W. 32 12S 149 28E **93 Ci**
Tallebung, N.S.W. 32 42S 146 34E **93 Cf**
Tallering Peak, W.A. 28 6S 115 37E **117 Db**
Tallimba, N.S.W. 33 58S 146 54E **93 Df**
Talmalmo, N.S.W. 35 55S 147 29E **93 Fg**
Talu, Indonesia 0 12N 99 50E **134 Da**
Talwood, Qld. 28 29S 149 29E **127 Dd**
Talyawalka Anabranch, N.S.W. 32 28S 142 22E **92 Cb**
Tamala, W.A. 26 35S 113 40 **117 Da**
Tamar, R., Tas. 41 5S 146 47E **107 Be**
Tamarang, N.S.W. 31 27S 150 5E **95 Ea**
Tambar Springs, N.S.W. 31 20S 149 51E **93 Bi**
Tambelan Is., Indonesia 1 0N 107 30E **134 Dc**
Tambellup, W.A. 34 4S 117 37E **119 Hd**
Tambo, Qld. 24 54S 146 14E **127 Cd**
Tambo, R., Vic. 37 50S 147 50E **101 Eh**
Tambo Crossing, Vic. 37 29S 147 50E **101 Eh**
Tamborine, Qld. 27 53S 153 10E **131 Ed**
Tamboritha, Mt., Vic. 37 31S 146 51E **101 Eg**
Tammie, W.A. 31 39S 117 29E **119 Ed**
Tamworth, N.S.W. 31 0S 150 58E **95 Ea**
Tanahdjampea I., Indonesia 7 10S 120 35 E **135 Ff**
Tanahgrogot, Indonesia 1 55S 116 15E **135 Ee**
Tanahmasa, I., Indonesia 0 5S 98 29E **134 Ea**
Tanahmerah, Indonesia 6 0S 140 7E **135 Fi**
Tanami, N.T. 19 59S 129 43E **123 Ba**
Tanami Desert, N.T. 18 50S 132 0E **123 Bb**
Tanbar, Qld. 25 55S 142 0E **127 Dc**
Tandag, Philippines 9 4N 126 9E **135 Cg**
Tandjung, Indonesia 2 10S 115 25E **135 Ee**
Tandjung Datu I., Indonesia 2 23N 118 3E **134 Dc**
Tandjung Selatan, Indonesia 4 10S 114 40E **135 Ed**
Tandjungbalai, Indonesia 2 55N 99 44E **134 Da**
Tandjungbatu, Indonesia 2 23N 118 3E **135 De**
Tandjungenim, Indonesia 3 51S 103 35E **134 Eb**
Tandjungkarang, Indonesia 5 20S 105 10E **134 Fc**
Tandjungpandan, Indonesia 2 43S 107 38E **134 Ec**

Gazetteer

Tirua Pt. N.Z. 38 25S 174 40E **144 Ec**
Tiverton, S.A. 32 44S 139 42E **113 Be**
Tjilatjap, Indonesia 7 43S 109 0E **134 Fc**
Tjirebon, Indonesia 6 45S 108 32E **134 Fc**
Tjurup, Indonesia 4 26S 102 13E **134 Eb**
Toatoa, N.Z. 38 7S 177 32E **144 Ef**
Tobelo, Indonesia 1 25N 127 56E **135 Dg**
Tobermorey, N.T. 22 12S 138 0E **123 Cc**
Tobin, L., W.A. 21 45S 125 40E **117 Cd**
Toboali, Indonesia 3 0S 106 25E **134 Ec**
Toboli, Indonesia 0 38S 120 12E **135 Ef**
Tocal Telegraph Office, Qld.
23 55S 143 33E **128 Eb**
Tocumwal, N.S.W. 35 45S 145 31E **92 Fe**
Todd R., N.T. 24 52S 135 48E **123 Cc**
Todjo, Indonesia 1 20S 121 15E **135 Ef**
Toetoes B., N.Z. 46 42S 168 41E **145 Gc**
Tofua, I., Tonga 19 45S 175 5W **139 Nn**
Toga, I., New Hebrides 13 26S 166 42E **139 Ff**
Togian Is., Indonesia 0 20S 121 50E **135 Ef**
Tokaanu, N.Z. 38 58S 175 46E **144 Ed**
Tokala Mt., Indonesia 1 30S 121 40E **135 Ef**
Tokanui, N.Z. 46 34S 168 56E **145 Gc**
Tokarahi, N.Z. 44 56S 170 39E **145 e**
Tokatu Pt., N.Z. 36 22S 174 52E **144 Cc**
Toko, N.Z. 39 20S 174 24E **144 Fc**
Toko Range, Qld. 23 5S 138 20E **127 Cb**
Tokomaru, N.Z. 38 7S 178 15E **144 Gd**
Tokomaru Bay, N.Z. 38 7S 178 15E **144 Eg**
Tokoroa, N.Z. 38 20S 175 50E **144 Ed**
Toku, Tonga 18 20S 174 24E **139 Nn**
Tolaga Bay, N.Z. 38 21S 178 20E **144 Eg**
Tolarno, N.S.W. 32 46S 142 24E **92 Cb**
Tolga, Qld. 17 15S 145 29E **129 Xw**
Tolitoli, Indonesia 1 5N 120 50E **135 Df**
Tolmie, Vic. 36 57S 146 15E **101 Dg**
Tom Price, Mt., W.A. 22 40S 117 48E **117 Cb**
Tomanlivi, Fiji 17 37S 178 1E **139 Ab**
Tomerong, N.S.W. 35 3S 150 35E **93 Fj**
Tomingley, N.S.W. 32 31S 148 16E **93 Ch**
Tomini, Indonesia 0 30N 120 30E **135 Df**
Tompkinson Ra., S.A. 26 11S 129 5E **111 Ba**
Toms Lake, N.S.W. 33 43S 144 47E **92 Dd**
Tone R., W.A. 34 23S 116 25E **119 Hc**
Tone R. Mill, W.A. 34 25S 116 29E **119 Hc**
Tonga, S-W Pacific 20 0S 173 0W **139 Nn**
Tongala, Vic. 36 14S 144 56E **100 De**
Tongaporutu, N.Z. 38 50S 174 36E **144 Ec**
Tongariro, N.Z. 39 7S 175 50E **144 Fd**
Tongariro Nat. Pk., N.Z. 39 8S 175 33E **144 Fd**
Tongatapu Group, Tonga 20 0S 174 0W **139 On**
Tongio, Vic. 37 14S 147 44E **101 Eh**
Tongoa, I., New Hebrides 16 54S 168 34E **139 Ih**
Tonkoro, Qld. 23 57S 142 31E **128 Ea**
Tonumea, I., Tonga 20 0S 174 0W **139 On**
Toodyay, W.A. 31 34S 116 28E **119 Ec**
Toogong, N.S.W. 33 19S 148 38E **93 Dh**
Toogoolawah, Qld. 27 5S 152 23E **131 Ec**
Toolara Forest, Qld. 26 0S 152 53E **131 Cc**
Toolibin, W.A. 32 59S 117 37E **119 Fd**
Tooligie, S.A. 33 52S 135 43E **113 Ca**
Toolleen, Vic. 36 45S 144 42E **100 De**
Toolondo, Vic. 36 58S 141 5E **100 Db**
Tooloom, N.S.W. 28 36S 152 27E **95 Bc**
Tooloon N.S.W. 30 59S 148 10E **93 Ah**
Tooma, N.S.W. 35 57S 148 3E **93 Fh**
Toomba, Qld. 19 58S 145 33E **128 Ad**
Toompine, Qld. 27 15S 144 19E **127 Dc**
Toongi, N.S.W. 32 28S 148 30E **93 Ch**
Toonpan, Qld. 19 28S 146 48E **129 Ae**
Toonumbar, N.S.W. 28 34S 152 46E **95 Bc**
Toora, Vic. 38 39S 146 23E **101 Fg**
Tooraweenah, N.S.W. 31 26S 148 52E **93 Bh**
Toowoomba, Qld. 27 32S 151 56E **131 Eb**
Top Hut, N.S.W. 33 40S 142 57E **92 Db**
Torbaniea, Qld. 25 21S 152 37E **131 Cc**
Torbay, W.A. 35 2S 117 36E **119 Hd**
Torbreck Mt., Vic. 37 23S 145 58E **101 Ef**
Torere, N.Z. 37 57S 177 29E **144 Df**
Torington, N.S.W. 29 19S 151 44E **95 Cb**
Toronto, N.S.W. 33 0S 151 30E **93 Ck**
Torquay, Vic. 38 20S 144 19E **100 Fe**
Torrens Creek, Qld. 20 48S 145 3E **128 Bd**
Torrens Ck., Qld. 22 23S 145 9E **128 Cd**
Torres Is., New Hebrides 13 15S 166 37E **139 Ff**
Tostaree, Vic. 37 44S 148 10E **101 Ei**
Totoya, I., Fiji 18 57S 179 50W **139 Bc**
Tottenham, N.S.W. 32 14S 147 21E **93 Cg**
Touho, New Caledonia 20 47S 165 14E **139 A₁c₁**
Toukley, N.S.W. 33 14S 151 31E **93 Dk**
Tourville, C., Tas. 42 6S 148 21E **107 Dg**
Towai, N.Z. 35 30S 174 9E **144 Bc**

Tower Peak, N.Z. 46 1S 167 3E **145 Gb**
Towerhill Ck., Qld. 22 28S 144 35E **128 Cc**
Townshend, C., Qld. 22 18S 150 30E **129 Di**
Townshend I., Qld. 22 16S 150 31E **129 Di**
Townson, Qld. 27 53S 152 23E **131 Ec**
Townsville, Qld. 19 15S 146 45E **129 Ae**
Towong, Vic. 36 8S 147 59E **101 Dh**
Trafalgar, Vic. 38 14S 146 12E **101 Fg**
Tragowel, Vic. 35 50S 144 0E **100 Cd**
Trang, Thailand 7 33N 99 38E **134 Ca**
Trangan I., Indonesia 6 40S 134 20E **135 Fh**
Trangie, N.S.W. 32 42S 148 0E **93 Bg**
Traralgon, Vic. 38 12S 146 34E **101 Fg**
Trat, Thailand 12 14N 102 33E **134 Bb**
Traveller's L., N.S.W. 33 20S 142 0E **92 Db**
Travers, Mt., N.Z. 42 1S 172 45E **145 Cg**
Trawalla, Vic. 37 25S 143 28E **100 Ed**
Trayning, W.A. 31 7S 117 46E **119 Ed**
Treasury Is., Solomon Is. 7 22S 155 37E **139 Pp**
Trebonne, Qld. 18 37S 146 5E **129 Yx**
Treesville, W.A. 33 10S 116 18E **119 Gc**
Tregrasse Is. 17 41S 150 43E **128 Be**
Trelega, N.S.W. 33 30S 142 9E **92 Db**
Trentham, Vic. 37 23S 144 21E **100 Ee**
Tressillian, Qld. 23 22S 146 39E **129 Ee**
Triabunna, Tas. 42 30S 147 55E **107 Df**
Trial B., N.S.W. 30 48S 153 2E **95 Dd**
Tribulation, C., Qld. 16 5S 145 29E **127 Bd**
Trida, N.S.W. 33 1S 145 1E **92 De**
Troubridge Pt., S.A. 35 10S 137 39E **113 Ec**
Trowutta, Tas. 41 1S 145 6E **107 Cd**
Trundle, N.S.W. 32 53S 147 42E **93 Cg**
Truro, S.A. 34 24S 139 9E **113 De**
Truslove, W.A. 33 20S 121 45E **117 Ec**
Tryphena, N.Z. 36 18S 175 28E **144 Cd**
Tuai, N.Z. 38 47S 177 15E **144 Ef**
Tuakau, N.Z. 37 16S 174 59E **144 Dc**
Tual, Indonesia 5 30S 132 50E **135 Fh**
Tuamarino, N.Z. 41 25S 173 59E **145 Bi**
Tuao, Philippines 17 47N 121 30E **135 Af**
Tuapeka Mouth, N.Z. 46 1S 169 31E **145 Gd**
Tuapere, N.Z. 48 7S 167 43E **145 Gb**
Tuban, Indonesia 6 57S 112 4E **134 Fd**
Tubau R., Malaysia 3 10N 113 40E **134 Dd**
Tuckanarra, W.A. 27 8S 118 1E **117 Db**
Tuckey, S.A. 33 39S 136 4E **113 Cb**
Tuen, P.O., Qld. 28 33S 145 37E **127 Dd**
Tuena, N.S.W. 34 1S 149 19E **93 Ei**
Tufi, Papua N.G. 9 8S 149 19E **141 Ee**
Tuggerah, L., N.S.W. 33 18S 151 30E **93 Dk**
Tukangbesi Is., Indonesia 6 0S 124 0E **135 Ff**
Tukituki, N.Z. 39 36S 176 56E **144 Ff**
Tuli, Indonesia 1 24S 122 26E **135 Ef**
Tullah, Tas. 41 43S 145 38E **107 Cd**
Tullamore, N.S.W. 32 39S 147 36E **93 Cg**
Tullibigeal, N.S.W. 33 25S 146 44E **93 Df**
Tulmur, Qld. 22 40S 142 20E **128 Da**
Tully, Qld. 17 56S 145 55E **129 Xw**
Tulungagung, Indonesia 8 5S 111 54E **134 Fd**
Tum, Indonesia 3 28S 130 21E **135 Eh**
Tumbarumba, N.S.W. 35 44S 148 0E **93 Fh**
Tumblong, N.S.W. 35 6S 148 1E **93 Fg**
Tumbulgum, N.S.W. 28 17S 153 27E **95 Bd**
Tumby Bay, S.A. 34 21S 136 8E **113 Db**
Tumorrrama, N.S.W. 35 11S 148 28E **93 Fh**
Tumpat, Thailand 6 11N 102 10E **134 Cb**
Tumut, N.S.W. 35 16S 148 13E **93 Fh**
Tunbridge, Tas. 42 5S 147 28E **107 Df**
Tuncurry, N.S.W. 32 9S 152 29E **95 Fc**
Tungamal, Vic. 36 10S 145 54E **101 Df**
Tunnack, Tas. 42 28S 147 28E **107 Df**
Turakina, N.Z. 40 3S 175 16E **144 Gd**
Turakirae Hd., N.Z. 41 26S 174 56E **144 Hc**
Turangi, N.Z. 38 59S 175 48E **144 Ed**
Turkey, Qld. 24 6S 151 38E **131 Bb**
Turkey Creek P.O., W.A. 17 2S 128 12E **117 Bd**
Turlee, N.S.W. 33 56S 143 5E **92 Dc**
Turnagain, C., N.Z. 40 28S 176 38E **144 Ge**
Turner, W.A. 35 16S 149 8E **117 Bd**
Turner Pt., N.T. 11 47S 133 32E **123 Ab**
Turon R., N.S.W. 33 0S 150 8E **93 Gj**
Turtle Head I., Qld. 10 50S 142 37E **127 Ac**
Tutong, Malaysia 4 47N 114 34E **135 Dd**
Tutuila, I., Eastern Samoa 14 19S 170 50 W **139 Dd**
Tutye, Vic. 35 12S 141 29E **100 Cb**
Tuvutha, I., Fiji 17 40S 178 48W **139 Ac**
Tweed Heads, N.S.W. 28 10S 153 31E **95 Bd**
Two People B., W.A. 34 58S 118 15E **119 He**
Two Thumbs Ra., N.Z. 43 45S 170 44E **145 De**
Two Wells, S.A. 34 34S 138 30E **113 Dd**
Tyagong, N.S.W. 34 4S 148 15E **93 Eh**
Tyalgum, N.S.W. 28 22S 153 10E **95 Bd**

Tyndall, Mt., N.Z. 43 15S 170 55E **145 De**
Tyrrell, L., Vic. 35 20S 142 50E **100 Cc**
Tyrell R., Vic. 35 26S 142 51E **100 Cd**
Tyrendarra, Vic. 38 12S 141 50E **100 Fb**
Tyringham, N.S.W. 30 15S 152 35E **95 Dc**

U

Uanda, Qld. 21 37S 144 55E **128 Cc**
Uarbry, N.S.W. 32 3S 149 49E **93 Ci**
Ubaba, Qld. 24 24S 151 17E **131 Bb**
Ubon Ratchathani, Thailand 15 15N 104 50E **134 Ab**
Ubuna, Solomon Is. 10 11S 161 21E **139 Rs**
Ucolta, S.A. 32 56S 138 59E **113 Bd**
Udon Thani, Thailand 17 29N 102 46E **134 Ab**
Ugi, I., Solomon Is. 10 14S 161 44E **139 Rs**
Uiha, I., Tonga 19 54S 174 25W **139 Nn**
Ujung Pandang, Indonesia 5 10S 119 20E **135 Ee**
Uki, N.S.W. 28 26S 153 20E **95 Bd**
Ulalie, N.S.W. 31 9S 143 38E **92 Bc**
Ulamambri, N.S.W. 31 19S 149 23E **93 Bi**
Ulan, N.S.W. 32 16S 149 46E **93 Ci**
Ulawa, I., Solomon Is. 9 46S 161 57E **139 Qt**
Ulinda, N.S.W. 31 35S 149 30E **93 Bi**
Ulladulla, N.S.W. 35 21S 150 29E **93 Fj**
Ulmarra, N.S.W. 29 37S 153 4E **95 Cd**
Ulong, N.S.W. 30 14S 152 54E **95 Dc**
Ultima, Vic. 35 22S 143 18E **100 Cd**
Ulverstone, Tas. 41 11S 146 11E **107 Ce**
Umatac, Guam 13 18N 144 39E **139 Tu**
Umboi I., Papua N.G. 5 40S 148 0E **141 Cd**
Umbrella Mts., N.Z. 45 35S 169 5E **145 Fd**
Umera, Indonesia 0 12S 129 30E **135 Eg**
Una, Mt., N.Z. 42 13S 172 36E **145 Cg**
Unanderra, N.S.W. 34 27S 150 49E **93 Ej**
Undera, Vic. 36 18S 145 13E **101 Df**
Underbool, Vic. 35 10S 141 51E **100 Cb**
Undercliff, Qld. 21 53S 149 8E **129 Ch**
Undu Pt., Fiji 16 8S 179 57W **139 Ac**
Ungarie, N.S.W. 33 38S 146 56E **93 Df**
Ungarra, S.A. 34 12S 136 2E **113 Db**
Uno, S.A. 32 40S 136 39E **113 Bb**
Unumgar, N.S.W. 28 25S 152 47E **95 Bc**
Upolu I., Eastern Samoa 13 58S 172 0W **139 Dd**
Upper Blessington, Tas. 41 28S 147 35E **107 Cf**
Upper Castra, Tas. 41 18S 146 9E **107 Ce**
Upper Horton, N.S.W. 30 6S 150 26E **95 Da**
Upper Hutt, N.Z. 41 8S 175 5E **144 Hd**
Upper Manilla, N.S.W. 30 38S 150 40E **95 Da**
Upper Moutere, N.Z. 41 16S 172 57E **145 Bg**
Upper Natone, Tas. 41 14S 145 55E **107 Cd**
Upper Pilton, Qld. 27 54S 152 6E **131 Ec**
Upper Rouchel, N.S.W. 32 6S 151 5E **93 Ck**
Upper Stone, Qld. 18 44S 145 58E **129 Yw**
Upper Swan, W.A. 31 46S 116 1E **119 Eb**
Upper Takaka, N.Z. 41 3S 172 51E **145 Bg**
Upstart, C., Qld. 19 41S 147 45E **129 Af**
Ural, Mt., N.S.W. 33 21S 146 12E **93 Df**
Uralla, N.S.W. 30 37S 151 29E **95 Db**
Urana, N.S.W. 35 15S 146 21E **93 Ef**
Urana, L., N.S.W. 35 16S 146 10E **93 Ff**
Urandangie, Qld. 21 32S 138 14E **127 Cb**
Urangan, Qld. 25 17S 152 53E **131 Cc**
Urangeline East, N.S.W. 35 30S 146 40E **93 Ff**
Urania, S.A. 34 32S 137 37E **113 Dc**
Uranquinty, N.S.W. 35 6S 147 12E **93 Fg**
Urbenville, N.S.W. 28 29S 152 34E **95 Bc**
Urenui, N.Z. 39 0S 174 23E **144 Fc**
Ure Para Para, I., New Hebrides
13 32S 167 20E **139 Fg**
Urewera Nat. Pk., N.Z. 38 47S 177 8E **144 Ef**
Uriah, Mt., N.Z. 42 1S 171 39E **145 Cf**
Urunga, N.S.W. 30 31S 153 1E **95 Dd**
Uruti, N.Z. 38 56S 174 32E **144 Ec**
'Uta Vava'u, I., Tonga 18 36S 174 0W **139 Nn**
Utiku, N.Z. 39 44S 175 52E **144 Fd**
Uttaradit, Thailand 17 36N 100 5E **134 Ab**
Uvea, I., New Caledonia 20 30S 166 35E **139 A₁d₁**

V

Vaitogi, Eastern Samoa 14 21S 170 44W **139 Dd**
Valentine Plains, Qld. 24 25S 150 36E **131 Ba**
Van Diemen, C., N.T. 11 9S 130 24E **123 Ab**
Van Diemen, C., Qld. 16 30S 139 46E **127 Bb**
Van Diemen G., N.T. 11 45S 131 50E **123 Ab**

Gazetteer

Watalgan, Qld. 24 38S 152 1E **131 Bc**
Watampone, Indonesia 4 29S 120 25E **135 Ef**
Watchem, Vic. 36 9S 142 52E **100 Dc**
Water Park Pt., Qld. 22 56S 150 47E **129 Di**
Waterhouse I. 40 47S 147 37E **107 Bf**
Watervale, S.A. 33 57S 138 38E **113 Cd**
Waterview, Qld. 21 31S 144 35E **128 Cc**
Watheroo, W.A. 30 15S 116 0E **119 Dc**
Watheroo Observatory, W.A. 30 19S 115 52E **119 Db**
Watraba, S.A. 31 58S 133 13E **111 Cb**
Watson, S.A. 30 19S 131 41E **111 Cb**
Watsons Creek, N.S.W. 37 40S 145 13E **95 Db**
Watten, Qld. 21 1S 144 3E **128 Cc**
Wattiwarriganna Cr., S.A. 28 57S 136 10E **111 Bc**
Wattle Flat, N.S.W. 33 8S 149 43E **93 Di**
Watubela Is., Indonesia 4 28S 131 54E **135 Eh**
Wau, Papua N.G. 7 21S 146 47E **141 Dd**
Waubra, Vic. 37 21S 143 39E **100 Ed**
Wauchope, N.S.W. 31 28S 152 45E **95 Ec**
Waukaringa, S.A. 32 18S 139 27E **113 Be**
Wave Hill, N.T. 17 32S 131 0E **123 Bb**
Waverley, N.Z. 39 46S 174 37E **144 Fc**
Wawoi R., Papua N.G. 7 48S 143 16E **141 Db**
Way, L., W.A. 26 45S 120 16E **117 Dc**
Wayatinah, Tas. 42 19S 146 27E **107 De**
Wé, New Caledonia 20 55S 167 16E **139 A₁e₁**
Weber, N.Z. 40 24S 176 20E **144 Ge**
Weda, Teluk, Indonesia 0 30N 127 50E **135 Dg**
Wedderburn, N.Z. 45 2S 170 2E **145 Fd**
Wedderburn, Vic. 36 20S 143 33E **100 Dd**
Wedge I., W.A. 30 50S 115 11E **119 Dd**
Wednesday Peak, N.Z. 46 8S 166 50E **145 Ga**
Wee Elwah, N.S.W. 32 2S 145 14E **92 De**
Wee Jasper, N.S.W. 35 8S 148 1E **93 Fh**
Wee Waa, N.S.W. 30 11S 149 26E **91 Bg**
Weemelah, N.S.W. 29 2S 149 7E **91 Ag**
Weetaliba, N.S.W. 31 35S 149 39E **93 Bi**
Weethalle, N.S.W. 33 52S 146 36E **93 Df**
Weetulta, S.A. 34 18S 137 37E **113 Dc**
Weipa, Qld. 12 24S 141 50E **127 Ac**
Weir R., Qld. 28 20S 149 50E **131 Ea**
Weja, N.S.W. 33 31S 146 50E **93 Df**
Welbourn Hill, S.A. 27 21S 134 6E **111 Bb**
Welbungin, W.A. 30 49S 117 59E **119 Dd**
Wellesley Is., Qld. 17 20S 139 30E **127 Bb**
Wellington, S.A. 35 16S 139 21E **113 Ee**
Wellington, Prov., N.Z. 40 8S 175 36E **144 Gd**
Wellington, N.S.W. 32 35S 148 59E **93 Ci**
Wellington, N.Z. 41 19S 174 46E **144 Hc**
Wellington, L., Vic. 38 6S 147 20E **101 Fh**
Wellington, Mt., N.Z. 36 55S 174 52E **144 Cd·**
Wells, L., W.A. 26 43S 123 10E **117 Dc**
Wellsford, N.Z. 36 16S 174 32E **144 Cc**
Wellshot, Qld. 23 55S 144 28E **128 Ec**
Welshpool, Vic. 38 42S 146 26E **101 Fg**
Wellstead, W.A. 34 7S 119 10E **119 Hf**
Wengenville, Qld. 26 50S 151 42E **131 Db**
Wenlock, Qld. 13 6S 142 58E **127 Ac**
Wenloch, R., Qld. 12 2S 141 55E **127 Ac**
Wentworth, N.S.W. 34 2S 141 54E **92 Ea**
Wentworth, N.S.W. 34 2S 141 54E **92 Ea**
Weonaworri, Qld. 23 4S 142 52E **128 Ea**
Weri, Indonesia 3 10S 132 30E **135 Eh**
Werombi, N.S.W. 33 58S 150 34E **93 Dj**
Werribee, Vic. 37 54S 144 40E **100 Ee**
Werrimull, Vic. 34 25S 141 38E **100 Bb**
Werris Creek, N.S.W. 31 18S 150 38E **95 Ea**
Wersar, Indonesia 1 30S 131 55E **135 Eh**
W.C. Howe, W.A. 35 8S 117 36E **119 Hd**
West Baines R., N.T. 15 36S 129 58E **123 Ba**
West I., W.A. 34 5S 120 28E **119 Hg**
West Morawa Hill, W.A. 29 11S 115 50E **119 Cb**
West Pt., S.A. 34 5S 120 28E **113 Ea**
West Pt., Tas. 40 56S 144 37E **107 Bc**
West, R., W.A. 33 47S 119 54E **119 Gf**
W. Sister I., Aust. 39 42S 147 55E **107 Af**
West Wyalong, N.S.W. 33 56S 147 10E **93 Dg**
Wessel, C., N.T. 10 59S 136 46E **123 Ac**
Wessel Is., N.T. 11 10S 136 45E **123 Ac**
Westall, Pt., S.A. 32 55S 134 4E **111 Cb**
Westbury, Tas. 41 30S 146 51E **107 Ce**
Westerfield, N.Z. 43 50S 171 37E **145 Df**
Western River, S.A. 35 42S 136 56E **113 Eb**
Western R., Qld. 22 20S 142 25E **128 Da**
Western Samoa, S-W Pacific 14 0S 172 0W **139 Cc**
Westerway, Tas. 42 37S 146 42E **107 De**
Westland, Prov., N.Z. 43 33S 169 59E **145 Dd**
Westland Bight, N.Z. 42 55S 170 5E **145 Dd**
Westland Nat. Pk., N.Z. 43 26S 169 56E **145 Dd**
Westmere, Vic. 37 42S 142 58E **100 Ec**
Weston, Malaysia 5 10N 115 35E **135 Ce**
Westonia, W.A. 31 18S 118 42E **119 Ee**

Westport, N.Z. 41 46S 171 37E **145 Bf**
Westwood, Qld. 23 36S 150 10E **131 Aa**
Wetar, I., Indonesia 7 30S 126 30E **135 Fg**
Wewak, Papua N.G. 3 38S 143 41E **141 Bb**
Weymouth, C., Qld. 12 37S 143 27E **127 Ac**
Whakamaru, N.Z. 38 23S 175 63E **144 Ed**
Whakapara, N.Z. 35 32S 174 16E **144 Bc**
Whakatane, N.Z. 37 57S 177 1E **144 Df**
Whangamomona, N.Z. 39 8S 174 44E **144 Fc**
Whangape L., N.Z. 37 28S 175 3E **144 Dc**
Whangara, N.Z. 38 34S 178 14E **144 Eg**
Whangarei, N.Z. 35 43S 174 21E **144 Bc**
Whangarei Harbour, N.Z. 35 45S 174 28E **144 Bc**
Whangaroa Harbour, N.Z. 35 4S 173 46E **144 Ab**
Wharanui, N.Z. 41 55S 174 6E **145 Bi**
Wharminda, S.A. 33 57S 136 12E **113 Cb**
Whataroa R., N.Z. 43 7S 170 6E **145 De**
Whatatutu, N.Z. 38 23S 177 52E **144 Ef**
Whatawhata, N.Z. 37 48S 175 9E **144 Dc**
Wheatlands, Qld. 26 15S 151 52E **131 Db**
Wherrol Flat, N.S.W. 31 46S 152 15E **95 Ec**
Whetstone, Qld. 28 30S 150 56E **131 Fa**
Whiporie, N.S.W. 29 18S 152 58E **95 Cc**
Whistleduck Ck., N.T 20 15S 135 18E **123 Cc**
Whitbarrow Ck., N.S.W. 31 45S 146 34E **93 Bf**
Whitcombe, Mt., N.Z. 43 12S 171 0E **145 De**
Whitcombe Pass, N.Z. 43 12S 171 0E **145 Df**
White I., N.Z. 37 30S 177 13E **144 Df**
White, L., N.T. 224 43S 121 44E **123Ca**
White Cliffs, N.S.W. 30 50S 143 10E **92 Ac**
Whitecliffs, N.Z. 43 26S 171 55E **145 Df**
Whiteman Ra., Papua N.G. 5 55S 150 0E **141 Ce**
Whitemark, Tas. 40 7S 148 3E **107 Bg**
Whitesands, New Hebrides 19 28S 169 25E **139 Li**
Whitewood, Qld. 21 28S 143 30E **128 Cb**
Whitfield, Vic. 36 44S 146 24E **101 Dg**
Whitianga, N.Z. 36 47S 175 41E **144 Cd**
Whitsunday I., Qld. 20 15S 149 4E **129 Bh**
Whitsunday Pass, Qld. 20 15S 148 53E **129 Bg**
Whittlesea, Vic. 37 27S 145 9E **100 Ef**
Whitton, N.S.W. 34 30S 146 6E **93 Ef**
Whorouly, Vic. 36 31S 146 35E **101 Dg**
Whyalla, S.A. 33 2S 137 30E **113 Cc**
Whyte Yarcowie, S.A. 33 13S 138 54E **113 Cd**
Wialki, W.A. 30 28S 118 7E **119 Ee**
Wiangaree, N.S.W. 28 30S 152 59E **95 Bd**
Wickepin, W.A. 32 50S 117 30E **119 Fd**
Wickham, C., King Island 39 35S 143 57E **107 Ab**
Widgiemooltha, W.A. 31 30S 121 34E **117 Ec**
Wietalaba, Qld. 24 17S 151 15E **131 Bb**
Wigton, Qld. 25 57S 151 37E **131 Cb**
Wilangee, N.S.W. 31 28S 141 20E **90 Bc**
Wilcannia, N.S.W. 31 30S 143 26E **92 Bc**
Wilga, N.S.W. 31 26S 143 50E **92 Bc**
Wilga, W.A. 33 42S 116 12E **119 Gc**
Wilga Downs, N.S.W. 30 48S 146 8E **93 Af**
Wilgaroon, N.S.W. 30 52S 145 42E **92 Ae**
Wilhelm, Mt., Papua N.G. 5 50S 145 1E **141 Cc**
Wilkawatt, S.A. 35 22S 140 22E **113 Ef**
Wilkinson L., S.A. 29 40S 132 39E **111 Bb**
Willamulka, S.A. 33 55S 137 52E **113 Cc**
Willandra Ck., N.S.W. 33 22S 145 52E **92 De**
Willandspey, Qld. 21 45S 146 45E **129 Ce**
Willaura, Vic. 37 31S 142 45E **100 Ec**
Willawa, Qld. 24 51S 150 3E **131 Ba**
Willawarrin, N.S.W. 30 55S 152 37E **95 Dc**
Willeroo, N.T. 15 14S 131 37E **123 Bb**
William B., W.A. 35 2S 117 7E **119 Hd**
William, Mt., Vic. 37 17S 142 35E **100 Ec**
William Creek, S.A. 28 58S 136 22E **111 Bc**
Williambury, W.A. 23 45S 115 12E **117 Cb**
Williams, W.A. 33 0S 117 0E **119 Gc**
Williams R., W.A. 32 58S 116 24E **119 Gc**
Williamsford, Tas. 41 48S 145 30E **107 Cd**
Williamstown, S.A. 34 40S 138 54E **113 Dd**
Williamstown, Vic. 37 51S 144 52E **100 Ee**
Willis Group 16 18S 150 0E **127 Be**
Willochra, S.A. 32 13S 138 10E **113 Bd**
Willow Tree, N.S.W. 31 40S 150 45E **95 Ea**
Willows, Qld. 23 45S 147 25E **129 Ef**
Wills Cr., Qld. 22 43S 140 2E **127 Cb**
Wills, L., W.A. 21 25S 128 51E **117 Cd**
Willson River, S.A. 35 51S 137 55E **113 Ec**
Willunga, S.A. 33 15S 138 30E **113 Ed**
Wilmington, S.A. 32 30S 138 0E **113 Bd**
Wilmot, Tas. 41 23S 146 10E **107 Ce**
Wilmot Pass, N.Z. 45 31S 167 13E **145 Fb**
Wilpeena Park, Qld. 23 6S 148 56E **129 Eg**
Wilpena Ck., S.A. 31 25S 139 29E **113 Ae**
Wilroy, W.A. 28 38S 115 38E **119 Bb**
Wilson, R., Qld. 27 38S 141 24E **127 Dc**
Wilson R., W.A. 16 48S 128 16E **117 Bd**

Wilson Inlet, W.A. 35 0S 117 20E **119 Hd**
Wilson Str., Solomon Is. 8 0S 156 39E **139 Pq**
Wilson's Promontory, Vic. 38 55S 146 25E **101 Fg**
Wilton, R., N.T. 14 45S 33E **123 Ab**
Wiluna, W.A. 26 36S 120 14E **117 Dc**
Wimbledon, N.Z. 40 27S 176 33E **144 Ge**
Wimmera, R., Vic. 36 8S 141 56E **100 Db**
Winchelsea, Vic. 38 10S 144 1E **100 Fd**
Winchester, N.Z. 44 11S 171 17E **145 Ef**
Winchester, W.A. 29 47S 115 56E **119 Cb**
Windalle, N.S.W. 32 18S 142 29E **92 Cb**
Windeyer, N.S.W. 32 46S 149 32E **93 Ci**
Windorah, Qld. 25 24S 142 36E **127 Dc**
Windsor, N.Z. 44 59S 170 49E **145 Fe**
Windsor, N.S.W. 33 37S 150 50E **93 Dj**
Windsor, S.A. 34 26S 138 19E **113 Dd**
Wingate Mts., N.T. 14 25S 130 40E **123 Ab**
Wingello, N.S.W. 34 42S 150 10E **93 Ej**
Wingen, N.S.W. 31 54S 150 54E **93 Bj**
Wingham, N.S.W. 31 48S 152 22E **95 Ec**
Winnaleah, Tas. 41 5S 147 49E **107 Cf**
Winnecke, Ck., N.T. 18 35S 131 34E **123 Bb**
Winnijup, W.A. 33 58S 116 20E **119 Gc**
Winton, N.Z. 46 8S 168 20E **145 Gc**
Winton, Qld. 22 24S 143 3E **128 Db**
Winton, Vic. 26 32S 146 7E **101 Df**
Winton Swamp, Vic. 36 27S 146 5E **101 Df**
Wirha, S.A. 25 8S 140 32E **113 Ef**
Wirrabara, S.A. 33 2S 138 17E **113 Cd**
Wirrapa, S.A. 31 26S 136 58E **113 Ab**
Wirrealpa, S.A. 31 6S 138 57E **113 Ad**
Wirrega, S.A. 36 12S 140 38E **113 Ff**
Wirrinya, N.S.W. 33 39S 147 48E **93 Dg**
Wirrulla, S.A. 32 24S 134 31E **111 Cb**
Wisemans Ferry, N.S.W. 33 22S 150 59E **93 Dj**
Witchcliffe, W.A. 34 2S 115 5E **119 Hb**
Withersfield, Qld. 23 34S 147 34E **129 Ef**
Wittenoom, W.A. 22 15S 118 20E **117 Cb**
Wodonga, Vic. 36 5S 146 50E **101 Dg**
Wokalup, W.A. 33 7S 115 52E **119 Gb**
Wokam I., Indonesia 5 45S 134 28E **135 Fh**
Wokingham Ck., Qld. 22 19S 142 30E **128 Ca**
Woldston, Qld. 19 48S 146 47E **129 Ae**
Wollar, N.S.W. 32 20S 149 56E **93 Ci**
Wollogorang, N.T. 17 13S 137 57E **123 Bc**
Wollombi, N.S.W. 32 56S 151 8E **93 Ck**
Wollomombi, N.S.W. 30 30S 152 4E **95 Dc**
Wollondilly R., N.S.W. 34 12S 150 18E **93 Ej**
Wollongong, N.S.W. 34 25S 150 54E **93 Ej**
Wolseley, S.A. 36 23S 140 54E **113 Ff**
Wolvi, Qld. 26 10S 152 52E **131 Dc**
Wombat, N.S.W. 34 24S 148 16E **93 Eh**
Wombeyan Caves, N.S.W. 34 17S 149 59E **93 Ei**
Wonaran P.O., N.T. 19 55S 136 20E **123 Bc**
Wondai, Qld. 26 20S 151 49E **131 Db**
Wondalga, N.S.W. 35 24S 148 8E **93 Fh**
Wongalarroo L., N.S.W. 31 32S 144 0E **92 Bd**
Wongalee, Qld. 20 38S 144 25E **128 Bc**
Wongan Hills, W.A. 30 53S 116 42E **119 Dc**
Wongamine, W.A. 31 30S 116 35E **119 Ec**
Wongarbon, N.S.W. 32 20S 148 45E **93 Ch**
Wongawal, W.A. 25 5S 121 55E **117 Dc**
Wongoondy, W.A. 28 50S 115 30E **119 Bb**
Wonnangatta, R., Vic. 37 32S 147 15E **101 Eh**
Wonnerup, W.A. 33 38S 115 26E **119 Gb**
Wonthaggi, Vic. 38 37S 145 37E **101 Ff**
Wonwron, Vic. 38 27S 146 45E **101 Fg**
Woocalla, S.A. 31 42S 137 12E **113 Ac**
Wood Is., W.A. 16 24S 123 19E **117 Bc**
Woodah I., N.T. 13 27S 136 10E **123 Ac**
Woodanilling, W.A. 33 31S 117 24E **119 Gd**
Woodbridge, Tas. 43 10S 147 14E **107 Ef**
Woodburn, N.S.W. 29 6S 153 23E **95 Cd**
Wooded Bluff, N.S.W. 29 24S 153 23E **95 Cd**
Woodenbong, N.S.W. 28 24S 152 39E **95 Bc**
Woodend, N.Z. 43 19S 173 40E **145 Dg**
Woodend, Vic. 37 20S 144 33E **100 Ee**
Woodford, Qld. 26 58S 152 47E **131 Dc**
Woodgate, Qld. 25 7S 152 35E **131 Cc**
Woodlands, W.A. 24 46S 118 8E **117 Cb**
Woodlark I., Papua N.G. 9 10S 152 50E **141 Eg**
Woodroffe, Mt., S.A. 26 20S 131 45E **111 Bb**
Woods, L., N.T. 17 50S 133 30E **123 Bb**
Woods Point, Vic. 37 32S 146 16E **101 Eg**
Woods Reef, N.S.W. 30 22S 150 45E **95 Da**
Woodside, S.A. 34 58S 138 52E **113 Dd**
Woodside, Vic. 38 31S 146 52E **101 Fg**
Woodstock, N.S.W. 33 45S 148 53E **93 Dh**
Woodstock, Qld. 19 35S 146 57E **128 Aa**
Woodstock, Qld. 22 15S 141 57E **129 Ae**
Woodstock, W.A. 21 41S 118 57E **117 Cb**
Woodville, N.Z. 40 20S 175 53E **144 Gd**

Gazetteer

Woogenellup, W.A. 34 31S 117 48E **119 Hd**
Wooka Wooka, W.A. 30 43S 115 18E **119 Db**
Woolamai, C., Vic. 38 30S 145 23E **101 Ff**
Woolbrook, N.S.W. 30 56S 151 25E **95 Db**
Woolgangie, W.A. 31 12S 120 35E **119 Eg**
Woolgooga, N.S.W. 30 6S 153 11E **95 Dd**
Wooli, N.S.W. 29 52S 153 17E **95 Cd**
Woolooga, Qld. 26 3S 152 24E **131 Dc**
Woolsthorpe, Vic. 38 11S 142 26E **100 Fc**
Woomargama, N.S.W. 35 45S 147 15E **93 Fg**
Woombye, Qld. 26 40S 152 55E **131 Dc**
Woomelang, Vic. 35 37S 142 40E **101 Cc**
Woomera, S.A. 31 11S 136 47E **113 Ab**
Woonona, N.S.W. 34 21S 150 54E **903 Ej**
Woorabinda Aboriginal Sett., Qld.
24 8S 149 28E **129 Fh**
Wooramel, W.A. 25 45S 114 40E **117 Da**
Wooramel, R., W.A. 25 45S 114 40E **117 Da**
Woorinen, Vic. 35 14S 143 27E **100 Cd**
Wooroloo, W.A. 31 48S 116 18E **119 Ec**
Wooroolin, Qld. 26 25S 151 49E **131 Db**
Woorragee, Vic. 36 16S 146 44E **101 Dg**
Wootton, N.S.W. 32 17S 152 18E **95 Fc**
Worsley, W.A. 33 15S 116 2E **119 Gb**
Wowan, Qld. 23 54S 150 12E **131 Aa**
Wowoni I., Indonesia 4 5S 123 5E **135 Ef**
Woy Woy, N.S.W. 33 30S 151 19E **93 Dk**
Wright, Philippines 11 42N 125 2E **135 Bg**
Wubin, W.A. 30 6S 116 37E **119 Dc**
Wubin West, W.A. 30 9S 116 30E **119 Dc**
Wumalgi, Qld. 22 30S 149 34E **129 Dh**
Wundowie, W.A. 31 47S 116 23E **119 Ec**
Wunghu, Vic. 36 9S 145 27E **101 Df**
Wunkar, S.A. 34 30S 140 17E **113 Df**
Wurarga, W.A. 28 25S 116 15E **119 Bc**
Wuruma Dam, Qld. 25 8S 150 59E **131 Cb**
Wurung, Qld. 19 13S 140 38E **127 Bc**
Wutul, Mt., Qld. 27 4S 151 44E **131 Eb**
Wyaaba Cr., Qld. 16 27S 141 35E **127 Bc**
Wyaga, Qld. 28 11S 150 37E **131 Fa**
Wyalkatchem, W.A. 31 8S 117 22E **119 Ed**
Wyalong, N.S.W. 33 54S 147 16E **93 Dg**
Wyan, N.S.W. 29 5S 152 52E **95 Cc**
Wyandra, Qld. 27 12S 145 56E **127 Dd**
Wyangala Res., N.S.W. 33 54S 149 0E **93 Di**
Wyara, L., Qld. 28 42S 144 14E **127 Dc**
Wycheproof, Vic. 36 0S 143 17E **100 D**
Wydgee, W.A. 28 50S 117 45E **119 Bd**
Wyemandoo, Mt., W.A. 28 28S 118 29E **119 Be**
Wyening, W.A. 31 6S 116 28E **119 Ec**
Wynarka, S.A. 35 7S 139 44E **113 Ee**
Wynbring, S.A. 30 33S 133 32E **111 Cb**
Wyndham, N.Z. 46 20S 168 51E **145 Gc**
Wyndham, W.A. 15 33S 128 3E **117 Bd**
Wynnum, Qld. 27 27S 153 9E **131 Ed**
Wynyango, W.A. 27 56S 118 9E **119 Ae**
Wynyard, Tas. 40 59S 145 45E **107 Bd**
Wyola L., S.A. 29 8S 130 17E **111 Bb**
Wyong, N.S.W. 33 14S 151 24E **93 Dk**
Wyreema, Qld. 27 39S 151 52E **131 Eb**

X

Xantippe T.O., W.A. 30 15S 117 2E **119 Dd**

Y

Yaamba, Qld. 23 8S 150 22E **131 Aa**
Yabba North, Vic. 36 13S 145 42E **101 Df**
Yacamunda, Qld. 21 53S 147 7E **129 Cf**
Yacka, S.A. 33 34S 138 28E **113 Cd**
Yackandandah, Vic. 36 18S 146 52E **101 Dg**
Yala, Thailand 6 33N 101 18E **134 Cb**
Yalbalgo, W.A. 25 10S 114 45E **117 Da**
Yalboroo, Qld. 20 50S 148 40E **129 Bg**
Yalgoo, W.A. 28 16S 116 39E **119 Bc**
Yalgorin, N.S.W. 33 51S 146 50E **93 Df**
Yallakool, N.S.W. 35 33S 144 26E **92 Fd**
Yalleroi, Qld. 24 3S 145 42E **128 Fd**
Yallingup, W.A. 33 39S 115 2E **119 Gb**
Yallock, N.S.W. 32 25S 144 48E **92 Cd**
Yallourn, Vic. 38 10S 146 18E **101 Fg**
Yalunda Flat, S.A. 34 21S 135 53E **113 Da**
Yamba, N.S.W. 29 26S 153 23E **95 Cd**
Yamba, S.A. 34 10S 140 52E **113 Df**
Yambacoona, Tas. 39 43S 143 57E **107 Ab**
Yambah, N.T. 34 10S 133 50E **123 Cb**
Yambarran Ra., N.T. 15 10S 130 25E **123 Bb**
Yamboyna, Qld. 23 23S 148 7E **129 Eg**
Yambuk, Vic. 38 18S 142 5E **100 Fc**
Yamma Yamma, L., Qld. 26 16S 141 20E **127 Dc**
Yampi Sd., W.A. 16 8S 123 38E **117 Bc**
Yanac, Vic. 36 8S 141 25E **100 Db**
Yanburra, Qld. 23 5S 144 26E **128 Ec**
Yancannia, N.S.W. 30 12S 142 35E **90 Bd**
Yanchep, W.A. 31 30S 115 45E **119 Eb**
Yanco, N.S.W. 34 38S 146 27E **93 Ef**
Yanco Ck., N.S.W. 35 14S 145 35E **92 Fe**
Yandal, W.A. 27 35S 121 10E **117 Dc**
Yandanooka, W.A. 29 18S 115 29E **119 Cb**
Yandaran, Qld. 24 43S 152 6E **131 Bc**
Yande I., New Caledonia 20 3S 163 49E **139 Tu**
Yandembah, N.S.W. 33 23S 144 54E **92 Dd**
Yandina, Qld. 26 33S 152 58E **131 Dc**
Yandina, Solomon Is. 9 7S 159 13E **139 Qr**
Yankalilla, S.A. 35 28S 138 17E **113 Ed**
Yanmah, W.A. 34 12S 116 1E **119 Hc**
Yanna, Qld. 26 58S 146 0E **127 Dd**
Yantabulla, N.S.W. 29 21S 145 0E **91Ae**
Yanyarrie, S.A. 32 18S 138 29E **113 Bd**
Yappar, R., Qld. 18 22S 141 16E **127 Bc**
Yardea P.O., S.A. 32 23S 135 32E **111 Cc**
Yarloop, W.A. 32 58S 115 55E **119 Fb**
Yarra R., Vic.37 50S 144 53E **101 Ef**
Yarra Glen, Vic. 37 40S 145 22E **101 Ef**
Yarra Yarra Lakes, W.A. 29 40S 115 45E **119 Cb**
Yarrabandai, N.S.W. 33 6S 147 36E **93 Dg**
Yarraden, Qld. 14 28S 143 15E **127 Ac**
Yarraloola, W.A. 21 33S 115 52E **117 Cb**
Yarram, Vic. 38 29S 146 40E **101 Fg**
Yarraman, Qld. 26 50S 152 0E **131 Db**
Yarranvale, Qld. 26 50S 145 20E **127 Dd**
Yarras, N.S.W. 31 25S 152 20E **95 Ec**
Yarrawonga, Vic. 36 0S 146 0E **101 Dd**
Yarrill Cr., Qld. 28 20S 150 8E **131 Fa**
Yarrowee, R., Vic. 38 18S 144 30E **100 Ed**
Yarrowmere, Qld. 21 27S 145 53E **128 Cd**
Yarrowyck, N.S.W. 30 27S 151 20E **95 Db**
Yarto, Vic. 35 28S 142 16E **100 Cc**
Yarwun, Qld. 23 50S 151 8E **131 Ab**
Yasawa Group, Fiji 17 0S 177 23E **139 Aa**
Yass, N.S.W. 34 49S 148 54E **93 Eh**
Yates Pt., N.Z. 44 29S 167 49E **145 Eb**
Yathong, N.S.W. 32 37S 145 33E **92 Ce**

Yea, Vic. 37 14S 145 26E **101 Ef**
Yealering, W.A. 32 36S 117 36E **119 Fd**
Yednia, Qld. 26 46S 152 28E **131 Dc**
Yeeda P.O., W.A. 17 31S 123 38E **117 Bc**
Yeelanna, S.A. 34 9S 135 45E **113 Da**
Yelarbon, Qld. 28 33S 150 49E **131 Fa**
Yelbeni, W.A. 31 10S 117 39E **119 Ed**
Yellow Mt., N.S.W. 32 31S 146 52E **93 Cf**
Yellowdine, W.A. 31 17S 119 40E **119 Ef**
Yelvertoft, Qld. 20 13S 138 53E **127 Cb**
Yenda, N.S.W. 34 13S 146 14E **93 Ef**
Yeo, L., W.A. 28 0S 124 30E **117 Dc**
Yeoval, N.S.W. 32 41S 148 39E **93 Ch**
Yeppoon, Qld. 23 5S 150 47E **131 Aa**
Yericoin, W.A. 30 55S 116 24E **119 Dc**
Yerilla, W.A. 29 24S 121 47E **117 Dc**
Yerong Creek, N.S.W. 35 23S 147 5E **93 Fg**
Yerrinbool, N.S.W. 34 28S 144 34E **92 Ed**
Yetman, N.S.W. 28 56S 150 48E **95 Ba**
Yetna, W.A. 28 38S 114 44E **119 Ba**
Yilliminning, W.A. 32 55S 117 21E **119 Fd**
Yindarlgooda, L., W.A. 30 40S 121 52E **117 Ec**
Yinkanie, S.A. 34 22S 140 17E **113 Df**
Yinnietharra, W.A. 24 39S 116 12E **117 Cb**
Yog Point, Philippines 13 55N 124 20E **135 Bf**
Yolla, Tas. 41 7S 145 43E **107 Cd**
Yongala, S.A. 33 1S 138 44E **113 Cd**
Yoogali, N.S.W. 34 21S 146 7E **93 Ef**
Yoongarilup, W.A. 33 47S 115 39E **119 Gb**
York, W.A. 31 52S 116 47E **119 Ec**
York, C. Pen., Qld. 13 30S 142 30E **127 Ac**
York Plains, Tas. 42 15S 147 27E **107 Df**
Yorke Pen., S.A. 34 50S 137 40E **113 Dc**
Yorketown, S.A. 35 0S 137 33E **113 Ec**
Yorkrakine, W.A. 31 23S 117 35E **119 Ed**
Yornaning, W.A. 32 45S 117 8E **119 Fd**
Yornup, W.A. 34 2S 116 10E **119 Hc**
Yoting, W.A. 31 58S 117 35E **119 Ed**
Youangarra, W.A. 28 45S 118 50E **119 Be**
Youanmi, W.A. 28 37S 118 49E **119 Be**
Young, N.S.W. 34 19S 148 18E **93 Eh**
Young Ra., N.Z. 44 10S 169 30E **145 Ed**
Younghusband Pen., S.A. 36 0S 139 25E **113 Ee**
Young's Siding, W.A. 35 2S 117 30E **119 Hd**
Yoweragabie, W.A. 28 14S 117 39E **119 Bd**
Yuat R., Papua N.G. 4 10S 143 52E **141 Cb**
Yuendumu, N.T. 22 16S 131 49E **123 Cb**
Yuin, W.A. 27 59S 116 2E **119 Ac**
Yule, R., W.A. 20 24S 118 12E **117 Cb**
Yuluma, N.S.W. 35 9S 146 29E **93 Ff**
Yumali, S.A. 35 32S 139 45E **113 Ee**
Yuna, W.A. 28 20S 115 0E **119 Ba**
Yuna East, W.A. 28 20S 115 6E **119 Bb**
Yungaburra, Qld. 17 17S 145 35E **129 Xw**
Yungera, Vic. 34 42S 143 3E **100 Bd**
Yunndaga, W.A. 29 45S 121 0E **117 Dc**
Yunta, S.A. 32 34S 139 36E **113 Be**
Yuraraba, Qld. 28 20S 151 25E **131 Fb**
Yurgo, S.A. 35 10S 140 3E **113 Ef**

Z

Zamboanga, Philippines 6 59N 122 3E **135 Cf**
Zanthus, W.A. 31 2S 123 34E **117 Ec**
Zeehan, Tas. 41 52S 145 25E **107 Cd**
Zeil, Mt., N.T. 23 24S 132 23E **123 Cb**
Zelee, C., Solomon Is. 9 44S 161 34E **139 Qs**